About the Cover Image

Archibald J. Motley, Jr. (1891–1981), *The Picnic*, 1936 (oil on canvas)

Archibald Motley used vibrant colors and modernist techniques to capture the energy of Black urban life. Although associated with the Harlem Renaissance, Motley turned to Chicago's Bronzeville neighborhood as his frequent subject. He graduated from the Art Institute of Chicago and spent several years living and painting in Paris.

Howard University Gallery of Art, Washington DC, USA / Bridgeman Images.

The

American Promise

A CONCISE HISTORY

The
American Promise
A CONCISE HISTORY

VOLUME 2: SINCE 1865

NINTH EDITION

James L. Roark
Emory University

Michael P. Johnson
Johns Hopkins University

François Furstenberg
Johns Hopkins University

Patricia Cline Cohen
University of California, Santa Barbara

Sarah Stage
Arizona State University

Susan M. Hartmann
The Ohio State University

Sarah E. Igo
Vanderbilt University

bedford/st.martin's
Macmillan Learning
Boston | New York

Vice President: Leasa Burton
Program Director: Erika Gutierrez
Program Manager: William J. Lombardo
Director of Content Development: Jane Knetzger
Senior Development Editor: Rachel Goldberg
Editorial Assistant: Josie Cruea
Director of Media Editorial: Adam Whitehurst
Media Editor: Cara Kaufman
Marketing Manager: Melissa Rodriguez
Senior Director, Content Management Enhancement: Tracey Kuehn
Senior Managing Editor: Michael Granger
Senior Content Project Manager: Kendra LeFleur
Workflow Project Manager: Lisa McDowell
Production Supervisor: Robin Besofsky
Director of Design, Content Management: Diana Blume
Cover Design: William Boardman
Cartographer: Mapping Specialists, Ltd.
Director, Rights and Permissions: Hilary Newman
Text Permissions Researcher: Michael McCarty
Text Permissions Researcher: Elaine Kosta, Senior Manager, Lumina Datamatics, Inc.
Executive Permissions Editor: Cecilia Varas
Photo Researcher: Cheryl Dubois, Senior Manager, Lumina Datamatics, Inc.
Director of Digital Production: Keri deManigold
Assistant Director Digital Production: Michelle Camisa
Copyeditor: Rosemary Winfield
Indexer: Lakshmi Suresh, Lumina Datamatics, Inc.
Composition: Lumina Datamatics, Inc.
Printing and Binding: Lakeside Book Company

Library of Congress Control Number: 2022933093

ISBN 978-1-319-32993-8 (Combined Edition)
ISBN 978-1-319-34372-9 (Volume 1)
ISBN 978-1-319-34373-6 (Volume 2)

Printed in Canada.
1 2 3 4 5 6   27 26 25 24 23 22

Acknowledgments Acknowledgments and copyrights appear on the same page as the text and art selections they cover; these acknowledgments and copyrights constitute an extension of the copyright page.

For information, write: Bedford/St. Martin's, 75 Arlington Street, Boston, MA 02116

PREFACE: Why This Book This Way?

We are delighted to present the ninth edition of *The American Promise*, Concise Edition. From the outset we have sought to meet this challenge by providing a story students enjoy for its **readability, clear chronology, and lively voices of ordinary Americans**. *The American Promise* delivers a narrative with political backbone, documents and features for analysis and discussion, and overall support for teaching. The Concise Edition provides our signature approach to history in a smaller, more affordable trim size. Featuring the unabridged narrative, full map program, and select features of the parent text, the Concise Edition tells the story of the American promise in an accessible, student-friendly manner.

For the first time, *The American Promise* is available with **Achieve**—a fully mobile, accessible, and flexible learning platform. Achieve offers powerful assessment tools and content to support students of all levels of preparation in an intuitive and user-friendly system. These tools easily integrate with your school's learning management system for a seamless experience. For more information, see page xi.

The American Promise grew out of many conversations among ourselves and with others about the teaching and learning of history. We know that instructors want a U.S. history text that introduces students to overarching trends and developments and, at the same time, gives voice to the diverse people who have made American history. We know that students of history often come away overwhelmed and confused about what information is most important to know. We seek to provide a text that does not overwhelm them with detail, offers clear signposts about the key questions to focus on, and introduces them to historical thinking skills.

Our title, *The American Promise*, demonstrates our conviction that the essence of America has been its promise. For millions, the nation has held out the promise of a better life, unfettered worship, equality before the law, representative government, democratic politics, and other freedoms seldom found elsewhere. But none of these promises has come with any guarantees. Throughout our history, the promise has been marred by disappointments, compromises, and denials, but it lives on. The narrative of *The American Promise* demonstrates how much of American history is a continuing struggle over the definition and realization of the nation's promise.

An Inquiry-Based Model

The unique pedagogical design of *The American Promise* reinforces the book's approach to **history as a discipline rooted in debate and inquiry**. All chapter headings are now phrased as analytical questions, aiding students' understanding of the book's major arguments and familiarizing them with the **question-driven methodology** at the heart of the historian's craft.

Highlighting Individual Voices of the Past

To engage students in this American story and to portray fully the diversity of the American experience, we stitch into our narrative **the voices of hundreds of Americans**, both ordinary people and notable figures. Evocative quotations call attention to the experiences of Americans from all walks of life. Moreover, each chapter opens by focusing on an individual story that emphasizes human agency, such as Deborah Sampson (chapter 7), Alexander Hamilton (chapter 9), Robert Smalls (chapter 15), Frances Willard (chapter 20), and Lieutenant Frederick Downs Jr. (chapter 29).

A Focus on Primary Sources

Because primary sources form the heart of historical study, the **Analyzing Historical Evidence** feature in each chapter invites students to strengthen their skills of historical interpretation. The feature juxtaposes two to four primary documents, including visual sources, to portray varying perspectives on major events. Each feature concludes with questions for analysis to help students understand the significance of the featured topic, its context, and ways it might be viewed from different angles. The questions fit in one of the following Historical Skill categories: Summarize the Argument, Analyze the Evidence, Consider the Context, Recognize Viewpoints, and Ask Historical Questions. Topics include "Enslavement by Marriage" (chapter 3), "The Nation's First Formal Declaration of War" (chapter 10), "The Meaning of Freedom" (chapter 16), "The Final Push for Woman Suffrage" (chapter 22), and "Protecting Gay and Lesbian Rights" (chapter 30).

Useful Apparatus That Supports Student Learning

Helpful tools throughout each chapter signal what students should focus on. A clear **chronology** at the beginning of the chapter provides context for key events. **Key terms** highlighted in the text are defined in the margins to remind students of what's most important to know. The **Chapter Review** section helps students solidify their understanding of the material and invites students to consider change over time and make connections between past and present.

A Vivid Art and Map Program

Because many students are visual learners, *The American Promise*, Concise Edition, boasts more than 165 maps in all. A **map activity** in each chapter engages students in geographical literacy and encourages active learning. The book contains more than 240 images, many of which are historical artifacts that underscore the importance of material culture. A **visual activity** in each chapter help students sharpen their visual interpretation skills. Some narrative material has been represented as figures and tables to underscore certain developments and provide an alternative mode of learning.

Amplifying Diversity, Equity, and Inclusion

Based on thoughtful feedback from instructors, the ninth edition of *The American Promise* strives to represent the difficult and complicated parts of our history with accuracy and sensitivity to multiple perspectives. We have paid deeper attention to the culture and experiences of Black people, Native Americans, and Latinos, along with transgender and nonbinary individuals, people with disabilities, and other marginalized Americans. We have carefully rethought the language that describes enslavement in order to emphasize the humanity and dignity of enslaved people and to place agency for enslavement upon those who perpetrated it. Similarly, the language used to describe Native Americans and the names of Native American nations has been updated. The book chronicles the dispossession of Native American peoples from their lands with honesty and accuracy, and several maps in chapters 6, 8, and 10 have been revised with deliberate attention to the presence of Native American nations prior to and during colonial settlement.

Updated and Revised Coverage in the Narrative

The new edition draws on recent scholarship and offers important updates to the narrative. Opening with an entirely new American Story, chapter 1 examines the recent archaeological finds at White Sands National Park, showing that ancient Americans were living in the area thousands of years earlier than previously believed. The chapter also highlights ancient Native American practices, including the creation of burial mounds. Chapters 6–11 expand the coverage of Native American and Black experiences during the colonial era. Chapter 6 offers more material on the global conflicts that led to the Seven Years' War, and a restructured section addresses how enslaved people reacted to the colonial rebellion. In chapter 7, new details and quotations elaborate on the 1778 attack of American militias on the Cherokee, while chapter 8 recounts how the Haudenosaunee lost more land after the Revolution. Chapter 9 features new coverage of the Haitian Revolution, including primary source quotations. Chapter 10 provides specific information on the powerful Native American nations west of the Mississippi.

In chapter 12, more coverage of desegregated schools in Boston includes new quotations by Black activist William C. Nell. Chapters 17–19 delve deeper into the experiences of Native Americans and Chinese Americans during the settlement of the West, covering Sinophobia and updating coverage of the Ghost Dance religion. Chapter 20 offers additional coverage of the labor wars and Homestead Strike, as well as the war in the Philippines.

The final chapters of the book (chapters 30 and 31) have been updated to address more fully global political developments, social movements, and the increasing polarization between liberals and conservatives. Chapter 30 offers a broader context for the economy of the Internet age and dot-com boom as well as the onset of the "culture wars" that continue to rage in the twenty-first century. Chapter 31 looks back on the judicial and legislative accomplishments of the Donald J. Trump administration along with its challenges, such as Trump's impeachments. It covers the early crises of the Joseph R. Biden administration, from the January 6, 2021, U.S. Capitol insurrection to the Russian invasion of Ukraine, as well as the stunning social and economic changes wrought by the COVID-19 pandemic. This chapter also extends the coverage of how transgender and nonbinary individuals have advocated for greater recognition of their full identities and new practices in the language used to refer to them.

Acknowledgments

We gratefully acknowledge all of the helpful suggestions from those who have read and taught from previous editions of *The American Promise* and cared enough to take the time to advise us. We hope that our many classroom collaborators will be pleased to see their influence in the ninth edition. In particular, we wish to thank the talented scholars and teachers who gave generously of their time and knowledge to review the previous edition in preparation for its revision: Jeanette Belle, *Ozarks Technical Community College*; Lori Buchanan, *Los Angeles Mission College*; Sally Cahalan, *Western Technical College*; Charles E. Delgadillo, *California State Polytechnic Pomona*; Chuck Dendy, *Stephen F. Austin State University*; Michael Dickinson, *Virginia Commonwealth University*; Alicia Duffy, *University of Central Florida*; Stephen Gibson, *Allegany College of Maryland*; Alexander J. Goodrich, *North Carolina State University at Raleigh*; Worth Hayes, *Tuskegee University*; Victoria L. Johnson, *Lawson State Community College*; Eric Jurgens, *College of Menominee Nation*; Eben Miller, *Southern Maine Community College*; Carlos Mujal, *De Anza College*; G. Patrick O'Brien, *Kennesaw State University*; Michael A. Ridge Jr., *The University of Texas Rio Grande Valley*; Laura Walikainen Rouleau, *Michigan Technological University*; Joel D. Rudewicz, *Erie Community College–South Campus*; Natalia Starostina, *Oklahoma City University*; Katherine Sturdevant, *Pikes Peak Community College*; Cyrana Wyker, *Middle Tennessee State University*.

A project as complex as this requires the talents of many individuals. First, we would like to acknowledge our families for their support, forbearance, and toleration of our textbook responsibilities. We would also like to thank the many people at Bedford/St. Martin's and Macmillan Learning who have been crucial to this project. Thanks are due to Rachel Goldberg, senior developmental editor, who shepherded the project from start to finish, always with good humor; William J. Lombardo, senior program manager for history; Erika Gutierrez, senior program director for history; and Leasa Burton, vice president, for their support and guidance. Thanks are also due to Cara Kaufman, media editor; Stephanie Sosa, associate editor; and Josie Cruea, editorial assistant. We thank history marketing manager Melissa Rodriguez as well as senior content project manager Kendra LeFleur, who pulled together the many pieces related to copyediting, design, and composition. Thanks are also due to Cheryl DuBois and Cecilia Varas for their diligent photo research; workflow manager Lisa McDowell; designer Diana Bloom; copy editor Rosemary Winfield; proofreader Paula Pyburn; indexer Lakshmi Suresh; cover designer William Boardman; and executive media project manager Michelle Camisa, who oversaw the production of Achieve with *The American Promise*.

Achieve with *The American Promise*

Achieve sets a new standard for driving student learning in your U.S. history course by way of powerful learning content, engaging activities, and actionable student insights and analytics. Achieve brings together all of the features that instructors and students loved about our previous platform, LaunchPad—interactive e-book, LearningCurve adaptive quizzing and other assessments, interactive learning activities, and extensive instructor resources—all within a new, enhanced technology platform.

Proven Student Success

Macmillan Learning's Learning Science & Insights team has conducted extensive research to inform the development of Achieve. Their research has shown that students who completed more of the assigned material and received higher grades on those assignments in Achieve also had higher exam scores.* In addition,

- 88 percent of students said that Achieve was easy to use.
- 82 percent of students agreed that Achieve helped them develop, practice, and apply skills associated with their course.
- 80 percent of instructors agreed that Achieve helped students improve their knowledge of the course material.

To learn more about Learning Science and Insights, please visit macmillanlearning.com/learning-science

Benefits

Powerful Learning Content

- **E-book.** Macmillan Learning's e-book is an interactive version of the textbook that offers highlighting, bookmarking, and note-taking. Students can download the e-book to read offline or to have it read aloud to them. Achieve allows instructors to assign chapter sections as homework.

---

*Based on a fall 2021 survey of Achieve users with over two hundred instructor responses and over three thousand student responses.

▶ **Adaptive Quizzing.**
LearningCurve Adaptive
Quizzing provides
personalized question
sets and clear feedback
based on each student's
correct and incorrect
answers—offering an
easy way for students
to prepare for class by
reviewing the e-book
and then assessing their
understanding of the key
concepts.

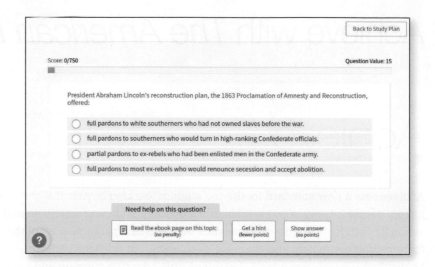

■ **Integrated companion reader.** *Reading the American Past*, the integrated companion reader for *The American Promise*, contains at least five additional primary source readings for each chapter. Auto-graded comprehension quizzes test students' understanding of each primary source.

BEDFORD TUTORIAL FOR HISTORY - U.S.

Working with Primary Sources

As a student in a history course, you probably have some preconceived ideas about what you will be studying and how you will study it. But your college-level history may surprise you. You may have thought that the study of history is about "facts," when the study of history has as much to do with working with and evaluating sources and as evidence as it does with learning dates, names, events, and places from the past. In this tutorial, you will learning the following:

- What exactly are historical sources
- The difference between primary and secondary sources
- How to read and analyze a written source
- How to read and analyze a visual source

What Are Historical Sources?

The stories historians tell in books, articles, and lectures are pieced together from hundreds, often thousands, of

Which of the following is an example of a primary source that would shed light on a research question about American soldiers' experiences during World War II?

○ A children's picture book about World War II soldiers written by a young mother during the 1960s

○ A letter written during World War II by an American soldier in France to his fiancé

○ A book, written and published by a historian in 2020, about American soldiers' experiences during World War II

○ A documentary film focusing on the American military during World War II

◀ **Guided tutorials.**
*Bedford Tutorials
for U.S. History* are
thirteen guided
tutorials with
assessment that
help students build
essential skills for
the course, such as
avoiding plagiarism,
working with
primary sources,
and learning to
think and read like a
historian.

Engaging Activities

Primary Source Activity for Analyzing Historical Evidence: The Meaning of Freedom

Although the Emancipation Proclamation itself did not free any enslaved men, women, or children, it transformed the character of the war. Black people resolutely focused on the possibilities of freedom even before the war ended.

Instructions: Read the following documents, and then respond to the questions.

Document 1

Letter from John Q. A. Dennis to Edwin M. Stanton, July 26, 1864

John Q. A. Dennis, formerly enslaved in Maryland, wrote to ask Secretary of War Edwin M. Stanton for help in reuniting his family.

Boston. Dear Sir I am Glad that I have the Honour to Write you a few line I have been in troble for about four yars my Dear wife was taken from me Nov 19th 1859 and left me with three Children and I being a Slave At the time Could Not do Anny thing for the poor little Children for my master it was took me Carry me some forty mile

Why does the petition by Black Tennesseans (Document 3) refer to the bayonet in its final paragraph?

◯ The petitioners remind their audience that Black soldiers had successfully fought on behalf of the Union, armed with the bayonet, and should therefore be entrusted with the right to vote.

◯ The petitioners invoke the bayonet as a way of threatening violence unless their requests are met.

◯ The petitioners invoke the bayonet as a symbol of the suffering Black people suffered during their years of enslavement.

◀ **Primary source activities.** Building on the Analyzing Historical Evidence feature in *The American Promise*, these critical reading activities encourage students to compare, contrast, and analyze the primary source documents in each chapter and demonstrate their knowledge in online assessments.

▶ **Video activities.** Brief, engaging videos offer a multimodal glimpse into some of America's most dramatic moments, from the Seneca Falls Convention on woman suffrage to D-Day. Online assessments reinforce the content and invite reflection.

The Reconstruction Amendments

Chapter 16 in *The American Promise* examines the years after the Civil War that we call Reconstruction. The nation struggled with questions about the fate of the South after its rebellion and the future of formerly enslaved Black men and women. The South's stubborn commitment to white supremacy caused northerners to seek regime change in the former rebel states and to find new ways to protect vulnerable freedmen.

A vital part of the Federal government's efforts were the three Reconstruction amendments to the Constitution. The 13th Amendment (adopted in 1865) abolished slavery, ending the more than 250-year-old institution. The 14th Amendment (adopted in 1868) made Black men citizens of the United States, overturning the Dred Scott decision of 1857, and granted them due process and equal protection under the law. The 15th Amendment (adopted in 1870) forbade the denial of a citizen's right to vote because of "race, color, or previous condition of servitude." The amendments had immediate effect, especially the provision to enfranchise Black men. White southerners condemned the amendments and claimed they were evidence of the tyranny of Reconstruction.

In this video, you will hear how white southerners successfully counterattacked, assuring that the regime change was temporary. In a very few years, they succeeded in restoring the South's traditional racial and political hierarchies. To complete this activity, watch the video and answer the questions.

What does Professor Barbara Fields mean when she says Reconstruction is not over? Do you agree?

+25 ◯

In order to receive credit for this question, your response must meet a minimum character count. Refer to the character counter to see how many characters are required for this question.

- **Instructor Activity Guides.** Ten Instructor Activity Guides provide instructors with a structured plan for using Achieve's active learning opportunities in both face-to-face and remote learning courses. Each guide offers step-by-step instructions—from preclass reflection to in-class engagement to postclass follow-up. The guides include suggestions for discussion questions, group work, presentations, and simulations, with estimated class time, implementation effort, and Bloom's taxonomy level for each activity.

© Macmillan Learning

- ▲ **iClicker classroom response system.** Achieve seamlessly integrates iClicker, Macmillan Learning's highly acclaimed classroom response system. iClicker can help make any classroom—in-person or virtual—more lively, engaging, and productive.

- **Instructor resources.** Achieve provides a full suite of instructor resources to foster active learning, all in one place. These include the Instructor's Resource Manual, Lecture Slides, iClicker Slides, map quizzes, and more.

Actionable Data and Insights

- **Summative assessment.** Chapter quizzes and test bank questions provided in Achieve allow students to demonstrate what they've learned. Results report to a gradebook that lets instructors monitor student progress individually and classwide. The test bank contains thousands of questions meticulously checked against the updated content of the text. Instructors can assign out-of-the-box exams or create their own by

    - Choosing from the questions in our database.

    - Filtering questions by type, topic, difficulty, and Bloom's level.

    - Customizing multiple-choice questions.

    - Integrating their own questions into the exam.

- **Goal-Setting and Reflection Surveys.** These checkpoint surveys help the instructor learn how students are doing beyond just their grade achievement to target interventions and accommodations that can help them achieve more in the course.

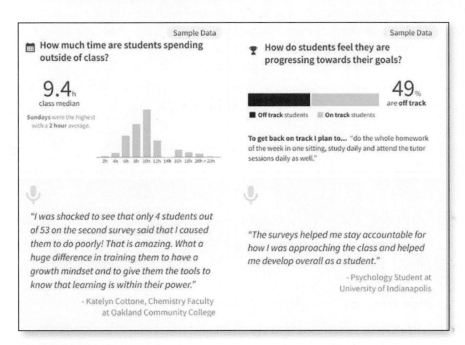

◀ **Learning Objectives, Reports, and Insights.** Achieve's Reports and its Insights provide powerful analytics, viewable in an elegant dashboard, that offer instructors a window into student progress against Learning Objectives and facilitate lessons that are specifically tailored to students' needs.

Enhanced Platform

- **Next-generation technology.** Achieve provides a cleaner, more intuitive, mobile-friendly interface. Designed for the Cloud, it has better monitoring tools and allows faster response to issues, allowing us to improve our uptime. It is generally more scalable and extensible, so it can support future products and customer needs.

- **Integration.** Achieve can all be integrated with the tools of your choice—including the iClicker Student Response system or your learning management system (Blackboard, Canvas, D2L, or Moodle). For more information, visit macmillanlearning.com/solutions/LMS-Integration or talk to your local sales representative.

- **Accessibility.** Macmillan Learning strives to create products that are usable by all learners and meet universally applied accessibility standards. For more information, visit macmillanlearning.com/accessibility.

Learn more: macmillanlearning.com/achieve

Customer support: macmillanlearning.com/Contact-Us/Training-and-Demos

Ordering information: store.macmillanlearning.com or talk to your local sales representative

BRIEF CONTENTS

CONTENTS

16
RECONSTRUCTION,
1863–1877 450

Photo: From the New York Public Library.

17
THE CONTESTED WEST,
1865–1900   480

18
THE GILDED AGE,
1865–1900   510

19
THE CITY AND ITS WORKERS,
1870–1900 540

20
DISSENT, DEPRESSION, AND WAR,
1890–1900 572

21
PROGRESSIVE REFORM,
1890–1916   602

22
WORLD WAR I: THE PROGRESSIVE CRUSADE,
1914–1920   634

Photo: Jane Addams Memorial Collection (JAMC_8000_0005_0014), Special Collections, University of Illinois at Chicago, photographer: Max Platz.

Photo: Courtesy of Janet W. Hansen.

23

FROM NEW ERA TO GREAT DEPRESSION,

1920–1932   666

24

THE NEW DEAL EXPERIMENT,

1932–1939   698

Photo: Getty Images.

Photo: Library of Congress Prints and Photographs Division [LC-DIG-fsa-8b29516].

25
THE UNITED STATES AND THE SECOND WORLD WAR,
1939–1945 730

26
THE NEW WORLD OF THE COLD WAR,
1945–1960 764

Photo: Bettmann/Getty Images.

Photo: Bettmann/Getty Images.

27
POSTWAR CULTURE AND POLITICS,
1945–1960 792

28
RIGHTS, REBELLION, AND REACTION,
1960–1974 822

29
CONFRONTING LIMITS AT HOME AND ABROAD,
1961–1979   854

30
POLITICAL DIVISIONS IN A CONSERVATIVE ERA,
1980–2000   886

Photo: AP Photo/Henri Huet.

Photo: Bettmann/Getty Images.

31

AMERICA IN A NEW CENTURY,

SINCE 2000 920

APPENDICES

I. DOCUMENTS A-1

II. GOVERNMENT AND DEMOGRAPHICS A-25

Photo: AP Photo/Susan Walsh.

MAPS, FIGURES, AND TABLES

Map Activities are listed in blue.

SPECIAL FEATURES

ANALYZING HISTORICAL EVIDENCE

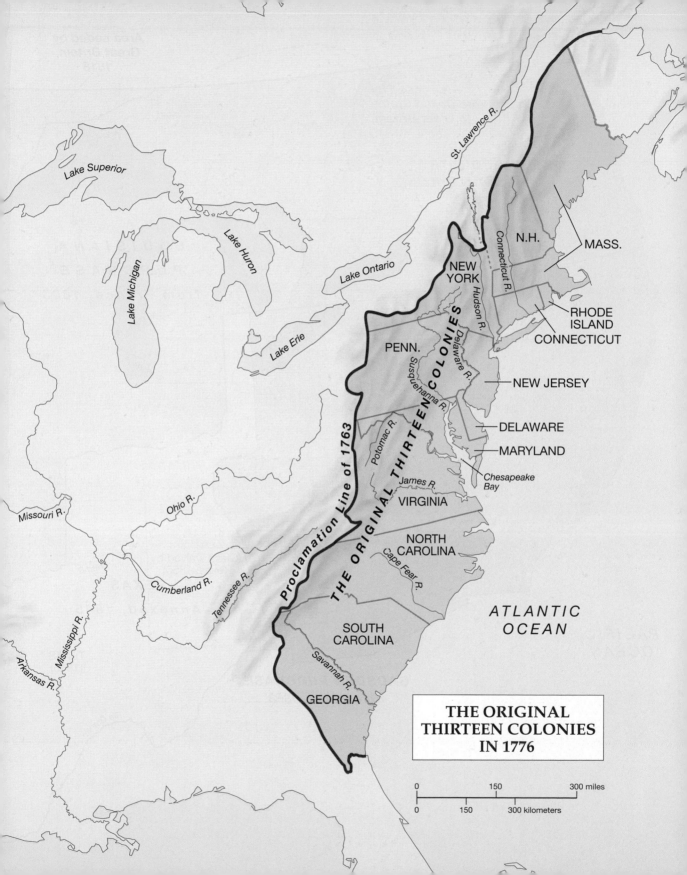

Lake Superior

Lake Michigan

Lake Huron

Lake Ontario

Lake Erie

St. Lawrence R.

Connecticut R.

N.H.

MASS.

NEW
YORK

Hudson R.

RHODE
ISLAND

CONNECTICUT

PENN.

Delaware R.

Susquehanna R.

NEW JERSEY

DELAWARE

MARYLAND

THE ORIGINAL THIRTEEN COLONIES

Proclamation Line of 1763

Potomac R.

James R.

Chesapeake
Bay

VIRGINIA

Missouri R.

Ohio R.

NORTH
CAROLINA

Cape Fear R.

Cumberland R.

Tennessee R.

ATLANTIC
OCEAN

Mississippi R.

Arkansas R.

SOUTH
CAROLINA

Savannah R.

GEORGIA

**THE ORIGINAL
THIRTEEN COLONIES
IN 1776**

0   150   300 miles

0   150   300 kilometers

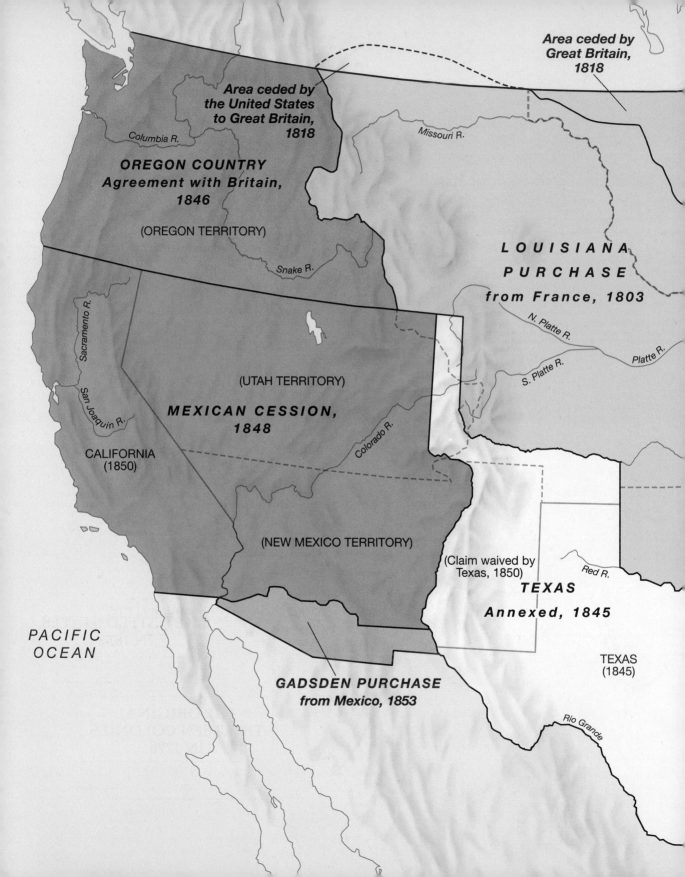

Area ceded by
Great Britain,
1818

Area ceded by
the United States
to Great Britain,
1818

Columbia R.

Missouri R.

OREGON COUNTRY
Agreement with Britain,
1846

(OREGON TERRITORY)

LOUISIANA
PURCHASE
from France, 1803

Snake R.

Sacramento R.

N. Platte R.

Platte R.

(UTAH TERRITORY)

S. Platte R.

San Joaquin R.

MEXICAN CESSION,
1848

Colorado R.

CALIFORNIA
(1850)

(NEW MEXICO TERRITORY)

(Claim waived by
Texas, 1850)

Red R.

TEXAS
Annexed, 1845

TEXAS
(1845)

PACIFIC
OCEAN

GADSDEN PURCHASE
from Mexico, 1853

Rio Grande

Areas ceded by Britain, 1842 (Webster-Ashburton Treaty)

Lake Superior

St. Lawrence R.

MAINE (1820)

VERMONT (1791)

Lake Huron

(MINNESOTA TERRITORY)

WISCONSIN (1848)

Lake Michigan

MICHIGAN (1837)

Lake Ontario

NEW YORK (1788)

Connecticut R.

N.H. (1788)

MASS. (1788)

Hudson R.

RHODE ISLAND (1790)

CONNECTICUT (1788)

Lake Erie

IOWA (1846)

Missouri R.

ILLINOIS (1818)

INDIANA (1816)

OHIO (1803)

PENN. (1787)

Susquehanna R.

Delaware R.

NEW JERSEY (1787)

DELAWARE (1787)

Ohio R.

KENTUCKY (1792)

Gained by treaty with Britain, 1783

Proclamation Line of 1763

Potomac R.

THE ORIGINAL THIRTEEN COLONIES

James R.

VIRGINIA (1788)

MARYLAND (1788)

Chesapeake Bay

MISSOURI (1821)

Cumberland R.

Tennessee R.

TENNESSEE (1796)

NORTH CAROLINA (1789)

Cape Fear R.

ARKANSAS (1836)

Mississippi R.

(INDIAN TERRITORY)

SOUTH CAROLINA (1788)

ATLANTIC OCEAN

ALABAMA (1819)

Savannah R.

MISSISSIPPI (1817)

GEORGIA (1788)

LOUISIANA (1812)

THE UNITED STATES IN 1853

0   150   300 miles

0   150   300 kilometers

FLORIDA (1845)

FLORIDA Treaty with Spain, 1819

Areas taken from Spain in 1810, 1813

Gulf of Mexico

(1789) Date of statehood

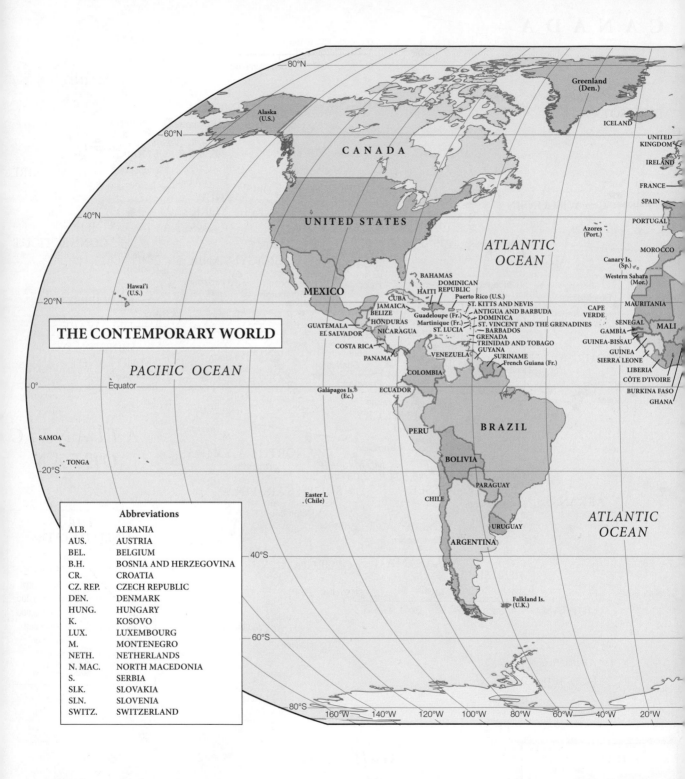

THE CONTEMPORARY WORLD

PACIFIC OCEAN

ATLANTIC OCEAN

ATLANTIC OCEAN

80°N

Greenland
(Den.)

ICELAND

Alaska
(U.S.)

60°N

UNITED
KINGDOM

IRELAND

C A N A D A

FRANCE

SPAIN

40°N

PORTUGAL

UNITED STATES

Azores
(Port.)

MOROCCO

Canary Is.
(Sp.)

Western Sahara
(Mor.)

Hawai'i
(U.S.)

20°N

MEXICO

BAHAMAS

DOMINICAN
REPUBLIC

HAITI

CUBA

Puerto Rico (U.S.)

ST. KITTS AND NEVIS

MAURITANIA

JAMAICA

BELIZE

Guadeloupe (Fr.)

ANTIGUA AND BARBUDA

DOMINICA

CAPE
VERDE

GUATEMALA

HONDURAS

Martinique (Fr.)

ST. VINCENT AND THE GRENADINES

ST. LUCIA

SENEGAL

MALI

EL SALVADOR

NICARAGUA

BARBADOS

GRENADA

GAMBIA

COSTA RICA

TRINIDAD AND TOBAGO

GUINEA-BISSAU

GUYANA

GUINEA

PANAMA

VENEZUELA

SURINAME

SIERRA LEONE

French Guiana (Fr.)

LIBERIA

COLOMBIA

CÔTE D'IVOIRE

Galápagos Is.
(Ec.)

0°   Equator

ECUADOR

BURKINA FASO

GHANA

PERU

B R A Z I L

SAMOA

BOLIVIA

TONGA

20°S

PARAGUAY

Easter I.
(Chile)

CHILE

ARGENTINA

URUGUAY

40°S

Falkland Is.
(U.K.)

60°S

80°S

160°W   140°W   120°W   100°W   80°W   60°W   40°W   20°W

Abbreviations

ALB.	ALBANIA
AUS.	AUSTRIA
BEL.	BELGIUM
B.H.	BOSNIA AND HERZEGOVINA
CR.	CROATIA
CZ. REP.	CZECH REPUBLIC
DEN.	DENMARK
HUNG.	HUNGARY
K.	KOSOVO
LUX.	LUXEMBOURG
M.	MONTENEGRO
NETH.	NETHERLANDS
N. MAC.	NORTH MACEDONIA
S.	SERBIA
SLK.	SLOVAKIA
SLN.	SLOVENIA
SWITZ.	SWITZERLAND

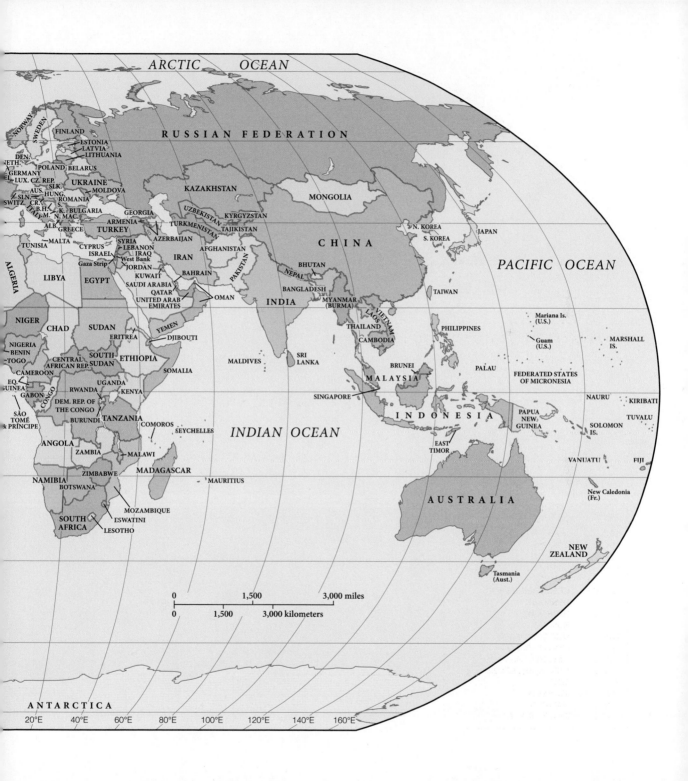

The
American Promise

A CONCISE HISTORY

16

RECONSTRUCTION
1863–1877

This chapter discusses the following questions:

- How did competing plans for wartime reconstruction differ?
- What did early reconstruction reveal about the North's and South's intentions?
- How radical was congressional reconstruction?
- How successful were the South's Republican governments?
- Why did Reconstruction collapse?
- Conclusion: Was Reconstruction "a revolution but half accomplished"?

▶ **James T. Rapier** In 1874, when Representative James T. Rapier spoke before Congress on behalf of a civil rights bill, he described the humiliation of being denied service at inns all along his route from Montgomery to Washington. Elsewhere in the world, he said, class and religion were invoked to defend discrimination. But in America, "our distinction is color." From the New York Public Library.

AN AMERICAN STORY

In 1856, John Rapier, a free Black barber in Florence, Alabama, urged his four freeborn sons to flee the increasingly repressive and dangerous South. Nineteen-year-old James T. Rapier chose Canada, where he went to live with his uncle in a largely Black community and studied in a log schoolhouse. In a letter to his father, he vowed, "I will endeavor to do my part in solving the problems [of African Americans] in my native land."

The Union victory in the Civil War gave James Rapier the opportunity to redeem his pledge. In 1865, after more than eight years of exile, Rapier returned to Alabama, where he presided over the first political gathering of formerly enslaved people in the state. He soon discovered, however, that Alabama's white population found it agonizingly difficult to accept defeat and Black freedom. They responded to the revolutionary changes under the banner "White Man—Right or Wrong—Still the White Man!"

During the elections of 1868, when Rapier and other Black Alabama residents vigorously supported the Republican ticket, the recently organized Ku Klux Klan went on a bloody rampage. A mob of 150 outraged whites raced through Rapier's neighborhood seeking four Black politicians they claimed were trying to "Africanize Alabama." They caught and hanged three, but the "n----- carpetbagger from Canada" escaped. After briefly considering fleeing the state, Rapier decided to stay and fight for his rights. In 1872, Rapier won election to the House of Representatives, where he joined six other Black congressmen in Washington, D.C. Defeated for reelection in 1874 in a campaign marked by ballot-box stuffing, Rapier turned to cotton farming. But unrelenting racial violence convinced him that Black people could never achieve equality and prosperity in the South. He purchased land in Kansas and urged Alabama's Blacks to escape with him. In 1883, however, before he could leave Alabama, the forty-five-year-old Rapier died of tuberculosis.

In 1865, Union general Carl Schurz had foreseen many of the troubles Rapier encountered in the postwar South. The Civil War, Schurz observed, was "a revolution but half accomplished." He meant that while northern victory had freed enslaved people, it had not changed former slaveholders' minds about Blacks' unfitness for freedom. Left to themselves, white people would "introduce some new system of forced labor, not perhaps exactly slavery in its old form but something similar to it," Schurz predicted. To defend their freedom, Blacks would need federal protection, land of their own, and voting rights. Until white Americans "cut loose from the past, it will be a dangerous experiment to put Southern society upon its own legs."

As Schurz understood, the end of the war did not mean peace. Indeed, the nation entered one of its most turbulent and violent eras—Reconstruction.

1863	Proclamation of Amnesty and Reconstruction pardons most rebels.
1864	Lincoln refuses to sign Wade-Davis bill.
1865	Freedmen's Bureau established. Lincoln assassinated; Andrew Johnson becomes president. First black codes enacted. Thirteenth Amendment passes.
1866	Civil Rights Act passes. Fourteenth Amendment passes. American Equal Rights Association founded. Ku Klux Klan founded.
1867	Military Reconstruction Act passes. Tenure of Office Act passes. Southern Black Americans gain voting rights under Military Reconstruction Act. Southern states hold elections for state convention delegates.
1868	President Johnson impeached. Ulysses S. Grant elected president.
1869	Congress approves Fifteenth Amendment.
1871	Ku Klux Klan Act passes.
1872	Liberal Party formed. President Grant reelected.
1873	Economic depression sets in. *Slaughterhouse* cases decided. Colfax massacre kills more than eighty Black people.

1874	Democrats win majority in House of Representatives.
1875	One-half of South Carolina's and Mississippi's children, the majority Black, attend school. Sharecropping is dominant labor system for rural southern Black farmers.
1877	Rutherford B. Hayes elected president and Reconstruction ends.

Answers to the era's central questions—about the defeated South's status within the Union and the meaning of freedom for former slaves—came from many directions and often clashed. In Washington, D.C., the federal government played an active role, passing the Fourteenth and Fifteenth Amendments to the Constitution that strengthened the claim of Black Americans to equal rights. But state legislatures and county seats across the South also featured Black and white people vigorously disagreeing about the future of the South. The struggle over the future also took place on the South's farms and plantations, where former slaves sought to become free workers while former slaveholders sought to retain as much of slavery as they could. Whites often backed their opinions with racial violence. In the end, the efforts of Black Americans and their allies to secure full citizenship and racial equality failed. In the contest to determine the consequences of Confederate defeat and emancipation, white southerners prevailed.

How did competing plans for wartime reconstruction differ?

Reconstruction did not wait for the end of war. As the odds of a northern victory increased, thinking about reunification quickened. But who had authority to devise a plan for reconstructing the Union? President Abraham Lincoln firmly believed that reconstruction was a matter of executive responsibility. Congress just as firmly asserted its jurisdiction. Fueling the argument were significant differences about the terms of reconstruction.

In their eagerness to formulate a plan for political reunification, neither Lincoln nor Congress gave much attention to the South's land and labor problems. Yet the war rapidly eroded slavery, and Yankee military commanders in the Union-occupied areas of the Confederacy had no choice but to oversee the emergence of a new labor system.

Why did Congress object to Lincoln's plan "to bind up the nation's wounds?"

As early as 1863, Lincoln began contemplating how "to bind up the nation's wounds" and achieve "a lasting peace." While deep compassion for the enemy guided his thinking about peace, his plan for reconstruction aimed primarily at shortening the war and ending slavery.

Lincoln's Proclamation of Amnesty and Reconstruction in December 1863 set out his terms. He offered a full pardon, restoring property (except enslaved people) and political rights, to most rebels willing to renounce secession and to accept emancipation. When 10 percent of a state's voting population had taken an oath of allegiance, the state could organize a new government and be readmitted into the Union.

Lincoln's plan did not extend civil rights to formerly enslaved people, nor did it anticipate a program of long-term federal assistance to freedmen. Clearly, the president looked forward to the rapid, forgiving restoration of the broken Union.

Lincoln's easy terms enraged abolitionists such as Wendell Phillips of Boston, who charged that the president "makes the negro's freedom a mere sham." He "is willing that the negro should be free but seeks nothing else for him." Comparing Lincoln to the Union's most passive general, Phillips declared, "What McClellan was on the battlefield—'Do as little hurt as possible!'—Lincoln is in civil affairs—'Make as little change as possible!'" Phillips and other northern Radicals called instead for a thorough overhaul of southern society. Their ideas proved to be too drastic for most Republicans during the war years, but Congress agreed that Lincoln's plan was inadequate.

In July 1864, Congress put forward a plan of its own. Congressman Henry Winter Davis of Maryland and Senator Benjamin Wade of Ohio jointly sponsored a bill that demanded that at least half of the voters in a conquered rebel state take the oath of allegiance before reconstruction could begin. The Wade-Davis bill also banned almost all ex-Confederates from participating in the drafting of new state constitutions. Finally, the bill guaranteed the equality of freedmen before the law. Congress's reconstruction would be neither as quick nor as forgiving as Lincoln's. When Lincoln refused to sign the bill and let it die, Wade and Davis charged the president with tyranny.

Undeterred, Lincoln continued to nurture the formation of loyal state governments under his own plan. Four states—Arkansas, Louisiana, Tennessee, and Virginia—fulfilled the president's requirements, but Congress refused to seat representatives from the "Lincoln states." Lincoln admitted that a government based on only 10 percent was not ideal, but he argued, "We shall sooner have the fowl by hatching the egg than by smashing it." Massachusetts senator Charles Sumner responded, "The eggs of crocodiles can produce only crocodiles." In his last public address in April 1865, Lincoln defended his plan but expressed his endorsement of voting rights for southern Black men, at least "the very intelligent, and . . . those who serve our cause as soldiers." The announcement demonstrated that Lincoln's thinking about reconstruction was still evolving. Four days later, he was dead.

How did land and labor systems change?

Of all the problems raised by the North's victory in the war, none proved more critical than the South's transition from slavery to free labor. As federal armies occupied the Confederacy, hundreds of thousands of enslaved people became free workers. In addition, Union armies controlled vast territories in the South where legal title to land had become unclear. The Confiscation Acts passed during the war punished "traitors" by taking away their property. The question of what to do with federally occupied land and how to organize labor on it engaged ex-slaves, ex-slaveholders, Union military commanders, and federal government officials long before the war ended.

In the Mississippi valley, occupying federal troops announced a new labor code. It required landholders to give up whipping, sign contracts with formerly enslaved men and women, pay wages, and provide food, housing, and medical care. The code also required Black laborers to enter into contracts, work diligently, and remain subordinate and obedient. The Union military clearly had no intention of promoting a

VISUAL ACTIVITY

▶ *The Lord Is My Shepherd* by Eastman Johnson,
1863 Maine-born Eastman Johnson (1824–1906) did this
painting only months after the Emancipation Proclamation.
Its title comes from Psalm 23, which begins, "The Lord is
my shepherd; I shall not want." The painting captures a
humble Black man quietly reading his Bible and reminds
us of one of the reasons freedmen struggled so hard for
literacy. FineArt/Alamy.

READING THE IMAGE: What is the artist saying about the
capacity of those who had been enslaved to live as free
people?

CONNECTIONS: Why did southern whites in the
Reconstruction era consider literacy for formerly enslaved
people less a religious impulse than a dangerous
political act?

social or economic revolution. Instead, they sought to restore traditional plantation
agriculture with wage labor. The effort resulted in a hybrid system that one contemporary called "compulsory free labor," which satisfied no one.

Planters complained because the new system fell short of slavery. They were
particularly exercised by the requirement to end violent force against workers. Black
people could not be "transformed by proclamation," a Louisiana sugar planter
declared. Without the right to whip, he argued, the new labor system did not have a
chance. Either Union soldiers must "*compel* the negroes to work," or the planters
themselves must "be authorized and sustained in using force."

Black people found the new regime too similar to slavery to be called free labor.
Its chief deficiency, they believed, was the failure to provide them with land of their
own. Freedmen believed they had a moral right to land because they and their
ancestors had worked it without pay for centuries. "What's the use of being free if
you don't own land enough to be buried in?" one man asked. Several wartime
developments led freedmen to believe that the federal government planned to defend
Black freedom with landownership.

In January 1865, General William Tecumseh Sherman set aside part of the coast south of Charleston for Black settlement. By June, some forty thousand freedmen sat on 400,000 acres of "Sherman land." In addition, in March 1865, Congress passed a bill establishing the Bureau of Refugees, Freedmen, and Abandoned Lands. The **Freedmen's Bureau**, as it was called, distributed food and clothing to destitute southerners and eased the transition of Black people from enslaved to free persons. Congress also authorized the agency to divide abandoned and confiscated land into forty-acre plots, to rent them to freedmen, and eventually to sell them "with such title as the United States can convey." By June 1865, the Bureau had situated nearly ten thousand Black families on one-half million acres.

Freedmen's Bureau
Government organization created in March 1865 to distribute food and clothing to destitute southerners and to ease the transition of enslaved to free persons.

Despite the flurry of activity, wartime reconstruction failed to produce agreement about whether the president or Congress had the authority to devise policy or what proper policy should be.

What did formerly enslaved people want from freedom?

News of emancipation did not reach all parts of the Confederacy at the same time. Indeed, the news did not reach Texas until June 19, more than two months after the war ended. (African Americans have celebrated June 19 as "Juneteenth" ever since, but in 2021, Juneteenth became a national holiday commemorating the end of American slavery.) No matter when Black southerners heard the news, they never had any doubt about what they wanted from freedom. They had only to contemplate what they had been denied when enslaved. **(See "Analyzing Historical Evidence: The Meaning of Freedom" on page 456.)** Slaves had to remain on their plantations; freedom allowed Black people to see what was on the other side of the hill. Slaves had to be at work in the fields by dawn; freedom permitted Blacks to sleep through a sunrise. Freedmen also tested the etiquette of racial subordination. "Lizzie's maid passed me today when I was coming from church *without speaking to me*," huffed one plantation mistress.

To white people, emancipation looked like pure anarchy. Black people, they claimed, had reverted to their natural condition: lazy, irresponsible, and wild. Actually, formerly enslaved people were experimenting with long-awaited freedom—freedom to control their own time, labor, language, and behavior. Such actions were considered presumptuous by white planters, who responded angrily. Soon, though, most Black people were back at work in white people's kitchens and fields.

But they continued to dream of land and independence. "The way we can best take care of ourselves is to have land," one former slave declared in 1865, "and turn it and till it by our own labor." A South Carolina freedman agreed, declaring that formerly enslaved people wanted land—"not a Master or owner[,] Neither a driver with his Whip."

Slavery had deliberately kept Black people illiterate, and freedmen emerged from bondage eager to learn to read and write. "I wishes the Childern all in School," one Black military veteran asserted. "It is beter for them then [than] to be their Surveing a mistes [mistress]." Freedmen looked on schools as "first proof of their *independence*."

The restoration of broken families was another persistent Black aspiration. Thousands of freedmen took to the roads in 1865 to look for kin who had been sold or to free those who were being held illegally as slaves. A Black soldier from Missouri

ANALYZING HISTORICAL EVIDENCE

The Meaning of Freedom

A lthough the Emancipation Proclamation itself did not free any enslaved men, women, or children, it transformed the character of the war. Black people resolutely focused on the possibilities of freedom even before the war ended.

DOCUMENT 1
Letter from John Q. A. Dennis to Edwin M. Stanton, July 26, 1864

John Q. A. Dennis, formerly enslaved in Maryland, wrote to ask Secretary of War Edwin M. Stanton for help in reuniting his family.

Boston. Dear Sir I am Glad that I have the Honour to Write you a few line I have been in troble for about four yars my Dear wife was taken from me Nov 19th 1859 and left me with three Children and I being a Slave At the time Could Not do Anny thing for the poor little Children for my master it was took me Carry me some forty mile from them So I Could Not do for them and the man that they live with half feed them and half Cloth them & beat them like dogs & when I was admitted to go to see them it use to brake my heart & Now I say again I am Glad to have the honour to write to you to see if you Can Do Anny thing for me or for my poor little Children I was keap in Slavy untell last Novr 1863. then the Good lord sent the Cornel borne [federal colonel William Birney?] Down their in Marland in worsester Co So as I have been recently freed I have but letle to live on but I am Strieving Dear Sir but what I went too know of you Sir is it possible for me to go & take my Children from those men that keep them in Savery if it is possible will you please give me a permit from your hand then I think they would let them go. . . . I want get the little Children out of Slavery. . . .

Source: *Freedom: A Documentary History of Emancipation, 1861–1867,* ser. 1, vol. 1, *The Destruction of Slavery,* edited by Ira Berlin, Joseph P. Reidy, and Leslie S. Rowland, 386. Copyright © 1985.

DOCUMENT 2
Report from the Reverend A. B. Randall, February 28, 1865

A. B. Randall, the white chaplain of a Black regiment stationed in Little Rock, Arkansas, affirmed the importance of legal marriage to freed slaves and emphasized their conviction that emancipation was only the first step toward full freedom.

Weddings, just now, are very popular, and abundant among the Colored People. They have just learned, of the Special Order No. 15. of Gen Thomas [Adjutant General Lorenzo Thomas] by which, they may not only be lawfully married, but have their Marriage Certificates, Recorded; in a book furnished by the Government. . . . I have married, during the month, at this Post; Twenty five couples; mostly, those, who have families; & have been living together for years. . . . The Colord People here, generally consider, this war not only; their exodus, from bondage; but the road, to Responsibility; Competency; and an honorable Citizenship—God grant that their hopes and expectations may be fully realized.

Source: *Freedom: A Documentary History of Emancipation, 1861–1867,* ser. 2, vol. 1, *The Black Military Experience,* edited by Ira Berlin, Joseph P. Reidy, and Leslie S. Rowland, 712. Copyright © 1982.

DOCUMENT 3
Petition "to the Union Convention of Tennessee Assembled in the Capitol at Nashville," January 9, 1865

In January 1865, Black Tennesseans petitioned a convention of white Unionists debating the reorganization of state government.

We the undersigned petitioners, American citizens of African descent, natives and residents of Tennessee, and devoted friends of the great National cause, do most respectfully ask a patient hearing of your honorable body in regard to matters deeply affecting the future condition of our unfortunate and long suffering race. . . .

In the contest between the nation and slavery, our unfortunate people have sided, by instinct, with the former. . . . We will work, pray, live, and, if need be, die for the Union, as cheerfully as ever a white patriot died for his country. The color of our skin does not lessen in the least degree, our love either for God or for the land of our birth. . . .

We know the burdens of citizenship, and are ready to bear them. We know the duties of the good citizen, and are ready to perform them cheerfully, and would ask to be put in a position in which we can discharge them more effectually. . . .

This is a democracy—a government of the people. It should aim to make every man, without regard to the color of his skin, the amount of his wealth, or the character of his religious faith, feel personally interested in its welfare. Every man who lives under the Government should feel that it is his property, his treasure, the bulwark and defence of himself and his family. . . .

This is not a Democratic Government if a numerous, law-abiding, industrious, and useful class of citizens, born and bred on the soil, are to be treated as aliens and enemies, as an inferior degraded class, who must have no voice in the Government which they support, protect and defend, with all their heart, soul, mind, and body, both in peace and war. . . .

The possibility that the negro suffrage proposition may shock popular prejudice at first sight, is not a conclusive argument against its wisdom and policy.

No proposition ever met with more furious or general opposition than the one to enlist colored soldiers in the United States army. The opponents of the measure exclaimed on all hands that the negro was a coward; that he would not fight; that one white man, with a whip in his hand could put to flight a regiment of them. . . . Yet the colored man has fought so well. . . .

The Government has asked the colored man to fight for its preservation and gladly has he done it. It can afford to trust him with a vote as safely as it trusted him with a bayonet.

Source: *Freedom: A Documentary History of Emancipation, 1861–1867,* ser. 2, vol. 1, *The Black Military Experience,* edited by Ira Berlin, Joseph P. Reidy, and Leslie S. Rowland, 811–16. Copyright © 1982.

Questions for Analysis

ANALYZE THE EVIDENCE: What does John Q. A. Dennis's interpretation of his responsibility as a father say about slavery's ability to destroy slave families?

CONSIDER THE CONTEXT: Why was legal marriage so important to formerly enslaved men and women?

RECOGNIZE VIEWPOINTS: According to petitioners to the Union Convention of Tennessee, why was the experience of Black soldiers relevant to Black voting rights?

▶ **Harry Stephens and Family, 1866** The seven members of the Stephens family sit proudly for a photograph just after the Civil War ended. Most Black families were not as fortunate as these Virginians. Separated by slavery or war, formerly enslaved people desperately sought news of missing family members through newspaper advertisements and taking to the roads. Heritage Images/Getty Images.

wrote his daughters that he was coming for them. "I will have you if it cost me my life," he declared. "Your Miss Kitty said that I tried to steal you," he told them. "But I'll let her know that god never intended for a man to steal his own flesh and blood." And he swore that "if she meets me with ten thousand soldiers, she [will] meet her enemy."

Independent worship was another dream. Black southerners greeted freedom with a mass exodus from white churches, where they had been required to worship when enslaved. Some joined the newly established southern branches of all-Black northern churches, such as the African Methodist Episcopal Church. Others formed Black versions of the major southern denominations, Baptists and Methodists.

REVIEW

To what extent did Lincoln's wartime plan for reconstruction reflect the concerns of newly freed enslaved people?

What did early reconstruction reveal about the North's and South's intentions?

Abraham Lincoln died on April 15, 1865, just hours after John Wilkes Booth shot him at a Washington, D.C., theater. Vice President Andrew Johnson of Tennessee became president. Congress had adjourned in March and would not reconvene until December. Throughout the summer and fall, Johnson drew up and executed a plan of reconstruction without congressional advice.

Congress returned to the capital in December to find that, as far as the new president and former Confederates were concerned, reconstruction was over. Most Republicans, however, thought Johnson's plan made far too few demands of ex-rebels and made a mockery of the sacrifice of Union soldiers. They claimed that Johnson's leniency had encouraged the rebirth of the Old South, that he had achieved political reunification at the cost of Black freedom. Republicans in Congress then proceeded to dismantle Johnson's program and substitute a program of their own.

What was Johnson's program of reconciliation?

Born in 1808 in Raleigh, North Carolina, Andrew Johnson was the son of illiterate parents. Self-educated and ambitious, Johnson moved to Tennessee, where he worked as a tailor, accumulated a fortune in land and five slaves, and built a career in politics championing the South's common white people and assailing its planter class. The only senator from a Confederate state to remain loyal to the Union, Johnson held planters responsible for secession. Less than two weeks before he became president, he announced what he would do to planters if he ever had the chance: "I would arrest them—I would try them—I would convict them and I would hang them."

A Democrat all his life, Johnson occupied the White House only because the Republican Party in 1864 had needed a vice presidential candidate who would appeal to Union-supporting Democrats. Johnson vigorously defended states' rights (but not secession) and opposed Republican efforts to expand the power of the federal government. A steadfast supporter of slavery, Johnson had owned slaves until 1862, when Tennessee rebels, angry at his Unionism, confiscated them. When he grudgingly accepted emancipation, it was more because he hated planters than sympathized with slaves. "Damn the negroes," he said. "I am fighting those traitorous aristocrats, their masters." The new president harbored unshakable racist convictions. Africans, Johnson said, were "inferior to the white man in point of intellect—better calculated in physical structure to undergo drudgery and hardship."

Like Lincoln, Johnson stressed the rapid restoration of civil government in the South. Like Lincoln, he promised to pardon most, but not all, ex-rebels. Johnson recognized the state governments created by Lincoln but set out his own requirements for restoring the other rebel states to the Union. All that the citizens of a state had to do was to renounce the right of secession, repudiate the debts of the Confederacy, and ratify the Thirteenth Amendment abolishing slavery, which became part of the Constitution in December 1865.

Johnson also returned all confiscated and abandoned land to pardoned ex-Confederates, even if it was in the hands of freedmen. Reformers were shocked. Instead of punishing planters as he had promised, Johnson canceled the promising beginnings made by General Sherman and the Freedmen's Bureau to settle Black farmers on land of their own.

How did white southerners react to Johnson's reconciliation efforts?

In the summer of 1865, white southerners drew up the new state constitutions Johnson's plan of reconstruction required. But they refused to accept even the president's mild requirements. Refusing to renounce secession, the South Carolina and Georgia conventions merely "repudiated" their secession ordinances, preserving in principle their right to secede in the future. South Carolina and Mississippi refused to disown their Confederate war debts. Mississippi rejected the Thirteenth Amendment, and Alabama rejected it in part. Despite this defiance, Johnson did nothing. White southerners began to think that by standing up for themselves they could shape the terms of reconstruction.

New state governments across the South adopted a series of laws known as **black codes**, which denied Black people basic rights. The codes sought to keep formerly enslaved people subordinate to whites by subjecting them to every sort of discrimination. Several states made it illegal for Blacks to own a gun. Mississippi made insulting gestures and language by Black people a criminal offense. The codes barred Black men from jury duty. Not a single southern state granted any Black man the right to vote.

At the core of the black codes, however, lay the matter of labor. Legislators sought to hustle freedmen back to the plantations. South Carolina attempted to limit freedmen and women to either farmwork or domestic service by requiring them to pay annual taxes of $10 to $100 to work in any other occupation. Mississippi declared that Black people who did not possess written evidence of employment could be declared vagrants and be subject to involuntary plantation labor. Under so-called apprenticeship laws, courts bound thousands of Black children—orphans and others whose parents were deemed unable to support them—to work for planter "guardians." According to the black codes, emancipation did not confer the right to exit plantations.

black codes
Laws passed by state governments in the South in 1865 and 1866 that sought to keep formerly enslaved people subordinate to white people. At the core of the black codes lay the desire to force freedmen back to the plantations.

▶ **The Black Codes** Titled *Selling a Freeman to Pay His Fine at Monticello, Florida*, this 1867 drawing from a northern magazine equates black codes with the reinstitution of slavery. The laws stopped short of reenslavement but sharply restricted Black people's freedom. In southern states, certain acts, such as breaking a labor contract, were made criminal offenses, the penalty for which could be involuntary plantation labor for a year. GRANGER–Historical Picture Archive.

Johnson refused to intervene. A staunch defender of states' rights, he believed that citizens of every state should be free to write their own constitutions and laws. Furthermore, he was as eager as other white southerners to restore white supremacy. "White men alone must manage the South," he declared.

Johnson also recognized that his do-nothing response offered him political advantage. A conservative Tennessee Democrat at the head of a northern Republican Party, he had begun to look southward for political allies. Despite tough talk about punishing traitors, he personally pardoned fourteen thousand wealthy or high-ranking ex-Confederates. By pardoning powerful white men, by accepting state governments even when they failed to satisfy his minimal demands, and by acquiescing to the black codes, he won useful southern friends.

In the fall elections of 1865, white southerners dramatically expressed their mood. To represent them in Congress, they chose former Confederates. Of the eighty senators and representatives they sent to Washington, fifteen had served in the Confederate army, ten of them as generals. Another sixteen had served in civil and judicial posts in the Confederacy. Nine others had served in the Confederate Congress. One—Alexander Stephens—had been vice president of the Confederacy. As one Georgian remarked, "It looked as though Richmond had moved to Washington."

How did Republicans respond to the South's black codes?

White southerners had blundered monumentally. They had assumed that what Andrew Johnson was willing to accept, northern Republicans would accept as well. But southern resistance compelled even moderates to conclude that ex-rebels were a "generation of vipers," still disloyal and dangerous. The black codes became a symbol of southern intentions to "restore all of slavery but its name." "We tell the white men of Mississippi," the *Chicago Tribune* roared, "that the men of the North will convert the State of Mississippi into a frog pond before they will allow such laws to disgrace one foot of the soil in which the bones of our soldiers sleep and over which the flag of freedom waves."

The moderate majority of the Republican Party wanted only assurance that slavery and treason were dead. They did not champion Black equality, the confiscation of plantations, or Black voting, as did the Radical minority within the party. But southern resistance to even modest Republicans goals had succeeded in forging unity (at least temporarily) among Republican factions. In December 1865, Republicans refused to seat the southerners elected in the fall elections. Rather than accept Johnson's claim that the "work of restoration" was done, Congress challenged Johnson's reconstruction.

Republican senator Lyman Trumbull declared that the president's policy meant that a formerly enslaved man would "be tyrannized over, abused, and virtually reenslaved without some legislation by the nation for his protection." Early in 1866, the moderates produced two bills that strengthened the federal shield. The Freedmen's Bureau bill prolonged the life of the agency established by the previous Congress. Arguing that the Constitution never contemplated a "system for the support of indigent persons," President Andrew Johnson vetoed the bill. Congress failed by a narrow margin to override the president's veto.

Civil Rights Act of 1866
Legislation passed by Congress in 1866 that nullified the black codes and affirmed that Black Americans should have equal benefit of the law. President Andrew Johnson vetoed this expansion of Black rights and federal authority, but Congress later overrode his veto.

The moderates designed their second measure, the **Civil Rights Act of 1866**, to nullify the black codes by affirming the rights of Black people to "full and equal benefit of all laws and proceedings for the security of person and property as is enjoyed by white citizens." The act boldly required the end of racial discrimination in state laws and represented an extraordinary expansion of Black rights and federal authority. The president argued that the civil rights bill amounted to "unconstitutional invasion of states' rights" and vetoed it. In essence, he denied that the federal government had the authority to protect the civil rights of Black Americans.

In April 1866, an outraged Republican Party again pushed the civil rights bill through Congress and overrode the presidential veto. In July, it passed another Freedmen's Bureau bill and overrode Johnson's veto. For the first time in American history, Congress had overturned presidential vetoes of major legislation. As a worried South Carolinian observed, Johnson's vetoes would probably touch off "a fight this fall such as has never been seen."

REVIEW

When the southern states passed the black codes, how did the U.S. Congress respond?

How radical was congressional reconstruction?

By the summer of 1866, President Andrew Johnson and Congress had dropped their gloves and stood toe-to-toe in a bare-knuckle contest unprecedented in American history. Johnson made it clear that he would not budge on either executive authority or policy. Moderate Republicans responded by amending the Constitution. But Johnson's and white southerners' stubbornness pushed Republican moderates ever closer to the Radicals and to acceptance of additional federal intervention in the South. To end presidential interference, Congress voted to impeach the president for the first time in the nation's history. Soon after, Congress debated whether to make voting rights color-blind, while women championed making voting sex-blind as well.

What did Republicans hope to achieve with the passage of the Fourteenth Amendment?

In June 1866, Congress passed the Fourteenth Amendment to the Constitution, and two years later, the states ratified it. President Johnson's continued commitment to bringing former Confederate states back into the Union with few changes in their government or politics had convinced anxious Republicans that something fundamental was required to permanently transform the South. The most important provisions of this complex amendment made all native-born or naturalized persons American citizens and prohibited states from abridging the "privileges and immunities" of citizens, depriving them of "life, liberty, or property without due process of law," and denying them "equal protection of the laws." By making Black people national citizens, the amendment provided a national guarantee of equality before the law. In essence, it protected Blacks against violation by southern state governments.

The **Fourteenth Amendment** also dealt with voting rights. It gave Congress the right to reduce the congressional representation of states that withheld suffrage from some of its adult male population. In other words, white southerners could either allow Black men to vote or see their representation in Washington slashed. Whatever happened, Republicans stood to benefit. If southern whites granted voting rights to freedmen, Republicans would gain valuable Black votes. If whites refused, the number of southern Democrats in Congress would plunge.

The Fourteenth Amendment's suffrage provisions ignored the small band of women who had emerged from the war demanding "the ballot for the two disenfranchised classes, negroes and women." Founding the American Equal Rights Association in 1866, Susan B. Anthony and Elizabeth Cady Stanton lobbied for "a government by the people, and the whole people; for the people and the whole people." They felt betrayed when their old antislavery allies refused to work for woman suffrage. "It was the Negro's hour," Frederick Douglass explained. Senator Charles Sumner suggested that woman suffrage could be "the great question of the future."

Tennessee approved the Fourteenth Amendment in July, and Congress promptly welcomed the state's representatives and senators back. Had President Johnson counseled other southern states to ratify the amendment, they might have listened. Instead, Johnson advised southerners to reject the Fourteenth Amendment and to rely on him to trounce the Republicans in the fall congressional elections.

Johnson had decided to make the Fourteenth Amendment the overriding issue of the 1866 elections and to gather its white opponents into a new conservative party, the National Union Party. The president's strategy suffered a setback when white people in several southern cities went on rampages against Black residents. Mobs killed thirty-four Black people in New Orleans and forty-six in Memphis. The slaughter shocked northerners and renewed skepticism about Johnson's claim that white southerners could be trusted.

Fourteenth Amendment Constitutional amendment passed in 1866 that made all native-born or naturalized persons U.S. citizens and prohibited states from abridging the rights of national citizens. The amendment hoped to provide a guarantee of equality before the law for Black citizens.

◀ **Memphis Riots, May 1866** On May 1, 1866, two carriages, one driven by a white man and the other by a Black man, collided on a busy street in Memphis, Tennessee. This minor incident led to three days of bloody racial violence in which dozens of Black and two white people died. South Memphis, pictured in this lithograph from *Harper's Weekly*, was a shantytown where the families of Black soldiers stationed at nearby Fort Pickering lived. The army commander refused to send troops to protect soldiers' families and property, and white mobs ran wild. GRANGER–Historical Picture Archive.

The 1866 elections resulted in an overwhelming Republican victory. Johnson had bet that northerners would not support federal protection of Black rights and that a racist backlash would punish the Republican Party. But the war was still fresh in northern minds, and as one Republican explained, southern whites "with all their intelligence were traitors, the Blacks with all their ignorance were loyal."

Why did Congress pass the Military Reconstruction Act?

When Johnson continued to urge southerners to reject the Fourteenth Amendment, every southern state except Tennessee voted it down. "The last one of the sinful ten," thundered Representative James A. Garfield of Ohio, "has flung back into our teeth the magnanimous offer of a generous nation." After the South rejected the moderates' program, the Radicals seized the initiative.

Each act of defiance by white southerners had boosted the standing of the Radicals within the Republican Party. Except for freedmen themselves, no one did more to make freedom the "mighty moral question of the age." Radicals such as Massachusetts senator Charles Sumner and Pennsylvania representative Thaddeus Stevens united in demanding civil and political equality for Black Americans. Southern states were "like clay in the hands of the potter," Stevens declared in January 1867, and he called on Congress to begin reconstruction all over again.

In March 1867, Congress overturned the Johnson state governments and initiated military rule of the South. The **Military Reconstruction Act** (and three subsequent acts) divided the ten unreconstructed Confederate states into five military districts. Congress placed a Union general in charge of each district and instructed him to "suppress insurrection, disorder, and violence" and to begin political reform. After the military had completed voter registration, which would include Black men, voters in each state would elect delegates to conventions that would draw up new state constitutions. Each constitution would guarantee Black suffrage. When the voters of each state had approved the constitution and the state legislature had ratified the Fourteenth Amendment, Congress could seat the state's senators and representatives, and political reunification would be completed.

Radicals proclaimed the provision for Black suffrage "a prodigious triumph," for it extended far beyond the limited voting provisions of the Fourteenth Amendment. When combined with the disfranchisement of thousands of ex-rebels, it promised to cripple any neo-Confederate resurgence and guarantee Republican state governments in the South.

Despite its bold suffrage provision, the Military Reconstruction Act of 1867 disappointed those who also advocated the confiscation of southern plantations and their redistribution to formerly enslaved people. Thaddeus Stevens agreed with the freedman who said, "Give us our own land and we take care of ourselves, but without land, the old masters can hire us or starve us, as they please." But most Republicans believed they had provided Black Americans with all they needed: equal legal rights and the ballot. Besides, confiscation was too radical, even for some Radicals. Taking private property, declared the *New York Times*, "strikes at the root of all property rights in both sections. It concerns Massachusetts quite as much as Mississippi." If Black people were to get land, they would have to gain it themselves.

Reconstruction Military Districts, 1867

Military Reconstruction Act
Congressional act of March 1867 that initiated military rule of the South. Congressional reconstruction divided the ten unreconstructed Confederate states into five military districts, each under the direction of a Union general. It also established the procedure by which unreconstructed states could reenter the Union.

Declaring that he would rather sever his right arm than sign such a formula for "anarchy and chaos," Andrew Johnson vetoed the Military Reconstruction Act, but Congress overrode his veto. With the passage of the Reconstruction Acts of 1867, congressional reconstruction was virtually completed. Congress left white people owning most of the South's land but, in a departure that justified the term *radical reconstruction*, had given Black men the ballot.

Why was President Johnson impeached?

Despite his defeats, Andrew Johnson had no intention of yielding control of reconstruction. In a dozen ways, he sabotaged Congress's will and encouraged white southerners to resist. He issued a flood of pardons, waged war against the Freedmen's Bureau, and replaced Union generals eager to enforce Congress's Reconstruction Acts with conservative officers eager to block them. Johnson claimed that he was merely defending the "violated Constitution." At bottom, however, the president acted to protect southern white people from what he considered the horrors of "Negro domination."

Radicals argued that Johnson's abuse of his power and his failure to fulfill constitutional obligations to enforce the law were impeachable offenses. According to the Constitution, the House of Representatives can impeach and the Senate can try any federal official for "treason, bribery, or other high crimes and misdemeanors." But moderates interpreted the Constitution to mean violation of criminal statutes. As long as Johnson refrained from breaking the law, impeachment (the process of bringing formal charges of wrongdoing against the president or another federal official) remained stalled.

In August 1867, Johnson suspended Secretary of War Edwin M. Stanton from office. As required by the Tenure of Office Act, which demanded the approval of the Senate for the removal of any government official who had been appointed with Senate approval, the president requested the Senate to consent to Stanton's dismissal. When the Senate declined, Johnson removed Stanton anyway. "Is the President crazy, or only drunk?" asked a dumbfounded Republican moderate. "I'm afraid his doings will make us all favor impeachment."

News of Johnson's open defiance of the law convinced every Republican in the House to vote for a resolution impeaching the president. Supreme Court chief justice Salmon Chase presided over the Senate trial, which lasted from March until May 1868. When the vote came, thirty-five senators voted guilty and nineteen not guilty. Impeachment fell one vote short of the two-thirds needed to convict.

After his trial, Johnson called a truce, and for the remaining ten months of his term, congressional reconstruction proceeded unhindered by presidential interference. Without interference from Johnson, Congress revisited the suffrage issue.

Why did the Fifteenth Amendment snub women?

In February 1869, Republicans passed the **Fifteenth Amendment** to the Constitution, which prohibited states from depriving any citizen of the right to vote because of "race, color, or previous condition of servitude." The Reconstruction Acts of 1867 already required Black suffrage in the South; the Fifteenth Amendment extended Black voting nationwide.

Fifteenth Amendment
Constitutional amendment passed in February 1869 prohibiting states from depriving any citizen of the right to vote because of "race, color, or previous condition of servitude." It extended Black suffrage nationwide.

Some Republicans, however, found the final wording of the Fifteenth Amendment "lame and halting." Rather than guaranteeing the right to vote, the amendment merely prohibited exclusion on grounds of race. The distinction would prove to be significant. In time, white southerners would devise tests of literacy and property and other apparently nonracial measures that would effectively disfranchise Black people yet not technically violate the Fifteenth Amendment. But an amendment that guaranteed the right to vote courted defeat outside the South. Facing rising antiforeign sentiment—against the Chinese in California and European immigrants in the Northeast—states held tight to suffrage requirements. In March 1870, after three-fourths of the states had ratified it, the Fifteenth Amendment became part of the Constitution.

Woman suffrage advocates, however, condemned the Fifteenth Amendment's failure to extend voting rights to white women. Elizabeth Cady Stanton and Susan B. Anthony rejected the Republicans' "negro first" strategy and pointed out that women remained "the only class of citizens wholly unrepresented in the government." Activist women concluded that woman "must not put her trust in man." The Fifteenth Amendment severed the early feminist movement from its abolitionist roots. Over the next several decades, feminists established an independent suffrage crusade that drew millions of women into political life.

After the Fifteen Amendment, Republicans concluded that Black suffrage was the "last great point that remained to be settled of the issues of the war" and promptly scratched the "Negro question" from the agenda of national politics. Even that steadfast crusader for equality Wendell Phillips reasoned that the Black man now held "sufficient shield in his own hands. . . . Whatever he suffers will be largely now, and in future, his own fault." Northerners had no idea of the violent struggles that lay ahead in the South.

REVIEW

Why did Congress impeach President Andrew Johnson?

How successful were the South's Republican governments?

Northerners believed they had discharged their responsibilities with the Reconstruction Acts and the amendments to the Constitution, but southerners knew that the battle had just begun. Black suffrage had destroyed traditional southern politics and established the foundation for the rise of the Republican Party. Gathering outsiders and outcasts, southern Republicans won elections, wrote new state constitutions, and formed new state governments.

Challenging the established class for political control was dangerous business. Equally dangerous were the confrontations that took place on southern farms and plantations, where Black people sought to give fuller meaning to their newly won legal and political equality. Former slaveholders had their own ideas about the labor system that should replace slavery, and freedom remained contested territory. Southerners fought pitched battles with one another to determine the contours of their new world.

Who were the southern Republicans?

Black people made up the majority of southern Republicans. After gaining voting rights in 1867, nearly all eligible Black men registered to vote as Republicans, grateful to the party that had freed them and granted them the franchise. "It is the hardest thing in the world to keep a negro away from the polls," observed a critical Alabama white man. Southern Black people did not all have identical political priorities, but they united in their desire for education and equal treatment before the law.

Northern whites who made the South their home after the war were a second element of the South's Republican Party. Most white southerners called them **carpetbaggers**, opportunists who stuffed all their belongings in a single carpet-sided suitcase and headed south to "fatten on our misfortunes." But most northerners who moved south were young men who looked upon the South as they did the West—as a promising place to make a living. Northerners in the southern Republican Party supported programs that encouraged vigorous economic development along the lines of the northern free-labor model.

Southern whites made up the third element of the South's Republican Party. Approximately one out of four white southerners voted Republican. The other three condemned the one who did as a traitor to his region and his race and called him a **scalawag**, a term for runty horses and low-down, good-for-nothing rascals. Yeoman farmers accounted for the majority of southern white Republicans. Some were Unionists who emerged from the war with bitter memories of Confederate persecution. Others were small farmers who wanted to end state governments' favoritism toward plantation owners. Yeomen supported initiatives for public schools and for expanding economic opportunity in the South.

The South's Republican Party, then, was made up of freedmen, Yankees, and yeomen—an improbable coalition. The mix of races, regions, and classes inevitably meant friction as each group maneuvered to define the party. Still, Reconstruction represented an extraordinary moment in American politics: Blacks and whites joined together in the Republican Party to pursue political change. Formally, only men participated in politics—casting ballots and holding offices—but white and Black women also played a part in the political struggle by joining in parades and rallies, attending stump speeches, and even campaigning.

Most whites in the South condemned southern Republicans as illegitimate and felt justified in doing whatever they could to stamp them out. Violence against Blacks—the "white terror"—took brutal institutional shape in 1866 with the formation in Tennessee of the **Ku Klux Klan**, a group of Confederate veterans that quickly developed into a paramilitary organization supporting Democrats. The Klan went on a rampage of whipping, hanging, shooting, burning, and throat-cutting Black southerners and the whites who allied with them to defeat Republicans and restore white supremacy.

Rapid demobilization of the Union army after the war left only a handful of troops to patrol the entire South. Without effective military protection, southern Republicans had to take care of themselves.

carpetbaggers
Southerners' pejorative term for northern migrants who sought opportunity in the South after the Civil War. Northern migrants formed an important part of the southern Republican Party.

scalawag
A derogatory term that southerners applied to southern white Republicans, who were seen as traitors to the South. Most were yeoman farmers.

Ku Klux Klan
A social club of Confederate veterans that quickly developed into a paramilitary organization supporting Democrats. With too few Union troops in the South to control the region, the Klan went on a rampage of violence to defeat Republicans and restore white supremacy.

What did southern Republican governments do?

In the fall of 1867, southern states held elections for delegates to state constitutional conventions, as required by the Reconstruction Acts. About 40 percent of the white electorate stayed home because they had been disfranchised or because they had decided to boycott politics. Republicans won three-fourths of the seats. About 15 percent of the Republican delegates to the conventions were northerners who had moved south, 25 percent were Black southerners, and 60 percent were white southerners. As a British visitor observed, the delegate elections reflected "the mighty revolution that had taken place in America."

The conventions brought together serious, purposeful men who hammered out the legal framework for a new society. The reconstruction constitutions introduced two broad categories of changes in the South: those that reduced aristocratic privilege and increased democratic equality and those that expanded the state's responsibility for the general welfare. In the first category, the constitutions adopted universal male suffrage, abolished property qualifications for holding office, and made more offices elective and fewer appointed. In the second category, they enacted prison reform; made the state responsible for caring for orphans, those with mental illness, and deaf individuals; and exempted debtors' homes from seizure.

To Democrats, these progressive constitutions looked like wild revolution. They ignored the fact that no constitution confiscated and redistributed land, as virtually every formerly enslaved person wished, or disfranchised ex-rebels whole-sale, as most southern Unionists advocated. Yet Democrats were convinced that the new constitutions initiated "Negro domination." In fact, although 80 percent of Republican voters were Black men, only 6 percent of southerners in Congress during Reconstruction were Black (**Figure 16.1**). The sixteen Black men in Congress included exceptional men, such as Representative James T. Rapier of Alabama. No state legislature experienced "Negro rule," despite Black majorities in the populations of some states.

Southern voters ratified the new state constitutions and swept Republicans into power. When the former Confederate states ratified the Fourteenth Amendment, Congress readmitted them. Southern Republicans then turned to a staggering array of problems at home. Wartime destruction littered the landscape. Making matters worse, racial harassment and reactionary violence dogged southerners who sought reform. Democrats mocked Black officeholders as ignorant field hands who had only "agricultural degrees" and "brick yard diplomas," but in reality Republicans began a serious effort to rebuild and reform the region.

Activity focused on three areas—education, civil rights, and economic development. Every state inaugurated a system of public education. Before the Civil War, white people had deliberately kept enslaved people illiterate, and planter-dominated governments rarely spent tax money to educate the children of yeomen. By 1875, half of Mississippi's and South Carolina's eligible children were attending school. Although schools were underfunded, literacy

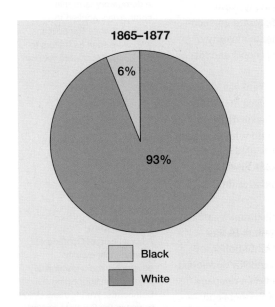

FIGURE 16.1 ▲ Southern Congressional Delegations, 1865–1877 The statistics contradict the myth of Black domination of congressional representation during Reconstruction.

rates rose sharply. Public schools were racially segregated, but education remained for many Black people a deeply satisfying benefit of freedom and Republican rule.

State legislatures also attacked racial discrimination and defended civil rights. Republicans resisted efforts to segregate Blacks from whites, especially in public transportation. Mississippi levied fines and jail terms for owners of railroads and steamboats that pushed Black passengers into "smoking cars" or to lower decks. But passing color-blind laws was one thing; enforcing them was another. A Mississippian complained: "Education amounts to nothing, good behavior counts for nothing, even money cannot buy for a colored man or woman decent treatment and the comforts that white people claim and can obtain." Despite the laws, segregation—later called Jim Crow—developed at white insistence. Determined to underscore the social inferiority of Black people, white southerners saw to it that separation by race became a feature of southern life long before the end of the Reconstruction era.

Republican governments also launched ambitious programs of economic development. They envisioned a South of diversified agriculture, roaring factories, and booming towns. State legislatures chartered scores of banks and industrial companies, appropriated funds to fix ruined levees and drain swamps, and went on a railroad-building binge. These efforts fell far short of solving the South's economic troubles, however. Republican spending to stimulate economic growth meant rising taxes and enormous debt that siphoned funds from schools and other programs.

The southern Republicans' record was mixed. To their credit, the biracial party adopted an ambitious agenda to change the South. But money was scarce, the Democrats continued their vicious harassment, and differences threatened the Republican Party from within. Serious corruption also infected Republican governments. Nonetheless, the Republican Party made headway in its efforts to purge the South of aristocratic privilege and racist oppression. Black children went to school and Black men voted. Republican governments had less success in overthrowing the long-established white oppression of Black farm laborers in the rural South.

How did plantations and labor systems change?

Formerly enslaved men and women who refused to return to slave labor conditions and ex-masters who wanted to reinstitute old oppressions clashed repeatedly. Except for having to pay subsistence wages, planters had not been required to offer many concessions to emancipation. Moreover, they continued to believe that Black laborers would not work without coercion. A Tennessee man declared two years after the war ended that Black people were "a trifling set of lazy devils who will never make a living without Masters."

Some planters were so discouraged about the prospect of farming with free Black labor that they fled the South. Their determination "to get away from the free Negro" carried them around the world but especially to Brazil, which seemed to offer the best chance of resurrecting antebellum southern society because slavery was still legal there. Firsthand experience in Brazil shocked most southern migrants, however. They found "decay" everywhere, race relations that challenged their notions of white supremacy, and most important, abolition on the horizon. By 1870, most migrating planters were back home, where they joined those who had stayed in their efforts to restore as much of slavery as they could get away with.

▶ **Students at a Freedmen's School in Virginia, ca. 1870s**   "The people are hungry and thirsty after knowledge," a formerly enslaved person observed immediately after the Civil War. Black leader Booker T. Washington remembered "a whole race trying to go to school." Students at this Virginia school stand in front of their log-cabin classroom, reading books. For people long forbidden to learn to read and write, literacy symbolized freedom.   Photo12/UIG/Getty Images.

Formerly enslaved people resisted every effort to turn back the clock. They argued that if any class could be described as "lazy," it was the planters, who, as one former slave noted, "lived in idleness all their lives on stolen labor." Freedmen believed that land of their own would anchor their economic independence and end planters' interference in their personal lives. They could then, for example, make their own decisions about whether women and children would labor in the fields. Indeed, within months after the war, perhaps one-third of Black women abandoned field labor to work on chores in their own cabins just as poor white women did. Black women also negotiated with wealthy white women about domestic work. Hundreds of thousands of Black children enrolled in school. But without their own land, former slaves had little choice but to work on plantations.

Although forced to return to the planters' fields, they resisted efforts to restore slavelike conditions. Instead of working for wages, a South Carolinian observed, "the negroes all seem disposed to rent land," which increased their independence from white planters but had its own drawbacks. Out of this tug-of-war between white landlords and Black laborers emerged a new system of southern agriculture.

sharecropping
Labor system that emerged in the South during Reconstruction. Under this system, planters divided their plantations into small farms that freedmen rented, paying with a share of each year's crop. Sharecropping gave Black farmers some freedom, but they remained dependent on white landlords and country merchants.

Sharecropping was a compromise that offered something to both former slaveholders and enslaved people but satisfied neither. Under the new system, planters divided their cotton plantations into small farms that freedmen rented, paying with a share of each year's crop, usually half. Sharecropping gave Black workers more freedom than the system of wages and labor gangs and released them from day-to-day supervision by white planters. Black families abandoned the old slave quarters and built separate cabins for themselves on the land they rented (**Map 16.1**). Still, most Black families remained dependent on white landlords, who had the power to evict them at the end of each growing season. For planters, sharecropping offered a labor force to resume agricultural production on their land, but it did not allow them to restore the old slave plantation.

MAP ACTIVITY

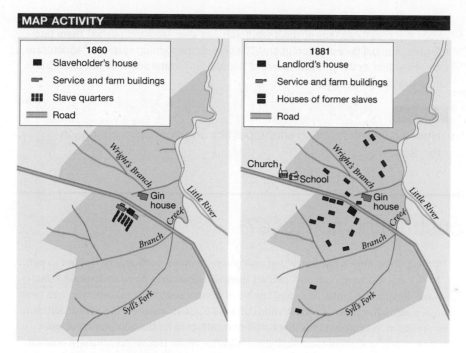

MAP 16.1 ▲ A Southern Plantation in 1860 and 1881 These maps of the Barrow cotton plantation in Georgia illustrate some of the ways in which formerly enslaved men and women expressed their freedom. Freedmen and freedwomen deserted the clustered living quarters behind the slaveholder's house, scattered over the plantation, built family cabins, and farmed rented land. The freedmen and women also worked together to build a school and a church.

READING THE MAP: Compare the number and size of the slave quarters in 1860 with the homes of the former slaves in 1881. How do they differ? Which buildings were prominently located along the road in 1860, and which could be found along the road in 1881?

CONNECTIONS: How might the former master feel about the new configuration of buildings on the plantation in 1881? In what ways did the new system of sharecropping replicate the old system of plantation agriculture? In what ways was it different?

Sharecropping introduced the country merchant into the agricultural equation. Landlords supplied sharecroppers with land, mules, seeds, and tools, but sharecroppers also needed credit to obtain essential food and clothing before they harvested their crops. Under an arrangement called a *crop lien*, a merchant would advance goods in exchange for a lien, or legal claim, on the sharecropper's future crop. Some white merchants charged exorbitant rates of interest, as much as 60 percent, on the goods they sold. At the end of the growing season, after the landlord had taken half of the farmer's crop for rent, the merchant took most of the rest. Sometimes, the farmer did not earn enough to repay the debt to the merchant, so he would have to borrow more from the merchant and begin the cycle again.

An experiment at first, sharecropping soon dominated the cotton South. Lien merchants forced tenants to plant cotton, which was easy to sell, instead of food crops.

The result was excessive production of cotton and falling cotton prices, developments that cost thousands of small white farmers their land and pushed them into the great army of poor sharecroppers. The new sharecropping system of agriculture took shape just as the political power of Republicans in the South began to buckle under Democratic pressure.

REVIEW

How did Reconstruction shape politics and economic change in the South?

Why did Reconstruction collapse?

By 1870, after a decade of war and reconstruction, northerners wanted to put "the southern problem" behind them. Businessmen came to dominate the Republican Party, replacing the band of reformers and idealists who had been prominent in the 1860s. Civil War hero Ulysses S. Grant succeeded Andrew Johnson as president in 1869 and quickly proved that brilliance on the battlefield does not necessarily translate into accomplishment in the White House. As northern commitment to defend Black freedom eroded, southern commitment to white supremacy intensified. Without northern protection, southern Republicans were no match for the Democrats' economic coercion, political fraud, and bloody violence. One by one, Republican state governments fell in the South. The election of 1876 both confirmed and completed the collapse of reconstruction.

What struggles did Grant's troubled presidency face?

In 1868, the Republican Party's presidential nomination went to Ulysses S. Grant, the North's favorite general. His Democratic opponent, Horatio Seymour of New York, ran on a platform that blasted reconstruction as "a flagrant usurpation of power . . . unconstitutional, revolutionary, and void." The Republicans answered by "waving the bloody shirt"—that is, they reminded voters that the Democrats were "the party of rebellion." Despite a reign of terror in the South, costing hundreds of Republicans their lives, Grant gained a narrow 309,000-vote margin in the popular vote and a substantial victory (214 votes to 80) in the electoral college (**Map 16.2**).

The talents Grant had demonstrated on the battlefield—decisiveness, clarity, and resolution—were less obvious in the White House. While Grant sought both justice for Blacks and sectional reconciliation, he surrounded himself

Candidate	Electoral Vote	Popular Vote	Percent of Popular Vote
Ulysses S. Grant (Republican)	214	3,012,833	52.7
Horatio Seymour (Democrat)	80	2,703,249	47.3
Nonvoting states (Reconstruction)			

MAP 16.2 ▲ The Election of 1868

with fumbling kinfolk and old friends from his army days and made a string of dubious appointments that led to a series of damaging scandals. Charges of corruption tainted his vice president, Schuyler Colfax, and brought down two of his cabinet officers. Though never personally implicated in any scandal, Grant was naive and blind to the rot that filled his administration. Republican congressman James A. Garfield declared: "His imperturbability is amazing. I am in doubt whether to call it greatness or stupidity."

In 1872, anti-Grant Republicans bolted and launched the Liberal Party. To clean up the corruption, Liberals proposed ending the spoils system, by which victorious parties rewarded loyal workers with public office, and replacing it with a nonpartisan civil service commission that would oversee competitive examinations for appointment to office. Liberals also demanded that the federal government remove its troops from the South and restore "home rule" (southern white control). Democrats liked the Liberals' southern policy and endorsed the Liberal presidential candidate, Horace Greeley, the longtime editor of the *New York Tribune*. The nation, however, still felt enormous affection for the man who had saved the Union and reelected Grant with 56 percent of the popular vote.

How did northern resolve wither?

Although Grant genuinely wanted to protect the civil and political rights of Black Americans, he understood that most northerners had grown weary of reconstruction. Citizens shifted their attention to other issues, especially after the nation slipped into a devastating economic depression in 1873. More than eighteen thousand businesses collapsed, leaving more than a million workers on the streets. Northern businessmen wanted to invest in the South but believed that repeated federal intrusion was itself a major cause of instability in the region. Republican leaders began to question the wisdom of their party's alliance with the South's lower classes—its small farmers and sharecroppers. One member of Grant's administration proposed allying with the "thinking and influential native southerners . . . the intelligent, well-to-do, and controlling class."

Congress, too, wanted to leave reconstruction behind, but southern Republicans made that difficult. When the South's Republicans begged for federal protection from increasing Klan violence, Congress enacted three laws in 1870 and 1871 that were intended to break the back of white terrorism. The severest of the three, the Ku Klux Klan Act (1871), made interference with voting rights a felony. Federal marshals arrested thousands of Klansmen and came close to destroying the Klan, but they did not end terrorism against Black people. Congress also passed the Civil Rights Act of 1875, which boldly outlawed racial discrimination in transportation, public accommodations, and juries. Federal authorities never enforced the law aggressively, however, and segregation remained the rule throughout the South.

By the early 1870s, the Republican Party had lost its leading champions of Black rights to death or defeat at the polls. Other Republicans concluded that the quest for Black equality was mistaken or hopelessly naive. In May 1872, Congress restored the right of officeholding to all but three hundred ex-rebels. Many Republicans had come to believe that white leaders offered the best hope for honesty, order, and prosperity in the South.

Underlying the North's abandonment of reconstruction was unyielding racial prejudice. Northerners had learned to accept Black freedom during the war, but deep-seated prejudice prevented many from accepting Black equality. Even the actions they took on behalf of Black people often served partisan political advantage. Northerners generally supported Indiana senator Thomas A. Hendricks's harsh declaration that "this is a white man's Government, made by the white man for the white man."

The U.S. Supreme Court also did its part to undermine reconstruction. The Court issued a series of decisions that significantly weakened the federal government's ability to protect Black southerners. In the *Slaughterhouse* cases (1873), the Court distinguished between national and state citizenship and ruled that the Fourteenth Amendment protected only those rights that stemmed from the federal government, such as voting in federal elections and interstate travel. Since the Court decided that most rights derived from the states, it sharply curtailed the federal government's authority to defend Black citizens. Even more devastating, the *United States v. Cruikshank* ruling (1876) said that the reconstruction amendments gave Congress the power to legislate against discrimination only by states, not by individuals. The "suppression of ordinary crime," such as assault, remained a state responsibility. The Supreme Court did not declare reconstruction unconstitutional but eroded its legal foundation.

The mood of the North found political expression in the election of 1874, when for the first time in eighteen years the Democrats gained control of the House of Representatives. As one Republican observed, the people had grown tired of the "negro question, with all its complications, and the reconstruction of Southern States, with all its interminable embroilments." Rather than defend reconstruction from its southern enemies, northerners steadily backed away from the challenge. By the early 1870s, southern Republicans faced the forces of southern racism largely on their own.

How did white supremacy triumph in the South?

To most white southerners, Reconstruction meant intolerable insults: Black militiamen patrolled town streets, Black laborers negotiated contracts with former masters, Black maids stood up to former mistresses, Black voters cast ballots, and Black legislators such as James T. Rapier helped enact laws. White southerners fought back by extolling the "great Confederate cause," or Lost Cause. They celebrated their soldiers, "the noblest band of men who ever fought," and made an idol of Robert E. Lee, the embodiment of the southern gentleman.

But the most important way white southerners responded to reconstruction was their assault on Republican governments in the South. These biracial governments attracted more hatred than did any other political regime in American history. The northern retreat from reconstruction permitted southern Democrats to seize control. Taking the name **Redeemers**, Democrats in the South promised to replace "bayonet rule" (a few federal troops continued to be stationed in the South) with "home rule." They promised that honest, thrifty white Democrats would supplant corrupt tax-and-spend Republicans. Above all, Redeemers swore to save southern civilization from a descent into "African barbarism." As one man put it, "We must render this either a white man's government, or convert the land into a Negro man's cemetery."

Southern Democrats adopted a multipronged strategy to overthrow Republican governments. First, they sought to polarize the parties around race. They went about

Redeemers
Name taken by southern Democrats who harnessed white rage in order to overthrow Republican rule and Black political power and thus, they believed, save southern civilization.

gathering all the South's white voters into the Democratic Party, leaving the Republicans to depend on Black voters, who made up a minority of the population in almost every southern state. To dislodge white people from the Republican Party, Democrats fanned the flames of racism. A South Carolina Democrat crowed that his party appealed to the "proud Caucasian race, whose sovereignty on earth God has proclaimed."

Democrats also exploited the severe economic plight of small white farmers by blaming it on Republicans. Government spending soared during Reconstruction, and small farmers saw their tax burden skyrocket. "This is tax time," a South Carolinian reported. "They are so high & so little money to pay with" that farmers were "selling every egg and chicken they can get." In 1871, Mississippi reported that one-seventh of the state's land—3.3 million acres—had been forfeited for nonpayment of taxes. The small farmers' economic distress had a racial dimension. Because few freedmen succeeded in acquiring land, they rarely paid taxes. In 1874, Black Georgians made up 45 percent of the population but paid only 2 percent of the taxes. From the perspective of a small white farmer, Republican rule meant that he was not only paying more taxes but paying them to aid Black farmers.

If racial pride and financial hardship proved insufficient to drive yeomen from the Republican Party, Democrats turned to terrorism. "Night riders," white vigilantes, targeted white as well as Black Republicans for beatings and assassination. Whether white or Black, a "dead Radical is very harmless," South Carolina Democratic leader Martin Gary told his followers.

Still, the primary victims of white violence were Black Republicans. Violence escalated to an unprecedented ferocity on Easter Sunday in 1873 in tiny Colfax, Louisiana. When Democrats turned to fraud to win a local election, Black Republicans refused to accept the result and occupied the courthouse. After three weeks, 165 white men attacked and set the courthouse on fire. When the Black people tried to surrender,

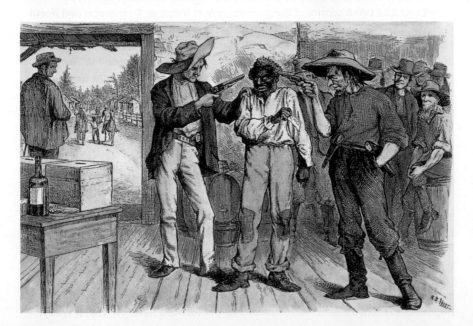

◄ *"Of Course He Wants to Vote the Democratic Ticket"* **by B. Frost** This Republican cartoon from the October 21, 1876, issue of *Harper's Weekly* comments sarcastically on the possibility of honest elections in the South. The caption reads: "You're free as air, ain't you? Say you are or I'll blow yer black head off." The cartoon demonstrates not only some northerners' concern that violence would deliver the election to the Democrats but also the perception that white southerners were crude, drunken, ignorant brutes. GRANGER–Historical Picture Archive.

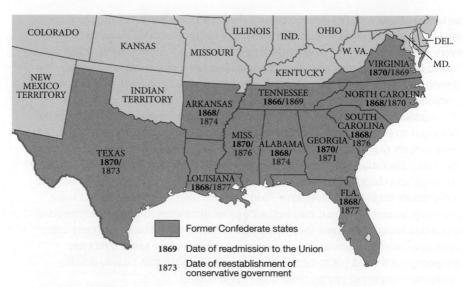

MAP 16.3 ▲ The Reconstruction of the South Myth has it that Republican rule of the former Confederacy was not only harsh but long. In most states, however, conservative white southerners stormed back into power in months or just a few years. By the election of 1876, Republican governments could be found in only three states, and they soon fell.

the attackers murdered them. At least 81 Black men were slaughtered that day. Although the federal government indicted the white killers, the Supreme Court ruled that it did not have the right to prosecute. And since local whites would not prosecute neighbors who killed Blacks, the defendants in the Colfax massacre went free.

Even before adopting the all-out white supremacist tactics of the 1870s, Democrats had taken control of the governments of Virginia, Tennessee, and North Carolina. The new campaign brought fresh gains. The Redeemers retook Georgia in 1871, Texas in 1873, and Arkansas and Alabama in 1874. As the state election approached in Mississippi in 1876, the Republican governor appealed to Washington for federal troops to control the violence, only to hear from the attorney general that the "whole public are tired of these annual autumnal outbreaks in the South." Abandoned, Mississippi Republicans succumbed to the Democratic onslaught in the fall elections. By 1876, only three Republican state governments survived in the South (**Map 16.3**).

How did the election of 1876 end in compromise?

The year 1876 witnessed one of the most chaotic elections in American history. The election took place in November, but not until March 2 of the following year did the nation know who would be inaugurated president on March 4. Sixteen years after Lincoln's election, Americans feared that a presidential election would again precipitate civil war.

The Democrats nominated New York's governor, Samuel J. Tilden, who targeted the corruption of the Grant administration and the "despotism" of Republican reconstruction. The Republicans put forward Rutherford B. Hayes, governor of Ohio. Privately, Hayes considered "bayonet rule" a mistake but concluded that waving the bloody shirt remained the Republicans' best political strategy.

On election day, Tilden tallied 4,288,590 votes to Hayes's 4,036,298. But in the all-important electoral college, Tilden fell one vote short of the majority required for victory. The electoral votes of three states—South Carolina, Louisiana, and Florida, the only remaining Republican governments in the South—remained in doubt because both Republicans and Democrats in those states claimed victory. To win, Tilden needed only one of the nineteen contested votes. Hayes had to have all of them.

Congress had to decide who had actually won the elections in the three southern states and thus who would be president. The Constitution provided no guidance. Democrats controlled the House, and Republicans controlled the Senate. Congress created a special electoral commission to arbitrate the disputed returns. All of the commissioners voted their party affiliation, giving every state to the Republican Hayes and putting him over the top in electoral votes (**Map 16.4**).

Some outraged Democrats vowed to resist Hayes's victory. Rumors flew of an impending coup and renewed civil war. But the impasse was broken when negotiations behind the scenes resulted in an informal understanding known as the **Compromise of 1877**. In exchange for a Democratic promise not to block Hayes's inauguration and to deal fairly with the freedmen, Hayes vowed to refrain from using the army to uphold the remaining Republican regimes in the South and to provide the South with substantial federal subsidies for railroads.

Stubborn Tilden supporters bemoaned the "stolen election" and damned "His Fraudulency," Rutherford B. Hayes. Old-guard Radicals such as William Lloyd Garrison denounced Hayes's bargain as a "policy of compromise, of credulity, of weakness, of subserviency, of surrender." But the nation as a whole celebrated, for the country had weathered a grave crisis. The last three Republican state governments in the South fell quickly once Hayes withdrew the U.S. Army. Reconstruction came to an end.

Candidate	Electoral Vote	Popular Vote	Percent of Popular Vote
Rutherford B. Hayes (Republican)	185*	4,036,298	47.9**
Samuel J. Tilden (Democrat)	184	4,288,590	51.0

*19 electoral votes were disputed.

**Percentages do not total 100 because some popular votes went to other parties.

MAP 16.4 ▲ The Election of 1876

Compromise of 1877 Informal agreement in which Democrats agreed not to block Rutherford Hayes's inauguration and to deal fairly with freedmen; in return, Hayes vowed not to use the army to uphold the remaining Republican regimes in the South and to provide the South with substantial federal subsidies for railroads. The compromise brought the Reconstruction era to an end.

REVIEW

What major factors explain the ending of Reconstruction?

Conclusion: Was Reconstruction "a revolution but half accomplished"?

In 1865, when General Carl Schurz visited the South, he discovered, he said, "a revolution but half accomplished." White southerners resisted the passage from slavery to free labor, from white racial despotism to equal justice, and from white political monopoly to biracial democracy. The old elite wanted to get "things back as near to slavery as possible," Schurz reported, while Black Americans such as James T. Rapier and some white people were eager to exploit the revolutionary possibilities of Confederate defeat and emancipation.

Although the northern-dominated Republican Congress refused to provide for Blacks' economic welfare, it employed constitutional amendments to require ex-Confederates to accept legal equality and share political power with Black men. Congress was not willing to extend such power to women, however. Conservative southern whites fought ferociously to recover their power and privilege. When Democrats regained control of politics, white people used both state power and private violence to wipe out many of the gains of Reconstruction, leading one observer to conclude that the North had won the war but the South had won the peace.

The Redeemer counterrevolution, however, did not mean a return to slavery. Northern victory in the Civil War ensured that formerly enslaved people no longer faced the auction block and could send their children to school, worship in their own churches, and work independently on rented farms. Sharecropping, with all its hardships, provided more autonomy and economic welfare than bondage had. It was limited freedom, to be sure, but it was not slavery.

The Civil War and emancipation set in motion the most profound upheaval in the nation's history. War destroyed the largest slave society in the New World. The world of slaveholders and slaves gave way to that of landlords and sharecroppers. Washington increased its role in national affairs, and the victorious North set the nation's compass toward the expansion of industrial capitalism and the final conquest of the West.

Despite massive changes, however, the Civil War remained only a "half accomplished" revolution. As General Schurz saw clearly in 1865, defeat had not budged white southerners' racism or their commitment to white supremacy. By not fulfilling the promises the nation seemed to hold out to Black Americans at war's end, Reconstruction represents a tragedy of enormous proportions. The failure to protect Blacks and guarantee their rights had enduring consequences. It was the failure of the first reconstruction that made the modern civil rights movement necessary.

CHAPTER REVIEW

EXPLAIN WHY IT MATTERS

Freedmen's Bureau (p. 455)

black codes (p. 460)

Civil Rights Act of 1866 (p. 462)

Fourteenth Amendment (p. 463)

Military Reconstruction Act (p. 464)

Fifteenth Amendment (p. 465)

carpetbaggers (p. 467)

scalawag (p. 467)

Ku Klux Klan (p. 467)

sharecropping (p. 470)

Redeemers (p. 474)

Compromise of 1877 (p. 477)

PUT IT ALL TOGETHER

PRESIDENTIAL AND CONGRESSIONAL RECONSTRUCTION

- What role did the black codes play in shaping the course of Reconstruction?
- What steps did Congress take between 1865 and 1869 to assist formerly enslaved people in their lives as freedmen? Were these actions effective?

SOUTHERN RECONSTRUCTION IN ACTION

- How did white southerners respond during Reconstruction? Consider both Democrats and Republicans in your response.
- How did southern Black Americans attempt to shape their own lives during Reconstruction?

THE END OF RECONSTRUCTION

- How and why did the decline of northern support for Reconstruction help southern Democrats "redeem" the South?
- Why did white supremacy become the foundation of southern politics in the 1870s?

LOOKING BACKWARD, LOOKING AHEAD

- How did long-held racist views among whites, in both the South and the North, shape Reconstruction?
- What were the lasting accomplishments of Reconstruction? What were its most important failures?

17

THE CONTESTED WEST

1865–1900

This chapter discusses the following questions:

- What did U.S. expansion mean for Native Americans?
- In what ways did Native American groups defy and resist colonial rule?
- How did mining shape American expansion?
- How did the fight for land and resources in the West unfold?
- Conclusion: How did the West help set the tone for the Gilded Age?

▼ **Buffalo Bill Poster** Buffalo Bill Cody used colorful posters to advertise his Wild West show during the 1880s and 1890s. The show included 100 cowboys, 97 Indians, 180 horses, and 18 American bison. The troupe performed "Attack on a Settler's Cabin" and "Custer's Last Stand." Sitting Bull, who had fought at the Battle of the Little Big Horn, toured with Cody in 1885 and signed autographs styling him as "the Indian who killed Custer." Cody's show indiscriminately mixed the authentic and the romantic until it blurred into the mythic West of the imagination. Library of Congress Prints and Photographs Division Washington, D.C. [LC-DIG-ppmsca-13514].

AN AMERICAN STORY

To celebrate the 400th anniversary of Columbus's voyage to the New World, Chicago hosted the World's Columbian Exposition in 1893, creating a magical White City on the shores of Lake Michigan. Among the organizations vying to hold meetings at the fair was the American Historical Association, whose members gathered on a warm July evening to hear Frederick Jackson Turner deliver his landmark essay "The Significance of the Frontier in American History." Turner began by noting that the 1890 census no longer discerned a clear frontier line. His tone was elegiac: "The existence of an area of free land, its continuous recession, and the advance of settlement westward," he observed, "explained American development."

Turner, who studied the old frontier east of the Mississippi, viewed the West as a process as much as a place. The availability of land provided a "safety valve," releasing social tensions and providing opportunities for social mobility that worked to Americanize Americans. Turner's West demanded strength and nerve, fostered invention and adaptation, and produced self-confident, individualistic Americans. His frontier thesis underscored the exceptionalism of America's history, highlighting its difference from the colonialism practiced by European powers in Asia and Africa.

Yet the historians who applauded Turner in Chicago had short memories. That afternoon, many had crossed the midway to attend Buffalo Bill Cody's Wild West extravaganza — a cowboys-and-Indians shoot-'em-up. The historians cheering in the stands that hot afternoon no doubt dismissed Buffalo Bill's history as amateur, but he made a point that Turner glossed over: The West was neither free nor open. It was the story of a fierce and violent contest for land and resources.

In the decades following the Civil War, the United States pursued empire in the American West through Indian wars that lasted until 1890. Pushed off their land and onto reservations, Native Americans resisted as they faced waves of miners and settlers as well as the degradation of their environment by railroads, mines, barbed wire, and mechanized agriculture. The Sioux, the Comanche, and the Cherokee were just a few of the tribes who suffered devastating losses in the fierce world contest for land and resources that fueled imperial adventures.

The mythic pastoral agrarianism Turner celebrated in his frontier thesis clashed with the reality of the urban, industrial West emerging on the Comstock Lode in Nevada and in the commercial farms of California. Turner's rugged white "frontiersman" masked the racial diversity of the West and failed to acknowledge the role of women in community building.

Yet in the waning decade of the nineteenth century, as history blurred with nostalgia, Turner's evocation of the frontier as a crucible for American identity hit a nerve in a population facing rapid changes. A major depression started even before the Columbian Exposition opened its doors. Americans worried about the economy, immigration, and urban industrialism found in Turner's message a new cause for concern. Would America continue to be America now that the frontier was closed?

What did U.S. expansion mean for Native Americans?

While the European powers expanded their authority and wealth through imperialism and colonialism in far-flung empires abroad, the United States focused its attention on its own western lands. From the U.S. Army attack on the Dakota Sioux in the Santee Uprising to the expropriation of the Black Hills, white people pushed Indians aside as they moved west. Frederick Jackson Turner's American exceptionalism stressed how the history of the United States differed from that of European nations, citing America's western frontier as a cause. Yet expansion in the trans-Mississippi West involved the conquest, displacement, and rule over native peoples—a process best understood in the global context of imperialism and colonialism.

The U.S. government, through trickery and conquest, forced tribes off their lands (**Map 17.1**) and onto designated Indian territories or reservations. The Indian wars depleted the Native American population and handed most Indian land to white settlers. The decimation of the bison herds pushed the Plains Indians onto reservations, where they lived as wards of the state.

How did the U.S. government remove Native Americans from their land and establish the reservation system?

Manifest destiny—the belief that the United States had a "God-given" right to aggressively spread the values of white civilization and expand the nation from ocean to ocean—dictated U.S. policy toward Native Americans and other nations. In the name of manifest destiny, Americans demanded the removal of the Five Civilized Tribes of the South (the Cherokee, Choctaw, Chickasaw, Creek, and Seminole peoples) to Oklahoma in the 1830s; colonized Texas and won its independence from Mexico in 1836; conquered California, Arizona, New Mexico, and parts of Utah and Colorado in the Mexican-American War of 1846–1848; invaded Oregon in the mid-1840s; and paid Mexico for land in Arizona and New Mexico in the Gadsden Purchase of 1854.

MAP ACTIVITY

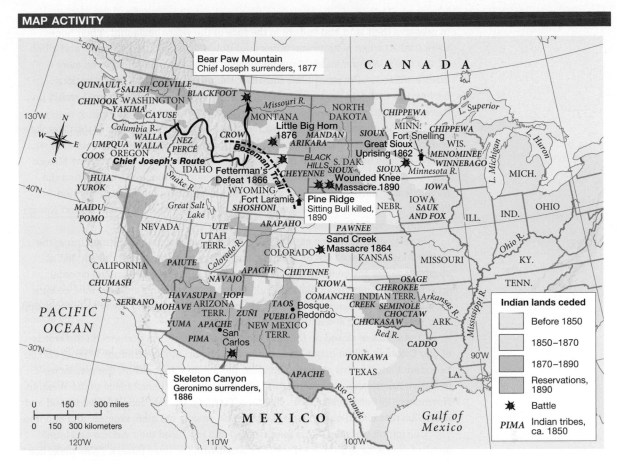

MAP 17.1 ▲ The Loss of Indian Lands, 1850–1890 By 1890, western Indians were isolated on small, scattered reservations. Native Americans had struggled to retain their land in major battles, from the Great Sioux Uprising in Minnesota in 1862 to the massacre at Wounded Knee, South Dakota, in 1890.

READING THE MAP: Where was the largest reservation located in 1890? Which states on this map show no reservations in 1890? Compare this map to Map 18.2.

CONNECTIONS: Why did the federal government force Native Americans onto reservations? What developments prompted these changes?

By midcentury, western lands no longer seemed inexhaustible. Hordes of settlers crossed the Great Plains on their way to the goldfields of California or the rich farmland of Washington and Oregon. In their path stood a solid wall of Indian land. To solve this "Indian problem," the U.S. government took Indian lands with the promise to pay annuities in return and put the Native Americans on lands reserved for their use—reservations. In 1851, some ten thousand Plains Indians came together at Fort Laramie in Wyoming to negotiate a treaty that ceded a wide swath of their land to allow white settlers passage to the West. In return, the government lavished the Native Americans with gifts and promised to prevent settlers from trespassing onto Indian land.

reservations
Land assigned by the federal government to American Indians in the 1860s to reduce tensions between Indians and western settlers. With meager government rations, Native Americans faced a life of poverty and starvation.

The Indians who "touched the pen" to the 1851 Treaty of Fort Laramie hoped to preserve their land and culture in the face of the white onslaught. Their hopes were dashed when settlers and miners cut down trees, polluted streams, and killed off the bison. White men had brought alcohol, guns, and something even more deadly—disease. Between 1780 and 1870, the population of the Plains nations declined by half. "If I could see this thing, if I knew where it came from, I would go there and fight it," a Cheyenne warrior anguished.

In the Southwest, the Navajo people, in a removal similar to that of the Cherokee, endured a forced 400-mile march called the "Long Walk" from their homeland in what is now Arizona to the desolate Bosque Redondo Reservation in eastern New Mexico in 1864. "This ground we were brought on, it is not productive," complained the Navajo leader Barboncito. "All the stock we brought here have nearly all died." Fighting malnutrition, disease, drought, and grasshoppers, over two thousand Navajo perished at Bosque Redondo.

Poverty and starvation stalked the reservations. Confined by armed force, the Native Americans eked out an existence on stingy government rations. Styled as stepping-stones to "civilization," Indian reservations closely resembled colonial societies where native populations, ruled by outside bureaucrats, saw their culture assaulted, their religious practices outlawed, their children sent away to schools, and their way of life attacked in the name of progress.

To Americans raised on theories of racial superiority, the Indians, in the words of one Colorado militia major, constituted "an obstacle to civilization . . . [and] should be exterminated." This attitude pervaded the military. As a result, the massacre of Native American men, women, and children became commonplace in the West. In November 1864 at Sand Creek in Colorado Territory, Colonel John M. Chivington and his militia descended on a village of Cheyenne, mostly old men, women, and children.

Chivington watched as his men scalped and mutilated their victims and later justified the killing of Native American children with the terse remark, "Nits make lice."

The city of Denver feted Chivington and his men as heroes, but a congressional inquiry eventually castigated the soldiers for their "fiendish malignity" and condemned the "savage cruelty" of the massacre. Four years later, Black Kettle, one of the few survivors of Sand Creek, died in another massacre when George Armstrong Custer slaughtered more than one hundred people on the banks of the Washita River in Oklahoma.

What led to the decimation of the great bison herds?

After the Civil War, the accelerating pace of industrial expansion brought about the near extinction of the American bison (buffalo). By 1850, the dynamic ecology of the Great Plains, with its droughts, fires, and blizzards, along with the demands of Indian buffalo-robe traders as well as whites and their cattle, had already driven the bison herds onto the far western plains.

In the 1870s, industrial demand for heavy leather belting used in machinery along with the development of a larger, more accurate rifle combined to hasten the bison's demise. The nation's transcontinental railroad systems cut the buffalo range in two and divided the dwindling herds. For the Sioux and other nomadic tribes of the plains, the buffalo constituted a way of life—a source of food, fuel, and shelter and a central part of religion and ritual. Railroad owners, however, considered bison a nuisance—at best a cheap source of meat for their workers and a target for sport.

Although the army took credit for the conquest of the Plains Indians, the decimation of the great bison herds contributed to the Indians' fate. With their food supply gone, Native Americans had to choose between starvation and the meager provisions supplied by the reservations. "A cold wind blew across the prairie when the last buffalo fell," the great Sioux leader Sitting Bull lamented, "a death wind for my people."

On the southern plains in 1867, more than five thousand warring Comanches, Kiowas, and Southern Arapahos gathered at Medicine Lodge Creek in Kansas to negotiate the Treaty of Medicine Lodge, hoping to preserve limited land and hunting by moving to a reservation. Three years after the treaty became law, hide hunters poured into the region; within a decade, they had nearly exterminated the southern bison herds. White hunters took about four million hides from herds south of the Platte River between 1872 and 1874. Luther Standing Bear recounted the sight and stench: "I saw the bodies of hundreds of dead buffalo lying about, just wasting, and the odor was terrible. . . . They were letting our food lie on the plains to rot." Once an estimated forty million bison roamed the West; by 1895, fewer than a thousand remained. With the buffalo gone, the Plains Indians faced starvation and reluctantly moved onto the reservations.

What led to the collapse of Comanchería?

The Indian wars in the West marked the last resistance of a Native American population devastated by disease and demoralized by the federal government's reservation policy. The Dakota Sioux in Minnesota went to war in 1862. For years, under the leadership of Chief Little Crow, the Dakota—also known as the Santee—had pursued a policy of accommodation, ceding land in return for the promise of annuities. But with his people on the verge of starvation (the local Indian agent told the hungry Dakota, "Go and eat grass"), Little Crow led his angry warriors in a desperate campaign against the intruders, killing more than a thousand settlers. American troops quelled the Great Sioux Uprising (also called the Santee Uprising) and marched seventeen hundred Sioux to Fort Snelling, where four hundred Indians went on trial for murder and thirty-eight died in the largest mass execution in American history.

Further west, the great Indian empire of **Comanchería** had once stretched from the Canadian plains to Mexico. By 1865, after two decades of what one historian has labeled "ethnic cleansing," fewer than five thousand Comanches remained in west Texas and Oklahoma.

After the Civil War, President Ulysses S. Grant faced the prospect of protracted Indian war. Reluctant to spend more money and sacrifice more lives, Grant adopted a "peace policy" designed to segregate and control Native Americans while opening land to white settlers. This policy won the support of both friends of the Indians and those who coveted the Indians' land. The army herded the Indians onto reservations (see Map 17.1), where the U.S. Bureau of Indian Affairs hired agents who, in the words of Paiute Sarah Winnemucca, did "nothing but fill their pockets." Grant thought to improve the situation by hiring Quakers and other religious men as agents, but they proved just as venal as their predecessors.

Comanchería
Native American empire based on trade in horses, hides, guns, and captives that stretched from the Canadian plains to Mexico in the eighteenth century. By 1865, fewer than five thousand Comanches lived in the empire, which ranged from west Texas north to Oklahoma.

In 1871, Congress determined to quit treating Indians as sovereign nations, to eliminate treaties, and to make Indians wards of the state. Grant's peace policy in the West gave way to all-out warfare, as the U.S. Army dispatched three thousand soldiers to wipe out the remains of Comanchería. The president's decision to deploy the army in the West effectively eliminated federal enforcement of Reconstruction in the South and left Black people without protection from mounting violence and intimidation.

To defeat the Comanche, the army adopted the practice of burning and destroying everything in its path, using the tactics that General William Tecumseh Sherman had perfected in his march through Georgia during the Civil War. Sherman, along with his fellow general, Philip Sheridan, led the assault in Texas with brutal efficiency. At the decisive battle of Palo Duro Canyon in 1874, only three Comanche warriors died in battle, but U.S. soldiers took the Indians' camp; burned more than two hundred tepees, hundreds of robes and blankets, and thousands of pounds of winter supplies; and shot more than a thousand horses. Coupled with the decimation of the bison, the army's scorched-earth policy led to the final collapse of the Comanche people—more an economic than a military defeat. The surviving Indians of Comanchería, now numbering fewer than fifteen hundred, reluctantly retreated to the reservation at Fort Sill. Sherman and Sheridan wanted the Indians executed, but cooler heads prevailed.

How did the Sioux fight to keep the Black Hills?

Lakota Sioux chief Red Cloud surveyed the situation in 1866. "When the Great Father at Washington sent us his chief soldier to ask for a path through our hunting ground, a way for his iron road to the mountains and the western sea, we were told that they wished merely to pass through our country, not to tarry among us, but to seek for gold in the far west." But the 1851 Treaty of Fort Laramie fell casualty to gold discoveries in Montana. Migrants flocked to the Powder River basin, the traditional hunting grounds of the Lakota, Cheyenne, and Arapaho. "[T]he Great Father is building his forts among us. You have heard the sound of the white soldier's ax upon the Little Piney," Red Cloud lamented. Incensed by this "insult and threat to the spirits of our ancestors," the great chief sounded the war cry. "Are we then to give up their sacred graves to be plowed for corn? Dakotas, I am for war!"

For the next year, Red Cloud, with the help of the legendary Crazy Horse and other young warriors, waged a tormenting campaign of guerrilla warfare against the army and its forts along the Bozeman Trail, known as **Red Cloud's War**. Taunting warriors lured cavalry into ambush time and again. Although early on the Native Americans lacked guns, they were rarely outshot. A skilled fighter could fire off a dozen arrows in the time it took a hapless soldier to reload his single-shot rifle. Eyewitness accounts told of one battlefield corpse riddled with over 120 arrows. As the Indians obtained modern firearms through battle and in trade, they became even more formidable foes.

Native Americans took revenge for the Sand Creek massacre in December 1866, when they wiped out Ft. Kearney's cavalry led by Captain William Fetterman, a decorated soldier who had boasted that with eighty men he could ride though Sioux territory. Fetterman and his troops faced slaughter when they followed Crazy Horse

Red Cloud's War
A conflict touched off when gold discoveries in Montana led settlers to invade Lakota lands. Chief Red Cloud, along with Crazy Horse, fought the incursion and was successful in forcing the army to abandon its forts on the Bozeman Trail and sign the second Treaty of Fort Laramie in 1868 reserving the Black Hills for the Lakota.

and a small decoy force into a mass of Sioux, Cheyenne, and Arapaho estimated at up to a thousand fighters. In the wake of the battle, women mutilated the army corpses. The Native Americans believed that gouging out eyeballs and cutting off noses and genitals would prevent the sprits of the dead from enjoying the afterlife.

After the Fetterman massacre the army capitulated, abandoning its forts and the Bozeman Trail. Red Cloud could claim to be the only Indian chief to successfully wage war against the United States. The Indians' impressive victories led to the second Treaty of Fort Laramie in 1868, in which the United States guaranteed the Indians control of the **Black Hills**, land sacred to the Lakota Sioux.

The government's fork-tongued promises induced some tribes to accept the treaty. Red Cloud led many of his people onto the reservation, but he soon regretted his action. "Think of it!" he told a visitor to the Pine Ridge Reservation. "I, who used to own . . . country so extensive that I could not ride through it in a week . . . must tell Washington when I am hungry. I must beg for that which I own." On a visit to Washington, D.C., in 1870, Red Cloud told the secretary of the interior, "We are melting like snow on the hillside, while you are grown like spring grass. . . . When the white man comes in my country, he leaves a trail of blood behind him." Sioux leadership passed to Crazy Horse and Sitting Bull, who refused to sign the treaty and called for armed resistance. Crazy Horse later declared that he wanted no part of the "piecemeal penning" of his people.

In 1874, the discovery of gold in the Black Hills led the government to break its promise to Red Cloud. Miners began pouring into the Dakotas, and the Northern Pacific Railroad made plans to lay tracks. At first, the government offered to purchase the Black Hills. But the Sioux refused to sell. The army responded by issuing an ultimatum ordering all Lakota Sioux and Northern Cheyenne bands onto the Pine Ridge Reservation and threatening to hunt down those who refused. The northern Lakota Sioux constituted the only armed threat remaining to westward expansion and the army, in defiance of the Treaty of Fort Laramie, saw the chance to get rid of them once and for all.

In the summer of 1876, the army launched a three-pronged attack led by Lieutenant Colonel George Armstrong Custer, General George Crook, and Colonel John Gibbon. Crazy Horse stopped Crook at the Battle of the Rosebud. Custer, leading the second prong of the army's offensive, divided his Seventh Cavalry troops and ordered an attack. On June 25, he spotted signs of the Indians' camp. Crying "Hurrah boys, we've got them," he charged into the largest gathering of Indians ever assembled on the Great Plains — more than eight thousand — camped along the banks of the Greasy Grass River, also known as the Little Big Horn River. Native American warriors led by Sitting Bull and Crazy Horse set upon Custer and his two hundred troopers and quickly annihilated them. "It took us about as long as a hungry man to eat his dinner," the Cheyenne chief Two Moons recalled. **(See "Analyzing Historical Evidence: 'Custer's Last Stand'" on page 488.)**

"Custer's Last Stand," or the **Battle of the Little Big Horn**, soon became part of national mythology. When word of the battle reached the World's Fair in Philadelphia, Americans greeted the news with incredulity and outrage. The defeat of "civilized" American soldiers by "savage" Indians was unthinkable. Custer's loss soon became a rallying cry that glossed over white encroachment on Native American land, transforming invasion, conquest, and empire into something that seemed more like self-defense.

Black Hills
Mountains in western South Dakota and northeast Wyoming that are sacred to the Lakota Sioux. In the 1868 Treaty of Fort Laramie, the United States guaranteed Indians control of the Black Hills, but it broke its promise after gold was discovered there in 1874.

Battle of the Little Big Horn
1876 battle begun when American cavalry under George Armstrong Custer attacked an encampment of Native Americans from several tribes who refused to remove to a reservation. Indian warriors led by Crazy Horse and Sitting Bull annihilated the American soldiers, but their victory was short lived.

ANALYZING HISTORICAL EVIDENCE

"Custer's Last Stand"

In the aftermath of Custer's defeat at the Little Big Horn, Americans created a myth of bravery and valor in which "civilization stood against savagery." The Native Americans who won the battle knew better but mainly stayed silent.

DOCUMENT 1

Artist William Cary was among the first to imagine the *Death Struggle of Custer* (see top right). This wood engraving appeared in the *New York Daily Graphic*. Cary sketched the cavalry leader on foot in the midst of a melee, single-handedly holding off a horde of mounted savages. Demonizing Native Americans, the artist depicts a hellish scene of fiendish savages and writhing cavalry corpses. As the Cheyenne Wooden Leg remembered, "It looked like thousands of dogs might look if all of them were mixed together in a fight." George Custer, wounded by a bullet in the chest, died of a second gunshot to the temple. Historians have speculated that his brother Tom shot Custer to prevent his capture and torture at the hands of the Sioux. The Anheuser-Busch Brewing Association distributed thousands of similar scenes to barrooms across America. Many of the battle depictions by white artists were little more than romantic idealism, with Custer on horseback leading a valiant charge.

▲ *The Battle on the Little Big Horn River; The Death Struggle of General Custer* by William Cary, 1876
Library of Congress Prints and Photographs Division Washington, D.C. [LC-USZ62-60760].

DOCUMENT 2

In an 1889 lithograph of the battle (see bottom right), Custer and his men are shown dismounted, firing at Native Americans on horseback. A much more accurate portrayal than many of the others in circulation at the time, the lithograph shows how badly Custer was outnumbered when he divided his forces and led a contingent into a force of two thousand warriors.

▲ *The Battle of Little Big Horn, June 25th 1876* (1889 lithograph) Bridgeman Images.

DOCUMENT 3

Amos Bad Heart Bull, an Oglala Sioux from the Pine Ridge Reservation, dramatized the battle at the river the Indians called the Greasy Grass in pictograph style, drawing with pen and crayon in a ledger book he purchased at a trading post (see below). Although the artist was only eight years old in 1876 when the battle occurred, he based his pictures on the recollections of his uncle and other Oglala elders. Crazy Horse appears in the center of the action wearing his distinctive hailstone war paint and single eagle feather and carrying a rifle. According to an Arapaho warrior who fought beside him, Crazy Horse "was the bravest man he ever saw."

Today the development of disaster archaeology — utilizing metal detectors, forensic science, and ballistic technology — has made it possible to re-create the battle scene with painstaking accuracy. The evidence supports the Indian view. Over half of the warriors carried guns in addition to clubs, knives, and stone hatchets. The wide dispersal of men and metal points to a rout. Outmanned, outmaneuvered, and outgunned, Custer and his soldiers fought not one last battle but a series of desperate, deadly encounters. According to one account, the last remnants of Custer's battalion ran into a ravine with "wooping warriors running them down . . . striking them to the ground, looking for more until there were no more."

Like the West itself, the battlefield in Montana remains a contested site of historical memory. In 1991, it was renamed the Little Bighorn Battlefield National Monument, dropping Custer's name. Today, in addition to the cemetery for the fallen white soldiers, there is a sculpture memorial to the Indian dead.

▲ *Crazy Horse at the Little Big Horn* **by Amos Bad Heart Bull** GRANGER - Historical Picture Archive.

Questions for Analysis

ANALYZE THE EVIDENCE: Compare the portrayals of "Custer's Last Stand." What strikes you about the Native American version in relationship to the Anglo lithographs?

RECOGNIZE VIEWPOINTS: Who is the center of focus for the Native Americans? Who for the Anglos? How does this reflect the two sides' different interpretations of this dramatic encounter?

CONSIDER THE CONTEXT: In what ways does the comparison of the depictions of the Battle of the Little Big Horn point to conflicting interpretations of the larger history of the American West?

Custer's last stand soon proved to be the last stand for the Sioux. The nomadic bands that had massed at the Little Big Horn scattered, and the army hunted them down. "Wherever we went," wrote the Oglala holy man Black Elk, "the soldiers came to kill us." In 1877, Crazy Horse was captured and bayoneted to death. Four years later, Sitting Bull surrendered. The government took the Black Hills and confined the Lakota to reservations. The Sioux never accepted the loss of the Black Hills. In 1923, they filed suit, demanding the return of the land taken from them. After a protracted court battle lasting nearly sixty years, the U.S. Supreme Court ruled in 1980 that the government had illegally violated the Treaty of Fort Laramie. Declaring that "a more ripe and rank case of dishonorable dealings will never, in all probability, be found in our history," the Court awarded the tribes $122.5 million. The Sioux refused the settlement and continue to press for the return of the Black Hills.

REVIEW

How did the slaughter of the bison contribute to the Plains Indians' removal to reservations?

In what ways did Native American groups defy and resist colonial rule?

Imperialistic attitudes of white people toward Indians, aiming to extend U.S. rule, continued to evolve in the late nineteenth century. To "civilize" the Native Americans, the U.S. government sought to force assimilation on their children. As reservations became increasingly unpopular among whites who coveted Indian land and among friends of the Indians appalled by starvation on the reservations, a new policy of allotment gained favor. It promised to put Native Americans on parcels of land, forcing them into farming, and then to redistribute the remaining land to white settlers. In the face of this ongoing assault on their way of life, Indians actively resisted, contested, and adapted to colonial rule.

How were Indian schools used to wage war on Native American culture?

Indian schools constituted the cultural battleground of the Indian wars in the West, their avowed purpose being, in the words of one of their supporters, to "kill the Indian . . . and save the man." In 1877, Congress appropriated funds for Indian education, reasoning, in the words of one congressman, that it was "less expensive to educate Indians than to kill them." That education effort focused on Native American boys and girls from toddlers to teenagers. Virginia's Hampton Institute, created in 1868 to school newly freed enslaved people, accepted its first Native

American students in 1878. Although many Indian schools operated on the reservations, authorities much preferred boarding facilities that isolated students from what white people saw as the "contamination" of tribal values.

Many Native American parents resisted sending their children away. When all else failed, the military kidnapped the children and sent them off to school. An agent at the Mescalero Apache Agency in Arizona Territory reported in 1886 that "it became necessary to visit the camps unexpectedly with a detachment of police, and seize such children as were proper and take them away to school, willing or unwilling." The parents put up a struggle. "Some hurried their children off to the mountains or hid them away in camp, and the police had to chase and capture them like so many wild rabbits," the agent observed. "This unusual proceeding created quite an outcry. The men were sullen and muttering, the women loud in their lamentations and the children almost out of their wits with fright."

Once at school, the children were stripped and scrubbed, their clothing and belongings confiscated, and their hair hacked off and doused with kerosene to kill lice. Issued stiff new uniforms, shoes, and what Luther Standing Bear recalled as the "torture" of woolen long underwear, the children often lost not only their possessions but also their names. Children were asked to stand at the blackboard, take a pointer, and select a proper English name, recalled Standing Bear, who immediately became Luther.

The **Carlisle Indian School** in Pennsylvania, founded in 1879, became the model for later institutions. To encourage assimilation, Carlisle pioneered the "outing system"—sending students to live with white families during summer vacations. The policy reflected the school's slogan: "To civilize the Indian, get him into civilization. To keep him civilized, let him stay." The curriculum featured agricultural and manual arts for boys and domestic skills for girls, training designed to eliminate Indians' dependence on government support.

Carlisle Indian School Institution established in Pennsylvania in 1879 to educate and assimilate Native Americans. It pioneered the "outing system," in which Indian students were sent to live with white families in order to accelerate acculturation.

◀ **Pueblo (Laguna) Students at the Carlisle Indian School** Almost all students brought to the Carlisle Indian School were photographed on their arrival. These photos, taken in the studio of photographer John Nicholas Choate, show Benjamin Thomas (Wat-ye-eh), Mary Perry (Ki-ot-se), and John Menaul (Kowsh-te-ah) of the Pueblo (Laguna) nation in their traditional dress in 1880 and again in their school uniforms in 1883. Dickinson College Archives & Special Collections.

Merrill Gates, a member of the Board of Indian Commissioners, summed up the goal of Indian education: "To get the Indian out of the blanket and into trousers,—and trousers with a pocket in them, *and with a pocket that aches to be filled with dollars*!" Gates's faith in the "civilizing" power of the dollar reflected the unabashed materialism of the age. But the cultural annihilation that Gates cheerfully predicted did not prove so easy.

Despite white authorities' efforts, Indians continued being Indians. Even in the "iron routine" of the "civilizing machine" at boarding school, Zitkala-Sa recounted how Indians retained their tribal loyalties and Indian identities. Students continued to speak tribal languages and attend tribal dances, even though the punishment was whipping with a leather belt. The schools themselves ultimately subverted their goal by creating generations of Indians who shared a common language, English, and would later create a pan-Indian reform movement in the Progressive Era.

How did the Dawes Allotment Act mark a new departure in Indian policy?

In the 1880s, the practice of rounding up and herding Indians onto reservations lost momentum in favor of allotment—a new policy designed to encourage assimilation through farming and the ownership of private property. Americans vowing to avenge Custer's defeat urged the government to get tough with the Indians. Reservations, they argued, took up too much good land that white settlers coveted and forced Americans to support "lazy" reservation Indians. At the same time, people sympathetic to the Indians were appalled at the desperate poverty on the reservations and feared for the Indians' survival. Helen Hunt Jackson, in her classic work *A Century of Dishonor* (1881), convinced many readers that the Indians had been treated unfairly. "Our Indian policy," the *New York Times* concluded, "is usually spoilation behind the mask of benevolence."

The Indian Rights Association, a group of mainly white easterners formed in 1882, campaigned for the dismantling of the reservations, now viewed as obstacles to progress. To "cease to treat the Indian as a red man and treat him as a man" meant putting an end to tribal communalism and fostering individualism. "Selfishness," declared Senator Henry Dawes of Massachusetts, "is at the bottom of civilization." Dawes called for "allotment in severalty"—the institution of private property.

Dawes Allotment Act
1887 law that divided up reservations and allotted parcels of land to individual Native Americans as private property. In the end, the U.S. government sold almost two-thirds of "surplus" Indian land to white settlers. The Dawes Act dealt a crippling blow to traditional tribal culture.

In 1887, Congress passed the **Dawes Allotment Act**, which divided up reservations and allotted parcels of land to individual Indians as private property. Indians who took allotments earned U.S. citizenship. By fostering individualism through land distribution, the Indian allotment policy ultimately dealt a crippling blow to traditional tribal culture. Eventually, many Native Americans sold their allotments and moved to urban areas, where they lost touch with tribal ways.

Since the government reserved the right to sell the "surplus" land to white settlers, the Dawes Act effectively reduced Indian land from 138 million acres to a scant 48 million. The legislation, in the words of one critic, worked "to despoil the Indians of their lands and to make them vagabonds on the face of the earth." By 1890, the United States controlled 97.5 percent of the territory formerly occupied by Native Americans.

How did Native Americans resist and survive white encroachment?

Faced with the extinction of their entire way of life, different groups of Indians responded in different ways. In the 1870s, Comanche and Kiowa raiding parties frustrated the U.S. Army by brazenly using the reservations as a seasonal supply base during the winter months. When spring came, they resumed their nomadic hunting so long as there were buffalo left to hunt.

Some tribes, including the Crow and Shoshoni, chose to fight alongside the army against their old enemies, the Sioux. The Crow chief Plenty Coups explained why he allied with the United States: "Not because we loved the white man . . . or because we hated the Sioux . . . but because we plainly saw that this course was the only one which might save our beautiful country for us." The Crow and Shoshoni got to stay in their homelands and avoided the fate of other tribes shipped to reservations far away.

Native Americans who refused to stay on reservations risked being hunted down. The Nez Percé war is perhaps the most harrowing example of the army's policy. In 1863, the government dictated a treaty drastically reducing Nez Percé land. Most of the chiefs refused to sign the treaty and did not move to the reservation. When the army cracked down in 1877, some eight hundred Nez Percé people, many of them women and children, fled across the mountains of Idaho, Wyoming, and Montana, heading for the safety of Canada. After a 1,300-mile trek, 50 miles from freedom, they stopped in the Bear Paw Mountains to rest in the snow. The U.S. Army caught up with them and attacked. Fewer than three hundred of the Indians escaped and made it to Canada. Yellow Wolf recalled the plight of those trapped: "Children crying with cold. No fire. There could be no light. Everywhere the crying, the death wail." After a five-day siege, the Nez Percé leader, Heinmot Tooyalakekt, or Chief Joseph, surrendered. His speech, reported by a white soldier, would become famous. "I am tired of fighting," he supposedly said as he surrendered his rifle. "Our chiefs are killed. It is cold and we have no blankets. The little children are freezing to death. . . . I am tired. My heart is sick and sad. From where the sun now stands, I will fight no more forever." General Sherman wanted to hang Chief Joseph, but instead he exiled the Nez Percé to Indian Territory, where they faced slow annihilation.

In the Southwest, the Apache resorted to armed resistance. They roamed the Sonoran Desert of southern Arizona and northern Mexico, perfecting a hit-and-run guerrilla warfare that terrorized white settlers and bedeviled the army in the 1870s and 1880s. General George Crook combined a policy of dogged pursuit with judicious diplomacy. Crook relied on Native American scouts to track the raiding parties, recruiting nearly two hundred Apache, Navajo, and Paiute. By 1882, Crook had succeeded in persuading most of the Apache to settle on the San Carlos Reservation in Arizona Territory. A desolate piece of desert inhabited by scorpions and rattlesnakes, San Carlos, in the words of one Apache, was "the worst place in all the great territory stolen from the Apaches."

Geronimo, a respected shaman (medicine man) of the Chiricahua Apache, refused to stay at San Carlos and repeatedly led raiding parties in the early 1880s. His warriors attacked ranches to obtain ammunition and horses. Among Geronimo's band was Lozen, a woman who rode with the warriors, armed with a rifle and a cartridge belt. Lozen's brother, a great chief, described her as being as "strong as a man, braver than most, and cunning in strategy." In the spring of 1885, Geronimo and his band went on a ten-month offensive, moving from the Apache sanctuary in the Sierra Madre to raid and burn ranches and towns on both sides of the Mexican border. General Crook caught up with Geronimo in the fall and persuaded him to return to San Carlos, only to have him slip away on the way back to the reservation. Chagrined, Crook resigned his post. General Nelson Miles, Crook's replacement, adopted a policy of search and destroy.

Geronimo's band consisted of only eighteen men and some twenty women and children. Miles commanded a force of five thousand. Yet the Apaches managed to elude Miles's troops for more than five months. Eventually, Miles's scouts cornered Geronimo in 1886 at Skeleton Canyon, where he agreed to march north and negotiate a settlement. "We have not slept for six months," he admitted, "and we are worn out."

Although fewer than three dozen Apache had been considered "hostile," the government rounded up nearly five hundred and sent them as prisoners to the South. Among them were the two scouts who had tracked Geronimo, still wearing their Army uniforms when they were thrown on the train. By 1889, more than one-quarter of the Apaches had died, some from malaria contracted in the damp lowland climate of Florida and Alabama and some by suicide. Their plight roused public opinion, and in 1892, those that remained were moved to Oklahoma and later to New Mexico.

Geronimo lived to become something of a celebrity. The "Scourge of the Sierra Madre" appeared at the St. Louis Exposition in 1904 and rode in President Theodore Roosevelt's inaugural parade in 1905. In a newspaper interview, he confessed, "I want to go to my old home before I die. . . . Want to go back to the mountains again. I asked the Great White Father to allow me to go back, but he said no." None of the Apaches were permitted to return to Arizona; when Geronimo died of pneumonia in 1909, he was buried in Oklahoma.

On the plains, many tribes turned to a nonviolent form of resistance — a compelling new religion called the **Ghost Dance**. A Nevada ranch hand named Jack Fisher, whose Paiute name was Wovoka, founded the Ghost Dance in 1889, promising it would bring rain to the drought-stricken region. Drawing on a cult developed in the 1870s, Wovoka received a vision in which the Great Spirit spoke through him to all Indians, prophesying that if they would unite in the Ghost Dance ritual the land would be restored, the buffalo would return, their dead ancestors would be resurrected, and whites would vanish. This religion, born of despair with its message of hope, spread like wildfire over the plains. In Idaho, Montana, Utah, Wyoming, Colorado, Nebraska, Kansas, the Dakotas, and Indian Territory, tribes as diverse as the Sioux, Arapaho, Cheyenne, Pawnee, and Shoshoni practiced the new religion. In the Ghost Dance, a circle of men, women, and children held hands and moved clockwise, often singing but without drums for accompaniment. The dance, performed both by Indians educated at Carlisle and by their uneducated brethren, had some variations. Dancers often wore special ghost shirts or dresses decorated with symbols, fringe, and beads. The Lakota Sioux claimed their white ghost shirts could magically stop bullets. Participants often went into hypnotic trances, dancing until they dropped from exhaustion and later recounting their visions.

Ghost Dance
Religion founded in 1889 by Paiute shaman Wovoka. It combined elements of Christianity and traditional Native American religion and served as a nonviolent form of resistance for Indians in the late nineteenth century. The Ghost Dance frightened white people and was violently suppressed.

Recent scholarship suggests that the Ghost Dance constituted a peaceful, legitimate attempt to accommodate to the changing world the Native Americans faced. Rather than emphasizing its backward-looking elements and dismissing it as desperate, militant, and futile, the Ghost Dance may be seen as a messianic, millenarian system of belief—"a forward looking, pragmatic religion." Wovoka told his followers "they must not fight; there must be peace all over the world." He urged Indians to "work all the time" and warned them "not to lay down in idleness." His message urged Indians to adapt to the white world. The Ghost Dance religion was itself distinctly modern. It spread rapidly not by magic but on iron rails as Native Americans moved throughout the west on railroads and through newspapers, telegrams, and letters that shared the promise among the newly literate that they could persist as Indians while surviving conquest and the reservation era.

Despite the peacefulness of the Ghost Dance, white reaction at the time became hysterical. "Indians are dancing in the snow and are wild and crazy," wrote the Bureau of Indian Affairs agent at the Pine Ridge Reservation in South Dakota. Frantic, he pleaded for reinforcements. "We are at the mercy of these dancers. We need protection, and we need it now." President Benjamin Harrison dispatched several thousand federal troops to Sioux country to handle any outbreak. With more than a third of the U.S. Army engaged on a remote reservation, the "Ghost Dance War" marked the largest military offensive since the Civil War while their adversaries numbered only four thousand Native Americans, mostly women, children, and old people.

In December 1890, when revered Chief Sitting Bull attempted to join the Ghost Dance religion, Indian police shot and killed him in his cabin on the Standing Rock Reservation. His people, fleeing the scene, joined with a larger group of Miniconjou Sioux, who were apprehended by the Seventh Cavalry, Custer's old regiment, near Wounded Knee Creek, South Dakota. Five hundred soldiers faced off against 120 Lakota men and boys and demanded that the Indians turn over their guns. As a soldier attempted to take a rifle from a deaf Miniconjou man, the gun went off and the soldiers opened fire, instantly killing eighty-three men and boys. In the ensuing massacre, more than two hundred Indian men, women, and children were slaughtered, some mowed down in minutes by the army's brutally efficient Hotchkiss machine guns and the rest, mainly women and children, pursued for up to three miles before being cut down. Swiss settler Jules Sandoz surveyed the scene the day after the massacre at **Wounded Knee**. "Here in ten minutes an entire community was as the buffalo that bleached on the plains," he wrote. "There was something loose in the world that hated joy and happiness as it hated brightness and color, reducing everything to drab agony and gray."

It had taken Euro-Americans 250 years to wrest control of the eastern half of the United States from the Indians. It took them only forty years to take the western half.

▲ **Ghost Dance Dress, 1904** An Arapaho woman poses in a Ghost Dance Dress at the 1904 Louisiana Purchase Exhibition in St. Louis, just fourteen years after the Ghost Dance religion spread over the West. White panic over the growing religion led to the killing of Sitting Bull and the massacre at Wounded Knee in 1890, the battle that officially ended the "Indian wars." Note the bird and stars motif, common in Ghost Dance dresses and shirts.   Field Museum Library/Getty Images.

Wounded Knee
1890 massacre of Sioux Indians by the Seventh Cavalry at Wounded Knee Creek, South Dakota. Sent to suppress the Ghost Dance, the soldiers opened fire on the Sioux as they attempted to surrender. More than two hundred Sioux men, women, and children were killed in this last episode in the "Indian Wars."

The subjugation of the Native Americans marked the first chapter in a national mission of empire that would anticipate U.S. overseas imperialistic adventures in Asia, Latin America, the Caribbean, and the Pacific islands.

REVIEW

How and why did U.S. Indian policy change between 1870 and 1890?

How did mining shape American expansion?

Comstock Lode
Silver ore deposit discovered in 1859 in Nevada. Discovery of the Comstock Lode touched off a mining rush that brought a diverse population into the region and led to the establishment of a number of boomtowns, including Virginia City, Nevada.

Mining stood at the center of the quest for empire in the West. The California gold rush of 1849 touched off the frenzy. The four decades following witnessed equally frenetic rushes for gold and other metals, most notably on the **Comstock Lode** in Nevada and later in New Mexico, Colorado, the Dakotas, Montana, Idaho, Arizona, and Utah (**Map 17.2**). At first glance, the mining West may seem much different from the East, but by the 1870s the term *urban industrialism* described Virginia City, Nevada, as accurately as it did Pittsburgh or Cleveland. A close look at life on the Comstock Lode indicates some of the patterns and paradoxes of western mining. The diversity of peoples drawn to the West by the promise of mining riches and land made the region the most cosmopolitan in the nation, as well as the most contested. And although mining was often a tale of boom and bust, it was also a story of community building.

What was life like on the Comstock Lode?

By 1859, refugees from California's played-out goldfields flocked to the Washoe basin in Nevada. While searching for gold, miners stumbled on the richest vein of silver ore on the continent—the legendary Comstock Lode, named for prospector Henry Comstock.

To exploit even potentially valuable silver claims required capital and expensive technology well beyond the means of the prospector. An active San Francisco stock market sprang up to finance operations on the Comstock. Shrewd businessmen soon recognized that the easiest way to get rich was to sell their claims or to form mining companies and sell shares of stock. The most unscrupulous mined the wallets of gullible investors by selling shares in bogus mining companies. Speculation, misrepresentation, and outright thievery ran rampant. In twenty years, more than $300 million poured from the earth in Nevada alone, most of it going to speculators in San Francisco.

The promise of gold and silver drew thousands to the mines of the West. As Mark Twain observed in Virginia City's *Territorial Enterprise*, "All the peoples of the earth had representative adventures in the Silverland." Irish, Chinese, Germans, English, Scots, Welsh, Canadians, Mexicans, Italians, Scandinavians, French, Swiss, Chileans, and other South and Central Americans came to share in the bonanza. With them came a sprinkling of Russians, Poles, Greeks, Japanese, Spaniards, Hungarians,

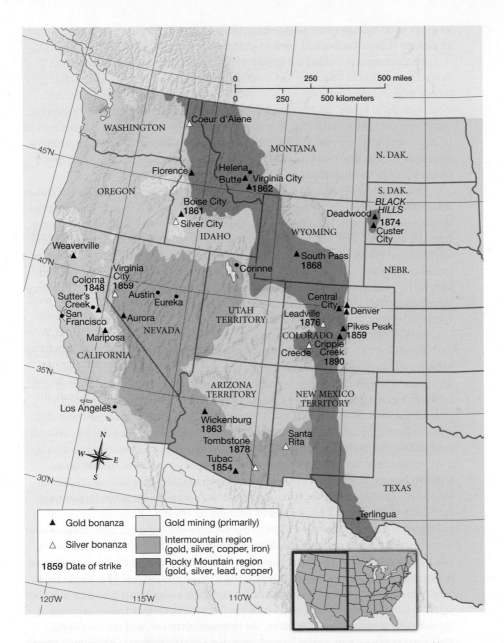

MAP 17.2 ▲ Western Mining, 1848–1890 Rich deposits of gold, silver, copper, lead, and iron larded the mountains of the West. Miners from all over the world flocked to the region. Few struck it rich, but many stayed on as paid workers in the increasingly mechanized corporate mines.

Portuguese, Turks, Pacific Islanders, and Moroccans, as well as other North Americans, African Americans, and Native Americans. This polyglot population, typical of mining boomtowns, made Virginia City in the 1870s more cosmopolitan than New York or Boston. In the part of the Utah Territory that eventually became Nevada, as many as 30 percent of the people came from outside the United States, compared to 25 percent in New York and 21 percent in Massachusetts.

Irish immigrants formed the largest ethnic group among the mining district's residents. In Virginia City, fully one-third of the population claimed at least one parent from Ireland. Irish women constituted the largest group of women on the Comstock. As servants, boardinghouse owners, and washerwomen, they made up a significant part of the workforce. In contrast, the Chinese community, numbering 642 in 1870, remained overwhelmingly male. Virulent anti-Chinese sentiment barred the men from work in the mines; nevertheless, the mining community came to depend on the Chinese for domestic labor.

The discovery of precious metals on the Comstock spelled disaster for the Native American way of life. No sooner had the miners struck pay dirt than they demanded that army troops "hunt Indians" and establish forts to protect transportation to and from the diggings. This sudden and dramatic intrusion left Nevada's native tribes— the Northern Paiute and Bannock Shoshoni—exiles in their own land. These hunter gatherers survived on a mix of wage labor and food foraged from town dumps and alleyways. They scavenged for firewood and combed through refuse piles. Over time they managed to adapt and preserve their culture and identity despite the havoc wreaked by western mining and settlement.

In 1873, Comstock miners uncovered a new vein of ore, a veritable cavern of gold and silver. This "Big Bonanza" speeded the transition from small-scale industry to corporate oligopoly, creating a radically new social and economic environment. The Comstock became a laboratory for new mining technology. Huge stamping mills pulverized rock with piston-like hammers driven by steam engines. Enormous Cornish pumps sucked water from the mine shafts, and giant ventilators circulated air in the underground chambers. No backwoods mining camp, Virginia City was an industrial center with more than twelve hundred stamping mills working on average a ton of ore every day. Almost four hundred men worked in milling, nearly three hundred labored in manufacturing industries, and roughly three thousand toiled in the mines. The Gould and Curry mine covered sixty acres. Most of the prospectors who came to the Comstock ended up as laborers for the big companies.

New technology eliminated some of the dangers of mining but often created new ones. In the hard-rock mines of the West, accidents in the 1870s disabled one out of every thirty miners and killed one in eighty. Ross Moudy, who worked as a gold miner in Cripple Creek, Colorado, recalled how a stockholder visiting the mine nearly fell to his death. The terrified visitor told the miner that "instead of being paid $3 a day, they ought to have all the gold they could take out." On the Comstock Lode—because of the difficulty of obtaining skilled labor, the richness of the ore, and the need for a stable workforce—labor unions formed early and held considerable bargaining power. Comstock miners commanded $4 a day, the highest wage in the mining West.

The mining towns of the "Wild West" are often portrayed as lawless outposts, filled with saloons and rough gambling dens and populated almost exclusively by men. The truth is more complex, as Virginia City's development attests. As an established urban community built to serve an industrial giant, Virginia City in its first decade boasted churches, schools, theaters, an opera house, and hundreds of families. By 1870, women composed 30 percent of the population, and 75 percent of the women listed their occupation in the census as housekeeper. Mary McNair Mathews, a widow from Buffalo, New York, who lived on the Comstock in the 1870s, worked as a teacher, nurse, seamstress, laundress, and lodging-house operator. She later published a book about her adventures.

By 1875, Virginia City boasted a population of 25,000 people, making it one of the largest cities between St. Louis and San Francisco. The city, dubbed the "Queen of the Comstock," hosted American presidents and legions of lesser dignitaries. Virginia City represented, in the words of a recent chronicler, "the distilled essence of America's newly established course—urban, industrial, acquisitive, and material-istic, on the move, 'a living polyglot' of cultures that collided and converged."

What groups fought for the West?

The West of the late nineteenth century was a polyglot place, as much so as the big cities of the East. The sheer number of peoples who mingled in the West produced a complex blend of racism and prejudice. One historian has noted, not entirely facetiously, that there were at least eight oppressed "races" in the West—Indians, Latinos, Chinese, Japanese, Blacks, Mormons, strikers, and radicals.

Determined to keep the Golden State for "white men only," mobs set upon and murdered any hapless group they deemed a threat. The numbers of Native Americans in California dropped precipitously; historians agree that if genocide occurred anywhere in the United States, it happened in California. Other groups faced similar treatment. In 1871, vigilantes in Los Angeles torched Chinatown. In the resulting melee, the crowd lynched seventeen Chinese immigrants, including one woman. The scene would repeat in towns and hamlets across the West. No act was judged too ruthless or too bloody in the attempt to drive out the Chinese. American slang underscored a grim reality: Someone facing overwhelming odds was said not to have "a Chinaman's chance."

African Americans who ventured out to the territories responded to racism by forming all-Black communities such as Nicodemus, Kansas. That settlement, founded by thirty Black Kentuckians in 1877, grew to a community of seven hundred by 1880. Isolated and often separated by great distances, small Black settlements grew up throughout the West, in Nevada, Utah, and the Pacific Northwest, as well as in Kansas. Black soldiers who served in the West during the Indian wars often stayed on as settlers. Called "buffalo soldiers" because Native Americans thought their hair resembled that of the bison, these Black troops numbered up to twenty-five thousand. Black people, along with immigrants—mostly Irish and German—and the nation's poor, constituted the frontier army. Underfed and often poorly armed, soldiers deserted in large numbers—up to 33 percent in 1871–1872. In the face of discrimination, poor treatment, and harsh conditions, the buffalo soldiers served with distinction and boasted the lowest desertion rate in the army.

Hispanic peoples had lived in Texas and the Southwest since Juan de Oñate led pioneer settlers up the Rio Grande in 1598. Hispanics had occupied the Pacific coast since San Diego was founded in 1769. Overnight, they were reduced to a minority after the United States annexed Texas in 1845 and took land stretching to California after the Mexican-American War ended in 1848. At first, the Hispanic owners of large *ranchos* in California, New Mexico, and Texas greeted conquest as an economic opportunity. But racial prejudice soon ended their optimism. *Californios* (Mexican residents of California), who had been granted American citizenship by the Treaty of Guadalupe Hidalgo (1848), faced discrimination by Anglos who sought to keep them out of California's mines and commerce.

On the Texas borderland in 1891, Caterino Estanza Garza led hundreds of border residents in challenging both the Mexican and American governments who sought to formalize what had been the permeable boundary between Texas and Mexico. Riding into the battle with the motto *libros fronterizos* (free border people), Garza's followers included wealthy merchants and landowners, poor farmers, landless ranchers, and a smattering of professionals—Mexicans, Texas-Mexicans, as well as a few Anglos and Italians. The military, refining tactics used against the Apache, brutally put down the rebellion.

In California, whites illegally squatted on *rancho* land while protracted litigation over Spanish and Mexican land grants forced the Californios into court. Although the U.S. Supreme Court eventually validated most of their claims, it took so long—seventeen years on average—that many Californios sold their property to pay taxes and legal bills.

Swindles, trickery, and intimidation dispossessed scores of Californios. Many ended up segregated in urban barrios (neighborhoods) in their own homeland. Their percentage of California's population declined from 82 percent in 1850 to 19 percent in 1880 as Anglos migrated to the state. In New Mexico and Texas, Mexicans remained a majority of the population but became increasingly impoverished as Anglos dominated business and took the best jobs. Skirmishes between Hispanics and whites in northern New Mexico over the fencing of the open range lasted for decades. Groups of Hispanics with names such as *Las Manos Negras* (the Black Hands) cut fences and burned barns. In Texas, violence along the Rio Grande pitted *Tejanos* (Mexican residents of Texas) against the Texas Rangers, state-supported vigilantes who saw their role as enforcing white supremacy, fighting Indians and "keeping Mexicans in their place."

Mormons, too, faced prejudice and hostility. The followers of Joseph Smith, the founder and prophet of the Church of Jesus Christ of Latter-Day Saints, fled west to the Utah Territory in 1844 to avoid religious persecution. They believed they had a divine right to the land, and their messianic militancy made others distrust them. The Mormon practice of polygamy (church leader Brigham Young had twenty-three wives) also came under attack. To counter the criticism of polygamy, the Utah territorial legislature gave women the right to vote in 1870, the first universal woman suffrage act in the nation. (Wyoming had granted suffrage to white women in 1869.) Although women's rights advocates expected the newly enfranchised women to "do away with the horrible institution of polygamy," it remained in force. Not until 1890 did the church hierarchy yield to pressure and renounce polygamy. The fierce controversy over polygamy postponed statehood for Utah until 1896.

Legislation as well as intimidation sought to keep Chinese out of California. As early as the 1850s California's governor called for laws curtailing Chinese immigration. Some twenty thousand Chinese had joined the rush to California by 1852. Miners succeeded in passing prohibitive foreign license laws to keep the Chinese out

◀ **Filling in the Secret Town Trestle, 1876** This iconic photo by Charlton Watkins is one of the most famous of the Chinese railroad workers. It shows Chinese laborers, recognizable by their characteristic hats, completing infill work on the great trestle near Colfax. On the right, more workers are busy breaking down hills, filling carts, and pulling them where fill was needed. Eventually they filled in the entire stretch, making the wood trestle unnecessary, and it was removed. PhotoQuest/Getty Images.

of the mines. But Chinese immigration continued. In the 1860s, when white workers moved on to find riches in the bonanza mines of Nevada, Chinese laborers took jobs abandoned by the whites. Railroad magnate Charles Crocker hired Chinese gangs to work on the Central Pacific, reasoning that "the race that built the Great Wall" could lay tracks across the treacherous Sierra Nevada. Some ten thousand Chinese, representing 90 percent of Crocker's workforce, completed America's first transcontinental railroad in 1869.

The Railroad Chinese proved frugal and resourceful. With the completion of the Central Pacific their skills commanded decent wages, and many Chinese saved enough to start small businesses. By 1870, more than 63,000 Chinese immigrants lived in America, 77 percent of them in California. A 1790 federal statute that limited naturalization to "white persons" was modified after the Civil War to extend naturalization to Blacks ("persons of African descent"). But the Chinese and other Asians continued to be denied access to citizenship. As perpetual aliens, they constituted what many saw as a threat to American labor.

In 1876, the Workingmen's Party formed to fight for Chinese exclusion. Racial and cultural animosities stood at the heart of anti-Chinese agitation. Denis Kearney, the fiery San Francisco leader of the movement, made clear this racist bent when he urged legislation to "expel every one of the moon-eyed lepers." Nor was California alone in its anti-immigrant nativism. As the country confronted growing ethnic and racial diversity with the rising tide of global immigration in the decades following the Civil War, many questioned the principle of racial equality and argued against the assimilation of "nonwhite" groups. In this climate, Congress passed the **Chinese Exclusion Act** in 1882, effectively barring Chinese immigration and setting a precedent for further immigration restrictions.

Chinese Exclusion Act
1882 law that effectively barred Chinese immigration and set a precedent for further immigration restrictions. The Chinese population in America dropped sharply as a result of the passage of the act, which was fueled by racial and cultural animosities.

Surveying the West in the decades following the gold rush, a stark pattern emerges. Whether called genocide, ethnic cleansing, lynching, or simply murder, the actions of white vigilantes against people of color deemed undesirable reached shocking proportions, while those in the East in positions of authority largely turned their backs on the bloodshed.

REVIEW

What role did mining play in shaping the society and economy of the American West?

How did the fight for land and resources in the West unfold?

I n the three decades following 1870, more land was settled than in all the previous history of the country. Americans by the hundreds of thousands packed up and moved west, goaded if not by the hope of striking gold then by the promise of owning land to farm or ranch. The agrarian West shared with the mining West a persistent restlessness, an equally pervasive addiction to speculation, and a penchant for exploiting natural resources and labor.

Two factors stimulated the land rush in the trans-Mississippi West. The **Homestead Act of 1862** promised 160 acres free to any citizen or prospective citizen, male or female, who settled on the land for five years. Even more important, transcontinental railroads opened new areas and actively recruited settlers. After the completion of the **first transcontinental railroad** in 1869, homesteaders abandoned the covered wagon, and by the 1880s, rampant railroad overbuilding meant that settlers could choose from four competing rail lines and make the trip in six days.

Although the country was rich in land and resources wrested from the Native Americans, not all who wanted to own land achieved their goal. As large commercial farming took hold, small farms and ranches gave way to vast spreads worked by migrant labor or paid farmworkers and cowhands. Just as industry corporatized and consolidated in the East, the period from 1870 to 1900 in the West witnessed corporate consolidation in mining, ranching, and agriculture.

What role did homesteaders and speculators play in the development of the West?

A Missouri homesteader remembered packing as her family pulled up stakes and headed west to Oklahoma in 1890. "We were going to God's Country," she wrote. "You had to work hard on that rocky country in Missouri. I was glad to be leaving it. . . . We were going to a new land and get rich."

Settlers who headed west in search of "God's Country" faced hardship, loneliness, and deprivation. To carve a farm from the raw prairie of Iowa, the plains

---

Homestead Act of 1862
An act that promised 160 acres in the trans-Mississippi West free to any citizen or prospective citizen who settled on the land for five years. The act spurred American settlement of the West. Altogether, nearly one-tenth of the United States was granted to settlers.

first transcontinental railroad
Railroad completed in 1869 that was the first to span the North American continent. Built in large part by Chinese laborers in the West, this railroad, followed soon by others, opened access to new areas in the West, fueling land speculation and actively recruiting settlers.

of Nebraska, or the forests of the Pacific Northwest took more than fortitude and backbreaking toil. It took luck. Blizzards, tornadoes, grasshoppers, hailstorms, drought, prairie fires, accidental death, and disease were only a few of the catastrophes that could befall even the best farmer. Homesteaders on free land still needed as much as $1,000 for a house, a team of farm animals, a well, fencing, and seed. Poor farmers called "sodbusters" did without even these basics, living in houses made from sod (blocks of grass-covered earth) or dugouts carved into hillsides and using muscle instead of machinery.

"Father made a dugout and covered it with willows and grass," one Kansas girl recounted. When it rained, the dugout flooded, and "we carried the water out in buckets, then waded around in the mud until it dried." Rain wasn't the only problem. "Sometimes the bull snakes would get in the roof and now and then one would lose his hold and fall down on the bed. . . . Mother would grab the hoe . . . and after the fight was over Mr. Bull Snake was dragged outside."

For women on the frontier, obtaining simple daily necessities such as water and fuel meant backbreaking labor. Out on the plains, where water was scarce, women often had to trudge to the nearest creek or spring. "A yoke was made to place across

VISUAL ACTIVITY

▲ **Norwegian Immigrant and Sod House** Norwegian immigrant Beret Olesdater sits in front of her sod house in Lac qui Parle, Minnesota, in 1896. On the plains, where trees were scarce, settlers carved dugouts into a hillside or built huts like the one here, carved from blocks of sod.
Minnesota Historical Society/Corbis via Getty Images.

READING THE IMAGE: What do the woman's dress and her expression tell us about the life of women on the plains?

CONNECTIONS: What expectations did homesteaders have for their lives on the plains, and how did these compare to the realities they faced?

[Mother's] shoulders, so as to carry at each end a bucket of water," one daughter recollected, "and then water was brought a half mile from spring to house."

Despite the hardships, some homesteaders succeeded in building comfortable lives. The dugout made way for the sod hut—a more substantial dwelling; the log cabin yielded to a white clapboard home with a porch and a rocking chair. For others, the promise of the West failed to materialize. Already by the 1870s, much of the best land had been taken. Too often, homesteaders found that only the least desirable tracts were left—poor land, far from markets, transportation, and society. "There is plenty of land for sale in California," one migrant complained in 1870, but "the majority of the available lands are held by speculators, at prices far beyond the reach of a poor man." The railroads, flush from land grants provided by the state and federal governments, owned huge swaths of land in the West and actively recruited buyers. Altogether, the land grants totaled approximately 180 million acres—an area as large as Texas. The vast majority of this land sold for a profit.

As land grew scarce on the prairie in the 1870s, farmers began to push farther west, moving into western Kansas, Nebraska, and eastern Colorado—the region called the Great American Desert by settlers who had passed over it on their way to California and Oregon. Many agricultural experts warned that the semiarid land (where less than twenty inches of rain fell annually) would not support a farm on the 160 acres allotted to homesteaders. But their words of caution were drowned out by the extravagant claims of western promoters, many employed by the railroads to sell off land grants. "Rain follows the plow" became the slogan of western boosters, who insisted that cultivation would alter the climate of the region and bring more rainfall.

Instead, drought followed the plow. Droughts were a cyclical fact of life on the Great Plains. Plowed up, the dry topsoil blew away in the wind. A period of relatively good rainfall in the early 1880s encouraged farming; then a protracted drought in the late 1880s and early 1890s forced thousands of starving farmers to leave, some in wagons carrying the slogan "In God we trusted, in Kansas we busted."

Fever for fertile land set off a series of spectacular land runs in Oklahoma. When two million acres of land in former Indian Territory opened for settlement in 1889, thousands of homesteaders massed on the border. At the opening pistol shot, "with a shout and a yell the swift riders shot out, then followed the light buggies or wagons," a reporter wrote. "Above all, a great cloud of dust hover[ed] like smoke over a battlefield." By nightfall, Oklahoma boasted two tent cities with more than ten thousand residents. In the last frenzied land rush on Oklahoma's Cherokee strip in 1893, several settlers were killed in the stampede, and nervous men guarded their claims with rifles. As public land dwindled, the hunger for land grew fierce for both farmers and ranchers.

Barbed wire, invented in 1874, revolutionized the cattle business and sounded the death knell for the open range. As the largest ranches in Texas began to fence, nasty fights broke out between big ranchers and "fence cutters," who resented the end of the open range. One old-timer observed, "Those persons, Mexicans and Americans, without land but who

Midwestern Settlement before 1862

had cattle were put out of business by fencing." Fencing forced small-time ranchers who owned land but could not afford to buy barbed wire or sink wells to sell out for the best price they could get. The displaced ranchers, many of them Mexicans, ended up as wageworkers on the huge spreads owned by Anglos or by European syndicates.

On the range, the cowboy gave way to the cattle king and, like the miner, became a wage laborer. Many cowboys were Black (as many as five thousand in Texas alone). Writers of western literature chose to ignore the presence of Black cowboys like Deadwood Dick (Nat Love), who was portrayed as a white man in the dime novels of the era. Nor was the cowboy's life romantic. George Schafer, who grew up on a ranch and later became governor of North Dakota, knew firsthand the hardships of ranch life. "Nearly every cowboy," he confessed, "is a physical wreck at the age of thirty-five years."

By the 1880s, cattle overcrowded the range. Severe blizzards during the winter of 1886–87 decimated the herds. "A whole generation of cowmen," wrote one chronicler, "went dead broke." Fencing worsened the situation. During blizzards, cattle stayed alive by keeping on the move. But when they ran up against barbed wire fences, they froze to death. In the aftermath of the "Great Die Up," new labor-intensive forms of cattle ranching replaced the open-range model.

What was life like for those who did not own land — tenants, sharecroppers, and migrants?

In the post–Civil War period, as agriculture became a big business tied by the railroads to national and global markets, an increasing number of laborers worked land that they would never own. In the southern United States, farmers labored under particularly heavy burdens. The Civil War wiped out much of the region's capital, which had been invested in enslaved persons, and crippled the plantation economy. "The colored folks stayed with the old boss man and farmed and worked on the plantations," a Black Alabama sharecropper observed bitterly. "They were still slaves, but they were free slaves." Some freedpeople did manage to pull together enough resources to go west. In 1879, more than fifteen thousand Exodusters, as the Black settlers were known, moved from Mississippi and Louisiana to take up land in Kansas.

California's Mexican cowboys, or *vaqueros*, commanded decent wages through-out the Southwest. But by 1880, as the coming of the railroads ended the long cattle drives and as large feedlots began to replace the open range, the value of their skills declined. Many vaqueros ended up as migrant laborers, often on land their families had once owned. Similarly, in Texas, Tejanos found themselves displaced. After the heyday of cattle ranching ended in the late 1880s, cotton production rose in the southeastern regions of the state. Ranchers turned their pastures into sharecroppers' plots and hired displaced cowboys, most of them Mexicans, as seasonal laborers for as little as seventy-five cents a day.

Land monopoly and large-scale farming fostered tenancy and migratory labor on the West Coast. By the 1870s, less than 1 percent of California's population owned half the state's available agricultural land. The rigid economics of large-scale commercial agriculture and the seasonal nature of the crops spawned a ragged army of migratory agricultural laborers. Derisively labeled "blanket men" or "bindle stiffs," these transients worked the fields in the growing season and wintered in the flophouses of San Francisco. After passage of the Chinese Exclusion Act of 1882, Mexicans, Filipinos, and Japanese immigrants filled the demand for migratory workers.

How did commercial farming give rise to industrial cowboys?

In the late nineteenth century, the population of the United States remained overwhelmingly rural. The 1870 census showed that nearly 80 percent of the nation's people lived on farms and in villages of fewer than eight thousand inhabitants. By 1900, the figure had dropped to 60 percent (**Figure 17.1**). At the same time, the number of farms rose. Rapid growth in the West increased the number of farms from 2 million in 1860 to more than 5.7 million in 1900.

New technology and farming techniques revolutionized American farm life. Mechanized farm machinery halved the time and labor cost of production and made it possible to cultivate vast tracts of land. Meanwhile, urbanization provided farmers with expanding markets for their produce, and railroads carried crops to markets thousands of miles away. Even before the start of the twentieth century, American agriculture had entered the era of what would come to be called agribusiness— farming as a big business—with the advent of huge commercial farms.

As farming moved onto the prairies and plains, mechanization took command. Steel plows, reapers, mowers, harrows, seed drills, combines, and threshers replaced human muscle. Horse-drawn implements gave way to steam-powered machinery. By 1880, a single combine could do the work of twenty men, vastly increasing the acreage a farmer could cultivate. Mechanization spurred the growth of bonanza

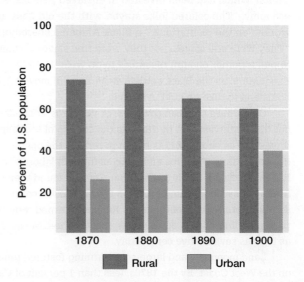

FIGURE 17.1 ▶ Changes in Rural and Urban Populations, 1870–1900 Between 1870 and 1900, both the number of urban dwellers and the number of farms increased, even as the number of rural inhabitants fell. Mechanization made it possible to farm with fewer hands, fueling the exodus from farm to city throughout the second half of the nineteenth century.

wheat farms, some more than 100,000 acres, in California and the Red River Valley of North Dakota and Minnesota. This agricultural revolution meant that Americans raised more than four times the corn, five times the hay, and seven times the wheat and oats they had before the Civil War.

Like cotton farmers in the South, western grain and livestock farmers increasingly depended on foreign markets for their livelihood. A fall in global market prices meant that a farmer's entire harvest went to pay off debts. In the depression that followed the panic of 1893, many heavily mortgaged farmers lost their land to creditors. As a Texas cotton farmer complained, "By the time the World Gets their Liveing out of the Farmer as we have to Feed the World, we the Farmer has nothing Left but a Bear Hard Liveing." Commercial farming, along with mining, represented another way in which the West developed its own brand of industrialism. The far West's industrial economy sprang initially from California gold and the vast territory gained following the Mexican-American War. In the ensuing rush on land and resources, environmental factors interacted with economic and social forces to produce enterprises as vast in scale and scope as anything found in the East.

Two German immigrants, Henry Miller and Charles Lux, pioneered the West's mix of agriculture and industrialism. With a labor force of migrant workers, a highly coordinated corporate system, and large sums of investment capital, the firm of Miller & Lux became one of America's industrial behemoths. Eventually, these "industrial cowboys" grazed a herd of 100,000 cattle on 1.25 million acres of company land in California, Oregon, and Nevada and employed more than 1,200 migrant laborers on their corporate ranches.

Miller & Lux dealt with the labor problem by offering free meals to migratory workers, thus keeping wages low while winning goodwill among an army of unemployed who competed for the work. When the company's Chinese cooks rebelled at washing all the dishes, the migrant laborers ate off dirty plates. By the 1890s, more than eight hundred migrants a year followed what came to be known as the "Dirty Plate Route" on Miller & Lux ranches throughout California.

Since the days of Thomas Jefferson, agrarian life had been linked with the highest ideals of a democratic society. But by the end of the nineteenth century, agrarianism had been transformed. The farmer was no longer a self-sufficient yeoman but often a businessman or a wage laborer tied to a global market. And even as farm production soared, industrialization outstripped it. More and more farmers left the fields for urban factories or found work in the "factories in the fields" of the new industrialized agribusinesses. Now that the future seemed to lie not with small farmers but with industrial enterprises, was democracy itself at risk? This question would ignite a farmers' revolt in the 1880s and dominate political debate in the 1890s.

REVIEW

Why did many homesteaders find it difficult to acquire good land in the West?

Conclusion: How did the West help set the tone for the Gilded Age?

I n 1871, author Mark Twain published *Roughing It*, a chronicle of his days spent in mining towns in California and Nevada. There he found the same corrupt politics, vulgar display, and mania for speculation that he later skewered in *The Gilded Age* (1873), his biting satire of greed and corruption in the nation's capital. Far from being an antidote to the tawdry values of the East—an innocent idyll out of place and time—the American West, with its get-rich-quick ethos, addiction to gambling and speculation, and virulent racism, set the tone for the Gilded Age.

Twain's view countered that of historian Frederick Jackson Turner. Turner, intent on promoting what was unique about the frontier, failed to note that the same issues that came to dominate debate east of the Mississippi—the growing power of big business, the exploitation of land and labor, corruption in politics, and ethnic and racial tensions exacerbated by colonial expansion and unparalleled immigration—also took center stage in the West at the end of the nineteenth century.

CHAPTER REVIEW

EXPLAIN WHY IT MATTERS

reservations (p. 483)

Comanchería (p. 485)

Red Cloud's War (p. 486)

Black Hills (p. 487)

Battle of the Little Big Horn (p. 487)

Carlisle Indian School (p. 491)

Dawes Allotment Act (p. 492)

Ghost Dance (p. 494)

Wounded Knee (p. 495)

Comstock Lode (p. 496)

Chinese Exclusion Act (p. 501)

Homestead Act of 1862 (p. 502)

first transcontinental railroad (p. 502)

PUT IT ALL TOGETHER

NATIVE AMERICANS

- How did Native Americans respond to the flood of westward migration after the Civil War?
- How did Native Americans respond to changes in federal Indian policy between 1865 and 1900?

NATURAL RESOURCES AND TRANSPORTATION IN THE WEST

- Why was mining so important in the economy and society of the West and of the nation?
- What role did the railroads play in the development of the West?

THE WEST AND ETHNIC DIVERSITY

- What was the impetus for and impact of the Chinese Exclusion Act?
- How did racial and ethnic prejudice affect relations among westerners?

LOOKING BACKWARD, LOOKING AHEAD

- How did western expansion before the Civil War differ from western expansion after the Civil War?
- What new political and economic issues and tensions did American expansion raise?
- How did American lives and livelihoods change as a result of migration to the West?

18

THE GILDED AGE

1865–1900

This chapter discusses the following questions:

- How did the railroads stimulate big business?
- Why did the ideas of social Darwinism appeal to wealthy Americans?
- What factors influenced political life in the late nineteenth century?
- What issues shaped party politics in the late nineteenth century?
- What role did economic issues play in party realignment?
- Conclusion: How did business dominate the Gilded Age?

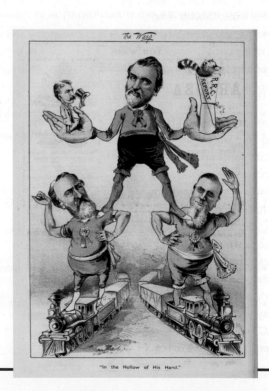

"In the Hollow of His Hand."

▶ **"In the Hollow of His Hand"** In this February 1881 political cartoon that appeared in *The Wasp*, a San Francisco illustrated weekly, Central Pacific Railroad mogul Leland Stanford stands on the shoulders of his partners, Collis P. Huntington (left) and Richard Croker (right). In his hand he holds the railroad commissioner and his report, with a racoon popping out the top. The so-called "Big Three" built the road, in the words of Croker, "for the profits we could make in building it," profits estimated at over $200 million — billions in today's currency. *The Wasp* (San Francisco, California) Vol. 6, 1881.

AN AMERICAN STORY

In 1861, four Sacramento store owners — Collis P. Huntington and his partner Mark Hopkins (hardware), Leland Stanford (groceries), and Charles Crocker (dry goods) — created the Central Pacific Railroad. A year later, Congress passed the Pacific Railroad Act, authorizing a transcontinental railroad and granting a right-of-way to the Union Pacific to build west from Omaha and to the Central Pacific to build east from Sacramento. The government provided both companies with a lavish package of loans, bonds, cash payments, and massive grants of public land — 6,400 acres for every mile of track. Four obscure California storekeepers had managed to score one of the biggest government contracts in history. In time, they would take at least $200 million from the enterprise — billions in today's dollars.

"None of us knew anything about railroad building," the red-faced, 250-pound Crocker admitted, "but at the same time [we] were enterprising men." The Big Four, as they became known, quickly settled into their respective roles. Stanford managed relationships with the state of California, Huntington took care of lobbying in Washington, Hopkins kept the books, and Charles Crocker supervised construction.

Crocker was born in Troy, New York, in 1822, and came west with the forty-niners. He failed at prospecting but excelled as a ruthless railroad manager. For a dollar a day, Crocker hired Chinese emigrant workers to tunnel through the Sierra Nevada mountains. When the crews reached the eastern slope, the cry became "a mile a day!" Construction subsidies depended on miles of track laid, and Crocker pushed his men hard. On May 10, 1869, after some six years, the Central Pacific and the Union Pacific railroads met at Promontory Summit, Utah.

Years later, Crocker declared, "We built that road for the profits we could make in building it." Not much interested in moving people and goods, the Big Four were instead experts at lining their own pockets. They organized a sham construction company and paid construction costs from government funds to themselves. A suit against the Central Pacific charged that of the $240 million the company received in government subsidies, only $19 million actually went to railroad construction.

On the eve of a congressional investigation, Hopkins burned the Central Pacific's books to hide the plunder. The Big Four forged maps and surveys, tricked inspectors, and laid miles of bad track. They bought newspapermen, created phony stockholders, and lied to banks when they borrowed. They provoked conflict with Native Americans, bullied ranchers off their lands, and may even have condoned murder. Huntington spent five years in Washington, D.C., carrying a leather satchel crammed with cash. "There are more hungry men in Congress this session than I have ever known before," he complained.

1892	Ida B. Wells launches anti-lynching campaign.
1893	Wall Street panic touches off national depression.
1895	J. P. Morgan bails out U.S. Treasury.
1901	U.S. Steel incorporated and capitalized at $1.4 billion.

Late in his career, Crocker mused: "One man works hard all his life and ends up a pauper. Another man, no smarter, makes twenty million dollars. Luck has a hell of a lot to do with it." Luck no doubt played a part, but ruthless disregard for the law, cruel exploitation of labor, and unremitting greed also figured in the success of the Big Four. One rival described Crocker as "a living, breathing, waddling monument of the triumph of vulgarity, viciousness and dishonesty."

While working furiously to get rich, the Big Four also built a railroad. The Iron Horse — the transcontinental railroad — marked one of the great triumphs of the Gilded Age.

How did the railroads stimulate big business?

I n the years following the Civil War, the American economy underwent a transformation. Where once wealth had been measured in tangible assets—property, livestock, and buildings—the economy now ran on money and the new devices of business—paper currency, securities, and anonymous corporate entities. Wall Street, the heart of the country's financial system, increasingly affected Main Street, as became evident in the depression following the panic of 1873. Driving the transition was the building of a transcontinental railroad system, which radically altered the scale and scope of American industry. Old industries like iron transformed into modern industries such as the behemoth U.S. Steel. Discovery and invention stimulated new industries, from oil refining to electric light and power. The overbuilding of railroads in the decades after the Civil War played a key role in transforming the American economy as business came to rely on huge government subsidies, "friends" in Congress, and complicated financial transactions.

Jay Gould in railroads, Andrew Carnegie in steel, and John D. Rockefeller in oil pioneered new strategies to seize markets and consolidate power. With keen senses of self-interest, these tycoons set the tone in the get-rich-quick era of freewheeling capitalism that came to be called the **Gilded Age**.

Gilded Age
A period of enormous economic growth and ostentatious displays of wealth during the last quarter of the nineteenth century. Industrialization dramatically changed U.S. society and created a newly dominant group of rich entrepreneurs and an impoverished working class.

How did the railroads become America's first big business?

The military conquest of America's inland empire and the dispossession of Native Americans (see chapter 17) was fed by an elaborate new railroad system in the West built on speculation and government giveaways. Between 1870 and 1880, the amount of track in the country doubled, and it nearly doubled again in the following decade. The railroads, built in advance of settlement, provoked Indian wars that resulted in a vast spatial rearrangement that some called nation building but later generations have labeled ethnic cleansing. By 1900, the nation boasted more than 193,000 miles of railroad track—more than in all of Europe and Russia combined (**Map 18.1**). Credit fueled the railroad boom. Privately owned but publicly financed and subsidized by enormous land grants from the federal government and the states, the railroads epitomized the insidious nexus of business and politics in the Gilded Age.

To understand how the railroads came to dominate American life, there is no better place to start than with the career of Jay Gould, the era's most notorious speculator. Jason "Jay" Gould bought his first railroad before he turned twenty-five. It was only sixty-two miles long, in bad repair, and on the brink of failure, but within two years he sold it at a profit of $130,000 (over $2.5 million in today's dollars).

The secretive Gould operated in the stock market like a shark, looking for vulnerable railroads, buying enough stock to take control, and threatening to undercut his competitors until they bought him out at a profit. The railroads that fell into his hands often went bankrupt. Gould's genius lay not in providing transportation but in

MAP ACTIVITY

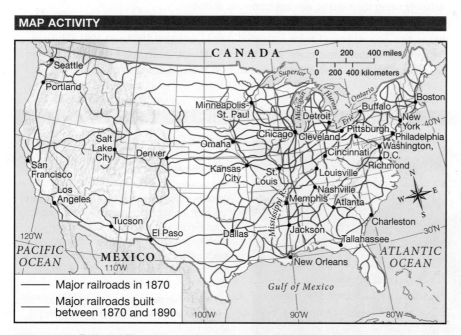

MAP 18.1 ▲ Railroad Expansion, 1870–1890 Railroad mileage nearly quadrupled between 1870 and 1890, with the greatest growth occurring in the trans-Mississippi West. The western lines were completed in the 1880s. Fueled by speculation and built ahead of demand, the western railroads made fortunes for individual speculators. But they rarely paid for themselves and speeded the demise of Native Americans.

READING THE MAP: Where were most of the railroad lines located in 1870? What was the end point of the only western route? By 1890, how many railroads reached the West Coast?
CONNECTIONS: Why were so many rails laid between 1870 and 1890? How did the railroads affect the nation's economy?

cleverly buying and selling railroad stock on Wall Street. Gould soon realized that a corporate failure could still mean financial success. His strategy of expansion and consolidation encouraged overbuilding even as it stimulated a new national market.

The first transcontinental railway had been completed in 1869 at Promontory Point, Utah. In the 1880s, Gould moved to put together a second transcontinental railroad. To defend their interests, his competitors had little choice but to adopt his strategy of expansion. The railroads built ahead of demand, regardless of the social and environmental costs. Soon more railroads drove into the West—by 1893, Kansas alone had at least six competing lines.

The railroad barons put up little of their own money to build the roads and instead relied on the largesse of government and the sale of railroad bonds and stock. Bondholders were creditors who required repayment at a specific time. Stockholders bought a share in the company and received dividends if the company prospered. Thus, railroad investors received money from these sales of financial interests but did not need to pay out until later. If the railroad failed, a court-appointed receiver determined how many pennies on the dollar shareholders received. The owners, astutely using the market, always came out ahead.

With help from railroad growth and speculation, the New York Stock Exchange expanded. The volume of stock increased sixfold between 1869 and 1901. The line between investment and speculation blurred, causing many Americans to question whether speculators fueled the boom and bust cycles that led to panic and

VISUAL ACTIVITY

JUSTICE IN THE WEB.

◄ **Jay Gould as a Spider** In this famous 1885 political cartoon titled "Justice in the Web," artist Frederick Burr Opper portrays Jay Gould as a hideous spider whose web, formed by Western Union telegraph lines, has entrapped "Justice" through its monopoly of the telegraph industry. Gould made his fortune through speculation on railroads, which often ran with telegraph lines alongside the tracks. Images like this one fueled the public's hatred of Gould. GRANGER – Historical Picture Archive.

READING THE IMAGE: By portraying Gould as a spider, what is the cartoonist trying to say about him?

CONNECTIONS: In what ways did wealthy industrialists use manipulative techniques for personal gain?

depression in 1873 and again twenty years later. The dramatic growth of the railroads created the country's first big business. Before the Civil War, even the largest textile mill in New England employed no more than 800 workers. By contrast, the Pennsylvania Railroad by the 1870s boasted a payroll of more than 55,000 employees. Capitalized at more than $400 million, the Pennsylvania Railroad constituted the largest private enterprise in the world.

The big business of railroads bestowed enormous riches on a handful of tycoons. Both Gould and his competitor "Commodore" Cornelius Vanderbilt amassed fortunes estimated at $100 million. Such staggering wealth eclipsed the power and influence of upper-class Americans from previous generations and created an abyss between the nation's rich and poor. In its wake, it left a legacy of lavish spending for an elite crop of ultrarich heirs.

The Republican Party, firmly entrenched in Washington after the Civil War, worked closely with business interests, subsidizing the transcontinental railroad system. Significant amounts of money changed hands to move bills through Congress. Along with "friends," often on the railroads' payrolls, lobbyists worked to craft legislation favorable to railroad interests. State legislatures and Congress lavished the new western roads with land grants of a staggering 100 million acres (taken from Native American land) and $64 million in tax incentives and direct aid. States and local communities joined the railroad boom, betting that only those towns and villages along the tracks would flourish.

A revolution in communication accompanied and supported the growth of the railroads. The telegraph, developed by Samuel F. B. Morse, marched across the continent alongside the railroad. By transmitting coded messages along electrical wire, the telegraph formed the nervous system of the new industrial order. Telegraph service quickly replaced Pony Express mail carriers in the West and transformed business by providing instantaneous communication. Once again Jay Gould took the lead. In 1879, through stock manipulation, he seized control of Western Union, the company that monopolized the telegraph industry.

The railroads soon fell on hard times. Already by the 1870s, lack of planning led to overbuilding. Across the nation, railroads competed fiercely for business. Manufacturers in areas served by competing railroads could get substantially reduced shipping rates in return for promises of steady business. Because railroad owners lost money through this kind of competition, they tried to set up agreements, or "pools," to divide up territory and set rates. But these informal gentlemen's agreements invariably failed because men like Gould, intent on undercutting all competitors, refused to play by the rules.

How did Andrew Carnegie pioneer vertical integration in steel?

If Jay Gould was the man Americans loved to hate, Andrew Carnegie became one of America's heroes. Unlike Gould, Carnegie turned his back on speculation and worked to build something enduring — Carnegie Steel, the biggest steel business in the world during the Gilded Age.

The growth of the steel industry proceeded directly from railroad building. The first railroads ran on iron rails, which cracked and broke with alarming frequency.

Steel, both stronger and more flexible than iron, remained too expensive for use in rails until Englishman Henry Bessemer developed a process to make steel more cheaply. Andrew Carnegie, among the first to champion the new "King Steel," came to dominate the emerging industry.

Carnegie, a Scottish immigrant, landed in New York in 1848 at the age of twelve. He rose from a job cleaning bobbins in a textile factory to become one of the richest men in America. Before he died, he gave away more than $300 million, most notably to public libraries. His generosity, combined with his own rise from poverty, burnished his public image.

When Carnegie was seventeen, his skill as a telegraph operator caught the attention of Tom Scott, superintendent of the Pennsylvania Railroad. Scott hired Carnegie, soon promoted him, and lent him the money for his first foray into Wall Street investment. As a result of this crony capitalism, Carnegie became a millionaire before his thirtieth birthday. At that point, Carnegie turned away from speculation. "My preference was always manufacturing," he wrote. "I wished to make something tangible." By applying the lessons of cost accounting and efficiency that he had learned with the Pennsylvania Railroad, Carnegie turned steel into the nation's first manufacturing big business.

In 1872, Andrew Carnegie built the world's largest, most up-to-date steel mill in Braddock, Pennsylvania. At that time, steelmakers produced about seventy tons a week. Within two decades, Carnegie's blast furnaces poured out an incredible ten thousand tons a week. His formula for success was simple: "Cut the prices, scoop the market, run the mills full; watch the costs and profits will take care of themselves." Carnegie pioneered a system of business organization called vertical integration in which all aspects of the business were under his control—from the mining of iron ore, to its transport on the Great Lakes, to the production of steel. As one observer noted, "there was never a price, profit, or royalty paid to any outsider."

The great productivity Carnegie encouraged came at a high price. He deliberately pitted his managers against one another, firing the losers and rewarding the winners with a share in the company. Carnegie's mills were deadly. Workers achieved the output Carnegie demanded by enduring low wages, dangerous working conditions, and twelve-hour days, six days a week and sometimes seven. One worker, observing the contradiction between Carnegie's generous endowment of public libraries and his labor policy, complained, "After working twelve hours, how can a man go to a library?"

By 1900, Andrew Carnegie had become the best-known manufacturer in the nation, and the age of iron had yielded to an age of steel (**Figure 18.1**). Steel from Carnegie's mills supported the elevated trains in New York and Chicago, formed the skeleton of the Washington Monument, supported the first steel bridge to span the Mississippi, and girded America's first skyscrapers. As a captain of industry, Carnegie's only rival was the titan of the oil industry, John D. Rockefeller.

What means did John D. Rockefeller use to create the Standard Oil trust?

In the days before the automobile and gasoline, crude oil was refined into lubricating oil for machinery and kerosene for lamps, the major source of lighting in the nineteenth century. The amount of capital needed to buy or build an oil refinery in

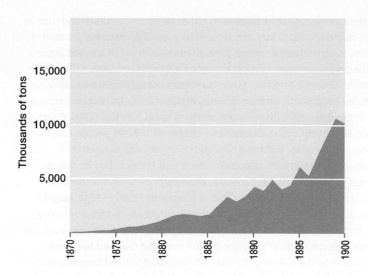

FIGURE 18.1 ◄ Iron and Steel Production, 1870–1900 Iron and steel production in the United States grew from nearly none in 1870 to ten million tons a year by 1900. The secrets to such a great increase were the use of the Bessemer process and vertical integration, pioneered by Andrew Carnegie. By 1900, Carnegie's mills alone produced more steel than all of Great Britain. With corporate consolidation after 1900, the rate of growth in steel proved even more spectacular.

the 1860s and 1870s remained relatively low—roughly what it cost to lay one mile of railroad track. As a result, the new petroleum industry experienced riotous competition. Ultimately, John D. Rockefeller and his Standard Oil Company succeeded in controlling nine-tenths of the oil-refining business.

Rockefeller grew up the son of a shrewd Yankee who peddled quack cures for cancer. Under his father's rough tutelage, Rockefeller learned how to drive a hard bargain. In 1865, at the age of twenty-five, he controlled the largest oil refinery in Cleveland. Like a growing number of business owners, Rockefeller abandoned partnership or single proprietorship to embrace the corporation as the business structure best suited to maximize profit and minimize personal liability. In 1870, he incorporated his oil business, founding the Standard Oil Company.

Given the size of his business, Rockefeller was able to demand illegal rebates from the railroads in exchange for his steady business. The secret rebates enabled Rockefeller to drive out his competitors through predatory pricing. The railroads needed Rockefeller's business so badly that they even gave him a share of the rates that his competitors paid. A Pennsylvania Railroad official later confessed that Rockefeller extracted such huge rebates that the railroad sometimes ended up paying him to transport Standard's oil. Rebates enabled Rockefeller to undercut his competitors and pressure competing refiners to sell out or face ruin.

To legitimize Standard Oil's secret deals, Rockefeller in 1882 pioneered a new form of corporate structure—the **trust**. The trust differed markedly from Carnegie's vertical approach in steel. Rockefeller used horizontal integration to control not the entire process but only a single aspect of oil production—refining. Several trustees held stock in various refinery companies in trust for Standard's stockholders. This elaborate stock swap allowed the trustees to coordinate policy among the refineries by gobbling up all the small, competing refineries. Often buyers did not know they were selling to Standard. By the end of the century, Rockefeller enjoyed a virtual monopoly of the oil-refining business. The Standard Oil trust, valued at more than $70 million, paved the way for trusts in sugar, whiskey, matches, and many other products.

trust
A system in which corporations give shares of their stock to trustees who hold the stocks "in trust" for their stockholders, thereby coordinating the industry to ensure profits to the participating corporations and to curb competition.

When the federal government responded to public pressure to outlaw the trust in 1890, Standard Oil changed tactics and reorganized as a holding company. Instead of stockholders in competing companies acting through trustees to set prices and determine territories, the holding company simply brought competing companies under one central administration. Now one business, not an assortment of individual refineries, Standard Oil controlled competition without violating antitrust laws that forbade competing companies from forming "combinations in restraint of trade." By the 1890s, Standard Oil ruled more than 90 percent of the oil business, employed 100,000 people, and was the biggest, richest, most feared, and most admired business organization in the world.

John D. Rockefeller enjoyed enormous success in business, but he was not popular. Editor and journalist Ida M. Tarbell's *The History of the Standard Oil Company*, which ran in serial form in *McClure's Magazine* (1902–1904), largely shaped the public's harsh view of Rockefeller. Her father had owned a refinery squeezed out by Rockefeller, and Tarbell scrupulously chronicled the illegal methods Rockefeller used to take over the oil industry. By the time she finished her story, Rockefeller slept with a loaded revolver by his bed. Standard Oil and the man who created it had become the symbol of heartless monopoly.

How did new inventions like the telephone and electricity transform American life?

The second half of the nineteenth century was an age of invention. Men like Thomas Alva Edison and Alexander Graham Bell became folk heroes. But no matter how dramatic the inventions, the new electric and telephone industries pioneered by Edison and Bell soon eclipsed their inventors and fell under the control of bankers and industrialists.

Alexander Graham Bell came to America from Scotland at the age of twenty-four with a passion to find a way to teach the deaf to speak (his wife and mother were deaf). Instead, he developed a way to transmit voice over wire—the telephone. Bell's invention astounded the world when he demonstrated it at the Philadelphia Centennial Exposition in 1876. In 1880, Bell's company, American Bell, pioneered "long lines" (long-distance telephone service), creating American Telephone and Telegraph (AT&T) as a subsidiary.

In 1900, AT&T developed a complicated structure that enabled Americans to communicate not only locally but also across the country. And unlike a telegraph message, the telephone connected both parties immediately and privately. Bell's invention proved a boon to business, contributing to speed and efficiency. The number of telephones soared, reaching 310,000 in 1895 and more than 1.5 million in 1900.

Even more than Alexander Graham Bell, inventor Thomas Alva Edison embodied the old-fashioned virtues of Yankee ingenuity and rugged individualism that Americans most admired. A self-educated dynamo, Edison worked twenty hours a day in his laboratory in Menlo Park, New Jersey, vowing to turn out "a minor invention every ten days and a big thing every six months or so." He made good on his promise. At the height of his career, he averaged a patent every eleven days and invented such "big things" as the phonograph, the motion picture camera, and the filament for the incandescent lightbulb.

▶ **Telephone Operator** The first telephone operators in the 1880s were young boys. But they were often rude and rowdy and soon replaced with women, who were expected to be better behaved. The operators worked twelve-hour shifts, often using both hands to connect calls. They were monitored for deportment and not allowed to cross their legs or even blow their noses without permission. Nevertheless, white middle-class women welcomed the new job opportunity, a step up from school teacher, and by 1900, New York City alone boasted over six thousand women telephone operators. Topical Press Agency/Getty Images.

Edison, in competition with George W. Westinghouse, pioneered the use of electricity as an energy source. By the late nineteenth century, electricity had become a part of American urban life. It powered trolley cars and lighted factories, homes, and office buildings. Indeed, electricity became so prevalent in urban life that it symbolized the city, whose bright lights contrasted with rural America, left largely in the dark.

The day of the inventor quietly yielded to the heyday of the corporation. In 1892, the electric industry consolidated. Reflecting a nationwide trend in business, Edison General Electric dropped the name of its inventor, becoming simply General Electric (GE). For years, an embittered Edison refused to set foot inside a GE building. GE, a prime example of the trend toward business consolidation, soon dominated the market.

REVIEW

What tactics and strategies did American business owners employ during the Gilded Age?

Why did the ideas of social Darwinism appeal to wealthy Americans?

E ven as Rockefeller and Carnegie built their empires, the era of the "robber barons," as their detractors dubbed them, was drawing to a close. Increasingly, businesses replaced partnerships and sole proprietorships with the anonymous corporate structure that would come to dominate the twentieth century. At the same time, mergers led to the creation of huge new corporations.

Banks and financiers played key roles in this consolidation, so much so that the decades at the turn of the twentieth century can be characterized as a period of

finance capitalism
Investment sponsored by banks and bankers that typified the American business scene at the end of the nineteenth century. After the panic of 1893, bankers stepped in and reorganized major industries to stabilize them, leaving power concentrated in the hands of a few influential capitalists.

finance capitalism — the economic and political dominance of financial institutions and financiers. When the depression that followed the panic of 1893 bankrupted many businesses, bankers stepped in to bring order and to reorganize major industries. During these years, a new social philosophy developed that helped to justify consolidation and to inhibit state or federal regulation of business. A conservative Supreme Court further frustrated attempts to control business by consistently declaring unconstitutional legislation designed to regulate railroads or to outlaw trusts and monopolies.

How did J. P. Morgan come to dominate finance capitalism?

John Pierpont Morgan, the preeminent finance capitalist of the late nineteenth century, loathed competition and sought whenever possible to eliminate it by substituting consolidation and central control. Morgan's passion for order made him the architect of business mergers. At the turn of the twentieth century, he dominated American banking, exerting an influence so powerful that his critics charged he controlled a vast "money trust" even more insidious than Rockefeller's Standard Oil.

Morgan acted as a power broker in the reorganization of the railroads and the creation of industrial giants such as General Electric. When the railroads collapsed, Morgan took over and eliminated competition by creating what he called "a community of interest." By the time he finished "Morganizing" the railroads, a handful of directors controlled two-thirds of the nation's track. His directors were bankers, not railroad men, and they saw the roads as little more than "a set of books." Their conservative approach aimed at short-term profit and discouraged the technological and organizational innovation necessary to run the railroads effectively.

In 1898, Morgan moved into the steel industry, directly challenging Andrew Carnegie. The pugnacious Carnegie cabled his partners in the summer of 1900: "Action essential: crisis has arrived . . . have no fear as to the result; victory certain." The press trumpeted news of the impending fight between the feisty Scot and the haughty Wall Street banker. But for all his belligerence, the sixty-six-year-old Carnegie yearned to retire to Scotland. Morgan, who disdained haggling, agreed to pay Carnegie's asking price, $480 million (the equivalent of about $10 billion in today's currency). According to legend, when Carnegie later teased Morgan, saying that he should have asked $100 million more, Morgan replied, "You would have got it if you had."

Morgan's acquisition of Carnegie Steel signaled the passing of the old entrepreneurial order personified by Andrew Carnegie and the arrival of a new anonymous corporate world. Morgan quickly moved to pull together Carnegie's chief competitors to form a huge new corporation, United States Steel, known today as USX. Created in 1901 and capitalized at $1.4 billion, U.S. Steel was the largest corporation in the world. Morgan, observed one of his contemporaries, "is apparently trying to swallow the sun."

Even more than Carnegie or Rockefeller, Morgan left his stamp on the twentieth century and formed the model for corporate consolidation that economists and social scientists justified with a new social theory later called social Darwinism.

What was the relationship between the theories of social Darwinism and laissez-faire?

John D. Rockefeller Jr., the son of the founder of Standard Oil, once remarked to his Baptist Bible class that the Standard Oil Company, like the American Beauty rose, resulted from "pruning the early buds that grew up around it." The elimination of competition, he declared, was "merely the working out of a law of nature and a law of God."

The comparison of the business world to the natural world resembled the theory of evolution formulated by the British naturalist Charles Darwin. In his monumental work *On the Origin of Species* (1859), Darwin theorized that in the struggle for survival, adaptation to the environment triggered among species a natural selection process that led to evolution. Herbert Spencer in Britain and William Graham Sumner in the United States developed the theory of **social Darwinism**. The social Darwinists insisted that societal progress came about as a result of relentless competition in which the strong survived and the weak died out.

In social terms, the idea of the "survival of the fittest," a phrase coined by Spencer, had profound significance. Sumner, a professor of political economy at Yale University, stated the principle baldly in his book *What Social Classes Owe to Each Other* (1883). "The drunkard in the gutter is just where he ought to be, according to the fitness and tendency of things," Sumner insisted. Conversely, "millionaires are the product of natural selection," and although "they get high wages and live in luxury," Sumner claimed, "the bargain is a good one for society."

Social Darwinists equated wealth and power with "fitness" and believed that any efforts by the rich to aid the poor would tamper with the laws of nature and slow down evolution. Social Darwinism acted to curb social reform while glorifying great wealth. In an age when Rockefeller and Carnegie amassed hundreds of millions of dollars (billions in today's currency) and the average worker earned $500 a year, social Darwinism justified economic inequality and stood as a solid barrier to reform.

Carnegie softened some of the harshness of social Darwinism in his essay "The Gospel of Wealth," published in 1889. The millionaire, Carnegie wrote, acted as a "mere trustee and agent for his poorer brethren, bringing to their service his superior wisdom, experience, and ability to administer, doing for them better than they could or would do for themselves." Carnegie preached philanthropy and urged the rich to "live unostentatious lives" and "administer surplus wealth for the good of the people." His **gospel of wealth** earned much praise but won few converts. Most millionaires followed the lead of Morgan, who contributed to charity but hoarded private treasures in his marble library.

With its emphasis on the free play of competition and the survival of the fittest, social Darwinism encouraged the economic theory of laissez-faire (French for "let it alone"). Business leaders argued that government should not meddle in economic affairs, except to protect private property (or support high tariffs and government subsidies). A conservative Supreme Court agreed. During the 1880s and 1890s, the Court increasingly reinterpreted the Constitution, judging corporations to be "persons" in order to protect business from taxation, regulation, labor organization, and antitrust legislation.

social Darwinism
A social theory popularized in the late nineteenth century by Herbert Spencer and William Graham Sumner. Proponents believed that only relentless competition could produce social progress and that wealth was a sign of "fitness" and poverty a sign of "unfitness" for survival.

gospel of wealth
The idea that the financially successful should use their wisdom, experience, and wealth to help the poor. Andrew Carnegie promoted this view in an 1889 essay in which he maintained that the wealthy should serve as stewards to society as a whole.

Only in the arena of politics did Americans tackle the social issues raised by corporate capitalism.

How did social Darwinism shape American society and business in the late nineteenth century?

What factors influenced political life in the late nineteenth century?

For many Americans, politics provided a source of identity, a means of livelihood, and a ready form of entertainment. No wonder voter turnout averaged a hefty 77 percent (compared to roughly 67 percent in the 2020 presidential election). A variety of factors contributed to the complicated interplay of politics and culture. Patronage provided an economic incentive for voter participation, but ethnicity, religion, sectional loyalty, race, and gender all influenced the political life of the period.

Why was party loyalty so important to America's voters?

Political parties in power doled out federal, state, and local government jobs to their loyal supporters. Money greased the wheels of the politics of patronage, dubbed the **spoils system** from the adage "To the victor go the spoils." With the expansion of the federal government necessitated by the Civil War, hundreds of thousands of jobs needed to be filled. The choice of party affiliation could mean the difference between a paycheck and an empty pocket. Salaries might be low, but many benefited from **fee-based governance**, where public officials received a portion of monies collected from fees and taxes. Lawman Wyatt Earp wanted to be sheriff in Arizona because the 10 percent of the fees and taxes the sheriff collected amounted to tens of thousands of dollars a year. Political parties took their cut, but even honest officials made money under the system. With their livelihoods tied to their party identity, government employees had a powerful incentive to vote in great numbers.

Political affiliation provided a sense of group identity for many voters proud of their loyalty to the Democrats or the Republicans. Democrats, who traced the party's roots back to Thomas Jefferson, called theirs "the party of the fathers." The Republican Party, founded in the 1850s, still claimed strong loyalties in the North because of its alignment with the Union during the Civil War. Republicans proved particularly adept at evoking Civil War loyalty, using a tactic called "waving the bloody shirt."

Religion and ethnicity also played significant roles in politics. In the North, Protestants from the old-line denominations, particularly Presbyterians and Methodists, flocked to the Republican Party, which championed a series of moral reforms,

spoils system
System in which politicians doled out government positions to their loyal supporters. This patronage system led to widespread corruption during the Gilded Age.

fee-based governance
System where public employees receive a percentage of fees, taxes, bounties, and subsidies collected. For example, postmasters got a small percentage on the stamps they sold.

including local laws requiring business to close on Sunday. In the cities, the Democratic Party courted immigrants and working-class Catholic and Jewish voters and charged, rightly, that Republican moral crusades often masked attacks on immigrant culture.

What role did sectionalism and the New South play in national politics?

After the end of Reconstruction, most white voters in the former Confederate states remained loyal Democrats, creating the so-called solid South that lasted for the next seventy years. Labeling the Republican Party the agent of "Negro rule," Democrats urged white southerners to "vote the way you shot." Yet the South proved far from solid for the Democrats on the state and local levels, leading to shifting political alliances and to third-party movements that challenged Democratic attempts to define politics along race lines and maintain the Democrats as the white man's party.

The South's economy, devastated by the war, foundered at the same time the North experienced an unprecedented industrial boom. Soon an influential group of southerners called for a "New South" modeled on the industrial North. Henry Grady, the ebullient young editor of the *Atlanta Constitution*, used his paper's influence to exhort the South to use its natural advantages — cheap labor and abundant natural resources — to go head-to-head in competition with northern industry. And even as southern Democrats took back control of state governments, they embraced northern promoters who promised prosperity and profits.

The railroads came first, opening the region for industrial development. Southern railroad mileage grew fourfold from 1865 to 1890. The number of cotton spindles also soared as textile mill owners abandoned New England in search of the cheap labor and proximity to raw materials promised in the South. By 1900, the South had become the nation's leading producer of cloth, and more than 100,000 southerners, two-thirds of them women and children, worked in the region's textile mills.

The New South prided itself most on its iron and steel industry, which grew up in the area surrounding Birmingham, Alabama. During this period, the smokestack replaced the white-pillared plantation as the symbol of the New South. Andrew Carnegie toured the region in 1889 and observed, "The South is Pennsylvania's most formidable industrial enemy." But southern industry remained controlled by northern investors, who had no intention of letting the South beat the North at its own game. Elaborate mechanisms rigged the price of southern steel, inflating it, as one northern insider confessed, "for the purpose of protecting the Pittsburgh mills and in turn the Pittsburgh steel users." Similarly, in the lumber and mining industries, investors in the North and abroad, not southerners, reaped the lion's share of the profits.

In only one industry did the South truly dominate — tobacco. Capitalizing on the invention of a machine for rolling cigarettes, the American Tobacco Company, founded by the Duke family of North Carolina, eventually dominated the industry. As cigarettes replaced chewing tobacco in popularity at the turn of the twentieth century, a booming market developed for Duke's "ready mades." Soon the company sold 400,000 cigarettes a day and happy wives threw out the odious, ubiquitous spittoon.

In practical terms, the industrialized New South proved an illusion. Much of the South remained agricultural, caught in the grip of the insidious crop lien system (see chapter 16). White southern farmers, desperate to get out of debt, sometimes joined Black voters to pursue mutual political goals. Between 1865 and 1900, voters in every southern state experimented with political alliances that crossed the color line and threatened the status quo.

How did gender and race influence politics?

Gender—society's notion of what constitutes acceptable masculine or feminine behavior—influenced politics throughout the nineteenth century. From the early days of the Republic, citizenship had been defined in male terms. Citizenship and its prerogatives (voting and officeholding) served as a badge of manliness and rested on its corollary, patriarchy—the power and authority men exerted over their wives and children. With the advent of universal white male suffrage in the early nineteenth century, gender eclipsed class as the defining feature of citizenship; men's dominance over women provided the common thread that knit all white men together politically. The concept of separate spheres dictated political participation for men only. Once the public sphere of political participation became equated with manhood, women found themselves increasingly restricted to the private sphere of the home.

Jim Crow
System of racial segregation in the South lasting from after the Civil War into the twentieth century. Jim Crow laws segregated Black people in public facilities such as trains and streetcars, curtailed their voting rights, and denied other basic civil rights.

Women were not alone in their limited access to the public sphere. Black people continued to face discrimination well after Reconstruction, especially in the New South. Segregation, commonly practiced through **Jim Crow** laws (as discussed in chapter 21), prevented freed Black people from riding in the same train cars as whites, from eating in the same restaurants, or from using the same toilet facilities.

Amid the turmoil of the post-Reconstruction South, some groups struck cross-racial alliances. In Virginia, the "Readjusters," a coalition of Blacks and whites determined to "readjust" (lower) the state debt and spend more money on public education, captured state offices from 1879 to 1883. Groups like the Readjusters believed universal political rights could be extended to Black males while maintaining racial segregation in the private sphere. Democrats fought back by arguing that Black voting would lead to racial mixing and urged whites to return to the Democratic fold to protect "white womanhood."

The notion that Black men threatened white southern women reached its most vicious form in the practice of lynching—the killing and mutilation of Black men by white mobs. By 1892, the practice had become so prevalent that a courageous Black editor, Ida B. Wells, launched an anti-lynching movement. That year, a white mob lynched three of Wells's friends when their grocery store competed too successfully with a white-owned store. Wells shrewdly concluded that lynching served "as an excuse to get rid of Negroes who were acquiring wealth and property and thus keep the race terrorized." **(See "Analyzing Historical Evidence: Ida B. Wells and Her Campaign to Stop Lynching" on page 526.)**

She began to collect data on lynching and discovered that in the decade between 1882 and 1892, lynching rose in the South by an overwhelming 200 percent, with more than 241 Black people killed. The vast increase in lynching testified to the retreat of the federal government following Reconstruction and to white southerners' determination to maintain supremacy through terrorism and intimidation.

► **Ida B. Wells** Ida B. Wells began her anti-lynching campaign in 1892 after the murder of three friends led her to examine lynching in the South. Through lectures and pamphlets, she brought the horror of lynching to national and international audiences, and she became a founding member of the National Association for the Advancement of Colored People (NAACP). Special Collections Research Center, University of Chicago Library.

Wells articulated lynching as a problem of gender as well as race. She insisted that the myth of Black attacks on white southern women masked the reality that mob violence had more to do with economics and the shifting social structure of the South than with rape. She demonstrated in a sophisticated way how the southern patriarchal system, having lost its control over Black people with the end of slavery, used its control over white women to circumscribe the liberty of Black men. Wells's outspoken stance immediately resulted in reprisal. While she was traveling in the North, vandals ransacked her office in Tennessee and destroyed her printing equipment. Yet the warning that she would be killed on sight if she ever returned to Memphis only stiffened her resolve. As she wrote in her autobiography, *Crusade for Justice* (1928), "Having lost my paper, had a price put on my life and been made an exile . . . , I felt that I owed it to myself and to my race to tell the whole truth now that I was where I could do so freely."

Lynching did not become a federal crime until 2022, but Wells's forceful voice brought the issue to national and international prominence a century earlier. Black leader W. E. B. Du Bois eulogized Wells as the woman who "began the awakening of the conscience of the nation" at her funeral in 1931. Wells's determined campaign against lynching provided just one example of women's political activism during the Gilded Age. The suffrage and temperance movements, along with the growing popularity of women's clubs, dramatized how women refused to be relegated to a separate sphere that kept them out of politics.

How were women active in politics before they got the vote?

In 1869, Elizabeth Cady Stanton and Susan B. Anthony formed the National Woman Suffrage Association (NWSA), the first independent women's rights organization in the United States, to fight for the vote for women. Already women had found ways to act politically before they voted and used their moral authority as wives and mothers to move from the domestic sphere into the realm of politics.

The extraordinary activity of women's clubs in the period following the Civil War provides just one example. Women's clubs proliferated beginning in the 1860s. Newspaper reporter Jane Cunningham Croly (pen name Jennie June) founded the

ANALYZING HISTORICAL EVIDENCE

Ida B. Wells and Her Campaign to Stop Lynching

Ida B. Wells fearlessly crusaded to stop lynching in the South by researching and reporting lynchings in detail and by comparing coverage from Black and white sources.

DOCUMENT 1

Ida B. Wells, Editorial Protesting the Lynching of Friends in Memphis, 1892

The lynching in 1892 of three friends who ran a grocery store outside of Memphis touched Wells deeply. She wrote an outraged editorial in the Free Press. *Later she would repeat the details in her first pamphlet,* Southern Horrors: Lynch Law in All Its Phases *(1892).*

On March 9, 1892, there were lynched in this same city three of the best specimens of young since-the-war Afro-American manhood. They were peaceful, law-abiding citizens and energetic business men. . . . They owned a flourishing grocery business in a thickly populated suburb of Memphis, and a white man named Barrett had one on the opposite corner. After a personal difficulty which Barrett sought by going into the "People's Grocery" drawing a pistol and was thrashed by Calvin McDowell, he (Barrett) threatened to "clean them out." These men were a mile beyond the city limits and the police protection; hearing that Barrett's crowd was coming to attack them Saturday night, they mustered forces and prepared to defend themselves against the attack.

When Barrett came he led a posse of officers, twelve in number, who afterward claimed to be hunting a man for whom they had a warrant. That twelve men in citizen's clothes should think it necessary to go in the night to hunt one man who had never before been arrested, or made any record as a criminal has never been explained. When they entered the back door the young men thought the threatened attack was on, and fired into them. Three of

the officers were wounded, and when the defending party found it was officers of the law upon whom they had fired, they ceased and got away.

Thirty-one men were arrested and thrown in jail as "conspirators," although they all declared more than once they did not know they were firing on officers. Excitement was at fever heat until the morning papers, two days after, announced that the wounded deputy sheriffs were out of danger. This hindered rather than helped the plans of the whites. There was no law on the statute books which would execute an Afro-American for wounding a white man, but the "unwritten law" did. Three of these men, the president, the manager and the clerk of the grocery — "the leaders of the conspiracy" — were secretly taken from jail and lynched in a shockingly brutal manner. "The Negroes are getting too independent," they say, "we must teach them a lesson."

What lesson? The lesson of subordination. "Kill the leaders and it will cow the Negro who dares to shoot a white man, even in self-defense."

Source: *Southern Horrors and Other Writings*, edited by Jacqueline Jones Royster (Boston: Bedford/St. Martin's, 1997), 64–65.

DOCUMENT 2

Ida B. Wells, On Lack of Justice and Due Process for Accused Blacks, 1894

In her 1894 pamphlet The Red Record, *Wells insisted that lynching assumed all Black men were guilty, thus denying them the constitutional right to defend themselves in front of a judge and jury.*

In lynching, opportunity is not given the Negro to defend himself against the unsupported accusations of white men and women. The word of the accuser is held to be true and the excited blood-thirsty mob demands that the rule of law be reserved and instead of proving the accused to be guilty, the victim of their hate and revenge must prove himself innocent. No evidence he can offer will satisfy the mob; he is bound hand and foot and swung into eternity. Then to excuse its infamy, the mob almost invariably reports the monstrous falsehood that its victim made a full confession before he was hanged.

Source: Royster, *Southern Horrors*, 153.

DOCUMENT 3
Ida B. Wells, On Mob Rule in New Orleans, 1900

In her last pamphlet, Mob Rule in New Orleans, *Wells describes the riot that occurred when a Black man, Robert Charles, attacked by a police officer with a billy club, retaliated. This led to a duel that then brought on further violence.*

During the entire time the mob held the city in its hands and went about holding up street cars and searching them, taking from them colored men to assault, shoot and kill, chasing colored men upon the public square, through alleys and into houses of anybody who would take them in, breaking into the homes of defenseless colored men and women and beating aged and decrepit men and women to death, the police and the legally-constituted authorities showed plainly where their sympathies were, for in no case reported through the daily papers does there appear the arrest, trial and conviction of one of the mob for any of the brutalities which occurred. The ringleaders of the mob were at no

time disguised. Men were chased, beaten, and killed by white brutes, who boasted of their crimes, and the murderers still walk the streets of New Orleans, well known and absolutely exempt from prosecution. Not only were they exempt from prosecution by the police while the town was in the hands of the mob, but even now that law and order is supposed to resume control, these men, well known, are not now, nor ever will be, called to account for the unspeakable brutalities of that terrible week. On the other hand, the colored men who were beaten by the police and dragged into the station for purposes of intimidation were quickly called before the courts and fined or sent to jail upon the statement of the police.

Source: Royster, *Southern Horrors*, 181–82.

Questions for Analysis

ANALYZE THE EVIDENCE: In her campaign to end lynching, how does Wells seek to generate sympathy for the victims and to build an outraged anti-lynching coalition that will end the practice?

RECOGNIZE VIEWPOINTS: How did the white people involved in lynching defend their actions?

CONSIDER THE CONTEXT: In addition to lynching, what else did white southerners do to keep Blacks in subordinate positions?

◀ **"Woman's Holy War"** This political cartoon styles the temperance campaign as "Woman's Holy War" and shows a woman knight in armor (demurely seated sidesaddle on her charger), wielding a battle-ax and trampling on barrels of liquor. The image of temperance women as ax-wielding Amazons proved a popular satiric image. The cartoon appeared in 1874, the year the Woman's Christian Temperance Union formed. Picture Research Consultants & Archives.

Sorosis Club in New York City in 1868 after the New York Press Club denied entry to women journalists wishing to attend a banquet honoring the British author Charles Dickens. In 1890, Croly brought state and local clubs together under the umbrella of the General Federation of Women's Clubs (GFWC). Not wishing to alienate southern women, the GFWC barred Black women's clubs from joining, despite vehement objections. Women's clubs soon abandoned literary pursuits to devote themselves to "civic usefulness," endorsing an end to child labor, supporting the eight-hour workday, and helping pass pure food and drug legislation.

The temperance movement (the movement to end drunkenness) attracted by far the largest number of organized women in the late nineteenth century. In the late 1860s and the 1870s, the liquor business flourished, with about one saloon for every fifty males over the age of fifteen. During the winter of 1873–74, temperance women adopted a radical new tactic. Armed with Bibles and singing hymns, they marched on taverns and saloons and refused to leave until the proprietors signed a pledge to quit selling liquor.

Known as the Woman's Crusade, the movement spread through small towns in Ohio, Indiana, Michigan, and Illinois and soon moved east into New York, New England, and Pennsylvania. Before it was over, more than 100,000 women had marched in more than 450 cities and towns.

The women's tactics may have been new, but the temperance movement dated back to the 1820s. Originally, Protestant men led the movement, organizing clubs to pledge voluntary abstinence from liquor. By the 1850s, temperance advocates won significant victories when states, starting with Maine, passed laws to prohibit the sale of liquor. The Woman's Crusade dramatically brought the issue of temperance back into the national spotlight and led to the formation of a new organization, the **Woman's Christian Temperance Union (WCTU)**, in 1874. Composed entirely of women, the WCTU advocated total abstinence from alcohol.

Temperance provided women with a respectable outlet for their increasing resentment of women's inferior status and their growing recognition of women's capabilities. In its first five years, the WCTU relied on education and moral suasion, but when Frances Willard became president in 1879, she politicized the organization (see chapter 20).

When the women of the WCTU joined with the Prohibition Party (formed in 1869 by a group of evangelical clergymen), one wag observed, "Politics is a man's game,

Woman's Christian Temperance Union (WCTU)
All-women organization founded in 1874 to advocate total abstinence from alcohol. The WCTU provided important political training for women, which many used in the suffrage movement.

an' women, childhern, and prohyibitionists do well to keep out iv it." By sharing power with women, the prohibitionist men violated the old political rules and risked attacks on their honor and manhood.

Even though women found ways to affect the political process, especially in third parties, it remained true that politics, like chewing tobacco, constituted an exclusively male prerogative.

REVIEW

How did race and gender influence politics?

What issues shaped party politics in the late nineteenth century?

The presidents of the Gilded Age, from Rutherford B. Hayes (1877–1881) to William McKinley (1897–1901), are largely forgotten men, primarily because so little was expected of them. The dominant creed of laissez-faire, coupled with the dictates of social Darwinism, warned the presidents and the government to leave business alone (except when government worked in business's interests). Thanks to the spoils system, political parties mattered much more than presidents. Still, reformers struggled toward the creation of new political ethics designed to replace patronage with a civil service system that promised to award jobs on merit, not party loyalty.

How did corruption and party strife come to dominate American politics?

The political corruption and party factionalism that characterized the administration of Ulysses S. Grant (1869–1877) (see chapter 16) continued to trouble the nation in the 1880s. The spoils system remained the driving force in party politics at all levels of government. Pro-business Republicans generally held a firm grip on the White House, while Democrats had better luck in Congress. Both parties relied on patronage and fee-based governance to cement party loyalty.

A small but determined group of reformers championed a new ethics that would preclude politicians from getting rich from public office. The selection of U.S. senators particularly concerned them. Under the Constitution, senators were selected by state legislatures, not directly elected by the voters. Powerful business interests often contrived to control state legislatures and, through them, U.S. senators. As journalist Henry Demarest Lloyd quipped, Standard Oil "had done everything to the Pennsylvania legislature except to refine it." In this climate, a constitutional amendment calling for the direct election of senators faced stiff opposition from entrenched interests.

Republican president Rutherford B. Hayes came to the presidency following a disputed election determined by a special electoral commission. He owed the presidency to his promise to the Democrats to back off on Republican reconstruction policies and remove troops from the South. Although his political rivals dismissed him as "Rutherfraud," Hayes proved a hardworking, well-informed executive who wanted peace, prosperity, and an end to party strife. The Republican Party remained divided into factions led by strong party bosses, who boasted that they could make or break any president.

Foremost among the Republican Senate bosses stood Roscoe Conkling of New York. An imposing six foot three with a luxurious blonde beard, Conkling led a faction called the "Stalwarts." He and his followers fiercely supported the patronage system, dismissing reform as "snivel service." Conkling's rival Senator James G. Blaine of Maine led the "Half Breeds," who were less openly corrupt yet still tainted by their involvement in financial scandals. A third group, called the "Mugwumps," consisted of reformers from Massachusetts and New York who deplored the spoils system and advocated civil service reform.

President Hayes appeased his Democratic opponents but alienated his own party. Few were surprised when he announced that he would not seek reelection in 1880. To avoid choosing among its factions, the Republicans in 1880 nominated a dark-horse candidate, Representative James A. Garfield of Ohio. To foster party unity, they picked Stalwart Chester A. Arthur as the vice-presidential candidate. The Democrats attempted to overcome sectionalism by selecting former Union general Winfield Scott Hancock, who garnered only lukewarm support, receiving just 155 electoral votes to Garfield's 214, although the popular vote proved less lopsided.

How did Garfield's assassination lead to civil service reform?

"My God," Garfield swore after only a few months in office, "what is there in this place that a man should ever want to get into it?" Garfield, like Hayes, faced the difficult task of remaining independent while pacifying the party bosses and placating the reformers. On July 2, 1881, less than four months after taking office, Garfield was shot and died two months later. His assailant, Charles Julius Guiteau, though clearly insane, turned out to be a disappointed office seeker, motivated by political partisanship. He told the police officer who arrested him, "I did it; I will go to jail for it: Arthur is president, and I am a Stalwart."

The press almost universally condemned Republican factionalism for creating the political climate that produced Guiteau. Attacks on the spoils system increased, and both parties claimed credit for passage of the Pendleton Civil Service Act of 1883, ushering in **civil service reform**. The law established a permanent Civil Service Commission consisting of three members appointed by the president. Some fourteen thousand jobs came under a merit system that required examinations for office and made it impossible to remove jobholders for political reasons. The new law also prohibited federal employees from contributing to political campaigns, thus drying up the major source of the party bosses' revenue. Whether by intention or accident, the new merit system favored the white and educated over immigrants and people of color. And business soon stepped in as the nation's chief political contributor, giving already powerful interests an even greater influence in political life.

civil service reform
Effort in the 1880s to end the spoils system and reduce government corruption. The Pendleton Civil Service Act of 1883 created the Civil Service Commission to award government jobs under a merit system that required examinations for office and made it impossible to remove jobholders for political reasons.

What role did reform and scandal play in the presidential campaign of 1884?

James G. Blaine assumed leadership of the Republican Party and at long last captured the presidential nomination in 1884. A magnetic Irish American, Blaine inspired such devotion that his supporters called themselves Blainiacs. But Mugwump reformers bolted the party and embraced the Democrats' presidential nominee, Governor Grover Cleveland of New York. The burly, beer-drinking Cleveland distinguished himself from a generation of politicians by the simple motto "A public office is a public trust."

First as mayor of Buffalo and later as governor of New York, he built a reputation for honesty, economy, and administrative efficiency. The Democrats, who had not won the presidency since 1856, had high hopes for his candidacy, especially after the Mugwumps threw their support to Cleveland, announcing, "The paramount issue this year is moral rather than political."

They soon regretted their words. In July, Cleveland's hometown paper, the *Buffalo Telegraph*, dropped the bombshell that a decade earlier the candidate had raped a local widow and fathered an illegitimate child. Cleveland, a bachelor, stoically accepted responsibility for the child, although some speculated that one of his married friends had fathered the boy. Crushed by the scandal, the Mugwumps lost much of their enthusiasm. At public rallies, Blaine's partisans taunted Cleveland, chanting, "Ma, Ma, where's my Pa?"

Blaine set a new campaign style by launching a whirlwind national tour. On a last-minute stop in New York City, the exhausted candidate committed a misstep that may have cost him the election. He overlooked a remark by a supporter, a local clergyman who cast a slur on Catholic voters by styling the Democrats as the party of "rum, Romanism, and rebellion." Linking drinking (rum) and Catholicism (Romanism) offended Irish Catholic voters, whom Blaine had counted on to desert the Democratic Party and support him because of his Irish background.

With less than a week to go until the election, Blaine had no chance to recover from the negative publicity. He lost New York State by fewer than 1,200 votes and with it the election. In the final tally, Cleveland defeated Blaine by a scant 23,005 votes nationwide but won with 219 electoral votes to Blaine's 182, ending twenty-four years of Republican control of the presidency. Cleveland's followers had the last word. To the chorus of "Ma, Ma, where's my Pa?" they retorted, "Going to the White House, ha, ha, ha."

How did Henry George use the issue of inequality to campaign for mayor of New York?

While Democrats and Republicans squabbled over spoils or worked to reform the corrupt process, disaffected working men and women looked to new leaders. With the ostentatious mansions of Fifth Avenue just blocks from the rancid tenements of lower Manhattan, New York City starkly mirrored the growing disparity of wealth that marked the Gilded Age. A yawning gap divided the haves and the have-nots. Fewer than 1 percent of Americans had scooped up 51 percent of the nation's wealth, a percentage approached again only in the early twenty-first century, when the top 1 percent accounted for 40 percent of the nation's wealth.

Economist and writer Henry George pointed to the paradox of poverty amid plenty in a surprise best seller he titled *Progress and Poverty*. "It is as though an immense wedge were being forced through society," he wrote in 1879. "Those who are above the point of separation are elevated but those who are below are crushed down." Something was wrong, and he called on the government to fix it through

▶ **Henry George Campaign**
Mayoral candidate Henry George mounted a "tailboarding" campaign in New York in 1886, giving speeches from the back of a wagon as he tore through the city. George lost to the Tammany Hall candidate but succeeded in spreading his reform message that the huge disparity in wealth evident in the Gilded Age posed a threat to democracy. His book *Progress and Poverty* was a runaway best seller. GRANGER – Historical Picture Archive.

taxation. His cause attracted the support of labor, who backed him in New York's 1886 mayoral race. George waged a strenuous campaign, speaking six or seven times a day from the tailboard of a wagon.

The size and enthusiasm of his crowds frightened moneyed New Yorkers, who saw in any working-class alliance the potential for bloody revolution. No wonder they quaked in fear when thirty thousand marchers braved a driving rain to march in a "Monster Parade" days before the election. A record number of voters turned out for the contest. Democrats managed to eke out a victory, largely thanks to the political dirty tricks of Tammany Hall, the center of New York's Democratic Party. George captured 68,000 votes, however, significantly more than the Republican candidate, a political up-and-comer named Theodore Roosevelt.

REVIEW

How did the question of civil service reform contribute to divisions within the Republican Party?

What role did economic issues play in party realignment?

On the national level in the election of 1888, fickle voters turned Cleveland out, electing Republican Benjamin Harrison, the grandson of President William Henry Harrison. Then, in the only instance in American history when a president once defeated at the polls returned to office, the voters brought Cleveland back in the election of 1892. What factors account for such a surprising turnaround? The 1880s witnessed a remarkable political realignment as economic concerns replaced appeals to Civil War sectional loyalties. The tariff, federal regulation of the railroads and trusts, and the campaign for free silver restructured American politics. In 1893, a Wall Street panic set off a major depression that further fed political unrest.

Why was the tariff such a potent political issue in the 1880s and 1890s?

The concept of a protective tariff to raise the price of imported goods and stimulate American industry dated back to the founding days of the Republic. Republicans turned the tariff to political ends in 1861 by enacting a measure that both raised revenues for the Civil War and rewarded their industrial supporters, who wanted protection from foreign competition. After the war, the pro-business Republicans continued to raise the tariff, which in the era before income tax, provided the lion's share of government revenue. Manufactured goods (such as steel and textiles) and some agricultural products (including sugar and wool) benefited from protection. Most farm products, notably wheat and cotton, did not. By the 1880s, the tariff produced more than $2.1 billion in revenue. Not only did the high tariff pay off the nation's Civil War debt and fund pensions for Union soldiers, but it also created a huge surplus that sat idly in the Treasury's vaults while the government argued about how (or even whether) to spend it.

To many Americans, particularly southern and midwestern farmers, who sold their crops in a world market but had to buy goods priced artificially high because of the protective tariff, the answer was simple: Reduce the tariff. But the Republican Party seized on the tariff question to forge a new national coalition. "Fold up the bloody shirt and lay it away," Blaine advised a colleague in 1880. "It's of no use to us. You want to shift the main issue to protection." By encouraging an alliance among industrialists, labor, and western producers of raw materials—groups seen to benefit from the tariff—Blaine hoped to solidify the North, Midwest, and West against the solidly Democratic South. Although the tactic failed for Blaine in the presidential election of 1884, it worked for the Republicans four years later.

Cleveland, who had straddled the tariff issue in the election of 1884, startled the nation in 1887 by calling for tariff reform. The president attacked the tariff as a tax levied on American consumers by powerful industries. And he pointed out that high tariffs impeded the expansion of American markets abroad at a time when American industries needed to expand. The Republicans countered by arguing that "tariff tinkering" would unsettle prosperous industries, drive down wages, and shrink the farmers' home market. Republican Benjamin Harrison, who supported the high tariff, ousted Cleveland from the White House in 1888, carrying all the western and northern states except Connecticut and New Jersey.

Back in power, the Republicans brazenly passed the highest tariff in the nation's history in 1890. The new tariff, sponsored by Republican representative William McKinley of Ohio, stirred up a hornet's nest of protest across the United States. The American people had elected Harrison to preserve protection, not to enact a higher tariff. Democrats condemned the McKinley tariff and labeled the Republican Congress that passed it the "Billion Dollar Congress" for its carnival of spending, which depleted the nation's surplus by enacting a series of pork barrel programs—legislation shamelessly designed to bring federal money to congressmen's constituencies. In the congressional election of 1890, angry voters swept the hapless Republicans, including tariff sponsor McKinley, out of office. Two years later, Harrison himself was defeated, and Grover Cleveland returned to the White House. Such were the changes in the political winds whipped up by the tariff issue.

Controversy over the tariff masked deeper divisions in American society. Conflict between workers and farmers on the one side and bankers and corporate giants on the other erupted throughout the 1880s and came to a head in the 1890s. Both sides in the tariff debate spoke to concerns over class conflict when they insisted that their respective plans, whether McKinley's high tariff or Cleveland's tariff reform, would bring prosperity and harmony. For their part, many working people shared the sentiment voiced by one labor leader that the tariff was "only a scheme devised by the old parties to throw dust in the eyes of laboring men."

How did the federal government regulate trusts and railroads?

American voters may have divided on the tariff, but increasingly they agreed on the need for federal regulation of the railroads and federal legislation to curb the power of the "trusts" (a term loosely applied to all large business combinations). As early as the 1870s, angry farmers in the Midwest who suffered from the unfair shipping practices of the railroads organized to fight for railroad regulation. The Patrons of Husbandry, or the Grange, founded in 1867 as a social and educational organization for farmers, soon became an independent political movement. By electing Grangers to state office, farmers made it possible for several midwestern states to pass laws in the 1870s and 1880s regulating the railroads.

At first, the Supreme Court ruled in favor of state regulation (*Munn v. Illinois*, 1877). But in 1886, the Court reversed itself, ruling that because railroads crossed state boundaries, they fell outside state jurisdiction (*Wabash v. Illinois*). With more than three-fourths of railroads crossing state lines, the Supreme Court's decision effectively quashed the states' attempts at railroad regulation.

Interstate Commerce Commission (ICC)
Federal regulatory agency designed to oversee the railroad industry. Congress created it through the 1887 Interstate Commerce Act after the Supreme Court decision in *Wabash v. Illinois* (1886) effectively denied states the right to regulate railroads. The ICC proved weak and did not immediately pose a threat to the industry.

Anger at the *Wabash* decision finally led to the first federal law regulating the railroads, the Interstate Commerce Act, passed in 1887 during Cleveland's first administration. The act established the nation's first federal regulatory agency, the **Interstate Commerce Commission (ICC)**, to oversee the railroad industry (**Map 18.2**). Railroad lobbyists worked furiously behind the scenes to make the new agency palatable to business leaders, many of whom felt a federal agency would be more lenient than state regulators. In its early years, the ICC was never strong enough to pose a serious threat to the railroads. For example, it could not end rebates to big shippers. In its early decades, the ICC proved more important as a precedent than effective as a watchdog.

Sherman Antitrust Act
1890 act that outlawed pools and trusts, ruling that businesses could no longer enter into agreements to restrict competition. Government inaction, combined with the Supreme Court's narrow reading of the act in the *United States v. E. C. Knight Company* (1895) decision, undermined the law's effectiveness.

Concern over the growing power of the trusts led Congress to pass the **Sherman Antitrust Act** in 1890. The act outlawed pools and trusts, ruling that businesses could no longer enter into agreements to restrict competition. It did nothing to restrict huge holding companies such as Standard Oil, however, and proved to be a weak sword against the trusts. In the following decade, the government successfully struck down only six trusts but used the law four times against labor by outlawing unions as a "conspiracy in restraint of trade."

In 1895, the conservative Supreme Court dealt the antitrust law a crippling blow in *United States v. E. C. Knight Company*. In its decision, the Court ruled that "manufacture" did not constitute "trade." This semantic quibble drastically narrowed the law, in this case allowing the American Sugar Refining Company, which had bought out other sugar companies (including E. C. Knight) and

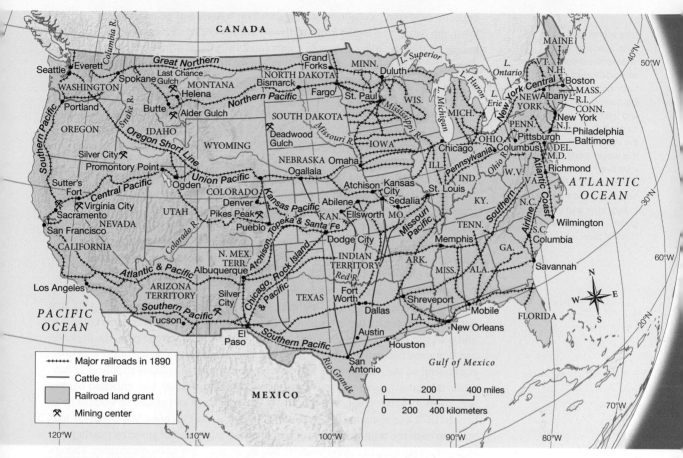

MAP 18.2 ▲ Federal Land Grants to Railroads and the Development of the West, 1850–1900 Railroads received more than 180 million acres, an area as large as Texas. Built well ahead of demand, the western railroads courted settlers, often onto land not fit for farming.

controlled 98 percent of the production of sugar, to continue its virtual monopoly. Yet the Court insisted the law could be used against labor unions.

Both the ICC and the Sherman Antitrust Act testified to the nation's concern about corporate abuses of power and to a growing antimonopolist reform movement willing to use federal measures to intervene on behalf of the public interest. As corporate capitalism became more and more powerful, public pressure toward government intervention grew. Yet not until the twentieth century would more active presidents sharpen and use these weapons effectively against the large corporations.

What was the fight for free silver about?

While the tariff and regulation of the trusts gained many backers, the silver issue stirred passions like no other issue of the day. On one side stood those who believed that gold constituted the only honest money. Many who supported the gold standard were eastern creditors who did not wish to be paid in devalued dollars. On the

free silver
Term used in the late nineteenth century by those who advocated minting silver dollars in addition to supporting the gold standard and the paper currency backed by gold. Poor farmers from the West and South hoped this would result in inflation, effectively providing them with debt relief. Western silver barons wanted the government to buy silver and mint silver dollars, thereby raising the price of silver.

opposite side stood a coalition of western silver barons and poor farmers from the West and South who called for **free silver**. Farmers hoped to increase the money supply by minting silver dollars to create inflation, which would give them some debt relief by enabling them to pay off their creditors with cheaper dollars. The mining interests, who had seen the silver bonanza in the West drive down the price of the precious metal, wanted the government to buy silver and mint silver dollars.

During the depression following the panic of 1873, critics of hard money organized the Greenback Labor Party, an alliance of farmers and urban wage laborers. The Greenbackers favored issuing paper currency not tied to the gold supply, citing the precedent of the greenbacks issued during the Civil War. The government had the right to define what constituted legal tender, the Greenbackers reasoned: "Paper is equally money, when . . . issued according to law." They proposed that the nation's currency be based on its wealth—land, labor, and capital—and not simply on its reserves of gold. The Greenback Labor Party captured more than a million votes and elected fourteen members to Congress in 1878. Although conservatives considered the Greenbackers dangerous cranks, their views eventually prevailed in the 1930s, when the country abandoned the gold standard.

After the Greenback Labor Party collapsed, proponents of free silver came to dominate the monetary debate in the 1890s. Advocates of free silver pointed out that until 1873 the country had enjoyed a system of bimetallism—the minting of both silver and gold into coins. In that year, at the behest of those who favored gold, the Republican Congress had voted to stop buying and minting silver, an action silver supporters denounced as the "crime of '73." By sharply contracting the money supply at a time when the nation's economy was burgeoning, the Republicans had enriched bankers and investors at the expense of cotton and wheat farmers and industrial wageworkers.

In 1878 and again in 1890, with the Sherman Silver Purchase Act, Congress took steps to ease the tight money policy and appease advocates of silver by passing legislation requiring the government to buy silver and issue silver certificates. Though good for the mining interests, the laws did little to promote the inflation desired by farmers. Soon monetary reformers began to call for "the free and unlimited coinage of silver," a plan whereby nearly all the silver mined in the West would be minted into coins circulated at the rate of sixteen ounces of silver equal in value to one ounce of gold.

By the 1890s, the silver issue crossed party lines. The Democrats hoped to use it to achieve a union between western and southern voters. Unfortunately for them, Democratic president Grover Cleveland supported the gold standard as vehemently as any Republican. After a panic on Wall Street in the spring of 1893, Cleveland called a special session of Congress and bullied the legislature into repealing the Silver Purchase Act because he believed it threatened economic confidence. Repeal proved disastrous for Cleveland. It did nothing to bring prosperity and dangerously divided the country. Angry farmers warned Cleveland not to travel west of the Mississippi River if he valued his life.

What caused the depression of the 1890s and how did it affect Americans?

President Cleveland had scarcely begun his second term in 1893 when the country plunged into the worst depression it had yet seen. In the face of economic disaster,

Cleveland clung to the economic orthodoxy of the gold standard. The subtreasury in lower Manhattan witnessed a dangerous drain on the gold reserves as cartloads of bullion were loaded on ships destined for nervous European investors. In the winter of 1894–95, the president walked the floor of the White House, sleepless over the prospect that the United States might go bankrupt. The Treasury's gold reserves had dipped so low that unless they could be buttressed, the unthinkable might happen: The U.S. Treasury might not be able to meet its obligations.

At this juncture, J. P. Morgan stepped in. Under Morgan's direction, a syndicate of bankers pledged to purchase millions in U.S. government bonds, paying in gold. An obscure Reconstruction-era statute made such a deal possible without congressional approval. Cleveland knew that the scheme would unleash a thunder of protest, yet to save the gold standard the president had no choice. Morgan and Cleveland managed to stop the drain of gold, but their deal did little to save the country from hardship.

In the winter of 1894–95, people faced unemployment, cold, and hunger. Cleveland, a firm believer in limited government, insisted that nothing could be done: "I do not believe that the power and duty of the General Government ought to be extended to the relief of individual suffering which is in no manner properly related to the public service or benefit." Nor did it occur to Cleveland that his great faith in the gold standard prolonged the depression, favored creditors over debtors, and caused immense hardship for millions of Americans.

REVIEW

What role did the gold standard play in the economic crisis of the 1890s?

Conclusion: How did business dominate the Gilded Age?

"We are the rich," boasted one of New York's newly minted millionaires. "We own America; we got it God knows how, but we intend to keep it if we can." To Mark Twain, who saw the era with his acerbic clarity, the new riches represented not a golden age but a gilded age. Twain, who himself had fallen prey to the get-rich-quick ethos of the era and ended up bankrupt, knew better than to trust the shiny surface. Underneath lay crasser stuff—greed, exploitation, waste, and corruption.

The gold deal between J. P. Morgan and Grover Cleveland in 1895 underscored a dangerous reality: The federal government had become so weak that its solvency depended on a private banker. This lopsided power relationship signaled the dominance of business in the era. Birthed by the railroads, the new economy spawned greed, corruption, and vulgarity on a grand scale. California's Big Four built railroads but also wreaked havoc to turn paper profits; the get-rich-quick ethic of the gold rush infused the whole continent; and businessmen like Collis Huntington boasted openly of buying politicians, who in turn lined their pockets at the public's expense.

Nevertheless, the Gilded Age was not without its share of solid achievements. Where dusty roads and cattle trails once sprawled across the continent, steel rails now

▶ **Mark Twain and *The Gilded Age***
Humorist and social critic Samuel Langhorne Clemens, writing under the pen name Mark Twain, made his name as a chronicler of the West. In the 1870s, he moved east and stormed the citadels of polite society, boasting a spacious mansion in Hartford, Connecticut, and a New York townhouse. Twain gave in to the reckless speculation of his era, losing his fortune and having to lecture his way out of bankruptcy. His novel *The Gilded Age*, written with Charles Dudley Warner in 1873, provided an apt title for an era whose glittering surface covered the rot of corruption. Photo of Twain: ullstein bild via Getty Images; book cover: From The New York Public Library.

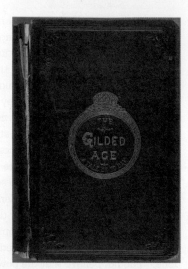

bound the country together, creating a national market that enabled America to make the leap into the industrial age. Factories and refineries poured out American steel and oil at unprecedented rates. Businessmen like Carnegie, Rockefeller, and Morgan developed new strategies to consolidate American industry. New inventions, including the telephone and electric light and power, transformed Americans' everyday lives.

By the end of the nineteenth century, the United States had achieved industrial maturity. It boasted the largest, most innovative, most productive economy in the world. The rise of Gilded Age industry came at a cost, however. The rampant railway building changed the nature of politics in the United States, entwining the state and the corporations and making a mockery of a free market economy. As one historian speculated, had railroad magnates waited to build western railroads to meet demand, their restraint might have resulted in less waste, less environmental degradation, and less human suffering for Native Americans and white settlers alike.

The power of American industry worried many Americans and gave rise to the era's political turmoil. Race, class, and gender profoundly influenced American politics, leading to new political alliances. Fearless activist Ida B. Wells fought racism in its most brutal form—lynching. Women's organizations championed causes, notably suffrage and temperance, and challenged prevailing views of woman's proper sphere. Reformers fought corruption by instituting civil service. Henry George attracted a mass following in New York's 1886 mayoral race by pointing to the inequity of progress and poverty. As the old parties, Democrat and Republican, faced the 1890s, new issues—the tariff, the regulation of the trusts, and currency reform—restructured the nation's politics.

The Gilded Age grappled with issues familiar to our own time: income inequality, new technologies, immigration, environmental crisis, political stalemate, and increasing social, cultural, and racial diversity. The turn of the twentieth century witnessed a nation transformed. Fueled by railroad building and expanding industry, cities grew exponentially, bulging at the seams with new inhabitants from around the globe and bristling with new bridges, subways, and skyscrapers. The frenzied growth of urban America brought wealth and opportunity but also the exploitation of labor, racism toward natives and newcomers, and social upheaval that lent a new urgency to calls for social reform.

CHAPTER REVIEW

EXPLAIN WHY IT MATTERS

Gilded Age (p. 512)

trust (p. 517)

finance capitalism (p. 520)

social Darwinism (p. 521)

gospel of wealth (p. 521)

spoils system (p. 522)

fee-based governance (p. 522)

Jim Crow (p. 524)

Woman's Christian Temperance Union (WCTU) (p. 528)

civil service reform (p. 530)

Interstate Commerce Commission (ICC) (p. 534)

Sherman Antitrust Act (p. 534)

free silver (p. 536)

PUT IT ALL TOGETHER

THE RISE OF BIG BUSINESS

• What role did railroads and new technologies play in the rise of American big business?

• How did the business pioneers of the late nineteenth century organize and grow their businesses?

LATE-NINETEENTH-CENTURY POLITICS

• How did ideas about gender and race shape late-nineteenth-century politics?

• How did new social philosophical theories justify business and political practices in the late nineteenth century?

• How did Henry George challenge ideas of inequality in New York City's 1886 mayoral race?

ECONOMIC ISSUES AND POLITICAL CONFLICT

• How did each Gilded Age president react to economic issues? How did Supreme Court decisions affect economic issues?

• What made free silver such a powerful and emotional issue in the late nineteenth century?

LOOKING BACKWARD, LOOKING AHEAD

• How did the role of business in politics in the late nineteenth century differ from its role in the first half of the century?

• How did the rise of big business affect the economic and political landscape of early-twentieth-century America? In what ways did Americans try to deal with the excesses of big business?

19

THE CITY AND ITS WORKERS

1870–1900

This chapter discusses the following questions:

- Why did American cities experience explosive growth in the late nineteenth century?
- What kinds of work did people do in industrial America?
- Why did the fortunes of the Knights of Labor rise in the late 1870s and 1880s only to decline in the 1890s?
- How did urban industrialism shape home life and the world of leisure?
- How did municipal governments respond to the challenges of urban expansion?
- Conclusion: Who built the cities?

▶ **Brooklyn Bridge** Here a group of men stand behind a sign warning not to "run, jump, or trot" on the cables. The first steel suspension bridge, with huge cables composed of five thousand individual steel wires, the Brooklyn Bridge was a marvel of nineteenth-century engineering, the only bridge of its kind when it opened in 1883. Hulton Archive/Getty Images.

AN AMERICAN STORY

" **A** town that crawled now stands erect, and we whose backs were bent above the hearths know how it got its spine," boasted a steelworker surveying New York City. Where once wooden buildings stood rooted in the mire of unpaved streets, cities of stone and steel sprang up in the last decades of the nineteenth century. The labor of millions of workers, many of them immigrants, laid the foundations for urban America.

No symbol better represented the new urban landscape than the Brooklyn Bridge, opened in May 1883. The great bridge soared over the East River in a single mile-long span. Building the Brooklyn Bridge took fourteen years and cost the lives of twenty-seven men. To sink the foundation in the riverbed, laborers tunneled through the mud and worked in boxes that were open at the bottom and pressurized to keep the water out. A scrawny sixteen-year-old from Ireland, Frank Harris, remembered the fearful experience of going to work on the bridge a few days after landing in America:

> The six of us were working naked to the waist in the small iron chamber with the temperature of about 80 degrees Fahrenheit: In five minutes the sweat was pouring from us, and all the while we were standing in icy water that was only kept from rising by the terrific pressure. No wonder the headaches were blinding.

When workers came up from the riverbed too quickly, they developed a deadly condition called "the bends." The first worker died when the foundation reached seventy-one feet. Other deaths followed. Washington Roebling, the bridge's chief engineer, fell victim to the bends and had to direct the completion of the bridge through a telescope from his bedroom. Emily Roebling, his wife, acted as site superintendent and chief engineer on the project.

At the end of the nineteenth century, the Brooklyn Bridge stood as a symbol of many things: the industrial might of the United States, the labor of the nation's immigrants, the ingenuity and genius of its engineers and inventors, the rise of iron and steel, and, most of all, the ascendancy of urban America. Poised on the brink of the twentieth century, the nation was shifting from a rural, agricultural society to an urban, industrial nation. The gap between the rich and the poor widened. In the burgeoning cities, tensions erupted into conflict as workers fought to organize into labor unions and to demand safer working conditions, shorter hours, and better pay, sometimes with violent and bloody results.

The explosive growth of the cities fostered political corruption as unscrupulous bosses and entrepreneurs cashed in on the building boom. Immigrants, political bosses, middle-class managers, manual laborers, and the very rich populated the nation's cities, crowding the streets, working in the stores and factories, and taking their leisure at the new ballparks, amusement parks, dance halls, and municipal parks. As the new century dawned, the city and its workers moved to center stage in American life.

Why did American cities experience explosive growth in the late nineteenth century?

" We cannot all live in cities, yet nearly all seem determined to do so," *New York Tribune* editor Horace Greeley complained. The last three decades of the nineteenth century witnessed an urban explosion. Cities and towns grew more than twice as rapidly as the total population. By 1900, the United States boasted three cities with more than a million inhabitants—New York, Chicago, and Philadelphia.

global migration
Movement of populations across large distances such as oceans and continents. In the late nineteenth century, large-scale immigration from southern and eastern Europe into the United States contributed to the growth of cities and changes in American demographics.

Patterns of **global migration** contributed to the rise of the city. In the port cities on the East Coast, more than fourteen million people arrived, many from southern and eastern Europe, and huddled together in dense urban ghettos. The word *slum* entered the American vocabulary along with a growing concern over the rising tide of newcomers. In the city, the widening gap between the rich and the poor became not just financial but physical. Changes in the city landscape brought about by advances in transportation and technology accentuated the great divide in wealth at the same time they put physical distance between the rich and the poor.

How did the urban explosion in the United States reflect a global migration?

The United States grew up in the country and moved to the city, or so it seemed by the end of the nineteenth century. Between 1870 and 1900, eleven million people had moved into cities. Burgeoning industrial centers such as Pittsburgh, Chicago, New York, and Cleveland acted as giant magnets, attracting workers from the countryside. But rural Americans were not the only ones migrating to cities. Millions of immigrants moved from their native countries to America. Worldwide in scope, the movement from rural areas to urban industrial centers attracted millions of immigrants to American shores.

By the 1870s, the world could be conceptualized as three interconnected geographic regions (**Map 19.1**). At the center stood an industrial core that encompassed the eastern United States and western Europe. Surrounding this industrial core lay a vast agricultural domain from the Canadian wheat fields to the hinterlands of northern China. Capitalist development in the late nineteenth century shattered

MAP ACTIVITY

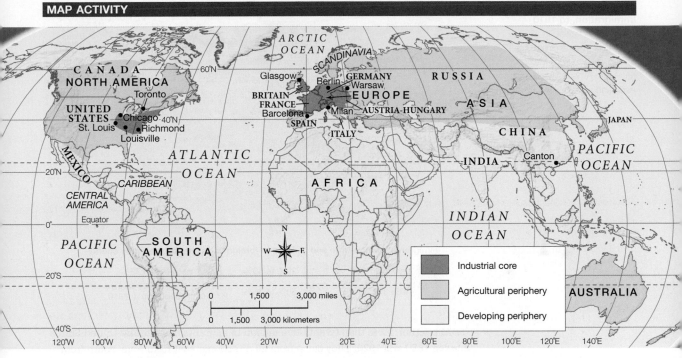

MAP 19.1 ▲ Economic Regions of the World, 1890 The global nature of the world economy at the turn of the twentieth century is indicated by three interconnected geographic regions. At the center stands the industrial core — western Europe and the northeastern United States. The second region — the agricultural periphery — supplied immigrant laborers to the industries in the core. Beyond these two regions lay a vast area tied economically to the industrial core by colonialism.

READING THE MAP: What types of economic regions were contained in the United States in this period? Which continents held most of the industrial core? Which held most of the agricultural rural domain? Which held the greatest portion of the developing periphery?

CONNECTIONS: Which of these three regions provided the bulk of immigrant workers to the United States? What major changes prompted the global migration at the end of the nineteenth century?

---

traditional patterns of economic activity in this rural periphery. As old patterns broke down, these rural areas exported, along with other raw materials, new recruits for the industrial labor force.

Beyond this second circle lay an even larger developing periphery. Colonial ties between this part of the world and the industrial core strengthened in the late nineteenth century, but most of the people living there stayed put. They worked on plantations and railroads and in mines and ports as part of a huge export network managed by foreign powers that staked out spheres of influence and colonies in this vast region.

In the 1870s, railroad expansion and low steamship fares gave the world's peoples a newfound mobility, enabling industrialists to draw on a global population for cheap labor. When Andrew Carnegie opened his first steel mill in 1872, his superintendent hired workers he called "buckwheats" — young American boys just off the farm. By the 1890s, however, Carnegie's workforce was liberally sprinkled with other rural boys, Hungarians and Slavs who had migrated to the United States and were willing to work for low wages.

MAP 19.2 ▶ The Impact of Immigration, to 1910

Immigration flowed in all directions — south from Canada, north from Mexico and Latin America, east from Asia, and west from Europe.

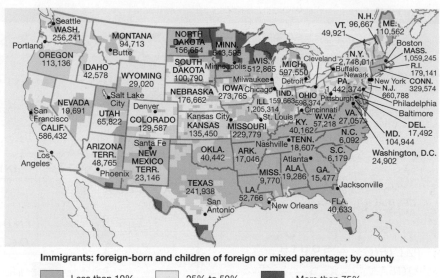

Immigrants: foreign-born and children of foreign or mixed parentage; by county

- Less than 10%
- 10% to 25%
- 25% to 50%
- 50% to 75%
- More than 75%
- N.Y. 2,748,011 Total foreign-born population in 1910

Altogether, more than twenty-five million immigrants came to the United States between 1850 and 1920. They came from all directions: east from Asia, south from Canada, north from Latin America, and west from Europe (**Map 19.2**). Part of a worldwide migration, emigrants traveled to South America and Australia as well as to the United States. Yet more than 70 percent of all European emigrants chose North America as their destination.

Historically, the largest number of immigrants to the United States came from the British Isles and from German-speaking lands (**Figure 19.1**), and the vast majority were white. Asians accounted for fewer than one million immigrants, and other people of color numbered even fewer. Yet ingrained racial prejudices increasingly

FIGURE 19.1 ▶ Global Comparison: European Emigration, 1870–1890

European emigration between 1870 and 1890 shows that people from Germany, Austria, and the British Isles formed the largest group of out-migrants. After 1890, the origin of European emigrants tilted south and east, with Italians and eastern Europeans growing in number. The United States took in nearly two-thirds of the European emigrants. What factors account for the popularity of the United States?

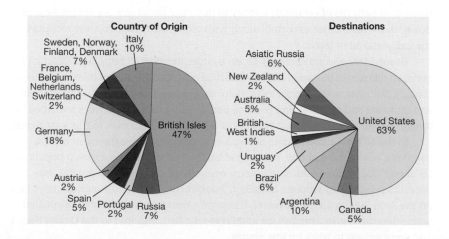

influenced the country's perception of immigration patterns. One of the classic formulations of the history of European immigration divided immigrants into two distinct waves that have been called the "old" and the "new" immigration. According to this theory, before 1880, the majority of immigrants came from northern and western Europe, with Germans, Irish, English, and Scandinavians making up approximately 85 percent of the newcomers.

After 1880, the pattern shifted, with more and more ships carrying passengers from southern and eastern Europe. Italians, Hungarians, eastern European Jews, Turks, Armenians, Poles, Russians, and other Slavic peoples accounted for more than 80 percent of all immigrants by 1896 (**Figure 19.2**). Implicit in the distinction was an invidious comparison between "old" pioneer settlers and "new" unskilled laborers. Yet this sweeping generalization spoke more to perception than to reality. In fact, many of the earlier immigrants from Ireland, Germany, and Scandinavia came not as settlers or farmers but as wageworkers, and they were met with much the same prejudice as the Italians and Slavs who followed them.

During good financial times, the need for cheap, unskilled labor for America's industries stimulated demand for immigrant workers. In 1873 and again in 1893, when the United States experienced economic depressions, immigration slowed, only to pick up again when prosperity returned. Steamship companies courted immigrants—a highly profitable, self-loading cargo. By the 1880s, the price of a ticket from Liverpool to New York City had dropped to less than $25. Would-be immigrants eager for information about the United States relied on letters from friends and relatives, advertisements, and word of mouth—sources that were not always dependable or

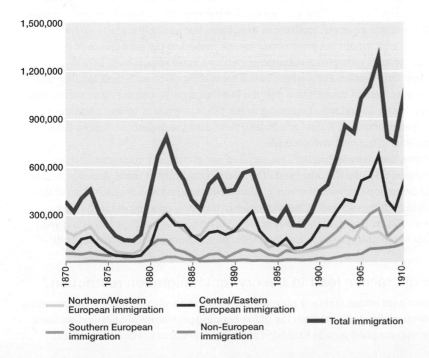

FIGURE 19.2 ◄ European Emigration, 1870–1910

Before 1880, more than 85 percent of U.S. immigrants came from northern and western Europe — Germany, Ireland, England, and the Scandinavian countries. After 1880, 80 percent of the "new" immigrants came from Italy, Turkey, Hungary, Armenia, Poland, Russia, and other Slavic countries.

truthful. As one Italian immigrant recalled, "News was colored, success magnified, comforts and advantages exaggerated beyond all proportions."

Even photographs proved deceptive: Workers dressed in their Sunday best looked more prosperous than they actually were to relatives in the old country, where only the very wealthy wore white collars or silk dresses. No wonder people left for the United States believing, as one Italian immigrant joked, "that if they were ever fortunate enough to reach America, they would fall into a pile of manure and get up brushing the diamonds out of their hair."

Most of the newcomers stayed in the nation's cities. By 1900, almost two-thirds of the country's immigrant population resided in cities. Many of the immigrants were too poor to move on. (The average laborer immigrating to the United States carried only about $21.50.) Although the foreign-born rarely outnumbered the native-born population, taken together immigrants and their American-born children did constitute a majority in some areas, particularly in the nation's largest cities: Philadelphia, 55 percent; Boston, 66 percent; Chicago, 75 percent; and New York City, a whopping 80 percent in 1900.

Not all the newcomers came to stay. Perhaps eight million European immigrants—most of them young men—worked for a year or a season and then returned to their homelands. Immigration officers called these immigrants, many of them Italians, "birds of passage" because they followed a regular pattern of migration to and from the United States. By 1900, almost 75 percent of the new immigrants were young, single men. Willing to accept conditions other workers regarded as intolerable, these young migrants showed little interest in labor unions. They organized only when the dream of returning home faded, as it did for millions who ultimately remained in the United States.

Women generally had less access to funds for travel and faced tighter family control. Because the traditional gendered division of labor relied on women's unpaid domestic work and care of the very young and the very old, women most often came to the United States as wives, mothers, or daughters, not as single wage laborers. Only among the Irish, where the great potato famine presented the grim choice of starve or leave, did women immigrants outnumber men by a small margin from 1871 to 1891.

Jews from eastern Europe and Russia most often came with their families and came to stay. Fear of conscription into the Russian army motivated many young men to leave Russia. In addition, beginning in the 1880s, a wave of violent pogroms, or bloody persecutions, in Russia and Poland prompted the departure of more than a million Jews in the next two decades.

Anzia Yezierska, a Russian Jew, recalled her excitement upon immigrating: "Ach! America! From the other end of the earth from where I came, America was a land of living hope, woven of dreams, aflame with longing and desire." Most of the Jewish immigrants settled in the port cities of the East, creating distinct ethnic enclaves. Hester Street, in the heart of New York City's Lower East Side, rang with the calls of pushcart peddlers hawking their wares, from pickles to feather beds.

How did racism lead to the cry for immigration restriction?

Prejudice over ethnic diversity played a role in dividing skilled workers (those with a craft or specialized ability) from the globe-hopping proletariat of unskilled workers (those who supplied muscle or tended machines). Members of older immigrant groups frequently criticized the newcomers. One Irish worker complained, "There should be a law . . . to keep all the Italians from comin' in and takin' the bread out of the mouths of honest people."

The Irish worker's resentment brings into focus the impact of racism on America's immigrant laborers. Throughout the nineteenth century and into the twentieth, members of the educated elite as well as the uneducated viewed ethnic and even religious differences as racial characteristics, referring, for example, to the Polish or the Jewish "race." Americans judged immigrants from southern and eastern Europe as inferior to earlier immigrants from northern and western Europe. Ironically, the Irish who criticized the Italians so harshly had themselves been stigmatized as a lesser "race" a generation earlier.

Immigrants not only brought their own religious and racial prejudices to the United States but also absorbed the popular prejudices of American culture. Social Darwinism, with its strongly racist overtones, decreed that whites stood at the top of the evolutionary ladder (see chapter 18). But who was "white"? Skin color supposedly served as a marker for the "new" immigrants—the "swarthy" Italians and dark-haired, olive-skinned Jews. But even blond, blue-eyed Poles were not considered "white." The social construction of race is nowhere more apparent than in the testimony of an Irish dockworker, who boasted that he hired only "white men," a category that he insisted excluded "Poles and Italians." For the new immigrants, Americanization and assimilation would prove inextricably part of becoming "white."

For Black people, the cities of the North promised not just economic opportunity but an escape from institutionalized segregation and persecution. Throughout the South, Jim Crow laws—restrictions that segregated Black people—became common in the decades following reconstruction. Intimidation and lynching terrorized Blacks. "To die from the bite of frost is far more glorious than at the hands of a mob," proclaimed the *Defender*, Chicago's largest African American newspaper. In the 1890s, many Black people moved north, settling for the most part in the growing cities. Racism relegated them to poor jobs and substandard living conditions, but by 1900 New York, Philadelphia, and Chicago had the largest Black communities in the nation. Although the most significant African American migration out of the South would occur during and after World War I, the great exodus had already begun.

On the West Coast, Chinese immigrants once again became scapegoats of the changing economy. Hard times in the 1870s made them a target for disgruntled workers, who dismissed them as "coolie" labor. In the West, the issue spawned violence as angry mobs torched "Chinatowns." Prohibited from owning land, the Chinese migrated to the cities. **Sinophobia**, or hostility toward the Chinese, was by no means limited to the West Coast. Labor leaders across the country joined the attack, arguing that American workers (unlike the Chinese) couldn't live on "rice and rats." In 1882, Congress yielded to the pressure and passed the Chinese Exclusion Act (see chapter 17). For the first time in the nation's history, U.S. law excluded an immigrant group on the basis of race.

Some Chinese managed to come to America using a loophole in the exclusion law that allowed relatives to join their families. Meanwhile, the number of Japanese immigrants rapidly grew until pressure to keep out all Asians led in 1910 to the creation of an immigration station at Angel Island in San Francisco Bay, where immigrants were quarantined until judged physically or mentally fit to enter the United States.

Sinophobia
Hostility and discrimination toward Chinese people, often based in racial prejudice and fear.

VISUAL ACTIVITY

◀ **Anti-Chinese Cartoon, 1886** Immigration restriction has always been about race. This 1886 anti-Chinese cartoon does double duty, attacking Chinese immigration and promoting "the George Dee automatic washer" — presumably superior to the Chinese laundry. The Chinese were the first to be barred with the Chinese Exclusion Act of 1882. By the 1890s, as immigration shifted from western to southern and eastern Europeans, many believed the newcomers — Jews, Italians, Hungarians, Polish — were not "white" and could never be assimilated. Attempts to block immigration passed only to be vetoed by Democrat Grover Cleveland. Library of Congress, Prints & Photographs Division, Reproduction number LC-DIG-pga-02758.

READING THE IMAGE: In both text and images, how does the cartoon stereotype Chinese immigrants?

CONNECTIONS: Before the Chinese Exclusion Act, how had western expansion depended on Chinese workers?

On the East Coast, the volume of immigration from Europe in the last two decades of the century proved unprecedented. In 1888 alone, more than half a million Europeans landed in America, 75 percent of them in New York City. The Statue of Liberty, erected in 1886 as a gift from the people of France, stood sentinel in the harbor.

The tide of immigrants to New York City soon swamped the immigration office at Castle Garden in lower Manhattan. After the federal government took over immigration in 1890, it built a facility on **Ellis Island** in New York harbor. When fire gutted the wooden building, a new brick edifice replaced it in 1900. Able to process five thousand immigrants a day, it was already inadequate by the time it opened. Its overcrowded halls became the gateway to the United States for millions of immigrants.

To many Americans, the new southern and eastern European immigrants appeared backward, uneducated, and outlandish in appearance—impossible to assimilate. "These people are not Americans," editorialized the popular journal *Public Opinion*: "they are the very scum and offal of Europe." Terence V. Powderly, head of the broadly inclusive Knights of Labor, complained that the newcomers "herded together like animals and lived like beasts." Blue-blooded Yankees led by Senator Henry Cabot Lodge of Massachusetts formed an unlikely alliance with leaders of organized labor—who feared that immigrants would drive down wages—to press for immigration restrictions. In 1896, Congress approved a literacy

Ellis Island
Immigration facility opened in 1892 in New York harbor that processed new immigrants coming into New York City. In the late nineteenth century, some 75 percent of European immigrants to America came through New York.

test for immigrants, but President Grover Cleveland promptly vetoed it. "It is said," the president reminded Congress, "that the quality of recent immigration is undesirable. The time is quite within recent memory when the same thing was said of immigrants who, with their descendants, are now numbered among our best citizens."

How did the city magnify extremes of wealth and poverty?

During the Gilded Age, the social geography of the city changed enormously. Cleveland, Ohio, provides a good example. In the 1870s, Cleveland was a small city in both population and area. Oil magnate John D. Rockefeller could, and often did, walk from his large brick house on Euclid Avenue to his office downtown. On his way, he passed the small homes of his clerks and other middle-class families. Behind these homes ran miles of alleys crowded with the dwellings of Cleveland's working class. Farther out, on the shores of Lake Erie, close to the factories and foundries, clustered the shanties of the city's poor and destitute.

Within two decades, the Cleveland that Rockefeller knew no longer existed. The coming of mass transit transformed the walking city. In its place emerged a central business district surrounded by concentric rings of residences organized by ethnicity and income. First the horsecar in the 1870s and then the electric streetcar in the 1880s made it possible for those who could afford the five-cent fare to work down-town and flee after work to the "cool green rim" of the city. Social segregation—the separation of rich and poor and of ethnic and old-stock Americans—became one of the major social changes engendered by the rise of the industrial metropolis.

Race and ethnicity affected the way cities evolved, too. Newcomers to the nation's cities faced hostility and, not surprisingly, sought out their kin and countryfolk. Distinct ethnic neighborhoods often formed around a synagogue or church. Black people typically experienced the greatest residential segregation, but every large city had areas—Little Italy, Chinatown, Bohemia Flats, Germantown—where English was rarely spoken.

Poverty, crowding, dirt, and disease constituted the daily reality of New York City's immigrant poor—a plight documented by photojournalist Jacob Riis in his best-selling book *How the Other Half Lives* (1890). By taking his camera into the hovels of the poor, Riis took his readers slumming from the safety of their armchairs, opening the nation's eyes to the filthy, overcrowded conditions of the city's poor. **(See "Analyzing Historical Evidence: Seeing How the Other Half Lives: Jacob Riis, the Flash, and the Birth of Photojournalism" on page 550.)**

Riis's book, like his photographs, presented a world of black and white. There were many layers to the population Riis labeled "the other half"—distinctions deepened by ethnicity, religion, race, and gender. *How the Other Half Lives* must be read more as a reformer's call to conscience than as an accurate portrayal of the varied and complex lives of "the other half." Still, Riis illuminated the plight of the poor. Tenement reform and city playgrounds grew out of Riis's exposé.

While Riis's audience shivered at his revelations about the "other half," many middle-class Americans worried equally about the excesses of the wealthy. The popular press fed the public's seemingly insatiable appetite for stories on the comings and goings of America's newly minted millionaires—their mansions and parties, their European excursions and Newport holidays. The growing chasm between the rich and

ANALYZING HISTORICAL EVIDENCE

Seeing How the Other Half Lives: Jacob Riis, the Flash, and the Birth of Photojournalism

Photography changed the way Americans viewed their world. By the 1890s, any amateur could purchase the Kodak camera that George Eastman marketed with the slogan "You push the button, we do the rest." As the poet Oliver Wendell Holmes observed, the camera became not just "the mirror of reality" but "the mirror with a memory."

Yet for Jacob Riis, a reporter for the *New York Tribune* who wished to document the grim horrors of tenement life, photography was useless because it required daylight or careful studio lighting. He could only crudely sketch the dim hovels, the criminal nightlife, and the windowless tenement rooms of New York. Then came the breakthrough: "One morning scanning my newspaper at my breakfast table, I put it down with an outcry. . . . There it was, the thing I had been looking for all these years. . . . A way had been discovered to take pictures by flashlight."

The new technology involved a pistol lamp that fired magnesium cartridges to provide light for instantaneous photography. Armed with the new flash pistols, Riis set out to shine light on the dark corners of New York's tenements. "Our party carried terror wherever it went," Riis recalled. "The spectacle of strange men invading a house in the midnight hours armed with [flash] pistols which they shot off recklessly was hardly reassuring . . . and it was not to be wondered that the tenants bolted through the windows and down fire escapes." Delighted with the results, Riis laid out $25 for his first box camera in 1888 and set about taking

▲ **Five Cents a Spot (line drawing)** Widener Library, Harvard University.

pictures he used in lantern slides to illustrate his lectures on the need for tenement reform. The results marked a giant step forward for photojournalism.

Riis's book *How the Other Half Lives* (1890) made photographic history. Along with Riis's text and line drawings, it contained seventeen halftone prints of Riis's photographs taken with his camera and flash. By looking at Riis's drawing side by side with the corresponding photograph, we can compare the impact of the two mediums.

DOCUMENT 1

In his early work, Riis had to rely on his own sketches of the conditions he encountered in New York's tenements.

Riis pictured the lodgers in a Bayard Street tenement in this line drawing (left) illustrating overcrowded, dirty, and dilapidated housing. Most of the men were lodgers who paid five cents a spot. Riis is a careful draughtsman, but how much detail can you see in the line drawing?

DOCUMENT 2

On a police raid to evict tenement lodgers, Riis describes the room as "not thirteen feet either way," in which "slept twelve men and women, two or three in bunks in a sort of alcove, the rest on the floor." Note how the flash catches the sleepy faces and tired bodies, the crowding, dirt, and disorder (right). Once Riis adopted the flash, he was able to show more graphically life in the tenements. What details are visible in the photograph that are missing in the line drawing?

▲ **Five Cents a Spot (photograph)** Library of Congress Prints and Photographs Division Washington, D.C. [LC-USZ62-16348].

DOCUMENT 3

Riis took his camera into Baxter Street Court and recorded these observations: "I counted the other day the little ones up to ten years old in a . . . tenement that for a yard has a . . . space in the center with sides fourteen or fifteen feet long, just enough for a row of ill-smelling closets [toilets] . . . and a hydrant. There was about as much light in the 'yard' as in the average cellar. . . . I counted one hundred twenty eight [children] in forty families." Riis's pioneering photojournalism shocked the nation and led not only to tenement reform but also to the development of city playgrounds, neighborhood parks, and child labor laws.

Questions for Analysis

SUMMARIZE THE ARGUMENT: How significant is the advent of flash photography? Compare the drawn image with the photograph. Why is the photo so much more dramatic?

ANALYZE THE EVIDENCE: Would you agree that Riis's photographs are "a mirror of reality," or did he interpret and frame the reality he photographed?

ASK HISTORICAL QUESTIONS: How do you think photography affected Americans' views of their society?

◄ **Alva Vanderbilt, 1886** Alva Vanderbilt greeted her guests as a Venetian princess at the legendary ball that marked the social ascendancy of new money in 1886. As a highlight of the evening, flocks of wild doves were released into the ballroom. New York Historical Society/Bridgeman Images.

the poor fueled class antagonism, and many shared Riis's view that "the real danger to society comes not only from the tenements, but from the ill-spent wealth which reared them."

The excesses of the Gilded Age's millionaires were nowhere more visible than in the monstrous wealth of the Vanderbilts. Cornelius "Commodore" Vanderbilt, the uncouth ferryman who built the New York Central Railroad, died in 1877. Today, he still holds first place among the richest men in America (when wealth is adjusted for inflation). He left his son William $90 million. William doubled that sum, and his two sons proceeded to spend it on Fifth Avenue mansions and "cottages" in Newport, Rhode Island, that rivaled the palaces of Europe. Yet despite her millions (or perhaps because of them), Alva Vanderbilt, Willie Vanderbilt's southern bride, found herself spurned socially by the old-money matrons of New York, notably the redoubtable Mrs. Caroline Astor.

In the aftermath of the Civil War, New York's old merchant elite found itself increasingly displaced by new moneyed manufacturers. Try as they might, the old-money matrons could not keep out the group they scorned as *nouveau riche*. Alva Vanderbilt launched herself into society by building the most ostentatious mansion in the city—a veritable Versailles occupying a city block on Fifth Avenue at 52nd Street. In her palace with its gargoyles, gables, and marble (naked!) statuary, Alva lived large. Her opulent ballroom accommodated over a thousand guests, and she lost no time putting it to use. Her triumph came when Mrs. Astor capitulated, accepting an invitation to Alva's housewarming—a fancy-dress ball for 750 partygoers. "We have no right to exclude those whom this great country has brought forward," Astor proclaimed. "The time has come for the Vanderbilts." A triumphant Alva greeted her guests dressed as a Venetian noble. But her sister-in-law Alice eclipsed her, appearing as that miraculous new invention, the electric light, resplendent in a white satin evening dress studded with diamonds. The *New York World* speculated that Alva's party cost more than a quarter of a million dollars, more than $5 million in today's currency.

Such ostentatious displays of wealth became especially alarming when they were coupled with disdain for the well-being of ordinary people. When a reporter in 1882 asked William Vanderbilt whether he considered the public good when running his railroads, he shot back, "The public be damned." The fear that America had become a **plutocracy**—a society ruled by the rich—gained credence from the fact that the wealthiest 1 percent of the population owned more than half the real and personal property in the country. The cost of one costume for a millionaire's fancy dress ball could

plutocracy
A society ruled by the rich.

feed hundreds of working-class families for over a year. As the new century dawned, reformers came together to build a progressive movement to address the problems of urban industrialism and the atrocious living and working conditions it produced.

REVIEW

What global trends were reflected in the growth of America's cities in the late nineteenth century?

What kinds of work did people do in industrial America?

The number of industrial wageworkers in the United States exploded in the second half of the nineteenth century, more than tripling from 5.3 million in 1860 to 17.4 million in 1900. These workers toiled in a variety of settings. Many skilled workers and artisans still earned a living in small workshops. But with the rise of corporate capitalism, large factories, mills, and mines increasingly dotted the landscape. Others, especially women, worked in sweatshops and did piece-work, such as finishing garments by hand. Pick-and-shovel labor constituted the lowest-paid work, while managers, as well as women "typewriters" and sales-clerks, formed a new white-collar segment of America's labor force. Children also worked for wages in growing numbers.

Who were America's diverse workers?

Common laborers formed the backbone of the American workforce. They built the railroads and subways, tunneled under New York's East River to anchor the Brooklyn Bridge, and helped lay the foundation of industrial America. These "human machines" generally came from the most recent immigrant groups. Initially, the Irish wielded the picks and shovels that built American cities, but by the turn of the century, as the Irish bettered their lot, Slavs and Italians took up their tools.

At the opposite end of labor's hierarchy stood skilled craftsmen like iron puddler James J. Davis, a Welsh immigrant who worked in the Pennsylvania mills. Using brains along with brawn, puddlers earned good wages—Davis drew up to $7 a day at a time when streetcar fare was 3 cents—when there was work. But most industry and manufacturing work in the nineteenth century remained seasonal; few workers could count on year-round pay. In addition, two major depressions twenty years apart, beginning in 1873 and 1893, brought unemployment and hardship. With no social safety net, even the best worker could not guarantee security for his family. "The fear of ending in the poor-house is one of the terrors that dog a man through life," Davis confessed. The working poor quickly learned mutualism was preferable to individualism. They banded together to form mutual aid societies where for pennies a month a man could guarantee that his funeral would be paid for and some help provided for his family.

Technological advances meant that employers replaced men with machines, breaking down skilled work into ever-smaller tasks that could be performed by unskilled factory operatives. New England's textile mills provided a classic example. Mary, a weaver at the mills in Fall River, Massachusetts, went to work in the 1880s at the age of twelve. Mechanization of the looms had reduced the job of the weaver to watching for breaks in the thread. "At first the noise is fierce, and you have to breathe the cotton all the time, but you get used to it," Mary told a reporter from the *Independent* magazine. "When the bobbin flies out and a girl gets hurt, you can't hear her shout—not if she just screams, you can't. She's got to wait, 'till you see her. . . . Lots of us is deaf."

During the 1880s, the number of foreign-born mill workers almost doubled. At Fall River, Mary and her Scots-Irish family resented the new immigrants. "The Polaks learn weavin' quick," she remarked, using a common derogatory term to identify a rival group. Employers encouraged racial and ethnic antagonism because it inhibited labor organization.

Mechanization transformed the garment industry as well. The introduction of the foot-pedaled sewing machine in the 1850s and the use of mechanical cloth-cutting knives drove out independent tailors, who were replaced by pieceworkers. Sadie Frowne, a sixteen-year-old Polish Jew, worked in a Brooklyn **sweatshop** in the 1890s. Frowne sewed for eleven hours a day in a 20-by-14-foot room containing fourteen machines. "The machines go like mad all day, because the faster you work the more money you get," she recalled. She earned about $4.50 a week and, by rigid economy, tried to save $2. Young and single, Frowne typified the woman wage earner in the

sweatshop
A small room used for clothing piecework beginning in the late nineteenth century. As mechanization transformed the garment industry with the introduction of foot-pedaled sewing machines and mechanical cloth-cutting knives, independent tailors were replaced with sweatshop workers hired by contractors to sew pieces into clothing.

▶ **Women at Work** Women workers labor under bright lights in this tenement hat shop in New York City. Often sweatshop workers labored in dim tenements belonging to the contractor who hired them. Garment workers frequently worked with highly combustible fabric in unsafe buildings. GRANGER – Historical Picture Archive.

late nineteenth century. In 1890, the average workingwoman was twenty-two and had been working since the age of fifteen, laboring twelve hours a day, six days a week, and earning less than $6 a week.

What role did women and children play in the family economy?

In 1900, the typical male worker in manufacturing earned $500 a year, about $15,000 in today's dollars, well below the poverty level. For many working-class families, whether native-born or immigrant, economic survival depended on the contributions of all family members, regardless of sex or age. "Father," asked one young immigrant girl, "does everybody in America live like this? Go to work early, come home late, eat and go to sleep? And the next day again work, eat, and sleep?" Most did. The **family economy** meant that everyone chipped in to maintain even the most meager household.

In the cities, boys as young as six years old plied their trades as bootblacks and newsboys. Often working under an adult contractor, these children earned as little as fifty cents a day. Many of them were homeless—orphaned or cast off by their families. "We wuz six, and we ain't got no father," a child of twelve told reporter Jacob Riis. "Some of us had to go."

Child labor increased each decade after 1870. The percentage of children under fifteen engaged in paid labor did not drop until after World War I. The 1900 census estimated that 1,750,178 children ages ten to fifteen were employed, an increase of more than a million over thirty years. Children in this age range constituted more than 18 percent of the industrial labor force.

Women working for wages in nonagricultural occupations more than doubled in number between 1870 and 1900 (**Figure 19.3**). Yet white married women, even among the working class, rarely worked for wages outside the home. In 1890, only 3 percent were employed. Wives contributed by taking in washing, renting out rooms to lodgers, keeping animals, and doing handicraft work. Black women, both married and unmarried, worked out of the home for wages in much greater numbers. The 1890 census showed that 25 percent of married Black women were employed, often as domestics in the houses of white families.

Who were the white-collar workers?

In the late nineteenth century, a managerial revolution created a new class of white-collar workers who worked in offices and stores. As skilled workers saw their crafts replaced

family economy
Economic contributions of multiple members of a household that were necessary to the survival of the family. From the late nineteenth century into the twentieth, many working-class families depended on the wages of all family members, regardless of sex or age.

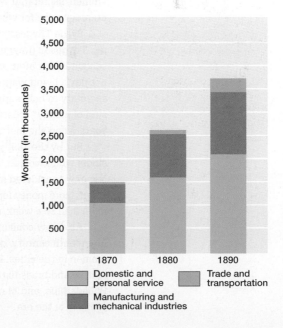

FIGURE 19.3 ▶ Women and Work, 1870–1890 In 1870, close to 1.5 million women worked in nonagricultural occupations. By 1890, that number had more than doubled to 3.7 million. More and more women sought work in manufacturing and mechanical industries, although domestic service still constituted the largest employment arena for women.

by mechanization, some moved into management positions. "The middle class is becoming a salaried class," a writer for the *Independent* magazine observed, "and is rapidly losing the economic and moral independence of former days."

As large business organizations consolidated, corporate development separated management from ownership, and the job of directing the firm became the province of salaried executives and managers, the majority of whom were white men drawn from the 8 percent of Americans who held high school diplomas.

Until late in the century, when engineering schools began to supply recruits, many skilled workers moved from the shop floor to positions of considerable responsibility. Captain William "Billy" Jones, son of a Welsh immigrant, grew up in the heat of the blast furnaces, where he worked as an apprentice at the age of ten. Jones, by all accounts the best steelman in the business, took as his motto "Good wages and good workmen." In 1872, Andrew Carnegie hired Jones as general superintendent of his new plant in Braddock, Pennsylvania.

Although Carnegie constantly tried to force down workers' pay, Jones resisted, and he succeeded in shortening the shift from twelve to eight hours by convincing Carnegie that shorter hours reduced absenteeism and accidents. Jones demanded and received "a hell of a big salary"—$25,000, the same as the president of the United States. He didn't enjoy his high pay for long; he died in a fiery furnace explosion in 1889. After Jones's death, Carnegie reinstituted the twelve-hour day.

"typewriters"
Women who were hired by businesses in the decades after the Civil War to keep records and conduct correspondence, often using equipment such as typewriters.

The new white-collar workforce included women **"typewriters"** and salesclerks. In the decades after the Civil War, as businesses became larger and more far-flung, more exact recordkeeping and a greater volume of correspondence led to the hiring of more office workers. The adding machine, the cash register, and the typewriter came into general use in the 1880s. Employers seeking literate workers soon turned to women. Educated men had many other career choices, but for middle-class white women, secretarial work constituted one of the few areas where they could put their literacy to use for wages.

Sylvie Thygeson was typical of the young women who went to work as secretaries. Thygeson grew up in an Illinois prairie town and went to work as a country schoolteacher after graduating high school in 1884. Realizing that teaching school did not pay a living wage, she mastered typing and stenography and found work as a secretary to help support her family. According to her account, she made "a fabulous sum of money" (possibly $25 a month). Nevertheless, she gave up her job after a few years when she met and married her husband.

But by the 1890s, secretarial work was the overwhelming choice of native-born, single white women, who constituted more than 90 percent of the female clerical force. Not only considered more genteel than factory work or domestic labor, office work also meant more money for shorter hours. In 1883, Boston's clerical workers on average made more than $6 a week, compared with less than $5 for women working in manufacturing.

As a new consumer culture came to dominate American urban life in the late nineteenth century, department stores offered another employment opportunity for women in the cities. Boasting ornate facades, large plate-glass display windows, and marble and brass fixtures, stores such as Macy's in New York, Wanamaker's in Philadelphia, and Marshall Field in Chicago stood as monuments to the material promise of the era.

Within these palaces of consumption, cash girls, stock clerks, and wrappers earned as little as $3 a week, while at the top of the scale, buyers like Belle Cushman of the fancy goods department at Macy's earned $25 a week, an unusually high salary for a woman in the 1870s. Salesclerks counted themselves a cut above factory workers. Their work was neither dirty nor dangerous, and even when they earned less than factory workers, they felt a sense of superiority. Race and ethnicity also played a role. Only white girls from old immigrant stock could become salesgirls. Women of color worked behind the scenes, cleaning and ironing.

REVIEW

How did business expansion and consolidation change workers' occupations in the late nineteenth century?

Why did the fortunes of the Knights of Labor rise in the late 1870s and 1880s only to decline in the 1890s?

By the late nineteenth century, industrial workers were losing ground in the workplace. In the fierce competition to reduce prices and cut costs, industrialists invested heavily in new machinery that replaced skilled workers with unskilled labor. The erosion of skills and the redefinition of labor as mere "machine tending" left the worker with a growing sense of individual helplessness that served as a spur to collective action. The 1870s and 1880s witnessed the emergence of two labor unions—the Knights of Labor and the American Federation of Labor. In 1877, in the midst of a depression, labor flexed its muscle in the Great Railroad Strike. But unionism would suffer a major setback after the Haymarket bombing in 1886.

What led to the Great Railroad Strike of 1877 and what were its results?

Economic depression following the panic of 1873 threw as many as three million people out of work. Those who were lucky enough to keep their jobs watched as pay cuts eroded wages until they could no longer feed their families. In the summer of 1877, the Baltimore and Ohio (B&O) Railroad announced a 10 percent wage cut at the same time it declared a 10 percent dividend to its stockholders.

Angry brakemen in West Virginia, whose wages had already fallen from $70 to $30 a month, walked out on strike. One B&O worker described the hardship that drove him to take such desperate action: "We eat our hard bread and tainted meat two days old on the sooty cars up the road, and when we come home, find our wives complaining that they cannot even buy hominy and molasses for food."

Great Railroad Strike

A violent multicity strike that began in 1877 with West Virginia railroad brakemen who protested against sharp wage reductions and quickly spread to include roughly 600,000 workers. President Rutherford B. Hayes used federal troops to break the strike. Following the strike's failure, union membership surged.

The West Virginia brakemen's strike touched off the **Great Railroad Strike** of 1877, a nationwide uprising that spread rapidly to Pittsburgh and Chicago, St. Louis and San Francisco (**Map 19.3**). Within a few days, nearly 100,000 railroad workers had walked off the job. An estimated 500,000 sympathetic railway workers soon joined the strikers. In Reading, Pennsylvania, militiamen refused to fire on the strikers, saying, "We may be militiamen, but we are workmen first."

Although there was no coordinated national leadership, the strike soon rode the rails from Pennsylvania through Chicago to the Midwest and on to San Francisco, paralyzing the country's rail system. Owners labeled the strike "an insurrection" and clamored for troops to run the trains and protect strikebreakers. President Rutherford B. Hayes, after hesitating briefly, called out the army—setting a precedent for the use of government troops against strikers.

Violence erupted as the strike spread. In Pittsburgh, militia brought in from Philadelphia marched on the crowd with fixed bayonets. In the resulting melee, ten to twenty died and scores were wounded. The crowd—including the wives and children of the strikers, joined by the unemployed and even clerks and professionals—made the strike as much a community rebellion as a labor action. The militia's bloody spree enraged the city, and a swelling crowd drove out the troops and looted and burned two thousand railroad cars and forty buildings, reducing an area two miles long beside the tracks to rubble. Before the day ended, the railroad sustained more than $2 million in property damage.

By the time Hayes's troops arrived, the violence had run its course. Federal troops did not shoot a single striker in 1877. But they struck a blow against labor by

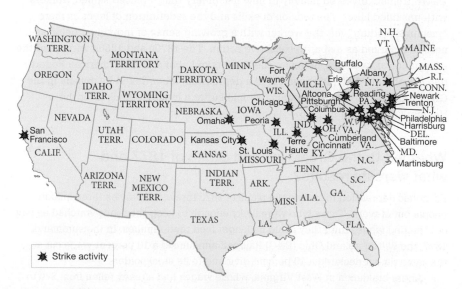

MAP 19.3 ▲ The Great Railroad Strike of 1877 Starting in West Virginia and Pennsylvania, the strike spread as far north as Albany, New York, and as far west as San Francisco, bringing rail traffic to a standstill. Called the Great Uprising, the strike heralded the beginning of a new era of working-class protest and trade union organization.

acting as strikebreakers. The troops opened rail traffic and protected nonstriking (derogatorily called "scab") train crews, maintaining peace along the line. In three weeks, the strike was put down. The use of state militia and federal troops in the Great Railroad Strike signaled a militarization of class conflict that would lead historians to call the strikes at the end of the century "labor wars."

Middle-class Americans initially sympathized with the conditions that led to the strikes. But they quickly condemned the strikers for the violence and property damage that occurred. The *New York Times* editorialized about the "dangerous classes," and the *Independent* magazine offered the following advice on how to deal with "rioters": "If the club of a policeman, knocking out the brains of the rioter, will answer then well and good; but if it does not promptly meet the exigency, then bullets and bayonets . . . constitutes the one remedy and one duty of the hour."

The hostility of the middle class toward labor only intensified in the 1880s and 1890s. The country's most famous minister, Henry Ward Beecher, complained that railroad workers spent too much on beer. "[T]he man who cannot live on bread and water is not fit to live," opined the reverend, who collected jewels and liked to fondle a handful of rubies in his pocket. The partisan press, often controlled by business interests, lost no opportunity to label crowds of workers "rioters" and to invoke bloody images of the French Revolution and the Paris Commune. That many of the workers were immigrants racialized labor issues at the same time that fears of European anarchism and radicalism made it difficult for even the most American of workmen to escape suspicion.

"The strikes have been put down by force," President Hayes noted in his diary. "But now for the real remedy. Can't something be done by education of the strikers, by judicious control of the capitalists, by wise general policy to end or diminish the evil? The railroad strikers, as a rule, are good men, sober, intelligent, and industrious." While Hayes acknowledged the workers' grievances, most businessmen condemned the idea of labor unions as agents of class warfare. For their part, workers quickly recognized that they held little power individually and flocked to join unions. As labor leader Samuel Gompers noted, the nation's first national strike dramatized the frustration and unity of the workers and served as an alarm bell to labor "that sounded a ringing message of hope to us all."

What were the philosophical and strategic differences between the Knights of Labor and the American Federation of Labor?

The **Knights of Labor**, the first mass organization of America's working class, proved the chief beneficiary of labor's newfound consciousness. The Noble and Holy Order of the Knights of Labor had been founded in 1869 as a secret society of workers who envisioned a "universal brotherhood" of all workers, from common laborers to master craftsmen. Secrecy and ritual served to bind Knights together at the same time that they discouraged company spies and protected members from reprisals.

Although the Knights played no active role in the 1877 railroad strike, membership swelled as interest in labor organizing grew following the strike. In 1878, the Knights abandoned secrecy and launched an ambitious public campaign to organize workers.

Knights of Labor
The first mass organization of America's working class. Founded in 1869, the Knights of Labor attempted to bridge the boundaries of ethnicity, gender, ideology, race, and occupation to build a "universal brotherhood" of all workers.

The Knights attempted to bridge the boundaries of ethnicity, gender, ideology, race, and occupation. And, although they shared the West Coast's Sinophobia and attacked "coolie labor," they recruited women and Black people. Leonora Barry served as general investigator for women's work from 1886 to 1890, helping the Knights recruit teachers, waitresses, housewives, and domestic workers, along with factory and sweatshop workers. Women composed perhaps 20 percent of the membership. The Knights also recruited more than 95,000 Black workers. That the Knights of Labor often fell short of its goals to unify the working class proved less surprising than the scope of its efforts.

Under the direction of Grand Master Workman Terence V. Powderly, the Knights became the dominant force in labor during the 1880s. The organization advocated a kind of workers' democracy that embraced reforms including public ownership of the railroads, an income tax, equal pay for women workers, and the abolition of child labor. The Knights called for one big union to create a cooperative commonwealth that would supplant the wage system and remove class distinctions. Only the "parasitic" members of society—gamblers, stockbrokers, lawyers, bankers, and liquor dealers—were barred from membership.

The Knights of Labor was not without rivals. Many skilled workers belonged to craft unions organized by trade. Among the largest and richest of these unions stood the Amalgamated Association of Iron and Steel Workers, founded in 1876 and counting twenty thousand skilled workers as members. Trade unionists spurned the broad reform goals of the Knights of Labor and focused on workplace issues. Samuel Gompers founded the Federation of Organized Trades and Labor Unions in 1881 and reorganized it in 1886 into the **American Federation of Labor (AFL)**, which coordinated the activities of craft unions throughout the United States. His plan was simple: Organize skilled workers such as machinists and locomotive engineers—those with the most bargaining power—and use strikes to gain immediate objectives such as higher pay and better working conditions. Gompers at first drew few converts. The AFL had only 138,000 members in 1886, compared with 730,000 for the Knights of Labor. But events soon brought down the Knights, and Gompers's brand of unionism came to prevail.

American Federation of Labor (AFL)
Organization created by Samuel Gompers in 1886 that coordinated the activities of craft unions throughout the United States. The AFL worked to achieve immediate benefits for skilled workers. Its narrow goals for unionism became popular after the Haymarket bombing.

What was the Haymarket bombing and what were its long-term effects?

While the AFL and the Knights of Labor competed for members, more radical labor groups, including socialists and anarchists, believed that reform was futile and called instead for social revolution. Sensitive to criticism that they preferred revolution in theory to improvements here and now, both of these groups rallied around the popular issue of the eight-hour day.

Since the 1840s, labor had sought to end the ten-hour workday, which was standard in industry and manufacturing. By the mid-1880s, it seemed clear to many workers that labor shared too little in the new prosperity of the decade, and pressure mounted for the eight-hour day. Supporters of the movement set May 1, 1886, as the date for a nationwide general strike in support of the eight-hour workday.

All factions of the labor movement came together in Chicago on May Day, though national leadership remained wary. A group of labor radicals led by *Mayflower* descendant Albert Parsons, an avowed anarchist, and August Spies, a German socialist, spearheaded the movement locally. Chicago's Knights of Labor rallied to the cause even though Powderly and the union's national leadership, worried about the increasing activism of the rank and file, refused to endorse the movement for shorter hours. Gompers went to Chicago to lead the city's trade unionists, although privately he urged his trade union assemblies not to participate in the general strike.

The cautious labor leaders in their frock coats and starched shirts stood in sharp contrast to the dispossessed workers out on strike across town at Chicago's huge McCormick reaper works. There strikers watched helplessly as the company brought in strikebreakers to take their jobs and marched the "scabs" to work under the protection of the Chicago police and security guards supplied by the Pinkerton Detective Agency. Cyrus McCormick Jr., son of the inventor of the mechanical reaper, viewed labor organization as a threat to his power as well as to his profits; he was determined to smash the union.

During the May Day rally, eighty thousand workers paraded peacefully down Michigan Avenue in support of the eight-hour day. The marchers sang the song that had become the workers' anthem:

We want to feel the sunshine;
We want to smell the flowers,
We're sure that God has willed it,
And we mean to have eight hours.
Eight hours for work, eight hours for rest,
Eight hours for what we will!

Trouble came two days later, when desperate strikers attacked strikebreakers outside the McCormick works and police opened fire, killing or wounding six men. Angry radicals urged workers to "arm yourselves and appear in full force" at a rally in Haymarket Square.

On the evening of May 4, the turnout at Haymarket proved disappointing. No more than two or three thousand gathered under threatening skies to hear Spies, Parsons, and the other speakers. Mayor Carter Harrison, known as a friend of labor, mingled conspicuously in the crowd, pronounced the meeting peaceable, and went home to bed. Albert Parsons and his wife, Lucy, ducked out early to avoid the rain. Only a few hundred stood in the drizzle when police inspector John "Blackjack" Bonfield marched a phalanx of men into Haymarket and ordered the crowd to disperse.

Suddenly, someone threw a bomb into the police ranks. After a moment of stunned silence, the police drew their revolvers and fired wildly. August Spies, who had jumped off the speakers' haywagon when he heard the blast, recounted, "Everybody was running, and people fell, struck by bullets, right and left." When the melee ended, one policeman lay dead from the explosion, and scores were wounded by gunfire, probably their own. An additional six policemen later died; the coroner reported three civilian deaths, although likely many more killed or wounded in the hail of police gunfire were dragged off to avoid arrest.

Haymarket bombing
May 4, 1886, conflict in which both workers and policemen were killed or wounded during a labor demonstration in Chicago. The violence began when someone threw a bomb into the ranks of police at the gathering. The incident created a backlash against labor activism.

◄ **"The Chicago Riot"** Inflammatory pamphlets published in the wake of the Haymarket bombing aimed to scare the public. In this charged atmosphere, the anarchist speakers at the rally were tried and convicted for the bombing, even though witnesses testified that none of them had thrown the bomb. Chicago History Museum/Bridgeman Images.

"NOW IT'S BLOOD," screamed the next day's headline. News of the "Haymarket riot" provoked a nationwide convulsion of fear, followed by blind rage directed at anarchists, labor unions, strikers, immigrants, and the working class in general. Eight men, including Parsons and Spies, went on trial in Chicago. "Convict these men," thundered the state's attorney, Julius S. Grinnell, "make examples of them, hang them, and you save our institutions." Although the state could not link any of the defendants to the **Haymarket bombing** (some like Parsons had not even been present), the jury nevertheless found them all guilty. Albert Parsons pronounced the verdict "judicial murder." In the end four men hanged, including Parsons and Spies; one committed suicide by swallowing dynamite; and three received prison sentences. On the gallows, Spies had the last word: "The time will come," he said, "when our silence will be more powerful than the voices you strangle today."

The bomb blast at Haymarket set off lasting repercussions. To commemorate the death of the Haymarket martyrs, labor made May 1 an annual international celebration of the worker. But the Haymarket bomb, in the eyes of one observer, proved "a godsend to all enemies of the labor movement." It scotched the eight-hour-day movement and dealt a fatal blow to the Knights of Labor. With labor everywhere under attack, many skilled workers turned to the AFL. Gompers's narrow economic strategy made sense at the time and enabled one segment of the workforce—the skilled—to organize effectively and achieve tangible gains. The sunny promise of the nonviolent parade for workers' rights in Chicago on May Day 1886 might have marked the start of a new era. Instead, the bomb exploded any hope of peace in the labor wars. Chicago would see worse violence in the Pullman strike in 1894, and it would take another fifty years before the Fair Labor Standards Act of 1938 guaranteed workers an eight-hour day.

REVIEW

What were the long-term effects of the Great Railroad Strike of 1877 and the Haymarket bombing of 1886?

How did urban industrialism shape home life and the world of leisure?

The growth of urban industrialism not only dramatically altered the workplace but also transformed home and family life and gave rise to new forms of commercialized leisure. Industrialization redefined the very concepts of work and home. Increasingly, men went out to work for wages, while most white married women stayed home, either working in the home without pay—cleaning, cooking, and rearing children—or supervising paid domestic servants (often immigrants and Black women) who did the housework.

What role did domesticity play in American culture in the nineteenth century?

The separation of the workplace and the home that marked the shift to industrial society led to a new ideology, one that sentimentalized the home and women's role in it. The cultural idea that dictated a woman's place was in the home, where she would create a haven for her family, began to develop in the early 1800s. Called the **cult of domesticity**, it prescribed an ideal of middle-class, white womanhood that predominated in the period from 1820 to the end of the nineteenth century.

The cult of domesticity around the middle-class home led to a major change in patterns of hiring household help. The live-in servant, or domestic, became a fixture in the North, replacing the hired girl of the previous century. In American cities by 1870, 15 to 30 percent of all households included live-in domestic servants, more than 90 percent of them women. Earlier in the mid-nineteenth century, native-born women increasingly took up other work and left domestic service to immigrants. In the East, the maid was so often Irish that "Bridget" became a generic term for female domestics. The South continued to rely on poorly paid Black female help. And in the far West, Chinese labor competed with Irish women for domestic work.

Servants by all accounts resented the long hours and lack of privacy. "She is liable to be rung up at all hours," one study of domestics reported. "Her very meals are not secure from interruption, and even her sleep is not sacred." Domestic service became the occupation of last resort, a "hard and lonely life" in the words of one female servant.

For women of the white middle class, domestics were a boon, freeing them from household drudgery and giving them more time to spend with their children, to pursue club work, or to work for reforms in the temperance and suffrage movements. Thus, while domestic service supported the cult of domesticity, it created for those women who could afford it opportunities to expand their horizons outside the home. Women's clubs, temperance, and suffrage all benefited from white, middle-class women's new leisure.

cult of domesticity
Nineteenth-century belief that women's place was in the home, where they should create havens for their families. This sentimentalized ideal led to an increase in the hiring of domestic servants and freed white middle-class women to spend time in pursuits outside the home.

What were the cheap amusements of working-class Americans?

Growing class divisions manifested themselves in patterns of leisure as well as in work and home life. The poor and working class took their leisure, when they had any, in the cities' new dance halls, music houses, ballparks, and amusement arcades, which by the 1890s formed a familiar part of the urban landscape.

Young working women no longer met prospective husbands only through their families. Fleeing crowded tenements, the young sought each other's company in dance halls and other commercial retreats. Young working women counted on being "treated" by men, a transaction that often implied sexual payback. Their behavior sometimes blurred the line between respectability and promiscuity, making the dance halls a favorite target of reformers who feared they lured teenage girls into prostitution.

For men, baseball became a national pastime in the 1870s—then, as now, one force in urban life capable of uniting a city across class lines. Cincinnati mounted the first entirely paid team, the Red Stockings, in 1869. Soon professional teams proliferated in cities across the nation, and Mark Twain hailed baseball as "the very symbol, the outward and visible expression, of the drive and push and rush and struggle of the raging, tearing, booming nineteenth century."

The increasing commercialization of entertainment in the late-nineteenth-century city was best seen at Coney Island. A two-mile stretch of sand nine miles from Manhattan by trolley or steamship, Coney Island in the 1890s was transformed into the site of some of the largest and most elaborate amusement parks in the country. Promoter George Tilyou built Steeplechase Park in 1897, advertising "10 hours of fun for 10 cents." With its mechanical thrills and fun-house laughs, the amusement park encouraged behavior that one schoolteacher aptly described as "everyone with the brakes off." By 1900, as many as a million New Yorkers flocked to Coney Island on any given weekend, making the amusement park the unofficial capital of a new mass culture.

REVIEW

How and why did recreation and leisure change in the last decades of the nineteenth century?

How did municipal governments respond to the challenges of urban expansion?

Private enterprise, not city planners, built the cities of the United States. With a few notable exceptions, cities simply mushroomed, formed by the dictates of profit and the exigencies of local politics. With the rise of the city came the need for public facilities, transportation, and services that would tax the imaginations of America's architects and engineers and set the scene for the rough-and-tumble of big-city government, politics, and bossism.

How did the landscape of American cities change?

Skyscrapers and mighty bridges dominated the imagination and the urban landscape. Less imposing but no less significant were the paved streets, the parks and public libraries, and the subways and sewers. In the late nineteenth century, Americans rushed to embrace new technology of all kinds, making their cities the most modern in the world.

Structural steel made enormous advances in building possible. A decade after the completion of the Brooklyn Bridge, engineers used the new technology to construct the Williamsburg Bridge. More prosaic and utilitarian than its neighbor, the new bridge was never as acclaimed, but it was longer by four feet and completed in half the time. It became the model for future building as the age of steel supplanted the age of stone and iron.

Chicago, not New York, gave birth to the modern skyscraper. Rising from the ashes of the Great Fire of 1871, which destroyed three square miles and left eighteen thousand people homeless, Chicago offered a generation of skilled architects and engineers the chance to experiment. Commercial architecture became an art form at the hands of a skilled group of architects who together constituted the "Chicago school." Employing the dictum "Form follows function," they built startlingly modern structures.

Across the United States, municipal governments undertook public works on a scale never before seen. They paved streets, built sewers and water mains, replaced gas lamps with electric lights, ran trolley tracks on the old horsecar lines, and dug underground to build subways, tearing down the unsightly elevated tracks that had clogged city streets. Boston completed the nation's first subway system in 1897, and New York and Philadelphia soon followed.

Cities became more beautiful with the creation of urban public parks to complement the new buildings that quickly rose. Much of the credit for America's greatest parks goes to one man—landscape architect Frederick Law Olmsted. New York City's Central Park, completed in 1873, became the first landscaped public park in the United States. Olmsted and his partner, Calvert Vaux, directed the planting of more than five million trees, shrubs, and vines to transform the eight hundred acres between 59th and 110th Streets into an oasis for urban dwellers. "We want a place," he wrote, where people "may stroll for an hour, seeing, hearing, and feeling nothing of the bustle and jar of the streets."

American cities did not overlook the mind in their efforts at improvement. A comprehensive free public school system educated everyone from the children of the middle class to the sons and daughters of immigrant workers. Yet the exploding urban population strained the system and led to crowded and inadequate facilities. In 1899, more than 544,000 pupils attended public school in New York's five boroughs. Although municipalities across the United States provided free secondary school education for all who wished to attend, only 8 percent of Americans completed high school.

To educate those who couldn't go to school, American cities created the most extensive free public library system in the world. In 1895, the Boston Public Library opened its bronze doors in its new Copley Square location under the inscription "Free to All." Designed in the style of a Renaissance palazzo, with more than 700,000 books on the shelves ready to be checked out, the library earned the description "a palace of the people."

Despite the Boston Public Library's legend "Free to All," the poor did not share equally in the advantages of city life. The parks, the libraries, and even the subways and sewers benefited some city dwellers more than others. Few library cards were held by Boston's laborers, who worked six days a week and found the library closed on Sunday. And in the 1890s, there was nothing central about New York's Central Park. It was a four-mile walk from the tenements of Hester Street to the park's entrance at 59th Street and Fifth Avenue. Then, as now, the comfortable, not the indigent, reaped a disproportionate share of the benefits in the nation's big cities.

Any story of the American city, it seems, must be a tale of two cities—or given the cities' great diversity, a tale of many cities within each metropolis. At the turn of the twentieth century, a central paradox emerged: The enduring monuments of America's cities—the bridges, skyscrapers, parks, and libraries—stood as the undeniable achievements of the same system of municipal government that reformers dismissed as boss-ridden, criminal, and corrupt.

How did American cities suffer from "boss rule"?

The physical growth of the cities required the expansion of public services and the creation of entirely new facilities: streets, subways, elevated trains, bridges, docks, sewers, and public utilities. There was work to be done and money to be made. The professional politician—the colorful big-city boss—became a phenomenon of urban growth and **bossism** a national concern. Though corrupt and often criminal, the boss saw to the building of the city and provided needed social services for new residents in return for their political support. Yet not even the big-city boss could be said to rule the unruly city. The governing of America's cities resembled more a tug-of-war than boss rule.

The most notorious of all the city bosses was William Marcy "Boss" Tweed of New York. At midcentury, Boss Tweed's Democratic Party "machine" held sway. A machine was really no more than a political party organized at the grassroots level. Its purpose was to win elections and reward its followers, often with jobs on the city's payroll. New York's citywide Democratic machine, Tammany Hall, commanded an army of party functionaries. They formed a shadow government more powerful than the city's elected officials.

As chairman of the Tammany general committee, Tweed kept the Democratic Party together and ran the city through the use of bribery and graft. "As long as I count the votes," he shamelessly boasted, "what are you going to do about it?" The excesses of the Tweed ring soon led to a clamor for reform and cries of "Throw the rascals out." Tweed's rule ended in 1871. Eventually, he was tried and convicted and later died in jail.

New York was not the only city to experience bossism and corruption. The British visitor James Bryce concluded in 1888, "There is no denying that the government of cities is the one conspicuous failure of the United States." More than 80 percent of the nation's thirty largest cities experienced some form of boss rule in the decades around the turn of the twentieth century. However, infighting among powerful ward bosses often meant that no single boss enjoyed exclusive power in the big cities.

bossism
Pattern of urban political organization that arose in the late nineteenth century in which an often corrupt "boss" maintains an inordinate level of power through command of a political machine that distributes services to its constituents.

Urban reformers and proponents of good government (derisively called "goo goos" by their rivals) challenged machine rule and sometimes succeeded in electing reform mayors. But the reformers rarely managed to stay in office for long. Their detractors called them "mornin' glories," observing that they "looked lovely in the mornin' and withered up in a short time." The bosses enjoyed continued success largely because the urban political machine helped the cities' immigrants and poor, who remained the bosses' staunchest allies. "What tells in holding your district," a Tammany ward boss observed, "is to go right down among the poor and help them in the different ways they need help. It's philanthropy, but it's politics, too — mighty good politics."

The big-city boss, through the skillful orchestration of rewards, exerted powerful leverage and lined up support for his party from a broad range of constituents, from the urban poor to wealthy industrialists. In 1902, when journalist Lincoln Steffens began "The Shame of the Cities," a series of articles exposing city corruption, he found that business leaders who fastidiously refused to mingle socially with the bosses nevertheless struck deals with them. "He is a self-righteous fraud, this big businessman," Steffens concluded. "I found him buying boodlers [bribers] in St. Louis, defending grafters in Minneapolis, originating corruption in Pittsburgh, sharing with bosses in Philadelphia, deploring reform in Chicago, and beating good government with corruption funds in New York."

For all his color and flamboyance, the big-city boss was simply one of many actors in the drama of municipal government. Old-stock aristocrats, new manufacturers, professionals, saloonkeepers, pushcart peddlers, and politicians all fought for their interests in the hurly-burly of city government. They didn't much like each other, and they sometimes fought savagely. But they learned to live with one another. Compromise and accommodation — not boss rule — best characterized big-city government by the turn of the twentieth century, although the cities' reputation for corruption left an indelible mark on the consciousness of the American public.

How did New York demonstrate the consolidation of the capitalist class?

New York City is neither the capital of the state nor the capital of the nation. But as the capital of capital, it holds a special place in American economic and social history. Its transition from a city run by merchants, largely rich through cotton and slavery, to an industrial and financial powerhouse demonstrates the workings of the consolidation of class. The Civil War struck the first blow by cutting the cotton threads that bound the Union economically and putting money in the pockets of a new group of manufacturers who financed and supplied the Union army. Their rise took place against the backdrop of class, race, and ethnic tensions that erupted spectacularly in the draft riots of 1863 (see chapter 15).

After Appomattox, as labor struggled to gain a portion of the prosperity that minted new railroad and industrial millionaires, New York's capitalist elite used fears of class war to solidify its power and to employ the state as an agent of its will. Wealthy New Yorkers formed local militia and built armories to protect private property from those they labeled "the dangerous classes." Through city ordinances they severely restricted urban workers' use of public space for organizing and protest. Most important, the capitalist elite utilized the power of the state—its militia and federal troops—to put down strikes.

New York City acted as a magnet for the rich. Those who had made their fortunes elsewhere, like Carnegie in Pittsburgh and Rockefeller in Cleveland, sooner or later moved to the city. By 1892, an amazing 27 percent of the country's millionaires lived in Manhattan. Once they wielded economic power, the new capitalist elite set out to legitimize itself through cultural hegemony by building libraries, endowing museums, and funding the arts—acquiring all the trappings of civilized society.

How was Chicago perceived as both the white city and city of sin?

Americans have always been of two minds about the city. They like to boast of its skyscrapers and bridges, its culture and sophistication, and they pride themselves on its bigness and bustle. At the same time, they fear it as the city of sin, the home of immigrant slums, the center of vice and crime. Nowhere did the divided view of the American city take form more graphically than in Chicago in 1893. In that year, Chicago hosted the **World's Columbian Exposition**, the grandest world's fair in the nation's history. The fairground, only five miles down the shore of Lake Michigan from downtown Chicago, offered a lesson in what Americans on the eve of the twentieth century imagined a city might be. Christened the "White City," it seemed light-years away from Chicago, with its stockyards, slums, and bustling terminals. Frederick Law Olmsted and architect Daniel Burnham supervised the transformation of a swampy wasteland into a pristine paradise of lagoons, fountains, wooded islands, gardens, and imposing white buildings.

"Sell the cookstove if necessary and come," novelist Hamlin Garland wrote to his parents on the farm. And come they did, in spite of the panic and depression that broke out only weeks after the fair opened in May 1893. In six months, fairgoers purchased more than twenty-seven million tickets, turning a profit of nearly a half million dollars for promoters. Visitors from home and abroad strolled the elaborate grounds and visited the exhibits—everything from a model of the Brooklyn Bridge carved in soap to the latest goods and inventions. Half carnival, half culture, the great fair offered something for everyone. On the Midway Plaisance, crowds thrilled to the massive wheel built by Mr. Ferris and watched agog as Little Egypt danced the hootchy-kootchy.

In October, the fair closed its doors in the midst of the worst depression the country had yet seen. During that winter, Chicago's unemployed and homeless took over the grounds, vandalized the buildings, and frightened the city's comfortable citizens out of their wits. When reporters asked Daniel Burnham, its chief architect, what should be done with the moldering remains of the White

World's Columbian Exposition
World's fair held in Chicago in 1893 that attracted millions of visitors. The elaborately designed pavilions of the "White City" included exhibits of technological innovation and of cultural exoticism. They embodied an urban ideal that contrasted with the realities of Chicago life.

▲ *Chicago's White City* This painting by H. D. Nichols captures the monumental architecture of the White City built for the World's Columbian Exposition in 1893. In the foreground, the central Court of Honor features a Frederick MacMonnies fountain, with Christopher Columbus at the prow of his ship. In the distance stands Daniel Chester French's sixty-foot gilded statue *Republic*. The awe-inspiring exposition drew millions of visitors from America and abroad. Chicago History Museum/Bridgeman Images.

City, he responded, "It should be torched." It was. In July 1894, in a clash between federal troops and striking railway workers, incendiaries set fires that leveled the fairgrounds.

In the end, the White City remained what it had always been, a dreamscape. Buildings that looked like marble were actually constructed of staff, a plaster substance that began to crumble even before fire destroyed the fairgrounds. Perhaps it was not so strange, after all, that the legacy of the White City could be found on Coney Island, where two new amusement parks, Luna and Dreamland, sought to combine, albeit in a more tawdry form, the beauty of the White City and the thrill of the Midway Plaisance. More enduring than the White City itself was what it represented: the emergent industrial might of the United States, at home and abroad, with its inventions, manufactured goods, and growing consumer culture.

REVIEW

How did city life change in the late nineteenth century?

Conclusion: Who built the cities?

As great a role as industrialists, financiers, and engineers played in building the nation's cities, common workers—most of them immigrants—provided the muscle. The unprecedented growth of urban, industrial America resulted from the labor of millions of men, women, and children who toiled in workshops and factories, in sweatshops and mines, and on railroads and construction sites across America.

America's cities in the late nineteenth century teemed with life. Townhouses and tenements jostled for space with skyscrapers and great department stores, while parks, ball fields, amusement arcades, and public libraries provided the city masses with recreation and entertainment. Municipal governments, straining to build the new cities, experienced the rough-and-tumble of machine politics as bosses and their constituents looked to profit from city growth.

For America's workers, urban industrialism, along with the rise of big business and corporate consolidation, drastically changed the workplace. Industrialists replaced skilled workers with new machines that could be operated by cheaper unskilled labor. During hard times, employers did not hesitate to cut workers' already meager wages. As the Great Railroad Strike of 1877 demonstrated, when labor united, it could bring the nation to attention. Organization held out the best hope for the workers; first the Knights of Labor and later the AFL won converts among the nation's working class.

The rise of urban industrialism challenged the American promise, which for decades had been dominated by Jeffersonian agrarian ideals. Could such a promise exist in the changing world of cities, tenements, immigrants, and huge corporations? In the Great Depression that came in the 1890s, mounting anger and frustration would lead farmers and workers to join forces and create a grassroots movement to fight for change under the banner of a new People's Party.

EXPLAIN WHY IT MATTERS

global migration (p. 542)

Sinophobia (p. 547)

Ellis Island (p. 548)

plutocracy (p. 552)

sweatshop (p. 554)

family economy (p. 555)

"typewriters" (p. 556)

Great Railroad Strike (p. 558)

Knights of Labor (p. 559)

American Federation of Labor (AFL) (p. 560)

Haymarket bombing (p. 562)

cult of domesticity (p. 563)

bossism (p. 566)

World's Columbian Exposition (p. 568)

PUT IT ALL TOGETHER

URBANIZATION

- What factors led immigrants to American cities in the late nineteenth century? How did their arrival change the cities in which they settled?

- How and why did the social geography of the American city change in the late nineteenth century?

INDUSTRY AND LABOR

- What new social divisions accompanied business expansion and industrialization?

- What kinds of organizations did workers form in the late nineteenth century, and what was their purpose? How successful were they?

CITY LIFE

- How did urban industrialism transform home and family life?

- What led to the rise of the big-city boss? Whose interests did late-nineteenth-century city governments serve?

LOOKING BACKWARD, LOOKING AHEAD

- How did early-twentieth-century American cities differ from their early-nineteenth-century counterparts?

- How did the rise of urban industrialism change Americans' sense of themselves as a people?

20

DISSENT, DEPRESSION, AND WAR

1890–1900

This chapter discusses the following questions:

- Why did American farmers organize alliances in the late nineteenth century?
- What led to the labor wars of the 1890s?
- How were women involved in late-nineteenth-century politics?
- How did economic depression affect American politics in the 1890s?
- Why did the United States largely abandon its isolationist foreign policy in the 1890s?
- Conclusion: How did domestic strife influence foreign policy?

▶ **Frances Willard** Frances Willard, the forward-thinking leader of the Woman's Christian Temperance Union, learned to ride a bicycle at age fifty-three. Willard brought her progressive ideas to the People's Party 1892 convention, where she shared a place on the platform with the new party's leaders. WCTU Archives, Evanston IL.

AN AMERICAN STORY

Frances Willard traveled to St. Louis in February 1892 with high hopes. Political change was in the air, and Willard had helped to fashion a new reform party. As head of the Woman's Christian Temperance Union (WCTU), an organization with dues-paying members in every state and territory in the nation, Willard wielded considerable clout. At her invitation, twenty-eight of the country's leading reformers had met in Chicago to draft a set of principles to bring to St. Louis. No American woman before her had played such a central role in a political movement. At the height of her power, Willard took her place among the leaders onstage in St. Louis.

Exposition Music Hall presented a colorful spectacle. "The banners of the different states rose above the delegates throughout the hall, fluttering like the flags over an army encamped," wrote one reporter. The fiery orator Ignatius Donnelly attacked the money kings of Wall Street. Terence V. Powderly, head of the Knights of Labor, called on workers to join hands with farmers against the "nonproducing classes." And Frances Willard took the podium, urging the crowd to prohibit liquor and give women the vote.

Delegates hammered out a series of demands, breathtaking in their scope. They tackled the tough questions of the day — the regulation of business, the need for banking and currency reform, the right of labor to organize and bargain collectively, and the role of the federal government in regulating business, curbing monopoly, and giving the people greater voice. But the new party, determined to stick to economic issues, resisted endorsing either prohibition or woman suffrage. Disappointed, Willard complained of the "crooked methods . . . employed to scuttle these planks."

The convention ended its work amid a chorus of cheers. According to one eyewitness, "Hats, paper, handkerchiefs, etc., were thrown into the air; . . . cheer after cheer thundered and reverberated through the vast hall reaching the outside of the building where thousands who had been waiting the outcome joined in the applause till for blocks in every direction the exultation made the din indescribable."

What was all the shouting about? The crowd, fed up with the Democrats and the Republicans, celebrated the birth of a new People's Party. The St. Louis gathering marked an early milestone in one of the most turbulent decades in U.S. history. An agrarian revolt, labor strikes, a severe depression, and a war shook the 1890s. As the decade opened, Americans flocked to organizations including the Farmers' Alliance, the American Federation of Labor, and the Woman's Christian Temperance Union. Their political alliance gave birth to the People's (or Populist) Party. In a decade of unrest and uncertainty, the Populists insisted that the federal government play a more active role to ensure economic fairness in industrial America.

This challenge to the status quo culminated in 1896 in one of the most hotly contested presidential elections in the nation's history. At the close of the tumultuous decade, the Spanish-American War brought the country together, with Americans rallying to support the troops. American imperialism and overseas expansion raised questions about the nation's role on the world stage as the United States stood poised to enter the twentieth century.

Why did American farmers organize alliances in the late nineteenth century?

Hard times in the 1880s and 1890s created a groundswell of agrarian revolt. A bitter farmer wrote from Minnesota, "I settled on this Land in good Faith Built House and Barn. Broken up Part of the Land. Spent years of hard Labor in grubbing fencing and Improving." About to lose his farm to foreclosure, he lamented, "Are they going to drive us out like trespassers . . . and give us away to the Corporations?"

After the Civil War, a series of setbacks helped strip any sense of security from American agriculture, robbing farmers of personal autonomy. Farm prices fell decade after decade, even as American farmers' share of the world market grew. In parts of Kansas, corn sold for as little as ten cents a bushel, and angry farmers burned their crops for fuel rather than sell them on the market. At the same time, consumer prices soared (**Figure 20.1**). In Kansas alone, almost half the farms had fallen into the hands of the banks through mortgage foreclosures by 1894. Farmers soon banded together into Farmers' Alliances that gave birth to a broad political movement.

How did the Farmers' Alliance aim to protect family farmers?

At the heart of the farmers' problems stood a banking system dominated by eastern commercial banks committed to the gold standard, a railroad rate system both capricious and unfair, and rampant speculation that drove up the price of land. Absentee owners in the East and abroad controlled the lion's share of land and resources in the West. Western farmers rankled under a system over which they had little control. Railroads charged them exorbitant freight rates while granting rebates to large shippers (see chapter 18).

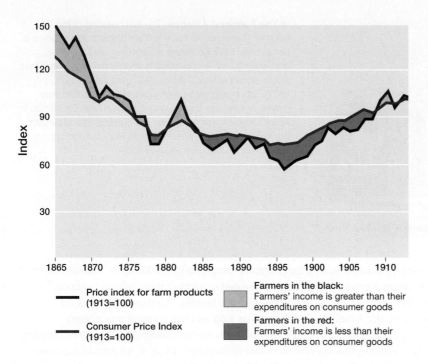

FIGURE 20.1 ◀ Consumer Prices and Farm Income, 1865–1910 Around 1870, consumer prices and farm income were about equal. During the 1880s and 1890s, however, farmers suffered great hardships as prices for their crops steadily declined and the cost of consumer goods continued to rise.

Price index for farm products
(1913=100)

Consumer Price Index
(1913=100)

Farmers in the black:
Farmers' income is greater than their expenditures on consumer goods

Farmers in the red:
Farmers' income is less than their expenditures on consumer goods

The practice of charging higher rates for short hauls than for long hauls meant that grain elevators could ship their wheat from Chicago to New York and across the Atlantic for less than a Dakota farmer paid to send his crop to mills in Minneapolis. The government's tight money policy meant that all together the southern states had less money in circulation than the state of Massachusetts. The lack of currency and credit drove southern farmers to the stopgap credit system of the crop lien. To pay for seed and supplies, farmers pledged their crops in advance as collateral to local creditors in a hopeless spiral of debt and tenancy. Determined to do something, farmers banded together to fight for change.

Farm protest was not new. In the 1870s, farmers had supported the Grange and the Greenback Labor Party. As the farmers' situation grew more desperate, they organized, forming regional alliances. The first **Farmers' Alliance** came together in Lampasas County, Texas, to fight "landsharks and horse thieves." In frontier farmhouses in Texas, in log cabins in the backwoods of Arkansas, and in the rural parishes of Louisiana, separate groups of farmers formed similar alliances for self-help.

Traveling lecturers spread throughout the South and West preaching the Alliance gospel of political education, social criticism, and economic collective action. Education was the hallmark of the Alliance. The sunburned men and careworn women who turned out by the tens of thousands did not need to be convinced that something was wrong. What they needed was a plan of action, and the Farmers' Alliance soon supplied it.

As the movement grew in the 1880s, farmers' groups consolidated into two regional alliances: the Northwestern Farmers' Alliance, active in Kansas, Nebraska, and other

Farmers' Alliance
Movement to form local organizations to advance farmers' collective interests that gained wide popularity in the 1880s. Over time, farmers' groups consolidated into the Northwestern Farmers' Alliance and the Southern Farmers' Alliance. In 1892, the Farmers' Alliance gave birth to the People's Party.

◀ **The Farmers' Alliance** The last meeting of the Southern Farmers' Alliance to take place in this building in Lampassas County, Texas, is captured here for the historical record. In this humble shack, the movement that would attract over 2.5 million followers was launched in 1877. This photo was taken just before the cabin was moved to Chicago for the World's Columbian Exposition in 1893. Once the fair was over, the building was chopped up, and pieces were passed out to Populist partisans like sacred relics. Wisconsin Historical Society.

"The Last Meeting of the First Farmers Alliance at their First House."

midwestern Granger states; and the more radical Southern Farmers' Alliance. By 1890, the Southern Farmers' Alliance alone counted more than three million members, with women as well as men rallying to the Alliance banner. "I am going to work for prohibition, the Alliance, and for Jesus as long as I live," swore one woman.

Radical in its inclusiveness, the Southern Alliance reached out to Black farmers, too. Through cooperation with the Colored Farmers' Alliance, an African American group founded in Texas in the 1880s, Black and white farmers attempted to make common cause. As Georgia's Tom Watson, a Southern Alliance stalwart, pointed out, "The colored tenant is in the same boat as the white tenant, . . . and . . . the accident of color can make no difference in the interests of farmers, croppers, and laborers." But at the same time Watson stressed economic justice, he made it clear that it was still a "white man's country" and would remain so.

The Alliance recruited industrial workers as well as farmers. During a major strike against Jay Gould's Texas and Pacific Railroad in 1886, the Alliance vocally sided with the workers and rushed food and supplies to the strikers. Labor support proved especially strong among miners and railroad workers—two of the most dynamic contingents of the labor movement.

At the heart of the Alliance stood a series of farmers' cooperatives. By "bulking" their cotton—that is, selling it together—farmers could negotiate a better price. And by setting up trade stores and exchanges, they sought to escape the grasp of the merchant/creditor. Through the cooperatives, the Farmers' Alliance promised to change the way farmers lived. "We are going to get out of debt and be free and independent people once more," exulted one Georgia farmer. But the Alliance faced insurmountable difficulties in running successful cooperatives. Opposition by merchants, bankers, wholesalers, and manufacturers made it impossible for the cooperatives to get credit. As the cooperative movement died, the Farmers' Alliance moved into politics.

How did the Farmers' Alliance become the Populist Party?

In the earliest days of the Alliance movement, a leader of the Southern Farmers' Alliance insisted, "The Alliance is a strictly white man's nonpolitical, secret business association." But by 1892, it was none of those things. Advocates of a third party carried the day at the convention of laborers, farmers, and common folk in 1892 in St. Louis, where the Farmers' Alliance gave birth to the **People's Party (Populist Party)** and launched the Populist movement.

The same spirit of religious revival that animated the Farmers' Alliance infused the People's Party. Convinced that the money and banking systems worked to the advantage of the wealthy few, Populists demanded economic democracy. To help get the credit they needed at reasonable rates, southern farmers hit on the ingenious idea of a subtreasury—a plan that would allow farmers to store their nonperishable crops until prices rose and to receive commodity credit from the federal government to obtain needed supplies. To the western farmer, the Populists promised land reform, championing a plan to reclaim excessive land granted to railroads or sold to foreign investors. The Populists' boldest proposal called for government ownership of the railroads and the telegraph system to put an end to discriminatory rates.

The Populists solidly supported free silver in the hope of increasing the nation's tight money supply. To empower the common people, the Populist platform called for the direct election of senators and for other electoral reforms, including the right to initiate legislation, to recall elected officials, and to submit issues to the people by means of a referendum. In support of labor, the Populists supported the eight-hour day.

The sweeping array of reforms enacted in the Populist platform changed the agenda of politics for decades to come. More than just a response to hard times, Populism presented an alternative vision of American economic democracy.

People's Party (Populist Party)
Political party formed in St. Louis in 1892 by the Farmers' Alliance to advance the goals of the Populist movement. Populists sought economic democracy, promoting land, electoral, banking, and monetary reform. Republican victory in the presidential election of 1896 effectively destroyed the People's Party.

REVIEW

Why did the Farmers' Alliance decide to form a political party?

What led to the labor wars of the 1890s?

W hile farmers united to fight for change, industrial laborers fought their own battles in a series of bloody strikes historians have called the "labor wars." By the 1890s, workers watched as their rights and what seemed their very manhood came under threat. They fought a losing battle for the control of production on the shop floor, a prerogative as important as wages and shorter hours. Only the ability to bargain collectively through unions promised a better life, and employers fought viciously to prevent them from achieving their goal. Three major conflicts—the lockout of steelworkers in Homestead, Pennsylvania, in 1892; the miners' strike in Cripple Creek, Colorado, in 1894; and the Pullman boycott that same year—brought into focus fundamental questions about the rights of labor and the sanctity of private property.

What precipitated the Homestead lockout and subsequent strike?

In 1892, steelworkers in Pennsylvania squared off against Andrew Carnegie in a decisive struggle over the right to organize in the Homestead steel mills. Carnegie resolved to crush the Amalgamated Association of Iron and Steel Workers, one of the largest and richest craft unions in the American Federation of Labor (AFL). When the Amalgamated attempted to renew its contract at Carnegie's Homestead mill, its leaders were told that since "the vast majority of our employees are Non-union, the Firm has decided that the minority must give place to the majority." While it was true that only skilled workers predominated in the elite Amalgamated, the union had begun to buttress its position by welcoming unskilled workers from the plant's four thousand employees. Slavs, who did much of the unskilled work, made common cause with the Welsh, Scottish, and Irish skilled workers in the union.

Carnegie, who in the past had supported labor unions, boasting he, too, was "a working man," preferred not to be directly involved in the union busting. That spring he sailed to Scotland and left Henry Clay Frick, the toughest antilabor man in the industry, in charge. By summer, a strike looked inevitable. Frick prepared by erecting a fifteen-foot fence around the Homestead plant and topping it with barbed wire. Workers aptly dubbed it "Fort Frick." Frick then hired 316 mercenaries from the Pinkerton National Detective Agency at the rate of $5 per day, more than double the wage of the average Homestead worker. The Pinkertons served as the advance agents and protectors of the strikebreakers Frick planned to import.

Homestead lockout
1892 lockout of workers at the Homestead, Pennsylvania, steel mill after Andrew Carnegie refused to renew the union contract and workers prepared to strike. Union supporters attacked the Pinkerton National Detective Agency guards hired to protect the mill, but the National Guard soon broke the strike.

On June 28, the **Homestead lockout** began. Frick locked the doors of the mills and prepared to bring in strikebreakers. Hugh O'Donnell, the young Irishman who led the union, vowed to prevent "scabs" from entering the plant. On July 6 at 4 a.m., a lookout spotted two barges moving up the Monongahela River in the fog. Frick was attempting to smuggle his Pinkertons into Homestead.

Workers sounded the alarm, and within minutes a crowd of more than a thousand, men, women, and children hastily armed with rifles, hoes, and fence posts, rushed to the riverbank. When the men on the barges attempted to come ashore, gunfire broke out, and more than a dozen Pinkertons and some thirty strikers fell, killed or wounded. Hastily abandoned by the tugboat that brought them, the barges wallowed helplessly at the dock. Inside the hapless Pinkertons hunkered down for a siege. For twelve hours, the crowd threw everything it had at the barges, from dynamite to fireworks left over from the Fourth of July. Finally, the Pinkertons hoisted a white flag and arranged with O'Donnell to surrender.

With three workers dead and scores wounded, the crowd, numbering perhaps ten thousand, was in no mood for conciliation. As the hated "Pinks" came up the hill, they were forced to run a gauntlet of screaming, cursing workers and their families. When a young guard dropped to his knees, crying for mercy, a woman used her umbrella to poke out his eye. One Pinkerton had been killed in the siege on the barges. In the grim rout that followed their surrender, not one avoided injury. The workers took control of the plant and elected a council to run the community. At first, public opinion favored their cause. A congressman castigated Carnegie for "skulking in his castle in Scotland." Populists, meeting in St. Louis, condemned the Pinkertons as "hireling armies."

The action of the Homestead workers struck at the heart of the capitalist system, pitting the workers' right to their jobs against the rights of private property. The workers' insistence that "we are not destroying the property of the company—merely protecting our rights" did not prove as compelling to the courts and the state as the property rights of the owners. Four days after the confrontation, Pennsylvania's governor, who sympathized with the workers, nonetheless yielded to pressure from

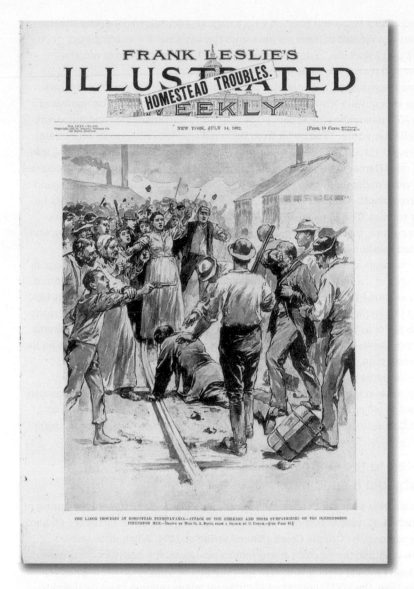

FRANK LESLIE'S
ILLUSTRATED
HOMESTEAD TROUBLES.
WEEKLY

NEW YORK, JULY 14, 1892.

THE LABOR TROUBLES AT HOMESTEAD, PENNSYLVANIA—ATTACK OF THE STRIKERS AND THEIR SYMPATHIZERS ON THE SURRENDERED
PINKERTON MEN.—DRAWN BY MISS G. A. DAVIS, FROM A SKETCH BY C. UPHAM.—[SEE PAGE 41.]

◄ **Homestead Workers Attack the Pinkertons** The nation's attention was riveted on labor strife at the Homestead steel mill in the summer of 1892. *Frank Leslie's Illustrated Weekly* ran a cover story on the violence that Pinkerton agents faced from an armed crowd of men, women, and children who were enraged that Frick had hired the Pinkertons to bring in strikebreakers. *Leslie's* illustrations exaggerated the violence of the strikers. Here, for example, a young man with a gun appears in the foreground. Although the Pinkertons were badly beaten, none were shot. The New York Society Library.

Frick and ordered eight thousand National Guard troops into Homestead to protect Carnegie's property. The workers, thinking they had nothing to fear from the militia, welcomed the troops with a brass band. But the troops' occupation not only protected Carnegie's property but also enabled Frick to reopen the mills and bring in strikebreakers. "We have been deceived," one worker complained bitterly. "We have stood idly by and let the town be occupied by soldiers who come here, not as our protectors, but as the protectors of non-union men. . . . If we undertake to resist the seizure of our jobs, we will be shot down like dogs."

Then, in a misguided effort to ignite a general uprising, Alexander Berkman, a Russian immigrant and anarchist, attempted to assassinate Frick. Berkman bungled his attempt. Shot twice and stabbed with a dagger, Frick allowed a doctor to remove the bullets but refused to leave his desk until the day's work was completed. "I do not think that I shall die," Frick remarked coolly, "but whether I do or not, the Company will pursue the same policy and it will win."

After the assassination attempt, public opinion turned against the workers. Berkman was quickly tried and sentenced to prison. Although the Amalgamated and the AFL denounced his action, Frick worked to link anarchism and unionism. O'Donnell later wrote, "The bullet from Berkman's pistol, failing in its foul intent, went straight through the heart of the Homestead strike." The union held out into the fall, with Carnegie taking substantial losses. But in the end strikers were forced back to work under an ironclad contract that forbade unions. Union leaders found themselves blacklisted in every steel mill in the country; Frick suggested they be tried for treason. The Homestead mill reopened in November. With the owners firmly in control, the company slashed wages, reinstated the twelve-hour day, and eliminated five hundred jobs.

The workers at Homestead had been taught a lesson. They would never again, in the words of the National Guard commander, "believe the works are theirs quite as much as Carnegie's." When journalist Hamlin Garland visited Homestead in 1894, he found the workers demoralized and "brutalized." The average steelworker made less than $2 for a twelve-hour day and lived "a dog's life." The death toll alone was staggering: Between 1870 and 1900, fatalities rose more than 25 percent, making the largely immigrant unskilled laborers little more than industrial "cannon fodder." Another forty-five years would pass before steelworkers successfully unionized.

In the meantime, Carnegie's production tripled, even in the midst of a depression. "Ashamed to tell you profits these days," Carnegie wrote a friend in 1899. And no wonder: Carnegie's profits had grown from $4 million in 1892 to $40 million in 1900.

What led to the Cripple Creek miners' strike of 1894 and why did it succeed?

Less than a year after the Homestead lockout, a panic on Wall Street in the spring of 1893 touched off a bitter economic depression. In the West, silver mines fell on hard times, leading to the **Cripple Creek miners' strike of 1894**. When mine owners moved to lengthen the workday from eight to ten hours, the newly formed Western Federation of Miners (WFM) vowed to hold the line in Cripple Creek, Colorado. In February 1894, the WFM threatened to strike all mines running more than eight-hour shifts. The mine owners divided: Some quickly settled with the WFM; others continued to demand ten hours, provoking a strike.

The striking miners received help from many quarters. Working miners paid $15 a month to a strike fund, and miners in neighboring districts sent substantial contributions. The miners enjoyed the support and assistance of local businesses and grocers, who provided credit to the strikers. With these advantages, the Cripple Creek strikers could afford to hold out for their demands.

Even more significant, Governor Davis H. Waite, a Populist elected in 1892, had strong ties to the miners and refused to use the power of the state against the strikers. Governor Waite asked the strikers to lay down their arms and demanded that the mine owners disperse their hired deputies. The miners agreed to arbitration

Cripple Creek miners' strike of 1894
Strike led by the Western Federation of Miners in response to an attempt to lengthen their workday to ten hours. With the support of local businessmen and the Populist governor of Colorado, the miners successfully maintained an eight-hour day.

and selected Waite as their sole arbitrator. By May, the recalcitrant mine owners capitulated, and the union won an eight-hour day.

Governor Waite's intervention demonstrated the pivotal power of the state in the nation's labor wars. Having a Populist in power made a difference. A decade later, in 1904, with Waite out of office, mine owners relied on state troops to take back control of the mines, defeating the WFM and blacklisting all its members. In retrospect, the Cripple Creek miners' victory in 1894 proved the exception to the rule of state intervention on the side of private property.

Why did Eugene V. Debs lead the Pullman strike?

The economic depression that began in 1893 swelled the ranks of the unemployed to three million, almost half of the working population. "A fearful crisis is upon us," wrote a labor publication. Nowhere were workers more demoralized than in the town of Pullman, on the outskirts of Chicago.

In the wake of the Great Railroad Strike of 1877, George M. Pullman, the builder of Pullman railroad cars, moved his plant nine miles south of Chicago and built a model town, which boasted parks, fountains, playgrounds, an auditorium, a library, a hotel, shops, and markets, along with eighteen hundred units of housing. Noticeably absent was a saloon.

The housing in Pullman was clearly superior to that in neighboring areas, but workers paid a premium to live there. Pullman's rents ran 10 to 20 percent higher than housing costs in nearby communities. In addition, George Pullman refused to "sell an acre under any circumstances." As long as he controlled the town absolutely, he held the powerful whip of eviction over his employees and could quickly get rid of "trouble-makers." Although observers at first praised the beauty and orderliness of the town, critics by the 1890s compared Pullman's model town to a "gilded cage" for workers.

The depression brought hard times to Pullman. Workers saw their wages slashed five times between May and December 1893, with cuts totaling at least 28 percent. At the same time, Pullman refused to lower the rents in his model town, insisting that "the renting of the dwellings and the employment of workmen at Pullman are in no way tied together." When workers went to the bank to cash their paychecks, they found that the rent had been taken out. One worker discovered only forty-seven cents in his pay envelope for two weeks' work. When the bank teller asked him whether he wanted to apply it to his back rent, he retorted, "If Mr. Pullman needs that forty-seven cents worse than I do, let him have it." At the same time, Pullman continued to pay his stockholders an 8 percent dividend, and the company accumulated a $25 million surplus.

At the heart of the labor problems at Pullman lay not only economic inequity but also the company's attempt to control the work process, substituting piecework for day wages and undermining skilled craftsworkers. During the spring of 1894, Pullman's desperate workers, seeking help, flocked to the ranks of the American Railway Union (ARU), led by the charismatic Eugene V. Debs. The ARU, unlike the skilled craft unions of the AFL, pledged to organize all railway workers—from engineers to engine wipers.

George Pullman responded to union organization at his plant by firing three of the union's leaders the day after they protested wage cuts. Angry men and women walked off the job in disgust. What began as a spontaneous protest in May 1894 quickly blossomed into a strike that involved more than 90 percent of Pullman's 3,300 workers. Pullman countered by shutting down the plant. In June, the strikers appealed to the ARU to come to their aid. Debs pleaded with the workers to find another solution. But when George Pullman refused arbitration, the ARU membership voted to boycott all Pullman cars. Beginning on June 29, switchmen across the United States refused to handle any train that carried Pullman cars.

The conflict escalated quickly. The General Managers Association (GMA), an organization of managers from twenty-four different railroads, acted in concert to quash the Pullman boycott. They recruited strikebreakers and fired all the protesting switchmen. Their tactics set off a chain reaction. Entire train crews walked off the job in a show of solidarity with the Pullman workers. By July 2, rail lines from New York to California lay paralyzed. Even the GMA was forced to concede that the railroads had been "fought to a standstill."

The boycott remained surprisingly peaceful. In contrast to the Great Railroad Strike of 1877, no major riots broke out, and no serious property damage occurred. Debs fired off telegrams to all parts of the country advising his followers to avoid violence and respect law and order. But the nation's newspapers, fed press releases by the GMA, distorted the issues and misrepresented the strike. Across the country, papers ran headlines like "Wild Riot in Chicago" and "Mob Is in Control." **(See "Analyzing Historical Evidence: The Press and the Pullman Strike: Framing Class Conflict" on page 584.)**

Pullman boycott
Nationwide railroad workers' boycott of trains carrying Pullman cars in 1894 after Pullman workers, suffering radically reduced wages, joined the American Railway Union (ARU) and union leaders were fired in response. The boycott ended after the U.S. Army fired on strikers and ARU leader Eugene Debs was jailed.

In Washington, Attorney General Richard B. Olney, a lawyer with strong ties to the railroads, determined to put down the strike. In his way stood the governor of Illinois, John Peter Altgeld, who, pointing out that the boycott remained peaceful, refused to call out troops. To get around Altgeld, Olney convinced President Grover Cleveland that federal troops had to intervene to "protect the mails." Two conservative Chicago judges further crippled the boycott by issuing an injunction so sweeping that it prohibited Debs from speaking in public. The injunction made the boycott a crime punishable by a jail sentence for contempt of court, a civil process that did not require a jury trial. Even the conservative *Chicago Tribune* judged the injunction "a menace to liberty . . . a weapon ever ready for the capitalist." Furious, Debs risked jail by refusing to honor it.

Olney's strategy worked. President Grover Cleveland called out the army. On July 5, nearly eight thousand troops marched into Chicago. Violence immediately erupted. In one day, troops killed twenty-five

◄ **A Pullman Car** In addition to his public railway cars, George Pullman built private cars for the wealthy. A private car generally featured an observation deck, a parlor, staterooms to sleep a dozen, and full bathrooms featuring marble sinks and gold-plated fixtures. George Pullman himself owned the most ostentatious car. He boasted that it took over fifteen woodcarvers to complete the various carving and moldings. Pullman's skilled woodcarvers would strike in 1894 as they sought greater control in the workplace as well as higher wages. ullstein bild Dtl./Getty Images.

workers and wounded more than sixty. In the face of bullets and bayonets, the strikers held firm. "Troops cannot move trains," Debs reminded his followers, a fact that was borne out as the railroads remained paralyzed despite the military intervention. But if the army could not put down the boycott, the injunction did.

Debs was arrested and imprisoned for contempt of court. With its leader in jail, its headquarters raided and ransacked, and its members demoralized, the ARU collapsed along with the boycott. Pullman reopened his factory, hiring new workers to replace many of the blacklisted strikers and leaving sixteen hundred workers without jobs.

In the aftermath of the strike, a special commission investigated the events at Pullman, taking testimony from 107 witnesses, from the lowliest workers to George M. Pullman himself. Stubborn and self-righteous, Pullman spoke for the business orthodoxy of his era, steadfastly affirming the right of business to safeguard its interests through confederacies such as the GMA and at the same time denying labor's right to organize. "If we were to receive these men as representatives of the union," he stated, "they could probably force us to pay any wages which they saw fit."

From his jail cell, Eugene Debs reviewed the events of the Pullman strike. With the courts and the government ready to side with industrialists in defense of private property, strikes seemed futile, and unions remained helpless. Workers would have to take control of the state itself. Debs went into jail a trade unionist and came out six months later a socialist. At first, he turned to the Populist Party, but after its demise he formed the Socialist Party in 1900 and ran for president five times.

> **REVIEW**
>
> Why were the labor conflicts of the 1890s so often marked by violence?

How were women involved in late-nineteenth-century politics?

"Do everything," Frances Willard urged her followers in 1881. The new president of the Woman's Christian Temperance Union (WCTU) meant what she said. The WCTU followed a trajectory that was common for women in the late nineteenth century. As women organized to deal with issues that touched their homes and families, they moved into politics, lending new urgency to the cause of woman suffrage. Urban industrialism dislocated women's lives no less than men's. Like men, women sought political change and organized to promote issues central to their lives, campaigning for temperance and woman suffrage.

What were the goals of the Woman's Christian Temperance Union?

A visionary leader, Frances Willard spoke for a group left almost entirely out of the U.S. electoral process. By 1890, only one state, Wyoming, allowed women to vote in

ANALYZING HISTORICAL EVIDENCE

The Press and the Pullman Strike: Framing Class Conflict

Newspaper coverage of the 1894 Pullman strike and the subsequent American Railway Union boycott provides a window into the way the press framed class conflict in the United States in the 1890s. The *Chicago Times*, for example, clearly supported the workers and the union. By contrast, the *Chicago Tribune* and most other Chicago newspapers sided with George M. Pullman and the General Managers Association. Elizabeth Jane Cochrane, who wrote under the byline Nellie Bly, was by far the era's most colorful investigative reporter. Bly published a personal account of her experience with the striking workers for the *New York World*.

DOCUMENT 1
Chicago Tribune, May 12, 1894

PULLMAN MEN OUT
Discharges the Cause

Two thousand employees in the Pullman car works struck yesterday, leaving 800 others at their posts. This was not enough to keep the works going, so a notice was posted on the big gates at 6 o'clock . . . saying: "These shops closed until further notice."

Mr. Pullman said last night he could not tell when work would be resumed. The American Railway Union, which has been proselytizing for a week among the workmen, announces that it will support the strikers . . . [intimating] that the trainmen on the railways on which are organized branches of the union might refuse to handle any of the Pullman rolling stock.

DOCUMENT 2
Chicago Times, May 12, 1894

PULLMAN MEN OUT
Firing Three Men Starts It

Almost the entire force of men employed in the Pullman shops went on strike yesterday. Out of the 4,800 men and women employed in the various departments there were probably not over 800 at work at 6 o'clock last evening. The immediate cause of the strike was the discharge or laying off of three men in the iron machine shop. The real but remote cause is the question of wages over which the men have long been dissatisfied and on account of which they had practically resolved to strike a month ago. . . .

The position of the company is that no increase in wages is possible. . . . President George M. Pullman

told the committee that the company was doing business at a loss even at the reduced wages paid the men and offered to show his books in support of his assertion.

DOCUMENT 3
Chicago Times, May 15, 1894

SKIMS OFF THE FAT
Pullman Company Declares a Dividend Today
Full Pockets Swallow $600,000 While Honest Labor Is Starving

Today the Pullman Company will declare a quarterly dividend of 2 per cent on its capital stock of $30,000,000 and President George M. Pullman is authority for the statement that his company owes no man a cent. This despite the assertion of Mr. Pullman that the works have been run at a loss for eight months. Six hundred thousand dollars to shareholders, while starvation threatens the workmen.

DOCUMENT 4
Chicago Tribune, July 1, 1894

MOBS BENT ON RUIN
Men Who Attempt to Work Are Terrorized and Beaten

Continued and menacing lawlessness marked the progress yesterday of Dictator Debs and those who obey his orders in their efforts at coercing the railroads of the country into obeying the mandates of the American Railway Union. . . . At Blue Island, anarchy reigned. The Mayor and police force of that town could do nothing to repress the riotous strikers and they did their own sweet will.

DOCUMENT 5
Chicago Tribune, July 7, 1894

YARDS FIRE SWEPT
Rioters Prevent Firemen from Saving the Property

From Brighton Park to Sixty-First Street the yards of the Pan-Handle road were last night put to the torch by the rioters. Between 600 and 700 freight cars have been destroyed, many of them loaded. Miles and miles of costly track are in a snarled tangle of heat-twisted rails. Not less than $750,000 — possibly a whole $1,000,000 of property — has been sacrificed to the caprice of a mob of drunken Anarchists and rebels.

DOCUMENT 6
Chicago Times, July 7, 1894

MEN NOT AWED BY SOLDIERS
Railway Union Is Confident of Winning against Armed Capital

Despite the presence of United States troops and the mobilization of five regiments of state militia, despite threats of martial law and total extermination of the strikers by bullet and bayonet, the great strike inaugurated by the American Railway Union holds three-fourths of the roads running out of Chicago in its strong fetters, and last night traffic was more fully paralyzed than at any time since the inception of the tie-up. . . .

    If the soldiers are sent to this district, bloodshed and perhaps death will follow today, for this is the most lawless element in the city, as is shown by their riotous work yesterday. . . . But the perpetrators are not American Railway Union men. The people engaged in this outrageous work of destruction are not strikers, most of them are not even grown men. The persons who set the fires yesterday on the authority of the firemen and police are young hoodlums . . . and the police on the scene apparently didn't care to or would not make arrests.

DOCUMENT 7
New York World, July 14, 1894

CHEERS FOR NELLIE BLY
Nellie Bly Covers the Strike

I found in my mail this morning an earnest request from the Pullman A. R. U. for me to be present at a meeting which was to be held in the Turner Hall, Kensington. . . .

    So I took my nerves in hand and my place before the table near where the speakers sat. I don't intend to repeat what I said, but I told them several truths. They were especially amused when I told them that I had come to Chicago very bitterly set against the strikers; that so far as I understood the question, I thought the inhabitants of the model town of Pullman hadn't a reason on earth to complain. With this belief I visited the town, intending in my articles to denounce the riotous and bloodthirsty strikers. Before I had been half a day in Pullman I was the most bitter striker in the town.

    That is true. I've [flip]flopped, as they call it, and I am brave enough to confess it. If ever men and women had cause to strike, those men and women are in Pullman. I also said to these men, sitting so quietly and peaceably before me, hungry for a word of sympathy or a word of hope, that if any of them wished to make any statements to me I would be glad to have them do so. After the meeting I was besieged. If I attempted to tell half the tales of wrong I've listened to I could fill an entire copy of *The World*.

Questions for Analysis

RECOGNIZE VIEWPOINTS: How do the *Chicago Tribune* and the *Chicago Times* articles differ in their portrayal of events and actors in the strike? Which version of the strike do you think most middle-class readers, who tended to be sympathetic to the strikers but fearful of violence, would have found more compelling?

CONSIDER THE CONTEXT: What economic and social conditions led workers to strike in the 1890s?

ASK HISTORICAL QUESTIONS: Do you think readers found Nellie Bly's *New York World* article persuasive? Why or why not?

national elections. But lack of the franchise did not mean that women were apoliti-cal. The WCTU demonstrated the breadth of women's political activity in the late nineteenth century.

Women supported the temperance movement because they felt particularly vulnerable to the effects of drunkenness. Dependent on men's wages, married women and their children suffered when money went for drink. The drunken, abusive husband epitomized the evils of a nation in which women remained second-class citizens. The WCTU, composed entirely of women, viewed all women's interests as essentially the same and therefore did not hesitate to use the singular *woman* to emphasize gender solidarity. Although mostly white and middle-class, WCTU members resolved to speak for their entire sex.

When Willard became president in 1879, she radically changed the direction of the organization. Social action replaced prayer as women's answer to the threat of drunkenness. Viewing alcoholism as a disease rather than a sin and poverty as a cause rather than a result of drink, the WCTU became involved in labor issues, joining with the Knights of Labor to press for better working conditions for women workers. Describing workers in a textile mill, a WCTU member wrote in the organiza-tion's *Union Signal* magazine, "It is dreadful to see these girls, stripped almost to the skin . . . and running like racehorses from the beginning to the end of the day." She concluded, "The hard slavish work is drawing the girls into the saloon."

Willard capitalized on the cult of domesticity as a shrewd political tactic. Using "home protection" as her watchword, she argued as early as 1884 that women needed the vote to protect home and family. By the 1890s, the WCTU's grassroots network of local unions included 200,000 dues-paying members and had spread to all but the most isolated rural areas of the country.

Willard worked to create a broad reform coalition in the 1890s, embracing the Knights of Labor, the People's Party, and the Prohibition Party. Until her death in 1898, she led, if not a women's rights movement, then the first organized mass movement of women united around a women's issue. By 1900, thanks largely to the WCTU, women could claim a generation of experience in political action—speaking, lobbying, organizing, drafting legislation, and running private charitable institutions. As Willard observed, "All this work has tended more toward the liberation of women than it has toward the extinction of the saloon."

National American Woman Suffrage Association (NAWSA)
Organization formed in 1890 that united the National Woman Suffrage Association and the American Woman Suffrage Association. The NAWSA pursued state-level campaigns to gain the vote for women. With successes in Idaho, Colorado, and Utah, woman suffrage had become more accepted by the 1890s.

How did Elizabeth Cady Stanton and Susan B. Anthony organize the movement for woman suffrage?

Unlike the WCTU, the organized movement for woman suffrage remained small and relatively weak in the late nineteenth century. In 1869, Elizabeth Cady Stanton and her ally Susan B. Anthony launched the National Woman Suffrage Association (NWSA) demanding the vote for women (see chapter 18). A more conservative group, the American Woman Suffrage Association (AWSA), formed the same year. Composed of men as well as women, the AWSA believed that women should stick with the Republican Party and make suffrage the Sixteenth Amendment. Their optimism proved misplaced.

By 1890, the split between the rival groups had healed, and the newly united **National American Woman Suffrage Association (NAWSA)** launched campaigns on the

◀ **Woman's Suffrage Campaigners** Two respectably attired middle-class suffragists from Long Island, New York, drove this cart to Boston to campaign for woman's suffrage. The boys standing behind the cart suggest the ridicule suffragists often encountered. One suffragist said driving the cart allowed them to stop frequently to explain their cause "to farmers and people in small towns." Buyenlarge/Getty Images.

state level to gain the vote for women. Twenty years had made a great change. Woman suffrage, though not yet generally supported, was no longer considered a crackpot idea, thanks in part to the WCTU's support of the "home protection" ballot. The NAWSA honored Elizabeth Cady Stanton by electing her its first president, but Susan B. Anthony, who took the helm in 1892, emerged as the leading figure in the new united organization.

Stanton and Anthony, both in their seventies, were coming to the end of their public careers. Since the days of the Seneca Falls woman's rights convention, they had worked for reforms for their sex, including property rights, custody rights, and the right to education and gainful employment. But the prize of woman suffrage still eluded them. Suffragists won victories in Colorado in 1893 and Idaho in 1896. One more state joined the suffrage column in 1896 when Utah entered the Union. But women suffered a bitter defeat in a California referendum on woman suffrage that same year. Never losing faith, Anthony remarked in her last public appearance in 1906, "Failure is impossible."

REVIEW

How did women's temperance activism contribute to the cause of woman suffrage?

How did economic depression affect American politics in the 1890s?

The depression that began in the spring of 1893 and lasted for more than four years put nearly half of the labor force out of work, a higher percentage than during the Great Depression of the 1930s. The human cost of the depression was staggering. "I Take my pen in hand to let you know that we are Starving to death," a Kansas farm woman wrote to the governor in 1894. "Last cent gone," wrote a young widow in her diary. "Children went to work without their breakfasts." Following the harsh dictates of social Darwinism and laissez-faire, the majority of America's elected officials believed that it was inappropriate for the government to intervene.

But the scope of the depression made it impossible for churches and local agencies to supply sufficient relief, and increasingly Americans called on the federal government to take action. Armies of the unemployed marched on Washington to demand relief, and the Populist Party experienced a surge of support as the election of 1896 approached.

What was "Coxey's army"?

Masses of unemployed Americans marched to Washington, D.C., in the spring of 1894 to call attention to their plight and to urge Congress to act. Jacob S. Coxey of Massilon, Ohio, led the most publicized contingent. Convinced that men could be put to work building badly needed roads for the nation, Coxey proposed a scheme to finance public works through non-interest-bearing bonds. "What I am after," he maintained, "is to try to put this country in a condition so that no man who wants work shall be obliged to remain idle." His plan won support from the AFL and the Populists.

Coxey's army
Unemployed men who marched to Washington, D.C., in 1894 to urge Congress to enact a public works program to end unemployment. Jacob S. Coxey of Ohio led the most publicized contingent. The movement failed to force federal relief legislation.

Starting out from Ohio with one hundred men, **Coxey's army**, as it was dubbed, swelled as it marched east through the spring snows of the Alleghenies. In Pennsylvania, Coxey recruited several hundred from the ranks of those left unemployed by the Homestead lockout. On May 1, Coxey arrived in Washington, D.C. When he defiantly marched his men onto the Capitol grounds, police set upon the demonstrators with nightsticks, cracking skulls and arresting Coxey and his lieutenants. Coxey went to jail for twenty days and was fined $5 for "walking on the grass."

But other armies of the unemployed, totaling possibly as many as five thousand people, were still on their way. In the West, the more daring contingents hijacked freight trains, stirring fears of revolution. Journalists who covered the march did little to quiet the nation's fright. They delighted in military terminology, describing themselves as "war correspondents." To boost newspaper sales, they gave to the episode a tone of urgency and heightened the sense of a nation imperiled.

By August, the leaderless, tattered armies dissolved. Although the "On to Washington" movement proved ineffective in forcing federal relief legislation, Coxey's army dramatized the plight of the unemployed and acted, in the words of one participant, as a "living, moving object lesson." Like the Populists, Coxey's army questioned the underlying values of the new industrial order and demonstrated how ordinary citizens turned to means outside the regular party system to influence politics in the 1890s.

Why is the election of 1896 considered one of the most important elections in U.S. history?

Even before the depression of 1893, the Populists had railed against the status quo. "We meet in the midst of a nation brought to the verge of moral, political, and material ruin," Ignatius Donnelly thundered in his keynote address at the creation of the People's Party in St. Louis in 1892. "The fruits of the toil of millions are boldly stolen to build up colossal fortunes for a few. . . . From the same prolific womb of governmental injustice we breed the two great classes—tramps and millionaires."

The fiery rhetoric frightened many who saw in the People's Party a call not to reform but to revolution. Throughout the country, the press denounced the Populists as "cranks, lunatics, and idiots." When one self-righteous editor dismissed them as "calamity howlers," Populist governor Lorenzo Lewelling of Kansas shot back, "If that is so I want to continue to howl until those conditions are improved."

The People's Party captured more than a million votes in the presidential election of 1892, a respectable showing for a new party (**Map 20.1**). As the presidential election of 1896 approached, the depression intensified cries for reform not only from the Populists but also throughout the electorate. Depression worsened the tight money problem caused by the deflationary pressure of the gold standard. Once again, proponents of free silver stirred rebellion in the ranks of the Democratic and Republican parties. When the Republicans nominated Ohio governor William McKinley on a platform pledging the preservation of the gold standard, western advocates of free silver representing miners and farmers walked out of the convention. Open rebellion also split the Democratic Party, as vast segments in the West and South repudiated President Grover Cleveland because of his support for gold. In South Carolina, Benjamin Tillman won his race for Congress by promising, "Send me to Washington and I'll stick my pitchfork into [Cleveland's] old ribs!"

The spirit of revolt animated the Democratic National Convention in Chicago in the summer of 1896. William Jennings Bryan of Nebraska, the thirty-six-year-old "boy orator from the Platte," whipped the convention into a frenzy, calling passionately for free silver with a ringing

Candidate	Electoral Vote	Popular Vote	Percent of Popular Vote
Grover Cleveland (Democrat)	277	5,555,426	46.1
Benjamin Harrison (Republican)	145	5,182,690	43.0
James B. Weaver (People's)	22	1,029,846	8.5

MAP 20.1 ▲ **The Election of 1892**

exhortation: "Do not crucify mankind upon a cross of gold." Pandemonium broke loose as delegates stampeded to nominate Bryan, the youngest candidate ever to run for the presidency.

The juggernaut of free silver rolled out of Chicago and on to St. Louis, where the People's Party met a week after the Democrats adjourned. Many western Populists urged the party to ally with the Democrats and endorse Bryan. A major obstacle, however, was Bryan's running mate, Arthur M. Sewall. A Maine railway director and bank president, Sewall, who had been placed on the ticket to appease conservative Democrats, embodied everything the Populists detested. Moreover, die-hard southern Populists wanted no part of fusion. Southern Democrats had resorted to fraud and violence to steal elections from the Populists in 1894, and support for a Democratic ticket proved hard to swallow.

Populists struggled to work out a compromise. To show that they remained true to their principles, delegates first voted to support all the planks of the 1892 platform, added to it a call for public works projects for the unemployed, and only narrowly defeated a plank for woman suffrage. To deal with the problem of fusion, the convention selected the vice presidential candidate first. The nomination of Tom Watson undercut opposition to Bryan's candidacy. And although Bryan quickly sent a telegram to protest that he would not drop Sewall as his running mate, mysteriously

VISUAL ACTIVITY

▲ **"Swallowed!"** This cartoon from 1900 shows William Jennings Bryan as a python swallowing the Democratic Party's donkey mascot. Bryan, who ran unsuccessfully for president in 1896, won the Democratic nomination again in 1900 and in 1908. Ironically, it was not the Democratic Party so much as the Populist Party that Bryan swallowed. By nominating the Democrat Bryan on its ticket in 1896, the Populist Party lost its identity. GRANGER – Historical Picture Archive.

READING THE IMAGE: Does the image of a Populist Bryan swallowing the Democratic Party accurately reflect what happened in 1896? What happened to the Populists after 1896?
CONNECTIONS: What issues did the Populists support?

his message never reached the convention floor. Fusion triumphed. Bryan won the nomination by a lopsided vote. The Populists did not know it, but their cheers for Bryan signaled the death knell for the People's Party.

Few contests in the nation's history have been as fiercely fought as the presidential election of 1896. On one side stood Republican William McKinley, backed by the wealthy industrialist and party boss Mark Hanna. Hanna played on the business community's fears of Populism to raise a Republican war chest more than double the amount of any previous campaign. An estimated $4 million to $16 million went to selling McKinley as "the advance agent of prosperity." William Jennings Bryan, with few assets beyond his silver tongue, struggled to make up in energy and eloquence what his party lacked in funds. Bryan crisscrossed the country in a whirlwind tour, by his own reckoning visiting twenty-seven states and speaking to more than six million Americans, often giving a dozen speeches a day.

As befitted a candidate whose platform called for public ownership of the railroads, Bryan got no free pass (common for many politicians) from the railroad barons. He bought his own tickets, carried his own bags, and rode in coach. McKinley stayed home in Canton, Ohio, waging a front-porch campaign that drew over 750,000 visitors. The Pennsylvania Railroad supplied cut-rate transport to contingents of up to fifty thousand people, who showed up on Saturdays to hear McKinley declare himself in favor of "the full dinner pail." His running mate, Theodore Roosevelt (the hero of San Juan Hill), added much-needed energy to the ticket. "He ain't running, he's galloping," quipped one observer.

In the battle of the standards, as the campaign came to be called, gold and silver became iconic. Gold stood for Wall Street, value, and the status quo, while silver represented the common people and common sense. The most popular silver pamphlet, *Coin's Financial School*, sold five thousand copies a day at its peak in 1895, not counting tens of thousands of copies distributed by silver supporters. The pamphlet's point was simple: The gold standard did not work. Lack of credit and an inflexible currency meant depression and deflation. On the other side, the goldbugs declared gold the only honest currency and decried silver supporters as no better than scofflaws seeking to shirk their debts. Big city newspapers kept up a drumbeat of alarmist rhetoric, predicting panic and depression if the Democrats won. Republicans denounced their rivals as "hayseed cranks," but their own partisanship verged on hysteria. In the heat of the race, Theodore Roosevelt proposed putting twelve Populist leaders against the wall and "shooting them dead."

On election day, four out of five voters went to the polls in an unprecedented turnout. The silver states of the Rocky Mountains lined up solidly for Bryan. The Northeast went for McKinley. The Midwest tipped the balance. In the end, the election hinged on between a hundred and a thousand votes in several key states, including Wisconsin, Iowa, and Minnesota. Although McKinley won twenty-three states to Bryan's twenty-two, the electoral vote showed a lopsided 271 to 176 in McKinley's favor (**Map 20.2**). The powerful economic warnings and charges that Bryan's inflated silver dollars would only lower their real wages scared away the

Candidate	Electoral Vote	Popular Vote	Percent of Popular Vote
William McKinley (Republican)	271	7,104,779	51.1
William J. Bryan (Democrat-People's)	176	6,502,925	47.7

MAP 20.2 ▲ The Election of 1896

labor vote. Democrats failed to carry a single big city, losing New York, Boston, Baltimore, Newark, Philadelphia, and San Francisco.

The biggest losers in 1896 turned out to be the Populists. On the national level, they polled fewer than 300,000 votes, a million less than in 1894. In the clamor to support Bryan, Populists in the South swallowed their differences and drifted back to the Democratic Party. As one Democratic governor exulted, "We stole their platform; we stole their candidate, we stole them out lock, stock, and barrel." But they couldn't steal victory. The real winner was the Republican Party, which successfully fought off the political alliance of the West and the South. The resulting Republican realignment claimed the North, Midwest, and West. Increasingly, the Democrats could count only on the white solid South.

Despite its defeat, the Populist movement signaled something momentous. It marked the attempt of ordinary men and women, farmers and laborers, to educate themselves and organize in an effort to seize the levers of power and make the capitalist state more equitable and just. Perhaps the true significance of the movement lay not in the success or failure of the People's Party, but simply in the act of trying.

REVIEW

Why was the People's Party unable to translate national support into victory in the 1896 election?

Why did the United States largely abandon its isolationist foreign policy in the 1890s?

Throughout much of the second half of the nineteenth century, U.S. interest in foreign policy took a backseat to territorial expansion in the American West. The United States fought the Indian wars while European nations carved empires in Asia, Africa, Latin America, and the Pacific.

At the turn of the twentieth century, the United States pursued a foreign policy consisting of two currents—isolationism and expansionism. Although the determination to remain detached from European politics had been a hallmark of U.S. foreign policy since the nation's founding, Americans simultaneously believed in manifest destiny—the "obvious" right to expand the nation from ocean to ocean. By the 1890s, with its own inland empire secured, the United States looked outward. Determined to protect its sphere of influence in the Western Hemisphere and to expand its trading in Asia, the nation turned away from isolationism and toward a more active role on the world stage that led to intervention in China's Boxer uprising and war with Spain.

How did both markets and missionaries promote U.S. expansion?

The depression of the 1890s provided a powerful impetus to American commercial expansion. As markets weakened at home, American businesses looked abroad for profits. As the depression deepened, one diplomat warned that Americans "must turn [their] eyes abroad, or they will soon look inward upon discontent."

Exports constituted a small but significant percentage of the profits of American business in the 1890s (**Figure 20.2**). And where American interests led, businessmen expected the government's power and influence to follow to protect their investments. Companies like Standard Oil actively sought to use the U.S. government as their agent, often putting foreign service employees on the payroll. "Our ambassadors and ministers and consuls," wrote John D. Rockefeller appreciatively, "have aided to push our way into new markets and to the utmost corners of the world."

America's foreign policy often appeared little more than a sidelight to business development. In Hawai'i (first called the Sandwich Islands), American sugar interests fomented a rebellion in 1893, toppling the increasingly independent Queen Lili'uokalani. They pushed Congress to annex the islands to avoid the high McKinley tariff on sugar. When President Cleveland learned that Hawai'ians opposed annexation, he withdrew the proposal from Congress. Yet expansionists still coveted the islands and looked for an opportunity to push through annexation.

Business interests alone did not account for the new expansionism that seized the nation during the 1890s. As Alfred Thayer Mahan, leader of a growing group of American expansionists, confessed, "Even when material interests are the original exciting cause, it is the sentiment to which they give rise, the moral tone which emotion takes that constitutes the greater force." Much of that moral tone was set by American missionaries' intent on spreading the gospel of Christianity to the "heathen." No area on the globe constituted a greater challenge than China.

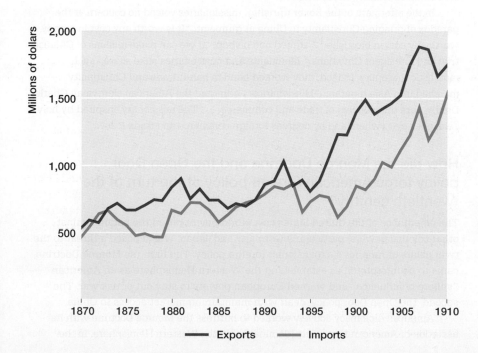

FIGURE 20.2 ◀ Expansion in U.S. Trade, 1870–1910 Between 1870 and 1910, American exports more than tripled. Imports generally rose, but they were held in check by the high protective tariffs championed by Republican presidents from Ulysses S. Grant to William Howard Taft. A decline in imports is particularly noticeable after the passage of the prohibitive McKinley tariff in 1890.

An 1858 agreement, the Tianjin (Tientsin) treaty, admitted foreign missionaries to China. Although Christians converted only 100,000 in a population of 400 million, the Chinese nevertheless resented the interference of missionaries in village life. Opposition to foreign missionaries took the form of antiforeign secret societies, most notably the Boxers, whose Chinese name translated to "Righteous Harmonious Fist." In 1899, the Boxers hunted down and killed Chinese Christians and missionaries in northwestern Shandong Province. With the tacit support of China's Empress Dowager Cixi, the Boxers shouted, "Uphold the Ch'ing Dynasty, Exterminate the Foreigners," and marched on the cities. Their rampage eventually led to the massacre of some 30,000 Chinese converts and 250 foreign nuns, priests, and missionaries.

As the Boxers spread terror throughout northern China, some eight hundred Americans and Europeans sought refuge in the foreign diplomatic buildings in Peking (today's Beijing). Along with missionaries from the countryside came thousands of their Chinese converts. Unable to escape and cut off from outside aid and communication, the Americans and Europeans in Beijing mounted a defense to face the Boxer onslaught.

For two months, the little group held out under siege, eating mule and horse meat and losing seventy-six men in battle. Sarah Conger, wife of the U.S. ambassador, wrote wearily, "[The siege] was exciting at first, but night after night of this firing, horn-blowing, and yelling, and the whizzing of bullets has hardened us to it."

In August 1900, 2,500 U.S. troops joined an international force sent to rescue the foreigners and put down the uprising in the Chinese capital. The European powers imposed the humiliating Boxer Protocol in 1901, granting themselves the right to maintain military forces in Beijing and requiring the Chinese government to pay an exorbitant indemnity of $333 million.

Boxer uprising
Uprising in China led by the Boxers, an antiforeign society, in which 30,000 Chinese converts and 250 foreign Christians were killed. An international force rescued foreigners in Beijing, and European powers imposed the humiliating Boxer Protocol on China in 1901.

In the aftermath of the **Boxer uprising**, missionaries voiced no concern at the paradox of bringing Christianity to China at gunpoint. "It is worth any cost in money, worth any cost in bloodshed," argued one bishop, "if we can make millions of Chinese true and intelligent Christians." Merchants and missionaries alike shared such moralistic reasoning. Indeed, they worked hand in hand; trade and Christianity marched into Asia together. "Missionaries," admitted the American clergyman Charles Denby, "are the pioneers of trade and commerce. . . . The missionary, inspired by holy zeal, goes everywhere and by degrees foreign commerce and trade follow."

How did the Monroe Doctrine and the Open Door policy forge American foreign policy at the turn of the twentieth century?

The emergence of the United States as a world power pitted the nation against other colonial powers, particularly Germany and Japan, which posed a threat to the twin pillars of America's expansionist foreign policy. The first, the Monroe Doctrine, came to be interpreted as establishing the Western Hemisphere as an American "sphere of influence" and warned European powers to stay out or risk war. The second, the Open Door policy, dealt with maintaining market access to China.

American diplomacy actively worked to buttress the Monroe Doctrine with its assertion of American hegemony (dominance) in the Western Hemisphere. In the

1880s, Republican secretary of state James G. Blaine promoted hemispheric peace and trade through Pan-American cooperation but at the same time used American troops to intervene in Latin American border disputes. In 1895, President Cleveland risked war with Great Britain to enforce the Monroe Doctrine when a conflict developed between Venezuela and British Guiana. After American sabers rattled, the British backed down and accepted U.S. mediation in the area despite their territorial claims in Guiana.

In Central America, American business triumphed in a bloodless takeover that routed French and British interests. The United Fruit Company of Boston virtually dominated the Central American nations of Costa Rica and Guatemala, while an importer from New Orleans turned Honduras into a "banana republic" (a country run by U.S. business interests). Thus, by 1895, the United States, through business as well as diplomacy, had successfully achieved hegemony in Latin America and the Caribbean, forcing even the British to concur that "the infinite resources [of the United States] combined with its isolated position render it master of the situation and practically invulnerable as against any or all other powers."

At the same time that American foreign policy warned European powers to stay out of the Western Hemisphere, the United States competed for trade in the Eastern Hemisphere. As American interests in China grew, the United States became more aggressive in defending its presence in Asia and the Pacific. In 1889, it risked war with Germany to guarantee the U.S. Navy access to Pago Pago in the Samoan Islands, a port for refueling on the way to Asia. Germany, seeking dominance over the islands, sent warships to the region. But before fighting broke out, a typhoon destroyed the German and American ships. The potential combatants later divided the islands amicably in the 1899 Treaty of Berlin.

In the 1890s, weakened by years of internal warfare, China was partitioned into spheres of influence by Britain, Japan, Germany, France, and Russia. Concerned about the integrity of China and no less about American trade, Secretary of State John Hay in 1899–1900 wrote a series of notes calling for an "open door" policy that would ensure trade access to all and maintain Chinese sovereignty. The notes were greeted by the major powers with polite evasion. Nevertheless, Hay skillfully managed to maneuver them into doing his bidding, and in 1900, he boldly announced the Open Door as international policy. The United States, by insisting on the **Open Door policy**, managed to secure access to Chinese markets, expanding its economic power while avoiding the problems of maintaining a far-flung colonial empire on the Asian mainland. But as the Spanish-American War soon demonstrated, Americans found it hard to resist the temptations of overseas empire.

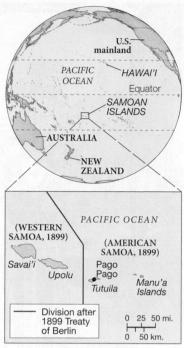

The Samoan Islands, 1889

Open Door policy
Policy successfully insisted upon by Secretary of State John Hay in 1899–1900 recommending that the major powers of the United States, Britain, Japan, Germany, France, and Russia all have access to trade with China and that Chinese sovereignty be maintained.

Spanish-American War
1898 war between Spain and the United States that began as an effort to free Cuba from Spain's colonial rule. This popular war left the United States an imperial power in control of Cuba and colonies in Puerto Rico, Guam, and the Philippines.

Why was the Spanish-American War called "a splendid little war"?

The **Spanish-American War** began as a humanitarian effort to free Cuba from Spain's colonial grasp. It ended, however, with the United States acquiring territory overseas and fighting a dirty guerrilla war with Filipino nationalists who, like the Cubans, sought independence from Spain. Behind the contradiction stood the twin

◄ **The Open Door** The trade advantage the United States gained by its Open Door policy is depicted in this political cartoon. Uncle Sam stands in the doorway to China, permitting access to representatives of Great Britain (left) and Russia (right) with the key of American diplomacy. In fact, the Open Door policy promised all foreign powers equal access to the China trade, not American control of access to the trade, as the cartoon suggests. GRANGER – Historical Picture Archive.

pillars of American foreign policy: The Monroe Doctrine made Spain's presence in Cuba unacceptable, and U.S. determination to keep open the door to Asia made control of the Philippines attractive. Precedent for the nation's imperial adventures also came from the recent Indian wars in the American West, which provided a template for the subjugation of native peoples in the name of civilization.

Looking back on the Spanish-American War of 1898, Secretary of State John Hay judged it "a splendid little war; begun with the highest motives, carried on with magnificent intelligence and spirit, favored by that fortune which loves the brave." At the close of a decade marred by bitter depression, social unrest, and political upheaval, the war offered Americans a chance to wave the flag and march in unison. War fever proved as infectious as the tune of a John Philip Sousa march. Few argued the merits of the conflict until it was over and the time came to divide the spoils.

The war began with moral outrage over the treatment of Cuban revolutionaries, who had launched a fight for independence against the Spanish colonial regime in 1895. In an attempt to isolate the guerrillas, the Spanish general Valeriano Weyler herded Cubans into crowded and unsanitary concentration camps, where thousands died of hunger, disease, and exposure. Starvation soon spread to the cities. By 1898, fully a quarter of the island's population had perished in the Cuban revolution.

As the Cuban rebellion dragged on, pressure for American intervention mounted. American newspapers fueled public outrage at Spain. A fierce circulation war raged in New York City between William Randolph Hearst's *Journal* and Joseph Pulitzer's *World*. Their competition provoked what came to be called **yellow journalism**, named for the colored ink used in a popular comic strip. The Cuban war provided a wealth of dramatic copy. Newspapers fed the American people a daily diet of "Butcher" Weyler and Spanish atrocities. Hearst sent artist Frederic Remington to document the horror, and when Remington wired home, "There is no trouble here. There will be no war," Hearst shot back, "You furnish the pictures and I'll furnish the war."

American interests in Cuba were, in the words of the U.S. minister to Spain, more than "merely theoretical or sentimental." American business had more than $50 million invested in Cuban sugar, and American trade with Cuba, a brisk $100 million a year

yellow journalism
Term first given to sensationalistic newspaper reporting and cartoon images rendered in yellow. A circulation war between William Randolph Hearst's *New York Journal* and Joseph Pulitzer's *New York World* provoked the tactics of yellow journalism that fueled popular support for the Spanish-American War in 1898.

before the rebellion, had dropped to near zero. Nevertheless, the business community balked, wary of a war with Spain. When industrialist Mark Hanna, the Republican kingmaker and senator from Ohio, urged restraint, a hotheaded Theodore Roosevelt exploded, "We will have this war for the freedom of Cuba, Senator Hanna, in spite of the timidity of commercial interests."

To expansionists like Roosevelt, more than Cuban independence was at stake. As assistant secretary of the navy, Roosevelt took the helm while his boss was on summer vacation, and in the summer of 1897, he audaciously ordered the U.S. fleet to be ready to steam to Manila. In the event of conflict with Spain, Roosevelt put the navy in a position to capture the islands and gain a stepping-stone to China.

President McKinley moved slowly toward intervention. In a show of American force, he dispatched the battleship *Maine* to Cuba. On the night of February 15, 1898, a mysterious explosion destroyed the *Maine*, killing 267 crew members. The source of the explosion remained unclear, but inflammatory stories in the press enraged Americans. Rallying to the cry "Remember the *Maine*," Congress declared war on Spain. In a surge of patriotism, more than a million men rushed to enlist. War brought with it a unity of purpose and national harmony that ended a decade of political dissent and strife. "In April, everywhere over this good fair land, flags were flying," wrote Kansas editor William Allen White. "At the stations, crowds gathered to hurrah for the soldiers, and to throw hats into the air, and to unfurl flags."

Five days after McKinley signed the war resolution, a U.S. Navy squadron destroyed the Spanish fleet in Manila Bay (**Map 20.3**). The stunning victory caught

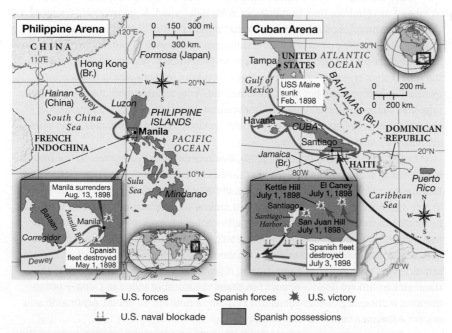

MAP 20.3 ▲ The Spanish-American War, 1898 The Spanish-American War was fought in two theaters, the Philippine Islands and Cuba. Five days after President William McKinley called for a declaration of war, Admiral George Dewey captured Manila. The war lasted only eight months. Troops landed in Cuba in mid-June, and by mid-July the American navy had destroyed the Spanish fleet.

most Americans by surprise. Few had ever heard of the Philippines. Even McKinley confessed that he could not locate the archipelago on the map. Nevertheless, he dispatched U.S. troops to secure the islands.

The war in Cuba ended almost as quickly as it began. The first troops landed on June 22, and after a handful of battles, the Spanish forces surrendered on July 17. The war lasted just long enough to elevate Theodore Roosevelt to the status of bona fide war hero. Roosevelt had resigned his navy post and formed the Rough Riders, a regiment composed of a sprinkling of Ivy League polo players and a number of western cowboys Roosevelt befriended during his stint as a cattle rancher in the Dakotas. The Rough Riders' charge up Kettle Hill and adjacent San Juan Hill and Roosevelt's role in the decisive battle made front-page news. Overnight, Roosevelt became the most famous man in America. By the time he sailed home from Cuba, a coalition of independent Republicans was already plotting his political future.

What was the debate over American imperialism following the war?

By the end of the Spanish-American War, the American people woke up in possession of an empire that stretched halfway around the globe. As part of the spoils of war, the United States acquired Cuba, Puerto Rico, Guam, and the Philippines. And Republicans quickly moved to annex Hawai'i in July 1898.

Contemptuous of the Cubans, whom General William Shafter declared "no more fit for self-government than gun-powder is for hell," the U.S. government imposed a Cuban constitution and refused to give up military control of the island until the Cubans accepted the so-called Platt Amendment—a series of provisions that granted the United States the right to intervene to protect Cuba's "independence," as well as the power to oversee Cuban debt so that European creditors would not find an excuse for intervention. For good measure, the United States gave itself a ninety-nine-year lease on a naval base at Guantánamo. In return, McKinley promised to implement an extensive sanitation program to clean up the island, making it more attractive to American investors.

In the formal Treaty of Paris (1898), Spain ceded the Philippines to the United States along with the former Spanish colonies of Puerto Rico and Guam (**Map 20.4**). Empire did not come cheap. When Spain initially balked at these terms, the United States agreed to pay an indemnity of $20 million for the islands. Nor was the cost measured in money alone. Filipino revolutionaries under Emilio Aguinaldo, who had greeted U.S. troops as liberators, bitterly fought the new masters. The war proved particularly brutal, with torture (the infamous water treatment) and atrocities sullying America's reputation. It would take seven years and four thousand American dead—almost ten times the number killed in Cuba—not to mention a shocking twenty thousand Filipino casualties, to defeat Aguinaldo and secure American control of the Philippines.

At home, a vocal minority, mostly Democrats and former Populists, resisted the country's foray into overseas empire, judging it unwise, immoral, and

MAP ACTIVITY

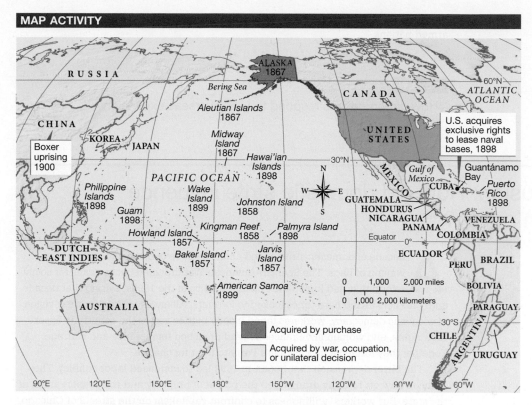

MAP 20.4 ▲ U.S. Overseas Expansion through 1900 The United States extended its interests abroad with a series of territorial acquisitions. Although Cuba was granted independence, the Platt Amendment kept the new nation firmly under U.S. control. In the wake of the Spanish-American War, the United States woke up to find that it held an empire extending halfway around the globe.

READING THE MAP: Does the map indicate that more territory was acquired by purchase or by war, occupation, or unilateral decision? How many purchases of land outside the continental United States did the government make?
CONNECTIONS: What foreign policy developments occurred in the 1890s? How did American political leaders react to them? Where was U.S. expansion headed, and why?

unconstitutional. William Jennings Bryan, who enlisted in the army but never saw action, concluded that American expansionism only distracted the nation from problems at home. Pointing to the central paradox of the war, Representative Bourke Cockran of New York admonished, "We who have been the destroyers of oppression are asked now to become its agents." But the expansionists won the day.

As Senator Knute Nelson of Minnesota assured his colleagues, "We come as ministering angels, not as despots." Fresh from its conquest of Native Americans in the West, the nation largely embraced the heady mixture of racism and missionary zeal that fueled American adventurism abroad. The *Washington Post* trumpeted, "The taste of empire is in the mouth of the people," thrilled at the prospect of "an imperial policy, the Republic renascent, taking her place with the armed nations."

REVIEW

How did Americans respond to U.S. overseas expansion?

Conclusion: How did domestic strife influence foreign policy?

A decade of domestic strife ended amid the blare of martial music and the waving of flags. The Spanish-American War drowned out the calls for social reform that had fueled the Populist politics of the 1890s. During that decade, angry farmers facing hard times looked to Farmers' Alliances to fight for their vision of economic democracy, workers staged bloody battles across the country to assert their rights, and women like Frances Willard preached temperance and suffrage. Together they formed a new People's Party to fight for change.

The bitter depression that began in 1893 led to increased labor conflict. The Pullman boycott brutally dramatized the power of property and the conservatism of the state. But workers' willingness to confront capitalism on the streets of Chicago, Homestead, Cripple Creek, and a host of other sites across America eloquently testified to labor's growing determination, unity, and strength.

As the depression deepened, the sight of Coxey's army of unemployed marching on Washington to demand federal intervention in the economy signaled a growing shift in the public mind against the politics of laissez-faire. The call for the government to take action to better the lives of workers, farmers, and the dispossessed manifested itself in the fiercely fought presidential campaign of William Jennings Bryan in 1896. With the outbreak of the Spanish-American War in 1898, the decade ended on a harmonious note with patriotic Americans rallying around the flag. But even though Americans basked in patriotism and contemplated empire, old grievances had not been laid to rest. The People's Party had been beaten, but the Populist spirit lived on in the demands for greater government involvement in the economy, expanded opportunities for direct democracy, and a more equitable balance of profits and power between the people and the big corporations. A new generation of progressive reformers would champion the unfinished reform agenda in the first decades of the twentieth century.

CHAPTER REVIEW

EXPLAIN WHY IT MATTERS

Farmers' Alliance (p. 575)

People's Party (Populist Party) (p. 577)

Homestead lockout (p. 578)

Cripple Creek miners' strike of 1894 (p. 580)

Pullman boycott (p. 582)

National American Woman Suffrage Association (NAWSA) (p. 586)

Coxey's army (p. 588)

Boxer uprising (p. 594)

Open Door policy (p. 595)

Spanish-American War (p. 595)

yellow journalism (p. 596)

PUT IT ALL TOGETHER

ECONOMICS

- What key issues fueled farm protest in the late nineteenth century? How did the Farmers' Alliance attempt to address these issues?

- What strategies and tactics did unions employ in the late nineteenth century? How did companies fight back?

POLITICS

- How did reform movements provide a vehicle for women's involvement in public political life?

- How did the depression of the mid-1890s shape the politics of the decade?

EMPIRE

- How did U.S. foreign policy reflect the tension between American tendencies toward isolationism and expansionism?

- How did the Spanish-American War change the place of the United States in global politics?

LOOKING BACKWARD, LOOKING AHEAD

- What were the United States' most important strengths and weaknesses in 1900? How had the nation's place in the world changed since 1800?

- Defend or refute the following statement: "With its victory in the Spanish-American War in 1898, the United States became an imperial power."

PROGRESSIVE REFORM

1890–1916

This chapter discusses the following questions:

- How did grassroots progressives attack the problems of urban industrial America?
- What were the key tenets of progressive theory?
- How did Theodore Roosevelt advance the progressive agenda?
- How did progressivism evolve during Woodrow Wilson's first term?
- What were the limits of progressive reform?
- Conclusion: How did the Progressive Era give rise to the liberal state?

▶ **Jane Addams** Jane Addams was twenty-nine years old when she founded Hull House on South Halsted Street in Chicago. Her desire to live among the poor and her insistence that settlement house work benefited educated women as well as their immigrant neighbors marked the distance from philanthropy to progressive reform. Jane Addams Memorial Collection (JAMC_8000_0005_0014), Special Collections, University of Illinois at Chicago, photographer: Max Platz.

AN AMERICAN STORY

In the summer of 1889, Jane Addams leased two floors of a dilapidated mansion on Chicago's West Side. Her immigrant neighbors must have wondered why this well-dressed young woman chose to live on South Halsted Street between a saloon and a funeral parlor. Yet the house, built by Charles Hull, precisely suited Addams's needs.

For Addams, personal action marked the first step in a search for solutions to the social problems created by urban industrialism. "No personal comfort nor individual development," Addams wrote, "can compensate a man for the misery of his neighbors."

She wanted to help her immigrant neighbors, and she wanted to offer meaningful work to educated women like herself. Addams's emphasis on the reciprocal relationship between the social classes made Hull House different from other philanthropic enterprises. She wished to do things *with*, not just *for*, Chicago's poor.

In the next decade, Hull House expanded from two rented floors in the old brick mansion to some thirteen buildings housing a remarkable variety of activities. Hull House did not provide rooms for the poor. Instead, it housed an extraordinary set of reformers who pioneered the scientific investigation of urban ills. Armed with statistics, they launched campaigns to improve housing, end child labor, fund playgrounds, and lobby for laws to protect workers.

First Addams set about to learn what her neighbors wanted. Then she set about to meet those needs. Hull House provided public baths, opened a restaurant for working women too tired to cook after their long shifts, and sponsored a nursery and kindergarten. Addams offered classes, lectures, art exhibits, musical instruction, and college extension courses. Before long, Hull House boasted a gymnasium, a theater, a manual training workshop, a labor museum, and the first public playground in Chicago. By 1900, over seventy women and men lived at Hull House working for reform.

Addams quickly learned that it was impossible to deal with urban problems without becoming involved in politics. Piles of decaying garbage overflowed South Halsted Street's wooden trash bins, breeding flies and disease. To fix the problem, Addams got the local ward boss to appoint her garbage inspector. Out on the streets at six in the morning, she rode atop the garbage wagon to make sure it picked up the trash. In her desire to aid the urban poor, Addams took on city hall and eventually carried her fight to the state capitol and to Washington, D.C. The transition from personal action to political activism that she personified became one of the hallmarks of the progressive period, which lasted from the 1890s to World War I.

CHRONOLOGY

1883	Lester Frank Ward champions reform Darwinism.
1889	Jane Addams opens Hull House in Chicago.
1893	Lillian Wald opens Henry Street settlement house in New York.
1896	*Plessy v. Ferguson* decided.
1900	Socialist Party founded.
1901	William McKinley assassinated; Theodore Roosevelt becomes president.
1902	Antitrust lawsuit filed against Northern Securities Company.
1903	Women's Trade Union League founded. Panama Canal construction begins.
1904	Roosevelt Corollary to Monroe Doctrine announced.
1905	Industrial Workers of the World founded.
1906	Pure Food and Drug Act and Meat Inspection Act enacted. Hepburn Act enacted. Atlanta race massacre kills several hundred Black people.
1907	Panic on Wall Street causes economic downturn. "Gentlemen's Agreement" made with Japan.
1908	*Muller v. Oregon* decided. William Howard Taft elected president.
1909	Garment workers strike. NAACP formed.
1910	Hiram Johnson elected California governor.

—chronology continued

1911	Triangle Shirtwaist Company fire.
1912	Roosevelt runs for president with Progressive Party. Woodrow Wilson elected president.
1913	Federal Reserve Act enacted. Suffragists march in Washington, D.C.
1914	Federal Trade Commission created. Clayton Antitrust Act enacted.
1916	Margaret Sanger opens first U.S. birth control clinic.

A sense of Christian mission inspired some reformers. Others feared social upheaval and sought to improve conditions for the urban poor. A belief in science and technical expertise infused the movement. But whatever their motives, progressives shared a willingness to use the power of the government to counterbalance special interests and big business. Their activism redefined liberalism in the twentieth century. Nevertheless, progressives shared the racism and prejudices of their time and attempted to restrict the rights of African Americans, Asians, and other immigrants in the name of reform.

Although progressives in the cities had rarely voted Populist in the 1890s, the People's Party platform (with the exception of its free silver plank) became the template for future reform, and populism's agrarian base continued to pursue reform into the 1930s. Taken together, the platform's elements — uplift and efficiency, social justice and social control, direct democracy and discrimination, urban professionals and agrarian rebels — all played a part in the progressive movement. Theodore Roosevelt became the movement's standard bearer, and Woodrow Wilson presided over the high tide of progressive legislation.

How did grassroots progressives attack the problems of urban industrial America?

progressivism
A reform movement that often advocated government activism to mitigate the problems created by urban industrialism. Progressivism reached its peak in 1912 with the creation of the Progressive Party. The term *progressivism* has come to mean any general effort advocating for social justice programs.

settlement houses
Settlements established in poor neighborhoods beginning in the 1880s. Reformers like Jane Addams and Lillian Wald believed that only by living among the poor could they help bridge the growing class divide. College-educated women formed the backbone of the settlement house movement.

Much of progressive reform began at the grassroots level and percolated upward into local, state, and eventually national politics as reformers attacked the social problems fostered by urban industrialism. Although **progressivism** flourished in many different settings across the country, urban problems inspired the progressives' greatest efforts. In their zeal to "civilize the city," middle-class reformers founded settlement houses, professed a new Christian social gospel, and campaigned against vice and crime in the name of "social purity." Allying with the working class, women progressives sought to better the lot of sweatshop garment workers and to end child labor. These local reform efforts often ended up being debated in state legislatures and in the U.S. Congress. At its heart, progressivism was at once audacious and thoroughly middle class.

How did reformers work to "civilize the city"?

Progressives attacked the problems of the city on many fronts. **Settlement houses**, which began in England, spread in the United States. By 1893, the needs of poor urban neighborhoods that had motivated reformer Jane Addams to open Hull House in Chicago led Lillian Wald to recruit others to move to New York City's Lower East Side "to live in the neighborhood as nurses, identify ourselves with it socially, and . . . contribute to it our citizenship." Wald's Henry Street settlement pioneered public health nursing.

Women, particularly college-educated women like Addams and Wald, formed the backbone of the settlement house movement. For the 85,000 women who had earned college degrees by 1900, the settlement house provided a way to put their skills to work in the service of society. Such reformers believed that only by living among the poor could they help bridge the growing class divide. Settlements like Hull House grew in number from six in 1891 to more than four hundred in 1911. In the process, settlement house women created a new profession—social work.

For their part, churches confronted urban social problems by enunciating a new **social gospel**, one that saw its mission as not simply to save individuals but to reform society. Social gospel ministers like Washington Gladden brought an abolitionist zeal to the problems of industrialism. After witnessing a coal miners' strike in Ohio, Gladden vigorously attacked social Darwinism and Andrew Carnegie's gospel of wealth, which fostered the belief that riches somehow signaled divine favor. The social gospel produced a stream of popular books. William Stead asked what might happen *If Christ Came to Chicago* (1893), and Charles M. Sheldon's *In His Steps* (1898) called on men and women to Christianize capitalism by asking, "What would Jesus do?"

social gospel
A vision of Christianity that saw its mission as not simply to reform individuals but to reform society. Emerging in the early twentieth century, it offered a powerful corrective to social Darwinism and the gospel of wealth, which fostered the belief that riches signaled divine favor.

Ministers also played an active role in the social purity movement, the campaign to attack vice. To end the "social evil," as reformers delicately referred to prostitution, social purity brought together ministers who wished to stamp out sin, doctors concerned about the spread of venereal disease, and women reformers whose husbands often unwittingly brought disease home from the brothel. Together, the social purity advocates waged a campaign to close red-light districts in cities across the country and lobbied to raise the age of consent for girls.

Attacks on alcohol went hand in hand with the push for social purity. The Anti-Saloon League, formed in 1895 under the leadership of Protestant clergy, added to the efforts of the Woman's Christian Temperance Union in campaigning to end the sale of liquor. Reformers pointed to links between drinking, prostitution, wife and child abuse, unemployment, and industrial accidents. The powerful liquor lobby fought back, spending liberally in election campaigns, fueling the charge that liquor corrupted the political process.

An element of nativism (dislike of foreigners) ran through the movement for prohibition, as it did in a number of progressive reforms. The Irish, the Italians, and the Germans were among the groups stigmatized by temperance reformers for their drinking. Progressives often failed to see that the tavern played an important role in many ethnic communities. Unlike the American saloon, an almost exclusively male space, the German beer garden was a family retreat, where workers socialized on Sunday after church. Nevertheless, progressives campaigned to enforce the Sunday closing of taverns, stores, and other commercial establishments and pushed for state legislation to outlaw the sale of liquor. By 1912, seven states were "dry."

Progressives' efforts to civilize the city demonstrated their willingness to take action; their belief that environment, not heredity alone, determined human behavior; and their optimism that conditions could be corrected through government action without radically altering America's economy or institutions. All these attitudes characterized the progressive movement.

How did middle-class progressives ally with the working class?

Day-to-day contact with their neighbors made settlement house workers particularly sympathetic to labor. When Mary Kenney O'Sullivan complained that her bookbinders' union met in a dirty, noisy saloon, Jane Addams invited them to meet at Hull House. And during the Pullman strike in 1894 (see chapter 20, "Analyzing Historical Evidence: The Press and the Pullman Strike—Framing Class Conflict"), Hull House residents organized strike relief. "Hull-House has been so unionized," grumbled one Chicago businessman, "that it has lost its usefulness and become a detriment and harm to the community." But to the working class, the support of middle-class reformers marked a significant gain.

Attempts to forge a cross-class alliance became institutionalized in 1903 with the creation of the Women's Trade Union League (WTUL). The WTUL brought together women workers and middle-class "allies." Its goal was to organize working women into unions under the auspices of the American Federation of Labor (AFL). However, the AFL provided little more than lip service to women workers. Given the union's attitude, it was not surprising that the money and leadership to organize women came largely from the wealthy allies in the WTUL. Although the alliance between working women, primarily immigrants and daughters of immigrants, and their middle-class allies was not without tension, the WTUL helped working women achieve significant gains.

The WTUL's most notable success came in 1909 in the "uprising of the twenty thousand," when women employees of the Triangle Shirtwaist Company in New York City went on strike to protest low wages, dangerous working conditions, and management's refusal to recognize their union, the International Ladies' Garment Workers Union. In support, an estimated twenty thousand garment workers, most of them teenaged girls and many of them Jewish and Italian immigrants, stayed out on strike through the winter, picketing in the bitter cold. Police and hired thugs harassed the picketing strikers, beating them up and arresting more than six hundred for "street walking" (prostitution). When WTUL allies, including J. P. Morgan's daughter Anne, joined the picket line, the harassment quickly stopped.

By the time the strike ended in February 1910, the workers had won important demands in many shops. The solidarity shown by the women workers proved to be the strike's greatest achievement. As Clara Lemlich, one of the strike's leaders, exclaimed, "They used to say that you couldn't even organize women. They wouldn't come to union meetings. They were 'temporary' workers. Well we showed them!"

The WTUL made enormous contributions to the strike. The league provided volunteers for the picket lines, posted more than $29,000 in bail, protested and publicized police brutality, organized a parade of ten thousand strikers, took part in the arbitration conference, arranged mass meetings, appealed for funds, and generated publicity for the strike. Under the leadership of the WTUL women from every class of society, from Madison Avenue socialites to socialists on New York's Lower East Side, found common cause in supporting the striking garment workers.

But for all its success, the uprising of the twenty thousand failed fundamentally to change conditions for women workers, as the tragic Triangle fire dramatized in 1911, a little over a year after the strike ended. The ramshackle building, full of lint and

◄ **Garment Workers on Strike** These two young women, both probably immigrants, walked the picket line during the successful "uprising of the twenty thousand" garment workers in 1909. The women's hats and dresses display their needlework skills and their respectability. The glowering men in the background suggest the conventional middle-class opposition to the working women's strike. Library of Congress Prints and Photographs Division Washington, D.C. [LC-DIG-ggbain-04505].

combustible cloth, burned to rubble in eighteen minutes. A WTUL member described the scene on the street: "Two young girls whom I knew to be working in the vicinity came rushing toward me, tears were running from their eyes and they were white and shaking as they caught me by the arm. 'Oh,' shrieked one of them, 'they are jumping. Jumping from ten stories up! They are going through the air like bundles of clothes.'"

The terrified Triangle workers had little choice but to jump. Flames blocked one exit, and the other door had been locked to prevent workers from pilfering. The flimsy, rusted fire escape collapsed under the weight of fleeing workers, killing dozens. The lucky ones made it out on the elevator or by climbing to the roof where they escaped to a neighboring building. For the rest, the building became a death-trap. Sixty-two workers jumped from the ninth-floor windows only to crash to their deaths on the sidewalks; forty-nine died from smoke inhalation; thirty-six died when the fire escape collapsed. Of 500 workers, 146 died—123 women and 23 men, the youngest two 14-year-old girls. The owners of the Triangle, who had managed to escape the fire, went to trial for negligence, but they avoided conviction when authorities determined that a careless smoker had started the blaze. The Triangle Shirtwaist Company reopened in another firetrap within a matter of weeks.

Outrage and a sense of futility overwhelmed Rose Schneiderman, a leading WTUL organizer, who made a bitter speech at the memorial service for the dead Triangle workers. "I would be a traitor to those poor burned bodies if I came here to talk good fellowship," she told her audience. "We have tried you good people of the public and we have found you wanting. . . . I know from my experience it is up to the working people to save themselves . . . by a strong working class movement." Schneiderman and other WTUL leaders determined that organizing and striking were no longer enough. Increasingly, the WTUL turned its efforts to lobbying for protective legislation—laws that would limit hours and regulate women's working conditions.

As a result of the Triangle tragedy, New York passed thirty-eight new laws that regulated and changed labor conditions. Statutes called for better building access, fireproofing requirements, availability of fire extinguishers, installation of fire alarm systems and automatic sprinklers, better eating and toilet facilities for workers, and limits on the number of hours women and children could work. Nevertheless, the Triangle fire severely tested the bonds of cross-class alliance.

The National Consumers League (NCL) sought to strengthen those bonds while at the same time advocating for protective legislation. When Hull House's Florence

▶ **Triangle Shirtwaist Fire** The Triangle Company occupied the eighth, ninth, and tenth floors of the ten-story Asch Building in the Greenwich Village neighborhood of New York City. On March 25, 1911, a fire burned the factory to the ground in eighteen minutes. A total of 146 workers perished in the fire — 123 women and 23 men. The owners were fined $20. Everett Collection, Inc.

Kelley took over the leadership of the NCL in 1899, she urged middle-class women to boycott stores and exert pressure for decent wages and working conditions for women employees. Frustrated by the reluctance of the private sector to reform, the NCL promoted protective legislation to better working conditions for women.

Advocates of protective legislation had won a major victory in 1908 when the U.S. Supreme Court, in *Muller v. Oregon*, reversed its previous rulings and upheld an Oregon law that limited the number of hours women could work in a day to ten. A mass of sociological evidence put together by Florence Kelley of the NCL and Josephine Goldmark of the WTUL convinced the Court that long hours endangered women and therefore the entire human race. The Court's ruling set a precedent that separated the well-being of women workers from that of men by arguing that women's reproductive role justified special treatment. Later generations of women fighting for equality would question the effectiveness of this strategy and argue that it ultimately closed good jobs to women. The WTUL, however, greeted protective legislation as a first step in the attempt to ensure the safety of all workers.

Reform also fueled the fight for woman suffrage. For women like Jane Addams, involvement in social reform led inevitably to support for woman suffrage. These new suffragists emphasized the reforms that could be accomplished if women had the vote. Addams insisted that in an urban, industrial society, a good homemaker could not be sure the food she fed her family or the water and milk they drank were pure unless she could vote. She needed the ballot as well as the broom to keep her home clean.

REVIEW

What types of people were drawn to the progressive movement, and why?

What were the key tenets of progressive theory?

P rogressivism emphasized action and experimentation. Dismissing the view that humans should leave progress to the dictates of natural selection, a new group of reform Darwinists argued that evolution could be advanced more rapidly if men and women used their intellects to improve society. In their zeal for action, progressives often showed an unchecked admiration for speed and efficiency that promoted scientific management, a new cult to improve productivity. These varied strands of progressive theory found practical application in state and local politics, where reformers challenged traditional laissez-faire government.

What was the theory of reform Darwinism?

The active, interventionist approach of the progressives directly challenged social Darwinism, with its insistence on survival of the fittest. A new group of sociologists argued that progress could be advanced more rapidly if people used their intellects

reform Darwinism
Sociological theory developed in the 1880s that argued humans could speed up evolution by altering their environment. A challenge to the laissez-faire approach of social Darwinism, reform Darwinism insisted that the liberal state should play an active role in solving social problems.

to alter their environment. The best statement of this **reform Darwinism** came from sociologist Lester Frank Ward in his book *Dynamic Sociology* (1883). Ward insisted the "blind natural forces in society must give way to human foresight." This theory condemned the laissez-faire approach, insisting that the liberal state should play a more active role in solving social problems.

Efficiency and *expertise* became progressives' watchwords. In *Drift and Mastery* (1914), journalist and critic Walter Lippmann called for skilled "technocrats" to use scientific techniques to control social change. Unlike the Populists, who advocated a greater voice for the masses, progressives, for all their interest in social justice, insisted that experts be put in charge. At its extreme, the application of expertise and social engineering took the form of scientific management, which workers dismissed as just another speedup.

What did progressive city and state government look like?

Progressivism burst forth at every level of government in 1900, but nowhere more forcefully than in Cleveland with the election of Democrat Thomas Loftin Johnson as mayor. A self-made millionaire by age forty, Johnson moved to Cleveland in 1899, where he began his career in politics. During his mayoral campaign, he pledged to reduce the streetcar fare from five cents to three cents. His election touched off a seven-year war between Johnson and the streetcar magnates. To get his three-cent fare, Johnson had Cleveland buy the streetcar system, a tactic of municipal ownership progressives called "gas and water socialism." Under Johnson's administration, Cleveland became, in the words of journalist Lincoln Steffens, the "best governed city in America."

In Wisconsin, Republican Robert M. La Follette converted to the progressive cause early in the 1900s. La Follette capitalized on the grassroots movement for reform to launch his long political career as governor (1901–1905) and U.S. senator (1906–1925). La Follette brought scientists and professors into his administration and used the university, just down the street from the statehouse in Madison, as a resource. As governor, La Follette lowered railroad rates, raised railroad taxes, improved education, preached conservation, established factory regulation and workers' compensation, instituted the first direct primary in the country, and inaugurated the first state income tax. Under his leadership, Wisconsin earned the title "laboratory of democracy."

West of the Rockies, progressivism arrived somewhat later and found a champion in Republican Hiram Johnson, who served as governor of California from 1911 to 1917 and later as U.S. senator. The Southern Pacific Railroad had dominated California politics since the 1870s. As governor, Johnson promised to "kick the Southern Pacific out of politics" and "return the government to the people," winning support from progressive voters. During Johnson's governorship, California adopted the direct primary; supported initiative, referendum, and recall; strengthened the state's railroad commission; and enacted an employer's liability law.

REVIEW

How did progressives justify their demand for more activist government?

How did Theodore Roosevelt advance the progressive agenda?

On September 6, 1901, anarchist Leon Czolgosz shot President William McKinley while the president was attending the Pan-American Exposition in Buffalo, New York. Eight days later, McKinley died. When news of the assassination reached Republican boss Mark Hanna, he is said to have growled, "Now that damned cowboy is president." He was speaking of Vice President Theodore Roosevelt, the colorful hero of San Juan Hill, who had indeed punched cattle in the Dakotas in the 1880s.

Roosevelt immediately reassured the shocked nation that he intended "to continue absolutely unbroken" the policies of McKinley. But Roosevelt was as different from McKinley as the nineteenth century from the twentieth. An activist and a moralist, imbued with the progressive spirit, Roosevelt would turn the Executive Mansion, which he dubbed the White House, into a "bully pulpit." As president, he achieved major reforms, advocated conservation and antitrust lawsuits, and championed the nation's emergence as a world power. In the process, Roosevelt would work to shift the nation's center of power from Wall Street to Washington.

After serving nearly two terms as president, Roosevelt left office at the height of his powers. Any man would have found it difficult to follow in his footsteps, but his handpicked successor, William Howard Taft, proved poorly suited to the task. Taft's presidency was marked by vigorous trust-busting, but it ended with a progressive stalemate and a bitter break with Roosevelt that split the Republican Party.

What was Roosevelt's Square Deal?

At age forty-two, Theodore Roosevelt became the youngest man ever to move into the White House. A patrician by birth and an activist by temperament, Roosevelt brought to the job enormous talent and energy. Early in his career, he had determined that the path to power did not lie in the good government leagues formed by his well-bred New York friends. "If it is the muckers that govern," he wrote, "then I want to see if I cannot hold my own with them." He served his political apprenticeship under a Republican ward boss in a grubby meeting hall above a saloon on Morton Street.

Roosevelt's rise in politics was swift and sure. He went from the New York assembly at the age of twenty-three to the presidency with time out as a cowboy in the Dakotas, police commissioner of New York City, assistant secretary of the navy, and colonel of the Rough Riders. Elected governor of New York in 1898, he alienated the Republican boss, who finagled to get him "kicked upstairs" as a candidate for the vice presidency in 1900. The party bosses reasoned Roosevelt could do little harm as vice president. But one bullet proved the error of their logic.

Once president, Roosevelt would harness his explosive energy to strengthen the power of the federal government, putting business on notice that it could no longer count on a weak federal government to give it free rein. In Roosevelt's eyes,

◄ **Theodore Roosevelt** Described by one journalist as "a steam engine in trousers," Theodore Roosevelt campaigns for the presidency in 1900. Bettmann/Getty Images.

self-interested capitalists like John D. Rockefeller, whose Standard Oil trust monopolized the refinery business, constituted "the most dangerous members of the criminal class—the criminals of great wealth."

The "absolutely vital question" facing the country, Roosevelt wrote to a friend in 1901, was "whether or not the government has the power to control the trusts." The Sherman Antitrust Act of 1890 had been badly weakened by a conservative Supreme Court and by attorneys general more willing to use it against labor unions than against monopolies. To determine whether the law had any teeth left, Roosevelt, in one of his first acts as president, ordered his attorney general to begin a secret antitrust investigation of the Northern Securities Company, a behemoth that monopolized railroad traffic in the Northwest.

Just five months after Roosevelt took office, Wall Street rocked with the news that the government had filed an antitrust suit against Northern Securities. As one newspaper editor sarcastically observed, "Wall Street is paralyzed at the thought that a President of the United States would sink so low as to try to enforce the law." Roosevelt's thunderbolt put Wall Street on notice that the new president expected to be treated as an equal and was willing to use government as a weapon to curb business excesses. Roosevelt later recounted how J. P. Morgan had come to him to suggest that "if we have done something wrong, send your man to my man and they can fix it up." Roosevelt responded, "That can't be done. We don't want to fix it up; we want to stop it." The president chortled over the exchange, noting "Mr. Morgan could not help regarding me as a big rival operator." And indeed he was. Perhaps sensing the new mood, the Supreme Court, in a significant turnaround, upheld the Sherman Act and called for the dissolution of Northern Securities in 1904.

"Hurrah for Teddy the Trustbuster," cheered the papers. Roosevelt went on to use the Sherman Act against forty-three trusts, including such giants as American Tobacco, Du Pont, and Standard Oil. Always the moralist, he insisted on a "rule of reason." He would punish "bad" trusts (those that broke the law) and leave "good" ones alone. In practice, he preferred regulation to antitrust suits. In 1903, he pressured Congress to pass the Elkins Act, outlawing railroad rebates. He created the new cabinet-level Department of Commerce and Labor with the subsidiary Bureau of Corporations to act as a corporate watchdog.

In his handling of the anthracite coal strike in 1902, Roosevelt again demonstrated his willingness to assert the authority of the presidency, this time to mediate between labor and management. In May, 147,000 coal miners in Pennsylvania went out on strike. The United Mine Workers (UMW) demanded a reduction in the workday from twelve to ten hours, an equitable system of weighing each miner's output, and a 10 percent wage increase, along with recognition of the union. When asked about the appalling conditions in the mines that led to the strike, George Baer, the mine operators' spokesman, scoffed, "The miners don't suffer, why they can't even speak English."

The strike dragged on through the summer and into the fall. Hoarding and profiteering more than doubled the price of coal. As winter approached, coal shortages touched off near riots in the nation's big cities. At this juncture, Roosevelt stepped in. Instead of sending in troops, he determined to mediate. His unprecedented intervention served notice that government counted itself an independent force in business and labor disputes. At the same time, it gave unionism a boost by granting the UMW a place at the table.

At the meeting, Baer and the mine owners refused to talk with the union representative—a move that angered the attorney general and insulted the president. Enraged over the "woodenheaded obstinacy and stupidity" of management, Roosevelt threatened to seize the mines and run them with federal troops. This quickly brought management to the table. In the end, the miners won a reduction in hours and a wage increase, but the owners succeeded in preventing formal recognition of the UMW.

Taken together, Roosevelt's actions in the Northern Securities case and the anthracite coal strike marked a dramatic departure from the use of federal troops to put down strikes that had characterized the Gilded Age. Roosevelt's actions demonstrated conclusively that government intended to act as a countervailing force to the power of the big corporations. Pleased with his role in the anthracite strike, Roosevelt announced that all he had tried to do was give labor and capital a "square deal."

The phrase "Square Deal" became Roosevelt's campaign slogan in the 1904 election. Roosevelt easily defeated the Democrats, who abandoned William Jennings Bryan to support Judge Alton B. Parker, a "safe" choice they hoped would lure business votes away from Roosevelt. In the months before the election, the president prudently toned down his criticism of big business. Roosevelt swept into office with the largest popular majority—57.9 percent—any candidate had polled up to that time.

How effective was Roosevelt as a reformer?

"Tomorrow I shall come into my office in my own right," Roosevelt is said to have remarked on the eve of his election. "Then watch out for me!" Roosevelt's stunning victory gave him a mandate for reform. He would need all the popularity and political savvy he could muster, however, to guide his reform measures through Congress. The Senate remained controlled by a staunchly conservative Republican "Old Guard," with many senators on the payrolls of the corporations Roosevelt sought to curb. As the *New York Times* suggested, "a millionaire could buy a Senate seat, just as he would buy an opera box, a yacht, or any other luxury."

Roosevelt's pet project remained railroad regulation. The Elkins Act prohibiting rebates had not worked. Roosevelt determined that the only solution lay in giving the Interstate Commerce Commission (ICC) real power to set rates and prevent discriminatory practices. But the right to determine the price of goods or services was an age-old prerogative of private enterprise and one that business had no intention of yielding to government.

The resulting legislation, the Hepburn Act of 1906, marked the crowning achievement of Roosevelt's presidency. It gave the ICC the power to set rates subject to court review. Committed progressives like La Follette judged the law a defeat for reform. Die-hard conservatives branded it a "piece of populism." Both sides exaggerated. The law left the courts too much power and failed to provide adequate means for the ICC to determine rates, but its passage proved a landmark in federal control of private industry. For the first time, a government commission had the power to investigate private business records and to set rates.

Always an apt reader of the public temper, Roosevelt witnessed a growing appetite for reform. Revelations of corporate and political wrongdoing as well as social injustice filled the papers and boosted the sales of popular magazines. Roosevelt counted many of the new investigative journalists among his friends. But he warned them against going too far, citing the allegorical character in *Pilgrim's Progress* who was too busy raking muck to notice higher things. Roosevelt's criticism gave the American vocabulary a new word, muckraker, which journalists soon appropriated as a title of honor.

muckraking
Early-twentieth-century style of journalism that exposed the corruption of big business and government. Theodore Roosevelt coined the term after a character in *Pilgrim's Progress* who was too busy raking muck to notice higher things.

Muckraking, as Roosevelt well knew, provided enormous help in securing progressive legislation. In the spring of 1906, muckrakers' reports about poisons in patent medicines goaded the Senate, with Roosevelt's backing, into passing a pure food and drug bill. Opponents in the House of Representatives hoped to keep the legislation locked up in committee.

There it would have died were it not for the publication of Upton Sinclair's novel *The Jungle* (1906), with its sensational account of filthy conditions in meatpacking plants. Roosevelt, who read the book over breakfast, was sickened by descriptions of rat feces and rotten meat. He invited Sinclair to the White House to discuss the problem. But the two were soon at loggerheads: Sinclair wanted socialism; Roosevelt wanted food inspection. He got it, thanks to the publicity generated by *The Jungle*. Congress passed the Pure Food and Drug Act and the Meat Inspection Act in 1906. As Sinclair ruefully observed, "I aimed at the public's heart, and by accident I hit it in the stomach."

In the waning years of his administration, Roosevelt allied with the more progressive elements of the Republican Party. In speech after speech, he attacked "malefactors of great wealth." Styling himself a "radical," he claimed credit for leading the "ultra conservative" party of McKinley to a position of "progressive conservatism and conservative radicalism."

When an economic panic developed in the fall of 1907, business interests quickly blamed the president, whom they judged a class traitor. Once again, J. P. Morgan stepped in to avert disaster, this time switching funds from one bank to another to prop up weak institutions. For his services, Morgan dispatched his lieutenants to Washington, where they told Roosevelt that the sale of the Tennessee Coal and Iron Company would aid the economy "but little benefit" U.S. Steel. Willing to take the word of a gentleman, Roosevelt tacitly agreed not to institute antitrust proceedings against U.S. Steel over the acquisition.

But as Roosevelt later learned, Morgan and his men had been less than candid. The acquisition of Tennessee Coal and Iron for a price below market value greatly strengthened U.S. Steel and undercut the economy of the Southeast. Roosevelt's promise would give rise to the charge that he acted as a tool of the Morgan interests.

The charge of collusion between business and government underscored the extent to which corporate leaders like Morgan found federal regulation preferable to unbridled competition or harsher state measures. During the Progressive Era, enlightened business leaders cooperated with government in the hope of avoiding antitrust prosecution.

Convinced that regulation and not trust-busting offered the best way to deal with big business, Roosevelt never acknowledged that his regulatory policies fostered an alliance between business and government that today is called corporate liberalism.

Why did Roosevelt champion conservation?

In the area of conservation, Roosevelt proved indisputably ahead of his time. When he took office, some 43 million acres of forestland remained as government reserves. He more than quadrupled that number to 194 million acres. To conserve natural resources, he fought western cattle barons, lumber kings, mining interests, and powerful leaders in Congress, including Speaker of the House Joseph Cannon, who vowed to spend "not one cent for scenery."

As the first president to have lived and worked in the West, Roosevelt came to the White House convinced of the need for better management of the nation's rivers and forests as well as the preservation of wildlife and wilderness. During his presidency, he placed the nation's conservation policy in the hands of scientifically trained experts like his chief forester, Gifford Pinchot. Pinchot preached conservation—the efficient use of natural resources. Willing to permit grazing, lumbering, and the development of hydroelectric power, conservationists fought private interests only when they felt business acted irresponsibly or threatened to monopolize water and electric power.

Unlike conservationists, preservationists like John Muir, founder of the Sierra Club, believed that the wilderness needed to be protected. Muir soon clashed with Roosevelt. After a devastating earthquake in 1906, San Francisco sought federal approval for a project that would supply fresh water and electric power to the city. The plan called for building a dam that would flood the spectacular Hetch Hetchy Valley in Yosemite National Park. Muir, who had played a central role in establishing the park, fiercely opposed the plan. After a protracted publicity battle, Roosevelt and the conservationists prevailed. To placate Muir, Roosevelt set aside a section of California's redwood forest as "Muir Woods."

In 1907, Congress attempted to put the brakes on Roosevelt's conservation program by passing a law limiting his power to create forest reserves in six western states. In the days leading up to the law's enactment, Roosevelt feverishly created twenty-one new reserves and enlarged eleven more, saving sixteen million acres from development. Once again, Roosevelt had outwitted his adversaries. "Opponents of the forest service turned handsprings in their wrath," he wrote, "but the threats . . . were really only a tribute to the efficiency of our action."

Worried that private utilities were gobbling up waterpower sites and creating a monopoly of hydroelectric power, he connived with Pinchot to withdraw 2,565 power sites from private use by designating them "ranger stations." Firm in his commitment to wild America, Roosevelt proved willing to stretch the law when it served his ends. His legacy is more than 234 million acres of American wilderness saved for posterity (**Map 21.1**).

Why did Roosevelt describe his foreign policy with the phrase "Speak softly but carry a big stick"?

Roosevelt's activism extended to his foreign policy. A fierce proponent of America's interests abroad, he relied on executive power to pursue a vigorous foreign policy, sometimes stretching the powers of the presidency beyond legal limits. In his relations

MAP ACTIVITY

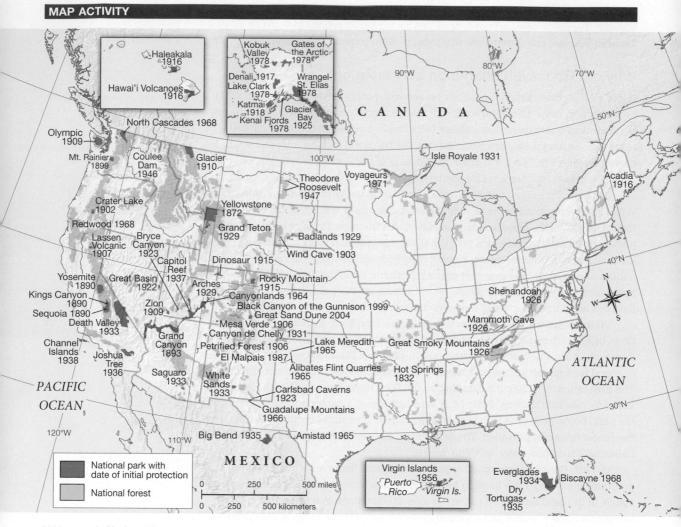

MAP 21.1 ▲ National Parks and Forests The national park system in the West began with Yellowstone in 1872. Grand Canyon, Yosemite, Kings Canyon, and Sequoia followed in the 1890s. During his presidency, Theodore Roosevelt added six parks — Crater Lake, Wind Cave, Petrified Forest, Lassen Volcanic, Mesa Verde, and Zion.

READING THE MAP: Collectively, do national parks or national forests encompass more land? According to the map, how many national parks were created before 1910? How many were created after 1910?

CONNECTIONS: How do conservation and preservation differ? Why did Roosevelt believe that saving land in the West was important? What principles guided the national land use policy of the Roosevelt administration?

with the European powers, he relied on military strength and diplomacy, a combination he aptly described with the aphorism "Speak softly but carry a big stick."

A strong supporter of the Monroe Doctrine, Roosevelt jealously guarded the U.S. sphere of influence in the Western Hemisphere. His proprietary attitude toward the Caribbean became evident in the case of the Panama Canal. Roosevelt

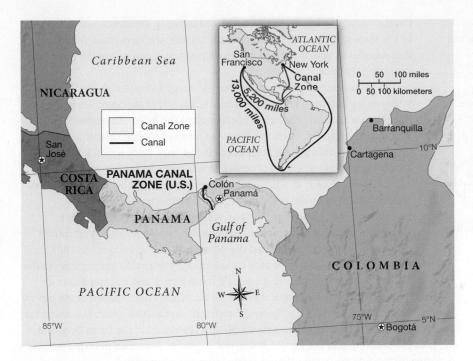

MAP 21.2 ◄ The Panama Canal, 1914 The Panama Canal, completed in 1914, bisects the isthmus in a series of massive locks and dams. As Theodore Roosevelt had planned, the canal greatly strengthened the U.S. Navy by allowing ships to move from the Atlantic to the Pacific in a matter of days.

had long been a supporter of a canal linking the Caribbean and the Pacific. By enabling ships to move quickly from the Atlantic to the Pacific, a canal would effectively double the U.S. Navy's power.

Having decided on a route across the Panamanian isthmus (a narrow strip of land connecting North and South America), Roosevelt in 1902 offered the Colombian government a one-time sum of $10 million and an annual rent of $250,000. When the government in Bogotá held out for more, Roosevelt became incensed at what he called the "homicidal corruptionists" in Colombia for trying to "blackmail" the United States.

At the prompting of a group of New York investors, the Panamanians staged an uprising in 1903, and with unseemly haste, the U.S. government recognized the new government within twenty-four hours. The Panamanians promptly accepted the $10 million, and the building got underway. The canal would take eleven years and $375 million to complete; it opened in 1914 (**Map 21.2**).

Roosevelt grew concerned that financial instability in Latin America would lead European powers to interfere. In 1904, he announced the **Roosevelt Corollary** to the Monroe Doctrine, in which he declared the United States had a right to act as "an international police power" in the Western Hemisphere. Roosevelt stated the United States would not intervene in Latin America as long as nations there conducted their affairs with "decency," but it would step in to stop "brutal wrongdoing." The Roosevelt Corollary served notice to the European powers that the United States would police the hemisphere. At the same time, it abrogated the sovereignty of Latin American nations and left a legacy of anti-Americanism.

In Asia, Roosevelt inherited the Open Door policy initiated by Secretary of State John Hay in 1899, designed to ensure U.S. commercial entry into China. As European

Roosevelt Corollary
Theodore Roosevelt's 1904 follow-up to the Monroe Doctrine in which he declared that the United States had the right to intervene in Latin America to stop "brutal wrongdoing" and protect American interests. The corollary warned European powers to keep out of the Western Hemisphere.

The Roosevelt Corollary in Action

powers raced to secure Chinese trade and territory, Roosevelt was tempted to use force to gain economic or possibly territorial concessions. Realizing that Americans would not support an aggressive Asian policy, the president sensibly held back.

In his relations with Europe, Roosevelt sought to establish the United States as a rising force in world affairs, often acting as mediator. He earned the Nobel Peace Prize in 1906 for his role in ending the Russo-Japanese War, which had broken out when the Japanese invaded Chinese Manchuria, threatening Russia's sphere of influence in the area. Once again, Roosevelt sought to maintain a balance of power, in this case working to curb Japanese expansionism. Roosevelt admired the Japanese as "the most dashing fighters in the world," but he did not want Japan to become too strong in Asia.

When good relations with Japan were jeopardized by California's blatantly racist, segregated public schools for Asians, Roosevelt smoothed over the incident and negotiated the "Gentlemen's Agreement" in 1907, which allowed the Japanese to save face by voluntarily restricting immigration to the United States. Then, to demonstrate America's naval power and counter Japan's growing bellicosity, Roosevelt dispatched the Great White Fleet, sixteen of the navy's most up-to-date battleships, on a "goodwill mission" around the world. U.S. relations with Japan improved, and the two nations pledged to maintain the Open Door and support the status quo in the Pacific. Roosevelt's show of American force constituted a classic example of his dictum "Speak softly but carry a big stick."

Why did William Howard Taft have such a troubled presidency?

Roosevelt promised on the eve of his election in 1904 that he would not seek another term. In 1909, at the age of fifty, he retired from the presidency and removed himself from the political scene by going on safari in Africa. Roosevelt turned the White House over to

◀ **"The World's Constable"** In this political cartoon from 1905, President Theodore Roosevelt, dressed as a constable, wields the club of "The New Diplomacy" in one hand with "Arbitration" tucked under his arm. The Roosevelt Corollary to the Monroe Doctrine made the United States the Western Hemisphere's marshal, a role Roosevelt relished. GRANGER – Historical Picture Archive.

READING THE IMAGE: How does this political cartoon visually represent Roosevelt's foreign policy? Does it appear to be supportive or critical of his policies? How does it treat the other peoples of the world?

CONNECTIONS: What aspects of Roosevelt's foreign policy ideas and actions are depicted in the cartoon?

his handpicked successor, William Howard Taft, a lawyer who had served as governor-general of the Philippines. Affectionately known as "Big Bill," Taft had served as Roosevelt's right-hand man in the cabinet. In the presidential election of 1908, Taft soundly defeated the perennial Democratic candidate William Jennings Bryan.

A genial man with a talent for law, Taft had no experience in elective office, no feel for politics, and no nerve for controversy. His ambitious wife coveted the office and urged him to seek it. He would have been better off listening to his mother, who warned, "Roosevelt is a good fighter and enjoys it, but the malice of politics would make you miserable." Sadly for Taft, his wife suffered a stroke in his first months in office, leaving him grieving and without his strongest ally.

Once in office, Taft proved a perfect tool in the hands of Republicans who yearned for a return to the days of a less active executive. A lawyer by training and instinct, Taft believed that it was up to the courts, not the president, to arbitrate social issues. Roosevelt had carried presidential power to a new level, often flouting the separation of powers and showing thinly veiled contempt for Congress and the courts. He believed that the president had the legal right to act as steward of the people and to do anything necessary "unless the Constitution or the laws explicitly forbid him to do it." Taft found such presidential activism difficult to condone. Although he pursued the trusts vigorously, he acted more as a judge than a steward. Wary of the progressive insurgents in Congress, Taft relied increasingly on conservatives in the Republican Party. As a progressive senator lamented, "Taft is a ponderous and amiable man completely surrounded by men who know exactly what they want."

Taft's troubles began on the eve of his inaugural, when he called a special session of Congress to deal with the tariff. Roosevelt had been too politically astute to tackle the troublesome tariff issue, even though he knew that rates needed to be lowered. Taft blundered into the fray, hoping to use public opinion to get a tariff reduction. But by the time Congress finished tinkering with the rate schedule, the Payne-Aldrich bill that emerged actually raised the tariff, benefiting big business and the trusts at the expense of consumers.

As if paralyzed, Taft neither fought for changes nor vetoed the measure. On a tour of the Midwest in 1909, he was greeted with jeers when he claimed, "I think the Payne bill is the best bill that the Republican Party ever passed." In the eyes of a growing number of Americans, Taft's praise of the tariff made him either a fool or a liar.

Taft's legalism soon got him into hot water in the area of conservation. He undid Roosevelt's work to preserve hydroelectric power sites when he learned that they had been improperly designated as ranger stations. And when Gifford Pinchot publicly denounced Taft's secretary of the interior as a pawn of western land-grabbers, Taft fired Pinchot, touching off a storm of controversy that damaged Taft and alienated Roosevelt.

When Roosevelt returned from Africa in June 1910, he received a hero's welcome and attracted a stream of visitors and reporters seeking his advice and opinions. Pinchot was among the first to greet him with a half dozen letters from progressives complaining about Taft's leadership. Hurt, Taft kept his distance. By late summer, Roosevelt had taken sides with the progressive insurgents in his party. "Taft is utterly hopeless as a leader," Roosevelt confided to his son as he set out on a speaking tour of the West. Reading the mood of the country, Roosevelt began to sound more and more like a candidate.

With the Republican Party divided, the Democrats swept the congressional elections of 1910. Branding the Payne-Aldrich tariff "the mother of trusts," they captured a majority in the House of Representatives and won several key governorships. The revitalized Democratic Party looked to new leaders, among them the progressive governor of New Jersey, Woodrow Wilson.

The new Democratic majority in the House, working with progressive Republicans in the Senate, achieved a number of key reforms, including legislation to regulate railroad safety, to create the Children's Bureau in the Department of Labor, and to establish an eight-hour day for federal workers and miners. Two significant constitutional amendments—the Sixteenth Amendment, which provided for a modest graduated income tax, and the Seventeenth Amendment, which called for the direct election of senators (formerly chosen by state legislatures)—went to the states, where they would win ratification in 1913. While Congress rode the high tide of progressive reform, Taft sat on the sidelines.

In foreign policy, Taft continued Roosevelt's policy of extending U.S. influence abroad, but here, too, Taft had a difficult time following Roosevelt. Taft's "dollar diplomacy" championed commercial goals rather than the strategic aims Roosevelt had pursued. Taft naively assumed he could substitute "dollars for bullets." In the Caribbean, he provoked anti-American feeling by dispatching U.S. Marines to Nicaragua and the Dominican Republic in 1912 pursuant to the Roosevelt Corollary. In Asia, he openly avowed his intent to promote "active intervention to secure for our merchandise and our capitalists opportunity for profitable investment." Lacking Roosevelt's understanding of power politics, Taft failed to recognize that an aggressive commercial policy could not exist without the willingness to use military might to back it up.

Taft faced the limits of dollar diplomacy when revolution broke out in Mexico in 1911. Under pressure to protect American investments, he mobilized troops along the border. In the end, however, with no popular support for a war with Mexico, he had to fall back on diplomatic pressure to salvage American interests.

Taft's greatest dream was to encourage world peace through the use of a world court and arbitration. He unsuccessfully sponsored a series of arbitration treaties that Roosevelt, who prized national honor more than international law, vehemently opposed as weak and cowardly. By 1910, Roosevelt had become a vocal critic of Taft's foreign policy.

The final breach between Taft and Roosevelt came in 1911, when Taft's attorney general filed an antitrust suit against U.S. Steel. In its brief against the corporation, the government cited Roosevelt's agreement with the Morgan interests in the 1907 acquisition of Tennessee Coal and Iron. The incident greatly embarrassed Roosevelt. Either he had been hoodwinked or he had colluded with Morgan. Neither idea pleased him. Thoroughly enraged, he lambasted Taft's "archaic" antitrust policy and hinted that he might be persuaded to run for president again.

Taft's "Dollar Diplomacy"

REVIEW

What advances in the progressive agenda were made at the federal level between 1901 and 1913?

How did progressivism evolve during Woodrow Wilson's first term?

Disillusionment with Taft resulted in a split in the Republican Party and the creation of a new Progressive Party that rallied to Theodore Roosevelt. In the election of 1912, four candidates styled themselves "progressives," but it was Democrat Woodrow Wilson, with a minority of the popular vote, who won the presidency. He would continue Roosevelt's presidential power and help enact progressive legislation.

How could all four presidential candidates in 1912 claim to be progressives?

Convinced that Taft was inept, in February 1912 Roosevelt declared his candidacy for the Republican nomination, announcing, "My hat is in the ring." Taft, with uncharacteristic strength, refused to step aside. As he bitterly told a journalist, "Even a rat in a corner will fight." Roosevelt took advantage of newly passed primary election laws and ran in thirteen states, winning 278 delegates to Taft's 48. But at the Chicago convention, Taft's bosses refused to seat the Roosevelt delegates. Fistfights broke out on the convention floor as Taft steamrolled the convention to win nomination on the first ballot. Crying robbery, Roosevelt's supporters bolted the party.

Seven weeks later, in the same Chicago auditorium, the hastily organized Progressive Party met to nominate Roosevelt. Full of reforming zeal, the delegates

◀ **Woodrow Wilson**
Woodrow Wilson, the Democrats' presidential nominee in 1912, speaks to an outdoor campaign rally in New York City. Note the absence of a microphone. Wilson, a former professor of political science and president of Princeton University and recently elected governor of New Jersey, gave carefully phrased, logical, and clear speeches in a somewhat professorial style that contrasted with the charisma of the Bull Moose candidate, Theodore Roosevelt. Library of Congress/Getty Images.

chose Roosevelt and Hiram Johnson to head the new party. Jane Addams seconded Roosevelt's nomination. "I have been fighting for progressive principles for thirty years," she told the enthusiastic crowd. "This is the first time there has been a chance to make them effective. This is the biggest day of my life." The new party lustily approved the most ambitious platform since that of the Populists. Planks called for woman suffrage, presidential primaries, conservation of natural resources, an end to child labor, workers' compensation, a living wage for both men and women workers, social security, health insurance, and a federal income tax.

Roosevelt arrived in Chicago to accept the nomination and announced that he felt "as fit as a bull moose," giving the new party a nickname and a mascot. With characteristic vigor, he launched his campaign with the exhortation, "We stand at Armageddon and do battle for the Lord!" But for all the excitement and the cheering, the new Progressive Party was doomed, and the candidate knew it. Privately he confessed to a friend, "I am under no illusion about it. It is a forlorn hope." The people may have supported Roosevelt, but the politicians, even progressives like La Follette, refused to back the new party. The Democrats, delighted at the split in the Republican ranks, nominated Woodrow Wilson, the governor of New Jersey.

Voters in 1912 could choose among four candidates who claimed to be progressives. Taft, Roosevelt, and Wilson each embraced the label, and even the Socialist candidate, Eugene V. Debs, styled himself a progressive. That the term *progressive* could stretch to cover these diverse candidates underscored major disagreements in progressive thinking about the relationship between business and government. Taft, in spite of his trust-busting, was generally viewed as the candidate of the Republican old guard. Debs urged voters to support the Socialist Party as the true spirit of the working class. The real contest for the presidency came down to a fight between Roosevelt and Wilson and the two political philosophies summed up in their respective campaign slogans: **"The New Nationalism"** and **"The New Freedom."**

The New Nationalism expressed Roosevelt's belief in federal planning and regulation. He accepted the inevitability of big business but demanded that government act as "a steward of the people" to regulate the giant corporations. Wilson, schooled in the Democratic principles of limited government and states' rights, set a markedly different course with his New Freedom. He promised to use antitrust legislation to get rid of big corporations and to give small businesses and farmers better opportunities in the marketplace.

The energy and enthusiasm of the Bull Moosers made the race seem closer than it was. In the end, the Republican vote split, while the Democrats remained united. No candidate claimed a majority in the race. Wilson captured a bare 42 percent of the popular vote. Roosevelt and his Bull Moose Party won 27 percent, an unprecedented tally for a new party. Taft came in third with 23 percent. The Socialist Party, led by Debs, captured a surprising 6 percent (**Map 21.3**). The Republican Party moved in a conservative direction, while the

"The New Nationalism" Theodore Roosevelt's 1912 campaign slogan, which reflected his commitment to federal planning and regulation. Roosevelt wanted to use the federal government to act as a "steward of the people" to regulate giant corporations.

"The New Freedom" Woodrow Wilson's 1912 campaign slogan, which reflected his belief in limited government and states' rights. Wilson promised to use antitrust legislation to eliminate big corporations and to improve opportunities for small businesses and farmers.

Candidate	Electoral Vote	Popular Vote	Percent of Popular Vote
Woodrow Wilson (Democrat)	435	6,293,454	41.9
Theodore Roosevelt (Progressive)	88	4,119,538	27.4
William H. Taft (Republican)	8	3,484,980	23.2
Eugene V. Debs (Socialist)	0	900,672	6.1

MAP 21.3 The Election of 1912

Progressive Party essentially collapsed after Roosevelt's defeat. It had always been, in the words of one astute observer, "a house divided against itself and already mortgaged."

Why did Wilson focus his progressive reforms on tariffs, banking, and trusts?

Born in Virginia and raised in Georgia, Woodrow Wilson became the first southerner elected president since 1844 and only the second Democrat to occupy the White House since Reconstruction. A believer in states' rights, Wilson nevertheless promised legislation to break the hold of the trusts. This lean, ascetic scholar was, as one biographer conceded, a man whose "political convictions were never as fixed as his ambition." Building on the base built by Roosevelt in strengthening presidential power, Wilson exerted leadership to achieve banking reform and worked through his party in Congress to accomplish the Democratic agenda. Before he was finished, Wilson lent his support to many of the Progressive Party's social reforms.

With the Democrats thoroughly in control of Congress, Wilson immediately called for tariff reform. "The object of the tariff," Wilson told Congress, "must be effective competition." The Democratic House of Representatives hastily passed the Underwood tariff, which lowered rates by 15 percent. To compensate for lost revenue, the House approved a moderate federal income tax made possible by the ratification of the Sixteenth Amendment a month earlier. In the Senate, lobbyists for industries quietly went to work to get the tariff raised, but Wilson rallied public opinion by attacking the "industrious and insidious lobby." In the harsh glare of publicity, the Senate passed the Underwood tariff.

Wilson next turned his attention to banking. The panic of 1907 led the government to turn once again to J. P. Morgan to avoid economic catastrophe. For years, Morgan had acted virtually as a fourth branch of the government, called in to keep the country's finances afloat in times of panic.

But by the time Wilson came to office, Morgan's legendary power had come under close scrutiny. In 1913, a Senate committee investigated the "money trust," calling Morgan himself to testify. The committee uncovered an alarming concentration of banking power. J. P. Morgan and Company and its affiliates held 341 directorships in 112 corporations, controlling assets of more than $22 million (billions in today's dollars). On the witness stand, Morgan adamantly refused to discuss his private financial transactions, insisting his power resulted from character, not cash. But Morgan's days as Wall Street's Jupiter were fading. Three months after testifying before the committee, Morgan died. His estate, valued at $68 million, led Andrew Carnegie to joke, "And to think, he was not a rich man!" Surely not compared to Carnegie, who had pocketed $225 million in the U.S. Steel merger Morgan orchestrated. Carnegie's jibe, however, missed the mark. Morgan's power came not from the millions he owned but from the many more millions he controlled. His death signaled the end of the "money trust" and the end of an era.

The Federal Reserve Act of 1913 marked the most significant piece of domestic legislation of Wilson's presidency. It established a national banking system composed of twelve regional banks, privately controlled but regulated and supervised by the Federal Reserve Board, appointed by the president. It gave the United States its first efficient banking and currency system and, at the same time, provided for a greater degree of government control over banking. The new system made currency more elastic and credit adequate for the needs of business and agriculture.

Wilson, flush with success, tackled the trust issue next. When Congress reconvened in January 1914, he supported the introduction and passage of the Clayton Antitrust Act to outlaw "unfair competition"—practices such as price discrimination and interlocking directorates (directors from one corporation sitting on the board of another). In the midst of the successful fight for the Clayton Act, Wilson changed course and threw his support behind the creation of the Federal Trade Commission (FTC), precisely the kind of federal regulatory agency that Roosevelt had advocated in his New Nationalism. The FTC, created in 1914, had not only wide investigatory powers but also the authority to prosecute corporations for "unfair trade practices" and to enforce its judgments by issuing "cease and desist" orders. Despite his campaign promises, Wilson's antitrust program worked to regulate rather than to break up big business.

Why has Wilson been called a reluctant progressive?

By the fall of 1914, Wilson declared that the progressive movement had fulfilled its mission and that the country needed "a time of healing." Progressives watched in dismay as Wilson repeatedly obstructed or obstinately refused to endorse further reforms. He rebuffed labor's demand for an end to court injunctions against labor unions. He refused to support child labor legislation or woman suffrage. Wilson used the rhetoric of the New Freedom to justify his actions, claiming that his administration would condone "special privileges to none." But in fact, his stance often reflected the interests of his small-business constituency.

In the face of Wilson's obstinacy, reform might have ended in 1913 had not politics intruded. In the congressional elections of 1914, the Republican Party, no longer split by Roosevelt's Bull Moose faction, won substantial gains. Democratic strategists recognized that Wilson needed to pick up support in the Midwest and the West by capturing votes from former Bull Moose progressives. Wilson responded belatedly by backing reform in the months leading up to the election of 1916.

In a sharp about-face, he cultivated union labor, farmers, and social reformers. To please labor, he appointed progressive Louis Brandeis to the Supreme Court. To woo farmers, he threw his weight behind legislation to obtain rural credits. And he won praise from labor by supporting workers' compensation and the Keating-Owen child labor law (1916), which outlawed the regular employment of children younger than sixteen. **(See "Analyzing Historical Evidence: Child Labor" on page 626.)** When a railroad strike threatened in the months before the election, Wilson ordered Congress to establish an eight-hour day on the railroads. He had moved a long way from his New Freedom of 1912, and, as Wilson noted, the Democrats had "come very near to carrying out the platform of the Progressive Party." Wilson's shift toward reform, along with his claim that he had kept the United States out of the war in Europe (discussed in chapter 22), helped him win reelection in 1916.

REVIEW

How did party politics change between 1912 and 1916, and what impact did this change have on progressivism?

What were the limits of progressive reform?

While progressivism called for a more active role for the liberal state, at heart it was a middle-class movement that sought reforms designed to preserve American institutions and stem the tide of more radical change. Its basic conservatism can be seen by comparing it with the more radical movements of socialism, radical labor, and birth control—and by looking at the groups progressive reform left out, including women, Asians, and African Americans.

What were some radical alternatives to progressive reform?

The year 1900 marked the birth of the Social Democratic Party in America, later called simply the **Socialist Party**. Like the progressives, the socialists were middle-class and native-born. They had broken with the older, more militant Socialist Labor Party precisely because of its dogmatic approach and immigrant constituency. The new group of socialists proved eager to appeal to a broad mass of disaffected Americans.

The Socialist Party chose as its presidential standard-bearer Eugene V. Debs, whose experience in the Pullman strike of 1894 (see chapter 20) convinced him that "there is no hope for the toiling masses of my countrymen, except by the pathways mapped out by Socialism." Debs would run for president five times, in every election (except 1916) from 1900 to 1920. The socialism Debs advocated preached cooperation over competition and urged men and women to liberate themselves from "the barbarism of private ownership and wage slavery." In the 1912 election, Debs indicted both old parties as each dedicated to the preservation of capitalism and the continuation of the wage system. Styling the Socialist Party the "revolutionary party of the working class," he urged voters to rally to his standard. Debs's best showing came in 1912, when his 6 percent of the popular vote totaled more than 900,000 votes.

Further to the left and more radical than the socialists stood the **Industrial Workers of the World (IWW)**, nicknamed the Wobblies. In 1905, Debs, along with Western Federation of Miners leader William Dudley "Big Bill" Haywood, created the IWW, "one big union" dedicated to organizing the most destitute segment of the workforce, the unskilled workers disdained by Samuel Gompers's AFL: western miners, migrant farmworkers, lumbermen, and immigrant textile workers. Haywood, a craggy-faced miner with one eye (he had lost the other in a childhood accident), was a charismatic leader and a proletarian intellectual. Seeing workers on the lowest rung of the social ladder as the victims of violent repression, the IWW advocated direct action, sabotage, and the general strike—tactics designed to trigger a workers' uprising and overthrow the capitalist state. The IWW claimed it had as many as 100,000 members. Although membership fluctuated greatly, the influence of the IWW extended far beyond its numbers (as discussed in chapter 22).

In contrast to political radicals like Debs and Haywood, Margaret Sanger promoted the **birth control movement** as a means of social change. Sanger, a nurse who had worked among the poor on New York's Lower East Side, coined the term

Socialist Party
Political party formed in 1900 that advocated cooperation over competition and promoted the breakdown of capitalism. Its members, who were largely middle-class and native-born, saw both the Republican and the Democratic parties as hopelessly beholden to capitalism.

Industrial Workers of the World (IWW)
Umbrella union and radical political group founded in 1905 that was dedicated to organizing unskilled workers to oppose capitalism. Nicknamed the Wobblies, the IWW advocated direct action by workers, including sabotage and general strikes, in hopes of triggering a widespread workers' uprising.

birth control movement
Movement launched in 1915 by Margaret Sanger in New York City's Lower East Side. Birth control advocates hoped that contraception would alter social and political power relationships: By having fewer babies, the working class could constrict the size of the workforce, thus making possible higher wages, and at the same time refuse to provide soldiers for the world's armies.

ANALYZING HISTORICAL EVIDENCE

Child Labor

By the early years of the twentieth century, as many as four million children between the ages of ten and fifteen toiled long hours for little pay. They worked in the depths of coal mines, in the seething heat of glass factories, in the canneries and textile mills, in cotton fields — wherever employers coveted small size and nimble fingers. Progressive reformers, often called "child savers," attempted to curb exploitation of children under the age of fourteen in sweatshops, mines, and mills across America. But they ran into solid opposition not only from employers, who had a vested interest in the cheap labor children performed, but also from parents, who counted on the meager wages of their children. In rural America, no one questioned parents' right to put children to hard tasks in the fields and on the farm. Similarly, immigrants from rural Italy, Germany, or Russia could see no harm in putting children to work in factories or sweatshops in America's industrial cities. They viewed it as the parents' prerogative to command their children's wages. Progressive reformers found themselves up against stiff opposition.

DOCUMENT 1

Lewis W. Parker, Testimony before the Congressional Committee on Labor, 1914

Not just immigrant but old-stock Americans relied on child labor, particularly in the South, where entire poor white families left the land to work in the textile mills. On May 22, 1914, a South Carolina mill owner testified before the House of Representatives Committee on Labor on why child labor was necessary in the South.

It is not possible for a man who has been working on a farm who is an adult — after the age of twenty-one years, for instance — to become a skilled employee in a cotton mill. His fingers are knotted and gnarled; he is slow in action, whereas activity is required in working in the cotton mills. Therefore, as a matter of necessity, the adult of the family had to come to the cotton mill as an unskilled employee, and it was the children of the family who became the skilled employees in the cotton mills. For that reason it was the children who had to support the families for the time being. I have seen instances in which a child of 12 years of age, working in the cotton mills, is earning one and one-half times as much as his father of 40 or 50 years of age.

DOCUMENT 2

Florence Kelley, Testimony before the Congressional Committee on Labor, 1914

Progressives countered these arguments with poignant testimony about the plight of young workers and the

failure of the states to enforce the law. At the same 1914 committee hearings, reformer Florence Kelley described her experiences investigating child labor practices in Illinois.

. . . I was at one time chief inspector of factories and workshops in the State of Illinois. I found great numbers of children working at night — working illegally. The superintendent of a glass-bottle company told me himself that this occurred once when he was rushed with work. A widow had come to him bringing two little boys, one still in kilts [baby skirts worn by small boys] and one in knee breeches. She told me that their father had just been killed on the railroad, and that they were penniless; and she wanted the older little boy to go to work in the glassworks, where he would get 40 cents a day. The superintendent was pressed for boys, and said, "I won't take the bigger fellow alone, but if you will take the baby back home and put him into knee pants, and then bring them both back in trousers, I will take them both." She did so, and those two little fellows, aged 9 and 7 years, began their work on the night shift.

DOCUMENT 3

Lowell Mellett, Interview with Reuben Dagenhart, 1923

Despite heavy odds against them, progressives achieved victory in 1916 when the National Child Labor Committee finally convinced Congress and President Woodrow Wilson to enact the Keating-Owen bill forbidding the regular employment of children under sixteen. The child savers' victory proved short-lived. In 1918, powerful business interests and a Supreme Court bent on preserving the sanctity of contracts struck down the law in Hammer v. Dagenhart *on the grounds that Congress could not regulate manufacturing within states. This decision made it legal for the chief plaintiff in the case, Roland Dagenhart, to continue having his young sons, aged thirteen and seven, work in a North Carolina cotton mill. It also protected the boys' "constitutional right" to work at the mill, where they put in twelve-hour days and sometimes worked night shifts as well.*

In 1923, reporter Lowell Mellett tracked down Reuben Dagenhart, one of the boys in whose favor the Supreme Court had ruled six years earlier. In an article published in Labor *in November 1923, Mellett recounted his meeting with Dagenhart.*

I found him at his home in Charlotte. He is about the size of the office boy — weighs 105 pounds, he told me. But he is a married man with a child. He is 20 years old.

"What benefit," I asked him, "did you get out of the suit which you won in the United States Supreme Court?"

"You mean the suit the Fidelity Manufacturing Company won? (It was the Fidelity Company for which the Dagenharts were working.) I don't see that I got any benefit. I guess I'd been a lot better off if they hadn't won it. . . .

"Look at me! A hundred and five pounds, a grown man and no education. I may be mistaken, but I think the years I've put in in the cotton mills have stunted my growth. They kept me from getting any schooling. I had to stop school after the third grade and now I need the education I didn't get."

"How was your growth stunted?"

"I don't know — the dust and the lint, maybe. But from 12 years old on, I was working 12 hours a day — from 6 in the morning till 7 at night, with time out for meals.

And sometimes I worked nights besides. Lifting a hundred pounds and I only weighed 65 pounds myself."

He explained that he and his sister worked together, "on section," spinning. They each made about a dollar a day, though later he worked up to where he could make $2. His father made $15 a week and infant John, at the time the suit was brought, was making close to $1 a day.

"Just what did you and John get out of the suit, then?"

"Why we got some automobile rides when them big lawyers from the North was down here. Oh, yes, and they brought both of us a coca-cola! That's all we got out of it."

Despite the efforts of committed reformers, child labor persisted into the 1920s, immune from federal law and condoned by states reluctant to exercise their authority against the force of private money and public indifference.

Source: Documents 1 and 2, House of Representatives Hearing before the Committee on Labor (1914), 93, 35–36; document 3, *Labor*, November 17, 1923.

Questions for Analysis

RECOGNIZE VIEWPOINTS: How does Lewis W. Parker justify child labor?

ANALYZE THE EVIDENCE: What does Florence Kelley testify about the presence of child labor in industry? How young are child workers?

ASK HISTORICAL QUESTIONS: What does Lowell Mellett's interview with Reuben Dagenhart tell us about the Supreme Court in the early 1900s?

birth control in 1915 and launched a movement with broad social implications. Sanger and her followers saw birth control not only as a sexual and medical reform but also as a means to alter social and political power relationships and to alleviate human misery. By having fewer babies, the working class could constrict the size of the workforce, make possible higher wages, and at the same time refuse to provide "cannon fodder" for the world's armies.

The desire to limit family size was widespread, and in this sense, birth control was nothing new. The birthrate in the United States had been falling consistently throughout the nineteenth century. The average number of children per white family dropped from 7.0 in 1800 to 3.6 by 1900. But the open advocacy of contraception (the use of artificial means to prevent pregnancy) struck many people as both new and shocking, and it was illegal. Anthony Comstock, New York City's commissioner of vice, promoted laws in the 1870s making it a felony not only to sell contraceptive devices like condoms and cervical caps but also to publish information on how to prevent pregnancy.

When Sanger used her militant feminist paper, the *Woman Rebel*, to promote birth control, the U.S. Post Office confiscated Sanger's publication and brought charges of obscenity against her. Facing arrest, she fled to Europe, only to return in 1916 as something of a national celebrity. In her absence, birth control had become linked with free speech and had been taken up as a liberal cause. Under public pressure, the government dropped the charges against Sanger, who undertook a nationwide tour to publicize the birth control cause.

Sanger then took direct action, opening the nation's first birth control clinic in the Brownsville section of Brooklyn in October 1916. Located in the heart of a Jewish and Italian immigrant neighborhood, the clinic attracted 464 clients. On the tenth day, police shut down the clinic and threw Sanger in jail. By then, she had become a national figure, and the cause she championed had gained legitimacy, if not legality. Sanger soon reopened her clinic. After World War I, the birth control movement would become much less radical. Altering her tactics to suit the conservative temper of the times, Sanger sought support from medical doctors and eugenicists. But in its infancy, birth control was part of a radical vision for reforming the world that made common cause with the socialists and the IWW in challenging the limits of progressive reform.

Why was progressivism for white men only?

The day before President Woodrow Wilson's inauguration in March 1913, the largest mass march to date in the nation's history took place as more than five thousand demonstrators took to the streets in Washington to demand the vote for women. A rowdy crowd on hand to celebrate the Democrats' triumph attacked the marchers. Men spat at the suffragists and threw lighted cigarettes and matches at their clothing. "If my wife were where you are," a burly cop told one suffragist, "I'd break her head." But for all the marching, Wilson pointedly ignored woman suffrage in his inaugural address the next day.

The march served as a reminder that the political gains of progressivism were not spread equally throughout the population. As the twentieth century dawned, women still could not vote in most states, although they had won major victories in the West. Increasingly, however, woman suffrage had become an international movement.

Alice Paul, a Quaker social worker who had visited England and participated in suffrage activism there, returned to the United States in 1910 in time to plan the mass march on the eve of Wilson's inauguration and to lobby for a federal amendment to give women the vote. Paul's dramatic tactics alienated many in the National American Woman Suffrage Association. In 1916, Paul founded the militant National Woman's Party, which became the radical voice of the suffrage movement.

Women weren't the only group left out in progressive reform. Progressivism, as it was practiced in the West and South, was tainted with racism by seeking to limit the rights of Asians and African Americans. Anti-Asian bigotry in the West led to a renewal of the Chinese Exclusion Act in 1902. At first, California governor Hiram Johnson stood against the strong anti-Asian prejudice of his state. But in 1913, he caved in to popular pressure and signed the Alien Land Law, which barred Japanese immigrants from purchasing land in California.

South of the Mason-Dixon line, the progressives' racism targeted Black southerners. Progressives preached the disfranchisement of Black voters as a reform. During the bitter electoral fights that had pitted Populists against Democrats in the 1890s, the party of white supremacy held its power by votes purchased or coerced from African Americans. Southern progressives proposed to reform the electoral system by eliminating Black voters. Beginning in 1890 in Mississippi, southern states curtailed the Black vote through devices such as poll taxes (fees required for voting) and literacy tests.

The Progressive Era also witnessed the rise of Jim Crow laws to segregate public facilities. The new railroads precipitated segregation in the South where it had rarely existed before, at least on paper. Soon, separate railcars, separate

◀ **Woman Suffrage Parade**
Suffragists staged a grand parade in Washington, D.C., in 1913, demanding, among other reforms, a constitutional amendment to enfranchise women, as depicted on the float shown here. Angry crowds tried unsuccessfully to break up the parade. The parade illustrated both the strong, organized support for woman suffrage and the implacable opposition.
Schlesinger Library, Radcliffe Institute, Harvard/Bridgeman Images.

waiting rooms, separate bathrooms, and separate dining facilities for Black people sprang up across the South. In courtrooms in Mississippi, Black witnesses were required to swear on a separate Bible.

In the face of this growing repression, Booker T. Washington, the preeminent Black leader of the day, urged caution and restraint. A former slave, Washington opened the Tuskegee Institute in Alabama in 1881 to teach vocational skills to African Americans. He emphasized education and economic progress for his race and urged Black people to put aside issues of political and social equality. In an 1895 speech in Atlanta that came to be known as the Atlanta Compromise, he stated, "In all things that are purely social we can be as separate as the fingers, yet one as the hand in all things essential to mutual progress." Washington's accommodationist policy appealed to whites and elevated "the wizard of Tuskegee" to the role of national spokesman for Black Americans.

The year after Washington proclaimed the Atlanta Compromise, the Supreme Court upheld the legality of racial segregation, affirming in *Plessy v. Ferguson* (1896) the constitutionality of the doctrine of "separate but equal." Black Americans could be segregated in separate schools, restrooms, and other facilities as long as the facilities were "equal" to those provided for whites. Of course, facilities for Black people rarely proved equal.

On issues of race and racial segregation, Woodrow Wilson brought to the White House southern attitudes. He instituted segregation in the federal workforce, especially the Post Office, and approved segregated drinking fountains and restrooms in the nation's capital. When critics attacked the policy, Wilson insisted that segregation was "in the interest of the Negro."

In 1906, a race massacre in Atlanta called into question Booker T. Washington's strategy of uplift and accommodation. Allegations that Black men had raped four white women inflamed the city. For three days in September, the streets of Atlanta ran red with blood as angry white mobs chased and cornered any Black resident they encountered. An estimated 250 African Americans died in the attacks—members of Atlanta's Black middle class along with the poor and derelict. Professor William Crogman of Clark College noted the central irony of the event: "Here we have worked and prayed and tried to make good men and women of our colored population," he observed, "and at our very doorstep the whites kill these good men." The massacre caused many Black people to question Washington's strategy of gradualism and accommodation.

Foremost among Washington's critics stood W. E. B. Du Bois, a Harvard graduate who urged Black people to fight for civil rights and racial justice. In *The Souls of Black Folk* (1903), Du Bois attacked the "Tuskegee Machine," comparing Washington to a political boss who used his influence to silence his critics and reward his followers. Du Bois founded the Niagara movement in 1905, calling for universal male suffrage, civil rights, and leadership composed of a Black intellectual elite or "talented tenth." The Atlanta riot only bolstered his resolve. In 1909, the Niagara movement helped found the National Association for the Advancement of Colored People (NAACP), a coalition of Black and white activists that sought legal and political rights for African Americans through the courts. In the decades that followed, the NAACP came to represent the future for Black people, while Booker T. Washington, who died in 1915, represented the past.

Plessy v. Ferguson
1896 Supreme Court ruling that upheld the legality of racial segregation. According to the ruling, Blacks could be segregated in separate schools, restrooms, and other facilities as long as the facilities were "equal" to those provided for whites.

EQUALITY

DINNER GIVEN AT THE WHITE HOUSE BY PRESIDENT ROOSEVELT TO BOOKER T. WASHINGTON, OCTOBER 17th, 1901

▲ **Booker T. Washington and Theodore Roosevelt Dine at the White House**
Theodore Roosevelt invited Booker T. Washington to the White House in 1901, stirring up a
hornet's nest of controversy that continued into the election of 1904. The Republican
campaign piece pictured shows Roosevelt and a light-skinned Washington sitting under a
portrait of Abraham Lincoln. Democrats' campaign buttons pictured Washington with
darker skin and implied that Roosevelt had "painted the White House black" and favored
"race mingling." The Frent Collection/Getty Images.

REVIEW

How did race, class, and gender shape the limits of progressive
reform?

Conclusion: How did the Progressive Era give rise to the liberal state?

Progressivism's goal was to reform the existing system—by government
intervention if necessary—but without uprooting any of the traditional
American political, economic, or social institutions. As Theodore Roosevelt,
the bellwether of the movement, insisted, "The only true conservative is the man

who resolutely sets his face toward the future." Roosevelt was such a man, and progressivism was such a movement. But although progressivism was never radical, progressives' willingness to use the power of government to regulate business and achieve a measure of social justice redefined liberalism in the twentieth century, tying it to the expanded power of the state.

Progressivism contained many paradoxes. A diverse coalition of individuals and interests, the progressive movement began at the grass roots but left as its legacy a stronger presidency and unprecedented federal involvement in the economy and social welfare. A movement that believed in social justice, progressivism often promoted social control. And while progressives called for greater democracy, they fostered elitism with their worship of experts and efficiency, often failed to champion equality for women, and adopted racist policies toward Asians and Black people.

Whatever its inconsistencies and limitations, progressivism took action to deal with the problems posed by urban industrialism. Progressivism saw grassroots activists address social problems on the local and state levels and search for national solutions. By increasing the power of the presidency, progressives worked to bring about greater social justice and to achieve a better balance between government and business. Jane Addams and Theodore Roosevelt could lay equal claim to the movement that redefined liberalism and launched the liberal state of the twentieth century. War on a global scale would provide progressivism with yet another challenge even before it had completed its ambitious agenda.

CHAPTER REVIEW

EXPLAIN WHY IT MATTERS

progressivism (p. 604)

settlement houses (p. 604)

social gospel (p. 605)

reform Darwinism (p. 610)

muckraking (p. 614)

Roosevelt Corollary (p. 617)

"The New Nationalism" (p. 622)

"The New Freedom" (p. 622)

Socialist Party (p. 625)

Industrial Workers of the World (IWW) (p. 625)

birth control movement (p. 625)

Plessy v. Ferguson (p. 630)

PUT IT ALL TOGETHER

PROGRESSIVES AND PROGRESSIVISM

• How did progressivism differ from earlier reform movements?

• Why was grassroots activism so important to the progressive movement?

THEODORE ROOSEVELT AND PROGRESSIVISM

• What progressive ideals were embodied in Roosevelt's Square Deal?

• What were the limits of progressive reform during Roosevelt's presidency?

WOODROW WILSON AND PROGRESSIVISM

• How did Wilson's progressivism differ from Roosevelt's?

• How did Wilson's progressive agenda change during his presidency?

LOOKING BACKWARD, LOOKING AHEAD

• To what extent, in both the short term and the long term, did progressivism reflect the interests of Black Americans, working-class Americans, and women?

• What progressive ideas and policies continue to influence American social and political life today?

22

WORLD WAR I: THE PROGRESSIVE CRUSADE

1914–1920

This chapter will explore the following questions:

- What was Woodrow Wilson's foreign policy agenda?
- What role did the United States play in World War I?
- What impact did the war have on the home front?
- Did Woodrow Wilson win the war but lose the peace?
- Why was America's transition from war to peace so turbulent?
- Conclusion: Victory, but at what cost?

▶ **George "Brownie" Browne** Training at Fort Slocum, New York, Brownie complained about the army's red tape, bad food, a shortage of equipment, inexperienced officers, lack of sleep, and physical exhaustion. Still, he enjoyed the camaraderie of the camp and was, as this photograph reveals, a happy soldier. When his unit arrived at Saint-Nazaire in October 1917, Brownie was proud to be one of the first doughboys in France. Courtesy of Janet W. Hansen.

AN AMERICAN STORY

George "Brownie" Browne was one of two million soldiers who crossed the Atlantic during World War I to serve in the American Expeditionary Force in France. The twenty-three-year-old civil engineer from Waterbury, Connecticut, volunteered in July 1917, three months after the United States entered the war, serving with the 117th Engineers Regiment, 42nd Division. Two-thirds of the "doughboys" (American soldiers in Europe) saw action during the war, and few white troops saw more than Brownie did.

When the 42nd arrived at the front, veteran French troops taught Brownie's regiment of engineers how to build and maintain trenches, barbed wire entanglements, and artillery and machine-gun positions. Although Brownie came under German fire each day, he wrote Martha Johnson, his girlfriend back home, "the longer I'm here the more spirit I have to 'stick it out' for the good of humanity and the U.S. which is the same thing."

Training ended in the spring of 1918 when the Germans launched a massive offensive in the Champagne region. The German bombardment made the night "as light as daytime, and the ground . . . was a mass of flames and whistling steel from the bursting shells." One doughboy from the 42nd remembered, "Dead bodies were all around me. Americans, French, Hun [Germans] in all phases and positions of death." Another declared that soon "the odor was something fierce. We had to put on our gas masks to keep from getting sick." Eight days of combat cost the 42nd nearly 6,500 dead, wounded, and missing, 20 percent of the division.

After only ten days' rest, Brownie and his unit joined in the first major American offensive, an attack against German defenses at Saint-Mihiel. On September 12, three thousand American artillery launched more than a million rounds against German positions. This time the engineers preceded the advancing infantry, cutting through or blasting any barbed wire that remained. The battle cost the 42nd another twelve hundred casualties, but Brownie was not among them.

At the end of September, the 42nd shifted to the Meuse-Argonne region, where it participated in the most brutal American fighting of the war. And it was there that Brownie's war ended. The Germans fired thousands of poison gas shells, and the gas, "so thick you could cut it with a knife," felled Brownie. When the war ended on November 11, 1918, he was recovering at a camp behind the lines. Discharged from the army in February 1919, Brownie returned home, where he and Martha married. Like the rest of the country, they were eager to get on with their lives.

When the Great War, as the Europeans called it, erupted in 1914, President Woodrow Wilson declared America's absolute neutrality. But trade and principle entangled the United States in Europe's troubles and gradually drew the nation into the conflict. Wilson claimed that America's participation would serve grand purposes and uplift both the United States and the entire world.

At home, the war helped progressives finally achieve their goals of national prohibition and woman suffrage, but it also promoted a vicious attack on Americans' civil liberties. Hyperpatriotism meant intolerance, repression, and vigilante violence. When the war ended, Wilson sailed for Europe to secure a just peace. Unable to dictate terms to the victors, he accepted disappointing compromises. Upon his return to the United States, he met a crushing defeat that marked the end of Wilsonian internationalism abroad. Crackdowns on dissenters, immigrants, racial and ethnic minorities, and unions also signaled the end of the Progressive Era at home.

What was Woodrow Wilson's foreign policy agenda?

Shortly after winning election to the presidency in 1912, Woodrow Wilson confided to a friend: "It would be an irony of fate if my administration had to deal with foreign affairs." Indeed, Wilson had focused his life and career on domestic concerns. In his campaign for the presidency, Wilson had hardly mentioned the world abroad.

Wilson, however, could not avoid the world and the rising tide of militarism, nationalism, and violence that beat against American shores. Trade and economic interests compelled the nation outward. Moreover, Wilson was drawn abroad by his own progressive political principles. He believed that the United States had a moral duty to champion peaceful free trade, national self-determination, and political democracy. "We have no selfish ends to serve," he proclaimed. "We desire no conquest, no dominion. . . . We are but one of the champions of the rights of mankind." Yet as president, Wilson was as ready as any American president to apply military solutions to problems of foreign policy. This readiness led Wilson and the United States into military conflict in Mexico and then in Europe.

How did Wilson seek to tame the Americas?

When he took office, Wilson sought to distinguish his foreign policy from that of his Republican predecessors. To Wilson, Theodore Roosevelt's "big stick" and William Howard Taft's "dollar diplomacy" appeared as crude flexing of military and economic muscle (see chapter 21). To signal a new direction, Wilson appointed William Jennings Bryan, a pacifist, as secretary of state.

But Wilson and Bryan, like Roosevelt and Taft, also believed that the Monroe Doctrine gave the United States special rights and responsibilities in the Western Hemisphere. Issued in 1823 to warn Europeans not to attempt to colonize the Americas again, the doctrine had become a cloak for U.S. domination. Wilson thus authorized U.S. military intervention in Nicaragua, Haiti, and the Dominican Republic, paving the way for U.S. banks and corporations to take financial control. All the while, Wilson believed that U.S. actions were promoting order and democracy (**Map 22.1**).

Wilson's most serious involvement in Latin America came in Mexico. When General Victoriano Huerta seized power by violent means in 1913, most European nations promptly recognized Mexico's new government, but Wilson refused, declaring that he would not support a "government of butchers." In April 1914, Wilson sent eight hundred Marines to seize the port of Veracruz to prevent the unloading of a large shipment of arms for Huerta. Huerta fled to Spain, and the United States welcomed a new government.

But a rebellion erupted among desperately poor farmers, who believed that the new government, aided by U.S. business interests, had betrayed the revolution's promise to help the common people. In January 1916, the rebel army, commanded by Francisco "Pancho" Villa, seized a train carrying gold to

U.S. Intervention in Mexico, 1916–1917

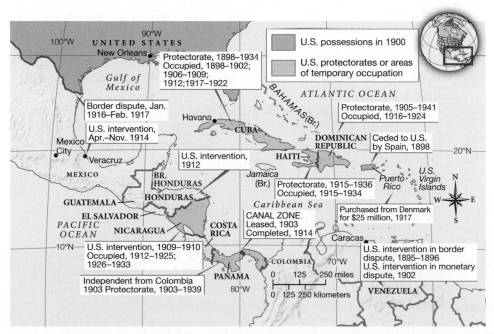

MAP 22.1 ▲ U.S. Involvement in Latin America and the Caribbean, 1895–1941 Victory against Spain in 1898 made Puerto Rico an American possession and Cuba a protectorate. The United States later gained control of the Panama Canal Zone. The nation protected its expanding economic interests with military force by propping up friendly, though not necessarily democratic, governments.

◀ **Francisco "Pancho" Villa** The dashing Mexican revolutionary Pancho Villa gallops along a column of his soldiers in 1914. After Villa's raid into New Mexico in 1916 to punish Americans for aiding his rivals, General John J. Pershing dove across the border, pursued Villa for three hundred miles into Mexico, and then returned home almost a year later empty-handed. Library of Congress, Prints & Photographs Division, Reproduction number LC-DIG-ggbain-15609 (digital file from original negative).

Texas from an American-owned mine in Mexico and killed the seventeen American engineers aboard. In March, Villa's men crossed the border for a predawn raid on Columbus, New Mexico, where they killed eighteen Americans.

Wilson promptly dispatched twelve thousand troops, led by Major General John J. Pershing. But Villa avoided capture, and in January 1917, Wilson recalled Pershing so that he might prepare the army for the possibility of fighting in the Great War.

How did Europe descend into war?

Before 1914, Europe had enjoyed decades of peace, but just beneath the surface lay the potentially destructive forces of nationalism and imperialism. The consolidation of the German and Italian states into unified nations and the similar ambition of Russia to create a Pan-Slavic union initiated new rivalries throughout Europe. As the conviction spread that colonial possessions were a mark of national greatness, competition expanded onto the world stage. Most ominously, Germany's efforts under Kaiser Wilhelm II to challenge Great Britain's world supremacy—by creating industrial muscle at home, an empire abroad, and a mighty navy—threatened the balance of power and thus the peace.

European nations sought to avoid an explosion by developing a complex web of military and diplomatic alliances. By 1914, Germany, Austria-Hungary, and Italy (the **Triple Alliance**) stood opposed to Great Britain, France, and Russia (the **Triple Entente**, also known as "the Allies"). But in their effort to prevent war, Europeans had actually magnified the possibility of large-scale conflict (**Map 22.2**). Treaties, some of them secret, obligated members of the alliances to come to the aid of another member if attacked.

The fatal sequence began on June 28, 1914, in the city of Sarajevo, when a Bosnian Serb terrorist assassinated Archduke Franz Ferdinand, heir to the Austro-Hungarian throne. On July 18, Austria-Hungary declared war on Serbia. Russia announced that it would back the Serbs. Compelled by treaty to support Austria-Hungary, on August 3, Germany attacked Russia and France. In response, on August 4, Great Britain, upholding its pact with France, declared war on Germany. Within weeks, Europe was engulfed in war. The conflict became a world war when Japan, seeing an opportunity to rid itself of European competition in China, joined the cause against Germany.

The evenly matched alliances would fight a disastrous war lasting more than four years, at a cost of 8.5 million soldiers' lives. A war that started with a solitary murder proved impossible to stop.

Triple Alliance
Early-twentieth-century alliance among Germany, Austria-Hungary, and Italy, which was formed as part of a complex network of military and diplomatic agreements intended to prevent war in Europe by balancing power.

Triple Entente
Early-twentieth-century alliance among Great Britain, France, and Russia. The Triple Entente stood opposed to the Triple Alliance.

MAP 22.2 ◀ European Alliances after the Outbreak of World War I
With Germany and Austria-Hungary wedged between their Entente rivals and all parties fully armed, Europe was poised for war when Archduke Franz Ferdinand of Austria-Hungary was assassinated in Sarajevo in June 1914.

What was Wilson's policy of neutrality?

Woodrow Wilson promptly announced that because the war engaged no vital American interest and involved no significant principle, the United States would remain neutral. Neutrality entitled the United States to trade safely with all nations at war, he declared. Unfettered trade, Wilson believed, was not only a right under international law but also a necessity, because in 1913, the U.S. economy had slipped into a recession that the wartime disruption of European trade could drastically worsen.

Although Wilson proclaimed neutrality, his sympathies, like those of most Americans, lay with Great Britain and France. Americans gratefully remembered crucial French assistance in the American Revolution and shared with the British a language, a culture, and a commitment to liberty. Germany, by contrast, was a monarchy with strong militaristic traditions. Still, Wilson insisted on neutrality, in part because he feared the conflict's effects on the United States as a nation of immigrants. As he told the German ambassador, "We definitely have to be neutral, since otherwise our mixed populations would wage war on each other."

Britain's powerful fleet controlled the seas and quickly set up an economic blockade of Germany. The United States vigorously protested, but Britain refused to give up its naval advantage. The blockade actually had little economic impact on the United States. Between 1914 and the spring of 1917, while U.S. trade with Germany evaporated, war-related exports to Britain—food, clothing, steel, and munitions—escalated by some 400 percent, enough to pull the American economy out of its slump. Although the British blockade violated American neutrality, the Wilson administration gradually accepted it, thus beginning the fateful process of alienation from Germany.

Germany retaliated with a submarine blockade of British ports. German *Unterseebooten*, or U-boats, threatened notions of civilized warfare. Unlike surface warships that could harmlessly prevent freighters from entering a war zone, submarines relied on sinking their prey. And once they sank a ship, the tiny U-boats could not pick up survivors. In February 1915, Germany announced that it intended to sink on sight enemy ships heading to the British Isles. On May 7, 1915, a German U-boat torpedoed the British passenger liner *Lusitania*, killing 1,198 passengers, 128 of them U.S. citizens.

Lusitania
British passenger liner torpedoed by a German U-boat on May 7, 1915. The attack killed 1,198 passengers, including 128 Americans, challenging American neutrality and moving the United States a step closer to entering World War I.

American newspapers featured drawings of drowning women and children, and some demanded war. Calmer voices pointed out that the *Lusitania* carried millions of rounds of ammunition and thus was a legitimate target. Secretary of State Bryan resisted the angry calls for war, declaring that a ship carrying war materiel "should not rely on passengers to protect her from attack—it would be like putting women and children in front of an army." He counseled Wilson to warn American citizens that they traveled on ships of warring countries at their own risk.

A peace coalition grew rapidly, promising a "war against war." Sickened by the struggle in Europe that had already cost millions their lives, antiwar Americans vowed to hold Wilson to his word: America must remain neutral. They had many reasons to lobby for peace, but they believed fervently that Germany posed no threat to the American homeland. One peace advocate declared that it would be a "crime" to "send thousands of husbands and fathers and sons to a useless slaughter." The most popular song in 1915 was "I Didn't Raise My Boy to Be a Soldier." Former president Theodore Roosevelt denounced the peace movement as "absolutely futile," as well as "silly." He claimed that it was motivated by "physical cowardice."

German submarine blockade

North Sea

NOR.

DEN.

GREAT BRITAIN

NETH.

BELG.

LUX.

GERMANY

Lusitania sunk May 7, 1915

ATLANTIC OCEAN

FRANCE

SWITZ.

ITALY

PORT.   SPAIN

Sinking of the *Lusitania*, 1915

Wilson sought a middle course that would retain his commitment to peace and neutrality without condoning German attacks on passenger ships. On May 10, 1915, he announced that any further destruction of ships would be regarded as "deliberately unfriendly" and might lead the United States to break diplomatic relations with Germany, essentially demanding that Germany abandon unrestricted submarine warfare. Bryan resigned, predicting that the president had placed the United States on a collision course with Germany. Wilson replaced Bryan with Robert Lansing, who believed that Germany's antidemocratic character and goal of "world dominance" meant that it "must not be permitted to win this war."

After Germany apologized for the civilian deaths on the *Lusitania*, tensions eased. In 1916, Germany went further, promising no more submarine attacks without warning and without provisions for the safety of civilians. Wilson's supporters celebrated the success of his middle-of-the-road strategy.

Wilson's diplomacy proved helpful in his bid for reelection in 1916. In the contest against Republican Charles Evans Hughes, the Democratic Party promoted Wilson under the slogan "He kept us out of war." Wilson felt uneasy with the claim, protesting that "they talk of me as though I were a god. Any little German lieutenant can push us into the war at any time by some calculated outrage." But the Democrats' case for Wilson gave him the victory, though only by the razor-thin margins of 600,000 popular and 23 electoral votes.

How did the United States enter the war?

Step by step, the United States backed away from "absolute neutrality." The consequence of protesting the German blockade of Great Britain but accepting the British blockade of Germany was that by 1916, the United States was supplying the Allies with 40 percent of their war materiel. When France and Britain ran short of money and asked for loans, Wilson argued that "loans by American bankers to any foreign government which is at war are inconsistent with the true spirit of neutrality." But rather than jeopardize America's wartime prosperity, he allowed billions of dollars in loans that kept American goods flowing to Britain and France.

In January 1917, Germany decided that it could no longer afford to allow American shipping to reach Great Britain while Britain's blockage gradually starved Germany. It announced that its navy would resume unrestricted submarine warfare and sink without warning any ship, enemy or neutral, found in the waters off Great Britain. Germany understood that the decision would probably bring the United States into the war, but gambled that its submarines would strangle the British economy and allow German armies to win a military victory in France before American troops arrived in Europe.

Resisting demands for war, Wilson only broke off diplomatic relations with Germany. On February 25, 1917, British authorities informed Wilson of a secret telegram sent by the German foreign secretary, Arthur Zimmermann, to the German minister in Mexico. It promised that in the event of war between Germany and the United States, Germany would see that Mexico regained its "lost provinces" of Texas, New Mexico, and Arizona if Mexico would declare war against the United States. Wilson angrily responded to the Zimmermann telegram by asking Congress to approve a policy of "armed neutrality" that would allow merchant ships to fight back against attackers.

In March, German submarines sank five American vessels off Britain, killing sixty-six Americans. On April 2, the president asked Congress to issue a declaration of war. Still, he called for a "war without hate" and declared that America fought only to "vindicate the principles of peace and justice." He promised a world made "safe for democracy." On April 6, 1917, by majorities of 373 to 50 in the House and 82 to 6 in the Senate, Congress voted to declare war.

Wilson feared what war would do at home. He said despairingly, "Once lead this people into war, and they'll forget there ever was such a thing as tolerance. To fight you must be brutal and ruthless, and the spirit of ruthless brutality will infect Congress, the courts, the policeman on the beat, the man in the street."

REVIEW

Why did President Wilson fail to maintain U.S. neutrality during World War I?

What role did the United States play in World War I?

American soldiers sailed for France eager to do their part in making the world safe for democracy. Although Black soldiers eventually won respect under the French, they faced discrimination under American commanders. Some doughboys maintained their idealism to the end. The majority of American soldiers found little that was noble in rats, lice, and poison gas and, despite the progressives' hopes, little to elevate the human soul in a landscape of utter destruction and death.

How did the United States build an army?

When America entered the war, Britain and France were nearly exhausted after almost three years of conflict. Millions of soldiers had perished; food and morale were dangerously low. Another Allied power, Russia, was in turmoil. In March 1917, a revolution had forced Czar Nicholas II to abdicate, and one year later, in a separate peace with Germany, the **Bolshevik** revolutionary government withdrew Russia from the war. Peace with Russia allowed Germany to withdraw hundreds of thousands of its soldiers from the eastern front and to deploy them against the Allies on the western front in France.

On May 18, 1917, Wilson signed a sweeping Selective Service Act, authorizing a draft of all young men into the armed forces. Conscription transformed a tiny volunteer military of 80,000 men into a vast army and navy. Draft boards eventually inducted 2.8 million men into the armed services, in addition to the 2 million who volunteered. Among the 4.8 million men under arms, 370,000 were Black Americans. Nearly 64,000 men became conscientious objectors, and remarkably, 3 million simply evaded service.

Training camps sought to transform raw white recruits into fighting men. Progressives in the government were also determined that the camps turn out soldiers with the highest moral and civic values. To provide recruits with "invisible armor," YMCA workers and veterans of the settlement house and playground movements led them in games, singing, and college extension courses. The army asked soldiers to stop thinking about sex, explaining that a "man who is thinking below the belt is not efficient." Wilson's choice to command the army on the battlefields of France, Major General John "Black Jack" Pershing, was as morally upright as he was militarily uncompromising. Described by one observer as "lean, clean, keen," he gave progressives perfect confidence.

What did Americans experience in France?

At the front, the **American Expeditionary Force (AEF)** discovered a desperate situation. The war had degenerated into a stalemate, with armies dug into trenches stretching hundreds of miles across France. Huddling in the mud among the corpses and rats, soldiers were separated from the enemy by only a few hundred yards of no-man's-land. When ordered "over the top," troops raced desperately toward the enemy's trenches, only to be entangled in barbed wire, enveloped in poison gas, and mowed down by machine guns. The three-day battle of the Somme in 1916 cost the

Bolshevik
Russian revolutionary. Bolsheviks forced Czar Nicholas II to abdicate and seized power in Russia in 1917. In a separate peace with Germany, the Bolshevik government withdrew Russia from World War I.

American Expeditionary Force (AEF)
U.S. armed forces under the command of General John Pershing who fought under a separate American command in Europe during World War I. They helped defeat Germany when they entered the conflict in full force in 1918.

French and British forces 600,000 dead and wounded, and the Germans 500,000. The deadliest battle of the war allowed the Allies to advance their trenches only a few meaningless miles.

Still, U.S. troops saw almost no combat in 1917. Troops continued to train and used much of their free time to explore places that most of them could otherwise never hope to see. True to the crusader image, American officials allowed only uplifting tourism. The temptations of Paris were off-limits. French premier Georges Clemenceau's offer to supply American troops with licensed prostitutes was declined with the half-serious remark that if Wilson found out, he would stop the war.

Black soldiers had a different experience. Rigidly segregated during training, Black recruits were usually assigned to labor battalions and faced crude abuse and miserable living conditions. When Black troops arrived in Europe, white commanders insisted on maintaining American racial standards and warned the French against "spoiling the Negroes."

In February 1918, General Pershing received an urgent call from the French for help on the front lines. Pershing sent what he considered less valuable Black regiments from the 92nd Division. At the front, they were integrated into the French army. The Black 369th Regiment spent 191 days in battle, longer than any other American outfit, and won more medals than any other American combat unit. Black soldiers recognized the irony of having to serve with the French to gain respect.

The vacation for white soldiers ended abruptly in March 1918 when a million German soldiers punched a hole in the Allied lines. Pershing finally committed the AEF to combat. In May and June, at Cantigny and then at Château-Thierry, the eager but green Americans checked the German advance with a series of assaults (**Map 22.3**). Then they headed toward the forest stronghold of Belleau

◀ **Black Participation in the War** This photograph captures the joy and pride African American troops felt when they arrived in New York City after the war. The ship carried the famous 369th New York Infantry, Black soldiers who served valiantly with the French but never fought alongside American troops. National Archives, photo no. 165-WW-127(42).

MAP 22.3 ▶ The American Expeditionary Force, 1918
In the last year of the war, the AEF joined the French army on the western front to respond to the final German offensive and pursue the retreating enemy until surrender.

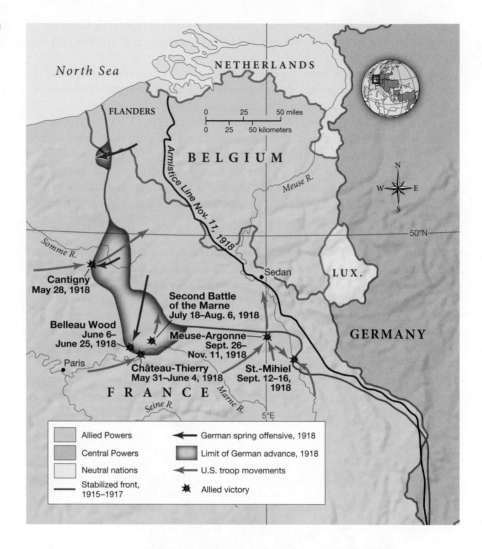

Wood. After charging through a wheat field against withering machine-gun fire, the Marines plunged into hand-to-hand combat. Victory came hard, but a German report praised the enemy's spirit, noting that "the Americans' nerves are not yet worn out." Indeed, it was German morale that was on the verge of cracking.

In the summer of 1918, the Allies launched a massive counteroffensive that would end the war. One-quarter of a million U.S. troops joined in the rout of German forces along the Marne River. In September, more than a million Americans took part in the assault that threw the Germans back from positions along the Meuse River. In four brutal days, the AEF sustained 45,000 casualties. In November, a revolt against the German government sent Kaiser Wilhelm II fleeing to Holland. On November 11, 1918, a delegation from the newly established German republic met with the French high command to sign an armistice that brought the fighting to an end.

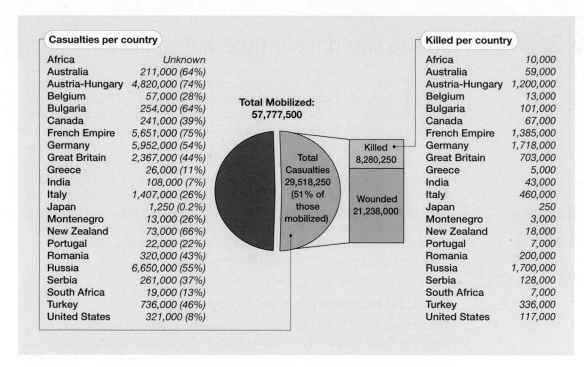

Casualties per country

Africa	Unknown
Australia	211,000 (64%)
Austria-Hungary	4,820,000 (74%)
Belgium	57,000 (28%)
Bulgaria	254,000 (64%)
Canada	241,000 (39%)
French Empire	5,651,000 (75%)
Germany	5,952,000 (54%)
Great Britain	2,367,000 (44%)
Greece	26,000 (11%)
India	108,000 (7%)
Italy	1,407,000 (26%)
Japan	1,250 (0.2%)
Montenegro	13,000 (26%)
New Zealand	73,000 (66%)
Portugal	22,000 (22%)
Romania	320,000 (43%)
Russia	6,650,000 (55%)
Serbia	261,000 (37%)
South Africa	19,000 (13%)
Turkey	736,000 (46%)
United States	321,000 (8%)

Total Mobilized:
57,777,500

Total
Casualties
29,518,250
(51% of
those
mobilized)

Killed
8,280,250

Wounded
21,238,000

Killed per country

Africa	10,000
Australia	59,000
Austria-Hungary	1,200,000
Belgium	13,000
Bulgaria	101,000
Canada	67,000
French Empire	1,385,000
Germany	1,718,000
Great Britain	703,000
Greece	5,000
India	43,000
Italy	460,000
Japan	250
Montenegro	3,000
New Zealand	18,000
Portugal	7,000
Romania	200,000
Russia	1,700,000
Serbia	128,000
South Africa	7,000
Turkey	336,000
United States	117,000

FIGURE 22.1 ▲ **Global Comparison: Casualties of the First World War** Historians disagree about the number of casualties in World War I. Record keeping in many countries was poor. The destructive nature of the war meant that countless soldiers were wholly obliterated or instantly buried. This chart shows estimates of casualties (the combined number of wounded and killed soldiers) per country. The percentage listed with each casualty figure represents the portion of soldiers mobilized who became casualties. However approximate, these figures make clear that the conflict that raged from 1914 to 1918 was a truly catastrophic world war. Although soldiers came from almost every part of the globe, the human devastation was not evenly distributed. Which country suffered the most casualties? Which country suffered the greatest percentage of casualties? What do you think was the principal reason that the United States suffered a smaller percentage of casualties than most other nations?

The history of the AEF was brief, bloody, and victorious. Germany had gambled that it could defeat Britain and France before the Americans could raise, train, and ship an army to France, but it had miscalculated badly. By the end, 112,000 AEF soldiers perished from wounds and disease, while another 230,000 Americans suffered casualties but survived. Only the Civil War, which lasted much longer, had cost more American lives. European nations, however, suffered much greater losses: 1.7 million Germans, 1.7 million Russians, 1.4 million French, and 700,000 Britons (**Figure 22.1**). Where they had fought, the landscape was as blasted and barren as the moon.

REVIEW

How did the AEF contribute to the defeat of Germany?

What impact did the war have on the home front?

Many progressives hoped that the war would improve the quality of American life as well as free Europe from tyranny and militarism. Troop mobilization helped propel the crusades for woman suffrage and prohibition to success. Progressives enthusiastically channeled industrial and agricultural production into the vast war effort. Labor shortages caused by workers entering the military provided new opportunities for women in the booming wartime economy. With labor at a premium, unionized workers gained higher pay and shorter hours. To instill loyalty in Americans whose ancestry was rooted in the belligerent nations, Wilson launched a campaign to foster patriotism, but fanning patriotism led to suppressing dissent. When the government launched a harsh assault on civil liberties, mobs gained license to attack those whom they considered disloyal. As Wilson feared, democracy took a beating at home when the nation undertook its crusade for democracy abroad.

What did progressives want from the war?

Progressives embraced the idea that the war could be an agent of national improvement. The Wilson administration, realizing that the federal government needed to mobilize the nation's human and physical resources, created new agencies to manage the war effort. Bernard Baruch, a Wall Street stockbroker, headed the War Industries Board, charged with stimulating and directing industrial production. Baruch brought management and labor together into a team that produced everything from boots to bullets and made U.S. troops the best-equipped soldiers in the world.

Herbert Hoover, a self-made millionaire engineer, headed the Food Administration. He led remarkably successful "Hooverizing" campaigns for "meatless" Mondays and "wheatless" Wednesdays and other ways of conserving resources. Guaranteed high prices, the American heartland not only supplied the needs of U.S. citizens and armed forces but also became the breadbasket of America's allies.

Wartime agencies multiplied: The Railroad Administration directed railroad traffic, the Fuel Administration coordinated the coal industry and other fuel suppliers, the Shipping Board organized the merchant marine, and the National War Labor Policies Board resolved labor disputes. Their successes gave most progressives reason to believe that, indeed, war and reform marched together. Still, skeptics like Wisconsin senator Robert La Follette declared that Wilson's promises of permanent peace and democracy were a case of "the blind leading the blind."

Industrial leaders found that wartime agencies enforced efficiency, which helped corporate profits triple. Some working people also had cause to celebrate: Mobilization meant high prices for farmers and plentiful jobs at high wages in the new war industries (**Figure 22.2**). Because increased industrial production required peaceful labor relations, the National War Labor Policies Board enacted the eight-hour day, a living minimum wage, and collective bargaining rights in some industries. The American Federation of Labor (AFL) saw its membership soar from 2.7 million to more than 5 million.

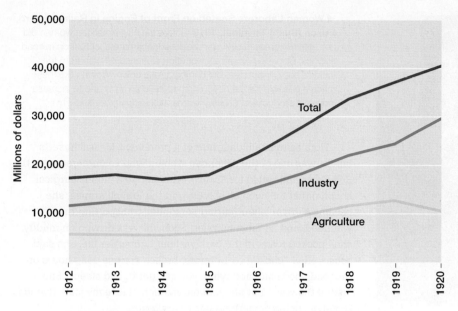

FIGURE 22.2 ◄ **Industrial Wages, 1912–1920**
With help from unions and progressive reformers, wageworkers gradually improved their economic condition. The entry of millions of young men into the armed forces during World War I caused labor shortages and led to a rapid surge in industrial wages.

Agriculture: cash receipts.
Industry: includes mining, electric power, manufacturing, construction, and communications.

The war also provided a huge boost to the crusade to ban alcohol. By 1917, prohibitionists had convinced nineteen states to go dry. Liquor's opponents now argued that banning alcohol would make the cause of democracy powerful and pure. At the same time, shutting down the distilleries would save millions of bushels of grain that could feed the United States and its allies. "Shall the many have food or the few drink?" the drys asked. Prohibition received an additional boost because many of the breweries had German names—Schlitz, Pabst, and Anheuser-Busch, for example. In December 1917, Congress passed the **Eighteenth Amendment**, which banned the manufacture, transportation, and sale of alcohol. After swift ratification by the states, the prohibition amendment went into effect on January 1, 1920.

How did the war aid the advance of women?

Women had made real strides during the Progressive Era, and war presented new opportunities. More than 25,000 women served in France. About half were nurses. The others drove ambulances; ran canteens for the Salvation Army, Red Cross, and YMCA; worked with French civilians in devastated areas; and acted as telephone operators and war correspondents. Like men who joined the war effort, they believed that they were taking part in a great national crusade. "I am more than willing to live as a soldier and know of the hardships I would have to undergo," one canteen worker declared when applying to go overseas, "but I want to help my country. . . . I want . . . to do the *real* work." And like men, women struggled against disillusionment in France. One woman explained: "Over in America, we thought we knew something about the war . . . but when you get here the difference is [like the one between] studying the laws of electricity and being struck by lightning."

Eighteenth Amendment (prohibition)
Constitutional amendment banning the manufacture, transportation, and sale of alcohol. Congress passed the amendment in December 1917, and it went into effect in January 1920.

◄ **Women Laborers Seated on Front of Engine in Railroad Yard, Busch (Bush) Terminal, 1918** Before the war, American women did not normally dress in overalls, wield sledgehammers, or rest on railroad engines. But when America's war effort siphoned off men from the nation's heavy industries, old barriers broke down. Women like these made it possible for the nation both to build an army and to increase industrial production. Courtesy National Archives, photo no. 86-G-6T(1).

Nora Saltonstall, daughter of a prominent Massachusetts family, was one of the American women who volunteered with the Red Cross and sailed for France. Attached to a mobile surgical hospital that followed closely behind the French armies, she became a driver, chauffeuring personnel, transporting the wounded, and hauling supplies. Soon she was driving on muddy, shell-pocked roads in the dark without lights. Her life, she said, consisted of "choked carburetors, broken springs, long hours on the road, food snatched when you can get it, and sleep." She "hated the war," but she told her mother, "I love my job." She was proud of "doing something necessary here."

At home, long-standing barriers against hiring women fell when millions of workingmen became soldiers and few new immigrant workers crossed the Atlantic. Tens of thousands of women found work with the railroads and in defense plants as welders, metalworkers, and heavy machine operators. A Black woman, a domestic before the war, celebrated her job as a laborer in a railroad yard: "We . . . do not have to work as hard as at housework which requires us to be on duty from six o'clock in the morning until nine or ten at night, with might[y] little time off and at very poor wages." Other women found white-collar work. Between 1910 and 1920, the number of women clerks doubled. Before the war ended, more than a million women had found work in war industries. One women's rights advocate exaggerated when she declared, "At last . . . women are coming into the labor and festival of life on equal terms with men," but women had made real economic strides.

The most dramatic advance for women came in the political arena. Before the war, suffragists had achieved some success adopting a state-by-state approach (**Map 22.4**). More commonly, voting rights for women met strong hostility and defeat. After 1910, suffrage leaders added a federal campaign to amend the Constitution to the traditional state-by-state strategy for suffrage.

The radical wing of the suffragists, led by Alice Paul, picketed the White House, where the marchers unfurled banners that proclaimed "America Is Not a Democracy. Twenty Million Women Are Denied the Right to Vote." They chained themselves to fences and went to jail, where many engaged in hunger strikes. "They seem bent on making their cause as obnoxious as possible," Woodrow Wilson declared. His wife, Edith, detested the idea of "masculinized" voting women. But membership in the mainstream organization, the National American Woman Suffrage Association (NAWSA), led by Carrie Chapman Catt, soared to some two million. Seeing the handwriting on the wall, the Republican and Progressive parties endorsed woman suffrage in 1916.

MAP ACTIVITY

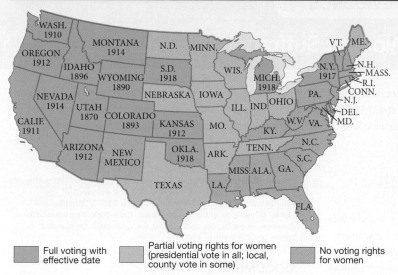

MAP 22.4 ◄ Women's Voting Rights before the Nineteenth Amendment The long campaign for women's voting rights reversed the pioneer epic that moved from east to west. From its first successes in the new democratic West, suffrage rolled eastward toward the entrenched, male-dominated public life of the Northeast and South.

READING THE MAP: What was the first state to grant woman suffrage? How many states extended full voting rights to women before 1914? How many extended these rights during World War I (1914–1918)?

CONNECTIONS: Suffragists redirected their focus during the war. What strategies did they use then?

Legend:
- Full voting with effective date
- Partial voting rights for women (presidential vote in all; local, county vote in some)
- No voting rights for women

In 1918, Wilson finally gave his support to suffrage, calling the amendment "vital to the winning of the war." He conceded that it would be wrong not to reward the wartime "partnership of suffering and sacrifice" with a "partnership of privilege and right." By linking their cause to the wartime emphasis on national unity, the advocates of woman suffrage finally triumphed. In 1919, Congress passed the **Nineteenth Amendment**, granting women the vote, and by August 1920 the required two-thirds of the states had ratified it. **(See "Analyzing Historical Evidence: The Final Push for Woman Suffrage" on page 650.)**

What happened to dissent in wartime?

When Congress committed the nation to war, only a handful of peace advocates resisted the tide of patriotism. A group of professional women, led by settlement house leader Jane Addams and economics professor Emily Greene Balch, denounced what Addams described as "the pathetic belief in the regenerative results of war." But after America entered the conflict, advocates for peace were labeled cowards and traitors.

To suppress criticism of the war, Wilson stirred up patriotic fervor. In 1917, the president created the Committee on Public Information under the direction of George Creel, a journalist who became the nation's cheerleader for war. Creel sent "Four-Minute Men," a squad of 75,000 volunteers, around the country to give brief pep talks that celebrated successes on the battlefields and in the factories. Posters, pamphlets, and cartoons depicted brave American soldiers and sailors defending freedom and democracy against the evil "Huns," the derogatory nickname applied to German soldiers.

America rallied around Creel's campaign. The film industry cranked out prowar melodramas and taught audiences to hiss at the German kaiser. Colleges and universities generated war propaganda in the guise of scholarship. When professor

Nineteenth Amendment (woman suffrage) Constitutional amendment granting women the vote. Congress passed the amendment in 1919, and it was ratified in August 1920. Like proponents of prohibition, the advocates of woman suffrage triumphed by linking their cause to the war.

ANALYZING HISTORICAL EVIDENCE

The Final Push for Woman Suffrage

By the early twentieth century, the women's movement had mobilized millions, who increasingly concentrated on the passage of an amendment to the U.S. Constitution to ensure women's voting rights. Nothing came easily to the suffragists, but in 1920 their passion and courage were rewarded by the ratification of the Nineteenth Amendment.

DOCUMENT 1
Politicking for Suffrage

While radical suffragists chained themselves to the White House fence and went on hunger strikes, other women followed more traditional political channels — methodically gathering petitions, lobbying legislators, building alliances, and rounding up votes. Mary Garrett Hay, vice president of the National American Woman Suffrage Association (NAWSA), reports her efforts with New York state legislators.

New York City, N.Y.
March 13th, 1919
Mrs. Maud Wood Park
1626 Rhode Island Avenue
Washington, D.C.

Dear Mrs. Park,
. . . I kept in very close touch on the telephone and telegraph wire with New York Congressmen and they reported to me, really twice a day what was going on, as far as Speaker, Floor Leader and Suffrage Committee was concerned. I can do more in the House than in the Senate, and I have asked Mr. Hays on the long distance telephone to try and see that things are perfectly straight for our Cause there.

    Things will be all right, I believe, but I have made up my mind not to trust either Democrats or Republicans, until the Suffrage Amendment is passed; however, I do not say this to the men[,] only to you, and I shall keep my eyes and ears open and busy, and on the job all I can.

Source: Kathryn Kish Sklar and Kathleen Hoerger, "How Did Suffragists Lobby to Obtain Congressional Approval of a Woman Suffrage Amendment to the U.S. Constitution, 1917–1920?," *Women and Social Movements in the United States, 1600–2000*, Document 10. Courtesy of the Schlesinger Library, Radcliffe Institute, Harvard University, Cambridge, MA.

DOCUMENT 2
The President Intervenes

Although some people urged suffragists to muffle their demands during the war so that the nation could concentrate on victory, Carrie Chapman Catt, president of the NAWSA since 1915, pressed on, recognizing that the war offered a special opportunity. Catt prodded President Woodrow Wilson quietly but persistently, and on September 30, 1918, Wilson finally intervened directly, urging the Senate to pass the Nineteenth Amendment. His argument on behalf of democracy mirrored precisely that of radical suffragists who were protesting in front of the White House.

[The Senate's] adoption is, in my judgment, clearly necessary to the successful prosecution of the war and the successful realization of the objects for which the war is being fought.
    . . . If we be indeed democrats and wish to lead the world to democracy, we can ask other peoples to accept in proof of our sincerity and our ability to lead them whither they wish to be led, nothing less persuasive and convincing than our actions.
    . . . They are looking to the great, powerful, famous democracy of the West to lead them to a new day for

which they have so long waited; and they think, in their logical simplicity, that democracy means that women shall play their part in affairs alongside men and upon an equal footing with them.

. . . We have made partners of the women in this war. Shall we admit them only to a partnership of suffering and sacrifice and toil and not to a partnership of privilege and right?

This war could not have been fought, either by the other nations engaged or by America, if it had not been for the services of the women — services rendered in every sphere. . . .

. . . I tell you plainly that this measure which I urge upon you is vital to the winning of the war and to the energies alike of preparation and of battle.

. . . And not to winning the war only. It is vital to the right solution of the great problems which we must settle, and settle immediately, when the war is over. We shall need in our vision of affairs, as we have never needed them before, the sympathy and insight and clear moral instinct of the women of the world. . . . We shall need their moral sense to preserve what is right and fine and worthy in our system of life as well as to discover just what it is that ought to be purified and reformed. Without their counsellings we shall be only half wise.

Source: "Appeal of President Wilson to the Senate of the United States to Submit the Federal Amendment for Woman Suffrage Delivered in Person Sept. 30, 1918," in *History of Woman Suffrage*, vol. 5, *1900–1920*, ed. Ida Husted Harper (New York: NAWSA, 1922), 761–63.

DOCUMENT 3
Reflections on Victory

Catt celebrates the passage of the Nineteenth Amendment in this letter to her staff at the NAWSA on Thanksgiving Day 1920. She reflects on the long road to victory and considers the satisfactions of the journey.

I have kept Thanksgiving sacred to reflections upon the long trail behind us, and the triumph which was its inevitable conclusion. John Adams said long after the Revolution that only about one third of the people were for it, a third being against it, and the remaining third utterly indifferent. Perhaps this proportion applies to all movements. At least a third of the women were for our cause at the end. . . . As I look back over the years . . . I realize that the greatest thing in the long campaign for us was not its crowning victory, but the discipline it gave us all. . . . It was a great crusade, the world has seen none more wonderful. . . . My admiration, love and reverence go out to that band which fought and won a revolution . . . with congratulations that we were permitted to establish a new and good thing in the world.

Source: Carrie Chapman Catt to NAWSA Office Staff, "Thanksgiving Day 1920," in *Women's Suffrage in America: An Eyewitness History*, ed. Elizabeth Frost and Kathryn Cullen-DuPont (New York: Facts on File, 1992), 335–36.

Questions for Analysis

ANALYZE THE EVIDENCE: What, according to Woodrow Wilson, would America's rejection of the Nineteenth Amendment have jeopardized?

CONSIDER THE CONTEXT: How did the First World War further the cause of woman suffrage in the United States?

ASK HISTORICAL QUESTIONS: What were the strategic differences between the NAWSA and the more radical wing of the woman suffrage movement? Which was more effective, and why?

James McKeen Cattell of Columbia University urged that America seek peace with Germany short of victory, university president Nicholas Murray Butler fired him on the grounds that "what had been folly is now treason."

A firestorm of anti-German passion erupted. Across the nation, "100% American" campaigns enlisted ordinary people to sniff out disloyalty. German, the most widely taught foreign language in 1914, practically disappeared from the nation's schools. Targeting German-born Americans, the *Saturday Evening Post* declared that it was time to rid the country of "the scum of the melting pot." Anti-German action reached its extreme with the lynching of Robert Prager, a German-born baker with socialist leanings. Persuaded by the defense lawyer who praised what he called a "patriotic murder," the jury at the trial of the killers took only twenty-five minutes to acquit.

As hysteria increased, the campaign reached absurd levels. Menus across the nation changed German toast to French toast and sauerkraut to liberty cabbage. In Milwaukee, vigilantes mounted a machine gun outside the Pabst Theater to prevent the staging of Schiller's *Wilhelm Tell*, a powerful protest against tyranny. The fiancée of one of the war's leading critics, caught dancing on the dunes of Cape Cod, was held on suspicion of signaling to German submarines.

The Wilson administration's zeal in suppressing dissent contrasted sharply with its war aims of defending democracy. In the name of self-defense, the Espionage Act (June 1917), the Trading with the Enemy Act (October 1917), and the Sedition Act (May 1918) gave the government sweeping powers to punish any opinion or activity it considered "disloyal, profane, scurrilous, or abusive." When Postmaster General Albert Burleson blocked mailing privileges for dissenting publications, dozens of journals were forced to close down. Of the fifteen hundred individuals eventually charged with sedition, all but a dozen had merely spoken words the government found objectionable.

One of them was Eugene V. Debs, the leader of the Socialist Party, who was convicted under the Espionage Act and sentenced to ten years. In a speech on June 16, 1918, Debs declared that the United States was not fighting a noble war to make the world safe for democracy but had joined greedy European imperialists seeking to conquer the globe. The government claimed that Debs had crossed the line between legitimate dissent and criminal speech. From the Atlanta penitentiary, Debs argued that he was just telling the truth, like hundreds of his friends who were also in jail.

The president hoped that national commitment to the war would silence partisan politics, but his Republican rivals used the war as a weapon against the Democrats. The trick was to oppose Wilson's conduct of the war but not the war itself. Republicans outshouted Wilson on the nation's need to mobilize for war but then complained that Wilson's War Industries Board was a tyrannical agency that crushed free enterprise. As the war progressed, Republicans gathered power against the Democrats, who had narrowly reelected Wilson in 1916.

In 1918, Republicans gained a narrow majority in both the House and the Senate. The end of Democratic control of Congress not only halted further domestic reform but divided political power between a Democratic president and a Republican Congress likely to challenge Wilson's plans for international cooperation.

REVIEW

How did progressive ideals fare during wartime?

Did Woodrow Wilson win the war but lose the peace?

Wilson decided to reaffirm his noble war ideals by announcing his peace aims before the end of the fighting. He hoped the victorious Allies would adopt his plan for international democracy, but he was sorely disappointed. America's allies understood that Wilson's principles jeopardized their own postwar plans for the acquisition of enemy territory, new colonial empires, and reparations. Wilson also faced strong opposition at home from those who feared that his enthusiasm for international cooperation would undermine American independence.

What were Wilson's Fourteen Points?

On January 8, 1918, ten months before the armistice in Europe, President Wilson revealed to Congress his **Fourteen Points**, his blueprint for a new democratic world order. The first five points affirmed basic liberal ideals: an end to secret treaties, freedom of the seas, removal of economic barriers to free trade, reduction of weapons of war, and recognition of the rights of colonized peoples. The next eight points supported the right to self-determination of European peoples who had been dominated by Germany or its allies. Wilson's fourteenth point called for a "general association of nations"—a **League of Nations**—to provide "mutual guarantees of political independence and territorial integrity to great and small states alike." A League of Nations reflected Wilson's lifelong dream of a "parliament of man." Only such an organization of "peace-loving nations," he believed, could justify the war and secure a lasting peace.

What part did Wilson play at the Paris peace conference?

From January to June 1919, the eyes of the world focused on Paris. Inspired by his mission, Wilson decided to head the U.S. delegation. He said he owed it to the American soldiers. "It is now my duty," he announced, "to play my full part in making good what they gave their life's blood to obtain." A dubious British diplomat retorted that Wilson was drawn to Paris "as a debutante is entranced by the prospect of her first ball." Leaving the country at a time when his political opponents challenged his leadership was risky enough, but his stubborn refusal to include prominent Republicans in the delegation eventually cost him his dream of a new world order.

After four terrible years of war, the common people of Europe almost worshipped Wilson, believing that he would create a safer, more decent world. When the peace conference convened at Louis XIV's magnificent palace at Versailles, however, Wilson encountered a different reception. To the Allied leaders, Wilson appeared a naive and impractical moralist. His desire to gather former enemies within a new international democratic order showed how little he understood hard European realities. Georges Clemenceau, premier of France, claimed that Wilson "believed you could do everything by formulas" and "empty theory." Disparaging the Fourteen Points, he added, "God himself was content with ten commandments."

Fourteen Points
Woodrow Wilson's plan, proposed in 1918, to create a new democratic world order with lasting peace. Wilson's plan affirmed basic liberal ideals, supported the right to self-determination, and called for the creation of a League of Nations. Wilson compromised on his plan at the 1919 Paris peace conference, and the U.S. Senate refused to ratify the resulting treaty.

League of Nations
International organization proposed in Woodrow Wilson's Fourteen Points that was designed to secure enduring peace and collective security through peaceful means. The U.S. Senate refused to ratify the Treaty of Versailles, and the United States never became a member of the league.

The Allies wanted to fasten blame for the war on Germany, totally disarm it, and make it pay so dearly that it would never threaten its neighbors again. The French demanded retribution in the form of territory containing Germany's richest mineral resources. The British made it clear that they were not about to give up the powerful weapon of naval blockade for the vague principle of freedom of the seas.

The Allies forced Wilson to make drastic compromises. In return for France's moderating its territorial claims, he agreed to support Article 231 of the peace treaty, assigning war guilt to Germany. Though saved from permanently losing Rhineland territory to the French, Germany was outraged at being singled out as the instigator of the war and being saddled with more than $33 billion in damages. Many Germans felt that their nation had been betrayed. After agreeing to an armistice in the belief that peace terms would be based in Wilson's generous Fourteen Points, they faced hardship and humiliation instead.

Wilson had better success in establishing the principle of national self-determination. But from the beginning, Secretary of State Robert Lansing knew that the concept was "simply loaded with dynamite." Lansing wondered, "What unit has he in mind? Does he mean a race, a territorial area, or a community?" Even Wilson was vague about what self-determination actually meant. "When I gave utterance to those words," he admitted, "I said them without the knowledge that nationalities existed, which are coming to us day after day." Lansing suspected that the notion "will raise hopes which can never be realized. It will, I fear, cost thousands of lives. In the end it is bound to be discredited, to be called the dream of an idealist who failed to realize the danger until it was too late."

Yet partly on the basis of self-determination, the conference redrew the map of Europe and parts of the rest of the world. Portions of Austria-Hungary were ceded to Italy, Poland, and Romania, and the remainder was reassembled into Austria, Hungary, Czechoslovakia, and Yugoslavia—independent republics whose boundaries were drawn with attention to concentrations of major ethnic groups.

More arbitrarily, the Ottoman empire was carved up into small mandates (including Palestine) run by local leaders but under the control of France and Great Britain. The conference reserved the mandate system for those regions it deemed insufficiently "civilized" to have full independence. Thus, the reconstructed nations—each beset with ethnic and nationalist rivalries—faced the challenge of making a new democratic government work (**Map 22.5**). Many of today's bitterest disputes—in the Balkans and Iraq, between Greece and Turkey, between Arabs and Jews—have roots in the decisions made in Paris in 1919.

Wilson hoped that self-determination would also dictate the fate of Germany's colonies in Asia and Africa. But the Allies, who had taken over the colonies during the war, merely allowed the League of Nations a mandate to administer them. Technically, the mandate system rejected imperialism, but in reality it allowed the Allies to maintain control. Thus, while denying Germany its colonies, the Allies added to their own empires.

The cause of democratic equality suffered another setback when the peace conference rejected Japan's call for a statement of racial equality in the treaty. Wilson's belief in the superiority of whites, as well as his apprehension about how white Americans would respond to such a declaration, led him to oppose the

MAP 22.5 ◄ Europe after World War I The post–World War I settlement redrew boundaries to create new nations based on ethnic groupings. Within defeated Germany and Russia, the outcome left bitter peoples who resolved to recover the territory taken from them.

clause. To soothe hurt feelings, Wilson agreed to grant Japan a mandate over the Shantung Peninsula in northern China, which had formerly been controlled by Germany. The gesture mollified Japan's moderate leaders, but the military faction preparing to take over the country used bitterness toward racist Western colonialism to build support for expanding Japanese power throughout Asia.

Closest to Wilson's heart was finding a new way to manage international relations. In Wilson's view, war had discredited the old strategy of balance of power. Instead, the League of Nations he proposed would provide collective security. It would establish rules of international conduct and resolve conflicts between nations through rational and peaceful means. When the Allies agreed to the league, Wilson was overjoyed. He believed that the league would rectify the errors his colleagues had forced on him in Paris.

To some Europeans and Americans, the **Versailles treaty** came as a bitter disappointment. Wilson's admirers were shocked that the president dealt in compromise like any other politician. But without Wilson's presence, the treaty that was signed on June 28, 1919, surely would have been more vindictive. Wilson returned

Versailles treaty
Treaty signed on June 28, 1919, that ended World War I. The agreement redrew the map of the world and assigned Germany sole responsibility for the war, saddling it with a debt of $33 billion in war damages. Many Germans felt betrayed by the treaty.

◄ *The Signing of Peace in the Hall of Mirrors, Versailles, 28th June 1919,* **by Sir William Orpen** Set in the dazzling Hall of Mirrors at Versailles, built for Louis XIV as a symbol of his power, this painting captures the moment when the treaty was signed in June 1919. The leaders in charge of putting the world back together after the Great War are gathered at the table. Wilson is seated fifth from the left, dignified but seemingly isolated, while the French premier Georges Clemenceau and the British prime minister David Lloyd George are huddled together at Wilson's left. VCG Wilson/ Corbis via Getty Images.

READING THE IMAGE: What might have been the artist's message in depicting Wilson, Clemenceau, and Lloyd George as he did?

CONNECTIONS: Diplomats and politicians hammered out the treaty. How did Americans back home respond to the work of Wilson and the other world leaders at Versailles?

home in July 1919 consoled that, despite his frustrations, he had gained what he most wanted—a League of Nations. In Wilson's judgment, "We have completed in the least time possible the greatest work that four men have ever done."

What were the sides in the fight for the treaty?

The tumultuous reception Wilson received when he arrived home persuaded him, probably correctly, that the American people supported the treaty. When the president submitted the treaty to the Senate in July 1919, he warned that failure to ratify it would "break the heart of the world." By then, however, criticism of the treaty was mounting, especially from Americans convinced that their countries of ethnic origin—Ireland, Italy, and Germany—had not been given fair treatment. Others worried that the president's concessions at Versailles had jeopardized the treaty's capacity to provide a workable plan for rebuilding Europe and to guarantee world peace.

In the Senate, Republican "irreconcilables" opposed the treaty because it entangled the United States in world affairs. A larger group of Republicans did not object to American participation in international politics but feared that membership in the League of Nations would jeopardize the nation's ability to act independently. No Republican, in any case, was eager to hand Wilson and the Democrats a foreign policy victory with the 1920 presidential election little more than a year away.

At the center of Republican opposition was Wilson's archenemy, Senator Henry Cabot Lodge of Massachusetts. Lodge was no isolationist, but he thought that much of the Fourteen Points was a "general bleat about virtue being better than vice." Lodge expected the United States' economic and military power to propel the nation into a major role in world affairs. But he insisted that membership in the League of Nations, which would require collective action to maintain peace, threatened the nation's freedom in foreign relations.

With Lodge as its chair, the Senate Foreign Relations Committee produced several amendments, or reservations, that sought to limit the consequences of American membership in the league. For example, several reservations required approval of both the House and the Senate before the United States could participate in league-sponsored economic sanctions or military action.

It gradually became clear that ratification of the treaty depended on acceptance of the Lodge reservations. Democratic senators, who overwhelmingly supported the treaty, urged Wilson to accept Lodge's terms, arguing that they left the essentials of the treaty intact. Wilson, however, insisted that the reservations cut "the very heart out of the treaty."

Wilson decided to take his case directly to the people. On September 3, 1919, still exhausted from the peace conference, he set out by train on the most ambitious speaking tour ever undertaken by a president. On September 25 in Pueblo, Colorado, Wilson collapsed and had to return to Washington. There, he suffered a massive stroke that partially paralyzed him. From his bedroom, Wilson sent messages instructing Democrats in the Senate to hold firm against any and all reservations. Wilson commanded enough loyalty to ensure a vote against the Lodge reservations. But when the treaty without reservations came before the Senate in March 1920, the combined opposition of the Republican irreconcilables and reservationists left Wilson six votes short of the two-thirds majority needed for passage.

The nations of Europe organized the League of Nations at Geneva, Switzerland. Although Woodrow Wilson received the Nobel Peace Prize in 1920 for his central role in creating the league, the United States never became a member. Whether American membership could have prevented the world war that would begin in Europe in 1939 is highly unlikely, but the United States' failure to join certainly weakened the league from the start. In refusing to accept relatively minor compromises with Senate moderates, Wilson lost his treaty and American membership in the league.

REVIEW

Why did the Senate fail to ratify the Versailles treaty?

Why was America's transition from war to peace so turbulent?

The defeat of Wilson's plan for international democracy proved the crowning blow to progressives, who had hoped that the war could boost reform at home. When the war ended, Americans wanted to demobilize swiftly. In the process, servicemen, defense workers, and farmers lost their war-related jobs. The volatile combination—of unemployed veterans returning home, a stalled economy, and leftover wartime patriotism looking for a new cause—threatened to explode. Wartime anti-German passion was quickly succeeded by the Red scare, an antiradical campaign broad enough to ensnare unionists, socialists, dissenters, and African Americans and Mexicans who had committed no offense but to seek an escape from rural poverty as they moved north.

How did labor fare after the war?

Americans demanded that the nation return to a peacetime economy. The government abruptly abandoned its wartime economic controls and canceled war contracts. In a matter of months, three million soldiers returned from the military and flooded the job market just as war production ceased. Unemployment soared. At the same time, consumers went on a postwar spending spree that drove inflation skyward. In 1919 alone, prices rose 75 percent over prewar levels.

Most of the gains workers had made during the war evaporated. Freed from government controls, business turned against the eight-hour day and attacked labor unions. With inflation eating up their paychecks, workers fought back. The year 1919 witnessed nearly 3,600 strikes involving four million workers. The most spectacular strike occurred in February 1919 in Seattle, where shipyard workers had been put out of work by demobilization. When a coalition of the radical Industrial Workers of the World (IWW, known as Wobblies) and the moderate American Federation of Labor (AFL) called a general strike, the largest work stoppage in American history shut down the city. Newspapers claimed that the walkout was "a Bolshevik effort to start a revolution." The suppression of the Seattle general strike by city officials cost the AFL many of its wartime gains and contributed to the destruction of the IWW soon afterward.

A strike by Boston policemen in the fall of 1919 underscored postwar hostility toward labor militancy. Although the police were paid less than pick-and-shovel laborers, they won little sympathy. Once the officers stopped walking their beats, looters sacked the city. Massachusetts governor Calvin Coolidge called in the National Guard to restore order and broke the strike. The public welcomed Coolidge's anti-union assurance that "there is no right to strike against the public safety by anybody, anywhere, any time."

Labor strife climaxed in the violent steel strike of 1919. Faced with the industry's plan to revert to seven-day weeks, twelve-hour days, and weekly wages of about $20, Samuel Gompers, head of the AFL, called for a strike. In September, 350,000 workers in fifteen states walked out. The steel industry hired 30,000 strikebreakers and convinced the public that the strikers were radicals bent on subverting democracy and capitalism. In January 1920, after 18 striking workers were killed, the strike collapsed. That devastating defeat initiated a sharp decline in the fortunes of the labor movement, a trend that would continue for almost twenty years.

What factors led to the Red scare?

Suppression of labor strikes was one response to the widespread fear of internal subversion that swept the nation in 1919. The **Red scare** ("Red" referred to the color of the Bolshevik flag) exceeded even the assault on civil liberties during the war. It had homegrown causes: the postwar recession, labor unrest, terrorist acts, and the difficulties of reintegrating millions of returning veterans. But unsettling events abroad also added to Americans' anxieties.

Two epidemics swept the globe in 1918. One was an influenza pandemic ("Spanish flu"), a disease that brought on a deadly accumulation of fluid in the lungs. A nurse near the front lines in France observed that victims "run a high temperature, so high that we can't believe it's true. . . . It is accompanied by vomiting and dysentery. When they die, as about half of them do, they turn a ghastly dark gray and are taken out at once and cremated." It was the deadliest outbreak of disease since the Black Death six centuries earlier that wiped out a third of Europe. Before the flu virus had run its course, 675,000 Americans had died. Science simply did not have the tools to develop a vaccine that would combat the virus, and officials proved unwilling to impose quarantines that might cripple the war effort. Unlike the normal seasonal flu, which mostly claimed victims among the very young and very old, this disease spiked with young people in their twenties and thirties. Worldwide, at least forty million people died, far more than in all the battles of World War I.

The other epidemic was Russian bolshevism, which seemed to most Americans equally contagious and deadly. Bolshevism became even more menacing in March 1919, when the new Soviet leaders created the Comintern, a worldwide association of Communists sworn to revolution in capitalist countries. A Communist revolution in the United States was extremely unlikely, but edgy Americans, faced with a flurry of terrorist acts, believed otherwise. Dozens of prominent individuals had received bombs through the mail. On September 16, 1920, a wagon filled with dynamite and iron exploded on Wall Street, killing 38 and maiming 143 others. Authorities never caught the terrorists, and the successful attack on America's financial capital fed the nation's anger and fear.

Even before the Wall Street bombing, the government had initiated a hunt for domestic revolutionaries. Led by Attorney General A. Mitchell Palmer, who believed that "there could be no nice distinctions drawn between the theoretical ideals of the radicals and their actual violations of our national laws," the campaign targeted men and women for their ideas, not their illegal acts. In January 1920, Palmer ordered a series of raids that netted six thousand alleged subversives. Finding no revolutionary conspiracies, Palmer nevertheless ordered five hundred noncitizens deported.

His action came in the wake of a campaign against the most notorious radical alien, Russian-born Emma Goldman. Before the war, Goldman's passionate support of labor strikes, women's rights, and birth control had made her a symbol of radicalism.

Red scare
The widespread fear of internal subversion and Communist revolution that swept the United States in 1919 and resulted in suppression of dissent. Wartime repression of free speech, labor unrest, postwar recession, the difficult peacetime readjustment, and the Soviet establishment of the Comintern all contributed to the scare.

In 1919, after she spent time in prison for denouncing military conscription, J. Edgar Hoover, the director of the Justice Department's Radical Division, ordered her deported. One observer remarked, "With Prohibition coming in and Emma Goldman goin' out, 'twill be a dull country."

The effort to rid the country of alien radicals was matched by efforts to crush troublesome citizens. Law enforcement officials and vigilante groups joined hands against so-called Reds. In November 1919, in the rugged lumber town of Centralia, Washington, a menacing crowd gathered in front of the IWW hall. Nervous Wobblies inside opened fire, killing three people. Three IWW members were arrested and later convicted of murder, but another, former soldier Wesley Everett, was carried off by the mob, which castrated him, hung him from a bridge, and then riddled his body with bullets. His death was officially ruled a suicide.

Public institutions joined the attack on civil liberties. Local libraries removed dissenting books. Schools fired unorthodox teachers. Police shut down radical newspapers. State legislatures refused to seat elected representatives who professed socialist ideas. And in 1919, Congress removed its lone socialist representative, Victor Berger, on the pretext that he was a threat to national safety.

Schenck v. United States
1919 Supreme Court decision that upheld the conviction of socialist Charles Schenck for urging resistance to the draft during wartime. It established a "clear and present danger" test for restricting free speech.

That same year, the Supreme Court provided a formula for restricting free speech. In upholding the conviction of socialist Charles Schenck for publishing a pamphlet urging resistance to the draft during wartime (*Schenck v. United States*), the Court established a "clear and present danger" test. Such utterances as Schenck's during a time of national peril, Justice Oliver Wendell Holmes wrote, were equivalent to shouting "Fire!" in a crowded theater.

In 1920, the assault on civil liberties provoked the creation of the American Civil Liberties Union (ACLU), which was dedicated to defending an individual's constitutional rights. One of the ACLU's founders, Roger Baldwin, declared, "So long as we have enough people in this country willing to fight for their rights, we'll be called a democracy." The ACLU championed the targets of Attorney General Palmer's campaign—politically radical immigrants, trade unionists, socialists and Communists, and antiwar activists who still languished in jail.

The Red scare eventually collapsed because of its excesses. In particular, the antiradical campaign lost credibility after Palmer warned that radicals were planning to celebrate the Bolshevik Revolution with a nationwide wave of violence on May 1, 1920. Officials called out state militias, mobilized bomb squads, and even placed machine-gun nests at major city intersections. When May 1 came and went without a single disturbance, the public mood turned from fear to scorn.

What stimulated the Great Migration of Black people and Mexicans?

Before the Red scare lost steam, the government raised alarms about the loyalty of African Americans. Black soldiers returned from the war determined to bring democracy to the United States, but nothing they had done in France persuaded white Americans that race relations should change. A Justice Department investigation concluded that Reds were fomenting racial unrest among Black citizens. Although the report was wrong about Bolshevik influence, it was correct in noticing a new stirring among Black Americans.

In 1900, nine of every ten Black Americans still lived in the South, where poverty, disfranchisement, segregation, and violence dominated their lives. A majority of Black men worked as dirt-poor tenant farmers or sharecroppers, while many Black women worked in the homes of white families as domestics. White southerners remained committed to keeping Black people down. "If we own a good farm or horse, or cow, or bird-dog, or yoke of oxen," a Black sharecropper in Mississippi observed in 1913, "we are harassed until we are bound to sell, give away, or run away, before we can have any peace in our lives."

The First World War provided Black Americans with the opportunity to escape the South's cotton fields and kitchens. When war channeled nearly five million American workers into military service and almost ended European immigration, northern industrialists turned to Black labor, beginning the **Great Migration**. Black

Great Migration
Movement of a half million Black people from their homes in the South to find economic and social opportunity in the North, spurred by acute labor shortages in northern industrial cities during World War I.

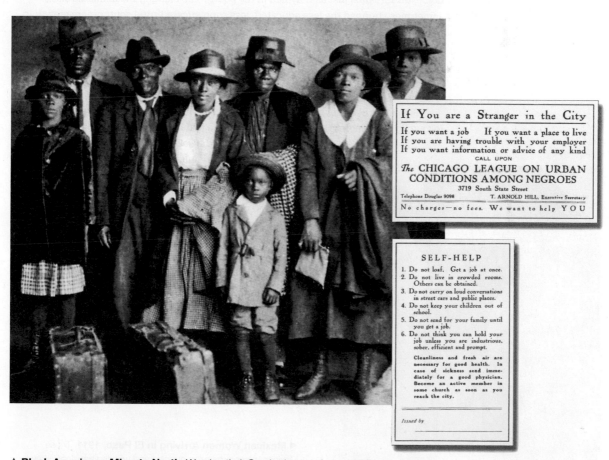

▲ **Black Americans Migrate North** Wearing their Sunday best and carrying the rest of what they own in two suitcases, three generations of this southern family wait to board a north-bound train in 1912. In Chicago, the League on Urban Conditions among Negroes, which became the Urban League, sought to ease the transition of southern Black people to life in the North by distributing cards such as the one shown here (front and back). Photo: Schomburg Center, NYPL/Art Resource, NY; cards: Arthur and Graham Aldis papers (APF_0001_0006a-01 a/b), Special Collections, The University Library, University of Illinois at Chicago.

men from the South found work in northern steel mills, shipyards, munitions plants, railroad yards, automobile factories, and mines. From 1915 to 1920, a half million Black people (approximately 10 percent of the South's Black population) boarded trains bound for Philadelphia, Detroit, Cleveland, Chicago, St. Louis, and other industrial cities.

Thousands of migrants wrote home to tell family and friends about their experiences in the North. One man announced proudly that he had recently been promoted to "first assistant to the head carpenter." He added, "I should have been here twenty years ago. I just begin to feel like a man. . . . My children are going to the same school with the whites and I don't have to [h]umble to no one. I have registered—will vote the next election and there ain't any 'yes sir'—it's all yes and no and Sam and Bill."

But the North was not the promised land. Black men stood on the lowest rungs of the labor ladder. Jobs of any kind proved scarce for Black women, and most worked as domestic servants, just as they had in the South. The existing Black middle class sometimes shunned the less educated, less sophisticated rural southerners crowding into northern cities. Many white people, fearful of losing jobs and status, lashed out against the new migrants. Savage race riots ripped through two dozen northern cities. The worst occurred in July 1917 when a mob of whites invaded a section of East St. Louis, Illinois, and murdered thirty-nine people. In 1918, the nation witnessed ninety-six lynchings of Black men, some of them decorated war veterans still in uniform.

Still, most Black migrants stayed in the North and encouraged friends and family to follow. By 1940, more than a million Black people had left the South, profoundly changing their own lives and the course of the nation's history. Black enclaves such as Harlem in New York and the South Side of Chicago, "cities within cities," emerged in the North. These assertive communities provided a foundation for Black protest and political organization in the years ahead.

At nearly the same time, another migration was under way in the American Southwest. Between 1910 and 1920, the Mexican-born population in the United States soared from 222,000 to 478,000. Mexican immigration resulted from developments on both sides of the border. When Mexicans revolted against dictator Porfirio Díaz in 1910, initiating a ten-year civil war, migrants flooded northward. In the United States, the Chinese Exclusion Act of 1882 and later the disruption of World War I cut off the supply of cheap foreign labor and caused western employers in the expanding rail, mining, construction, and agricultural industries to look south to Mexico for workers.

◀ **Mexican Women Arriving in El Paso, 1911** These Mexican women, carrying bundles and wearing traditional shawls, try to get their bearings upon arriving in El Paso, Texas — the Ellis Island for Mexican immigrants. They were part of the first modern wave of Mexican immigration to the United States. Women like them found work in the fields, canneries, and restaurants of the Southwest, as well as at home, taking in sewing, laundry, and boarders. New Mexico State University Library, Archives and Special Collections.

Like immigrants from Europe and Black migrants from the South, Mexicans in the American Southwest dreamed of a better life. And like the others, they found both opportunity and disappointment. Wages were better than in Mexico, but life in the fields, mines, and factories was hard, and living conditions—in boxcars, labor camps, or urban barrios—were dismal. Signs warning "No Mexicans Allowed" increased rather than declined. Mexicans were considered excellent prospects for manual labor but not for citizenship. By 1920, Mexicans made up about three-fourths of California's farm laborers.

Among Mexican Americans, some of whom had lived in the Southwest for more than a century, *los recién llegados* (the recent arrivals) encountered mixed reactions. One Mexican American expressed this ambivalence: "We are all Mexicans anyway because the *gueros* [Anglos] always treat all of us alike." But he also called for immigration quotas because the recent arrivals drove down wages and incited white prejudice that affected all ethnic Mexicans.

Despite friction, large-scale immigration into the Southwest meant a resurgence of the Mexican cultural presence, which became the basis for greater solidarity and political action for the ethnic Mexican population. In 1929 in Texas, Mexican Americans formed the League of United Latin American Citizens.

What did the election of 1920 signal?

A thousand miles away in Washington, D.C., President Woodrow Wilson, bedridden and paralyzed, ignored the mountain of domestic troubles—labor strikes, the Red scare, race riots, immigration backlash—and insisted that the 1920 election would be a "solemn referendum" on the League of Nations. Dutifully, the Democratic nominees for president, James M. Cox of Ohio, and for vice president, Franklin Delano Roosevelt of New York, campaigned on Wilson's international ideals. The Republican Party chose the handsome, friendly Warren Gamaliel Harding, senator from Ohio.

Harding found the winning formula when he declared that "America's present need is not heroics, but healing; not nostrums [questionable remedies], but normalcy." But what was "normalcy"? Harding explained: "By 'normalcy' I don't mean the old order but a regular steady order of things. I mean normal procedure, the natural way, without excess." Eager to put wartime crusades and postwar strife behind them, voters responded by giving Harding the largest presidential victory ever: 60.5 percent of the popular vote and 404 out of 531 electoral votes (**Map 22.6**). Harding's election lifted the national pall, signaling a new, more easygoing era.

Candidate	Electoral Vote	Popular Vote	Percent of Popular Vote
Warren G. Harding (Republican)	404	16,143,407	60.5
James M. Cox (Democrat)	127	9,130,328	34.2
Eugene V. Debs (Socialist)	0	919,799	3.4

MAP 22.6 ▲ The Election of 1920

REVIEW

How did the Red scare contribute to the erosion of civil liberties after the war?

Conclusion: Victory, but at what cost?

America's experience in World War I was exceptional. For much of the world, the Great War produced great destruction—blackened fields, ruined factories, and millions of casualties. But in the United States, war and prosperity marched hand in hand. America emerged from the war with the strongest economy in the world and a position of international preeminence.

Still, the nation paid a heavy price both at home and abroad. American soldiers and sailors encountered unprecedented horrors—submarines, poison gas, machine guns—and more than a hundred thousand died. But rather than redeeming their sacrifice, as Woodrow Wilson promised, the peace that followed tarnished it.

At home, rather than permanently improving working conditions, advancing public health, and spreading educational opportunity as progressives had hoped, the war threatened to undermine the achievements of the previous two decades. Rather than promoting democracy, the war bred fear, intolerance, and repression that led to a crackdown on dissent and a demand for conformity. Reformers could count only woman suffrage as a permanent victory.

Woodrow Wilson had promised more than anyone could deliver. Progressive hopes of extending democracy and liberal reform nationally and internationally were dashed. In 1920, a bruised and disillusioned society stumbled into a new decade. The era coming to an end had called on Americans to crusade and sacrifice. The new era promised peace, prosperity, and a good time.

CHAPTER REVIEW

EXPLAIN WHY IT MATTERS

Triple Alliance (p. 638)

Triple Entente (p. 638)

Lusitania (p. 640)

Bolshevik (p. 642)

American Expeditionary Force (AEF) (p. 642)

Eighteenth Amendment (prohibition) (p. 647)

Nineteenth Amendment (woman suffrage) (p. 649)

Fourteen Points (p. 653)

League of Nations (p. 653)

Versailles treaty (p. 655)

Red scare (p. 659)

Schenck v. United States (p. 660)

Great Migration (p. 661)

PUT IT ALL TOGETHER

THE PATH TO WAR

- Describe Woodrow Wilson's foreign policy during his first term in office. How did Wilson see the relationship between the United States and the rest of the world?

- Is it fair to describe the American people as isolationist prior to America's entry into World War I? Why or why not?

THE HOME FRONT

- How did the war affect the progressive agenda? How did progressives use the war to achieve their goals?

- How did the domestic efforts of the American people affect U.S. participation in World War I abroad?

A TROUBLED PEACE

- What vision did Wilson have of the postwar world? Why did the Senate refuse to endorse his vision, as embodied in the Treaty of Versailles?

- What led to the Red scare, and why did it eventually subside?

LOOKING BACKWARD, LOOKING AHEAD

- Why did Woodrow Wilson initially oppose the country's entry into World War I? What events and experiences helped change his mind?

- How did World War I change the place of the United States in the world? What role in world affairs was America poised to take as it entered the 1920s?

23

FROM NEW ERA TO GREAT DEPRESSION

1920–1932

This chapter discusses the following questions:

- How did big business shape the "New Era" of the 1920s?
- In what ways did the Roaring Twenties challenge traditional values?
- Why did the relationship between urban and rural America deteriorate in the 1920s?
- How did President Hoover respond to the economic crash of 1929?
- What impact did the economic depression have on everyday life?
- Conclusion: Why did the hope of the 1920s turn to despair?

▶ **Henry Ford and His Model T** When Henry Ford introduced his Model T in 1908, America thought of automobiles as toys for the rich. But by the 1920s when this photograph was taken, millions of Americans owned Fords, and their lives were never the same. Getty Images.

AN AMERICAN STORY

Born in 1863 on a farm in Dearborn, Michigan, Henry Ford at sixteen fled rural life for Detroit, where he became a journeyman machinist. In 1893, he put together one of the first successful gasoline-driven carriages in the United States. In 1903, Ford gathered twelve workers in a 250-by-50-foot shed and created the Ford Motor Company. By 1920, he had already produced six million automobiles; by 1927, the figure reached fifteen million. In 1920, a Ford car cost $845; in 1928, the price was less than $300, within range of most of the country's skilled workingmen. Henry Ford put America on wheels, and in the eyes of most Americans he was an authentic American hero.

Ford's early cars were custom-made one at a time. By 1914, his cars were being built along a continuously moving assembly line. Workers bolted on parts brought to them by cranes and conveyor belts. In 1920, one car rolled off the Ford assembly line every minute; in 1925, one appeared every ten seconds. Ford made only one kind of car, the Model T, which became synonymous with mass production (Map 23.1).

When Ford began his rise, progressive critics condemned the industrial giants of the nineteenth century as "robber barons" who lived in luxury while reducing their workers to wage slaves. Ford, however, identified with the common folk and saw himself as the benefactor of average Americans. But like the age in which he lived, Ford was more complex and more contradictory than this simple image suggests.

A man of genius whose compelling vision of modern mass production led the way in the 1920s, Ford was also cranky, tightfisted, and mean-spirited. He hated Jews and Catholics, bankers and doctors, liquor and tobacco, and his money allowed him to act on his prejudices. His automobile plants made him a billionaire, but their regimented assembly lines reduced workers to near robots. On the cutting edge of modern technology, Ford nevertheless remained nostalgic about rural values. He sought to revive the past in Greenfield Village, where he relocated buildings from a bygone era, including his parents' farmhouse. His museum contrasted sharply with the roaring Ford assembly plant at River Rouge. Yet Ford insisted that if Americans remained true to their farming past and managed to be modern and scientific at the same time, all would be well.

Tension between traditional values and modern conditions lay at the heart of the conflicted 1920s. For the first time, more Americans lived in urban than in rural areas, and cities seemed to harbor everything rural people opposed. While millions admired urban America's sophisticated new style and consumer products, others condemned postwar society for its loose

1931	Scottsboro Boys arrested.
	Harlan County, Kentucky, coal miners' strike.
1932	Reconstruction Finance Corporation established.
	River Rouge factory demonstration takes place.
	National Farmers' Holiday Association formed.

morals and vulgar materialism. The Ku Klux Klan and other discriminatory champions of an older America resorted to violence as well as words when they condemned the era's "new woman," "New Negro," and surging immigrant populations. Those who sought to dam the tide of change proposed prohibition, Protestantism, and patriotism.

The public, disillusioned with the outcome of World War I, turned away from the Christian moralism and idealism of the Progressive Era. In the 1920s, Ford and businessmen like him replaced political reformers such as Theodore Roosevelt and Woodrow Wilson as the models of progress. The U.S. Chamber of Commerce crowed, "The American businessman is the most influential person in the nation." The fortunes of the era rose, then in 1929 crashed, according to the values and practices of the business community. When prosperity collapsed, the nation entered the most serious economic depression of all time.

How did big business shape the "New Era" of the 1920s?

Once Woodrow Wilson left the White House, government activism and civic reform declined, and private economic endeavor took on new energy. The rise of a freewheeling economy and a heightened sense of individualism caused Secretary of Commerce Herbert Hoover to declare that America had entered a "New Era," one of many labels used to describe the complex 1920s.

Some terms focus on the decade's high-spirited energy and cultural change: Roaring Twenties, Jazz Age, Flaming Youth. Others echo the rising importance of money (Dollar Decade, Golden Twenties) or reflect the sinister side of gangster profiteering (Lawless Decade). Still others emphasize the lonely confusion of the Lost Generation and the stress and anxiety of the Aspirin Age.

America in the twenties was many things, but President Calvin Coolidge got at an essential truth when he declared, "The business of America is business." Politicians and diplomats proclaimed business the heart of American civilization as they promoted its products at home and abroad. Average men and women bought into the idea that business and its wonderful products were what made America great, as they snatched up the flood of new consumer items American factories sent forth. Nothing caught Americans' fancy more powerfully than the automobile.

What did it mean that the United States had a business government?

Republicans controlled the White House from 1921 to 1933. The first of the three Republican presidents was Warren Gamaliel Harding, the Ohio senator who in his

1920 campaign called for a "return to normalcy," by which he meant the end of public crusades. Harding appointed a few men of real merit to his cabinet. Herbert Hoover, for example, the former head of the wartime Food Administration, became secretary of commerce. But wealth and friendship also counted: Andrew Mellon, one of the richest men in America, became secretary of the treasury, and Harding handed out jobs to his friends, members of his old "Ohio gang." This curious combination of ability and favoritism made for an uneven administration.

When Harding was elected in 1920 (see chapter 22, Map 22.6), the unemployment rate hit 20 percent, the highest ever up to that point. The bankruptcy rate of farmers increased tenfold. Harding pushed measures to regain national prosperity—high tariffs to protect American businesses, price supports for agriculture, and the dismantling of wartime government control over industry in favor of unregulated private business. "Never before, here or anywhere else," the U.S. Chamber of Commerce said proudly, "has a government been so completely fused with business."

Harding's policies to boost American enterprise made him very popular, but ultimately his small-town friendliness and trusting ways did him in. Some of his friends in the Ohio gang were up to their necks in crime. Three of Harding's appointees went to jail. Interior Secretary Albert Fall was convicted of accepting bribes of more than $400,000 for leasing oil reserves on public land in Teapot Dome, Wyoming, and "**Teapot Dome**" became a synonym for political corruption.

On August 2, 1923, when Harding died from a heart attack, Vice President Calvin Coolidge became president. Coolidge, who once said that "the man who builds a factory builds a temple, the man who works there worships there," continued and extended Harding's policies of promoting business and limiting government. Secretary of the Treasury Andrew Mellon reduced government's control of the economy and cut taxes for corporations and wealthy individuals. New rules for the Federal Trade Commission severely restricted its power to regulate business. Secretary of Commerce Herbert Hoover hedged government authority by encouraging trade associations to keep business honest and efficient through voluntary cooperation.

Coolidge found an ally in the Supreme Court. For years, the Court had thwarted federal regulation of hours, wages, and working conditions on the grounds that such legislation was the proper concern of the states. In the 1920s, the Court found ways to limit even a state's ability to regulate business. It ruled against closed shops—businesses where only union members could be employed—while confirming the right of owners to form trade associations. In 1923, the Court declared unconstitutional the District of Columbia's minimum-wage law for women, asserting that the law interfered with the freedom of employer and employee to make labor contracts. The Court and the president attacked government intrusion in the free market, even when the prohibition of government regulation threatened the welfare of workers.

The election of 1924 confirmed the defeat of the progressive belief that the state should ensure the general welfare. To oppose Coolidge, the Democrats nominated John W. Davis, a corporate lawyer whose conservative views differed little from Republican principles. Only the Progressive Party and its presidential nominee, Senator Robert La Follette of Wisconsin, offered a genuine alternative. When La Follette championed labor unions, regulation of business, and protection of civil

Teapot Dome
Nickname for the scandal in which Interior Secretary Albert Fall accepted $400,000 in bribes for leasing oil reserves on public land in Teapot Dome, Wyoming. It was part of a larger pattern of corruption that marred Warren G. Harding's presidency.

liberties, Republicans coined the slogan "Coolidge or Chaos." Voters chose Coolidge in a landslide. Coolidge was right when he declared, "This is a business country, and it wants a business government." What was true of the government's relationship to business at home was also true abroad.

How did the government promote prosperity and peace abroad?

After leading the Senate's successful effort to block U.S. membership in the League of Nations, Henry Cabot Lodge boasted, "We have torn Wilsonism up by the roots." But repudiation of Wilson's internationalism and rejection of collective security through the League of Nations did not mean that the United States retreated into isolationism. The United States emerged from World War I with its economy intact and enjoyed a decade of stunning growth. New York replaced London as the center of world finance, and the United States became the world's chief creditor. Trade with the world and continuing chaos in Europe made withdrawal impossible.

One of the Republicans' most ambitious foreign policy initiatives was the Washington Disarmament Conference, which convened in 1921 to establish a global balance of naval power. Secretary of State Charles Evans Hughes shaped the **Five-Power Naval Treaty of 1922**, committing Britain, France, Japan, Italy, and the United States to reductions of their navies. The treaty led to the scrapping of more than two million tons of warships, by far the world's greatest success in disarmament. By fostering international peace, Hughes also helped make the world a safer place for American trade.

A second major effort on behalf of world peace came in 1928, when Secretary of State Frank Kellogg joined French foreign minister Aristide Briand to produce the Kellogg-Briand pact. Nearly fifty nations signed the solemn pledge to renounce war and settle international disputes peacefully.

But Republican administrations preferred private-sector diplomacy to state action. With the blessing of the White House, a team of American financiers led by Charles Dawes swung into action when Germany suspended its war reparation payments in 1923. Impoverished, Germany was staggering under the massive bill of $33 billion presented by the victorious Allies in the Versailles treaty. When Germany failed to meet its annual payment, France occupied Germany's industrial Ruhr Valley, creating the worst international crisis since the war. In 1924, the Dawes Plan halved Germany's annual reparation payments, initiated fresh American loans to Germany, and caused the French to retreat from the Ruhr. Although the United States failed to join the League of Nations, it continued to exercise significant economic and diplomatic influence abroad. These Republican successes overseas helped fuel prosperity at home.

How did the automobile shape the American economy?

The automobile industry emerged as the largest single manufacturing industry in the nation. Henry Ford shrewdly located his company in Detroit, knowing that key materials for his automobiles were manufactured in nearby states (**Map 23.1**). The heart of the American economy, the automobile industry not only employed

Five-Power Naval Treaty of 1922
Treaty that committed Britain, France, Japan, Italy, and the United States to a reduction of naval forces, producing the world's greatest success in disarmament up to that time.

MAP ACTIVITY

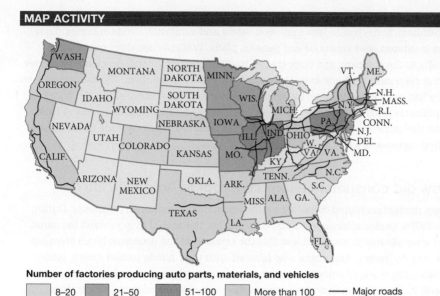

Number of factories producing auto parts, materials, and vehicles

8–20	21–50	51–100	More than 100	—— Major roads

MAP 23.1 ▲ Auto Manufacturing By the mid-1920s, the massive coal and steel industries of the Midwest had made that region the center of the new automobile industry. A major roadbuilding program by the federal government carried the thousands of new cars produced each day to every corner of the country.

READING THE MAP: How many states had factories involved with the manufacture of automobiles? In what regions was auto manufacturing concentrated?
CONNECTIONS: On what related industries did auto manufacturing depend? How did the integration of the automobile into everyday life affect American society?

hundreds of thousands of workers directly but also created whole new industries—filling stations, garages, fast-food restaurants, and "guest cottages" (motels). The need for tires, glass, steel, highways, oil, and refined gasoline for automobiles provided millions of related jobs. By 1929, one American in four found employment directly or indirectly in the automobile industry. "Give us our daily bread" was no longer addressed to the Almighty, one commentator joked, but to Detroit.

Automobiles changed where people lived, what work they did, how they spent their leisure, even how they thought. Hundreds of small towns decayed because the automobile enabled rural people to skip them on their way to cities. In cities, streetcars began to disappear as workers moved to the suburbs and commuted to work along crowded highways. Nothing shaped modern America more than the automobile, and efficient mass production made the automobile revolution possible.

Mass production by the assembly-line technique became standard in almost every factory, from automobiles to meatpacking to cigarettes. Corporations reduced assembly-line work to the simplest, most repetitive tasks. These changes, along with technological advances, significantly boosted overall efficiency. Between 1922 and 1929, productivity in manufacturing increased 32 percent. Average wages, however, increased only 8 percent.

welfare capitalism
Popular programs for workers sponsored by employers in the 1920s. Some businesses improved safety and sanitation inside factories. They also instituted paid vacations and pension plans. This encouraged loyalty to companies and discouraged independent labor unions.

Industries also developed programs for workers that came to be called **welfare capitalism**. Some businesses improved safety and sanitation inside factories. They also instituted paid vacations and pension plans. Welfare capitalism encouraged loyalty to the company and discouraged traditional labor unions. One labor organizer in the steel industry bemoaned the success of welfare capitalism. "So many workmen here had been lulled to sleep by the company union, the welfare plans, the social organizations fostered by the employer," he declared, "that they had come to look upon the employer as their protector, and had believed vigorous trade union organization unnecessary for their welfare."

How did consumer culture take root in American life?

Mass production fueled corporate profits and national economic prosperity. During the 1920s, personal income increased by a third, the cost of living stayed the same, and unemployment remained low. But the rewards of the economic boom were not evenly distributed. Americans who labored with their hands inched ahead, while white-collar workers enjoyed significantly more money and more leisure time to spend it. Mass production of new products—automobiles, radios, refrigerators, electric irons, washing machines—produced a consumer goods revolution.

In this new era of plenty, more people than ever conceived of the American dream in terms of the things they could acquire. *Middletown* (1929), a study of the inhabitants of Muncie, Indiana, revealed that Muncie had become, above all, "a culture in which everything hinges on money." Faced with technological and organizational change beyond their understanding, many citizens had lost confidence in their ability to play an effective role in civic affairs. More and more, they became passive consumers, deferring to the supposed expertise of leaders in politics and economics.

The rapidly expanding business of advertising stimulated the desire for new products and attacked the traditional values of thrift and saving. Advertising linked material goods to the fulfillment of every spiritual and emotional need. Americans increasingly measured their social status and, indeed, their personal worth on the yardstick of material possessions. Happiness itself depended on owning a car and choosing the right cigarettes and toothpaste. **(See "Analyzing Historical Evidence: Advertising in a Consumer Age" on page 674.)**

By the 1920s, the United States had achieved the physical capacity to satisfy Americans' material wants (**Figure 23.1**). The economic problem shifted from production to consumption: Who would buy the goods flying off American assembly lines? One solution was to expand America's markets in foreign countries, and government and business joined in that effort. Another solution to the problem of consumption was to expand the market at home.

Henry Ford realized early on that "mass production requires mass consumption." He understood that automobile workers not only could produce cars but also would buy them if they made enough money. "One's own employees ought to be one's own best customers," Ford said. In 1914, he raised wages in his factories to $5 a day, more than twice the

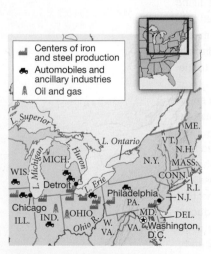

Centers of iron and steel production

Automobiles and ancillary industries

Oil and gas

Detroit and the Automobile Industry in the 1920s

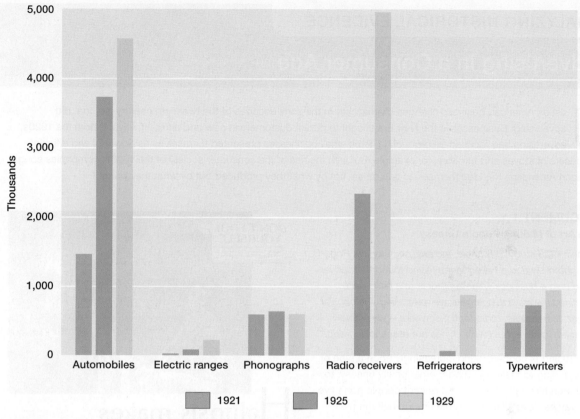

FIGURE 23.1 ▲ Production of Consumer Goods, 1921–1929 Transportation, communications, and entertainment changed the lives of consumers in the 1920s. Laborsaving devices for the home were popular, but the vastly greater sales of automobiles and radios showed how consumerism moved people's attention beyond their homes.

going rate. High wages made for workers who were more loyal and more exploitable, and high wages returned as profits when workers bought Fords.

Many people's incomes, however, could not satisfy the growing desire for consumer goods. The solution was installment buying—a little money down, a payment each month—which allowed people to purchase expensive items they could not otherwise afford or to purchase items before saving the necessary money. As one newspaper announced, "The first responsibility of an American to his country is no longer that of a citizen, but of a consumer." During the 1920s, America's motto became spend, not save. Old values—"Use it up, wear it out, make it do or do without"—seemed about as pertinent as a horse and buggy. American culture had shifted.

REVIEW

How did mass production transform the United States?

ANALYZING HISTORICAL EVIDENCE

Advertising in a Consumer Age

Just as American business changed dramatically in the early decades of the twentieth century, so, too, did advertising. Businesses in the New Era sought to attract customers in new and different ways. Before the 1920s, advertising had focused on production. Even small businesses presented themselves as powerful and efficient producers of stoves and furniture, for example. But with the rise of the consumer society of the 1920s, companies sought to teach Americans to judge themselves and others not by what they produced but by what they bought.

DOCUMENT 1

The Art of Making People Uneasy

In their 1929 study of Muncie, Indiana, sociologists Robert Staughton Lynd and Helen Merrell Lynd found that "advertising is to a business what fertilizer is to a farm" and examined the ways that large-scale advertising — in popular magazines, movies, radio, and elsewhere — was rapidly changing ideas about "what things are essential to living."

Advertising is concentrating increasingly upon a type of copy aiming to make the reader emotionally uneasy, to bludgeon him with the fact that decent people don't live the way *he* does: *decent* people ride on balloon tires, have a second bathroom, and so on. The copy points an accusing finger at the stenographer as she reads her *Motion Picture Magazine* and makes her acutely conscious of her unpolished finger nails, or of the worn place in the living room rug, and sends the housewife peering anxiously into the mirror to see if *her* wrinkles look like those that made Mrs. X— in the ad "old at thirty-five" because she did not have a Leisure Hour electric washer.

Source: Robert S. Lynd and Helen Merrell Lynd, *Middletown: A Study in Contemporary American Culture* (New York: 1929), 82.

DOCUMENT 2

Unmasking Advertising

Frederick Lewis Allen, a journalist and historian, was an acute observer of contemporary life. In his enormously popular Only Yesterday, *published two years after the 1920s ended, he contemplates an advertising campaign based on anxiety about bad breath.*

▲ **Ad for Breath** The message is clear: Bad breath could be keeping you on the sidelines while your friends are dancing! Buy Listerine and join in the fun! Bettmann/Getty Images.

By far the most famous of these dramatic advertisements of the Post-war Decade was the long series in which the awful results of halitosis were set forth through the depiction of a gallery of unfortunates whose closest friends would not tell them. "Often a bridesmaid but never a bride. . . . Edna's case was really a pathetic one." . . . "Why did she leave him that way?" . . . "*That's* why you're a failure," . . . and then that devilishly ingenious display which capitalized on the fears aroused by earlier tragedies in the series: the picture of a girl looking at a Listerine advertisement and saying to herself, "This *can't* apply to me!" Useless for the American Medical Association to insist that Listerine was "not a true deodorant," that it simply covered one smell with another. Just as useless as for the Life Extension Institute to find "one out of twenty with pyorrhea [gum disease], rather than Mr. Forhan's [a mouth product] famous four-out-of-five." . . . Halitosis had the power of dramatic advertising behind it, and Listerine swept to greater and greater profits on a tide of public trepidation.

Source: Frederick Lewis Allen, *Only Yesterday: An Informal History of the 1920s* (New York: 1931), 144–45.

DOCUMENT 3
"Messenger to the King"

Not every observer of the avalanche of new advertising found it objectionable. William Chenery, editor and publisher of Collier's, *a national magazine, sang advertising's praises in this 1930 article in his magazine.*

Advertising, essentially, is the awakening of human desire. There is no stronger force in this new world of ours.

The successful advertisement makes you crave new things. The motive is frankly commercial but the consequences reach far beyond trade. . . . The byproducts of the [advertiser's] efforts have had prodigious effects upon our opinions, our standards of taste, our habits, and even upon our picture of a good life.

We arise in the morning and we bathe. Why? Merely because soap makers have taught us the importance of cleanliness. . . .

Beards and even mustaches have gone out of fashion because razor manufacturers persuaded us to shave.

We clean our teeth because toothpaste manufacturers have made us believe in the importance of oral hygiene. They have saved us from more aches than the dentists could cure.

Our breakfast habits are the results of the teaching of food manufacturers. The old heavy American breakfast has gone the way of the hoop skirt. Our health is better. Advertising did it.

The clothes we wear, the houses we live in, the furniture we use, our very conception of a home is the product of advertising. . . .

If journalism is the little sister of literature, advertising began certainly as the Cinderella of selling. Now it is the great motive force in our commercial life. It is the life blood of public demand. Our material civilization has been made possible by it.

Source: William Chenery, "Messenger to the King," *Collier's*, May 3, 1930.

Questions for Analysis

ANALYZE THE EVIDENCE: According to the critics — Frederick Lewis Allen and the Lynds — what is the most damaging feature of modern advertising?

RECOGNIZE VIEWPOINTS: How might William Chenery's job have helped shape his positive opinion of advertising? How might the other writers included here dispute his argument?

CONSIDER THE CONTEXT: How did the rise of mass production translate into the rise of mass advertising and mass consumption?

In what ways did the Roaring Twenties challenge traditional values?

The theme of personal freedom resulted in a whirl of activity that earned the decade the name "Roaring Twenties." Prohibition made lawbreakers of millions of otherwise decent folk. Flappers and "new women" challenged traditional gender boundaries. Other Americans enjoyed the Roaring Twenties through the words and images of vastly expanded mass communication, especially radio and movies. In America's big cities, particularly New York, a burst of creativity produced the "New Negro," who disturbed white Americans. The "Lost Generation" of writers, profoundly disillusioned with mainstream America's culture, fled the country.

How successful was the experiment of prohibition?

Republicans generally sought to limit the powers of government, but the twenties witnessed a great exception to this rule when the federal government implemented one of the last reforms of the Progressive Era: the Eighteenth Amendment, which banned the manufacture and sale of alcohol. It took effect in January 1920 (see chapter 22). Enforcement of **prohibition** led to marked growth in the federal government, as it created a huge apparatus to fight crime and built new prisons to house the influx of convicts.

prohibition
The ban on the manufacture and sale of alcohol that went into effect in January 1920 with the Eighteenth Amendment. Prohibition proved almost impossible to enforce. By the end of the 1920s, most Americans wished it to end, and it was finally repealed in 1933.

Drying up the rivers of liquor that Americans consumed, supporters of prohibition claimed, would eliminate crime, boost production, and lift the nation's morals. Prohibition would destroy the saloon, which according to a leading "dry" was the "most fiendish, corrupt and hell-soaked institution that ever crawled out of the slime of the eternal pit." Instead, prohibition initiated a fourteen-year orgy of lawbreaking unparalleled in the nation's history.

The Treasury Department agents charged with enforcing prohibition faced a staggering task. Although they smashed more than 172,000 illegal stills in 1925 alone, loopholes in the law almost guaranteed failure. Sacramental wine was permitted, allowing fake clergy to party with fake congregations. Farmers were allowed to ferment their own "fruit juices." Doctors and dentists could prescribe liquor for medicinal purposes.

In 1929, a Treasury agent in Indiana reported intense local resistance to enforcement of prohibition. "Conditions in most important cities very bad," he declared. "Lax and corrupt public officials great handicap . . . prevalence of drinking among minor boys and the . . . middle or better classes of adults." The "speakeasy," an illegal nightclub, became common in American cities. Speakeasies' dance floors led to the sexual integration of the formerly all-male drinking culture, changing American social life forever. Detroit, probably America's wettest city, was home to more than twenty thousand illegal drinking establishments, making the alcohol business the city's second-largest industry, behind automobile manufacturing.

Eventually, serious criminals took over the liquor trade. During the first four years of prohibition, Chicago witnessed more than two hundred gang-related killings

▶ **Prohibition Action** Prohibition agents sometimes liked to do their work before appreciative audiences. Agents pour nine hundred gallons of confiscated wine down a drain in Los Angeles to the delight of a crowd of boys and others. But not even the criminalization of liquor could permanently defeat "Satan in a bottle." Bettmann/Getty Images.

as rival mobs struggled for control of the liquor trade. The most notorious event came on St. Valentine's Day 1929, when Alphonse "Big Al" Capone's Italian-dominated mob machine-gunned seven members of a rival Irish gang. Capone's bootlegging empire brought in $95 million a year, at a time when a chicken dinner cost 5 cents. Federal authorities finally sent Capone to prison for income tax evasion. "I violate the Prohibition law—sure," he told a reporter. "Who doesn't? The only difference is, I take more chances than the man who drinks a cocktail before dinner."

Capone's self-serving statement made a valid point. Enforcement of prohibition was less than evenhanded. Vigilante groups, including the Woman's Christian Temperance Union, the Anti-Saloon League, and the Ku Klux Klan, helped enforce prohibition and targeted immigrants, working people, and Blacks. Working-class Americans asked why "the poor man's club is raided while the rich man is left alone." The answer was that the war on alcohol was fueled by the same class, ethnic, and religious discrimination that permeated so much of life in the 1920s.

By the end of the "dry" years, Americans overwhelmingly favored the repeal of the Eighteenth Amendment—the "noble experiment," as Herbert Hoover called prohibition. In 1931, a panel of experts reported that the experiment had failed. The social and political costs of prohibition outweighed the benefits. Prohibition fueled criminal activity, corrupted the police, demoralized the courts, and caused ordinary citizens to break the law. In 1933, the nation ended prohibition, making the Eighteenth Amendment the only constitutional amendment to be repealed.

How did women's roles change in the 1920s?

Of all the changes in American life in the 1920s, none sparked more heated debate than changes in the traditional roles of women. Increasing numbers of women worked and went to college, defying older gender norms. Even mainstream magazines such as the *Saturday Evening Post* began publishing stories about young, college-educated women who drank gin cocktails, smoked cigarettes, and wore skimpy dresses and dangly necklaces. Before the Great War, the **new woman** dwelt in New York City's bohemian Greenwich Village, but afterward the mass media brought her into middle-class America's living rooms.

When the Nineteenth Amendment, ratified in 1920, granted women the vote, feminists felt liberated and expected women to reshape the political landscape. A Kansas woman declared, "I went to bed last night a *slave*[;] I awoke this morning a *free woman*." Women began pressuring Congress to pass laws that especially

new woman
Alternative image of womanhood that came into the American mainstream in the 1920s. The mass media frequently portrayed young, college-educated women who drank, smoked, and wore skimpy dresses. New women also challenged American convictions about separate spheres for women and men and the sexual double standard.

concerned women, including measures to protect women in factories. Black women lobbied particularly for federal courts to assume jurisdiction over the crime of lynching. But women's only significant national legislative success came in 1921 when Congress enacted the Sheppard-Towner Act, which extended federal assistance to states seeking to reduce high infant mortality rates.

A number of factors helped check women's political influence. Male domination of both political parties, the rarity of female candidates, and lack of experience in voting, especially among recent immigrants, kept many women away from the polls. In some places, male-run political organizations actually disfranchised women, despite the Nineteenth Amendment. In the South, poll taxes, literacy tests, and outright terrorism continued to decimate the vote of Black men and women alike.

Most important, rather than forming a solid voting bloc, feminists divided. Some argued for women's right to special protection; others demanded equal protection. The radical National Woman's Party fought for an Equal Rights Amendment that stated flatly: "Men and women shall have equal rights throughout the United States." The more moderate League of Women Voters feared that the amendment threatened state laws that provided women special protection, such as preventing them from working on certain dangerous machines. Congress defeated the Equal Rights Amendment in 1923, and radical women were forced to work for the causes of birth control, legal equality for minorities, and the end of child labor through other means.

Economically, more women worked for pay—approximately one in four by 1930—but they clustered in "women's jobs." Women almost monopolized the occupations of librarian, nurse, elementary school teacher, secretary, typist, and telephone operator. Women also represented 40 percent of salesclerks by 1930. More female white-collar workers meant that fewer women were interested in protective legislation for women; new women wanted salaries and opportunities equal to men's.

Increased earnings gave working women more buying power in the new consumer culture. A stereotype soon emerged of the flapper, so called because of the short-lived fad of wearing unbuckled rain boots. The flapper had short bobbed hair and wore lipstick and rouge. She spent freely on the latest styles, and she danced all night to wild jazz. As F. Scott Fitzgerald described her in his novel *This Side of Paradise* (1920), she was "lovely and expensive and about nineteen."

The new woman both reflected and propelled the modern birth control movement. Margaret Sanger, the crusading pioneer for contraception during the Progressive Era (see chapter 21), restated her principal conviction in 1920: "No woman can call herself free until she can choose consciously whether she will or will not be a mother." Shifting strategy in the twenties, Sanger courted the conservative American Medical Association and linked birth control with the eugenics movement, which advocated limiting reproduction among "undesirable" groups, such as women with physical disabilities or mental illness, immigrants, and Black women. By using a pseudo-scientific framework, albeit a racist one, she made contraception a respectable subject for discussion.

Flapper style and values spread from coast to coast through films, novels, magazines, and advertisements. New women challenged American convictions about separate spheres for women and men, the double standard of sexual conduct, and Victorian ideas of proper female appearance and behavior. Although only a minority of American women became flappers, all women, even those who remained at home, heard about girls gone wild and felt the great changes of the era.

How did the New Negro expand Black cultural life?

The 1920s witnessed the emergence not only of the "new woman" but also of the "New Negro." Black people challenged the caste system that confined dark-skinned Americans to the lowest levels of society, confronting whites who insisted that race relations would not change.

As southern Black people flooded northern cities (see chapter 22), they found decent housing in short supply, even if they had the money to pay. Property owners resolved to keep their neighborhoods all white. Although the U.S. Supreme Court struck down a law requiring segregated housing in 1917, inventive white homeowners created other means to draw racial boundaries. Real estate agents refused to show Black people houses in white neighborhoods. Banks turned them down for mortgages. White people signed agreements promising not to sell their homes to Blacks. If a Black family managed to slip through their defenses, white locals resorted to violence. Housing was only one area of life that sparked racial violence.

The prominent Black intellectual W. E. B. Du Bois and the National Association for the Advancement of Colored People (NAACP) aggressively pursued the passage of a federal antilynching law to counter mob violence against Black people in the South. At the same time, however, many disillusioned poor urban Blacks turned to the new leadership of the Jamaican-born Marcus Garvey, who urged Black Americans to rediscover the heritage of Africa, take pride in their own achievements, and maintain racial purity by avoiding miscegenation. In 1917, Garvey launched the Universal Negro Improvement Association (UNIA) to help African Americans gain economic and political independence entirely outside white society.

In 1919, the UNIA created its own shipping company, the Black Star Line, to support the "Back to Africa" movement among Black Americans. In 1927, the federal government pinned charges of illegal practices on Garvey and deported him to Jamaica. Nevertheless, the issues Garvey raised about racial pride, Black identity, and the search for equality persisted, and his legacy remains at the center of Black nationalist thought.

Still, most Black people maintained hope in the American promise. In New York City, hope and talent came together. The city's Black population jumped 115 percent (from 152,000 to 327,000) in the 1920s. In Harlem in uptown Manhattan, an extraordinary mix of Black artists, sculptors, novelists, musicians, and poets set out to create a distinctive African American culture that drew on their identities as Americans and Blacks. As scholar Alain Locke put it in 1925, they introduced to the world the "**New Negro**" to proclaim African Americans' creative genius.

The emergence of the New Negro came to be known as the Harlem Renaissance. Building on the achievement and pride displayed by Black soldiers during the war, Black artists sought to defeat the fresh assault of racial discrimination and violence with poems, paintings, and plays. "We younger Negro artists . . . intend to express our individual dark-skinned selves without fear or shame," poet Langston Hughes said of the Harlem Renaissance. "If white people are pleased, we are glad. If they are not, it doesn't matter. We know we are beautiful. And ugly, too."

New Negro
Term referring to Black artists who challenged American racial hierarchy. The New Negro emerged in New York City in the 1920s, in what became known as the Harlem Renaissance, which produced dazzling literary, musical, and artistic talent.

The Harlem Renaissance produced dazzling talent. Black writer James Weldon Johnson—who in 1903 had written the Negro national anthem, "Lift Every Voice and Sing"—wrote *God's Trombones* (1927), in which he expressed the wisdom and beauty of Black folktales from the South. The poetry of Langston Hughes, Claude McKay, and Countee Cullen celebrated the vitality of life in Harlem. Zora Neale Hurston's novel *Their Eyes Were Watching God* (1937) explored the complex passions of Black southerners. Black painters, led by Aaron Douglas, linked African art, which had recently inspired European artists, to the concept of the New Negro.

Despite such ferment, Harlem for most white people remained a separate Black ghetto known only for its lively nightlife. Fashionable white New Yorkers crowded into Harlem's segregated nightclubs, the most famous of which was the Cotton Club, where they believed they could hear "real" jazz, a relatively new musical form, in its "natural" surroundings. The vigor of the Harlem Renaissance left a powerful legacy for Black Americans, but the creative burst did little in the short run to dissolve the prejudice of white society.

What explains the rise of popular culture?

In the 1920s, popular culture, like consumer goods, was both mass-produced and mass-consumed. The rise of movies, radios, music, and sports meant that Americans found plenty to do, and in doing the same things, they helped create a national culture.

Nothing offered entertainment like the movies. Hollywood, California, discovered the successful formula of combining wealth, sex, and adventure. Admission was cheap, and by 1929, the movies were drawing more than eighty million people in a single week. Hollywood created "movie stars," glamorous beings whose every move

▶ **Duke Ellington Leads His Jazz Band** From 1927 to 1931, the Duke Ellington Orchestra was the house band at the Cotton Club in Harlem, where Black performers played for white audiences. The photograph captures something of the energy and exuberance that helped make Ellington America's greatest jazz composer and bandleader. Bettmann/Getty Images.

▶ **Warren G. Harding and Babe Ruth** President Warren G. Harding shakes hands with New York Yankee home run king George Herman "Babe" Ruth Jr. during an April 4, 1923, visit to Yankee Stadium. The 1920s were the Golden Age of Sports, and Ruth was the best paid and most highly acclaimed athlete of the decade. Even when he struck out, "the Babe" attracted more attention than any politician — even the president of the United States. Bettmann/Getty Images.

was tracked by fan magazines. Rudolph Valentino, described as "catnip to women," and Clara Bow, the "It Girl" (everyone knew what *it* was), became household names. Most loved of all was the comic Charlie Chaplin, whose famous character, the Little Tramp, showed an endearing inability to cope with the complexities of modern life.

Americans also found heroes in sports. Baseball became the national pastime in the 1920s. It remained essentially a game played by and for the working class. In George Herman "Babe" Ruth, baseball had the most cherished free spirit of the time. The rowdy escapades of the "Sultan of Swat" demonstrated that sports offered a way to break out of the ordinariness of everyday life. By "his sheer exuberance," one sportswriter declared, Ruth "has lightened the cares of the world."

The public also fell in love with a young boxer from the grim mining districts of Colorado. As a teenager, Jack Dempsey had made his living hanging around saloons betting he could beat anyone in the house. When he took the heavyweight crown just after World War I, he was revered as the people's champ, the hero of average Americans who felt increasingly confined by bureaucracy and routine. In Philadelphia in 1926, a crowd of 125,000 fans saw challenger Gene Tunney pound and defeat the people's champ.

Football, mostly a college sport, appealed to the upper classes. The most famous coach, Knute Rockne of Notre Dame, celebrated football for its life lessons of hard work and teamwork. Let the professors make learning as exciting as football, Rockne advised, and the problem of getting young people to learn would disappear. But in keeping with the times, football moved toward a more commercial enterprise. Harold "Red" Grange, "the Galloping Ghost," led the way by going from stardom at the University of Illinois to the Chicago Bears in the new professional football league.

The decade's hero worship reached its peak in the celebration of Charles Lindbergh, a young pilot who set out on May 20, 1927, to become the first person to fly solo nonstop across the Atlantic. Newspapers tagged Lindbergh "the Lone Eagle," the perfect hero for an age that celebrated individual accomplishment. "Charles Lindbergh," one journalist proclaimed, "is the stuff out of which have been made the pioneers that opened up the wilderness. His are the qualities which we, as a people, must nourish." Lindbergh realized, however, that technical and organizational complexity was fast reducing chances for solitary achievement. Consequently, he titled his book about the flight *We* (1927) to include the machine that had made it all possible.

Another machine, the radio, became crucial to mass culture in the 1920s. The nation's first licensed radio station, KDKA in Pittsburgh, began broadcasting in

◀ **Charles Lindbergh** Lindbergh's historic flight brought the handsome young aviator unprecedented adulation. One observer commented, people were "behaving as though Lindbergh had walked on water, not flown over it." But Lindbergh's charmed life ended in the 1930s when his infant son was kidnapped and murdered, and his statements about Jews led some to suspect him of being a Nazi sympathizer. Bettmann/Getty Images.

1920, and soon American airwaves buzzed with news, sermons, soap operas, sports, comedy, and music. Because they could now reach prospective customers in their own homes, advertisers bankrolled radio's rapid growth. Between 1922 and 1929, the number of radio stations in the United States increased from 30 to 606. In just seven years, homes with radios jumped from 60,000 to a staggering 10.25 million.

Why did the Lost Generation find a home abroad?

Some writers and artists felt alienated from America's mass-culture society, which they found shallow and materialistic. Silly movie stars disgusted them. They believed that business culture blighted American life. In their minds, Henry Ford made a poor hero. Young, white, and mostly college educated, these expatriates, as they came to be called, felt embittered by the war and renounced the progressives who had promoted it as a crusade. For them, Europe—not Hollywood or Harlem—seemed the place to seek their potential.

The American-born writer Gertrude Stein, long established in Paris, remarked famously as the young exiles gathered around her, "They are the lost generation." Most of the expatriates, however, believed to the contrary that they had finally found themselves. The Lost Generation helped launch the most creative period in American art and literature in the twentieth century. The novelist whose simple, clean style best illustrated the expatriate efforts to make art mirror basic reality was Ernest Hemingway. Admirers found the clipped language and hard lessons of his novel *The Sun Also Rises* (1926) to be perfect expressions of a world stripped of illusions.

Many writers who remained in America were expatriates in spirit. Before the war, intellectuals had eagerly joined progressive reform movements. Afterward, they were more likely critics of vulgar American culture. Novelist Sinclair Lewis in *Main Street* (1920) and *Babbitt* (1922) poked fun at his native Midwest as a cultural wasteland. Writers like James Thurber used humor to criticize America's ridiculous habits. And southern writers, led by William Faulkner, explored the South's tragic class and race heritage. Worries about alienation surfaced as well. F. Scott Fitzgerald spoke sadly in *This Side of Paradise* (1920) of a disillusioned generation "grown up to find all Gods dead, all wars fought, all faiths in man shaken."

REVIEW

How did the new freedoms of the 1920s challenge older conceptions of gender and race?

Why did the relationship between urban and rural America deteriorate in the 1920s?

Large areas of the country did not share in the wealth of the 1920s. By the end of the decade, 40 percent of the nation's farmers were landless, and 90 percent of rural homes lacked indoor plumbing, gas, or electricity. Rural America's traditional distrust of urban America turned to despair in the 1920s when the census reported that the majority of the population had shifted to the city (**Map 23.2**). Once the "backbone of the republic," rural Americans had become poor country cousins. Urban domination over the nation's political and cultural life and sharply rising economic difference drove rural Americans in often ugly, reactionary directions.

Cities seemed to stand for everything rural areas stood against. Rural America imagined itself as solidly Anglo-Saxon (despite the presence of millions of Black people in the South and Mexican Americans, Native Americans, and Asian

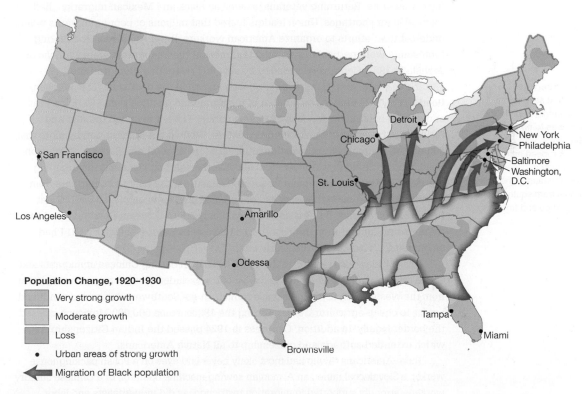

Population Change, 1920–1930

- Very strong growth
- Moderate growth
- Loss
- • Urban areas of strong growth
- ◄ Migration of Black population

MAP 23.2 ▲ The Shift from Rural to Urban Population, 1920–1930 The movement of white and Hispanic people toward urban and agricultural opportunity made Florida, the West, and the Southwest the regions of fastest population growth. By contrast, large numbers of Black people left the rural South to find a better life in the North. Almost all migrating Black Americans went from the countryside to cities in distant parts of the nation, while white and Hispanic migrants tended to move shorter distances toward familiar places.

Americans in the West), and the cities seemed to be filled with undesirable immigrants. Rural America was the home of old-time Protestant religion, and the cities teemed with Catholics, Jews, liberal Protestants, and atheists. Rural America championed old-fashioned moral standards—abstinence and self-denial—while the cities spawned every imaginable vice. In the 1920s, frustrated rural people sought to recapture their country by helping to push through prohibition, dam the flow of immigrants, revive the Ku Klux Klan, defend the Bible as literal truth, and defeat an urban Roman Catholic for president.

What were the consequences of the rising antiforeigner sentiment?

Before the war, when about a million immigrants arrived each year, some citizens warned that foreigners who would never become truly American were drowning the nation. War against Germany and its allies expanded nativist and antiradical sentiment. After the war, large-scale immigration resumed (another 800,000 immigrants arrived in 1921) at a moment when industrialists no longer needed new factory laborers. Returning veterans, as well as Black and Mexican migration, had relieved labor shortages. Union leaders feared that millions of poor immigrants would undercut their efforts to organize American workers. Rural America's God-fearing Protestants were particularly alarmed that most of the immigrants were Catholic or Jewish. In 1921, Congress responded by severely restricting immigration.

Johnson-Reed Act
1924 law that severely restricted immigration to the United States to no more than 161,000 a year, with quotas for each European nation. The racist restrictions were designed to staunch the flow of immigrants from southern and eastern Europe and from Asia.

Three years later, Congress very nearly slammed the door shut. The **Johnson-Reed Act** of 1924 limited the number of immigrants to no more than 161,000 a year and established quotas for each European nation. The act revealed the fear and racism that fueled anti-immigration legislation. While it cut immigration by more than 80 percent, it squeezed some nationalities far more than others. Backers of Johnson-Reed, who declared that America had become the "garbage can and the dumping ground of the world," manipulated quotas to ensure entry only to immigrants from western Europe, whom they saw as "good." The law, for example, allowed Great Britain 62,458 entries, but Russia could send only 1,992. Johnson-Reed reversed the trend toward immigration from southern and eastern Europe, which by 1914 had amounted to 75 percent of the yearly total.

The 1924 law also reaffirmed the 1880s legislation barring Chinese immigrants and added Japanese and other Asians to the list of the excluded. But it left open immigration from the Western Hemisphere because farmers in the Southwest demanded continued access to cheap agricultural labor. During the 1920s, some 500,000 Mexicans crossed the border legally. In addition, Congress in 1924 passed the Indian Citizenship Act, which extended suffrage and citizenship to all Native Americans.

Rural Americans—who had most likely never laid eyes on a Polish packinghouse worker, a Slovak coal miner, an Armenian sewing machine operator, or a Chinese laundry worker—strongly supported immigration restriction, as did industrialists and labor leaders. The laws of the 1920s marked the end of the era symbolized by the Statue of Liberty's open-armed welcome to Europe's "huddled masses yearning to breathe free."

Antiforeign hysteria climaxed in the trial of two anarchist immigrants from Italy, Nicola Sacco and Bartolomeo Vanzetti. Arrested in 1920 for robbery and murder in

◀ **Sacco and Vanzetti** Murder suspects Bartolomeo Vanzetti (left) and Nicola Sacco (right) talk with Sacco's wife, Rosina, while waiting in the prisoners' dock. Even today, the 1927 executions symbolize for some the shortcomings of American justice. Bettmann/Getty Images.

South Braintree, Massachusetts, the men were sentenced to death by a judge who openly referred to them as "anarchist bastards." In response to doubts about the fairness of the verdict, a blue-ribbon review committee found the trial judge guilty of a "grave breach of official decorum" but refused to recommend a motion for retrial. When Massachusetts executed Sacco and Vanzetti on August 23, 1927, fifty thousand American mourners followed the caskets, convinced that the men had died because they were immigrants and radicals, not because they were murderers.

How was the Ku Klux Klan reborn?

Members of the **Ku Klux Klan** shared the nation's sour antiforeign mood. The Klan first appeared in the South during Reconstruction to thwart Black freedom and ended with the reestablishment of white supremacy (see chapter 16). In 1915, the Klan was reborn at Stone Mountain, Georgia, but when the new Klan extended its targets beyond Black Americans, it quickly spread beyond the South. Under a banner proclaiming "100 percent Americanism," the Klan promised to defend family, morality, and traditional American values against the threats posed by Black people, immigrants, radicals, feminists, Catholics, and Jews.

Building on the frustrations of rural America, the Klan in the 1920s spread throughout the nation, helping to shape politics in Indiana, Illinois, California, Oregon, Texas, Louisiana, Oklahoma, and Kansas. The Klan believed that its America was under siege. "One by one all our traditional moral standards went by the boards or were so disregarded that they ceased to be binding," Klan imperial wizard Hiram Wesley Evans explained in 1926. "The sacredness of our Sabbath, of our homes, of

Ku Klux Klan
Secret society that first thwarted Black freedom after the Civil War but was reborn in 1915 to fight against perceived threats posed by Black people, immigrants, radicals, feminists, Catholics, and Jews. The new Klan spread well beyond the South in the 1920s.

chastity, and finally even our right to teach our own children in schools [represented] fundamental facts and truth torn away from us." The Klan cast its members as outcasts in their own land.

Eventually, social changes, along with criminal behavior, crippled the Klan. Immigration restrictions eased the worry about invading foreigners, and sensational wrongdoing by Klan leaders cost it the support of many supporters. Grand Dragon David Stephenson of Indiana, for example, went to jail for the kidnapping and rape of a woman who subsequently committed suicide. Yet the social grievances, economic problems, and religious anxieties of the countryside and small towns remained alive, ready to be ignited.

How did the Scopes trial reflect the divide between urban and rural America?

In 1925 in a Tennessee courtroom, old-time religion and the new spirit of science went head-to-head. The confrontation occurred after several southern states passed legislation against the teaching of Charles Darwin's theory of evolution in the public schools. Scientists and civil liberties organizations called for a challenge to the law, and John Scopes, a young biology teacher in Dayton, Tennessee, offered to test his state's ban on teaching evolution. Clarence Darrow, a brilliant defense lawyer from Chicago, volunteered to defend Scopes, taking on the prosecution's William Jennings Bryan, three-time Democratic nominee for president, fundamentalist Christian, and symbol of rural America.

Scopes trial
1925 trial of John Scopes, a biology teacher in Dayton, Tennessee, for violating his state's ban on teaching evolution. The trial created a nationwide media frenzy and came to be seen as a showdown between urban and rural values.

The **Scopes trial** quickly degenerated into a media circus. The first trial to be covered live on radio, it attracted a nationwide audience. When, under relentless questioning by Darrow, Bryan declared on the witness stand that he did indeed believe that the world had been created in six days and that Jonah had lived in the belly of a whale, most urban observers ridiculed Bryan as a simpleton. Nevertheless, the Tennessee court upheld the law and punished Scopes with a $100 fine. Although fundamentalism won the battle, it lost the war.

Baltimore journalist H. L. Mencken had the last word in a merciless obituary for Bryan, who died just a week after the trial ended. Portraying the "monkey trial" as a battle between the country and the city, Mencken denounced Bryan as a "charlatan, a mountebank, a zany without shame or dignity," motivated solely by "hatred of the city men who had laughed at him for so long."

As Mencken's acid words indicated, Bryan's humiliation was not purely a victory of reason and science. It also revealed the disdain urban people felt for country people and the values they clung to. The Ku Klux Klan revival and the Scopes trial dramatized and inflamed divisions between city and country, intellectuals and the uneducated, the privileged and the poor, the doubters and the faithful.

How did the election of 1928 reflect Republican strength?

The presidential election of 1928 brought many of the developments of the 1920s—prohibition, immigration, religion, and the clash of rural and urban values—into sharp focus. Republicans emphasized the economic success of their party's pro-business government and turned to Herbert Hoover, the energetic secretary of commerce and symbol of 1920s prosperity. But with both parties agreeing that the American economy was basically sound, the campaign turned on social issues that divided Americans.

The Democrats nominated four-time governor of New York Alfred E. Smith. Smith adopted "The Sidewalks of New York" as a campaign theme song and seemed to represent all that rural Americans feared and resented. A child of immigrants, Smith got his start in politics with the help of New York City's Irish-dominated Tammany Hall political machine, to many the worst example of big-city corruption. He denounced immigration quotas, signed New York State's anti-Klan bill, and opposed prohibition, believing that it was a nativist attack on immigrant customs. When Smith admitted enjoying an occasional beer, prohibition forces dubbed him "Alcohol Al." But Smith's greatest vulnerability in the heartland was his religion. He was the first Catholic to run for president. A Methodist bishop in Virginia denounced Roman Catholicism as "the Mother of ignorance, superstition, intolerance and sin" and begged Protestants not to vote for a candidate who represented "the kind of dirty people that you find today on the sidewalks of New York."

Hoover, who neatly combined the images of morality, efficiency, service, and prosperity, won the election by a landslide (**Map 23.3**). He received nearly 58 percent of the vote and gained 444 electoral votes to Smith's 87. The only bright spot for Democrats was the nation's cities, which voted Democratic. The decade-long war on alcohol had succeeded in bringing into the Democratic Party millions of new voters, especially immigrants and Black people, who previously voted Republican.

Candidate	Electoral Vote	Popular Vote	Percent of Popular Vote
Herbert Hoover (Republican)	444	21,391,381	57.4
Alfred E. Smith (Democrat)	87	15,016,443	40.3
Norman Thomas (Socialist)	0	881,951	2.3

MAP 23.3 ▲ The Election of 1928

REVIEW

How did some Americans resist cultural change?

How did President Hoover respond to the economic crash of 1929?

A t his inauguration in 1929, Hoover told the American people, "Given a chance to go forward with the policies of the last eight years, we shall soon with the help of God be in sight of the day when poverty will be banished from this nation." Those words came back to haunt Hoover when eight months later, the prosperity he celebrated collapsed in the stock market crash of 1929. The nation ended nearly three decades of barely interrupted economic growth. Like much of the world, the United States fell into the most serious economic depression of all time. Hoover's reputation was among the first casualties, along with the reverence for business that had been the hallmark of the New Era.

What did Herbert Hoover bring to the presidency?

When Hoover became president in 1929, he seemed the perfect choice to lead a prosperous business nation. His rise from poor Iowa orphan to one of the world's most celebrated mining engineers by the time he was thirty confirmed America's rags-to-riches ideal. His success in feeding civilian victims of the fighting during World War I won him acclaim as "the Great Humanitarian" and led Woodrow Wilson to name him head of the Food Administration once the United States entered the war. Hoover's reputation soared even higher as secretary of commerce in the Harding and Coolidge administrations.

Hoover belonged to the progressive wing of his party. "The time when the employer could ride roughshod over his labor[ers] is disappearing with the doctrine

VISUAL ACTIVITY

▲ **"It's an Elephant's Job"** This political cartoon from the 1928 election depicts Hoover's Republican Party as a powerful elephant successfully pushing the American economy (a loaded truck) out of the mud and toward the rising sun of prosperity. Found Image Press/Corbis via Getty Images.

READING THE IMAGE: What does the emaciated, carefree donkey represent, and how might it have resonated with some Americans?

CONNECTIONS: Why might Americans have responded positively to this characterization of the Republican Party?

of 'laissez-faire' on which it is founded," he declared in 1909. Hoover brought a reform agenda to the White House: "We want to see a nation built of home owners and farm owners. We want to see their savings protected. We want to see them in steady jobs. We want to see more and more of them insured against death and accident, unemployment and old age. We want them all secure."

But Hoover also had ideological and political liabilities. Principles that appeared strengths in the prosperous 1920s — individual self-reliance, industrial self-management, and a limited federal government — became straitjackets when economic catastrophe struck. Moreover, Hoover had never held an elected public office, had a poor political touch, and was too thin-skinned to be an effective politician. Even so, most Americans considered him "a sort of superman" able to solve any problem. But he confided to a friend his fear that "if some unprecedented calamity should come upon the nation . . . I would be sacrificed to the unreasoning disappointment of a people who expected too much." The distorted national economy set the stage for the calamity Hoover so feared.

What factors distorted the U.S. economy?

In the spring of 1929, the United States enjoyed a fragile prosperity. Although America had become the world's leading economy, it had done little to help rebuild Europe's shattered economy after World War I. Instead, the Republican administrations demanded that Allied nations repay their war loans, creating a tangled web of debts and reparations that sapped Europe's economic vitality. To boost American business, the United States enacted tariffs that prevented other nations from selling their goods to Americans. Fewer sales meant that foreign nations had less money to buy American goods. American banks propped up the nation's export trade by extending credit to foreign customers, deepening their debt.

America's domestic economy was also in trouble. Wealth was badly distributed. Farmers continued to suffer from low prices and chronic indebtedness. The average income of farm families was only $240 per year. The wages of industrial workers, though rising during the decade, failed to keep up with productivity and corporate profits. Overall, nearly two-thirds of all American families lived on less than the $2,000 per year that economists estimated would "supply only basic necessities." In sharp contrast, the wealthiest 1 percent of the population received 15 percent of the nation's income — the amount received by the poorest 42 percent. The Coolidge administration worsened the deepening inequality by cutting taxes on the wealthy.

By 1929, the inequality of wealth produced a serious problem in consumption. The rich, brilliantly portrayed in F. Scott Fitzgerald's novel *The Great Gatsby* (1925), spent lavishly, but they could absorb only a tiny fraction of the nation's output. For a time, the new device of installment buying — buying on credit — kept consumer demand up. By the end of the decade, four out of five cars and two out of three radios were bought on credit.

Signs of economic trouble began to appear at mid-decade. New construction slowed down. Automobile sales faltered. Companies began cutting back production and laying off workers. Between 1921 and 1928, as investment and loan opportunities faded, five thousand banks failed, wiping out the life savings of hundreds of thousands.

What caused the crash of 1929?

Even as the economy faltered, Americans remained upbeat. Hoping for even bigger slices of the economic pie, Americans speculated wildly in the stock market on Wall Street. Between 1924 and 1929, the values of stocks listed on the New York Stock Exchange increased by more than 400 percent. Buying stocks on margin—that is, putting up only part of the money at the time of purchase—accelerated. Some people got rich this way, but those who bought on credit could finance their loans only if their stocks increased in value. A Yale economist assured doubters that stock prices had reached "a permanently high plateau." Former president Calvin Coolidge declared that, at current prices, stocks were a bargain. But President Hoover observed, "The only trouble with capitalism is capitalists. They're too damned greedy."

Finally, in the autumn of 1929, the market hesitated. Investors nervously began to sell their overvalued stocks. The dip quickly became a panic on October 24, the day that came to be known as Black Thursday. More panic selling came on Black Tuesday, October 29, the day the market suffered a greater fall than ever before. In the next six months, the stock market lost six-sevenths of its total value.

It was once thought that the crash alone caused the Great Depression. It did not. In 1929, the national and international economies were already riddled with severe problems. But the dramatic losses in the stock market crash and the fear of risking what was left acted as a brake on economic activity. The collapse on Wall Street shattered the New Era's confidence that America would enjoy perpetually expanding prosperity.

How did Hoover respond to the economic crisis?

When the bubble broke, Americans expressed relief that Hoover sat in the White House. Not surprisingly for a man who had been such an active secretary of commerce, Hoover acted quickly to arrest the decline. In November 1929, to keep the stock market collapse from ravaging the entire economy, Hoover called a White House conference of business and labor leaders. He urged them to join in a voluntary plan for recovery: Businesses would maintain production and keep their workers on the job; labor would accept existing wages, hours, and conditions. Within a few months, however, the bargain fell apart. As demand for their products declined, industrialists cut production, sliced wages, and laid off workers. Poorly paid or unemployed workers could not buy much, and their decreased spending led to further cuts in production and further loss of jobs. Thus began the terrible spiral of economic decline.

To deal with the problems of rural America, Hoover got Congress to pass the Agricultural Marketing Act in 1929. The act created the Farm Board, which used its budget of $500 million to buy up agricultural surpluses and thus, it was hoped, raise prices. But prices continued to fall. To help end the decline, Hoover joined conservatives in urging protective tariffs on agricultural goods, and the Hawley-Smoot tariff of 1930 established the highest rates in history. The same year, Congress also authorized $420 million for public works projects to give the unemployed jobs and create more purchasing power. In three years, the Hoover administration nearly doubled federal public works spending.

But with each year of Hoover's term, the economy weakened. Tariffs did not end the suffering of farmers because foreign nations retaliated with increased tariffs of their own that crippled American farmers' ability to sell abroad. In 1932, Hoover hoped to help hard-pressed industry with the **Reconstruction Finance Corporation (RFC)**, a federal agency empowered to lend government funds to endangered banks and corporations. The theory was trickle-down economics: Pump money into the economy at the top, and in the long run the people at the bottom would benefit. Or, as one critic put it, "Feed the sparrows by feeding the horses." In the end, very little of what enemies of the RFC called a "millionaires' dole" trickled down to the poor.

Meanwhile, hundreds of thousands of workers lost their jobs each month. By 1932, an astounding one-quarter of the American workforce (nearly thirteen million people) was unemployed. There was no direct federal assistance, and state services and private charities were swamped. The depression that began in 1929 devastated much of the world, but no other industrialized nation provided such feeble support to the jobless. Cries grew louder for the federal government to give hurting people relief.

Hoover was no do-nothing president, but he believed there were limits to the government's proper role in fighting the economic disaster. He compared direct federal aid to the needy to the "dole" in Britain, which he thought destroyed the moral fiber of the chronically unemployed. "Prosperity cannot be restored by raids on the public Treasury," Hoover declared. Besides, he said, the poor could rely on their neighbors to protect them "from hunger and cold." In 1931, he allowed the Red Cross to distribute government-owned agricultural surpluses to the hungry. In 1932, he relaxed his principles further to offer small federal loans, not gifts, to the states to help them in their relief efforts. But Hoover's restricted notions of legitimate government action proved vastly inadequate to address the problems of restarting the economy and ending human suffering.

Reconstruction Finance Corporation (RFC)
Federal agency established by Herbert Hoover in 1932 to help American industry by lending government funds to endangered banks and corporations, which Hoover hoped would benefit people at the bottom through trickle-down economics. In practice, this strategy provided little help to the poor.

REVIEW

Why did the American economy collapse in 1929?

What impact did the economic depression have on everyday life?

I n 1930, suffering on a massive scale set in. Men and women hollow-eyed with hunger grew increasingly bewildered and angry in the face of cruel contradictions. They saw agricultural surpluses pile up in the countryside and knew that their children were going to bed hungry. They saw factories standing idle, yet they knew that they and millions of others were willing to work. The gap between the American people and leaders who failed to resolve these contradictions widened as the depression deepened. By 1932, America's economic problems had created a dangerous social and political crisis.

What was the human toll of the Great Depression?

Statistics only hint at the human tragedy of the Great Depression. When Hoover took office in 1929, the American economy stood at its peak. When he left in 1933, it had reached its twentieth-century low (**Figure 23.2**). In 1929, national income was $88 billion. By 1933, it had declined to $40 billion. In 1929, unemployment was 3.1 percent, or 1.5 million workers. By 1933, unemployment stood at 25 percent, almost 13 million workers. In Cleveland, Ohio, 50 percent of the workforce was jobless, and in Toledo, 80 percent. By 1932, more than nine thousand banks had shut their doors, wiping out millions of savings accounts.

Jobless, homeless victims wandered in search of work, and the tramp, or hobo, became one of the most visible figures of the decade. Riding the rails or hitchhiking, a million vagabonds moved southward and westward looking for seasonal agricultural work. Other unemployed men and women, sick or less hopeful, huddled in doorways, overcome, one man remembered, by "helpless despair and submission." Scavengers haunted alleys behind restaurants in search of food. One writer told of an elderly woman who always took off her glasses to avoid seeing the maggots crawling over the garbage she ate. In 1931, four New York City hospitals reported ninety-five deaths from starvation. "I don't want to steal," a Pennsylvania man wrote to the governor, "but I won't let my wife and boy cry for something to eat. . . . How long is this going to keep up? I cannot stand it any longer."

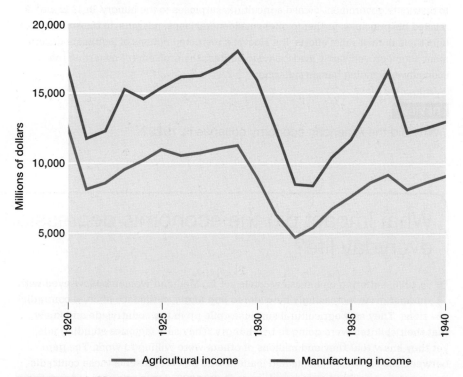

FIGURE 23.2 ▲ **Manufacturing and Agricultural Income, 1920–1940** After economic collapse, recovery in the 1930s began under New Deal auspices.

Rural poverty was most acute. Tenant farmers and sharecroppers, mainly in the South, revealed how poverty could crush the human spirit. Eight and a half million people, three million of them Black, crowded into cabins without plumbing, electricity, or running water. They subsisted—just barely—on salt pork, cornmeal, molasses, beans, peas, and whatever they could hunt or fish. When economist John Maynard Keynes was asked whether anything like this degradation had existed before, he replied, "Yes, it was called the Dark Ages and it lasted four hundred years."

There was no federal assistance to meet this human catastrophe, only a patchwork of strapped charities and broke state and local agencies. For a family of four without any income, the best the city of Philadelphia could do was provide $5.50 per week. That was not enough to live on, but better than Detroit, which allotted 60 cents a week before the city ran out of money altogether.

The deepening crisis roused old fears and caused some Americans to look for someone to blame. During the 1920s, cheap agricultural labor from Mexico flowed legally across the U.S. border, welcomed by the large farmers. In the 1930s, however, the public denounced the newcomers as dangerous aliens who took jobs from Americans. Government officials, most prominently those in Los Angeles County, targeted Mexican residents for deportation, regardless of citizenship status. As many as half a million Mexicans and Mexican Americans were deported or fled to Mexico.

The depression deeply affected the American family. Young people postponed marriage. When they did marry, they produced few children. White women, who generally worked in low-paying service areas, did not lose their jobs as often as men who worked in steel, automobile, and other heavy industries. Idle husbands suffered a loss of self-esteem. "Before the depression," one unemployed man reported, "I wore the pants in this family, and rightly so." Jobless, he lost self-respect and also "the respect of my children, and I am afraid that I am losing my wife." Employers discriminated against married women workers, but necessity continued to drive women into the marketplace. As a result, by 1940, some 25 percent more women were employed for wages than in 1930.

How did Americans try to escape the realities of the Great Depression?

President Hoover assured Americans that economic recovery was on its way, but makeshift shantytowns, called "Hoovervilles," that sprang up on the edges of America's cities contradicted the president's optimism. Newspapers, used as cover by those sleeping on the streets, were "Hoover blankets." An empty pocket turned inside out was a "Hoover flag," and jackrabbits caught for food were "Hoover hogs." Bitter jokes circulated about the increasingly unpopular president. One told of Hoover asking for a nickel to telephone a friend. Flipping him a dime, an aide said, "Here, call them both."

While Hoover practiced denial, most Americans sought refuge from reality at the movies. Throughout the depression, between 60 million and 75 million people (nearly two-thirds of the nation) scraped together enough change to fill the movie palaces every week. Box office hits such as *42nd Street* and *Gold Diggers of 1933* capitalized on the hope that prosperity lay just around the corner. But a few filmmakers grappled with realities rather than escape them. *The Public Enemy* (1931) taught hard lessons about gangsters' lawbreaking. Indeed, under the new production code of 1930, designed to protect public morals, all movies had to find some way to show that crime did not pay.

Despite Hollywood's efforts to keep Americans on the right side of the law, crime increased. In the countryside, the plight of people who had lost their farms to bank foreclosures led to the romantic idea that bank robbers were only getting back what banks had stolen from the poor.

Woody Guthrie, a folksinger from Oklahoma, captured the public's tolerance for outlaws in his tribute to a murderous bank robber with a choirboy face, "The Ballad of Pretty Boy Floyd." Guthrie sang that there were two kinds of robbers, those who used guns and those who used pens, and he observed that robbers with guns, like Pretty Boy Floyd, never drove families from their homes. Named Public Enemy No. 1, Floyd was shot and killed by police in 1934. His funeral in Oklahoma was attended by between twenty thousand and forty thousand people, many of whom viewed Floyd as a tragic figure, a victim of the hard times.

How did the working class rise up?

The nation's working class bore the brunt of the economic collapse. By 1931, William Green, head of the American Federation of Labor (AFL), had turned militant. "I warn the people who are exploiting the workers," he shouted, "that they can drive them only so far before they will turn on them and destroy them. They are taking no account of the history of nations in which governments have been overturned. Revolutions grow out of the depths of hunger."

The American people were slow to anger, but on March 7, 1932, several thousand unemployed autoworkers gathered at the gates of Henry Ford's River Rouge factory in Dearborn, Michigan, to demand work. Pelted with rocks, Ford's private security forces responded with gunfire, killing four demonstrators. Forty thousand outraged citizens turned out for the unemployed men's funerals.

Farmers mounted uprisings of their own. When Congress refused to guarantee farm prices, several thousand farmers created the National Farmers' Holiday Association in 1932, so named because its members planned to take a "holiday" from shipping crops to market. Farm militants also resorted to what they called "penny sales." When banks foreclosed and put farms up for auction, neighbors warned others not to bid, bought the foreclosed property for a few pennies, and returned it to the bankrupt owners. Activism won farmers little in the way of long-term solutions, but one individual observed that "the biggest and finest crop of revolutions you ever saw is sprouting all over the country right now."

Even those who had proved their patriotism by serving in World War I rose up in protest against the government. In 1932, tens of thousands of unemployed veterans traveled to Washington, D.C., to demand the immediate payment of the pension (known as a "bonus") that Congress had promised them in 1924. Hoover feared that the veterans would spark a riot and ordered the U.S. Army to evict the **Bonus Marchers** from their camp on the outskirts of the city. Tanks destroyed the squatters' camps while five hundred soldiers wielding bayonets and tear gas sent the protesters

Harlan County Coal Strike, 1931

Bonus Marchers
World War I veterans who marched on Washington, D.C., in 1932 to peacefully lobby for immediate payment of the pension ("bonus") promised them in 1924. President Herbert Hoover feared that the veterans would set off riots and sent the U.S. Army to evict them from the city.

◀ **"Scottsboro Boys"** Nine Black youths, ranging in age from thirteen to twenty-one, were convicted of the rape of two white women and sentenced to death by an all-white jury in March 1931. None was executed, and eventually the state dropped the charges against the youngest four and granted paroles to the others. The last Scottsboro Boy left jail in 1950.
Bettmann/Getty Images.

fleeing. The spectacle of the army driving peaceful, petitioning veterans from the nation's capital further undermined public support for the beleaguered Hoover.

The Great Depression—the massive failure of capitalism—catapulted the Communist Party to its greatest size and influence in American history. Some 100,000 Americans—workers, intellectuals, college students—joined the Communist Party believing that only an overthrow of the capitalist system could save the victims of the depression. In 1931, the party, through its National Miners Union, moved into Harlan County, Kentucky, to support a strike by brutalized coal miners. Mine owners unleashed thugs against the strikers and eventually beat the miners down. But the Communist Party gained a reputation as the most dedicated and fearless champion of the union cause.

The left also led the fight against racism. While both major parties refused to challenge segregation in the South, the Socialist Party, led by Norman Thomas, attacked the system of sharecropping that left many Black people in near servitude. The Communist Party also took action. When nine young Black men in Scottsboro, Alabama (the **Scottsboro Boys**), were arrested on trumped-up rape charges in 1931, a team of lawyers sent by the party saved the defendants from the electric chair.

Radicals on the left often sparked action, but protests by moderate workers and farmers occurred on a far greater scale. Breadlines, soup kitchens, foreclosures, unemployment, government violence, and cold despair drove patriotic men and women to question American capitalism. "I am as conservative as any man could be," a Wisconsin farmer explained, "but any economic system that has in its power to set me and my wife in the streets, at my age—what can I see but red?"

Scottsboro Boys
Nine Black youths who were arrested for the alleged rape of two white women in Scottsboro, Alabama, in 1931. After an all-white jury sentenced the young men to death, the Communist Party took action that saved them from the electric chair.

REVIEW

What was the human toll of the depression?

Conclusion: Why did the hope of the 1920s turn to despair?

In the aftermath of World War I, America turned its back on progressive crusades and embraced conservative Republican politics, the growing influence of corporate leaders, and business values. Changes in the nation's economy—Henry Ford's automobile revolution, mass production, advertising—propelled fundamental change throughout society. Living standards rose, economic opportunity increased, and Americans threw themselves into private pleasures—gobbling up the latest household goods and fashions, attending baseball and football games and boxing matches, gathering around the radio, and going to the movies. As big cities came to dominate American life, the culture of youth and flappers became the leading edge of what one observer called a "revolution in manners and morals." At home in Harlem and abroad in Paris, American literature, art, and music flourished.

For many Americans, however, none of the glamour and vitality had much meaning. Instead of seeking thrills at the speakeasies, plunging into speculation on Wall Street, or escaping overseas, the vast majority struggled to earn a decent living. Blue-collar America did not participate fully in white-collar prosperity. Rural America was almost entirely left out of the Roaring Twenties. Country folk, deeply suspicious and profoundly discontented, championed prohibition, revived the Klan, attacked immigration, and defended old-time Protestant religion.

The crash of 1929 and the depression that followed starkly revealed the economy's crises of international trade and consumption. Hard times swept high living off the front pages of the nation's newspapers. Different images emerged: hoboes hopping freight trains, strikers confronting police, malnourished sharecroppers staring blankly into the distance, empty apartment buildings alongside cardboard shantytowns, and mountains of food rotting in the sun while guards with shotguns chased away the hungry.

The depression hurt everyone, but the poor were hurt most. As farmers and workers sank into misery, businessmen rallied around Herbert Hoover to proclaim that private enterprise would get the country moving again. But things fell apart, and Hoover faced increasingly radical opposition. Membership in the Socialist and Communist parties surged, and more and more Americans contemplated desperate measures. By 1932, the depression had nearly brought the nation to its knees. America faced its greatest crisis since the Civil War, and citizens demanded new leaders who would save them from the "Hoover Depression."

CHAPTER REVIEW

EXPLAIN WHY IT MATTERS

Teapot Dome (p. 669)

Five-Power Naval Treaty of 1922 (p. 670)

welfare capitalism (p. 672)

prohibition (p. 676)

new woman (p. 677)

New Negro (p. 679)

Johnson-Reed Act (p. 684)

Ku Klux Klan (p. 685)

Scopes trial (p. 686)

Reconstruction Finance Corporation (RFC) (p. 691)

Bonus Marchers (p. 694)

Scottsboro Boys (p. 695)

PUT IT ALL TOGETHER

POSTWAR DEVELOPMENTS

• What place did big business hold in the politics and culture of the 1920s?

• How did the economic changes of the 1920s contribute to challenges to social, cultural, and ethical norms?

RESISTANCE TO CHANGE

• What explains the rising anti-immigrant mood of America in the 1920s?

• What cultural divisions between rural and urban America were highlighted by the election of 1928?

THE CRASH AND THE GREAT DEPRESSION

• What underlying weaknesses in the American and world economies led to the Great Depression?

• How did Herbert Hoover respond to the economic crisis that engulfed his presidency? Why were his efforts unsuccessful?

• What was the human toll of the Great Depression?

LOOKING BACKWARD, LOOKING AHEAD

• Were the 1920s truly a New Era? Why or why not?

• How were American life and culture challenged by the economic collapse of 1929? Why did economic disaster make political change possible?

24

THE NEW DEAL EXPERIMENT

1932–1939

This chapter discusses the following questions:

- Why was Franklin D. Roosevelt elected president in 1932?
- What were the goals and achievements of the first New Deal?
- Who opposed the New Deal?
- Why did the New Deal begin to create a welfare state?
- Why did the New Deal lose support during Roosevelt's second term as president?
- Conclusion: What were the achievements and limitations of the New Deal?

▶ **Florence Owens and Children** This classic photograph of migrant farm laborer Florence Owens and her children was taken by New Deal photographer Dorothea Lange in 1936 in the labor camp of a pea field in California. The photo depicts the privations common among working people during the depression, but it also evokes a mother's leadership, dignity, and affection — qualities that helped shelter her family from poverty and joblessness. Library of Congress Prints and Photographs Division [LC-DIG-fsa-8b29516].

AN AMERICAN STORY

In March 1936, Florence Owens piled her seven children into her old Hudson. They had been picking beets in southern California, near the Mexican border, but the harvest was over now. Owens headed north, where she hoped to find work picking lettuce. About halfway there, her car broke down. She coasted into a labor camp of more than two thousand migrant workers who were hungry and out of work. Owens set up a lean-to shelter and prepared food for her family while two of her sons worked on the car. They ate half-frozen peas from the field and small birds killed by the children. Owens recalled later, "I started to cook dinner for my kids, and all the little kids around the camp came in. 'Can I have a bite? . . .' And they was hungry, them people was."

Florence Owens was born in 1903 in Indian Territory, which became the state of Oklahoma. Both of Florence's parents were Cherokee. When she was seventeen, she married a farmer who moved his growing family to California, where he died of tuberculosis in 1931, leaving Florence a widow with young children.

To support herself and her children, Florence began to work as a farm laborer in California's Central Valley. She picked cotton, earning about $2 a day. "I'd leave home before daylight and come in after dark," she explained. "We just existed!" To survive, she worked nights as a waitress, making "50-cents a day and the leftovers." Sometimes, she remembered, "I'd carry home two water buckets full" of leftovers for her children.

Like tens of thousands of other migrant laborers, Owens followed the crops along the West Coast from California to Oregon and Washington. Joining Owens and other migrants — many of whom were Mexicans and Filipinos — were Okie refugees from the Dust Bowl, the large swath of Great Plains states that suffered drought, failed crops, and foreclosed mortgages during the 1930s.

Soon after Florence Owens fed her children at the pea pickers' camp, a car pulled up, and a woman with a camera got out and began to take photographs of Owens. The woman was Dorothea Lange, a photographer employed by a New Deal agency to document conditions among farmworkers in California. Lange snapped six photos of Owens, then climbed back in her car and headed to Berkeley. Owens and her family, their car now repaired, drove off to look for work in the lettuce fields.

Lange's last photograph of Owens, subsequently known as *Migrant Mother*, became an icon of the desperate Americans that President Franklin Roosevelt's New Deal sought to help. *Migrant Mother* became

Dorothea Lange's most famous photograph. But neither the publicity nor the New Deal did anything for Florence Owens. She continued to work in the fields, "ragged, hungry, and broke," as a San Francisco newspaper noted.

Unlike Owens, her children, and other migrant workers, many Americans received government help from Roosevelt's New Deal. They benefited from New Deal policies designed to provide relief for the needy, to speed economic recovery, and to reform basic institutions of government and economy. The New Deal provoked bitter opposition from critics on the right and the left. It failed to satisfy fully its own goals of relief, recovery, and reform. But it helped millions of Americans withstand the hardships of the Great Depression. It also energized a powerful political coalition within the Democratic Party that supported Roosevelt and the New Deal. In the process, the federal government became a major presence in the daily lives of most Americans.

Why was Franklin D. Roosevelt elected president in 1932?

Unlike most Americans, Franklin Roosevelt came from a wealthy family. His privileged background separated him from the struggles of ordinary people. In his political career, however, he sought to help less fortunate Americans. During the twelve years he served as president (1933–1945), many rich and powerful people came to hate him as a traitor to his class. Millions of other Americans, especially the poor and unemployed, revered him because he cared about them and their problems.

How did Roosevelt's background shape his political ideas?

Born in 1882, Franklin D. Roosevelt grew up in a mansion on the Hudson River, north of New York City. Roosevelt planned to go into politics, following in the political footsteps of his cousin, Theodore Roosevelt. When he married another cousin, Eleanor Roosevelt, the current president of the United States—Theodore Roosevelt—gave the bride away. Unlike cousin Teddy, Franklin Roosevelt joined the Democratic Party. In 1920, Democrats chose him as their candidate for vice president on the ticket of their presidential nominee, James M. Cox. Although Cox lost the election (see chapter 22), Roosevelt's energy as a campaigner impressed Democratic Party leaders.

In 1921, when he was thirty-nine, Roosevelt caught polio, which paralyzed both his legs. For the rest of his life, he used a wheelchair. He wore heavy steel braces that allowed him to walk only by leaning on another person. Tireless physical therapy helped him regain his strength and ambition for high political office.

After his polio attack, Roosevelt went to a therapy center at Warm Springs, Georgia. There he got to know southern Democrats, who helped make him a rare political creature: a New Yorker from the Democratic Party's urban, immigrant, northern wing who got along with white people from the party's powerful, rural, native-born, southern wing. By 1928, Roosevelt had recovered enough to campaign successfully for governor of New York. His term as governor showcased his activist policies and became a dress rehearsal for the New Deal.

Governor Roosevelt believed that government should take steps to protect citizens from economic hardships caused by the Great Depression rather than wait passively until the law of supply and demand eventually improved the economy. According to the laissez-faire views of many conservatives — especially Republicans but also numerous Democrats — the depression was the result of the market economy punishing losers and allowing winners in the competitive struggle to survive, as it was supposed to do.

Unlike Roosevelt, conservatives believed that government handouts sapped individual initiative and blocked the self-correcting forces of the market. Government help, they claimed, rewarded weak people instead of leaving them to sink or swim by their own efforts. Roosevelt lacked a full-fledged counterargument to these conservative claims, but he sympathized with the plight of poor people. "To these unfortunate citizens," he declared, "aid must be extended by governments, not as a matter of charity but as a matter of social duty. . . . [No one should go] unfed, unclothed, or unsheltered."

To his supporters, Roosevelt seemed to be a leader determined to attack the economic crisis without deviating from democracy or capitalism, unlike the fascists gaining strength in Europe and the Communists in the Soviet Union. Roosevelt's ideas about how to revive the economy were vague. A prominent journalist described him in 1931 as "a kind of amiable boy scout . . . who, without any important qualifications for the office, would very much like to be president." Roosevelt's many supporters, however, appreciated his energy and his conviction that government should do something to help Americans who were suffering from the economic collapse.

What contributed to FDR's victory in the 1932 election?

Democrats knew that President Herbert Hoover was very unpopular among voters, which gave them a historic opportunity to recapture the White House in 1932. Since Abraham Lincoln's election back in 1860, Republican presidents had occupied the White House three-fourths of the time. To reverse this trend, however, Democrats had to overcome warring factions that divided their own party by region, religion, culture, and commitment to the status quo. The conservative wing of the Democratic Party included southern, native-born, white, rural

Candidate	Electoral Vote	Popular Vote	Percent of Popular Vote
Franklin D. Roosevelt (Democrat)	472	22,821,857	57.4
Herbert C. Hoover (Republican)	59	15,761,841	39.7
Norman Thomas (Socialist)	0	881,951	2.2
William Z. Foster (Communist)	0	102,991	0.3

MAP 24.1 ▲ The Election of 1932

New Deal coalition
Political coalition that supported Franklin D. Roosevelt's New Deal and the Democratic Party.

Protestants. These Democrats found little common ground with the party's liberal wing, whose voters were mostly northern, urban, and immigrants, many of them Catholics. Eastern-establishment Democratic dignitaries shared few goals with angry urban factory workers or midwestern and southern farmers. Still, this unruly coalition managed to agree that Franklin Roosevelt should be the Democrats' presidential candidate.

In a series of speeches, Roosevelt vowed to help "the forgotten man at the bottom of the pyramid" with "bold, persistent experimentation." Highlighting his differences with Hoover and the Republicans, he pledged "a new deal for the American people." Few details about what Roosevelt meant by "a new deal" surfaced in the presidential campaign. He declared that "the people of America want more than anything else . . . two things: work . . . and a reasonable measure of security . . . for themselves and for their wives and children." Voters decided that whatever Roosevelt's new deal might be, it was better than reelecting Hoover.

Roosevelt won the 1932 presidential election in a historic landslide. He received 57 percent of the nation's votes, the first time a Democrat had won a majority of the popular vote since 1852 (**Map 24.1**). He piled up 472 electoral votes to Hoover's 59, carrying state after state that had voted Republican for years (**Map 24.2**). Roosevelt's coattails swept Democrats into control of Congress by large margins. The popular mandate for change was loud and clear.

Roosevelt's victory represented the emergence of what came to be known as the **New Deal coalition**. Attracting support from farmers, factory workers, immigrants, city folk, Black people, women, and progressive intellectuals, Roosevelt launched a realignment of the nation's political loyalties. The New Deal coalition dominated American politics throughout Roosevelt's presidency and remained powerful long after his death in 1945. United less by their ideas or support for specific policies, voters in the New Deal coalition came together around their faith in Roosevelt's promise of a government that would somehow change things for the better.

Nobody, including Roosevelt, knew exactly what the New Deal would change or whether the changes would revive the nation's ailing economy and improve Americans' lives. But as he said during the presidential campaign, "It is high time to admit with courage that we are in the midst of an emergency at least equal to that of war. Let us mobilize to meet it." Roosevelt and many others knew that the future of American capitalism and democracy was at stake.

REVIEW

Why did Roosevelt win by a landslide in 1932?

MAP ACTIVITY

Switched from Republican in 1928 to Democrat in 1932

Remained Republican, 1928 and 1932

Remained Democrat, 1928 and 1932

MAP 24.2 ▲ Electoral Shift, 1928–1932 The Democratic victory in 1932 signaled the rise of a New Deal coalition within which women and minorities, many of them new voters, made the Democrats the majority party for the first time in the twentieth century.

READING THE MAP. How many states voted Democratic in 1928? How many states voted Republican in 1932? How many states shifted from Republican to Democratic between 1928 and 1932?

CONNECTIONS: What factions within the Democratic Party opposed Franklin Roosevelt's candidacy in 1932, and why did they do so? To what do you attribute his landslide victory?

What were the goals and achievements of the first New Deal?

At noon on March 4, 1933, Americans gathered around their radios to hear Roosevelt's inaugural address. He began by declaring his "firm belief that the only thing we have to fear is fear itself—nameless, unreasoning, unjustified terror which paralyzes needed efforts to convert retreat into advance." He promised "direct, vigorous action." The first months of his administration, termed "the Hundred Days," fulfilled that promise in a whirlwind of New Deal initiatives.

Roosevelt and his advisers had three related objectives: First, they wanted to provide relief to poor people, especially the one out of four Americans who were unemployed. Second, they hoped to stimulate the economic recovery of farms and businesses, thereby creating jobs and reducing the need for relief. Third, they intended to reform the government and economy to try to reduce the risk of future economic depressions and thereby strengthen capitalism. The New Deal never fully achieved these goals of relief, recovery, and reform. But by aiming for them, Roosevelt's experimental programs greatly expanded government's role in the nation's economy and society.

Who were the New Dealers?

To design and implement the New Deal, Roosevelt needed ideas and people. He convened a "Brains Trust" of economists and other leaders to offer suggestions and advice about the problems facing the nation. He consulted Democratic leaders throughout the nation. But no New Dealers were more important than the president and his wife, Eleanor.

While the popular president radiated charm and good cheer, giving the New Deal's bureaucratic programs a friendly human face, Eleanor Roosevelt became the New Deal's unofficial ambassador. As she said, she served as "the eyes and ears of the New Deal," traveling throughout the nation meeting Americans of all colors and creeds. A North Carolina women's rights activist recalled, "One of my greatest pleasures was meeting Mrs. Roosevelt. . . . She was so free of prejudice . . . and she was always willing to take a stand, and there were stands to take about blacks and women."

As Roosevelt's programs swung into action, the millions who benefited from the New Deal became grassroots supporters voting Democratic on election day. In this way, the New Deal created a durable political coalition that reelected Roosevelt in 1936, 1940, and 1944, making him the only four-term president in American history.

Four guiding ideas shaped New Deal policies. First, Roosevelt and his advisers sought capitalist solutions to the economic crisis. They had no desire to eliminate private property or impose socialist programs, such as government ownership of productive resources. Instead, they hoped to save the capitalist economy by correcting its flaws.

underconsumption
When factories and farms produce more than consumers can buy, causing factories to lay off workers and farmers to lose markets for their crops.

Second, Roosevelt's Brains Trust persuaded him that the greatest flaw of America's capitalist economy was **underconsumption**, the root cause of the current economic paralysis. Underconsumption, New Dealers argued, resulted from the gigantic productive success of capitalism. Factories and farms produced more than they could sell to consumers, causing factories to lay off workers and farmers to lose money on bumper crops. Workers without wages and farmers without profits shrank consumption and choked the economy. Somehow, the balance between consumption and production needed to be restored.

Third, New Dealers believed that the immense size and economic power of American corporations needed to be counterbalanced by government and by organizations of workers and small producers. Unlike progressive trustbusters, New Dealers did not seek to splinter big businesses. Roosevelt and his advisers hoped to offset big economic institutions with government programs that focused on protecting individuals and the public interest.

Fourth, New Dealers believed that government must somehow moderate the imbalance of wealth created by American capitalism. Wealth concentrated in a few hands reduced consumption by most Americans and thereby contributed to the current economic gridlock. Government needed to find a way to permit ordinary working people to share more fully in the fruits of the economy. "Our task now," Roosevelt declared during the presidential campaign, "is . . . meeting the problem of underconsumption, . . . adjusting production to consumption, . . . [and] distributing wealth and products more equitably."

How did the New Deal reform banking and finance?

Roosevelt wasted no time making good on his inaugural pledge of "action now." When he took the oath of office, the nation's banking system was on the brink of collapse. Working round the clock, New Dealers drafted the Emergency Banking Act, which propped up banks with federal funds and required them to follow federal rules and regulations.

To secure the confidence of depositors, Congress passed the Glass-Steagall Banking Act, which started the **Federal Deposit Insurance Corporation (FDIC)**. The FDIC guaranteed that, if a bank failed, the federal government would reimburse people who had deposited their money in the bank. In addition, the Glass-Steagall Act required commercial banks (which accept deposits and make loans to individuals and small businesses) to be separated from investment banks (which make speculative investments with their funds). This provision protected the finances of Main Street America from the risky speculations of Wall Street wheeler-dealers.

On Sunday night, March 12, while the banks were still closed during the "bank holiday," Roosevelt broadcast the first of his **fireside chats**. Speaking in a friendly, informal manner, he explained the new banking legislation that made it "safer to keep your money in a reopened bank than under the mattress." With such plain talk, Roosevelt translated complex matters into common sense. His fireside chats forged a direct connection—via radio—between the president and millions of Americans. A man from Paris, Texas, expressed that connection by writing Roosevelt, "You are the one & only President that ever helped a Working Class of People. . . . Please help us some way I Pray to God for relief."

The banking legislation and fireside chat worked. Within a few days, most of the nation's major banks reopened, and they remained open as newly confident depositors switched funds from their mattresses to their bank accounts (**Figure 24.1**). One New Dealer boasted, "Capitalism was saved in eight days."

In his inaugural address, Roosevelt criticized financiers for their greed and incompetence. To prevent the fraud, corruption, and insider trading that had tainted Wall Street and contributed to the crash of 1929, the New Deal set up the Securities and Exchange Commission (SEC) in 1934 to oversee financial markets. The SEC licensed investment brokers, monitored all stock transactions, and required corporations to make full disclosures about their finances, opening a new era of public information about corporate balance sheets that persists today. To lead the SEC, Roosevelt appointed a successful Wall Street financier, Joseph P. Kennedy (father of the future president John F. Kennedy). Under Kennedy's leadership, the SEC helped clean up and regulate Wall Street.

Federal Deposit Insurance Corporation (FDIC)
Federal agency that guaranteed the government would reimburse bank depositors if their banks failed.

fireside chats
Series of informal radio addresses Franklin Roosevelt made to the nation in which he explained New Deal initiatives.

**FIGURE 24.1 ▶ Bank
Failures and Farm
Foreclosures, 1932–1942**
New Deal legislation to stabilize
the economy had its most
immediate effect in preventing
banks and their depositors
from going under and farmers
from losing their land.

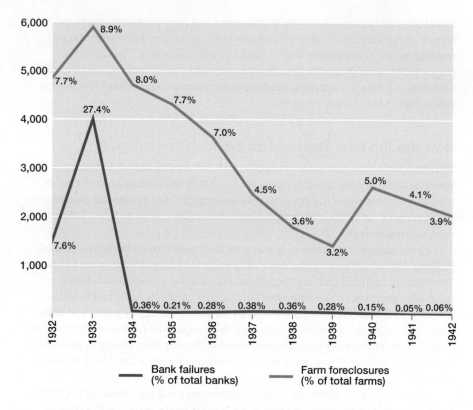

How did the New Deal provide relief and conserve natural resources?

Patching the nation's financial structure gave little relief to hungry and
unemployed citizens. A poor man from Nebraska asked Eleanor Roosevelt "if
the folk who was borned here in America . . . are this Forgotten Man, the
President had in mind, [and] if we are this Forgotten Man then we are still
Forgotten." The federal government had never assumed responsibility for needy
people, except in moments of natural disaster or in emergencies such as the
Civil War. Instead, churches, private charities, county and municipal
governments, and occasionally states shouldered the burden of poor relief,
usually with meager payments.

The crisis of the depression demanded new federal relief efforts, according to
New Dealers. A New Yorker who still had a job described the plight of millions:
"We work, ten hours a day for six days. In the grime and dirt of a nation [for] . . .
low pay [making us] . . . slaves—slaves of the depression!" In 1933, the Federal
Emergency Relief Administration (FERA) was established, supporting four million
to five million households with grants of $20 or $30 a month. FERA also created
jobs for the unemployed on thousands of public works projects. Organized under
the Civil Works Administration (CWA), these jobs put paychecks worth more than

$800 million into the hands of previously jobless workers. Laborers earned wages between 40 and 60 cents an hour working to renovate schools, dig sewers, and rebuild roads and bridges.

The most popular work relief program was the **Civilian Conservation Corps (CCC)**, set up in 1933. The CCC offered unemployed young men a chance to earn wages while working to conserve natural resources, a lifelong interest of Roosevelt. Women were excluded from the CCC until Eleanor Roosevelt demanded that a token number of women be hired. By the end of the program in 1942, three million CCC workers had left a legacy of vast new parks and recreation areas, along with roads that allowed millions of Americans to enjoy the outdoors. Just as important, the CCC, CWA, and other work relief efforts replaced the disgrace of welfare with the dignity of jobs. As one woman said about her husband's work relief job, "We aren't on relief anymore. My husband is working for the Government."

The New Deal's most ambitious and controversial natural resources project was the Tennessee Valley Authority (TVA). Created in 1933, the TVA built dams along the Tennessee River to supply poverty-stricken rural communities with cheap electricity (**Map 24.3**). Overcoming barriers erected by state governments and private enterprises, the TVA gave millions of local residents access to abundant natural resources as well as electric power, flood protection, soil reclamation, and jobs. Many Americans, however, believed the TVA violated the principles of free enterprise by allowing public ownership of dams and electricity-generating equipment.

New sources of hydroelectric power like the TVA helped the New Deal bring the wonders of electricity to country folk, fulfilling an old progressive dream. When Roosevelt became president, 90 percent of rural Americans lacked electricity. Private electric companies refused to build transmission lines into the sparsely settled countryside when they had a profitable market in more densely populated urban areas.

Beginning in 1935, the Rural Electrification Administration (REA) gave low-cost loans to rural communities for power plants and transmission lines. Within ten years, the REA delivered electricity to nine out of ten farms, giving rural Americans access for the first time to such modern conveniences as lightbulbs and electric appliances that urban people had enjoyed for decades.

Civilian Conservation Corps (CCC)
Federal relief program established in March 1933 that provided jobs on conservation projects to millions of unemployed young men and a token number of women.

▶ **Civilian Conservation Corps Workers**
These exuberant CCC workers posing for a photograph in the Shasta forest in northern California proudly display their work tools and their happiness about having jobs and earning money. The two men in military style uniforms on the left of the second row were CCC supervisors. In contrast to the racial and ethnic diversity in California, all these CCC men were white.
Historical/Getty Images.

MAP 24.3 ► The Tennessee Valley Authority The New Deal created the Tennessee Valley Authority to modernize a vast impoverished region with hydroelectric power dams and, at the same time, to reclaim eroded land and preserve old folkways.

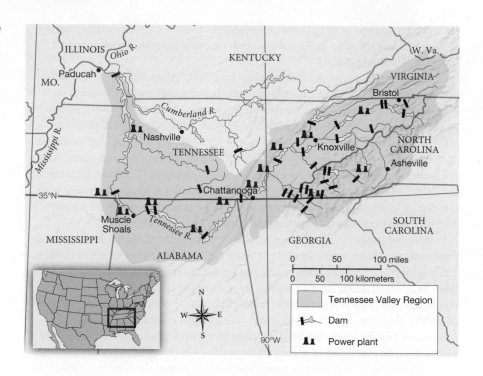

How did the New Deal address agricultural problems?

Farmers had been mired in agricultural depression since the end of World War I. New Dealers diagnosed the farmers' plight as a classic case of overproduction and underconsumption. Following age-old practices, farmers tried to compensate for low crop prices by growing more crops, but producing more crops pushed prices lower still. By 1932, a farmer's income sank to $167 a year, barely one-tenth of the national average.

New Dealers tried to cut agricultural production, thereby raising crop prices and farmers' income. With more money in their pockets, farm families—who made up a third of all Americans—would then buy more goods and lift consumption in the entire economy. To reduce production, the **Agricultural Adjustment Act (AAA),** passed in 1933, authorized the "domestic allotment plan." The plan paid farmers not to grow crops. Individual farmers who agreed not to plant crops on a portion of their fields (their "allotment") received a government payment compensating them for the crops they did not grow. To qualify for their allotment payments during the first year of the AAA, farmers slaughtered livestock and destroyed crops while millions of Americans went to bed hungry.

The Commodity Credit Corporation gave federal loans to farmers who held their harvested crops off the market and waited for a higher price. The Farm Credit Act (FCA) gave long-term credit on farm mortgages, allowing debt-ridden farmers to avoid foreclosures that were driving so many off their land (see Figure 24.1).

Crop allotments, commodity loans, and mortgage credit made farmers major beneficiaries of the New Deal. Crop prices rose impressively. Farm income jumped

Agricultural Adjustment Act (AAA)
New Deal legislation passed in May 1933 aimed at cutting agricultural production and raising crop prices.

VISUAL ACTIVITY

◀ **Water Pump in Rural Community** New Deal programs brought electricity and running water for the first time to many rural families, like the one shown here in east-central Tennessee. The Tennessee Valley Authority and the Rural Electrification Administration helped families in this and many other villages replace kerosene lamps with electric lights and gain access to clean, safe water. Franklin D. Roosevelt Presidential Library and Museum/NARA.

READING THE IMAGE: Where can you see evidence of New Deal benefits in this photo? What difference did electricity and running water make in the lives of people like the children depicted at the pump?

CONNECTIONS: Why did New Deal programs devote so much attention to improving the lives of rural Americans?

50 percent by 1936, and FCA loans financed 40 percent of farm mortgage debt by the end of the decade. These gains were distributed fairly equally among farmers in the corn, hog, and wheat region of the Midwest.

In the South's cotton belt, however, landlords controlled the distribution of New Deal agricultural benefits and shamelessly rewarded themselves. They took the land worked by Black and white sharecroppers and tenant farmers and assigned it to the allotment program. The president of the Oklahoma Tenant Farmers' Union explained that large farmers who got "Triple-A" payments often used the money to buy tractors and then "forced their tenants and [share] croppers off the land," causing these "Americans to be starved and dispossessed of their homes in our land of plenty."

How did the New Deal try to stimulate industrial recovery?

Unlike farmers, industrialists cut production with the onset of the depression. Between 1929 and 1933, industrial production fell more than 40 percent as businesses tried to maintain prices. But cutting industrial production meant that millions of workers lost their jobs. Mass unemployment also reduced consumer demand for industrial products, contributing to a downward spiral in both production and jobs, with no end in sight.

Businesses responded by cutting wages for employees who still had jobs, further reducing demand. Competition among industrial producers made the trend worse as one company after another cut labor costs to lower the prices they charged for their products. New Dealers struggled to find a way to break this cycle of unemployment and underconsumption—a way consistent with corporate profits and capitalism.

The New Deal's National Industrial Recovery Act offered a government-sponsored form of industrial self-government through the **National Recovery Administration (NRA)**, established in 1933. The NRA encouraged companies in every industry to agree

National Recovery Administration (NRA) Federal agency established in June 1933 to promote industrial recovery by the adoption of codes that set prices, minimized competition, and allowed workers to organize in unions.

on rules, known as "codes," that defined fair working conditions, set prices, and ideally reduced competition. The idea was to stabilize existing industries and save the jobs of their workers. Industry after industry wrote elaborate codes with detailed rules about production, pricing, and competition. In exchange for relaxing federal antitrust laws that prohibited such business agreements, participating companies promised to recognize the right of their workers to organize and engage in collective bargaining. To encourage consumers to patronize businesses with NRA codes, posters with the NRA's Blue Eagle appeared in shop windows throughout the nation.

Compliance with NRA codes was voluntary, and government enforcement efforts were weak to nonexistent. Consequently, the NRA did little to reduce unemployment, raise consumption, or relieve the depression. It was a New Deal peace offering to business leaders intended to show that Roosevelt did not want to wage war against profits or private enterprise. The peace offering failed, however. Most corporate leaders became bitter opponents of Roosevelt and the New Deal.

A second major industrial recovery initiative was far more successful. In 1933, the New Deal's Public Works Administration (PWA) launched a massive effort to construct dams, bridges, schools, post offices, and courthouses. These infrastructure projects supported heavy construction companies and employed thousands of workers in all but three of the nation's 3,071 counties. Spending on public works accounted for more than two-thirds of New Deal budgets. In addition to relieving unemployment, the PWA and its successor the WPA changed the built environment of America, a legacy that persists to the present.

REVIEW

How did the New Deal try to attack the Great Depression?

Who opposed the New Deal?

N ew Deal programs provoked fierce criticism. From the right, Republicans and businesspeople charged that the New Deal was too radical, undermining private property, economic stability, and democracy. Critics on the left faulted the New Deal for its failure to relieve the human suffering caused by the depression and for its caution in attacking corporate power and greed.

Why did business leaders oppose New Deal policies?

Even though their economic prospects improved more than those of most Americans during the 1930s, Republicans and business leaders lambasted Roosevelt and denounced New Deal efforts to regulate or reform what they considered their private enterprises.

By 1935, two major business organizations, the National Association of Manufacturers and the Chamber of Commerce, openly campaigned against the New Deal.

Their criticisms were echoed by the American Liberty League, founded in 1934, which blamed the New Deal for betraying basic constitutional guarantees of freedom and individualism. One League spokesman proclaimed that, "This administration has copied the autocratic tactics of fascism, Hitlerism and communism at their worst."

Economists who favored more direct intervention in the economy to moderate the failures of capitalism and union organizers who sought to raise wages and improve working conditions attacked the New Deal from the left. In their view, the NRA stifled competition by permitting monopolistic practices. They pointed out how industrial trade associations twisted NRA codes to suit their private interests and raise prices. Labor leaders especially resented the NRA's willingness to allow company-controlled unions while blocking workers from organizing their own unions.

The Supreme Court stepped into this crossfire of criticisms in May 1935 and declared that the NRA unconstitutionally conferred powers on an administrative agency that only Congress possessed. NRA codes soon lost the little authority they had. The failure of the NRA demonstrated many Americans' deep resistance to economic planning and most business leaders' stubborn refusal to tolerate government regulations and reforms.

Why did New Deal agricultural policies fail to help many rural people?

The AAA weathered opposition better than the NRA. Allotment checks for keeping land unplanted and crop prices high built loyalty among farmers with enough acreage to participate. As a white farmer in North Carolina said, "I stand for the New Deal and Roosevelt . . . , the AAA . . . and crop control."

Protests stirred, however, among those who did not qualify for allotments. The Southern Tenant Farmers' Union argued passionately that the AAA enriched large farmers while it impoverished small farmers who rented rather than owned their land. One Black sharecropper explained why few New Deal agricultural subsidies trickled down to her: "De landlord is landlord, de politicians is landlord, de judge is landlord, de shurf [sheriff] is landlord, ever'body is landlord, en we [sharecroppers] ain' got nothin'!'" Like the NRA, the AAA tended to help most those who least needed help. Because Roosevelt needed southern Democrats in Congress, he avoided confronting the deep-seated economic and racial inequities in the South.

Displaced tenants often joined the army of migrant workers like Florence Owens who straggled across rural America during the 1930s, some to flee Great Plains dust storms. Many migrants came from Mexico to work Texas cotton, Michigan beans, Idaho sugar beets, and California crops of all kinds. But since the number of people willing to take agricultural jobs usually exceeded the number of jobs available, wages fell, and native-born white migrants fought to reserve even these low-wage jobs for themselves.

Hundreds of thousands of "Okies" streamed out of the Dust Bowl of Oklahoma, Kansas, Texas, and Colorado, where chronic drought and harmful agricultural practices blasted crops and hopes. Parched, poor, and

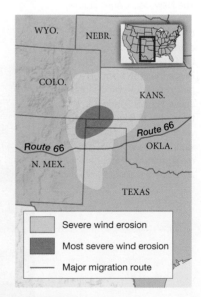

The Dust Bowl

windblown, Okies migrated to the lush fields and orchards of California, living in labor camps and hoping to find work and a future. But migrant laborers seldom found steady work. As one Okie said, "When they need us they call us migrants, and when we've picked their crop, we're bums and we got to get out."

What political challenges confronted New Deal policies?

Politically, the New Deal's staunchest opponents were in the Republican Party. Republicans were organized, well-heeled, mainstream, and determined to challenge Roosevelt at every turn. But the New Deal also faced challenges from the political fringes, fueled by the hardship of the depression and the hope for a cure.

Socialists and Communists accused the New Deal of being the handmaiden of business elites, seeking to rescue capitalism from its self-inflicted crisis. Socialist author Upton Sinclair ran for governor of California in 1934 on a plan for the state to take ownership of idle factories and unused land and then turn them over to cooperatives of working people, a first step toward putting the needs of people above profits. Sinclair lost the election, ending the most serious electoral challenge by socialists.

Some intellectuals and artists sought more radical change by joining left-wing organizations, including the American Communist Party. At its high point in the 1930s, the Communist Party had only about thirty thousand members, most of them immigrants, especially Scandinavians in the upper Midwest and eastern European

► **Evicted Sharecroppers**
The New Deal's Agricultural Adjustment Administration often resulted in the eviction of tenant farmers when the land they worked was left idle. These Black sharecroppers protested AAA policies that caused cotton farmers to evict them from their homes. They were among the many rural laborers whose lives were made worse by New Deal agricultural policies. Bettmann/ Getty Images.

Jews in major cities. Individually, Communists worked to organize labor unions, protect the civil rights of Black people, and help the destitute.

But Communist Party leaders preached the destruction of capitalism and the overthrow of "bourgeois democracy" in favor of Soviet-style communism. Such talk attracted few followers among the nation's millions of poor and unemployed. They wanted jobs and economic security within American capitalism and democracy, not violent revolution to establish a dictatorship of the Communist Party.

More powerful radical challenges to the New Deal sprouted from homegrown roots. Many Americans felt overlooked by New Deal programs that concentrated on finance, agriculture, and industry but did not do enough to create jobs or aid the poor. The merciless reality of the depression also eroded the security of people who had jobs but worried constantly that they, too, might be pushed into the ranks of the unemployed and penniless.

Charles Coughlin, a Catholic priest in Detroit, spoke to and for many Americans in his weekly radio broadcasts, which reached a nationwide audience of forty million. He expressed outrage at the suffering and inequities that he blamed on Communists, bankers, and "predatory capitalists." Coughlin appealed to widespread anti-Semitic sentiments with false claims that the economic predators were mostly Jews. At first, he championed the New Deal, proclaiming, "I will never change my philosophy that the New Deal is Christ's deal." Coughlin soon became frustrated by Roosevelt's refusal to grant him influence, and he turned against the New Deal. In 1935, he founded the National Union for Social Justice, or Union Party, to challenge Roosevelt in the 1936 presidential election.

Dr. Francis Townsend, of Long Beach, California, also criticized the timidity of the New Deal. Angry that many of his retired patients lived in misery, Townsend proposed in 1934 the creation of the Old Age Revolving Pension, which would pay every American over age sixty a pension of $200 a month. To receive the pension, senior citizens had to agree to spend the entire amount within thirty days, thereby stimulating the economy. Townsend organized pension clubs and petitioned the federal government to enact his scheme. When the major political parties ignored his impractical plan, he merged his forces with Coughlin's Union Party in time for the 1936 election.

A more potent challenge to the New Deal came from the powerful southern wing of the Democratic Party. Huey Long, son of a backcountry Louisiana farmer, was elected governor of the state in 1928 with his slogan "Every man a king, but no one wears a crown." Unlike nearly all other southern white politicians who harped on white supremacy, Long championed the poor over the rich, country people over city folk, and the humble over elites. As governor, "the Kingfish"—as he liked to call himself—delivered on his promises to provide jobs and build roads, schools, and hospitals.

Long delighted his supporters, who elected him to the U.S. Senate in 1932, where he introduced a sweeping "soak the rich" tax bill that would outlaw personal incomes of more than $1 million and inheritances of more than $5 million. When the Senate rejected his proposal, he decided to run for president, mobilizing more than five million Americans behind his "Share Our Wealth" plan. "Is that right," Long asked, "when . . . more [is] owned by 12 men than . . . by 120,000,000 people? . . . They own the banks, they own the steel mills, they own the railroads, they own the bonds, they own the mortgages, they own the stores, and they have chained the country from one end to

◄ **WPA Mural** The New Deal employed artists to create murals like this one in public buildings like post offices and courthouses throughout the nation. This mural, painted by San Francisco artist John Langley Howard, depicts the longshoremen's strike of May 1934. Thousands of longshoremen from Seattle to San Diego went on strike for wages of a dollar an hour and thirty hours of work a week, effectively shutting down West Coast ports. Strikers also sought to abolish the "shape-up" system they despised, which allowed port bosses absolute power to hire or fire workers arbitrarily. The strike lasted nearly three months, a sign of the solidarity among the striking workers portrayed. The mural emphasizes the common purpose of the strikers despite their racial and ethnic differences. Marmaduke St. John/Alamy.

the other." Like Townsend's scheme, Long's program promised far more than it could deliver. The Share Our Wealth campaign died when Long was assassinated in 1935, but his constituency and the wide appeal of a more equitable distribution of wealth persisted.

These challenges to the New Deal from both right and left stirred Democrats to preserve their winning coalition. In the midterm congressional elections of 1934 — normally a time when a president loses support — voters gave New Dealers a landslide victory. Democrats increased their majority in the House of Representatives and gained a two-thirds majority in the Senate.

REVIEW

Why did right-wing and left-wing groups criticize the New Deal?

Why did the New Deal begin to create a welfare state?

The popular mandate for the New Deal revealed by the 1934 congressional elections persuaded Roosevelt to press ahead with bold new efforts to achieve relief, recovery, and reform. Despite the initiatives of the Hundred Days, the depression still strangled the economy. In 1935, Roosevelt used his congressional majorities to enact major new programs that became the foundation of an American welfare state.

Taken together, these New Deal efforts stretched a safety net under the lives of millions of ordinary Americans. Landmark legislation included Social Security, which provided modest pensions for the elderly, and the Wagner Act, which encouraged the organization of labor unions. New Deal programs helped millions more with jobs, relief, and government support, although many citizens did not qualify for such help. Knitting together the safety net was the idea that when individual Americans suffered because of forces beyond their control, the federal government had the responsibility to support and protect them. The safety net of welfare programs tied the political loyalty of working people to the New Deal and the Democratic Party. As a North Carolina mill worker said, "Mr. Roosevelt is the only man we ever had in the White House who would understand that my boss is a sonofabitch."

How did the New Deal create jobs?

First and foremost, Americans still needed jobs. Since the private economy left eight million people jobless by 1935, Roosevelt and his advisers launched a massive work relief program. Roosevelt believed that direct government handouts crippled recipients with "spiritual and moral disintegration . . . destructive to the human spirit." Jobs, by contrast, bolstered individuals' "self-respect, . . . self-reliance and courage and determination." With a congressional appropriation of nearly $5 billion—more than all government revenues in 1934—the New Deal created the **Works Progress Administration (WPA)** to give unemployed Americans government-funded jobs on public works projects. The WPA put millions of jobless citizens to work on roads, bridges, parks, schools, post offices, courthouses, and more. In addition, over Roosevelt's veto, Congress passed the bonus that gave World War I veterans an average of $580, thereby stimulating the economy.

By 1936, the WPA provided jobs for 7 percent of the nation's labor force. In effect, the WPA made the federal government the employer of last resort, creating useful jobs when the capitalist economy failed to do so. In hiring, WPA officials tended to discriminate against women and racial minorities in favor of white men. Still, the WPA made major contributions to both relief and recovery, putting thirteen million men and women to work earning paychecks worth $10 billion. **(See "Analyzing Historical Evidence: Americans Encounter the New Deal" on page 716.)**

About three out of four WPA jobs involved construction and renovation of the nation's physical infrastructure. WPA workers built 572,000 miles of roads, 78,000 bridges, 67,000 miles of city streets, 40,000 public buildings, and much else. In addition, the WPA gave jobs to thousands of artists, musicians, actors, journalists, poets, and novelists. The WPA also organized sewing rooms for jobless women, giving them work and wages. These sewing rooms produced more than 100 million pieces of clothing that were donated to the needy. Throughout the nation, WPA projects displayed visible evidence of the New Deal's commitment to public welfare. In addition to relieving unemployment, the WPA changed the built environment of America, a legacy that persists to the present.

Works Progress Administration (WPA) Federal New Deal program established in 1935 that provided government-funded public works jobs to millions of unemployed Americans during the Great Depression.

How did the New Deal support workers?

During the Great Depression, factory workers who managed to keep their jobs often had their wages and working hours cut, and they worried constantly about being laid off. When workers tried to organize labor unions to protect themselves, municipal and state governments usually sided with employers. Since the Gilded Age, state and federal governments had been far more effective at busting unions than at busting trusts. The New Deal dramatically reversed the federal government's stance toward unions. With legislation and political support, the New Deal encouraged the organization of the nation's working people into unions.

When the head of the United Mine Workers, John L. Lewis, told coal miners that "the President wants you to join a union," he exaggerated only a little. New Dealers believed that unions would counterbalance the organized power of big corporations by defending working people, maintaining wages, and providing economic peace and commercial stability in place of the bloody violence that often accompanied labor strikes. In 1934, striking workers in Toledo, Minneapolis, San Francisco, and elsewhere were beaten and shot by police and the National Guard.

ANALYZING HISTORICAL EVIDENCE

Americans Encounter the New Deal

A mericans in all walks of life encountered New Deal measures in their daily lives. In 1938 and 1939, the Federal Writers Project, a part of the WPA, interviewed thousands of ordinary citizens throughout the nation, and many expressed their opinions of the New Deal. A sample of their views of the depression, Franklin Roosevelt, the WPA, and the CIO, as well as of political and economic power, can be found in the following excerpts from three interviews.

DOCUMENT 1

Charles Fusco, On the Value of Relief Work during the Depression, December 6, 1938

An Italian American machinist in a munitions plant in Hampden, Connecticut, explained the value of the relief work provided by the WPA.

I can get a job today even if we got a depression. I don't mean that I wasn't on relief when things got tough because there was a time when everything was shut down and I had to get on relief for a job. It isn't so long ago I was working on WPA. Believe me it was a big help. But it wasn't the kind of a job I should have had because this town is Republican and I am a Republican and I was a good worker for the party — making voters and helping a lot of people out. . . . Getting jobs for them. When it came my turn that I needed help the politicians told me that I had to go on relief — well, when I did I was handed a shovel and pick. . . . Roosevelt is a damn good man. . . . You know there shouldn't be a depression in this country . . . the Democrats are in power and the Republicans won't let loose with the money. Well I say that the money men started this thing and I believe the government should make laws to force these capitalists to bring back prosperity. They can do it if they wanted to.

Source: Interview with Charles Fusco, Manuscript, U.S. Works Progress Administration, Federal Writers Project. From Library of Congress, *Folklore Project, Life Histories, 1936–39*, GIF. http://www.loc.gov/resource/wpalh0.09030115/seq-1#seq-1 (accessed December 3, 2013).

DOCUMENT 2

Myron Buxton, The Benefits of WPA Projects, July 25, 1939

A native-born draftsman and assistant to an engineer working on WPA building projects in Newburyport, Massachusetts, illuminated the WPA's benefits to the community and to the individual workers.

One reason people here don't like WPA is because they don't understand it's not all bums and drunks and aliens! Nobody ever explains to them that they'd never have had the new High School they're so goddam proud of if it hadn't been for WPA. They don't stop to figure that new brick sidewalks wouldn't be there, the shade trees wouldn't be all dressed up to look at along High Street and all around town, if it weren't for WPA projects. To most in this town, and I guess it's not much different in this, than any other New England place, WPA's just a racket, set up to give a bunch of loafers and drunks steady pay to indulge in their vices! They don't stop to consider that on WPA are men and women who have traveled places and seen things, been educated and found their jobs folded up and nothing to replace them with. . . . The working guy in this country never had such a swell chance to get a toe-hold as he's had in the last four years! The louder the Republicans yell, the more of a toe-hold you can figure the ordinary guy's got!

Source: Seymour D. Buck, Interview with Myron Buxton, Manuscript, U.S. Works Progress Administration, Federal Writers Project. From Library of Congress, *Folklore Project, Life Histories, 1936–39*, GIF. http://www.loc.gov/resource/wpalh1.14030415/#seq-1 (accessed December 3, 2013).

DOCUMENT 3

Jim Cole, Overcoming Racism in the Unions, May 18, 1939

A Black packinghouse worker near Chicago, Illinois, explained how the CIO united workers from different racial and ethnic backgrounds when other unions turned them away.

I'm working in the Beef Kill section. Butcher on the chain. Been in the place twenty years, I believe. You got to have a certain amount of skill to do the job I'm doing. Long ago, I wanted to join the AFL union, the Amalgamated Butchers and Meat Cutters, they called it and wouldn't take me. Wouldn't let me in the union. Never said it to my face, but reason of it was plain. Negro. That's it. Just didn't want a Negro man to have what he should. That's wrong. You know that's wrong. Long about 1937 the CIO come. Well, I tell you, we Negroes was glad to see it come. Well, you know, some-times the bosses, or either the company stooges try to keep the white boys from joining the union. They say, "you don't want to belong to a black man's organization. That's all the CIO is." Don't fool nobody, but they got to lie, spread lyin' words around. There's a many different people, talkin' different speech, can't understand English very well, we have to have us union interpreters

for lots of our members, but that don't make no mind, they all friends in the union, even if they can't say nothin' except "Brother," an' shake hands. Well, my own local, we elected our officers and it's the same all over. We try to get every people represented. President of the local, he's Negro. First V[ice] President, he's Polish. Second V. President, he's Irish. Other officers, Scotchman, Lithuanian, Negro, German. . . . I don't care if the union don't do another lick of work raisin' our pay, or settling grievances about anything, I'll always believe they done the greatest thing in the world gettin' everybody who works in the yards together, and breakin' up the hate and bad feelings that used to be held against the Negro.

Source: Betty Burke, Interview with Jim Cole, Manuscript, U.S. Works Progress Administration, Federal Writers Project. From Library of Congress, *Folklore Project, Life Histories, 1936–39*, GIF. http://www.loc.gov/resource/wpalh0.07050602/seq-1#seq-1 (accessed December 3, 2013).

Questions for Analysis

ANALYZE THE EVIDENCE: What did Fusco, Buxton, and Cole see as successes and shortcomings of the New Deal? According to these men, how did New Deal programs influence the lives of ordinary American citizens?

CONSIDER THE CONTEXT: Whom did these men identify as opponents of New Deal measures, and why?

RECOGNIZE VIEWPOINTS: What attitudes did these men believe other Americans had about the WPA, the CIO, and the New Deal in general?

Wagner Act
1935 law that guaranteed industrial workers the right to organize into unions.

In Congress, labor leaders lobbied for the National Labor Relations Act, a bill sponsored by Senator Robert Wagner of New York that authorized the federal government to intervene in labor disputes and supervise the organization of labor unions. Roosevelt signed the **Wagner Act** in July 1935, for the first time providing federal support for labor organization—the most important New Deal reform of the industrial order. The Wagner Act guaranteed industrial workers the right to organize unions, putting the might of federal law behind the efforts of labor leaders. If the majority of workers at a company voted for a union, then the union became the sole bargaining agent for the entire workplace, and the employer was legally required to negotiate with the elected union leaders.

The achievements that flowed from the Wagner Act and renewed labor militancy were impressive. When Roosevelt became president in 1933, union membership stood at three million men who were almost entirely skilled workers in trade unions affiliated with the American Federation of Labor (AFL). With the support of the Wagner Act, union membership expanded to fourteen million by 1945. By then, 30 percent of the industrial workforce was unionized, the highest percentage in American history.

Most of the new union members were factory workers and unskilled laborers, many of them immigrants, women, and Black people. For decades, established AFL unions had no desire to organize unskilled factory workers. In 1935, under the aggressive leadership of the mine workers' John L. Lewis and the head of the Amalgamated Clothing Workers, Sidney Hillman, a coalition of unskilled workers formed the **Congress of Industrial Organizations (CIO)**. The CIO, helped by the Wagner Act, mobilized organizing drives in major industries, including the bitterly anti-union automobile and steel industries.

Congress of Industrial Organizations (CIO)
Coalition of mostly unskilled workers formed in 1935 that mobilized massive union organizing drives in major industries.

The bloody struggle by the CIO-affiliated United Auto Workers (UAW) to organize workers at General Motors climaxed in January 1937. Striking workers occupied the main assembly plant in Flint, Michigan, in a sit-down strike that slashed the plant's production of 15,000 cars a week to only 150. Stymied, General Motors eventually surrendered and agreed to make the UAW the sole bargaining agent for all the company's workers and to refrain from interfering with union activity. The UAW expanded its campaign until, after much violence, the entire auto industry was unionized by 1941.

The CIO hoped to ride organizing success in auto plants to victory in the steel mills. After unionizing the giant U.S. Steel, the CIO ran up against determined opposition from smaller steel companies. Following a police attack that killed ten strikers at Republic Steel outside Chicago in May 1937, the battered steelworkers halted their organizing campaign. In steel and other major industries, such as the stridently anti-union southern textile mills, organizing efforts stalled until after 1941, when military mobilization created labor shortages that gave workers greater bargaining power.

Social Security
New Deal program created in August 1935 that was designed to provide a modest income for elderly people as well as modest unemployment insurance.

Why did the New Deal create Social Security and increase taxes on wealth?

The single most important feature of the New Deal's emerging welfare state was **Social Security**. An ambitious, far-reaching, and permanent reform, Social Security was designed to provide a modest income to relieve the poverty of elderly people.

Only about 15 percent of older Americans had private pension plans. During the depression, corporations and banks often failed to pay the meager pensions they had promised. Corporations routinely fired or demoted employees to avoid or reduce pension payments. Prompted by the popular but impractical proposals of Dr. Townsend, Father Coughlin, and Huey Long, Roosevelt told Congress that "it is our plain duty to provide for that security upon which welfare depends . . . and undertake the great task of furthering the security of the citizen and his family through social insurance."

The political struggle for Social Security highlighted class differences among Americans. Support for the measure came from a coalition of groups advocating for the elderly and the poor, as well as from traditional progressives, leftists, social workers, and labor unions. Against them were economic conservatives, including the American Liberty League, the National Association of Manufacturers, the Chamber of Commerce, and the American Medical Association. Enact the Social Security system, these conservatives and other Republicans warned, and the government will ruin private property, destroy initiative, and reduce proud individuals to spineless loafers.

The large New Deal majority in Congress passed the Social Security Act in August 1935. The act took contributions from workers and their employers and used them to fund pensions for the elderly, giving workers who paid into the system a personal and political stake in the success of the program. When eligible workers reached retirement age, they did not have to prove that they were impoverished. Instead, they had earned Social Security benefits based on their contributions and years of work. Social Security also set up unemployment insurance that provided small benefits for workers who lost their jobs.

Millions of workers did not qualify to participate in Social Security. Domestic and agricultural workers like Florence Owens were excluded. In fact, about half of all Black people, more than half of all employed women, and workers in religious and nonprofit organizations such as schools and hospitals were not eligible to participate in Social Security.

Social Security also gave states multimillion-dollar grants to help support dependent children, blind people, and public health services. After the Supreme Court approved Social Security in 1937, the program was expanded to include benefits for dependent survivors of deceased recipients. The first Social Security check (for $41.30) was not issued until 1940. But the system gave millions of working people a guarantee that they would receive a small income from the federal government when they became too old to work. This safety net protected many ordinary working people from fears of a penniless and insecure old age.

Fervent opposition to Social Security persuaded New Dealers that rich people had learned little from the depression. Roosevelt had contempt for the moneyed elite who ignored the suffering of the poor. He looked for a way to redistribute wealth that would weaken conservative opposition, advance the cause of social equity, and defuse political challenges from Huey Long and Father Coughlin. Roosevelt declared in 1935 that large fortunes put "great and undesirable concentration of control in [the hands of] relatively few individuals." He urged a graduated tax on corporations, an inheritance tax, and an increase in maximum personal income taxes. Congress endorsed Roosevelt's basic principle by increasing taxes on those with high incomes.

Which Americans did the New Deal neglect?

The patchwork of New Deal reforms built a two-tier welfare state. In the top tier, farmers and organized workers in major industries were the greatest beneficiaries of New Deal initiatives. In the bottom tier, millions of neglected Americans fell through the New Deal safety net, including women, children, and the elderly, along with the unorganized, unskilled, uneducated, and unemployed. Many working people remained more or less untouched by New Deal benefits. The average unemployment rate for the 1930s stayed high—17 percent. Workers in industries that resisted unions received little help from the Wagner Act or the WPA. Tens of thousands of women in southern textile mills, for example, commonly received wages of less than ten cents an hour and were fired if they protested. Domestic workers, almost all of them women, and agricultural workers—many of them minorities—were neither unionized nor eligible for Social Security.

The New Deal neglected few citizens more than Black people. About half of Black Americans in cities were jobless, more than double the unemployment rate among white Americans. In the rural South, where the vast majority of Black men and women lived, conditions were worse. New Deal agricultural policies such as the AAA favored landowners, who often pushed Black tenants off the land they farmed. Only eleven of more than ten thousand WPA supervisors in the South were Black, even though African Americans accounted for a third of the region's population. Violence and intimidation prevented southern Blacks from protesting their plight at the ballot box. Protesters risked ruthless retaliation from local whites. Bitter critics charged that the New Deal's NRA stood for "Negro Run Around" or "Negroes Ruined Again."

Roosevelt responded to such criticisms with great caution, since New Deal reforms required the political support of powerful, conservative, segregationist southern white Democrats in Congress who opposed programs that aided Black people. Stymied by the political clout of entrenched white racism, New Dealers still attracted support from Black voters. Roosevelt's overtures prompted many northern Black voters in the 1934 congressional elections to shift from the Republican to the Democratic Party, helping elect New Deal Democrats.

Eleanor Roosevelt sponsored the appointment of Mary McLeod Bethune—the energetic cofounder of

◀ **National Youth Administration Workers** In 1935, the New Deal created the National Youth Administration (NYA) to help young people stay in school by providing part-time jobs that paid $10 to $25 a month. In all, more than 4.5 million young people — like these two young men shown here working on a NYA project in Riverside, California — received benefits from the NYA. Courtesy National Archives, photo no. 119-S-3C-25.

the National Council of Negro Women—as head of the Division of Negro Affairs in the National Youth Administration. The highest-ranking Black official in Roosevelt's administration, Bethune used her position to guide a small number of Black professionals and civil rights activists to posts within New Deal agencies. Ultimately, about one in four Black people got access to New Deal relief programs.

Despite these gains, by 1940 Black Americans still suffered severe handicaps. Most of the thirteen million Black workers toiled at low-paying menial jobs, unprotected by the New Deal safety net. Segregated and unequal schools were the norm. Only 1 percent of Black students earned college degrees. In southern states, vigilante violence against Blacks went unpunished. For Black Americans, the New Deal offered few remedies.

Hispanic Americans fared no better. About a million Mexican Americans lived in the United States in the 1930s, most of them first- or second-generation immigrants who worked crops throughout the West. During the depression, field workers saw their low wages plunge lower still, to about a dime an hour. Ten thousand Mexican American pecan shellers in San Antonio, Texas, earned only a nickel an hour. To preserve scarce jobs for U.S. citizens, the federal government choked off immigration from Mexico, while state and local officials deported tens of thousands of Mexican Americans, many with their American-born children. New Deal programs throughout the West often discriminated against Hispanics and other people of color. A New Deal study concluded that "the Mexican is . . . segregated from the rest of the community as effectively as the Negro . . . [by] poverty and low wages."

Asian Americans had similar experiences. Asian immigrants were still excluded from U.S. citizenship and in many states were not permitted to own land. By 1930, more than half of Japanese Americans had been born in the United States, but they still faced discrimination. One young Asian American expressed the frustration felt by many others: "I am a fruit-stand worker. I would much rather it were doctor or lawyer . . . but my aspirations [were] frustrated long ago by circumstances. . . . I am only what I am, a professional carrot washer."

Native Americans also suffered neglect from New Deal agencies. As a group, they remained the poorest of the poor. Since the Dawes Act of 1887 (see chapter 17), the federal government had encouraged Native Americans to abandon their Indian identities and adopt the cultural norms of white society. Under the leadership of the New Deal's commissioner of Indian affairs, John Collier, the Indian Reorganization Act (IRA) of 1934 largely reversed that policy. Collier claimed that "the most interesting and important fact about Indians" was that they "do not expect much, often they expect nothing at all; yet they are able to be happy." Given such views, the IRA provided little economic aid to Native Americans, but it did restore their right to own land communally and to have greater control over their own affairs. The IRA brought little immediate benefit to Native Americans, but it provided an important foundation for their economic, cultural, and political resurgence a generation later.

Voicing common experiences among Americans neglected by the New Deal, singer and songwriter Woody Guthrie traveled the nation for eight years during the 1930s and heard other rambling men tell him "the story of their life": "how the home went to pieces, how . . . the crops got to where they wouldn't bring nothing, work in factories would kill a dog . . . and—always, always [you] have to fight and argue and cuss and swear . . . to try to get a nickel more out of the rich bosses."

▲ **Antilynching Protesters** These Howard University students protested the New Deal's refusal to support antilynching legislation by standing outside the Washington, D.C., building of the Daughters of the American Revolution in 1935 with nooses around their necks and placards naming recent lynching victims. Roosevelt and his advisers never made federal antilynching laws a priority since they feared alienating white southerners in Congress whose votes were needed to pass other New Deal measures. Bettmann/Getty Images.

REVIEW

What did the New Deal's two-tier welfare state accomplish?

Why did the New Deal lose support during Roosevelt's second term as president?

To accelerate the sputtering economic recovery, Roosevelt shifted the emphasis of the New Deal in the mid-1930s. Instead of seeking cooperation from conservative business leaders, he decided to rely on the growing New Deal coalition to enact reforms over the entrenched opposition of the Supreme Court, Republicans, and corporate interests. Roosevelt's conservative opponents reacted by intensifying their opposition to the welfare state.

While Roosevelt continued to lose conservatives' support, he added new allies on the left in farm states and big cities. Throughout Roosevelt's first term, socialists and Communists denounced the slow pace of change and accused the New Deal of failing to serve the interests of the workers who produced the nation's wealth. But in 1935, the Soviet Union, worried about the threat of fascism in Europe, instructed Communists throughout the world to join hands with non-Communist progressives in a "Popular Front" to advance the fortunes of the working class. Many radicals soon embraced Popular Front politics and began supporting New Deal relief programs and encouraging labor unions.

Roosevelt won reelection in 1936 in another landslide and concluded mistakenly that the economy was improving. He reduced government spending in 1937, triggering a sharp recession that undermined economic recovery and prolonged the depression.

How did the election of 1936 influence Roosevelt's political outlook?

Roosevelt believed that the presidential election of 1936 would test his leadership and progressive ideals. The depression still choked the economy. Conservative leaders believed that the New Deal's failure to lift the nation out of the depression showed that Americans were ready for a change. Left-wing critics insisted that the New Deal had missed the opportunity to displace capitalism with a socialist economy and that voters would favor candidates who recommended more radical remedies.

Republicans turned to Kansas governor Alfred (Alf) Landon as their presidential nominee, a moderate who stressed mainstream Republican proposals to balance the federal budget and to reduce government bureaucracy. Landon recommended that the perils of sickness and old age should be eased by old-fashioned neighborliness instead of a government program like Social Security.

Roosevelt believed the New Deal would liberate the nation from the long era of privilege and wealth for a few and "economic slavery" for the rest. He proclaimed that "the forces of selfishness and lust for power met their match" in his first term as president, and he hoped it would be said about his second term that "these forces met their master."

Roosevelt triumphed spectacularly. He won 60.8 percent of the popular vote, making it the widest margin of victory in a presidential election to date. Third parties—including the Socialist and Communist parties—fell pitifully short of the support they expected and never again mounted a significant challenge to the New Deal. Congressional results were equally lopsided, with Democrats outnumbering Republicans more than three to one in both houses of Congress. In his inaugural address, Roosevelt announced, "I see one third of a nation ill-housed, ill-clad, [and] ill-nourished," and he promised to devote his second term to helping them.

Why did Roosevelt try to pack the Supreme Court?

In the afterglow of his reelection, Roosevelt pondered how to remove the remaining obstacles to New Deal reforms. He decided to target the Supreme Court. Conservative justices appointed by Republican presidents had declared unconstitutional eleven New Deal measures. Now, Social Security, the Wagner Act, the Securities and Exchange Commission, and other New Deal programs were about to be considered by the Supreme Court.

court-packing plan
Law proposed by Franklin
Roosevelt to add one new
Supreme Court justice for each
existing judge who had served
for ten years and who was over
the age of seventy.

To prevent the Supreme Court from dismantling these vital New Deal programs, Roosevelt proposed a **court-packing plan**. The plan would add one new Supreme Court justice for each current justice over the age of seventy who had served for at least ten years. This proposed plan gave Roosevelt the power to pack the Supreme Court with up to six New Dealers who could then outvote the elderly, conservative Republicans on the Court.

Roosevelt had not reckoned with Americans' deeply rooted belief in the constitutional separation of executive and judicial powers and the independent authority of the Supreme Court. More than two-thirds of Americans believed that the Court should be free from political interference by the president. Even some New Dealers were disturbed by the court-packing scheme. Many elderly members of Congress in both parties were offended by the plan's suggestion that officials older than seventy were mentally handicapped. The many opponents soundly defeated Roosevelt's plan in 1937.

Supreme Court justices still got the message. The four most conservative of the elderly justices—the "four horsemen of reaction," according to one New Dealer—retired. Roosevelt eventually named eight justices to the Court—more than any other president—ultimately giving New Deal laws safe passage through the Court, despite the failure of the court-packing plan.

How did politics and a new economic slump slow New Deal reforms?

Emboldened by their defeat of the court-packing plan, Republicans and southern Democrats rallied around their common conservatism to obstruct additional reforms. Former president Herbert Hoover proclaimed that the New Deal was the "repudiation of Democracy" and that "the Republican Party alone [was] the guardian of . . . the charter of freedom." Democrats' arguments over whether the New Deal needed to be expanded—and if so, how—undermined the coalition among reformers and sparked antagonism between Congress and the White House. The ominous rise of belligerent regimes in Germany, Italy, and Japan also slowed reform as some Americans began to worry more about defending the nation than changing it.

Roosevelt himself favored slowing the pace of the New Deal. He believed that existing New Deal measures had steadily boosted the economy and largely eliminated the depression crisis. He failed to appreciate the stubborn realities of unemployment and poverty. In fact, the gross national product in 1937 briefly equaled the 1929 level before dropping lower for the rest of the decade.

Unemployment declined to 14 percent in 1937 but quickly spiked upward and stayed higher until 1940. Even at the high-water mark of recovery in the summer of 1937, seven million people lacked jobs. In the following months, national income and production slipped so steeply that almost two-thirds of the economic gains since 1933 were lost by June 1938.

Roosevelt's mistaken optimism about the economic recovery persuaded him that additional deficit spending was no longer necessary. But his support for reducing federal spending pushed the improving economy into recession.

This economic reversal hurt the New Deal politically. Conservatives argued that this recession proved that New Deal measures produced only an illusion of progress.

▲ **Distributing Surplus Food to the Needy** When bountiful harvests produced surplus crops that would depress prices if they were sent to market, the New Deal arranged to distribute some of the surplus to needy Americans. Here, farmworkers in east-central Arizona near the New Mexico border line up to receive a ration of potatoes authorized by the New Deal agent checking the box of index cards. Library of Congress Prints and Photographs Division [LC-DIG-fsac-1a34185].

The way to weather the recession was to tax and spend less and wait for the natural laws of supply and demand to restore prosperity. Many New Dealers insisted instead that Roosevelt revive federal spending and redouble efforts to stimulate the economy. In 1938, Congress heeded such pleas and enacted a massive new program of federal spending.

The recession scare of 1937–1938 taught the president that economic growth had to be nurtured carefully. The English economist John Maynard Keynes argued that only government intervention could pump enough money into the economy to restore prosperity, a concept that became known as Keynesian economics. Roosevelt never had the interest or time to master Keynesian thought. But in a commonsense way, he understood that escape from the depression required a plan for large-scale spending to alleviate distress and stimulate economic growth (**Figure 24.2**).

What reforms were enacted while the New Deal lost steam?

From the moment he was sworn in, Roosevelt sought to expand the powers of the presidency. He believed that the president needed more authority to meet emergencies such as the depression and to administer the sprawling federal bureaucracy.

FIGURE 24.2 ▶ Global Comparison: National Populations and Economies, ca. 1938 Throughout the Great Depression, the United States remained more productive than any other nation in the world. By 1938, the United States produced more than twice as much as its closest competitors, Germany and the USSR. If Germany had gained control of the other European nations listed here, it would have become the biggest economy in the world. What do these data suggest about the relationship between population and product?

	Population (millions)	Gross Domestic Product (millions of dollars)
United States		
Britain		
British Colonies		
France		
French Colonies		
Italy		
Italian Colonies		
Netherlands		
Dutch Colonies		
USSR		
Japan		
Japanese Colonies		
Germany		
Austria		
Czechoslovakia		
Poland		
Hungary		
Yugoslavia		
Romania		

= 10 million people
= 10 million dollars

Combined with a Democratic majority in Congress, a now-friendly Supreme Court, and the revival of deficit spending, the newly empowered White House seemed to be in a good position to move ahead with a revitalized New Deal.

Resistance to further reform was also on the rise, however. Conservatives argued that the New Deal had pressed government centralization too far. Even the New Deal's friends became tired of one emergency program after another while economic woes continued to shadow their achievements. By the midpoint of Roosevelt's second term, many members of Congress balked at new initiatives. But enough support remained for one last burst of reform.

Agriculture still had strong claims on New Deal attention in the face of drought, declining crop prices, and impoverished sharecroppers and tenants. In 1937, the Agriculture Department created the Farm Security Administration (FSA) to provide housing and loans to help tenant farmers become independent. A Black tenant farmer in North Carolina who received an FSA loan told a New Deal interviewer, "I wake up in the night sometimes and think I must be half-dead and gone to heaven." For those who owned farms, the New Deal offered renewed prosperity with a second Agricultural Adjustment Act (AAA) in 1938, which placed production quotas on cotton, tobacco, wheat, corn, and rice while issuing food stamps to allow poor people to obtain surplus food. The AAA of 1938 brought stability to American agriculture and ample food to most—but not all—tables.

Advocates for the urban poor also made modest gains after decades of neglect. New York senator Robert Wagner convinced Congress to pass the National Housing Act in 1937. By 1941, some 160,000 residences had been made available to poor people at affordable rents. The program did not come close to meeting the need for affordable housing, but for the first time, the federal government took an active role in providing decent urban housing.

The last major piece of New Deal labor legislation, the Fair Labor Standards Act of 1938, honored the New Deal pledge to provide workers with a decent standard of living. The new law set wage and hours standards and at long last curbed the use of child labor. The minimum-wage level was twenty-five cents an hour for a maximum of forty-four hours a week.

Critics of the minimum-wage law said it was "government interference," to which one New Dealer (future president Lyndon Baines Johnson) responded, "It was. It interfered with the fellow running that pecan shelling plant . . . [and] told him he couldn't pay that little widow seven cents an hour." To attract enough conservative votes, the act did not apply to domestic help and farm laborers, thereby not raising the wages of most women and Black Americans. Enforcement of the minimum-wage standards was weak and haphazard. Still, the Fair Labor Standards Act slowly advanced Roosevelt's inaugural promise to improve the living standards of the poorest Americans.

The final New Deal reform effort failed to make much headway against the hide-bound system of racial injustice. Although Roosevelt denounced lynching as murder, he would not jeopardize his base of southern political support by demanding antilynching legislation. Congress voted down proposals to make lynching a federal crime. Laws to eliminate the poll tax—used to deny Black people the opportunity to vote—encountered the same overwhelming resistance. The New Deal refused to confront racial injustice with the same vigor it brought to bear on economic hardship.

By the end of 1938, the New Deal had lost steam and encountered stiff opposition. In the congressional elections of 1938, Republicans made gains that gave them more congressional influence than they had enjoyed since 1932. New Dealers could claim unprecedented achievements since 1933, but nobody needed reminding that those achievements had not ended the depression. In his annual message to Congress in January 1939, Roosevelt signaled a halt to New Deal reforms by speaking about preserving the progress already achieved rather than extending it. Roosevelt pointed to the ominous threats posed by fascist aggressors in Germany and Japan, and he proposed defense expenditures that surpassed New Deal appropriations for relief and economic recovery.

REVIEW

Why did political support for New Deal reforms decline?

Conclusion: What were the achievements and limitations of the New Deal?

The New Deal demonstrated that a growing majority of Americans agreed with Roosevelt that the federal government should help those in need. Through programs that sought relief, recovery, and reform, the New Deal greatly expanded the size and influence of the federal government and changed the way many Americans viewed Washington. New Dealers achieved significant victories, such as Social Security, labor's right to organize, and guarantees that farm prices would be maintained through controls on production and marketing. New Deal measures marked the emergence of a welfare state, but its limits left millions of needy Americans with little aid.

The New Deal did not achieve full-scale relief, recovery, and reform. Even though millions of Americans benefited from its initiatives, both relief and recovery were limited and temporary. In 1940, the depression still plagued the economy. Perhaps the most impressive achievement of the New Deal was what did not happen. Although authoritarian governments and anticapitalist policies were common outside the United States during the 1930s, they were shunned by the New Deal. The greatest economic crisis the nation had ever faced did not cause Americans to abandon democracy, as happened in Germany, where Adolf Hitler seized dictatorial power. Nor did the nation turn to radical alternatives such as socialism or communism.

Republicans and other conservatives claimed that the New Deal amounted to a form of socialism that threatened democracy and capitalism. But rather than attack capitalism, Roosevelt sought to save it, and he succeeded. That success also marked the limits of the New Deal's achievements. The New Deal stopped far short of challenging capitalism either by undermining private property or by imposing strict national planning. Roosevelt believed that a shift of authority toward the federal government would allow capitalist enterprises to be balanced by the nation's democratic traditions.

New Dealers repeatedly described their programs as a kind of warfare against the depression of the 1930s. In the next decade, Roosevelt had to turn from the economic crisis at home to participate in a worldwide conflagration to defeat the enemies of democracy abroad. Today, New Deal reforms still structure the basic institutions of banking, the stock market, union organizations, agricultural markets, Social Security, minimum-wage standards, and more. Opponents of these measures and of the New Deal notion of an activist government remain powerful, especially in the Republican Party. They claim that government is the problem, not the solution—a slogan that Republicans have championed since the 1980s. With the cooperation of some Democrats, Republicans have tried to dismantle New Deal programs that they believe interfere with the free market and stifle individual responsibility with government handouts. Although the New Deal was built during the 1930s, it continues to influence political debate more than eighty years later.

CHAPTER REVIEW

EXPLAIN WHY IT MATTERS

New Deal coalition (p. 702)

underconsumption (p. 704)

Federal Deposit Insurance Corporation (FDIC) (p. 705)

fireside chats (p. 705)

Civilian Conservation Corps (CCC) (p. 707)

Agricultural Adjustment Act (AAA) (p. 708)

National Recovery Administration (NRA) (p. 709)

Works Progress Administration (WPA) (p. 715)

Wagner Act (p. 718)

Congress of Industrial Organizations (CIO) (p. 718)

Social Security (p. 718)

court-packing plan (p. 724)

PUT IT ALL TOGETHER

FRANKLIN D. ROOSEVELT

• Why was Franklin Roosevelt so popular? Why did he win the elections of 1932 and 1936?

• Why was Eleanor Roosevelt a part of her husband's political career?

THE NEW DEAL

• What were the greatest achievements of the New Deal?

• How and why did the first phase of the New Deal differ from the second phase?

THE OPPOSITION

• Who initially opposed the New Deal, and why?

• Why did general support for the New Deal decline?

LOOKING BACKWARD, LOOKING AHEAD

• How did the New Deal compare to reforms enacted during the Progressive Era?

• What was the long-term significance of the New Deal?

25

THE UNITED STATES AND THE SECOND WORLD WAR

1939–1945

This chapter discusses the following questions:

- How did isolationism shape American foreign policy in the 1930s?
- How did war in Europe and Asia influence U.S. foreign policy?
- How did the United States mobilize for war?
- How did the Allies reverse Axis advances in Europe and the Pacific?
- How did war change the American home front?
- How did the Allies win the war?
- Conclusion: Why did the United States emerge as a superpower at the end of the war?

▶ **Colonel Paul Tibbets** Before taking off to drop the world's first atomic bomb on Hiroshima, Tibbets posed on the tarmac next to his customized B-29 Super Fortress bomber, named *Enola Gay* in honor of his mother. A crew of eleven handpicked airmen accompanied Tibbets on the top-secret mission. Bettmann/Getty Images.

AN AMERICAN STORY

On a sun-drenched Florida afternoon in 1927, twelve-year-old Paul Tibbets climbed into the front seat of the open cockpit of a biplane for his first airplane ride. While the pilot brought the plane in low over a racetrack in Miami, Florida, Tibbets pitched Baby Ruth candy bars tethered to small paper parachutes to racing fans below. After repeating this stunt, sales of Baby Ruths soared, and Tibbets was hooked on flying.

In 1937, Tibbets became a military pilot. Shortly after the Japanese attack on Pearl Harbor in December 1941 brought the United States into World War II, Tibbets flew antisubmarine patrols against German U-boats lurking along the East Coast. When heavily armored B-17 Flying Fortress bombers became available early in 1942, he took a squadron of the new planes to England. In August 1942, he led the first American daytime bombing raid on German-occupied Europe, releasing the first of 700,000 tons of explosives dropped by American bombers during the air war in Europe.

After numerous raids over Europe, Tibbets was reassigned to the North African campaign. After eight months of combat missions, he returned to the United States to test the new B-29 Super Fortress being built in Wichita, Kansas. The B-29 was much bigger than the B-17 and could fly higher and faster, making it ideal for the campaign against Japan. Tibbets's mastery of the B-29 caused him to be singled out in September 1944 to command a top-secret unit training for a special mission.

The mission was to be ready to drop on Japan a bomb so powerful that it might end the war. No such bomb existed, but American scientists and engineers were working around the clock to build one. In May 1945, Tibbets and his men went to Tinian Island in the Pacific, where they trained for their secret mission by flying raids over Japanese cities and dropping ordinary bombs. The atomic bomb arrived on Tinian on July 26, just ten days after a successful test explosion in the New Mexico desert. Nicknamed "Little Boy," the bomb packed the equivalent of forty million pounds of TNT, or 200,000 of the 200-pound bombs Tibbets and other American airmen had dropped on Europe.

On August 6, 1945, Tibbets, his crew, and their atomic payload took off in the B-29 bomber *Enola Gay* and headed for Japan. Less than seven hours later, over the city of Hiroshima, Tibbets and his men released Little Boy from the *Enola Gay*'s bomb bay. Three days later, airmen from Tibbets's command dropped a second atomic bomb on Nagasaki, and within five days, Japan surrendered.

Paul Tibbets's experiences traced an arc followed by millions of Americans during World War II. Like Tibbets, Americans joined their allies to fight the Axis powers in Europe and Asia. Like his *Enola Gay* crewmen — who hailed from New York, Texas, California, New Jersey, New Mexico, Maryland, North Carolina, Pennsylvania, Michigan, and Nevada — Americans from all regions united to help defeat the fascist aggressors in Asia and Europe. American industries mobilized to produce advanced bombers, along with enough other military equipment to supply the American armed forces and their allies. At enormous cost in human life and suffering — including millions of civilians killed in military actions and millions more exterminated in the Holocaust of the Nazis' racist death camps — the war resulted in employment and prosperity for most Americans at home, ending the depression, providing new opportunities for women and Black Americans, and ushering the nation into the postwar world as a triumphant economic and atomic superpower.

How did isolationism shape American foreign policy in the 1930s?

The First World War left a dangerous and deadly legacy. The victors—especially Britain, France, and the United States—sought to avoid future wars at almost any cost. The defeated nation, Germany, aspired to avenge its losses. Italy and Japan felt humiliated by the Versailles peace settlement and believed war would increase their global power. Japan invaded the northern Chinese province of Manchuria in 1931, with ambitions to expand throughout Asia. Italy, led by the fascist Benito Mussolini since 1922, hungered for an empire in Africa. In Germany, National Socialist Adolf Hitler rose to power in 1933, the first step in his quest to dominate Europe and the world. These aggressive, militaristic, antidemocratic governments seemed a smaller threat to most people in the United States during the 1930s than the economic crisis at home. Shielded by the Atlantic and Pacific oceans, Americans hoped to avoid entanglement in foreign disputes and to concentrate on climbing out of the Great Depression.

How did the depression influence U.S. isolationism?

Like most Americans during the 1930s, Franklin Roosevelt believed that the nation's highest priority was to attack the domestic causes and consequences of the depression. But unlike most Americans, Roosevelt had long believed the United States should actively engage in international relations.

The depression forced Roosevelt to retreat from his previous internationalism. He came to believe that foreign affairs threatened to divert resources and political support from New Deal efforts to promote domestic recovery. Once in office, Roosevelt sought to combine domestic economic recovery with a low-profile foreign policy that encouraged free trade and disarmament.

Roosevelt's pursuit of international cooperation was hindered by economic circumstances and American popular opinion. After an opinion poll demonstrated popular support for recognizing the Soviet Union—an international outcast since the Bolshevik Revolution in 1917—Roosevelt established formal diplomatic relations in 1933. But when the League of Nations condemned Japanese and German aggression, Roosevelt did not support the league's attempts to keep the peace. He feared isolationists would withdraw support for New Deal measures in Congress. America watched from the sidelines when Japan withdrew from the League of Nations and ignored the limitations on its navy imposed after World War I. The United States also looked the other way when Hitler rearmed Germany and recalled its representative to the League in 1933. Roosevelt worried that German and Japanese actions threatened world peace, but he told Americans that the nation would not "use its armed forces for the settlement of any [international] dispute anywhere."

Why did Roosevelt support the good neighbor policy?

In 1933, Roosevelt announced that the United States would pursue "the policy of the good neighbor" in international relations. This policy declared that no nation had the right to intervene in the internal or external affairs of another. Roosevelt emphasized that the **good neighbor policy** applied specifically to Latin America, where U.S. military forces had often intervened. The policy did not indicate a U.S. retreat from empire in Latin America, though. Instead, it declared that, unlike in the past, the United States' influence in the region would not depend on military force.

Roosevelt refrained from sending troops to defend the interests of American corporations when Mexico nationalized American oil properties and revolutions boiled over in Nicaragua, Guatemala, and Cuba during the 1930s. In 1934, Roosevelt withdrew American Marines from Haiti, where they had been stationed since 1916. Roosevelt's hands-off policy honored the principle of national self-determination, but it also permitted the rise of dictators in Nicaragua, Cuba, and elsewhere who exploited and terrorized their nations with private support from U.S. businesses.

Military nonintervention also did not prevent the United States from exerting its economic influence in Latin America. In 1934, Congress gave the president the power to reduce tariffs on goods imported into the United States from nations that agreed to lower their own tariffs on U.S. goods. By 1940, twenty-two nations had agreed to such reciprocal tariff reductions. This policy helped to double U.S. exports to Latin America and planted seeds of friendship and hemispheric solidarity while boosting the domestic economy through free trade.

good neighbor policy
Foreign policy announced by Roosevelt in 1933 that promised the United States would not interfere in the internal or external affairs of another country.

How did isolationism influence American foreign policy?

In Europe, fascist governments in Italy and Germany threatened military aggression. Britain and France made only verbal protests. Encouraged, Hitler plotted to recapture territories with German inhabitants, all the while accusing Jews of polluting the purity of the Aryan master race. The wild-eyed anti-Semitism of Hitler and the Nazi Party unified non-Jewish Germans and attracted sympathizers among many other Europeans, even in France and Britain.

In Japan, a militaristic government planned to follow the invasion of Manchuria in 1931 with conquests extending throughout Southeast Asia. The Manchurian invasion bogged down in a long and vicious war when Chinese Nationalists rallied around their leader, Jiang Jieshi (Chiang Kai-shek), to fight against the Japanese. Preparations for new Japanese conquests continued, however. In 1936, Japan openly violated naval limitation treaties and began to build a battle-ready fleet to seek naval superiority in the Pacific.

In the United States, the hostilities in Asia and Europe reinforced isolationist sentiments. Popular disillusionment with the failure of Woodrow Wilson's idealistic goals caused many Americans to question the nation's participation in World War I. In 1933, Gerald Nye, a Republican from North Dakota, chaired a Senate committee that declared greedy "merchants of death"—American weapons makers, bankers, and financiers—had dragged the nation into the war to line their own pockets. International tensions and the Nye Committee report prompted Congress to pass a series of **neutrality acts** between 1935 and 1937. Designed to keep the nation out of foreign wars, the neutrality acts prohibited making loans and selling weapons to nations at war.

neutrality acts
Legislation passed between 1935 and 1937 that sought to avoid entanglement in foreign wars while protecting trade.

By 1937, the growing conflicts overseas caused some Americans to call for a total embargo on all trade with warring countries. The Neutrality Act of 1937 imposed a "cash-and-carry" policy that required nations at war to pay cash for nonmilitary goods and to transport them in their own ships. This policy benefited the nation's economy, but it also helped foreign aggressors by supplying them with goods and thereby undermining peace.

Germany, Italy, and Japan launched military offensives because they believed that the Western democracies of France, Britain, and the United States lacked the will to oppose them. In March 1936, Nazi troops marched into the industry-rich Rhineland on Germany's western border, a blatant violation of the Versailles peace treaty. A month later, Italian armies completed their conquest of Ethiopia, projecting fascist power into Africa. In December 1937, Japanese invaders captured Nanjing (Nanking) and celebrated their triumph in the "Rape of Nanking," a deadly rampage that killed 200,000 Chinese civilians.

In Spain, a bitter civil war broke out in July 1936 when the Nationalists— fascist rebels led by General Francisco Franco—attacked the democratically elected Republicans, called Loyalists. Both Germany and Italy reinforced Franco, while the Soviet Union provided much less aid to the Republican Loyalists. The Loyalists did not receive help from European democracies or the U.S. government. But more than three thousand individual Americans fought alongside Republican Loyalists in the Russian-sponsored Abraham Lincoln Brigade. Abandoned by the Western democracies, the Republican Loyalists were defeated in 1939, and Franco built a fascist bulwark in Spain.

Hostilities in Europe, Africa, and Asia alarmed Roosevelt and some Americans. The president sought to persuade most Americans to moderate

ATLANTIC OCEAN

Germans bomb civilians, 1937

FRANCE
Guernica

PORTUGAL

Madrid   Barcelona

SPAIN

Surrendered March 28, 1939

Mediterranean Sea

SPANISH MOROCCO   ALGERIA

- Nationalist, July 1936
- Nationalist gains, Oct. 1937
- Nationalist gains, July 1938
- Nationalist gains, Feb. 1939
- Republican, Feb. 1939

Spanish Civil War, 1936–1939

their isolationism and find a way to support the victims of fascist aggression. He warned that an "epidemic of world lawlessness is spreading" and pointed out that "mere isolation or neutrality" offered no remedy. The popularity of isolationist sentiment caused Roosevelt to remark privately, "It's a terrible thing to look over your shoulder when you are trying to lead and find no one there." Roosevelt knew he needed to maneuver carefully to help prevent fascist aggressors from conquering Europe and Asia, which would leave the United States an isolated island of democracy.

REVIEW

Why did isolationism during the 1930s concern Roosevelt?

How did war in Europe and Asia influence U.S. foreign policy?

Between 1939 and 1941, fascist victories overseas slowly eroded American isolationism. At first, U.S. involvement in the war was limited to providing material support to Britain, China, and the Soviet Union, the principal enemies of Germany and Japan. But Japan's surprise attack on Pearl Harbor caused the nation to declare war and mobilize for an all-out assault on its European and Asian enemies.

How did Nazi aggression start war in Europe?

Under the spell of isolationism, Americans watched Hitler's campaign to dominate Europe (**Map 25.1**). In 1938, Hitler incorporated Austria into Germany and turned his attention to the Sudetenland, which had been granted to Czechoslovakia by the World War I peace settlement. Hoping to avoid war, British prime minister Neville Chamberlain offered Hitler terms of appeasement that would give the Sudetenland to Germany if Hitler agreed to leave the rest of Czechoslovakia alone. Hitler accepted the terms but did not keep his promise.

By 1939, Hitler had annexed Czechoslovakia and demanded that Poland return the German territory it had gained after World War I. Recognizing that **appeasement** of Hitler had failed, Britain and France promised Poland that, if Hitler attacked, they would go to war with Germany. In turn, Hitler tried to prevent the Soviet Union from joining Britain and France in support of Poland. Despite the enduring hatred between fascist Germany and the Communist Soviet Union, the two nations signed the Nazi-Soviet treaty of nonaggression in August 1939, exposing Poland to an onslaught by both the German and Soviet armies.

At dawn on September 1, 1939, Hitler unleashed his *blitzkrieg* (literally, "lightning war") on Poland. "Act brutally!" Hitler exhorted his generals. "Send [every] man, woman, and child of Polish descent and language to their deaths, pitilessly and remorselessly." The attack triggered Soviet assaults on eastern Poland and

appeasement
British strategy aimed at avoiding a war with Germany by not objecting to Hitler's territorial aggressions.

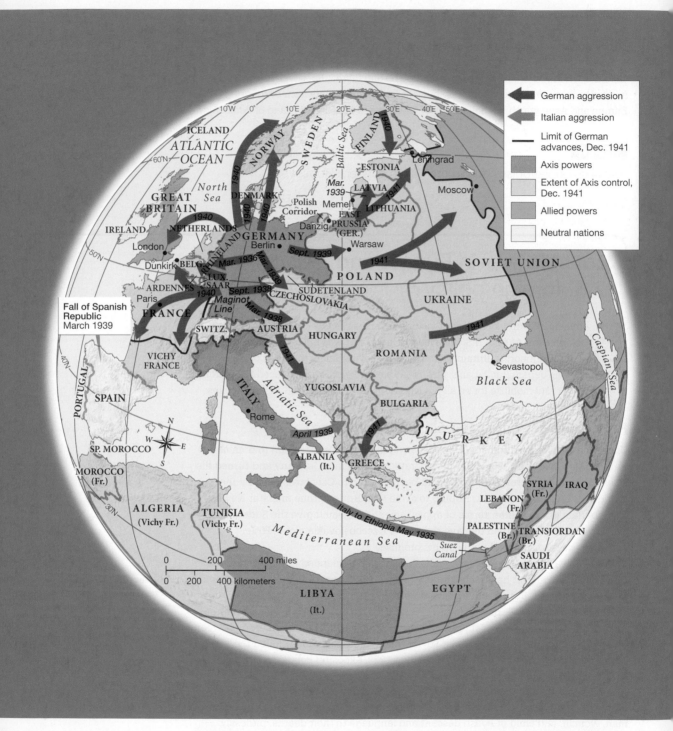

MAP 25.1 ▲ Axis Aggression through 1941 Through a series of surprise strikes before 1942, Mussolini sought to re-create the Roman empire in the Mediterranean while Hitler aimed to annex Austria and reclaim German territories occupied by France after World War I. World War II broke out when the German dictator attacked Poland.

declarations of war from France and Britain two days later, igniting a conflict that raced around the globe. In September 1939, Germany seemed invincible, causing many people to fear that all of Europe would soon share Poland's fate.

After the Nazis overran Poland, Hitler soon launched a westward blitzkrieg. In the first six months of 1940, German forces smashed through Denmark, Norway, the Netherlands, Belgium, and France. The speed of the German attack trapped more than 300,000 British and French soldiers, who retreated to the port of Dunkirk and ferried to safety across the English Channel. One observer noted that the British rescued "hardly enough tanks to fight a regiment of well armed Boy Scouts."

By mid-June 1940, France had surrendered the largest army in the world, signed an armistice that gave Germany control of nearly two-thirds of the countryside, and installed a collaborationist government at Vichy. With an empire that stretched across Europe from Poland to France, Hitler was poised to attack Britain.

The new British prime minister, Winston Churchill, vowed that Britain, unlike France, would never surrender to Hitler. "We shall fight on the seas and oceans [and] . . . in the air," he proclaimed, "whatever the cost may be, we shall fight on the beaches, . . . and in the fields and in the streets." Churchill's defiance stiffened British resolve against Hitler's attack, which began in mid-June 1940, when wave after wave of German bombers targeted British military installations and cities, killing tens of thousands of civilians. The outgunned Royal Air Force fought as doggedly as Churchill had predicted and finally won the Battle of Britain by November, clearing German bombers from British skies and handing Hitler his first defeat. Churchill praised the valiant British pilots, declaring that "never . . . was so much owed by so many to so few." Advance knowledge of German plans aided British pilots, who had access to the new technology of radar and to decoded top-secret German military communications. Battered and exhausted by German attacks, Britain needed American help to continue to fight, as Churchill repeatedly wrote Roosevelt in private.

How did America become the arsenal of democracy?

Most Americans condemned German aggression and favored Britain and France, but isolationism remained powerful. Roosevelt feared that if Congress did not repeal the arms embargo required by the Neutrality Act of 1937, France and Britain would soon fall to the Nazi onslaught. "What worries me," Roosevelt wrote a friend, "is that public opinion . . . is patting itself on the back every morning and thanking God for the Atlantic Ocean (and the Pacific Ocean)," and ignoring "the serious implications" of the European war "for our own future." Congress agreed in November 1939 to allow warring nations to buy arms and nonmilitary supplies on a cash-and-carry basis.

The revised neutrality law permitted Britain and France to purchase American war supplies and carry them across the Atlantic in their own ships, thereby shielding American vessels from attack by German submarines. Roosevelt searched for a way to aid Britain short of a formal alliance or declaring war against Germany. Churchill pleaded for American destroyers, aircraft, and munitions, but he had no money to buy them under the prevailing cash-and-carry neutrality law. As the Battle of Britain raged late in the summer of 1940, Roosevelt agreed to deliver fifty old destroyers to

Britain in exchange for American access to British bases in the Western Hemisphere, the first step toward building a firm Anglo-American alliance against Hitler.

The Anglo-American allies quickly cooperated to advance radar technology. The British had invented a top-secret radio-wave transmitter that allowed radar to identify an object as small as a few inches. British leaders desperately needed to use the new radar to attack German bombers and submarines, but they lacked the resources to make the technology widely available to the military. In September 1940, the British shared their technology with a top-secret group of American physicists and engineers in universities and corporate research labs to adapt the new radar to help fight the war.

One American scientist explained the significance of the new technology by saying, "If automobiles had been similarly improved, modern cars would cost about a dollar and go a thousand miles on a gallon of gas." With headquarters at the Radiation Lab of the Massachusetts Institute of Technology, American scientists across the nation worked feverishly to improve radar. Eventually, their efforts helped identify enemy aircraft and targets on land and sea, directed antiaircraft fire against enemy planes, and made possible the radar-based proximity fuse, which caused antiaircraft and artillery shells to explode when they neared a target. For example, a proximity fuse caused the atomic bomb used at Hiroshima to detonate at an altitude that created maximum destruction. These and many other military uses of radar technology contributed greatly to Allied military campaigns.

While German Luftwaffe (air force) pilots bombed Britain, Roosevelt decided to run for an unprecedented third term as president in 1940. When voters reelected Roosevelt, they sent a message of support for American involvement in the European war. The Republican presidential candidate, Wendell Willkie, who was ridiculed by New Dealers as a "simple, barefoot Wall Street lawyer," attacked Roosevelt as a warmonger. Willkie's accusations caused the president to promise voters, "Your boys are not going to be sent into any foreign wars," a pledge offset by his repeated warnings during the campaign about the threats to America posed by Nazi aggression.

Once reelected, Roosevelt maneuvered to support Britain in every way short of a declaration of war against Germany. In a fireside chat shortly after Christmas 1940, Roosevelt proclaimed that the United States had to become "the great arsenal of democracy" and send "every ounce and every ton of munitions and supplies that we can possibly spare to help the defenders who are in the front lines."

Lend-Lease Act
Legislation in 1941 that enabled Britain to obtain arms from the United States without cash but with the promise to reimburse the United States when the war ended.

In January 1941, Roosevelt proposed the **Lend-Lease Act**, which allowed the British to obtain weapons from the United States without paying cash but with the promise to reimburse the United States when the war ended. The purpose of Lend-Lease, Roosevelt proclaimed, was to defend democracy and human rights throughout the world, specifically the Four Freedoms: "freedom of speech and expression . . . freedom of every person to worship God in his own way . . . freedom from want . . . [and] freedom from fear." Isolationist opponents accused Roosevelt of concocting a "Triple A foreign policy" that would lead to war and "plow under every fourth American boy," as the New Deal's AAA had encouraged farmers to plow under part of their crops (see chapter 24). After fierce debates, Congress approved Lend-Lease, channeling more than $50 billion to Britain during the war, far more than all federal expenditures combined since Roosevelt had become president in 1933.

Hindered in his plans to invade Britain, Hitler turned his massive army eastward. On June 22, 1941, Germany launched a surprise attack on the Soviet Union, his ally in the 1939 Nazi-Soviet nonaggression pact. Neither Roosevelt nor Churchill had any love for Joseph Stalin or communism, but they welcomed the Soviet Union to the anti-Nazi cause. Both Western leaders understood that Hitler's attack on Russia would provide relief for the hard-pressed British. Roosevelt quickly persuaded Congress to extend Lend-Lease to the Soviet Union, beginning the shipment of millions of tons of trucks, jeeps, and other equipment that in all supplied about 10 percent of Russian war materiel.

As Hitler's army raced across the Russian plains and Nazi U-boats tried to choke off supplies to Britain and the Soviet Union, Roosevelt met with Churchill aboard a ship near Newfoundland to cement the Anglo-American alliance. In August 1941, the two leaders issued the Atlantic Charter, pledging the two nations to freedom of the seas and free trade as well as the right of national self-determination.

Why did Japan attack Pearl Harbor?

Although Roosevelt worried about war with Germany, Hitler avoided directly provoking the United States. Japanese ambitions in Asia clashed more openly with American interests and commitments, especially in China and the Philippines. Unlike Hitler, the Japanese high command planned to attack the United States in order to allow Japan to rule an Asian empire it termed the Greater East Asia Co-Prosperity Sphere.

The Japanese appealed to widespread Asian bitterness toward white colonial powers such as the British in India and Burma, the French in Indochina (now Vietnam), and the Dutch in the East Indies (now Indonesia). The Japanese claimed that they would preserve "Asia for the Asians." However, Japan's invasion of China—which had lasted for ten years by 1941—proved that its true goal was Asia for the Japanese (**Map 25.2**). Japan coveted the raw materials available from China and Southeast Asia, ignoring American demands to stop its campaign of aggression.

In 1940, Japan entered a defensive alliance with Germany and Italy—the Tripartite Pact. To obstruct Japanese plans to invade the Dutch East Indies, in July 1941 Roosevelt announced a trade embargo that denied Japan access to oil, scrap iron, and other goods essential for its war machine. Roosevelt hoped the embargo would strengthen Japan's moderate factions.

Instead, the American embargo played into the hands of Japanese militarists headed by General Hideki Tojo, who seized control of the government in October 1941 and persuaded other leaders, including Emperor Hirohito, that swift destruction of American naval bases in the Pacific would leave Japan free to achieve its war aims. On December 7, 1941, 183 aircraft lifted off from six Japanese carriers and attacked the U.S. Pacific Fleet at Pearl Harbor on the Hawai'ian island of Oahu. The devastating surprise attack sank all of the fleet's battleships, killed more than 2,400 Americans, and almost crippled U.S. forces in the Pacific. Luckily for the United States, Japanese pilots failed to destroy oil storage facilities at Pearl Harbor and the nation's aircraft carriers, which happened to be at sea during the attack.

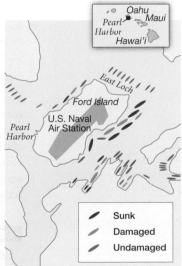

Bombing of Pearl Harbor, December 7, 1941

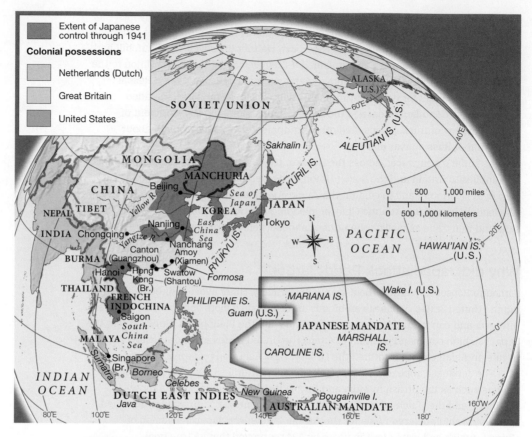

MAP 25.2 ▲ Japanese Aggression through 1941 Beginning with the invasion of Manchuria in 1931, Japan sought to extend its imperialist control over most of East Asia. Japanese aggression was driven by the need for raw materials for the country's expanding industries and by the government's devotion to militaristic values.

The Japanese scored a stunning tactical victory at Pearl Harbor. In the long run, however, the attack proved a colossal blunder. The victory made many Japanese commanders overconfident about their military strength. Worse, Americans instantly united in their desire to fight and avenge the attack. Roosevelt vowed that "this form of treachery shall never endanger us again." On December 8, Congress endorsed the president's call for a declaration of war. Both Hitler and Mussolini declared war against America three days later, bringing the United States into all-out war with the Axis powers in both Europe and Asia.

REVIEW

How did American isolationism influence Roosevelt's policies toward military aggression by Germany and Japan?

How did the United States mobilize for war?

The time had come, Roosevelt announced, for the prescriptions of "Dr. New Deal" to be replaced by the stronger medicines of "Dr. Win-the-War." Military and civilian leaders rushed to protect the nation against further attacks, causing Americans with Japanese ancestry to be stigmatized and sent to internment camps. Roosevelt and his advisers lost no time enlisting millions of Americans in the armed forces to bring the isolationist-era military to fighting strength for a two-front war. The war emergency also required economic mobilization unparalleled in the nation's history. As Dr. Win-the-War, Roosevelt set aside the New Deal goal of reform and plunged headlong into transforming the American economy into the world's greatest military machine. Wartime mobilization achieved full employment and economic recovery, goals the New Deal had never reached.

Why did the wartime emergency lead to internment of Japanese Americans?

Shortly after declaring war against the United States, Hitler sent German submarines to hunt American ships along the Atlantic coast, where Paul Tibbets and other American pilots tried to destroy them. The U-boats had devastating success for about eight months, sinking hundreds of U.S. ships and threatening to disrupt the Lend-Lease lifeline to Britain and the Soviet Union. By mid-1942, the U.S. Navy protected the U.S. coast and chased German submarines into the mid-Atlantic.

Within the continental United States, Americans remained sheltered from the chaos and destruction the war brought to hundreds of millions in Europe and Asia. Nevertheless, the government worried constantly about espionage and internal subversion. Posters warned Americans that "Loose lips sink ships" and "Enemy agents are always near; if you don't talk, they won't hear." The campaign for patriotic vigilance focused on German and Japanese foes, but Americans of Japanese descent became targets of persecution because of Pearl Harbor and long-standing racial prejudice against people of Asian descent.

About 320,000 people of Japanese ancestry lived in U.S. territory in 1941, two-thirds of them in Hawai'i, where they largely escaped wartime persecution because they were essential and valued members of society. On the mainland, however, Japanese Americans were a tiny minority—even along the West Coast, where most of them worked on farms and in small businesses. Although an official military survey concluded that Japanese Americans posed no danger, popular hostility fueled a campaign to round up all mainland Japanese Americans—two-thirds of them U.S. citizens. "A Jap's a Jap. . . . It makes no difference whether he is an American citizen or not," one official declared.

On February 19, 1942, Roosevelt issued Executive Order 9066, which sent all Americans of Japanese descent to ten makeshift **internment camps** located in

internment camps
Makeshift prison camps to which Americans of Japanese descent were sent as a result of Roosevelt's Executive Order 9066, issued in February 1942.

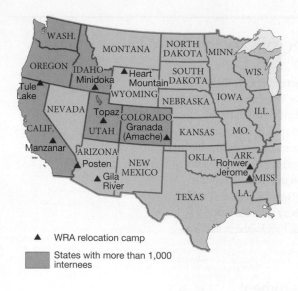

▲ WRA relocation camp

☐ States with more than 1,000
internees

MAP 25.3 ◄ Western Relocation Authority Centers
Responding to prejudice and fear of sabotage, President Roosevelt authorized the relocation of all Americans of Japanese descent in 1942. Taken from their homes in the cities and farmland of the far West, more than 120,000 Japanese Americans were confined in camps scattered as far east as the Mississippi River.

remote areas of the West and South (**Map 25.3**). Allowed little time to sell or protect their property, Japanese Americans lost homes and businesses worth about $400 million and lived out the war penned in by barbed wire and armed guards. (**See "Analyzing Historical Evidence: Japanese Internment" on page 744.**)

Several thousand Japanese Americans served with distinction in the U.S. armed forces, and no case of subversion by a Japanese American was ever uncovered. Still, the Supreme Court's 1944 *Korematsu* decision upheld Executive Order 9066's clear violation of Japanese Americans' constitutional rights as justified by "military necessity."

How did the United States build a citizen army?

As war raged in Europe and Asia, "the U.S. Army looked like a few nice boys with BB guns," according to one observer. In 1940, Roosevelt urged Congress to prepare for war by passing the **Selective Service Act**, which registered men of military age who could be drafted if the need arose. More than six thousand local draft boards registered more than thirty million men. When the war came, more than sixteen million men and women served in uniform, two-thirds of them draftees and most of them young men. Women were barred from combat duty, but they worked at nearly every noncombat task, eroding barriers to women's military service.

Selective Service Act
Law enacted in 1940 requiring all men who would be eligible for a military draft to register in preparation for the possibility of a future conflict.

The Selective Service Act prohibited discrimination "on account of race or color." Almost one million Black men and women donned uniforms, as did half a million Mexican Americans, 25,000 Native Americans, and 13,000 Chinese Americans. The racial insults and discrimination suffered by all people of color made some soldiers ask, as a Mexican American GI did on his way to the European front, "Why fight for America when you have not been treated as an American?"

Black Americans were trained in segregated camps, confined in segregated barracks, and assigned to segregated units. Most Black soldiers were assigned to manual labor. Few served in combat until late in 1944, when the need for military manpower in Europe increased. Then, as General George Patton told Black soldiers in a tank unit in Normandy, "I don't care what color you are, so long as you go up there and kill those Kraut sonsabitches."

Homosexuals also served in the armed forces, although in much smaller numbers than Black Americans. Allowed to serve as long as their sexual preferences

◄ Black Machine Gunners
Soldiers William Adam Leak and Adam Parham, shown here in May 1944, were among the first Black combat troops in the Pacific theater. They and thousands of other Black soldiers fought in the Bougainville campaign, which continued until August 1945, to retake the Japanese-occupied portions of the Solomon Islands, just north of Australia. GRANGER–Historical Picture Archive.

remained covert, gay Americans, like other minorities, sought to demonstrate their worth under fire. "I was superpatriotic," a gay combat veteran recalled. Another gay GI remarked, "Who in the hell is going to worry about [homosexuality]" in the midst of the life-or-death realities of war?

How did the United States convert to a war economy?

In 1940, the American economy remained mired in the depression. Nearly one worker in seven was still unemployed, factories operated far below their productive capacity, and the total federal budget was less than $10 billion. Shortly after the attack on Pearl Harbor, Roosevelt announced the goal of converting the economy to produce "overwhelming . . . , crushing superiority of equipment in any theater of the world war." Factories were overhauled for assembling tanks and airplanes, and production soared to record levels. By the end of the war, jobs exceeded workers, plants operated at full capacity, and the federal budget topped $100 billion.

To organize and oversee this tidal wave of military production, Roosevelt called upon business leaders to come to Washington and accept a token payment of a dollar a year to head new government agencies, such as the War Production Board, which set production priorities and pushed for maximum output. Contracts flowed to large corporations, often guaranteeing their profits. During the first half of 1942, the government issued contracts worth more than the entire gross national product in 1941.

Booming wartime employment swelled union membership. To speed production, the government asked unions to pledge not to strike. Despite the relentless pace of

ANALYZING HISTORICAL EVIDENCE

Japanese Internment

A fter the bombing of Pearl Harbor, Japanese Americans pledged their loyalty to the United States. Soon, however, military and political leaders targeted Japanese American citizens as enemy agents and confined them to intern-ment camps scattered across the West and South.

DOCUMENT 1
Japanese American Citizens League of Seattle Pledges Loyalty to the United States, December 22, 1941

Barely two weeks after Pearl Harbor, the Japanese Ameri-can Citizens League of Seattle held an Americanism rally and unanimously passed the following resolution pledging members' loyalty to the United States and their willingness to do their part in the war against Japan.

December 22, 1941

Whereas we are now in a war forced upon us by Japan, the prosecution of which toward a victorious end is the principal aim of the American people, and

Whereas this can be accomplished only by coop-eration with the President of the United States and our National Defense Agencies, now

Be it resolved that we Americans of Japanese ancestry and the members of our parent generation here assembled and elsewhere reaffirm our allegiance and loy-alty to the United States of America and pledge our effort toward a victorious prosecution of this war by extending unstinting co-operation to the President of the United States and the duly constituted defense authorities by:

1.   Volunteering for service in the United States military forces;
2.   Volunteering every service to eradicate subversive activities;
3.   Volunteering for service in the Civilian Defense Program;
4.   Volunteering for service in the American Red Cross;
5.   Purchasing National Defense Bonds and Stamps.

Source: Japanese American Citizens League, "Japanese American Citi-zens League Resolution regarding the Loyalty of Those with Japanese Ancestry to the United States, December 22, 1941," Digital Public Library of America, http://dp.la/item/ce377a7f62fd614f4be97ca96ed0fe6e.

DOCUMENT 2
General John DeWitt, Final Recommendations of the Commanding General, Western Defense Command and Fourth Army, Submitted to the Secretary of War, 1942

Early in 1942, General John DeWitt, commander of the Western Defense Command, persuaded President Franklin Roosevelt to round up Japanese people living in the United States and confine them to relocation camps for the duration of the war. DeWitt's recommendation expressed concern for military security and appealed to racist conceptions long used to curb Asian immigration. Japanese Americans and their supporters fought the internment order in the courts as a violation of fundamen-tal constitutional rights, an argument rejected during the war by the U.S. Supreme Court.

February 14, 1942
Memorandum for the Secretary of War

Subject: Evacuation of Japanese and Other Subversive Persons from the Pacific Coast . . .
Brief Estimate of the Situation.
1.   . . . The following are possible and probable enemy activities: . . .
   a.   Naval attack on shipping on coastal waters;
   b.   Naval attack on coastal cities and vital installations;
   c.   Air raids on vital installations, particularly within two hundred miles of the coast;
   d.   Sabotage of vital installations throughout the Western Defense Command. . . .

Hostile Naval and air raids will be assisted by enemy agents signaling from the coastline and the vicinity thereof; and by supplying and otherwise assisting enemy vessels and by sabotage. . . .

In the war in which we are now engaged racial affinities are not severed by migration. The Japanese race is an enemy race and while many second and third generation Japanese born on United States soil, possessed of United States citizenship, have become "Americanized," the racial strains are undiluted. To conclude otherwise is to expect that children born of white parents on Japanese soil sever all racial affinity and become loyal Japanese subjects, ready to fight and, if necessary, to die for Japan in a war against the nation of their parents. . . .

It, therefore, follows that along the vital Pacific Coast over 112,000 potential enemies, of Japanese extraction, are at large today. There are indications that these are organized and ready for concerted action at a favorable opportunity. The very fact that no sabotage has taken place to date is a disturbing and confirming indication that such action will be taken.

Source: General John Lesesne DeWitt, *Final Recommendations*, report to the United States Secretary of War, February 14, 1942.

DOCUMENT 3
Kenji Okuda, Letter from Camp Harmony, Puyallup, Washington, May 30, 1942

Kenji Okuda, his parents, Haji and Ura, and his sister Shizuko were interned at Camp Harmony in Puyallup, Washington, along with more than seven thousand other Japanese Americans from the West Coast. Okuda, who had hoped to be admitted to medical school, wrote his friend Norio Higano with news of the "concentration camp."

May 30, 1942
Dear Norio-san,

On this first Memorial Day after our fateful entrance into a frightening, devastating war. . . . thousands of young Americans have already perished and other thousands are fighting furiously dying and killing. . . . there is

nothing in this camp to remind us of that occasion except a memorial service this evening at 7. No military parade will we see; no valiant or half-hearted display of armed might. . . . just a quiet service for those Japanese pioneers who have died striving that we, their children, might inherit something of that Great American ideal, Democracy.

But how futile and hypocritical this all sounds . . . in concentration camps in a Democracy . . . to be kept herein at the sole discretion of the military . . . and yet to be expected to be willing to do our best to insure the defeat of a nation with which so many of us are connected only by facial and racial characteristics . . .

. . . Gordie refused to register for evacuation and surrendered to the F.B.I. . . . He's still in the Federal tank . . . with C. T. Takahashi, Kenji Iki, and another Japanese among others and seems to be making the best out of conditions. Almost enjoying himself! He is the only one all up and down the coast who has shown his refusal or dislike for the evacuation and may make a constitutional test of the whole procedure. More power to him.

Source: Kenji Okuda, letter to Norio Higano from Camp Harmony, Digital Public Library of America, http://dp.la/item /e0934a498297dd0d1a4c60068f3835fb.

Questions for Analysis

ANALYZE THE EVIDENCE: What views of citizenship and racial identity are expressed by the Japanese American Citizens League, General DeWitt, and Kenji Okuda?

CONSIDER THE CONTEXT: Why did General DeWitt insist on evacuating the Japanese after military investigators told him that no acts of sabotage had occurred?

RECOGNIZE VIEWPOINTS: Why did the Japanese American Citizens League express loyalty to the United States so soon after Pearl Harbor?

ASK HISTORICAL QUESTIONS: Why did the internment policy deny the rights of United States citizenship to Japanese Americans?

work, union members mostly kept their no-strike pledge. An important exception was the United Mine Workers, whose members walked out of the coal mines in 1943, demanding a pay hike and earning hostility from many Americans.

Overall, conversion to war production achieved Roosevelt's ambitious goal of "crushing superiority" in military goods. At a total cost of $304 billion (equivalent to about $4 trillion today) during the war, the nation produced an avalanche of military equipment, more than double the combined production of Germany, Japan, and Italy (**Figure 25.1**). This outpouring of military goods

FIGURE 25.1 ▶ Global Comparison: Weapons Production by the Axis and Allied Powers during World War II U.S. weapons dominated the air and the sea during World War II. Together, the three Allied powers produced about three times as many aircraft and five to eight times as many warships as the two Axis powers. The Soviet Union led the other Allies in the production of tanks and artillery. What does the chronology of weapons production suggest about the kind of warfare emphasized by each belligerent nation and the course of the war?

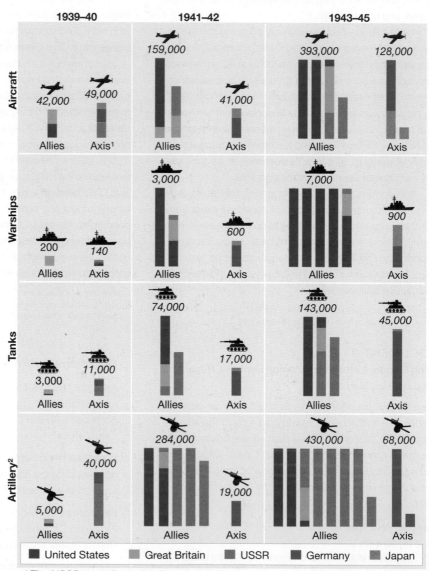

Legend: United States | Great Britain | USSR | Germany | Japan

[1] The USSR was allied with Germany 1939–40.
[2] No reliable data exist for Japan.

supplied not only U.S. forces but also America's allies, giving tangible meaning to
Roosevelt's pledge to make America the "arsenal of democracy."

How did the Roosevelt administration mobilize the human and
industrial resources necessary to fight a two-front war?

How did the Allies reverse Axis advances in Europe and the Pacific?

The United States confronted an intimidating military challenge in December
1941. The attack on Pearl Harbor destroyed much of its Pacific Fleet. In the
Atlantic, Hitler's U-boats sank American ships, while German armies occupied most of western Europe and steadily advanced into the Soviet Union. Roosevelt
and his military advisers believed that defeating Germany took top priority. That
meant the United States had to support its allies, Britain and the Soviet Union. If they
fell, Hitler would command all the resources of Europe and would be ready for an
assault on the United States.

To fight back against Germany and Japan, the United States had to coordinate
military and political strategy with its allies and muster all its human and economic
assets. Victory over the Japanese fleet at the Battle of Midway, the elimination of
Germany's menace to Allied shipping in the prolonged Battle of the Atlantic, and the
Allied assault on North Africa and then Italy established Allied naval superiority in the
Atlantic and Pacific and began to challenge German domination of southern Europe.

What turned the tide in the Pacific?

In the Pacific theater, Japan's leading military strategist, Admiral Isoroku Yamamoto,
believed that after Pearl Harbor his forces must quickly conquer and secure the
territories they targeted, or Japan would lose the war because of America's far
greater resources. Swiftly, the Japanese assaulted American airfields and captured
U.S. outposts on Guam and Wake Island. After occupying Singapore and Burma,
Japan sought to complete its domination of the southern Pacific with an attack in
January 1942 on the American stronghold in the Philippines (**Map 25.5**). American
defenders surrendered to the Japanese in May. The Japanese victors sent captured
American and Filipino soldiers on the infamous Bataan Death March to a concentration camp, killing thousands. By the summer of 1942, the Japanese had conquered
the Dutch East Indies and were poised to strike Australia and New Zealand.

In the spring of 1942, U.S. forces launched a major two-pronged counteroffensive
that military officials hoped would reverse Japanese advances. Forces led by General
Douglas MacArthur, commander of the U.S. armed forces in the Pacific, moved north
from Australia and attacked the Japanese in the Philippines. Far more decisively,

Admiral Chester W. Nimitz sailed his battle fleet west from Hawai'i to retake Japanese-held islands in the southern and mid-Pacific. On May 7–8, 1942, in the Coral Sea just north of Australia, the American fleet and carrier-based warplanes defeated a Japanese armada sailing around the coast of New Guinea.

Battle of Midway
June 3–6, 1942, naval battle in the Central Pacific in which American forces surprised and defeated the Japanese fleet planning to invade Midway Island.

Nimitz then learned from an intelligence intercept that the Japanese were massing an invasion force aimed at Midway Island, an outpost guarding the Hawai'ian Islands. Nimitz maneuvered his fleet to surprise the Japanese. In three days of furious fighting, American ships and planes crushed the Japanese navy. The **Battle of Midway** reversed the balance of naval power in the Pacific and put the Japanese at a disadvantage for the rest of the war. Japan managed to build only six more large aircraft carriers during the war, while the United States launched dozens, proving the wisdom of Yamamoto's prediction. But the Japanese still occupied and defended the many places they had conquered.

How did the Allies counterattack against Nazi advances in Europe and Africa?

After Pearl Harbor, Hitler's eastern-front armies marched ever deeper into the Soviet Union, while his western-front forces prepared to invade Britain. As in World War I, the Germans tried to starve the British into submission by destroying their seaborne supply routes. In 1941 and 1942, they sank Allied ships faster than new ones could be built. Overall, this U-boat campaign sank 4,700 merchant vessels and almost 200 warships and killed 40,000 Allied seamen.

Until mid-1943, the outcome of the war in the Atlantic remained in doubt. Then, newly invented radar detectors and increased production of destroyer escorts for merchant vessels allowed the Allies to prey upon the lurking U-boats. After suffering a 75 percent casualty rate among U-boat crews, Hitler withdrew German submarines from the North Atlantic in late May 1943. Winning the Battle of the Atlantic allowed the United States to supply its British and Soviet allies for the duration of the war and to reduce the threat of a German invasion of Britain.

The most important strategic questions confronting the United States and its allies were when and where to open a second front against the Nazis. To relieve the pressure on the Soviet Union, Stalin demanded that America and Britain mount an immediate and massive assault across the English Channel into western France and force Hitler to divert his armies. Churchill and Roosevelt delayed, however, allowing the Germans and the Soviets to slug it out. This drawn-out conflict weakened both the Nazis and the Communists and made an eventual Allied attack on western France more likely to succeed. Churchill and Roosevelt decided to strike first in North Africa to help secure Allied control of the Mediterranean.

In October and November 1942, British forces at El-Alamein in Egypt halted German general Erwin Rommel's drive to capture the Suez Canal, Britain's lifeline to the oil of the Middle East and to British colonies in India and South Asia (**Map 25.4**). In November, an American army under General Dwight D. Eisenhower landed far to the west, in French Morocco. Propelled by American tank units commanded by General George Patton, the Allied armies defeated the Germans in North Africa in May 1943. With the Germans out of Africa, the Mediterranean was safe for Allied shipping.

In January 1943, while the North African campaign was still under way, Roosevelt and Churchill met in Casablanca and announced that they would

▲ *Night Shift, Italy* **by Joseph Hirsch, 1944** Medics saved the lives of hundreds of thousands soldiers during World War II. Here, medical corps stretcher bearers carry a soldier wounded in the brutal Italian campaign over treacherously steep rocks in the dead of night. They were taking him to a portable surgical hospital very close to the front lines where his injuries could be diagnosed and treated. More than 320,000 Allied soldiers were wounded during the Italian campaign, roughly five times more than the men killed in combat. Overall, medics, nurses, and doctors managed to save the lives of all but 3 percent of the wounded, compared to 8 percent in World War I and 25 percent in the Civil War. Courtesy of the U.S. Army Center of Military History.

accept nothing less than the "unconditional surrender" of the Axis powers, ruling out peace negotiations. They agreed that they should strike next against Italy, forcing the Soviet Union to continue to bear the brunt of the Nazi war machine.

In July 1943, American and British forces landed in Sicily. Soon afterward, Mussolini was deposed in Italy, ending the reign of Italian fascism. Quickly, the Allies invaded the mainland, and the Italian government surrendered unconditionally. The Germans responded by rushing reinforcements to Italy, turning the Allies' Italian campaign into a series of battles to liberate Italy from German occupation.

German troops dug into strong fortifications and fought to defend every inch of Italy's rugged terrain. Allied forces continued to battle against stubborn German defenses for the remainder of the war, making the Italian campaign the war's deadliest for American infantrymen. One soldier in Italy wrote that his buddies "died like butchered swine."

REVIEW

How did U.S. military strategy against the Japanese and the Germans differ?

How did war change the American home front?

The war effort mobilized Americans as never before. Factories churned out bombs, bullets, tanks, ships, and airplanes, which workers rushed to assemble, leaving their farms and small towns and congregating in cities. Women took jobs with wrenches and welding torches, boosting the nation's workforce while violating traditional notions that a woman's place was in the home rather than on the assembly line. Despite rationing and shortages, gigantic government expenditures for war production brought prosperity to many Americans after years of depression-era poverty.

Although Americans in uniform risked their lives on battlefields in Europe and Asia, Americans on the U.S. mainland were immune to foreign attack—in sharp contrast to their Soviet and British allies. Wartime ideology contrasted Allied support for human rights with Axis tyranny and provided justification for the many sacrifices Americans were required to make. The ideology also established a standard of basic human equality that became a potent weapon in the campaign for equal rights at home and in condemning atrocities such as the Nazis' Holocaust.

How did American women and families contribute to the war effort?

Millions of American women gladly took their places on assembly lines in defense industries. At the start of the war, about a quarter of adult women worked outside the home, but few women worked in factories, except for textile mills and sewing industries. Wartime mobilization and the enlistment of millions of men in the armed forces left factories begging for women workers.

Government advertisements urged women to take industrial jobs by assuring them that their household chores had prepared them for work on the "Victory Line." One billboard proclaimed, "If you've sewed buttons, or made buttonholes, on a [sewing] machine, you can learn to do spot welding on airplane parts." Millions of women responded. Advertisers often referred to a woman who worked in a war industry as "Rosie the Riveter," a popular wartime term.

By the end of the war, women working outside the home numbered 50 percent more than in 1939. Contributing to the war effort also paid off in wages. A Kentucky woman remembered her job at a munitions plant, where she earned "the fabulous sum of $32 a week. To us it was an absolute miracle. Before that we made nothing." Although men were paid an average of $54 for similar wartime work, women welcomed their chance to earn wages and help win the war at the same time.

The majority of married women remained at home, occupied with domestic chores and child care. But they, too, supported the war effort by planting Victory Gardens, saving tin cans and newspapers for recycling into war materiel, and buying war bonds. Many families scrimped to cope with the 30 percent inflation

▲ **B-24 Bomber Assembly Plant** Workers swarm over B-24 bombers under construction at the enormous Consolidated Aircraft factory in Fort Worth, Texas. The B-24 was the workhorse American bomber, carrying eight thousand pounds of bombs and up to ten 50-caliber machine guns in the nose, tail, and body of the aircraft. Factory workers churned out more than eighteen thousand B-24s during the war using assembly-line methods perfected in the prewar automobile business. At peak production, a B-24 rolled off the assembly line every fifty-nine minutes, exemplifying Roosevelt's pledge for the United States to become the arsenal of democracy. Chronicle/Alamy.

during the war, but men and women in manufacturing industries enjoyed wages that grew twice as fast as inflation.

The war influenced how all families spent their earnings. Buying a new washing machine or car was out of the question, since factories that formerly built them now made military goods. Many other consumer goods—such as tires, gasoline, shoes, and meat—were rationed at home to meet military needs overseas. But most Americans readily found things to buy, including movie tickets, cosmetics, and music recordings.

The wartime prosperity and abundance enjoyed by most Americans contrasted with the experiences of their hard-pressed allies. Personal consumption fell by 22 percent in Britain, and food output plummeted to just a third of prewar levels in the Soviet Union, creating widespread hunger and even starvation. Few went hungry in the United States as farm output grew 25 percent annually during the war, providing a food surplus for export to the Allies.

VISUAL ACTIVITY

◀ **Riveting Rosies** Dora Miles (left) and Dorothy Johnson (right) were among the millions of women (nicknamed "Rosie the Riveter") who flocked to work in war industries at jobs formerly held by men. Like many other women war workers, Miles and Johnson helped build airplanes. Here they are depicted riveting the frame of an aircraft at a plant in Long Beach, California. Library of Congress Prints and Photographs Division Washington, D.C. [LC-USW33- 028626-C].

READING THE IMAGE: How does the work Miles and Johnson are doing compare to the conventional work routines of women before the war? What does the photo suggest about the relationship between Miles (driving the rivet into a hole) and Johnson (smashing the end of the rivet snug against the airframe)?

CONNECTIONS: What contributions did American women make to the war effort?

Why did Black activists support the Double V campaign?

Double V campaign
World War II campaign in America to attack racism at home and abroad.

While fighting against Nazi Germany and its ideology of white racial supremacy, Americans confronted extensive racial prejudice in their own country. The *Pittsburgh Courier*, a leading Black newspaper, asserted that the wartime emergency called for a **Double V campaign** seeking "victory over our enemies at home and victory over our enemies on the battlefields abroad." As a Mississippi-born Black combat veteran of the Pacific theater recalled, "We had two wars to fight: prejudice . . . and those Japs."

In 1941, Black organizations demanded that the federal government require companies receiving defense contracts to integrate their workforces. A. Philip Randolph, head of the Brotherhood of Sleeping Car Porters, promised that 100,000 Black protesters would march on Washington if the president did not eliminate discrimination in defense industries. Roosevelt decided to risk offending his white allies in unions and in the South. In mid-1941, FDR issued Executive Order 8802, which created the Committee on Fair Employment Practices to investigate and prevent racial discrimination in employment.

Progress came slowly, however. In 1940, nine out of ten Black Americans lived below the federal poverty line. Those who worked earned an average of just 39 percent of white Americans' wages. In search of better jobs and living conditions, 5.5 million Black Americans migrated from the South to war-industry jobs in the North and West. For the first time in U.S. history, the migration made a majority of Black Americans city dwellers. Severe labor shortages and government fair employment standards opened assembly-line jobs in defense plants to Blacks, causing Black unemployment to drop by 80 percent during the war. But more jobs did not mean equal pay for Black workers. The average income of Black families rose during the war, but by the end of the conflict it still stood at only half of what white families earned.

Blacks' migration to defense jobs intensified racial antagonisms, which boiled over in the hot summer of 1943, when 242 race riots erupted in forty-seven cities. The worst mayhem occurred in Detroit, where a long-simmering conflict between whites and Blacks over racially segregated housing ignited into a race war. In two days of violence, twenty-five Blacks and nine whites were killed, and scores more were injured.

Racial violence created the impetus for the Double V campaign, officially supported by the National Association for the Advancement of Colored People (NAACP). Double V activists argued that Black Americans deserved the same rights and privileges enjoyed by all other Americans, an argument that was reinforced by the Allies' wartime ideology of freedom and democracy. The NAACP focused largely on court challenges to segregation, while a new organization founded in 1942, the Congress of Racial Equality, staged pickets and sit-ins against racially segregated restaurants and theaters. Despite these efforts, the Double V campaign achieved only limited success against racial discrimination during the war.

How did the war influence the 1944 presidential election?

Americans rallied around the war effort almost unanimously. In June 1944, Congress recognized the sacrifices made by millions of veterans by unanimously passing the landmark **GI Bill of Rights**, which gave military veterans government funds for

GI Bill of Rights
Legislation passed in 1944 authorizing the government to provide World War II veterans with funds for education, housing, and health care, as well as loans to start businesses and buy homes.

▶ **Learning about the GI Bill of Rights** Staff Sergeant Herbert Ellison explains the provisions of the GI Bill to soldiers stationed in Italy while the war still raged in February 1945. Passed unanimously by Congress just a few weeks after D-Day, the GI Bill was a kind of thank you to the nearly 16 million Americans who had interrupted their lives to serve in uniform during the war. The GI Bill, the largest government program since the nation's founding, offered veterans monthly unemployment payments until they found a postwar job, paid for college or specialized training, and made loans available to buy a home, business, or farm. More than 12 million veterans directly benefited. Library of Congress, Prints & Photographs Division, Reproduction number LC-USZ62-94042 (b&w film copy neg.).

education, housing, and health care, as well as providing loans to start businesses and buy homes. The GI Bill put the financial resources of the federal government behind the abstract goals of freedom and democracy, and it empowered millions of GIs to better themselves and their families after the war.

After twelve turbulent years in the White House, Roosevelt was exhausted and ill with heart disease. Still, he was determined to remain president until the war ended. His poor health made the selection of a vice presidential candidate unusually important. Convinced that many Americans had soured on liberal reform, Roosevelt chose Senator Harry S. Truman of Missouri as his running mate. A reliable party man from a southern border state, Truman satisfied urban Democratic leaders while not worrying white southerners, who were nervous about any candidate who might challenge racial segregation.

The Republicans, confident of a strong conservative upsurge in the nation, nominated Thomas E. Dewey as their presidential candidate. The governor of New York, Dewey had made his reputation as a tough crime fighter. In the 1944 presidential campaign, Dewey failed to persuade most voters that the New Deal was a creeping socialist menace. Although Roosevelt's failing health alarmed many observers, it was outweighed by Americans' unwillingness to change presidents in the midst of the war. In his narrowest presidential victory, Roosevelt received a 53.5 percent majority, confirming his leadership as Dr. Win-the-War.

The Holocaust, 1933–1945

How did the United States respond to the Holocaust?

Since the 1930s, the Nazis had persecuted Jews in Germany and every German-occupied territory, causing many Jews to seek asylum beyond Hitler's reach. Thousands of Jews sought to immigrate to the United States, but 82 percent of Americans opposed admitting them, and the government turned them away. In 1942, numerous reports reached the United States that Hitler was sending Jews, Gypsies, religious and political dissenters, homosexuals, and others to concentration camps, where old people, children, and others deemed too weak to work were systematically killed and cremated, while the able-bodied were put to work at slave labor until they died of starvation, disease, and abuse.

Death camps were devoted almost exclusively to murdering and cremating Jews. Despite reports of the brutal slave labor and death camps, U.S. officials refused to grant asylum to Jewish refugees. Most Americans, including top officials, believed that reports about the Holocaust were exaggerated. Only 152,000 of Europe's millions of Jews managed to gain refuge in the United States before America's entry into the war. Afterward, U.S. immigration restrictions caused the number of Jewish refugees to plummet to just 2,400 by 1944.

Desperate to stop the atrocities, the World Jewish Congress appealed to the Allies to bomb the death camps and the railroad tracks leading to them. The Allies repeatedly turned down such bombing requests. Intent on achieving military victory as soon as possible, they argued that the air forces could not deviate from their military missions.

The nightmare of the **Holocaust** was all too real. When Russian troops arrived at Auschwitz in Poland in January 1945, they found emaciated prisoners, skeletal corpses, gas chambers, pits filled with human ashes, and loot the Nazis had stripped from the dead, including hair, gold fillings, and false teeth. At last, the truth about the Holocaust began to be known beyond the murdered men, women, and children and the Germans who had tolerated and participated in this genocide. By then, it was too late for the eleven million civilian victims—mostly Jews—of these Nazi crimes against humanity.

Holocaust
German genocide of Europe's Jews, along with others the Nazis deemed "undesirable."

REVIEW
How did the war influence American society?

How did the Allies win the war?

B y February 1943, Soviet troops had defeated the massive German offensive against Stalingrad, turning the tide of the war in Europe. After gargantuan sacrifices in fighting that lasted for eighteen months, the Red Army forced Hitler's Wehrmacht to turn back toward the west. In the Pacific, the Allies halted the expansion of the Japanese empire and now had the deadly task of dislodging Japanese defenders from their outposts. Allied military planners adopted a strategy to annihilate Axis resistance by taking advantage of America's industrial superiority. A secret plan to develop a superbomb that harnessed atomic power developed too late to use against Germany. But when the atomic bomb devastated the cities of Hiroshima and Nagasaki, Japan finally surrendered, canceling the planned assault on the Japanese homeland by hundreds of thousands of American soldiers and sailors and their allies.

How did the Allies' European campaign defeat Nazi Germany?

As an airborne substitute for the delayed second front on the ground, British and American pilots flew bombing missions from England to German-occupied territories and to Germany itself. During night raids, British bombers targeted general areas, hoping to hit civilians, create terror, and undermine morale. Beginning with Paul Tibbets's flight in August 1942, American pilots flew heavily armored B-17s from English airfields in daytime raids on industrial targets vital for the German war machine.

German air defenses took a fearsome toll on Allied pilots and aircraft. In 1943, two-thirds of American airmen did not survive to complete their twenty-five-mission tours of duty. In all, 85,000 American airmen were killed in the skies over Europe. Many others were shot down and held as prisoners of war. In February 1944, the arrival of America's durable and deadly P-51 Mustang fighter gave Allied bombers superior protection. The Mustangs slowly began to sweep the Luftwaffe from the skies, allowing Allied bombers to penetrate deep into Germany and pound civilian and military targets around the clock.

In November 1943, Churchill, Roosevelt, and Stalin met in Tehran to discuss wartime strategy and the second front. Roosevelt agreed to Stalin's demand that the Soviet Union would exercise control of the Eastern European countries that the Red Army occupied as it rolled back the still-potent German Wehrmacht. Stalin agreed to enter the war against Japan once Germany finally surrendered, in effect promising to open a second front in the Pacific theater. Roosevelt and Churchill agreed at last to launch a massive second-front assault in northern France, code-named Overlord, in May 1944.

General Eisenhower was assigned overall command of Allied forces. Mountains of military supplies were stockpiled in Britain. Most of Hitler's armies were in the east, trying to halt the Red Army's westward offensive, leaving relatively few German troops to defend against an Allied attack on occupied France. More decisive, years of Allied air raids had decimated the German Luftwaffe, which could send aloft only three hundred fighter planes against twelve thousand Allied aircraft.

▲ **D-Day Landing, June 6, 1944** Coast Guard photographer Robert F. Sargent took this photo of U.S. soldiers wading toward Omaha Beach on D-Day, a photo subsequently entitled *Into the Jaws of Death*. At about 5:30 that morning, the GIs of the 1st Infantry Division had climbed over the side of the U.S. Coast Guard's USS *Samuel Chase* positioned about ten miles offshore in the English Channel and into the Higgins boat shown here. They sloshed around in the rough seas — quiet, cold, soaked, and seasick — before disembarking at 7:40 a.m. Deadly German artillery and machine-gun fire swept the landing zone from the cliffs above the beach. Poor Allied intelligence had failed to identify and destroy German mines and concrete barriers, which prevented the boat from landing the GIs closer to the beach, and U.S. naval and air bombardment did not stop the entrenched Germans from inflicting heavy casualties among the GIs on the beach. National Archives and Records Administration.

After frustrating delays caused by stormy weather, Eisenhower launched the largest amphibious assault in world history on **D-Day**, June 6, 1944 (see Map 25.4). Allied soldiers finally succeeded in securing the beachhead at Normandy, France. An officer told his men, "The only people on this beach are the dead and those that are going to die—now let's get the hell out of here." They did, finally surmounting the cliffs that loomed over the beach and destroying the German defenses. One GI who made the landing recalled the soldiers "were exhausted and we were exultant. We had survived D-Day!"

D-Day
The Allied invasion of northern France, on June 6, 1944, opening a second front against the Germans.

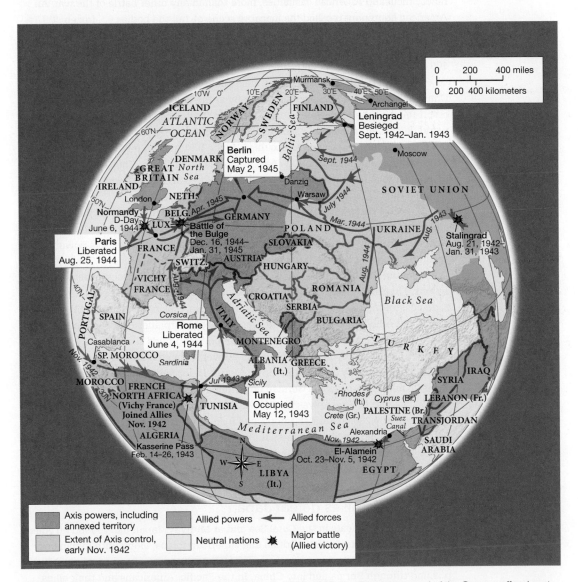

MAP 25.4 ▲ The European Theater of World War II, 1942–1945 The Russian reversal of the German offensive at Stalingrad and Leningrad, combined with Allied landings in North Africa and Normandy, trapped Germany in a closing vise of Allied armies on all sides.

Within a week, a flood of soldiers, tanks, and other military equipment pushed Allied forces toward Germany. On August 25, the Allies liberated Paris from four years of Nazi occupation. As the giant pincers of the Allied and Soviet armies closed on Germany in December 1944, Hitler ordered a counterattack to capture the Allies' essential supply port at Antwerp, Belgium. In the Battle of the Bulge (December 16, 1944, to January 31, 1945), as the Allies termed it, German forces drove fifty-five miles into Allied lines before being stopped at Bastogne. The battle caused nearly ninety thousand American casualties, more than in any other battle of the war. An American lieutenant recalled the macabre scene of "all the bodies . . . frozen stiff . . . many dead Americans and Germans . . . [many with] the ring finger . . . cut off in order to get the ring." The battle cost the Nazis hundreds of tanks and more than 100,000 men, fatally depleting Hitler's reserves.

In February 1945, while Allied armies pushed German forces backward, Churchill, Stalin, and Roosevelt met secretly at the Yalta Conference (named for the resort town on the Black Sea where it was held) to discuss their plans for the postwar world. Roosevelt managed to secure Stalin's promise to permit self-determination in the Eastern European countries occupied by the Red Army. The Allies pledged to support Jiang Jieshi (Chiang Kai-shek) as the leader of China. The Soviet Union obtained a role in the postwar governments of Korea and Manchuria in exchange for entering the war against Japan after the defeat of Germany.

The "Big Three" also agreed on the creation of a new international peacekeeping organization, the United Nations (UN). All nations would have a place in the UN General Assembly, but the smaller Security Council would wield decisive power. The Security Council's permanent representatives from the Allied powers—China, France, Great Britain, the Soviet Union, and the United States—would possess a veto over UN actions. The Senate ratified the United Nations Charter in July 1945 by a vote of 89 to 2, demonstrating the triumph of internationalism over isolationism during the war.

While Allied armies sped toward Berlin, Allied warplanes dropped more bombs after D-Day than in all the previous European bombing raids combined. By April 11, Allied armies reached the banks of the Elbe River, while the Soviets smashed into Berlin. The Red Army captured Berlin on May 2. Hitler had committed suicide on April 30, and the provisional German government surrendered unconditionally on May 7. The war in Europe was finally over, with the sacrifice of 135,576 American soldiers, nearly 250,000 British troops, and 9 million Russian combatants.

Roosevelt did not live to witness the end of the war. On April 12, he suffered a fatal stroke. Americans grieved for the man who had led them through years of depression and war, and they worried about his untested successor, Vice President Harry Truman.

How did the Allies defeat Japan?

After punishing defeats in the Coral Sea and at Midway, Japan had to fend off Allied naval and air attacks. In 1943, British and American forces, along with Indian and Chinese allies, launched an offensive against Japanese outposts in southern Asia, pushing through Burma and into China. In the Pacific, Americans and their allies attacked Japanese strongholds by sea, air, and land, moving island by island toward the Japanese homeland (see Map 25.5).

MAP ACTIVITY

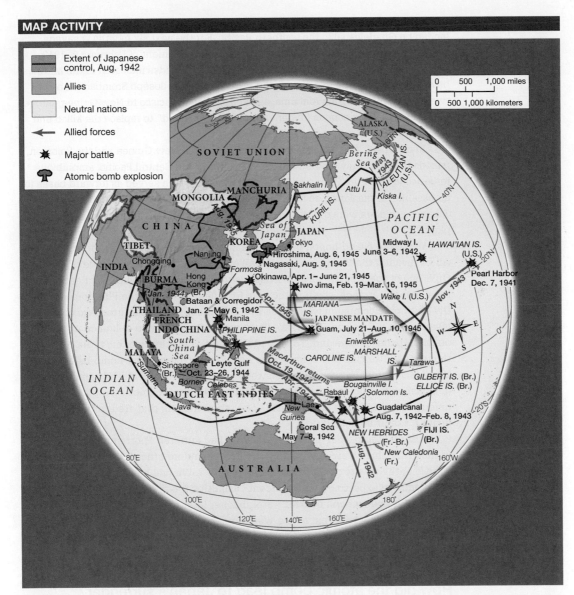

Legend:
- Extent of Japanese control, Aug. 1942
- Allies
- Neutral nations
- Allied forces
- Major battle
- Atomic bomb explosion

0 500 1,000 miles
0 500 1,000 kilometers

MAP 25.5 ▲ The Pacific Theater of World War II, 1941–1945 To drive the Japanese from their far-flung empire, the Allies launched two combined naval and military offensives — one to recapture the Philippines and then attack Japanese forces in China and the other to hop from island to island in the Central Pacific toward the Japanese mainland.

READING THE MAP: What was the extent of Japanese control up until August 1942? Which nations in the Pacific theater sided with the Allies? Which nations remained neutral?

CONNECTIONS: Describe the economic and military motivations behind Japanese domination of the region. How and when did Japan achieve this dominance? Judging from this map, what strategic and geographic concerns might have prompted Truman and his advisers to consider using the atomic bomb against Japan?

This island-hopping campaign began in August 1942, when American Marines landed on Guadalcanal in the southern Pacific. For the next six months, a savage battle raged for control of the island. Finally, during the night of February 8, 1943, Japanese forces withdrew. The terrible losses on both sides indicated to the Marines how costly it would be to defeat Japan. After the battle, Joseph Steinbacher, a twenty-one-year-old from Alabama, sailed from San Francisco to New Guinea, where he recalled, "all the cannon fodder waited to be assigned" to replace the killed and wounded.

In mid-1943, Allied forces launched offensives in New Guinea and the Solomon Islands that gradually secured the South Pacific. In the Central Pacific, amphibious forces conquered the Gilbert and Marshall islands, which served as forward bases for air assaults on the Japanese home islands. As the Allies attacked island after island, Japanese soldiers were ordered to refuse to surrender no matter how hopeless their plight.

While the island-hopping campaign kept pressure on Japanese forces, the Allies invaded the Philippines in the fall of 1944. In the four-day Battle of Leyte Gulf, one of the greatest naval battles in world history, the American fleet crushed the Japanese armada, clearing the way for Allied victory in the Philippines. While the Philippine campaign was under way, American forces captured two crucial islands—Iwo Jima and Okinawa—from which they planned to launch an attack on the Japanese homeland. To defend Okinawa, Japanese leaders ordered thousands of suicide pilots, known as *kamikaze*, to crash their bomb-laden planes into Allied ships. But instead of destroying the American fleet, the kamikaze demolished the Japanese air force. By June 1945, the Japanese were nearly defenseless on the sea and in the air. Still, their leaders prepared to fight to the death for their homeland.

Joseph Steinbacher and other GIs who had suffered "horrendous" casualties in the Philippines were now told by their commanding officer, "Men, in a few short months we are going to invade [Japan]. . . . We will be going in on the first wave and are expecting ninety percent casualties the first day. . . . For the few of us left alive the war will be over." Steinbacher later recalled his thoughts at that moment: "I know that I am now a walking dead man and will not have a snow-ball's chance in hell of making it through the last great battle to conquer the home islands of Japan."

How did the atomic bomb lead to Japan's surrender?

In mid-July 1945, as Allied forces prepared for the final assault on Japan, American scientists tested a secret weapon at an isolated desert site near Los Alamos, New Mexico. In 1942, Roosevelt had authorized the top-secret **Manhattan Project** to convert nuclear energy into a superbomb before the Germans added such a weapon to their arsenal. More than 100,000 Americans, led by scientists, engineers, and military officers, worked frantically to win the race for an atomic bomb. Germany surrendered two and a half months before the test on July 16, 1945, when scientists first witnessed an atomic explosion that sent a mushroom cloud of debris

Manhattan Project
Top-secret project authorized by Franklin Roosevelt in 1942 to develop an atomic bomb.

eight miles into the atmosphere. After watching the successful test of the bomb, J. Robert Oppenheimer, the head scientist at Los Alamos, remarked soberly, "Lots of boys not grown up yet will owe their life to it."

President Truman saw no reason not to use the atomic bomb against Japan if doing so would save American lives. Despite numerous defeats, Japan still had more than six million reserves to defend against the anticipated Allied assault, which U.S. military advisers estimated would kill at least 250,000 Americans. But first Truman issued an ultimatum: Japan must surrender unconditionally or face utter ruin. When the Japanese failed to respond by the deadline, Truman ordered that an atomic bomb be dropped on a Japanese city. The bomb that Colonel Paul Tibbets and his crew released over Hiroshima on August 6 leveled the city and incinerated about eighty thousand people. Many thousands more died later from injuries and radiation sickness. Three days later, after the Japanese government still refused to surrender, the second atomic bomb killed nearly as many civilians at Nagasaki.

With America's promise that the emperor could retain his throne after the Allies took over, Japan surrendered on August 14. On a ship departing from Europe for what would have been the final assault on Japan, an American soldier spoke for millions of others when he heard the wonderful news that the killing was over: "We are going to grow to adulthood after all."

While all Americans welcomed peace, some worried about the consequences of unleashing atomic power. Almost every American believed that the atomic bomb had brought peace in 1945, but nobody knew what it would bring in the future.

REVIEW

Why did Truman decide to use the atomic bomb against Japan?

Conclusion: Why did the United States emerge as a superpower at the end of the war?

At a cost of 405,399 American lives, the nation united with its allies to crush the Axis aggressors into unconditional surrender. Almost all Americans believed they had won a "good war" against totalitarian evil. The Allies saved Asia and Europe from conquest and finally halted the Nazis' genocidal campaign against Jews and many others whom the Nazis considered inferior. To secure human rights and protect the world against future wars, the Roosevelt administration took the lead in creating the United Nations.

Wartime production lifted the nation out of the Great Depression. The gross national product soared to four times what it had been when Roosevelt became president in 1933. Jobs in defense industries eliminated chronic unemployment, provided wages for millions of women workers and Black migrants from southern farms, and boosted Americans' prosperity. Ahead stretched the challenge of maintaining that prosperity while reintegrating millions of uniformed men and women, with help from the benefits of the GI Bill.

By the end of the war, the United States had emerged as a global superpower. Wartime mobilization made the American economy the strongest in the world, protected by the military clout of the nation's nuclear monopoly. Although the war left much of the world a rubble-strewn wasteland, the American mainland had remained safe from attack. The Japanese occupation of China had left fifty million people without homes, and millions more dead, maimed, or orphaned. The German offensive against the Soviet Union had killed more than twenty-seven million Russian soldiers and civilians. Germany and Japan lay in ruins, their economies and societies as shattered as their military forces. But in the gruesome balance sheet of war, the Axis powers had inflicted far more grief, misery, and destruction on the global victims of their aggression than they had suffered in return.

As the dominant Western nation in the postwar world, the United States led the reconstruction of Europe while overseeing Japan's economic and political recovery. America soon confronted new challenges in the tense aftermath of the war, as the Soviets seized political control of Eastern Europe, a Communist revolution swept China, and national liberation movements emerged in the colonial empires of Britain and France. The forces unleashed by World War II would shape the United States and the rest of the world for decades to come. Before the ashes of World War II had cooled, America's wartime alliance with the Soviet Union fractured, igniting a Cold War between the superpowers. To resist global communism, the United States became in effect the policeman of the free world, leaving behind the pre–World War II legacy of isolationism.

CHAPTER REVIEW

EXPLAIN WHY IT MATTERS

PUT IT ALL TOGETHER

THE ONSET OF WORLD WAR II

- Why were the American people as a whole reluctant to become involved in World War II?

- How did Roosevelt aid Britain and the Soviet Union, despite strong American isolationism?

THE HOME FRONT

- How did wartime mobilization influence the American home front?

- What were the most important social consequences of America's involvement in World War II?

VICTORY IN WORLD WAR II

- How did the Allies achieve victory?

- What led to the decision to drop atomic bombs on Japan?

LOOKING BACKWARD, LOOKING AHEAD

- How did America's experience of World War I shape U.S. involvement in World War II?

- How did World War II set the stage for the postwar period?

26

THE NEW WORLD OF THE COLD WAR

1945–1960

This chapter discusses the following questions:

- How did the Cold War begin?
- In what ways did anticommunism shape U.S. politics and policy?
- Why did the United States go to war in Korea?
- How did the U.S. approach to the superpower struggle evolve in the 1950s?
- Conclusion: What were the costs and consequences of the Cold War?

▶ **Helen Gahagan Douglas** Long accustomed as an actress to appearing before an audience, the member of Congress from California was a popular campaigner for Democratic candidates and a charismatic speaker. When soaring prices threatened ordinary Americans' budgets in 1948, she brought a basket of groceries to the House of Representatives to plead for the continuance of government price controls. Bettmann/Getty Images.

AN AMERICAN STORY

Member of Congress Helen Gahagan Douglas was a rare sight in the U.S. Capitol. A former Broadway star and opera singer, she was one of only ten female representatives in the 435-seat body. Douglas served in Congress from 1945 to 1951, when the fate of the New Deal hung in the balance and the nation charted an unprecedented course in foreign policy.

Born in 1900, Helen Gahagan grew up in Brooklyn, New York, and left college early for the stage. She quickly won fame on Broadway, starring in show after show until she married one of her leading men, Melvyn Douglas, in 1931. She followed him to Hollywood, where he hoped to advance his movie career, and the couple had two children.

Helen Gahagan Douglas admired Franklin D. Roosevelt's leadership during the depression. She visited migrant camps where she saw "faces stamped with poverty and despair." Her work on behalf of poor migrant farmworkers led her to testify before Congress and become a friend of the Roosevelts. In 1944, she won election to Congress, representing not the posh Hollywood district where she lived but a multiracial district in downtown Los Angeles, which cemented her dedication to progressive politics.

Like many liberals, Douglas was devastated by Roosevelt's death and initially unimpressed by his successor. "Who was Harry Truman anyway?" she asked. A compromise choice for the vice presidency, this "accidental president" lacked the charisma and political skills with which FDR had forged a winning Democratic Party coalition. Truman would confront domestic problems that the New Deal had not solved as well as major international challenges.

By 1947, a new term described the hostility that had emerged between the United States and its wartime ally, the Soviet Union: the Cold War. Truman and his advisers insisted that the Soviet Union posed a major threat to the United States, and they gradually crafted a policy to contain Soviet power and influence. As a member of the House Foreign Affairs Committee, Douglas initially urged cooperation with the Soviet Union. But she would become Truman's loyal ally, supporting the Marshall Plan, the creation of the North Atlantic Treaty Organization, and the war in Korea.

What came to be known as containment policy was successful in Europe, but communism spread in Asia, and the Truman and Eisenhower administrations alike sought to thwart its expansion. Some critics decried anticommunism as an "ideological crusade," but a second Red scare stifled dissent and debate at home.

CHRONOLOGY

1945	Roosevelt dies; Truman becomes president.
	Korea divided at thirty-eighth parallel after World War II.
	Vietnam claims independence from France; war breaks out.
1946	George F. Kennan drafts containment policy.
	United States grants independence to the Philippines.
1947	National Security Act passes forming Central Intelligence Agency.
	Truman Doctrine announced.
	United States sends aid to Greece and Turkey.
1948	Marshall Plan approved.
	United States recognizes Israel.
1948–1949	Berlin crisis leads to airlift.
1949	North Atlantic Treaty Organization formed.
	Soviet Union explodes atomic bomb.
	Truman approves hydrogen bomb.
1950	Senator Joseph McCarthy claims U.S. government harbors Communists.
	Korean War begins.
1951	U.S. military occupation of Japan ends.
1952	Dwight D. Eisenhower elected president.
1953	CIA organizes coup against Iranian government.
	Armistice ends Korean War.
1954	CIA organizes coup against Guatemalan government.
	Geneva accords end French presence in Vietnam.
1955	Eisenhower and Khrushchev meet.
1956	Suez crisis breaks out.

Douglas's earlier links with leftist groups and her advocacy of civil rights and social welfare programs made her an easy target for conservative politicians exploiting anti-Communist fervor. Running for the U.S. Senate in 1950, she faced Republican Richard M. Nixon, who had gained national attention for his efforts to expose Communists in government. Nixon's campaign labeled Douglas as "pink right down to her underwear" and sent thousands of voters the anonymous message, "I think you should know Helen Douglas is a Communist." Douglas's political career ended in defeat, just as much of Truman's domestic agenda would fall victim to the Red scare.

How did the Cold War begin?

After Japan's surrender in August 1945, Americans looked forward to the end of international crises and the dismantling of the large military establishment. Postwar realities played out differently. The wartime alliance of the United States, Great Britain, and the Soviet Union crumbled, giving birth to the Cold War. As tensions grew, the United States developed new policies to "contain" the spread of Soviet power around the globe, including a military buildup, new alliances, covert actions, and an enormous aid program for Europe.

Why did U.S.-Soviet tensions emerge after World War II?

"The guys who came out of World War II were idealistic," reported Harold Russell, a young paratrooper who had lost both hands in a training accident. "We felt the day had come when the wars were all over." But such hopes were dashed as old

◄ **Nuclear Testing at Bikini Atoll** An automatic camera positioned on a nearby island captured this image of a 1946 atomic bomb test, with its characteristic mushroom cloud shape, in the Bikini Atoll in the Marshall Islands. A total of twenty-three nuclear devices were detonated there by the U.S. government between 1946 and 1958, a project that entailed relocating indigenous residents of the Pacific Ocean island, radioactive contamination of surrounding islands, and ongoing claims of exposure from cancer victims. Bettmann/Getty Images.

antagonisms between the Soviet Union and the West resurfaced. No longer bound by a common enemy, the former allies would clash over their contrasting visions of the postwar world.

Hostility between the two nations was apparent even during the war. The Soviets, for instance, were angered by the Western Allies' delay in opening a second front in western Europe. After the war, these tensions came to the surface. The Soviet Union had made deep sacrifices, losing more than twenty million citizens and vast portions of its agricultural and industrial capacity. Soviet leader Joseph Stalin wanted to make Germany pay for his nation's economic reconstruction. Having been attacked on its borders in both world wars, the USSR also desired security in the form of friendly governments in neighboring countries in Eastern Europe. Stalin, a ruthless dictator who jailed or murdered his critics and sought to purge all his political opponents, aimed both to expand Soviet influence and to maintain his own power.

By contrast, American losses were light. The United States emerged from the war as the most powerful nation on the planet, with a vastly expanded economy and a monopoly on atomic weapons. That global position, along with U.S. economic interests and a belief in the superiority of American institutions and intentions, affected how Truman approached the Soviet Union and its system of state socialism.

With the depression still fresh in their minds, U.S. officials were intent on preserving economic opportunities abroad for American businesses. These included access to raw materials, markets for U.S. goods, and security for overseas investments. Believing Communist rule and state-controlled economies posed a fundamental threat, President Harry S. Truman urged in 1947 that "the American system can survive in America only if it becomes a world system."

U.S. leaders and citizens alike regarded their foreign policy not as a self-interested campaign for economic advantage but rather as a plank of national security and even a noble mission to extend freedom, democracy, and capitalism around the globe. Laura Briggs, a woman from Idaho, spoke for many Americans who believed "it was our destiny to prove that we were the children of God and that our way was right for the world."

Recent history also shaped postwar foreign policy. Many believed that World War II could have been avoided had Britain and France resisted rather than appeased Hitler's initial aggression. Navy Secretary James V. Forrestal opposed trying to "buy [the Soviets'] understanding and sympathy. We tried that once with Hitler." The man with ultimate responsibility for U.S. policy was a keen student of history but had little international experience beyond his service in World War I. Harry S. Truman was willing to cooperate with the Soviets only so long as the USSR accepted U.S. plans for the postwar world. Proud of his ability to make quick decisions and confident in America's nuclear advantage, Truman was determined to block Soviet expansion.

The Cold War first emerged over clashing Soviet and American interests in Eastern Europe. Stalin insisted that wartime agreements gave him a free hand in the countries defeated or liberated by the Red Army, just as the United States had moved to reconstruct governments in Italy and Japan. Facing Western pressure, however, Stalin removed troops from Iran on the Soviet Union's southwest border in 1946, allowing U.S. access to the rich oil fields there.

Stalin saw hypocrisy when U.S. officials demanded democratic elections in Eastern Europe while supporting dictatorships friendly to U.S. interests in Latin

America. The Soviet dictator initially tolerated non-Communist governments in Hungary and Czechoslovakia, but he would use harsh methods to install one-party rule in Poland and Bulgaria. Western Allies protested, but they did not use military force to prevent the Soviet Union from establishing Communist rule in satellite countries throughout Eastern Europe (**Map 26.1**).

In 1946, the wartime Allies sparred over Germany's future. Both sides wanted to demilitarize the country. U.S. policymakers sought rapid industrial revival there to foster European economic recovery. The Soviet Union, by contrast, wanted Germany weak both militarily and economically, and Stalin demanded that the Germans pay heavy reparations to help rebuild the devastated Soviet economy. Unable to settle their differences, the Allies divided the country. The Soviet Union installed a puppet Communist government in the eastern section, and Britain, France, and the United States began to unify their occupation zones, establishing the Federal Republic of Germany—West Germany—in 1949.

MAP ACTIVITY

MAP 26.1 ▲ The Division of Europe after World War II The "iron curtain," a term coined by Winston Churchill to refer to the Soviet grip on Eastern Europe, divided the continent for nearly fifty years.

READING THE MAP: Is the division of Europe among NATO, Communist, and neutral countries about equal? Why did the Soviet Union want Communist governments in control of the countries along its western border? How did the location of Berlin pose a problem for the Western Allies?

CONNECTIONS: When was NATO founded, and what was its purpose? How did the postwar division of Europe compare with the wartime alliances?

Conflict between the two superpowers only escalated. Boasting of the superiority of the Soviet system in February 1946, Stalin told a Moscow audience that capitalism inevitably produced war. One month later, in his home state of Missouri, Truman sat beside Winston Churchill, the former British prime minister, who denounced Soviet interference in Eastern Europe. "From Stettin in the Baltic to Trieste in the Adriatic, an **iron curtain** has descended across the Continent," Churchill warned. **(See "Analyzing Historical Evidence: The Emerging Cold War" on page 770.)** In turn, Stalin viewed Churchill's proposal for joint British-American action to combat Soviet aggression as "a call to war against the USSR."

In 1946, George F. Kennan, a career diplomat and expert on Russia, authored a rationale for what came to be called **containment**. Downplaying the influence of Communist ideology, he instead stressed Soviet insecurity and Stalin's need to maintain authority at home as the prime forces behind efforts to expand Soviet power abroad. Kennan believed that the Soviet Union would retreat if the United States responded with "unalterable counterforce." This approach, he predicted, would eventually end in "either the breakup or the gradual mellowing of Soviet power."

Not all public figures agreed. In late 1946, Secretary of Commerce Henry A. Wallace urged greater understanding of the Soviets' national security concerns, insisting that "we have no more business in the political affairs of Eastern Europe than Russia has in the political affairs of Latin America." State Department officials were furious at Wallace for challenging the administration's hard line against the Soviet Union, and Truman fired him.

How did the Truman Doctrine and the Marshall Plan reflect new U.S. priorities?

In 1947, the United States began to implement containment, a doctrine that would guide foreign policy for the next four decades. It was not an easy transition. Americans approved of resisting Soviet expansion but wanted to keep their soldiers and tax dollars at home. Truman not only had to sell containment to the public; he also had to gain the support of a Republican-controlled Congress, which included those staunchly opposed to a strong U.S. presence in Europe.

Crises in Greece and Turkey helped Truman make his case. In February 1947, Britain informed the United States that it could no longer sustain military assistance to Greece, where the autocratic government faced economic disaster and a leftist uprising, and to Turkey, which was trying to resist Soviet pressures. Unaware that the Soviet Union had deliberately avoided aiding the Greek Communists, Truman promptly sought congressional authority to send both countries military and economic aid. Meeting with congressional leaders, Undersecretary of State Dean Acheson predicted that if Greece and Turkey fell, communism would soon consume three-fourths of the world. After a stunned silence, one senator warned that to get approval for the aid, Truman would have to "scare the hell out of the country."

Truman did just that. He warned that if Greece fell to the rebels, "confusion and disorder might well spread throughout the entire Middle East" and create instability in Europe. According to the **Truman Doctrine**, the United States must not only resist Soviet military power but also "support free peoples who are resisting attempted subjugation by armed minorities or by outside pressures."

iron curtain
Metaphor coined by Winston Churchill in 1946 to describe the line dividing Soviet-controlled countries in Eastern Europe from democratic nations in Western Europe.

containment
Foreign policy strategy that committed the United States to resisting the expansion of the Soviet Union and communism during the Cold War.

Truman Doctrine
President Truman's pledge to "support free peoples who are resisting attempted subjugation by armed minorities or by outside pressures." First applied to Greece and Turkey in 1947, it became the justification for many U.S. interventions during the Cold War.

ANALYZING HISTORICAL EVIDENCE

The Emerging Cold War

Early in 1946, Soviet and Western leaders accused one another of hostile actions that endangered world peace. A close reading of early Cold War speeches reveals what public officials saw as the primary threats to their nations' security and how they viewed the interests and motives of other nations.

DOCUMENT 1
Joseph Stalin, Address on the Strengths of the Soviet Social System, Moscow, February 9, 1946

In the aftermath of World War II, Premier Joseph Stalin called on the Soviet people to support his program for economic development. Leaders in the West viewed his comments about communism and capitalism and his boasts about the strength of the Red Army as a threat to peace.

The [Second World War] arose as the inevitable result of the development of the world economic and political forces on the basis of monopoly capitalism. . . .

. . . The uneven development of the capitalist countries leads in time to sharp disturbances in their relations, and the group of countries which consider themselves inadequately provided with raw materials and export markets try usually to change this situation and to change the position in their favor by means of armed force. As a result of these factors, the capitalist world is split into two hostile camps and war follows. . . . The Soviet social system has proved to be more capable of life and more stable than a non-Soviet social system. . . .

. . . The Red Army heroically withstood all the adversities of the war, routed completely the armies of our enemies and emerged victoriously from the war. This is recognized by everybody — friend and foe.

[Stalin talks about his new Five-Year Plan.] Special attention will be focused on expanding the production of goods for mass consumption, on raising the standard of life of the working people by consistent and systematic reduction of the costs of all goods, and on wide-scale construction of all kinds of scientific research institutes to enable science to develop its forces. I have no doubt that if we render the necessary assistance to our scientists they will be able not only to overtake but also in the very near future to surpass the achievements of science outside the boundaries of our country.

Source: Excerpts from Joseph Stalin, "New Five-Year Plan for Russia," *Vital Speeches of the Day*, February 9, 1946, pp. 300–304.

DOCUMENT 2
Winston Churchill, "Iron Curtain" Speech, Westminster College, Fulton, Missouri, March 5, 1946

With Truman beside him, Winston Churchill, former prime minister of Great Britain, assessed Soviet actions in harsh terms. In response, Stalin equated Churchill with Hitler, a "firebrand of war."

. . . I have a strong admiration and regard for the valiant Russian people and for my war-time comrade, Marshal Stalin. . . . We understand the Russians' need to be secure on her western frontiers from all renewal of German aggression. . . . It is my duty, however, to place before you certain facts. . . .

From Stettin in the Baltic to Trieste in the Adriatic, an iron curtain has descended across the Continent. Behind that line lie all the capitals of the ancient states of central and eastern Europe. Warsaw, Berlin, Prague, Vienna, Budapest, Belgrade, Bucharest and Sofia, all these famous cities and the populations around them lie in the Soviet sphere and all are subject in one form or another, not only to Soviet influence but to a very high and increasing measure of control from Moscow. . . . The Communist parties, which were very small in all these eastern states of Europe, have been raised to preeminence and power far beyond their numbers and are seeking everywhere to obtain totalitarian control. Police governments are prevailing in nearly every case. . . .

. . . In a great number of countries, far from the Russian frontiers and throughout the world, Communist fifth columns are established and work in complete unity and absolute obedience to the directions they receive from the Communist center.

I do not believe that Soviet Russia desires war. What they desire is the fruits of war and the indefinite expansion of their power and doctrines. . . . Our difficulties and dangers will not be removed by . . . mere waiting to see what happens; nor will they be relieved by a policy of appeasement. . . . I am convinced that there is nothing [the Russians] admire so much as strength, and there is nothing for which they have less respect than for military weakness.

Source: Excerpts from "The Iron Curtain" speech by Sir Winston Churchill. Reproduced with permission of Curtis Brown, London, on behalf of the Estate of Sir Winston Churchill. Copyright © Estate of Winston S. Churchill.

DOCUMENT 3

Henry A. Wallace, Address on the Folly of the U.S. "Get Tough with Russia" Policy, Madison Square Garden, New York, September 12, 1946

Throughout 1946, Henry A. Wallace, Truman's secretary of commerce, urged the president to take a more conciliatory approach toward the Soviet Union, a position reflected in his speech to leftist and liberal groups.

We cannot rest in the assurance that we invented the atom bomb — and therefore that this agent of destruction will work best for us. He who trusts in the atom bomb will sooner or later perish by the atom bomb — or something worse. . . .

To achieve lasting peace, we must study in detail just how the Russian character was formed — by invasions of Tartars, Mongols, Germans, Poles, Swedes, and French; by the czarist rule based on ignorance, fear and force; by the intervention of the British, French and Americans in Russian affairs from 1919 to 1921; by the geography of the huge Russian land mass situated strategically between Europe and Asia; and by the vitality derived from the rich Russian soil and the strenuous Russian climate.

Add to all this the tremendous emotional power which Marxism and Leninism gives to the Russian leaders — and then we can realize that we are reckoning with a force which cannot be handled successfully by a "Get tough with Russia" policy. "Getting tough" never bought anything real and lasting — whether for schoolyard bullies or businessmen or world powers. The tougher we get, the tougher the Russians will get. . . .

We should recognize that we have no more business in the political affairs of Eastern Europe than Russia has in the political affairs of Latin America, Western Europe and the United States. . . . We have to recognize that the Balkans are closer to Russia than to us — and that Russia cannot permit either England or the United States to dominate the politics of that area. . . .

. . . Under friendly peaceful competition the Russian world and the American world will gradually become more alike. The Russians will be forced to grant more and more of the personal freedoms; and we shall become more and more absorbed with the problems of social-economic justice.

Source: Courtesy of Henry A. Wallace Papers. University of Iowa Libraries, Iowa City, Iowa.

Questions for Analysis

CONSIDER THE CONTEXT: What lessons did these three leaders draw from World War II? How were these lessons shaped by a longer history of relationships between the Soviet Union and the West?

RECOGNIZE VIEWPOINTS: What contrasts did these speakers draw between the political and economic systems of the Soviet Union and those of the United States and Western Europe? How did their predictions about these systems diverge?

ANALYZE THE EVIDENCE: What motives did these three leaders ascribe to Soviet actions? On what grounds did Churchill and Wallace disagree about the stance the West should adopt toward the Soviet Union?

The president failed to convince some liberal members of Congress who wanted the United States to work through the United Nations and who opposed propping up the authoritarian Greek government. But Truman won the day, setting a precedent for forty years of Cold War interventions that would aid any kind of government if the alternative appeared to be communism. Bipartisan support for this agenda helped Truman secure the presidency in 1948.

A much larger assistance program for Europe followed aid to Greece and Turkey. In 1947, Acheson described a war-ravaged Western Europe, with "factories destroyed, fields impoverished, transportation systems wrecked, populations scattered and on the borderline of starvation." Americans were sending generous amounts of private aid, but U.S. leaders were convinced that Europe needed large-scale assistance to keep desperate citizens from turning to socialism or communism.

Marshall Plan
Aid program begun in 1948 to help European economies recover from World War II. By 1953, the United States had provided $13 billion to sixteen Western European nations, boosting its own economy in the process.

In 1948, Congress approved the **Marshall Plan**, named for Secretary of State George C. Marshall, who proposed what a British official called "a lifeline to a sinking man." Over the next five years, the United States spent $13 billion ($151 billion in 2021 dollars) to restore the economies of sixteen Western European nations. Marshall invited all European nations and the Soviet Union to cooperate in a request for aid, but—as U.S. officials had expected—the Soviets rejected the offer and ordered their Eastern European satellites to do the same.

Humanitarian impulses and the goal of keeping Western Europe free of communism drove the enormous aid program. The Marshall Plan also helped boost the U.S. economy: Its beneficiaries used the aid to buy American products, and Europe's economic recovery created new markets and opportunities for American investment. In the longer term, by insisting that the recipient nations work together, the Marshall Plan marked the first step toward the European Union.

Berlin Divided, 1948

In early 1948, while Congress was debating the Marshall Plan, the Soviets brutally installed a Communist regime in Czechoslovakia, the only remaining democracy in Eastern Europe. Next, Stalin threatened Western access to Berlin. The former capital of Germany lay within Soviet-controlled East Germany but was jointly occupied by all four Allies. As the Western Allies moved to organize West Germany as a separate nation, the Soviets retaliated by blocking roads and rail lines between West Germany and the Western-held sections of Berlin, cutting off food, fuel, and other essentials to two million inhabitants (see Map 26.1).

"We stay in Berlin, period," Truman vowed. To avoid a confrontation with Soviet troops, U.S. and British pilots over the next year airlifted 2.3 million tons of goods to sustain the West Berliners. Stalin finally lifted the blockade in 1949. The city was then divided into East Berlin, under Soviet control, and West Berlin, which became part of West Germany.

What were the elements of the national security state?

During the Truman years, the United States fashioned a six-pronged defense strategy in the name of containment: (1) development of atomic weapons, (2) strengthened conventional military capacity, (3) military alliances, (4) military and economic aid to friendly nations, (5) an espionage network and covert actions to subvert Communist expansion, and (6) a global propaganda offensive.

The dawn of the nuclear age altered the nature of national defense. In 1949, the Soviet Union detonated its own atomic bomb at a test site, ending the U.S. monopoly on nuclear weapons. Truman then approved the development of a hydrogen bomb—equivalent to five hundred atomic bombs—rejecting the protests of several scientists who had worked on the atomic bomb and of George Kennan, who warned of an endless arms race. The "superbomb" was ready by 1954, but the U.S. advantage was brief. In 1955, the Soviets exploded their own hydrogen bomb.

From the 1950s through the 1980s, deterrence formed the basis of American nuclear strategy. To deter a Soviet attack, the United States strove to maintain a nuclear force more powerful than that of the USSR. Because the Russians pursued a similar policy, the superpowers became locked in an escalating nuclear arms race, amassing weapons that could destroy the earth many times over. Albert Einstein, whose mathematical discoveries had helped lay the foundations for nuclear weapons, commented grimly that the war that came after World War III would of necessity "be fought with sticks and stones."

A second U.S. strategy was to beef up conventional military power. The National Security Act of 1947 united the military branches under a single secretary of defense and created the National Security Council (NSC) to advise the president. During the Berlin crisis in 1948, Congress boosted military appropriations and enacted a peacetime draft. In addition, Congress granted permanent status to the women's military branches, although it limited the number of women, the jobs they could do, and the ranks they could attain. With 1.5 million men and women in uniform in 1950, the military strength of the United States had quadrupled since the 1930s, and defense expenditures claimed one-third of the federal budget.

Collective security, the third prong of containment strategy, marked a sharp reversal of the nation's traditional foreign policy. In 1949, the United States joined Canada and Western European nations in its first peacetime military alliance, the **North Atlantic Treaty Organization (NATO)**, designed to counter a Soviet threat to Western Europe. For the first time in its history, the United States pledged to go to war if any of its allies were attacked.

The fourth ingredient of defense strategy was foreign assistance programs to strengthen friendly countries, as with aid to Greece and Turkey and the Marshall Plan. In 1949, Congress approved $1 billion of military aid to its NATO allies, and the government pledged economic assistance to nations in other parts of the world.

The fifth element of containment provided for espionage and covert activities. The National Security Act of 1947 created the **Central Intelligence Agency (CIA)** to gather information and to take any actions "related to intelligence affecting the national security" that the NSC might authorize. Such functions included propaganda, sabotage, economic warfare, and support for "anti-communist elements in threatened countries of the free world." Secret CIA operations helped defeat Italy's Communist Party in 1948, and the agency would become an increasingly significant, if shadowy, player in U.S. foreign policy. In the coming years, its agents would be implicated in toppling legitimate foreign governments as well as violating the rights of U.S. citizens.

North Atlantic Treaty Organization (NATO)
Military alliance formed in 1949 among the United States, Canada, and Western European nations to counter any possible Soviet threat. It represented an unprecedented commitment by the United States to go to war if any of its allies were attacked.

Central Intelligence Agency (CIA)
Agency created by the National Security Act of 1947 to expand the government's espionage capacities. The CIA attempted to thwart communism through covert activities, including propaganda, sabotage, economic warfare, and support for anti-Communist forces around the world.

▶ **Cold War Spying** "Intelligence," the gathering of information about the enemy, took on new importance during the Cold War with the creation of the Central Intelligence Agency (CIA) in 1947. While much intelligence work took place in Washington, where analysts combed through Communist newspapers, official reports, and speeches, secret agents gathered information behind the iron curtain with bugs and devices, such as these cameras hidden in cigarette packs. Jack Naylor Collection/Picture Research Consultants & Archives.

Finally, the U.S. government created cultural exchanges and propaganda designed to win foreign populations' "hearts and minds." The Voice of America, established during World War II to broadcast U.S. propaganda abroad, was expanded, and the State Department sent books, exhibits, jazz musicians, and other performers around the world as "cultural ambassadors."

By 1950, the United States had abandoned many traditional tenets of its foreign policy. Isolationism and neutrality gave way to a peacetime military alliance and efforts to control events far beyond U.S. borders. The United States would not go to war to raise the iron curtain, but it aggressively and successfully promoted economic recovery and a military shield for the rest of Europe.

REVIEW

What was the Cold War, and how did it alter U.S. foreign policy?

In what ways did anticommunism shape U.S. politics and policy?

During the Cold War, anticommunism became a mainstay of U.S. foreign policy, coloring American reactions to anticolonial and independence movements around the world, and leading the United States to retreat from its stated commitment to national self-determination. Anticommunism would also loom large in domestic politics. Vigilance against subversion, many argued, was as important within as beyond U.S. borders. As the fight against communism extended around the globe, it also led to a new set of policies and practices affecting U.S. citizens.

How did superpower rivalry play out across the globe?

Containment policy soon expanded beyond Europe. In Africa, Asia, and the Middle East, World War II had accelerated a tide of national liberation movements against war-weakened imperial powers. By 1960, forty countries would win their independence. Unaligned with either the United States or the Soviet Union, they—along with Latin America—collectively came to be referred to as the "third world." These nations had their own priorities and typically did not view their struggles through a Cold War framework. Yet they would often be treated by the United States and the Soviet Union alike as pawns in the superpower struggle.

Like Woodrow Wilson during World War I, Roosevelt and Truman each publicly endorsed the ideal of national self-determination. The United States granted independence to the Philippines in 1946 and applauded the British withdrawal from India in 1947. Black leaders and many on the left called upon the United States to back other liberation struggles waged by colonized peoples and to hasten the end of imperial rule. The United States, after all, had fought its own war for independence and sharply opposed the forcible installation of communism in Eastern Europe. As the Cold War intensified, however, American policymakers proved willing to set aside the principle of self-determination when it conflicted with U.S. interests.

American leaders did promote democracy in emerging nations. They were equally intent on advancing American-style capitalism and trade, with U.S. corporations particularly focused on the vast oil reserves in the Middle East. Yet leaders of many national liberation movements around the world were impressed by Russia's rapid economic growth and professed commitment to improving the lot of the ordinary citizen. Some adopted socialist or Communist ideas, including the nationalization of industry and state control of the economy. Although few of these movements had formal ties with the USSR, American leaders viewed them as a threatening extension of Soviet power. Seeking to hold communism at bay by fostering economic development and political stability, in 1949 the Truman administration began a small program of aid to developing nations, including Iran, India, Pakistan, and Jordan.

Meanwhile civil war raged in China, where the Communists, led by Mao Zedong (Mao Tse-tung), fought the official Nationalist government under Jiang Jieshi (Chiang Kai-shek). The Communists gained popular support for their land reforms, whereas Jiang's corrupt, incompetent government alienated much of the population, and his military forces had been devastated by the Japanese. Failing to achieve a settlement between Jiang and Mao, the United States supplied $3 billion in aid to the Nationalists. Truman opted not to divert any further resources from Europe to China, however.

In October 1949, Mao established the People's Republic of China (PRC), and the Nationalists fled to the island of Taiwan. Fearing a U.S.-supported invasion, Mao signed a mutual defense treaty with the Soviet Union. The United States refused to recognize the PRC, blocked its admission to the United Nations, and supported the

Nationalist government in Taiwan. Only a massive U.S. military commitment could have shored up Jiang's inept government and defeated the Chinese Communists. But some Republicans charged that Truman and "pro-Communists in the State Department" had "lost" China. China became a political albatross for the Democrats, who resolved never again to be vulnerable to charges of being soft on communism.

With China in turmoil, the United States shifted to helping its former enemy, Japan, to reindustrialize. America's official military occupation there ended when the two nations signed a peace treaty and a mutual security pact in 1951. Like West Germany, Japan now sat squarely within the American orbit, serving as an economic hub in a vital area.

The one place where Cold War considerations did not control U.S. policy was Palestine. In 1943, then-senator Harry Truman spoke powerfully about Nazi Germany's annihilation of the Jews, asserting, "This is not a Jewish problem, it is an American problem—and we must . . . face it squarely and honorably." As president, he made good on his words. Jews had been migrating to Palestine, their biblical homeland, since the nineteenth century, resulting in tension and hostilities with the Palestinian Arabs. After World War II, as hundreds of thousands of European Jews sought refuge and a national homeland there, fighting and terrorism escalated on both sides.

Truman's foreign policy experts proposed cultivating Arab allies in order to contain Soviet influence in the Middle East and to secure access to Arabian oil. Defying his advisers, the president responded instead to pleas from Jewish organizations, a moral commitment to Holocaust survivors, and his interest in the American Jewish vote. When Jews in Palestine declared the state of Israel in May 1948, Truman quickly recognized the new country and made its defense the cornerstone of U.S. policy in the Middle East.

CYPRUS **SYRIA**
LEBANON
Mediterranean Sea
ISRAEL
Jerusalem
Dead Sea
JORDAN
EGYPT
SAUDI ARABIA

UN partition of Palestine, 1947
Jewish state
Arab state
Boundary of Israel, 1949

Israel, 1948

What contributed to the rise of McCarthyism?

The superpower struggle altered the political climate at home too. "Red-baiting"—attempts to link individuals or ideas with communism—and official retaliation against leftist critics of the government had flourished during the Red scare at the end of World War I. Some Republicans had also attacked the New Deal as a plot of radicals in the 1930s. A renewed Red scare followed World War II, this time the product of foreign policy setbacks, reports of Soviet espionage, and partisan politics. From the late 1940s onward, anticommunism would weaken liberals and undermine Truman's domestic agenda.

Republicans seized on events such as the Soviet takeover of Eastern Europe and the "loss" of China to accuse Democrats of Communist sympathies. Wisconsin senator Joseph R. McCarthy would catapult to fame based on his claim that the "traitorous actions of those who have been treated so well by this Nation," including scores of "bright young men" in the State Department, were paving the way for Communist takeover. McCarthy's charges—such as the allegation that retired general George C. Marshall belonged to a Communist conspiracy—were reckless and often ludicrous, but the press covered him avidly, and **McCarthyism** became a term synonymous with the anti-Communist crusade.

McCarthyism
Name given to Senator Joseph McCarthy's campaign in the early 1950s to expose Communist infiltration of the U.S. government. Many of those accused of Communist sympathies were blacklisted or lost their jobs, although most did not in fact belong to the Communist Party.

Revelations of Soviet espionage lent credibility to fears of internal subversion. A number of Americans who had once been Communists, including Whittaker Chambers and Elizabeth Bentley, testified that they and others had provided secret documents to the Soviets. Even more alarming, a British physicist working on the atomic bomb project confessed in 1950 that he was a spy and implicated several Americans, including Ethel and Julius Rosenberg. The Rosenbergs pleaded not guilty but were convicted of conspiracy to commit espionage and electrocuted in 1953.

Records opened in the 1990s disclosed that the Soviet Union did receive secret documents from Americans that probably sped up its development of nuclear weapons by a year or two. Yet the vast majority of individuals targeted in the Red scare had done nothing more than join the Communist Party, associate with suspected Communists, or support radical causes—usually long before the Cold War had made the Soviet Union an enemy.

What were the effects of the anti-Communist crusade at home?

The hunt for "internal subversives" was conducted by both Congress and the executive branch. Stung by charges of being weak on communism, Truman issued Executive Order 9835 in 1947, establishing loyalty review boards to investigate every federal employee. "A nightmare from which there [was] no awakening" was how State Department employee Esther Brunauer described it when she and her husband, a chemist in the navy, both lost their jobs because he had joined a Communist youth organization in the 1920s and associated with suspected radicals.

Government investigators used anonymous informers and placed the burden of proof on the accused. More than two thousand civil service employees lost their jobs, and another ten thousand resigned as Truman's loyalty program continued into the mid-1950s. Hundreds of alleged homosexuals resigned or were fired over charges of "sexual perversion," which anti-Communist crusaders said could subject them to blackmail. Years later, Truman privately conceded that the loyalty program had been a mistake.

The congressional **House Un-American Activities Committee (HUAC)** also investigated individuals' political associations—and assumed the guilt of those who refused to name names. These "unfriendly witnesses" lost their jobs and suffered public ostracism. In 1947, HUAC investigated radical activity in Hollywood. Some actors and directors cooperated, but ten individuals refused, citing their First Amendment rights. The "Hollywood Ten" served jail sentences for contempt of Congress and then found themselves blacklisted in the movie industry. Popular singer Frank Sinatra, a defender of the Hollywood Ten, wondered, "How long will it be before we're told what we cannot say into a radio microphone? If you make a pitch . . . for a square deal for the underdog, will they call you a Commie?"

The Truman administration went after the Communist Party directly, prosecuting its leaders under a 1940 law that made it a crime to "advocate the

House Un-American Activities Committee (HUAC)
Congressional committee prominent during the early years of the Cold War that investigated Americans for disloyalty to the government or associations with Communists.

◀ **Annie Lee Moss** Pentagon worker Annie Lee Moss, photographed next to her attorney, was brought before McCarthy's committee during its investigation of Communist infiltration of the U.S. Army in 1954. Her denials of Communist associations brought public applause, suggesting mounting opposition to McCarthy's crusade. AP Photo.

overthrow and destruction of the [government] by force and violence." Civil libertarians argued that the law violated First Amendment freedoms of speech, press, and association, but the Supreme Court ruled in 1951 that the Communist threat overrode constitutional guarantees.

The domestic Cold War spread beyond the nation's capital. State and local governments investigated citizens, demanded loyalty oaths, fired employees suspected of disloyalty, and banned "subversive" books from public libraries. Left-leaning college professors and public school teachers, accused of planting dangerous ideas in the minds of youth, lost their jobs in New York and California. Because the Communist Party had helped organize unions and championed racial justice, labor and civil rights activists often by association became victims of McCarthyism as well. Black activist Jack O'Dell remembered that segregationists pinned the tag of Communist on "anybody who supported the right of blacks to have civil rights."

Anti-Communist fervor outlasted the Truman years. The Eisenhower administration intensified Truman's loyalty program, allowing federal executives to dismiss thousands of employees on grounds of loyalty, security, or "suitability." Some Americans investigated for disloyalty effectively pursued their rights. Annie Lee Moss, an Army Signal Corps communications clerk at the Pentagon suspected of past Communist Party membership, managed to appeal her case to the army's loyalty board and remain employed. At a public hearing before McCarthy's committee in 1954, Moss's declaration of her innocence roused cheers, and publicity about the case led to fresh criticism of the anti-Communist crusade.

Indeed, McCarthy began to destroy himself that year by hurling reckless charges of communism against military personnel in televised hearings, leading the army's lawyer to demand of him, "Have you left no sense of decency?" A Senate vote in 1954 to censure McCarthy marked the end of his influence but not an end to the harassment of dissenters on the left. Annie Lee Moss's story stands out against many more of law-abiding individuals who lost their livelihoods, friends, and families—and their constitutional rights to free speech and association—during the Red scare.

REVIEW

What impact did the Red scare of the 1950s have on U.S. citizens' rights?

Why did the United States go to war in Korea?

The Cold War became a hot war in June 1950, when troops from Communist North Korea invaded South Korea. For the first time, Americans would go into battle to implement containment. Confirming the global reach of the Truman Doctrine, U.S. involvement in Korea also tightened the link between military might and American foreign policy. The United States, in cooperation with the United Nations, ultimately held the line in Korea but at a great cost in lives, dollars, and national unity.

How did containment lead to military intervention?

The Korean War stemmed from the artificial division of Korea after World War II. Having expelled the Japanese, the United States and the Soviet Union created two occupation zones separated by the thirty-eighth parallel (**Map 26.2**), with the USSR in the north and the United States in the south. When Moscow and Washington were unable to agree on unification, the United Nations sponsored elections in South Korea in 1948, and the American-backed candidate, Syngman Rhee, was elected president.

Although unsure whether Rhee's repressive government could sustain popular support, U.S. officials prioritized his anticommunism. After the election, the United States provided economic and military aid to South Korea but withdrew most of its troops. That same year, the Soviets established the People's Republic of North Korea under Kim Il-sung and also withdrew.

Skirmishes between North and South Korean troops at the thirty-eighth parallel began almost immediately. In June 1950, ninety thousand North Koreans swept into South Korea. Truman's advisers assumed that the Soviet Union or China had instigated the attack, an assumption later proven incorrect. The president quickly decided to intervene, viewing Korea as "the Greece of the Far East." With the Soviet

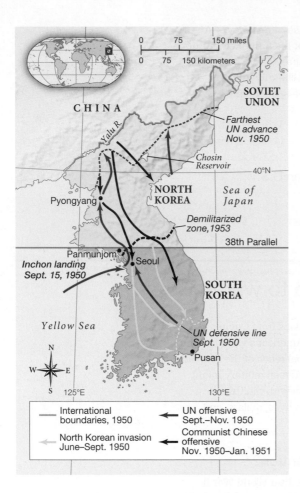

MAP 26.2 ◀ The Korean War, 1950–1953 Although each side had plunged deep into enemy territory, the war ended in 1953 with the dividing line between North and South Korea nearly unchanged from where it had been before the fighting began.

Union absent from the Security Council, the United States obtained UN sponsorship of a collective effort to repel the attack. Truman's choice for commander of the UN force was the World War II hero, General Douglas MacArthur.

Sixteen nations sent troops to Korea, but the United States furnished most of the weapons and personnel, deploying almost 1.8 million soldiers—a mere five years after the close of World War II. By dispatching troops on his own authority without asking Congress for a declaration of war, Truman violated the spirit if not the letter of the Constitution. While some legislators pushed back, Congress as a whole failed to defend its constitutional powers, leading to the expansion of executive power that would characterize the Cold War.

The first American soldiers rushed to Korea were unprepared and ill equipped: "I didn't even know how to dig a foxhole," recalled a nineteen-year-old army reservist, who was told by his sergeant to "Make it like a grave." As a result, U.S. forces suffered major defeats early in the war. The North Koreans took the capital of Seoul and drove deep into South Korea, forcing UN troops to retreat. Then in September 1950, General MacArthur launched a bold counteroffensive 180 miles behind North Korean lines. By October, UN and South Korean forces had retaken Seoul and pushed the North Koreans back to the thirty-eighth parallel. Now Truman had to decide whether containment or reunification was the goal.

He chose the latter. "Troops could not be expected . . . to march up to a surveyor's line and stop," remarked Secretary of State Dean Acheson. His comment reflected a transformation of the military objective from containment to elimination of the enemy and unification of Korea. It would be the only time during the entire Cold War that the United States tried to roll back communism by force. With UN approval, Truman authorized MacArthur to cross the thirty-eighth parallel. Concerned about possible intervention by China, the president directed him to keep UN forces away from the Korean-Chinese border. MacArthur disregarded that order. The general moved troops within forty miles of China, whereupon 300,000 Chinese soldiers crossed into Korea. With Chinese help, the North Koreans recaptured Seoul.

After three months of grueling battle, UN forces fought their way back to the thirty-eighth parallel. At that point, Truman decided to seek a negotiated settlement. MacArthur was furious, considering mere containment a defeat. Taking his case to the public, he challenged both the president's authority to conduct foreign policy and the principle of civilian control of the military. In response to this insubordination, Truman fired MacArthur in April 1951. All the top military leaders supported the president. Many Americans, however, agreed with the general. Why should Americans die simply to preserve the status quo? Why not destroy the enemy once and for all? Those siding with MacArthur blamed the stalemate in Korea on the government's ineptitude or softness toward communism.

What was the war's impact on domestic politics?

Truman never recovered from the political fallout. Nor was he able to end the war. Negotiations began in July 1951, but peace talks dragged on for two years while twelve thousand more U.S. soldiers and many more Korean soldiers and civilians died.

Truman had won the election of 1948 based on the continuing popularity of the New Deal and bipartisan consensus around foreign policy. The fall of China and the protracted war in Korea weakened both the president and the Democratic Party. Popular discontent with "Truman's war" boosted Republicans in the 1952 election. Their presidential nominee, General Dwight D. Eisenhower, was a popular military hero and the president of Columbia University. As supreme commander in Europe during World War II, he won widespread acclaim for leading the Allied armies to victory over Germany, and in 1950 he was Truman's choice for the first supreme commander of NATO forces.

Although Eisenhower believed that professional soldiers should stay out of politics, he found compelling reasons to run in 1952. He largely agreed with Truman's foreign policy, but he criticized Democrats for solving domestic problems with expensive federal programs. He also disliked the foreign policy views of Republican rivals, who attacked containment and sought to cut defense spending.

Eisenhower won the nomination, but the Republican Party platform condemned containment as immoral for its failure to turn back communism and charged the Truman administration with shielding "traitors." By choosing the thirty-nine-year-old California senator and anti-Communist crusader Richard M. Nixon for his running mate, Eisenhower helped to appease the right wing of the party. Elected to Congress in 1946, Nixon had quickly made a name for himself as a member of HUAC, defeating Helen Gahagan Douglas in the Senate race of 1950.

His public approval ratings plummeting, Truman decided not to run for reelection. The Democrats nominated Adlai E. Stevenson, the popular governor of Illinois, but he could neither escape the domestic fallout from the Korean War nor match Eisenhower's widespread appeal. Shortly before the election, Eisenhower announced dramatically, "I shall go to Korea." Voters registered their confidence in his ability to end the war. Cutting sharply into traditional Democratic territory, Eisenhower won several southern states and garnered 55 percent of the popular vote overall. His coattails carried a narrow Republican majority to Congress.

How did the Korean War shape U.S. defense policy?

Eisenhower made good on his pledge to end the Korean War. In July 1953, the two sides reached an armistice that left Korea divided, again roughly at the thirty-eighth parallel, with North and South separated by a demilitarized zone two-and-a-half miles wide. The war fulfilled the objective of containment: the United States had backed up its promise to aid nations resisting communism. The Truman and Eisenhower administrations had managed to contain what amounted to a world war—involving twenty nations altogether—within a single country and had avoided the use of nuclear weapons.

Yet what was described as a "limited war" took the lives of 36,000 Americans and wounded more than 100,000. Thousands of U.S. soldiers suffered as prisoners of war. South Korea lost more than one million people to war-related causes, and 1.8 million North Koreans and Chinese were killed or wounded. The war also set a precedent for "police actions" that bypassed the traditional U.S. requirement of a congressional declaration of war, even in cases involving extensive commitments of U.S. troops and treasure.

The border separating North and South Korea may not have budged as a result of the war, but the conflict had a pronounced effect on American defense policy and spending. In 1950, just before the war began, the National Security Council completed a top-secret report, known as **NSC 68**, which urged that national survival required a massive military buildup. The Korean War triggered nearly all of the military expansion called for in that document, vastly increasing U.S. capacity to act as a global power. Military spending shot up from $14 billion in 1950 to $50 billion in 1953 and remained above $40 billion thereafter. By 1952, defense spending claimed nearly 70 percent of the federal budget, and the size of the armed forces had tripled.

For Eisenhower and other military leaders, one lesson of Korea was that U.S. forces should never again fight a land war in Asia. But even before the war's end, the Truman administration was expanding its role in that region by increasing aid to the French, who were fighting to hang on to their colonial empire in Indochina. As U.S. Marines retreated from a battle against Chinese soldiers in 1950, they sang, prophetically, of the Vietnamese capital: "We're Harry's police force on call, / So put back your pack on, / The next step is Saigon."

NSC 68
Secret government report of 1950 warning that national survival required a massive military buildup. The Korean War led to nearly all of the expansion called for in the report, so that by 1952 defense spending consumed nearly 70 percent of the federal budget.

> **REVIEW**
>
> What were the causes and outcomes of the Korean War?

How did the U.S. approach to the superpower struggle evolve in the 1950s?

During the 1952 campaign, hard-line anti-Communists in the Republican Party vowed not just to end the Korean War but to liberate "enslaved" peoples under Soviet rule. Some, such as the new secretary of state John Foster Dulles, attacked containment as "negative, futile, and immoral." In practice,

► **Eisenhower for President** An early poster supporting "Ike" for president goes up in New York City at a restaurant founded by his former mess sergeants. Eisenhower's distinguished military credentials — signaled here by his uniform — appealed to many Americans in the midst of the Cold War and the ongoing "hot" war in Korea, and he would easily win the presidency in 1952. Keystone-France/Getty Images.

however, President Eisenhower pursued a containment policy much like that of his predecessor. His administration did not attempt to roll back communism but instead chose to intervene at the margins of Communist power in Asia, Latin America, and the Middle East and typically in places where U.S. economic interests were at stake. Eisenhower's defense strategy relied more on nuclear weapons and secret CIA operations than had Truman's. Toward the end of his presidency, Eisenhower also seized on political changes in the Soviet Union to reduce tensions between the superpowers.

What was the "New Look" in foreign policy?

In his inaugural address, Eisenhower warned that the "forces of good and evil are massed and armed and opposed as rarely before in history." Like Truman, he saw communism as a threat to the nation's security and economic interests, and he was intent on maintaining U.S. power around the globe. Eisenhower's foreign policy differed, however, in three areas: its rhetoric, its means, and, after Stalin's death in 1953, its steps toward accommodation with the Soviet Union.

Eisenhower was determined to control military expenditures in order to balance the budget and cut taxes. Reflecting American confidence in technology as well as public opposition to a large peacetime army, Eisenhower's "New Look" in defense concentrated U.S. military strength in nuclear weapons. Instead of maintaining large ground forces of its own, the United States would arm friendly nations and back them up with an ominous nuclear arsenal, providing, according to one defense official, "more bang for the buck." Dulles believed that America's willingness to "go to the brink" of war with nuclear weapons—a strategy termed "brinksmanship"—would block any Soviet efforts to expand.

There was no way for the United States to defend itself from a nuclear strike, but the certainty of "massive retaliation" was intended to deter the Soviets from launching an attack in the first place. Because the Soviet Union could respond similarly to an American strike, this nuclear standoff became known as **mutually assured destruction (MAD)**. Leaders of both nations joined an ever-escalating arms race, with the United States determined to outpace the Soviet Union in nuclear warheads and delivery missiles.

The growing U.S. nuclear stockpile did not alter the terms of the superpower struggle or reverse containment policy. When a revolt against the Soviet-controlled government broke out in Hungary in 1956, Dulles's liberation rhetoric proved hollow. A radio plea from Hungarian freedom fighters professed their hope that "American

mutually assured destruction (MAD)
Term for the standoff between the United States and the Soviet Union based on the assumption that a nuclear first strike by either nation would result in massive retaliation and mutual destruction.

troops will be here within one or two hours." But help did not come. Eisenhower was unwilling to risk U.S. soldiers and possible nuclear war, and Soviet troops soon suppressed the insurrection, killing or wounding thousands of Hungarians.

Why and how did the United States apply containment in Vietnam?

A major challenge for U.S. containment policy came in Southeast Asia, and specifically in French-occupied Indochina. During World War II, Ho Chi Minh and his nationalist coalition, the Vietminh, fought both the occupying Japanese forces and French colonial rulers. In 1945, the Vietminh—citing the American Declaration of Independence and the French Declaration of the Rights of Man and of the Citizen—claimed Vietnam's independence from France. When France fought back, the region plunged into war. Because Ho declared himself a Communist, the Truman administration quietly funneled aid to the French. Once again, American rhetoric in support of national self-determination took a backseat to the battle against communism.

domino theory
Theory of containment expressed by President Eisenhower in the context of Vietnam. Using the metaphor of dominoes, he warned that the fall of one government to communism would lead neighboring countries to topple as well.

Eisenhower viewed the Communist threat in Vietnam much as Truman had regarded it in Greece and Turkey. In what became known as the **domino theory**, Eisenhower explained, "You have a row of dominoes, you knock over the first one, and what will happen to the last one is the certainty that it will go over very quickly." A Communist victory in Southeast Asia, he warned, could lead to the toppling of Japan, Taiwan, and the Philippines. By 1954, the United States was paying 75 percent of the cost of France's war in Vietnam. But with the Korean War fresh in his mind, Eisenhower resisted a larger role for the United States. When the French asked for American troops and planes to avert almost certain defeat in the battle for Dien Bien Phu, the president declined.

Geneva Accords, 1954

Dien Bien Phu fell to the Vietminh in May 1954, and two months later in Geneva, a truce was signed. The Geneva accords recognized Vietnam's independence and temporarily partitioned it at the seventeenth parallel, separating the Vietminh in the north from the puppet government established by the French in the south. Within two years, the Vietnamese people were to elect a unified government. Some officials warned against the continued American involvement in Vietnam, envisioning "nothing but grief in store for us if we remained in that area." Eisenhower and Dulles nonetheless moved to shore up South Vietnam and put the CIA to work infiltrating and destabilizing North Vietnam. Fearing a Communist victory in the mandated elections, they supported South Vietnamese prime minister Ngo Dinh Diem when he refused to hold the vote.

Between 1955 and 1961, the United States provided $800 million to the South Vietnamese army. Those troops proved grossly unprepared for the guerrilla warfare that began in the late 1950s. With help from Ho Chi Minh's government in the north, Vietminh rebels in the south stepped up their attacks on Diem's government. The insurgents gained support from the largely Buddhist peasants, who were outraged by the repressive regime of the Catholic, Westernized Diem. Unwilling to abandon containment, Eisenhower left his successor with no clear path to resolution beyond the pledge to save South Vietnam from communism.

What prompted U.S. interventions in Latin America and the Middle East?

The Eisenhower administration propped up friendly governments in Asia, but it also sought to topple unfriendly ones in Latin America and the Middle East. Officials regularly—and often mistakenly—interpreted internal civil wars in terms of the Cold War conflict between the superpowers, treating homegrown nationalist movements as Communist challenges to democracy. The administration also acted forcefully against governments that threatened U.S. economic interests. Increasingly, such foreign policy decisions were enacted out of sight of Congress and the public, through the use of the CIA.

This was the case in Guatemala. Its government, under the popularly elected president Jacobo Arbenz, was not Soviet-controlled, although it did accept support from the local Communist Party. In 1953, Arbenz moved to help landless, poverty-stricken peasants by nationalizing—or claiming for the state—the land owned, but not cultivated, by the United Fruit Company, a U.S. corporation whose annual profits were twice the size of Guatemala's national budget. United Fruit rejected Arbenz's

VISUAL ACTIVITY

◀ **Anti-Castro Cuban Exiles** The Cuban Revolution of 1959 created the largest refugee flow to the United States in history, with 1,600 to 1,700 refugees arriving by commercial airline every week. Many of those who fled Castro's Cuba became fierce anti-Communists, urging a tough American stance toward their homeland; here, in a show of support for U.S. Cold War policy, exiles line up by the Lincoln Memorial in 1961. Bettmann/Getty Images.

READING THE IMAGE: What does the dress of these Cuban refugees suggest about their backgrounds and economic status and about the kinds of people who most feared the new revolutionary government? Why might exiles have chosen the Lincoln Memorial as a place to express their views? What about this photograph would have pleased U.S. policymakers?

CONNECTIONS: What made Fidel Castro's rise to power especially threatening to the United States? How did the Cold War shape migration patterns not just in Cuba but in other parts of the world?

offer to compensate the company. Equating Arbenz's reformist government with a Communist threat, the CIA supplied pilots and other support to an opposition army that overthrew the elected government and installed a military dictatorship in 1954. United Fruit kept its land, and Guatemala was beset by destructive civil wars that lasted through the 1990s.

In 1959, when Cuban opposition to an authoritarian government erupted into a revolution led by Fidel Castro, a CIA agent promised "to take care of Castro just like we took care of Arbenz." As in Guatemala, American companies controlled major Cuban resources, and the country's internal affairs were monitored closely in Washington. The Cuban revolution of 1959 drove out the U.S.-supported dictator Fulgencio Batista and led the CIA to warn Eisenhower that "Communists and other extreme radicals appear to have penetrated the Castro movement."

When the United States denied Castro's requests for loans, he turned to the Soviet Union. And when U.S. companies refused Castro's offer to purchase their Cuban holdings at their assessed value, he began to nationalize their property. Many anti-Castro Cubans fled to the United States and reported his atrocities. Before leaving office, Eisenhower broke off diplomatic relations with Cuba and authorized the CIA to train Cuban exiles for an invasion to overthrow Castro.

This pattern had been established early in Eisenhower's administration. In the Middle East, the CIA intervened in Iran to oust an elected government, support an unpopular dictatorship, and maintain Western access to Iranian oil (see Map 29.3). In 1951, the Iranian parliament, led by Prime Minister Mohammed Mosaddegh, nationalized the country's oil fields and refineries, the majority of which were held by a British company and from which Iran received less than 20 percent of the profits. Britain strongly objected to the takeover and eventually sought help from the United States.

Advisers convinced Eisenhower that Mosaddegh, whom *Time* magazine had called "the Iranian George Washington," left Iran vulnerable to communism. Moreover, the president was eager to keep oil-rich areas in friendly hands. With Eisenhower's authorization, CIA agents instigated a coup, bribing army officers and financing demonstrations in the streets. In August 1953, Iranian army officers captured Mosaddegh and reestablished the authority of the former shah (or monarch), Mohammad Reza Pahlavi, who was known for favoring Western interests and the Iranian wealthy classes. U.S. companies received a 40 percent share of Iran's oil concessions. Resentment over the intervention would poison U.S.-Iranian relations into the twenty-first century.

Elsewhere in the Middle East, Eisenhower continued Truman's policy of support for Israel. He also pursued friendships with Arab nations to secure access to oil and create a bulwark against communism in the region, demanding their allegiance to America's side in the Cold War even when they preferred neutrality. In 1955, as part of the effort to win Arab allies, U.S. officials began talks with Egypt about American support to build the Aswan Dam on the Nile River. The following year, Egypt's

The Suez Crisis, 1956

leader, Gamal Abdel Nasser, sought arms from Communist Czechoslovakia, formed a military alliance with other Arab nations, and recognized the People's Republic of China. In retaliation, the United States called off the deal for the dam.

In July 1956, Nasser responded by seizing the Suez Canal, then owned by Britain and France but scheduled to revert to Egypt within seven years. In turn, Israel attacked Egypt, with help from Britain and France. Eisenhower in this case opposed the intervention, recognizing that the Egyptians had claimed their own territory and that Nasser "embodie[d] the emotional demands of the people . . . for independence." Calling on the United Nations to arrange a truce, he pressured Britain and France to pull back, forcing Israel to retreat.

Despite staying out of the Suez crisis, Eisenhower made it clear in a January 1957 speech that the United States would actively combat communism in the Middle East. Two months later, Congress approved aid to any Middle Eastern nation "requesting assistance against armed aggression from any country controlled by international communism." The president invoked this Eisenhower Doctrine to send aid to Jordan in 1957 and troops to Lebanon in 1958 to counter anti-Western pressures on those governments.

Why did the United States and Soviet Union engage in a nuclear arms race?

Eisenhower firmly resisted Communist inroads abroad through overt and covert actions. But he also sought to reduce superpower tensions. After Stalin's death in 1953, Nikita Khrushchev emerged as a more moderate Soviet leader. Like Eisenhower, who remarked privately that the arms race would lead "at worst to atomic warfare, at best to robbing every people and nation on earth of the fruits of their own toil," Khrushchev wanted to reduce defense spending and the threat of nuclear devastation. Eisenhower and Khrushchev met in Geneva in 1955 at the first summit conference between the two nations since the end of World War II, symbolizing what Eisenhower called "a new spirit of conciliation and cooperation."

The race to develop new weapons and defenses continued, however. In August 1957, the Soviets test-fired their first intercontinental ballistic missile (ICBM), and two months later, they beat the United States into space by launching *Sputnik*, the first manmade satellite to circle the earth.

The United States launched a successful satellite of its own in 1958, but *Sputnik* raised fears that the Soviets led not only in missile development and space exploration but also in science and education. In response, Eisenhower established the National Aeronautics and Space Administration (NASA) with a huge budget increase for space exploration. He also signed the National Defense Education Act, providing support for students in math, foreign languages, and science and technology. As the legislation's title suggested, domestic policies even in areas seemingly far removed from the Cold War could be justified in national security terms.

Eisenhower assured the public of the United States' nuclear superiority—and during his presidency, the stockpile of American nuclear weapons more than

Sputnik
First manmade satellite to circle the earth, launched by the Soviets in 1957. It created fears that the Soviets were ahead of the United States not only in missile development and space exploration but also in science and education.

▲ **The Age of Nuclear Anxiety** Children directly experienced the insecurity of the Cold War nuclear arms race through routine school drills instructing them to "duck and cover" in the event of a Soviet strike. Although such techniques would not have offered much of a safeguard, civil defense agencies also distributed pamphlets about how to protect oneself in the event of an atomic attack. Photo: American Stock Archive/Getty Images; pamphlet: Lynn Museum and Historical Society.

quadrupled. Having installed ICBMs at home and in Britain, the United States was prepared to deploy more in Italy and Turkey. In 1960, it would launch the first Polaris submarine carrying nuclear missiles.

Yet nuclear weapons could not guarantee security for either superpower, each of which possessed sufficient capacity to devastate the other. In drills, American school children were trained to "duck and cover" in case of nuclear attack, and the Civilian Defense Administration issued similar guidelines for adults. Most Americans did not follow the recommendation to construct home bomb shelters, but they recognized the unprecedented perils of a nuclear age. A new organization, the Committee for a Sane Nuclear Policy, called the nuclear arms race "a danger unlike any danger that has ever existed."

Helped by the thaw in U.S.-Soviet relations, the superpowers began to discuss possible resolutions of the arms race in the Eisenhower years. By 1960, the two sides were close to a ban on nuclear testing. But just before a planned summit in Paris, a

Soviet missile shot down an American U-2 spy plane over Soviet territory. When the State Department denied that U.S. planes had been violating Soviet airspace, the Soviets produced the pilot and the photos taken on his flight. The incident dashed all prospects for a nuclear arms agreement.

In the name of deterrence, Eisenhower promoted the development of more destructive atomic weapons. But he was uneasy with the expansion of defense budgets. Indeed, as the president left office, he warned about the growing influence of the **military-industrial complex**, the insatiable demand of defense contractors and the U.S. military for newer, more powerful weapons systems. In his farewell address, he warned that the "conjunction of an immense military establishment and a large arms industry . . . exercised a total influence . . . in every city, every state house, every office of the federal government." His administration had done little, however, to curtail the defense industry's power. The Cold War had created a warfare state.

military-industrial complex
Term used by President Eisenhower to refer to the influence of the military establishment and defense contractors on U.S. government and policy.

REVIEW

Where, and with what tools, did Eisenhower practice containment?

Conclusion: What were the costs and consequences of the Cold War?

H oping for continued U.S.-Soviet cooperation rather than unilateral American intervention to resolve foreign crises, some liberal members of Congress, such as Helen Gahagan Douglas, initially opposed the implementation of containment. By 1948, however, most politicians and public figures had lined up squarely behind Truman's decision to fight communism throughout the world. It was perhaps the most momentous foreign policy initiative in the nation's history.

More than any other development in the postwar world, the Cold War defined American politics and society for decades to come. It changed the U.S. government itself, greatly expanding the federal budget and substantially increasing the power of the president and executive branch along with that of the military and the CIA. It altered policymaking, shifting priorities from internal to external affairs and linking domestic spending to national security. And it transformed the U.S. economy, which was boosted by the reconstruction of Western Europe and Japan as well as Cold War defense outlays. The nuclear arms race put the people of the world at risk, consumed resources that might have been used to improve living standards, and skewed the economy toward dependence on military projects.

Another cost of the early Cold War years was the anti-Communist wave that swept the nation, denying Douglas a Senate seat, intimidating radicals and liberals, and narrowing the range of ideas acceptable for political discussion. Partisan politics and Truman's warnings about the Communist menace fueled McCarthyism, as did popular frustrations over the failure of containment to defeat the nation's enemies. The Korean War, which ended in stalemate rather than victory, prompted the Eisenhower administration to seek new tools for winning the Cold War, including covert CIA operations and aid to authoritarian leaders around the world — in Guatemala, Iran, and Vietnam — so long as they promised to stave off communism. The conviction that the United States must fight communism everywhere led to infringements on the constitutional rights of U.S. citizens. As the basis for postwar foreign policy, it provoked anti-Americanism and led to military commitments and interventions that would plague future generations.

EXPLAIN WHY IT MATTERS

iron curtain (p. 769)

containment (p. 769)

Truman Doctrine (p. 769)

Marshall Plan (p. 772)

North Atlantic Treaty Organization (NATO) (p. 773)

Central Intelligence Agency (CIA) (p. 773)

McCarthyism (p. 776)

House Un-American Activities Committee (HUAC) (p. 777)

NSC 68 (p. 782)

mutually assured destruction (MAD) (p. 783)

domino theory (p. 784)

Sputnik (p. 787)

military-industrial complex (p. 789)

PUT IT ALL TOGETHER

THE UNITED STATES AND THE POSTWAR WORLD

- What interests did American and Soviet policymakers believe were at stake in Eastern Europe after World War II? How did events in the region contribute to the growing Cold War?

- What was the policy of containment? What assumptions did it make about Soviet power and intentions?

ANTICOMMUNISM AS POLICY AND POLITICS

- How did the United States address the Communist threat in Asia as compared to Europe? What impact did the Korean War have on American domestic politics and on future military decision making?

- What conditions explain the rise of McCarthyism? Why did some Americans believe that their country faced a grave internal threat to its security?

FOREIGN POLICY IN THE EISENHOWER YEARS

- How did Eisenhower's approach to the Cold War compare to Truman's?

- Why did the United States turn to military intervention and covert CIA activities as tools of foreign policy in the 1950s? What were the immediate and longer-term consequences in Asia, the Middle East, and Latin America?

LOOKING BACKWARD, LOOKING AHEAD

- How did American and Soviet experiences between 1918 and 1945 lay the groundwork for the Cold War?

- How did the Cold War redirect U.S. foreign and domestic priorities in the 1950s and beyond? What were its effects on the U.S. government and military?

27

POSTWAR CULTURE AND POLITICS

1945–1960

This chapter discusses the following questions:

- Why did domestic reform wane after World War II?
- What fueled postwar prosperity?
- How did economic growth shape American society?
- Why did civil rights struggles erupt in the 1950s?
- Conclusion: What challenges did prosperity mask?

▶ **The Kitchen Debate** Soviet premier Nikita Khrushchev (left) and Vice President Richard M. Nixon (center) debate the merits of their nations' economic systems at the American National Exhibition held in Moscow in 1959. "You are a lawyer for capitalism and I am a lawyer for communism," Khrushchev told Nixon as each tried to outdo the other. AP Photo.

AN AMERICAN STORY

T railed by reporters, Vice President Richard M. Nixon led Soviet premier Nikita Khrushchev through the American National Exhibition in Moscow in July 1959. The cultural exchange reflected a slight thaw in the Cold War but was nevertheless an excellent opportunity for propaganda. As they examined a display of American consumer goods, Khrushchev and Nixon took part in a slugfest of words that reporters dubbed "the kitchen debate."

Showing off a new color television set, Nixon remarked that the Soviet Union "may be ahead of us . . . in the thrust of your rockets" but insisted that the United States outpaced the Soviets in supplying consumer goods for its people. Linking capitalism and democracy, Nixon asserted that such products and "our right to choose" were the very substance of American freedom. As the two leaders walked through a model of a six-room ranch-style home, Nixon boasted that "any steelworker could buy this house." Khrushchev retorted that in his country citizens were "entitled to housing," whereas in the United States the homeless slept on the pavement. Moving on, Nixon declared that household appliances were "designed to make things easier for our women." Khrushchev disparaged this "capitalist attitude," maintaining that the Soviets appreciated women for their economic contributions, not their domesticity.

Nixon got Khrushchev to agree that it was "far better to be talking about washing machines than machines of war." Yet despite such exchanges, the two nations remained locked in Cold War animosity and an intense arms race throughout the postwar decades. Free enterprise and capitalist abundance would be enlisted in this struggle, providing a key justification for "the American way." This celebratory stance toward U.S. institutions signaled a retreat from the reform ambitions of the New Deal years.

Americans' soaring standard of living in the 1950s was unparalleled. It was also unanticipated. Many in the United States feared a recession as troops returned from Europe and Asia in 1945, and the conversion from a war footing was not easy. Even at the time of the kitchen debate, poverty clung stubbornly to one of every five Americans. Yet the Moscow display testified to the unheard-of material gains savored by many in the postwar era.

Cold War weapons production spurred the economy, whose vitality stimulated suburban development, contributed to the growth of the South and Southwest (the Sun Belt), and enabled millions of Americans to buy a host of new products. As new homes, television sets, and household appliances transformed living patterns, Americans took part in a consumer culture that promoted the family and traditional gender roles, even as growing numbers of married women took jobs outside the home.

The prosperity of the postwar period also made way for challenges to dominant norms and practices by dissenting writers known as the Beats and an emerging youth culture. Most dramatically, the Cold War and the economic boom of the 1950s created new opportunities for Black Americans to protest the system of segregation and disfranchisement that had replaced slavery. The organizations, leadership, and strategies that Black activists developed in this period built a civil rights movement of unprecedented size and influence.

Why did domestic reform wane after World War II?

Referring to the Civil War general who coined the phrase "War is hell," the newly installed president Harry S. Truman joked in 1945 that "Sherman was wrong. I'm telling you I find peace is hell." Challenged by crises abroad, Truman also faced shortages, strikes, and inflation as the economy shifted to peacetime production. The president had vowed to expand on New Deal reforms with his own "Fair Deal" program focused on health care, housing, civil rights, and education. But Cold War commitments around the globe, anticommunism at home, and Republican gains in Congress prevented Truman from enacting much of his domestic agenda. His successor, the moderate Republican Dwight D. Eisenhower, would mostly stay the course, neither rolling back New Deal programs nor extending them.

How did the United States reconvert to a peacetime economy?

As World War II came to a close, economic experts and ordinary citizens feared a peacetime recession. They also worried about providing jobs for millions of returning soldiers. To that end, Truman asked Congress for a twenty-one-point program of social and economic reforms for reconversion, as the nation adjusted to peacetime production, including the temporary continuation of wartime wage, rent, and price controls. He also called for new government support for housing and health care for those in need. "Not even President Roosevelt ever asked for as much at one sitting," exploded one Republican leader.

Congress approved just one of Truman's key proposals—full-employment legislation—and only after watering it down. The Employment Act of 1946 called on the federal government "to promote maximum employment, production, and purchasing power," thereby formalizing the state's responsibility for maintaining a healthy economy. It created the Council of Economic Advisors to assist the president but authorized no new powers to translate the government's obligations into action.

Inflation, not unemployment, turned out to be the biggest economic problem facing the postwar United States. Consumers had $30 billion in wartime savings to spend, but shortages of meat, automobiles, housing, and other items drove up prices. Some in Congress sought to maintain price and rent controls, but those efforts were dashed by pressures from business groups and others determined to trim government powers.

Labor relations were another thorn in Truman's side. Organized labor emerged from the war 14.5 million members strong, a full 35 percent of the nonagricultural workforce. Unions feared the erosion of wartime gains and turned to the weapon they had surrendered during the war. Five million workers went on strike in 1946, affecting nearly every major industry. One former Marine and his coworkers voted to strike after calculating that an executive had spent more on a party than they would earn in a whole year at the steel mill. "That sort of stuff made us realize, hell we had to bite the bullet. . . . The bosses sure didn't give a damn for us." Although most Americans approved of unions in principle, many became fed up with strikes and blamed unions for shortages and rising prices. When the strikes subsided, workers had won wage increases of about 20 percent, but the loss of overtime pay coupled with rising prices left their purchasing power only slightly higher than it was in 1942.

Women workers fared even worse. Polls indicated that 68 to 85 percent wanted to keep their wartime jobs, but most who remained in the workforce had to settle for relatively low-paying jobs in light industry or the service sector (**Figure 27.1**). Displaced from her shipyard work, Marie Schreiber took a cashier's job, lamenting, "You were back to women's wages, you know . . . practically in half." Women's organizations and union women called for bills to require equal pay for equal work, provide child care for employed mothers, and create a

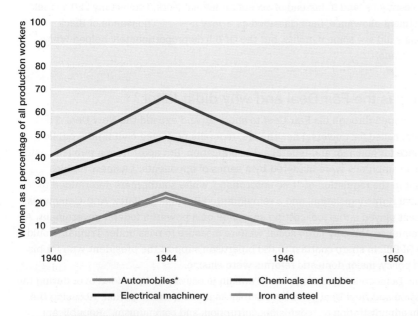

FIGURE 27.1 ◄ **Women Workers in Selected Industries, 1940–1950**
Women demolished the idea that some jobs were "men's work" during World War II, but they lost ground in the manufacturing sector after the war.

Legend:
Automobiles*
Electrical machinery
Chemicals and rubber
Iron and steel

*During World War II, this industry did not produce cars, but rather military transportation such as jeeps, tanks, and aircraft.

government commission to study women's status. But it was clear that many others viewed women primarily as wives and mothers—and their wartime work as temporary. Given rising opposition to expansion of federal powers, initiatives on equal pay and child care went nowhere.

Servicemen's Readjustment Act
Act, popularly known as the GI Bill, that provided tuition benefits, unemployment benefits, loan assistance, and medical care to World War II veterans in an attempt to ease the transition from a wartime to a peacetime economy.

The most successful of the reconversion measures was the **Servicemen's Readjustment Act**, or GI Bill, enacted in 1944. Addressing concerns about absorbing returning veterans into the postwar economy, it offered sixteen million veterans vocational training and education. It also provided unemployment compensation until they found jobs and low-interest loans to purchase homes, farms, and small businesses. By 1948, some 1.3 million veterans had bought houses with government loans. A drugstore clerk before his military service, Don Condren was able to pursue an engineering degree and buy his first house. "The GI Bill gave the whole country an upward boost economically," he recalled.

The impact of the GI Bill was uneven, however. As wives and daughters of veterans, women gained indirect support from GI subsidies, but few women qualified for employment and educational benefits. Soldiers dishonorably discharged for "homosexual conduct" were barred entirely from GI benefits. Because GI programs were administered at the state and local levels, they also resulted in systematic racial and ethnic discrimination, especially in the South, to the bitter disappointment of Black veterans.

The legislation reinforced existing inequalities in other ways. Southern universities remained segregated, and historically Black colleges could not accommodate demand. Federal housing loans also heavily favored white applicants. Despite the employment assistance offered by the GI Bill, Black veterans were often shuttled into low-skill jobs. One decorated WWII veteran reported that "my color bars me from most decent jobs, and if, instead of accepting menial work, I collect my $20 a week readjustment allowance, I am classified as a 'lazy n-----.' " Thousands of Black Americans did see some benefits, but the GI Bill disproportionately helped white male veterans.

What was the Fair Deal and why did it falter?

Fair Deal
President Truman's domestic agenda, little of it enacted, for extending the New Deal through universal health care, federally protected civil rights, public assistance for housing, and federal aid to education.

Truman hoped through his **Fair Deal** to shore up and expand the New Deal. The president called for universal health care, federally protected civil rights, public assistance for housing, and federal aid to education. But apart from a public housing act, these ambitions were hindered by a series of opponents: business lobbies resistant to the regulation of "free enterprise," white southerners determined to block civil rights legislation, and a reinvigorated Republican Party. Anti-Communist sentiment played a role too, casting suspicion on a powerful federal government. As a consequence, the only large social welfare measure to pass under Truman would be the GI Bill. In sharp contrast to the bipartisan support the president won for his foreign policy, major domestic reforms were elusive.

The Democratic dominance that Franklin Roosevelt had presided over during the depression and New Deal years hit roadblocks in the postwar period. Accusing the Truman administration of "confusion, corruption, and communism," Republicans capitalized on public frustrations with postwar strikes and shortages, capturing control of Congress in 1946 for the first time in fourteen years. Many had campaigned against the New Deal. Once elected, they weakened some reform programs and enacted tax cuts for higher-income groups.

Organized labor took the most severe blow when Congress passed the **Taft-Hartley Act** over Truman's veto in 1947. Called a "slave labor" law by unions, the measure amended the Wagner Act (see chapter 24), reducing unions' power to bargain with employers and making it more difficult to organize workers. States could now pass "right-to-work" laws, which banned the practice of requiring all workers to join a union once a majority had voted for it. Many states, especially in the South and West, rushed to enact such laws, encouraging industries to relocate there. Taft-Hartley maintained the New Deal principle of government protection for collective bargaining, but it tipped the balance of power toward management.

In the 1948 election, Truman faced not only a resurgent Republican Party headed by New York governor Thomas E. Dewey but also two revolts within his own party. On the left, Henry A. Wallace, whose foreign policy views had cost him his cabinet seat, led the new Progressive Party. On the right, South Carolina governor J. Strom Thurmond headed the States' Rights Party—the **Dixiecrats**—formed by southern Democrats who walked out of their party's 1948 convention when it passed a liberal civil rights plank.

Truman's prospects looked so bleak on election night that the *Chicago Daily Tribune* went to press with the headline "Dewey Defeats Truman." But even though the Dixiecrats won four southern states, Truman took 303 electoral votes to Dewey's 189, and his party regained control of Congress (**Map 27.1**). His unexpected victory attested to the broad support for his foreign policy and the enduring popularity of New Deal reform.

Most of the original New Deal programs survived Republican attacks, with Congress making modest improvements in Social Security and raising the minimum wage. But the only significant new reform measure to pass was the **Housing Act of 1949**, which authorized 810,000 units of government-constructed housing over the next six years and represented a landmark commitment by the government to address the lack of housing for poor Americans. Yet it fell far short of actual need, and it created new problems when slum clearance displaced people from their homes and neighborhoods without providing alternatives.

The rest of Truman's Fair Deal did not materialize. With southern Democrats playing a pivotal role, Congress rejected Truman's proposals for civil rights. A powerful medical lobby blocked plans for national health insurance, attacking it as "socialized medicine" and the Truman administration as "followers of the Moscow party line." Conflicts over race and religion thwarted federal aid to education. Truman's efforts to revise immigration policy were mixed. The McCarran-Walter Act of 1952 ended the outright ban on immigration and citizenship for Japanese

Taft-Hartley Act
Law passed by the Republican-controlled Congress in 1947 that amended the Wagner Act and placed restrictions on organized labor, making it more difficult for unions to organize workers.

Dixiecrats
Group of southern Democrats who defected from their party during the 1948 convention when it passed a liberal civil rights plank, suggesting the difficulty the Democratic Party would have in keeping both white southerners and Black Americans in its ranks.

Housing Act of 1949
Law authorizing the construction of 810,000 units of government housing. This landmark effort marked the first significant commitment of the federal government to meet the housing needs of the poor.

Candidate	Electoral Vote	Popular Vote	Percent of Popular Vote
Harry S. Truman (Democrat)	303	24,105,695	49.5
Thomas E. Dewey (Republican)	189	21,969,170	45.1
J. Strom Thurmond (States' Rights)	39	1,169,021	2.4
Henry A. Wallace (Progressive)	0	1,156,103	2.4

MAP 27.1 ▲ The Election of 1948

and other Asians, but it authorized the government to bar suspected Communists and homosexuals and maintained the discriminatory quota system established in the 1920s.

Truman's foreign policy also undermined his domestic proposals. By late 1950, the Korean War embroiled the president in controversy and depleted his power as a legislative leader. The failure to enact the Fair Deal set the United States apart from most European nations, which by the 1950s had established comprehensive health, housing, and employment programs to underwrite the material well-being and security of their populations.

How did the New Deal fare under Eisenhower?

Truman's successor was Dwight D. Eisenhower, a national military hero elected in 1952 in large part based on his promise to end the Korean War. The first Republican president to take office since 1928, he charted a path between progressive and conservative agendas. In 1953, Eisenhower pledged a "middle way between untrammeled freedom of the individual and the demands for the welfare of the whole Nation," promising that his administration would "avoid government by bureaucracy as carefully as it avoids neglect of the helpless."

Eisenhower generally resisted expanding the federal government's power. He only reluctantly stepped in when the Supreme Court ordered schools to desegregate, and his administration terminated the federal trusteeship of dozens of Native American tribes. As a moderate Republican, however, Eisenhower supported the continuation of existing social welfare programs. In the name of national defense, he even extended the reach of the federal government.

"Ike," as he was nicknamed, was very popular with the U.S. public, but so were Democratic social welfare programs. In contrast to the old guard conservatives in his party who wanted to repeal much of the New Deal, Eisenhower preached "modern Republicanism." This meant curbing additional federal intervention in economic life but not turning the clock back to the 1920s. "Should any political party attempt to abolish social security and eliminate labor laws and farm programs," he wrote privately in 1954, "you would not hear of that party again in our political history." Democratic control of Congress after the midterm elections of 1954 further contributed to Eisenhower's middle-of-the-road approach.

Eisenhower sometimes echoed conservative Republicans' conviction that government was best left to the states and economic decisions to private business. Yet he signed laws that brought ten million more workers under the umbrella of Social Security, increased the minimum wage, and created a new Department of Health, Education, and Welfare. When the spread of polio—a viral disease that could lead to paralysis—neared epidemic proportions, Eisenhower obtained funds from Congress to distribute a vaccine, a responsibility that conservatives thought individual states should bear.

Eisenhower's most significant domestic initiative was the **National Interstate and Defense Highways Act of 1956 (Map 27.2)**. Promoted as essential to the nation's defense and economic growth, the act authorized construction of a national highway system. The federal government shouldered most of the costs through fuel and

National Interstate and Defense Highways Act of 1956
Law authorizing the construction of a national interstate highway system. Promoted as essential to national defense and a spur to economic growth, the act accelerated the movement of people and goods and changed the nature of American communities.

MAP ACTIVITY

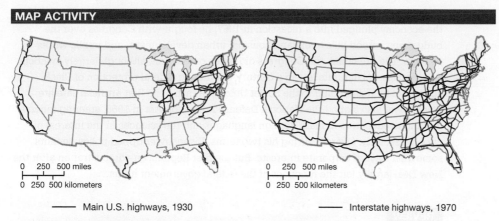

— Main U.S. highways, 1930   — Interstate highways, 1970

MAP 27.2 ▲ The Interstate Highway System, 1930 and 1970 Built with federal funds authorized in the National Interstate and Defense Highways Act of 1956, superhighways soon crisscrossed the nation. Trucking, construction, gasoline, and travel were among the industries that prospered, while railroads suffered from the subsidized competition.

READING THE MAP: What regions of the United States had main highways in 1930? What regions did not? How had the situation changed by 1970?

CONNECTIONS: What impact did the growth of the interstate highway system have on migration and housing patterns in the United States? What benefits did the new interstate highways bring to Americans, and at what costs?

vehicle taxes. The new highways were justified in part by the need for escape arteries in the case of nuclear attack. More immediately, the highway network accelerated the mobility of people and goods, spurring suburban expansion. It also benefited the trucking, construction, and automobile industries that had lobbied for the law. Eventually, the monumental highway project exacted unforeseen costs in the form of air pollution, energy consumption, declining railroads and mass transportation, and decay of central cities.

In other areas, however, Eisenhower reined in federal activity in favor of state governments and private enterprise. His large tax cuts benefited business and the wealthy, and he resisted federal aid to primary and secondary education. The president likewise opposed national health insurance, preferring the growing practice of private insurance provided by employers. And whereas Democrats sought to keep nuclear power in government hands, Eisenhower signed legislation authorizing the private manufacture and sale of nuclear energy. The first commercial nuclear power plant opened in 1958 in northwest Pennsylvania. Most consequentially, Eisenhower refused to endorse desegregation, believing such matters were best left to the states.

Eisenhower was easily reelected in 1956, defeating Adlai Stevenson and doubling his victory margin of 1952. Yet Democrats kept control of Congress, and in the midterm elections two years later, they all but wiped out the Republican Party, gaining a 64–34 majority in the Senate and a 282–135 advantage in the House. Although Ike captured voters' hearts, a majority of Americans appeared wedded to the programs and policies of the Democrats.

In his second term, Eisenhower faced more serious leadership challenges. When the economy plunged into a recession in 1957, he fought with Congress over the budget and vetoed bills to expand housing, urban development, and public works projects. The president and Congress did agree on the first, although largely symbolic and toothless, civil rights law in a century, stipulating federal protection of Black voting rights. Responding to the Soviet Union's launch of its first artificial satellite, Eisenhower also signed the National Defense Education Act in 1958, steering federal funding to education in math, foreign languages and the sciences in the interest of national security. Overall, during his two terms, Eisenhower tipped policy benefits somewhat toward corporate interests. But the first Republican administration after the New Deal largely left the functions of the federal government intact.

REVIEW

How did the context for domestic reform change between the 1930s and the 1950s?

What fueled postwar prosperity?

D espite scarcities and inflation, World War II delivered to most Americans a higher standard of living than ever before. By 1947, the economy had stabilized, escaping the postwar depression that so many had feared. Wartime profits enabled businesses to expand, and consumers could now spend their savings on items that had been beyond their reach during the depression and war.

By the 1950s, the economy was booming, in part a product of the Cold War defense buildup. As Nixon and Khrushchev's "kitchen debate" attested, American life would be transformed by an array of modern conveniences along with suburban development, federally funded highways, and broad access to higher education. Prosperity was far from universal, however. Rural deprivation was particularly pronounced, as was poverty among the older Americans, Black Americans, Native Americans, and Latinos. But a remarkable economic boom lasted through the 1960s, prompting economist John Kenneth Galbraith to label the United States "the affluent society."

How did technology transform agriculture and industry?

Stimulated by Cold War spending and technological advances, economic productivity increased enormously in the 1950s. Mechanization meant that work itself was changing in the postwar era. Fewer people labored on farms, service-sector employment overtook manufacturing jobs, women's employment grew, and union membership soared. These changes created prosperity for many; others, shut out of their old livelihoods, instead faced insecurity. Economic transformations also prompted far-reaching shifts in where—and how—Americans lived.

Between 1940 and 1960, agricultural output mushroomed even as the number of farmworkers declined by almost one-third. Farmers achieved unprecedented productivity through greater crop specialization, intensive use of fertilizers, and, above all, mechanization. A single mechanical cotton picker replaced fifty people and cut the cost of harvesting a bale of cotton from $40 to $5.

The decline of family farms and the growth of large commercial farming, or agribusiness, were causes as well as consequences of mechanization. Benefiting handsomely from federal price supports begun during the New Deal, larger farmers could afford technological improvements, but smaller producers lacked capital to purchase the machinery necessary to compete. Consequently, the average farm size more than doubled between 1940 and 1964, and the number of farms fell by more than 40 percent.

Many small farmers who hung on became the face of rural poverty. Others were forced off the land altogether as southern landowners replaced sharecroppers and tenants with machines. Hundreds of thousands of Black Americans moved to cities, where racial discrimination and a lack of jobs mired many in urban poverty. A Mississippi mother reported that most of her relatives headed for Chicago when they realized that "it was going to be machines now that harvest the crops." Worrying that "it might be worse up there" for her children, she agonized, "I'm afraid to leave and I'm afraid to stay."

New technologies also transformed industrial production. Between 1945 and 1960, the number of labor-hours needed to manufacture a car fell by 50 percent. Technology revolutionized industries from electronics to chemicals to air transportation. New industrial sectors emerged in television, plastics, and computers. American businesses benefited from U.S. global power in the form of access to cheap oil, ample markets abroad, and little foreign competition. Even with Eisenhower's conservative fiscal policies, government spending reached $80 billion annually and created new jobs.

The strength of labor unions contributed to prosperity by putting money into the hands of people who would spend it on consumer items. Real earnings for production workers shot up 40 percent. A steelworker's son marveled, "In 1946, we did not have a car, a television set, or a refrigerator. By 1952 we had all those things." In most other industrial nations, government programs underwrote their citizens' economic security, but the United States developed a mixed system in which company-funded programs won by unions provided for retirement, health care, paid vacations, supplementary unemployment benefits, and more. This system of worker welfare—privately rather than state-funded—resulted in wide disparities among workers. Those who did not belong to strong unions or who worked irregularly received fewer benefits.

While the number of organized workers continued to grow, union membership peaked at 27.4 percent of all workers in 1957. Technological advances eliminated jobs in heavy industry. "You are going to have trouble collecting union dues from all of these machines," commented a Ford manager to union leader Walter Reuther. The U.S. economy as a whole was shifting from the production of goods to services. Beginning in 1957, service and office jobs outnumbered factory jobs, as more workers distributed goods, performed services, provided education, and carried out government work. Unions made some headway in these fields, especially among government employees, but most service industries resisted unionization.

The growing clerical and service occupations swelled the demand for female workers, who held nearly one-third of all U.S. jobs by the end of the 1950s. The vast majority worked in offices, light manufacturing, domestic service, teaching, and nursing. Because these occupations were dominated by women, wages remained relatively low. In 1960, the average female full-time worker earned just 60 percent of the average male worker's wages. At the bottom of the employment ladder, Black women took home only 42 percent of what white men earned.

What led Americans to move to the suburbs?

Housing was another growth industry of the postwar era. Although suburbs had existed since the nineteenth century, nothing symbolized the affluent society more than their tremendous expansion in the 1950s. Eleven million new homes went up in suburbia; by 1960, one in four Americans lived in a suburban neighborhood.

As Vice President Nixon boasted to Khrushchev during the 1959 kitchen debate, these homes were accessible to families with modest incomes. Adapting the factory assembly line to home construction, builder William J. Levitt erected nearly identical units. In 1949, families could purchase mass-produced houses in his 17,000-home development, called Levittown, on Long Island, New York, for just under $8,000 each (approximately $93,000 in current dollars). Similar developments, as well as more luxurious ones, sprouted up across the country.

Suburbanization was underwritten by federal policy. The government subsidized home ownership by guaranteeing low-interest mortgages and by making interest on mortgages tax deductible. Government-funded interstate highways also encouraged suburban development. After years of depression and war, most families were thrilled to be able to own new homes. "It was a miracle to them," one man said of his working-class parents who moved to Levittown. They left behind dense urban neighborhoods and extended family networks. For the white working class, including many immigrants, private home ownership became a key piece of the American dream.

That opportunity was not open to all. Government loans were less available to aspiring Black homeowners, and the new housing tracts observed strict racial lines. Each Levittown resident, for example, signed a contract pledging not to rent or sell to a non-Caucasian. The Supreme Court had declared such covenants unenforceable in 1948, but the new suburbs would nevertheless be sharply—and deliberately—segregated.

Although some Black Americans joined the suburban migration, most headed to urban centers in search of economic opportunity, doubling their numbers in major cities during the 1950s. They moved to cities that were already in decline, losing not only population but also commerce, industry, and jobs to the suburbs or to southern and western states. Plant closings and unemployment in the urban core were the flip side of rapid suburbanization.

By the 1960s, suburbs came under attack for bulldozing the natural environment, creating groundwater contamination, and disrupting wildlife patterns. They were also the target of social critics, who decried the new communities as hothouses of conformity. Lewis Mumford, for example, disparaged suburbia as "a multitude of

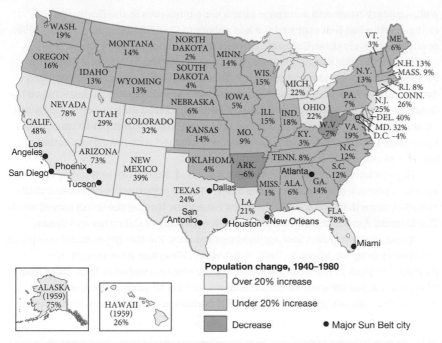

MAP 27.3 ◄ The Rise of the Sun Belt, 1940–1980 The growth of defense industries, interstate highways, a nonunionized labor force, and air-conditioning all helped spur economic development and population growth in the Southwest and the South. This made the Sun Belt the fastest-growing region of the country between 1940 and 1980.

Population change, 1940–1980

- Over 20% increase
- Under 20% increase
- Decrease   ● Major Sun Belt city

uniform, unidentifiable houses in a treeless communal wasteland, inhabited by people of the same class, the same income, the same age group." In the late 1940s, the suburbs were a symbol of economic security and class mobility; a decade later, suburbia would come to represent for some dissenters all that was wrong with American consumer society.

Why did the postwar Sun Belt grow so quickly?

Although every section of the nation witnessed rapid economic growth, the Southwest and South especially thrived in production, commerce, and population (**Map 27.3**). California overtook New York as the most populous state. Sports franchises followed fans: In 1958, the Brooklyn Dodgers moved to Los Angeles, joined by the Minneapolis Lakers three years later.

A temperate climate attracted new residents to the **Sun Belt**, but the real magnet was economic opportunity. Just as railroads had fueled western development in the nineteenth century, the automobile and the airplane spurred post–World War II growth. New technologies made the Sun Belt livable. Air-conditioning cooled nearly eight million homes by 1960, fostering industrial development and tourism. Asked a journalist: "Can you conceive a Walt Disney World in central Florida without its air-conditioned hotels?"

So important was the defense industry to the South and Southwest that the area was later referred to as the "Gun Belt." The aerospace industry boomed in Los Angeles and Dallas–Fort Worth, and military bases underwrote prosperity in San Diego and San Antonio. Although defense dollars flowed to other regions as

Sun Belt
Name applied to the Southwest and South, which grew rapidly after World War II as a center of defense industries and nonunionized labor.

well—military bases and aerospace plants were numerous in the Northwest, for example—the Sun Belt captured the lion's share of Cold War spending. By the 1960s, nearly one of every three California workers held a defense-related job.

Surging populations and industries soon presented environmental dilemmas. Providing sufficient water and power to cities and to agribusiness meant building dams and reservoirs on free-flowing rivers. Native Americans lost fishing sites on the Columbia River, and dams on the Upper Missouri displaced nine hundred American Indian families. Sprawling suburban settlement without efficient public transportation ensured that the new highway system was clogged with cars, contributing to blankets of smog over Los Angeles and other cities.

High-technology industries drew well-educated, skilled workers to the West, but economic promise also attracted those bereft of other opportunities. Between 1945 and 1960, more than one-third of the Black Americans leaving the South moved west. The Mexican American population also grew, especially in California and Texas.

To supply California's vast agribusiness industry, the U.S. government continued the *bracero* program begun in 1942, under which Mexicans were temporarily permitted to work in the United States. Until the program ended in 1964, more than 100,000 Mexicans entered the United States each year to labor in the fields—and many of them stayed, legally or illegally. But permanent Mexican immigration was

bracero program
Program begun in 1942 permitting Mexicans temporary entrance into the United States as agricultural laborers. Until the program ended in 1964, more than 100,000 Mexicans entered the United States each year.

VISUAL ACTIVITY

◀ **Air-Conditioning** The first air-conditioning systems were installed in factories, but room air-conditioning began to appear in homes in the 1930s and spread rapidly in the 1950s. Fewer than one million homes had room air conditioners in 1950, but nearly eight million did in 1960, and more than half of all homes had some form of air-conditioning by 1975, as its status changed from a luxury to a necessity. Picture Research Consultants & Archives.

READING THE IMAGE: What does this ad promise consumers? What negative effects of air-conditioning does it leave out?

CONNECTIONS: How was air-conditioning related to the rise of the Sun Belt? What other factors contributed to its growth?

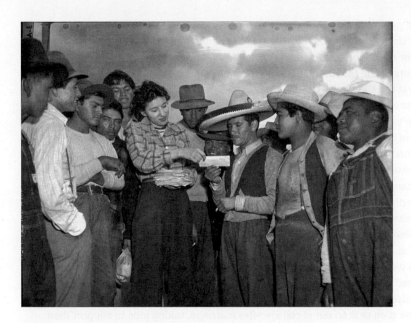

◀ **Mexican *Braceros*** Labor shortages during World War II prompted the creation of the *bracero* (Spanish for "manual laborer") program, an arrangement between the United States and Mexico allowing for the temporary importation of contract laborers. Here a group of Mexican farm workers receive their paychecks in 1943 in Skagit Valley, Washington. Seattle Post-Intelligencer Collection, Museum of History & Industry, Seattle; All Rights Reserved.

not as welcome as Mexicans' low-wage labor. In 1954, the government—using a derogatory term for those who entered the country by swimming across the Rio Grande River—launched a series of raids called "Operation Wetback," sending more than one million Mexicans back across the border.

Free of the discrimination faced by others, white Americans enjoyed the fullest prosperity in the West. In 1950, when California developers opened Lakewood, a 17,500-home development in Los Angeles County, thirty thousand people lined up to buy houses at prices averaging $101,000 in today's dollars. Many of the new homeowners were veterans, blue-collar and lower-level white-collar workers who worked in defense-based jobs at aerospace corporations. A huge shopping mall, Lakewood Center, displayed the fruits of a consumer culture, and the workers' children lived within commuting distance of community colleges and six state universities.

What role did higher education play in economic expansion?

California's postwar university system exemplified a spectacular transformation of higher education. A college education had once been reserved for the affluent. But between 1940 and 1960, college enrollments in the United States more than doubled, with more than 40 percent of young Americans attending college by the mid-1960s. State governments vastly expanded the number of public colleges and universities, while municipalities began to build two-year community colleges.

Higher education in these years would become central not only to individuals' economic prospects but also to a variety of state projects. The Cold War channeled millions of federal dollars to universities for defense-related research in fields ranging from engineering and chemistry to anthropology, linguistics, and psychology. College curricula were redesigned to prepare students for the responsibility of protecting, and leading, "the free world."

Like private home ownership, a college degree became newly accessible to working-class Americans. Thanks to the GI Bill, the federal government subsidized the higher education of more than two million veterans, many of whom were immigrants or the first in their family to attend college. As one servicewoman who enrolled at the University of Minnesota in 1946 put it, "Without the GI Bill, I never would have gone to college and I would have lived with disappointment." The following year, when photographer Margaret Bourke-White traveled to the University of Iowa on behalf of *Life* magazine, she found that a remarkable 60 percent of the student body had served in World War II. She discovered, too, that the new veteran-student was "getting better grades than the non-veteran and has forced higher standards on everyone else."

The democratization of higher education had its bounds. Although their college enrollments surged from 37,000 in 1941 to 90,000 in 1961, Black people constituted just 5 percent of all college students while comprising 10 percent of the U.S. population. Women's enrollments increased, but the educational gap between white men and women widened as veterans flocked to college campuses. In 1940, women had earned 40 percent of undergraduate degrees, but their proportion dropped to 25 percent after World War II, rising to just 33 percent by 1960. Women were also more likely than men to drop out of college after marriage, taking jobs to support their husbands in school. Reflecting gender norms of the 1950s, white college women were assured that "it is natural for a woman to be satisfied with her husband's success and not crave personal achievement."

These important limitations aside, the tremendous growth of universities opened up new pathways to the middle class for large numbers of Americans. A better-educated and higher-paid workforce was another ingredient fueling the extraordinary prosperity of the postwar years.

REVIEW

How did technology contribute to economic growth, suburbanization, and the rise of the Sun Belt?

How did economic growth shape American society?

The United States in the 1950s became a full-fledged consumer society. The easy availability of credit, the wide array of products on offer, and the growing centrality of purchasing power to social status and personal identity changed the way Americans lived. The new medium of television both reflected and stimulated a consumer culture focused less on work than on the fruits of one's labor. More certain of a stable future—the effect of federal programs as well as economic abundance—Americans married at earlier ages, and the birthrate soared. This "baby boom" led to celebrations of family life. Less predictably, reassertions of traditional gender roles accompanied a modern consumer culture. But undercurrents of rebellion, especially among young people, and women's growing participation in the workforce would defy these norms. So would an emerging critique of consumerism from environmentalists and social critics.

What characterized American consumer culture?

Scorned by Khrushchev during the kitchen debate as unnecessary gadgets, consumer items flooded American society in the 1950s. Although the purchase and display of consumer goods was not new (see chapter 23), consumption became a reigning value at midcentury, vital for continued economic prosperity and equated in some quarters with patriotism and the American way of life. In place of a traditional emphasis on work and savings, advertisements encouraged satisfaction and happiness through the acquisition of consumer goods. Marketers dreamed up campaigns to persuade Americans that their lives would be improved through new and better products.

U.S. consumer culture at midcentury rested on a firm material base. Between 1950 and 1960, both the gross national product (the value of all goods and services produced) and median family income grew by 25 percent in constant dollars (**Figure 27.2**). Economists claimed that 60 percent of Americans enjoyed middle-class incomes in 1960. By then, the vast majority of all families owned a television set, nearly all had a refrigerator, and most owned at least one car. The number of shopping centers quadrupled between 1957 and 1963.

This unparalleled abundance was linked both to the **baby boom** and to new financial practices. The U.S. population surged from 152 million to 180 million during the 1950s, heightening demand for products and boosting industries ranging from

baby boom
Surge in the American birthrate between 1946 and 1964, which peaked in 1957 with 4.3 million births. The baby boom both reflected and promoted America's postwar prosperity.

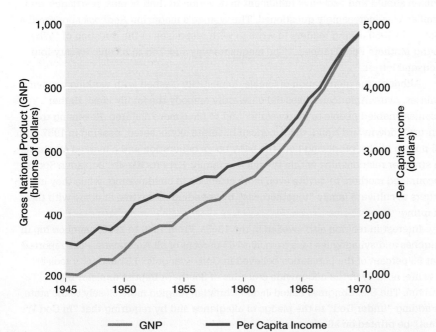

FIGURE 27.2 ◄ The Postwar Economic Boom: GNP and Per Capita Income, 1945–1970
Several factors — American dominance of the worldwide market, innovative technologies that led to new industries such as computers and plastics, population growth, and increases in worker productivity — contributed to the enormous economic growth of the United States after World War II.

suburban builders to toy manufacturers. Consumer borrowing also drove the economy, as buyers made purchases on installment plans and began to use credit cards. Increasingly, Americans enjoyed their possessions while they paid for them instead of waiting until they could buy items in full.

Although the sheer need to support themselves and their families motivated most women's employment, a desire to partake in "the good life" propelled growing numbers of women into the workforce. As one explained, "My Joe can't put five kids through college . . . and the washer had to be replaced, and Ann was ashamed to bring friends home because the living room furniture was such a mess, so I went to work." Anxiety about "keeping up with the Joneses," or staying up to date with the latest products and appliances, was a pressure peculiar to an affluent society. The rising cost—and standard—of living increasingly required a second income, even as television shows and magazine advertisements portrayed middle-class white women as homemakers first and foremost.

What explains the postwar revival of domesticity and religion?

In a reversal of—and partly in response to—the social trends of prior decades, traditional family life and gender roles were celebrated in the 1950s. Popular culture defined the ideal family as a male breadwinner, a full-time female homemaker, and three or four children. Feminist Betty Friedan gave a name to the idealization of women's domestic roles in her 1963 book *The Feminine Mystique*. Friedan criticized health professionals, scholars, advertisers, and public officials for assuming that biological differences dictated distinct roles for men and women. The belief that women should find exclusive fulfillment in devotion to their homes, marriages, and families was increasingly questioned. The women's magazine *Redbook* sponsored a contest in 1960 asking readers to write in with responses to the question of "Why Young Mothers Feel Trapped." The magazine was shocked to receive twenty-four thousand letters.

Although the glorification of female domesticity clashed with working women's realities, many Americans' lives did outwardly embody the family ideal. Higher incomes enabled people to marry earlier and to have more children. Reversing the century's downward trend, the American birthrate skyrocketed, peaking in 1957 with 4.3 million births, producing both the baby boom generation and a marked emphasis on stronger relationships within the nuclear family. Experts like Dr. Benjamin Spock encouraged mothers to devote even more attention to child rearing, while they urged fathers to cultivate family "togetherness" by spending more time at home with their offspring.

Interest in religion also swelled in the 1950s. From 1940 to 1960, membership in churches and synagogues rose from 50 to 63 percent of all Americans. Polls reported that 95 percent of the population believed in God. Evangelical Christianity took on new life, notably in the nationwide crusades of Southern Baptist minister Billy Graham. The U.S. Congress linked Judeo-Christian religion more closely to the state by adding "under God" to the pledge of allegiance and by requiring that "In God We Trust" be printed on all currency.

Religion helped many find meaning and comfort in the nuclear age. Ministers such as Graham linked spiritual faith to American victory in the Cold War, painting communism as a "sinister anti-Christian movement masterminded by Satan." Some critics questioned the depth of the religious revival, attributing the growth in church membership to a desire for conformity and a need for social outlets. One commentator noted that 53 percent of Americans could not name a single book of the Christian New Testament. Yet the trend was striking, countering earlier predictions of religion's waning significance in a scientific, secular nation.

How did television transform culture and politics?

The new medium of television altered American life as much as any other development in the 1950s. TV was both a product of midcentury consumer culture and a mirror held up to it, carrying Billy Graham's sermons as well as conventional gender norms into suburban living rooms. By 1960, nearly 90 percent of American homes contained a television set, and the average viewer spent more than five hours each day watching it. Situation comedies like *I Love Lucy* and *Father Knows Best* broadcasted the white nuclear family ideal alongside new leisure habits and consumer desires.

Television would also have a major impact on politics. Eisenhower's 1952 presidential campaign was the first to air TV ads, although he bewailed the fact that "an old soldier should come to this." By 1960, television played a central role in election campaigns. Reflecting on his narrow victory that year, president-elect John F. Kennedy remarked, "We wouldn't have had a prayer without that gadget." The expense of TV ads meant that fundraising would play an ever-larger role in politics. The ability to appeal directly to voters in their living rooms put a premium on personal attractiveness and encouraged candidates to build their own campaign organizations, relying less on political parties. While the declining strength of parties and the growing power of money in elections were not new trends, television greatly accelerated them.

◄ **Television Arrives in American Homes** A mother, father, and their children gather around the new family hearth in the mid-1950s. Television rapidly changed Americans' leisure habits; its programs also broadcast stereotypical images of the "standard" U.S. family. Harold M. Lambert/Getty Images.

Unlike government-financed television in Europe, private enterprise—meaning advertising—paid for American TV. What NBC called a "selling machine in every living room" became the major vehicle for fostering consumption. In 1961, Newton Minow, chairman of the Federal Communications Commission, called television a "vast wasteland." While acknowledging some of TV's achievements, particularly documentaries and drama, Minow depicted it as "a procession of game shows, . . . formula comedies about totally unbelievable families, blood and thunder, mayhem, violence, sadism, murder, . . . and cartoons." But viewers kept tuning in. In little more than a decade, television came to dominate Americans' leisure time, influence their consumption patterns, and shape their perceptions of public affairs.

Who were the critics of the affluent society?

Most Americans—recalling the deprivations of depression and war—embraced the bounty and convenience of a modern consumer society. Others, however, worried that the pursuit of new products and comforts had altered Americans' values as well as their habits. In *The Lonely Crowd* (1950), sociologist David Riesman lamented a shift from the "inner-directed" to the "other-directed" individual, as Americans seemingly replaced independent thinking with a desire to adapt to external standards of behavior and belief. William H. Whyte Jr., in his popular book *The Organization Man* (1956), likewise criticized Americans' quest for "belonging," blaming the modern corporation for making employees tailor themselves to the group. Best-selling exposés of subliminal advertising and the use of psychological manipulation to sell products reflected general unease with the priorities of a culture based around consumption.

A growing environmental critique blamed rapid development and unchecked consumerism for the pillage of natural resources and the American countryside. Other critics worried that Americans were privileging private life over public affairs. Economist John Kenneth Galbraith, who had described the United States as "the affluent society," warned in 1958 that the quest for private comforts was endangering public goods and public spaces. "The family which takes its . . . air-conditioned, power-steered and power-braked automobile out for a tour," he chided, "passes through cities that are badly paved" and "made hideous by litter."

Some critiques of 1950s culture stemmed from concern about the weakening of traditional masculinity, given that consumption was associated with women and that white-collar jobs no longer seemed to demand independence or aggressive action. The increase in married women's employment further undercut the presumed male role of breadwinner. Into this context arrived *Playboy*, which began publication in 1953 and quickly gained a circulation of one million. The new magazine redefined masculine independence as sophisticated bachelorhood and sexual freedom, pushing against middle-class norms of domesticity and respectability.

In fact, two best-selling studies published by Alfred Kinsey and other researchers at Indiana University—*Sexual Behavior in the Human Male* (1948) and *Sexual Behavior in the Human Female* (1953)—indicated that Americans' sexual practices regularly departed from the postwar family ideal. Large numbers of men and women reported that they had engaged in premarital sex and extramarital affairs; one-third of the men and one-seventh of the women reported homosexual experiences. The Kinsey Reports shocked many Americans but lent support to legal efforts to decriminalize homosexuality and to the midcentury homophile movement, which sought equal rights for individuals regardless of sexual orientation.

Challenges to mainstream standards also appeared in the everyday behavior of young Americans. "Roll over Beethoven and tell Tchaikovsky the news!" belted out Chuck Berry in his 1956 hit record celebrating rock and roll, a new form of music that grew out of Black rhythm and blues and mingled with the country and western traditions of the 1940s. White teenagers idolized Elvis Presley, who shocked their parents with his tight pants, hip-rolling gestures, and sensuous rock-and-roll music. "Before there was Elvis . . . I started going crazy for 'race music,'" recalled a white man of his teenage years. His words underscored African Americans' contributions to rock and roll, as well as the importance of Black music to the rebellions of white youth.

The most overt revolt against the social conformity of the 1950s came from the self-proclaimed Beat generation, a small group of mostly male literary figures based in New York City and San Francisco. Rejecting the values of the dominant culture—patriotism, consumerism, technology, and conventional family life—writers such as Allen Ginsberg and Jack Kerouac celebrated spontaneity and absolute personal freedom, including drug consumption and freewheeling sex. The Beats scandalized "square" Americans, but they would provide a model for a new movement of youthful dissidents in the 1960s.

Bold new styles in the visual arts also showed the 1950s to be much more than a decade of bland conformity. In New York City, action painting or abstract expressionism flowered, countering the idea that art should represent recognizable forms. Jackson Pollock and other abstract expressionists poured, dripped, and threw paint on canvases or substituted sticks and other implements for brushes. The new form of painting so captivated the Western art world that New York replaced Paris as its center.

REVIEW

What was the relationship between economic and cultural change in the 1950s?

Why did civil rights struggles erupt in the 1950s?

At the outset of the 1950s, every southern state mandated rigid segregation in public settings, ranging from schools to cemeteries. Segregation in practice, if not by law, was also commonplace in the North. Voting laws and practices in the South disfranchised the vast majority of Black people, who also faced systematic employment discrimination throughout the country.

Building on the civil rights initiatives begun during World War II, activists sought to topple discrimination and segregation. Although Black protest was as old as American racism, in the 1950s grassroots movements arose that forced change by capturing national attention and the support of white liberals. Ordinary Black people in substantial numbers sought their own liberation, launching a movement that would galvanize other disenfranchised groups and transform race relations in the United States. Pressed by civil rights activists, the Supreme Court delivered significant institutional reforms for Black and Mexican Americans. Native Americans, subject to shifting U.S. policies, faced their own struggles during these years—winning some claims against the government but losing tribal lands and some federal protections.

What was the status of race relations and civil rights in the postwar period?

"I spent four years in the army to free a bunch of Frenchmen and Dutchmen," a Black corporal declared, "and I'm hanged if I'm going to let the Alabama version of the Germans kick me around when I get home." Truman's civil rights legislation may have languished in Congress, but Black veterans and civilians alike resolved to root out the racial injustices of postwar America. The migration of two million African Americans to northern and western cities made the ballot a newly powerful tool, strengthening ongoing efforts to end discrimination in housing and education. Pursuing civil rights through the courts and Congress, the National Association for the Advancement of Colored People (NAACP) counted half a million members.

Individual Black Americans broke through the color barrier in the postwar years. Jackie Robinson integrated major league baseball, playing for the Brooklyn Dodgers and braving abuse from fans and players to win the Rookie of the Year Award in 1947. In 1950, Ralph J. Bunche received the Nobel Peace Prize for his United Nations work, and Gwendolyn Brooks won the Pulitzer Prize for poetry. Some organizations, such as the American Medical Association in 1949, opened their doors to Black members.

Still, little had changed for most Black people, especially in the South, where violence met their attempts to assert even the most basic rights of U.S. citizens. Armed white men prevented Medgar Evers—who would become a key civil rights leader in the 1960s—and four other veterans from voting in Mississippi. A mob lynched Isaac Nixon for voting in Georgia, and an all-white jury acquitted the men accused of his murder. White supremacy was not confined to the South. Segregation and economic discrimination were widespread in the North as well.

The Cold War, however, compelled U.S. leaders to pay fresh attention to racial issues. Soviet propaganda repeatedly highlighted racial injustice in the United States—a liability in the nation's quest for the allegiance of newly independent nations with nonwhite populations. Secretary of State Dean Acheson worried that segregation and racial discrimination jeopardized "our moral leadership of the free and democratic nations of the world." Black leaders pressed the argument, pointing to the human rights commitment of the new United Nations.

"My very stomach turned over when I learned that Negro soldiers just back from overseas were being dumped out of army trucks in Mississippi and beaten," wrote Truman. Risking the loss of support from southern white voters, Truman spoke more boldly on civil rights than had any previous president. In 1946, he created the President's Committee on Civil Rights, and in 1948, he asked Congress to enact its recommendations. The first president to address the NAACP, Truman

▶ **Desegregation of the Armed Services** Truman's 1948 executive order integrating the armed services met steely resistance from parts of the military and took years to implement fully. A photograph from that year shows Black and white soldiers together at a mess hall, but it was the Korean War that finally forced the U.S. armed services to fully integrate. In 1954, the army dissolved its last all-Black unit. National Archives photo no. 80-G-333985.

asserted that all Americans should have equal rights to housing, education, employment, and the ballot.

Truman did not match those words with effective action. Congress rejected his proposals for national civil rights legislation, although some states outside the South did pass laws against discrimination in employment and public accommodations. Truman's most significant step was an executive order desegregating the armed services. In part an appeal to northern Black and liberal voters leading up to the 1948 election, the order was not implemented until the Korean War, when the cost of segregation to military efficiency became apparent. Officers gradually integrated their ranks, so that by 1953, nearly all Black soldiers served in mixed units—making the military among the most integrated of all U.S. institutions. Truman's accomplishments fell far short of his proposals. But desegregation of the military and federal support of civil rights cases in the Supreme Court seeded far-reaching changes.

Mexican Americans fought injustices as well. In 1929, activists had formed the League of United Latin American Citizens (LULAC) to combat discrimination and segregation in the Southwest. Like Black soldiers, Mexican American veterans of World War II believed, as one insisted, that "we had earned our credentials as American citizens." Problems with obtaining their veterans' benefits spurred the formation of the American GI Forum in 1948 in Corpus Christi, Texas. Led by Dr. Héctor Peréz García, president of the local LULAC and a Bronze Star combat surgeon, the organization became a national force for battling discrimination and electing sympathetic officials.

Mexican American children were routinely subject to segregation in public schools. In 1945, with the help of LULAC, parents filed a class action suit in southern California, challenging school districts that barred their children from white schools. In the resulting decision, *Mendez v. Westminster* (1947), a federal court for the first time struck down school segregation, arguing that forced attendance at "Mexican schools" was unconstitutional and opposed to the principle of social equality. NAACP lawyer Thurgood Marshall filed a supporting brief in the case, which foreshadowed the landmark *Brown* decision.

In 1954, Mexican American citizens gained a victory in their ongoing struggle for civil rights in *Hernandez v. Texas*. The Supreme Court ruled unanimously that Mexican Americans were a distinct group entitled to equal protection under the Fourteenth Amendment and that their systematic exclusion from juries was unconstitutional. The lawyers who won the case were the first Mexican Americans in U.S. history to argue before the Supreme Court. Efforts to gain equal education, challenges to employment discrimination, and campaigns for political representation made evident the growing mobilization of Mexican Americans.

Hernandez v. Texas
1954 Supreme Court decision ruling that the systematic exclusion of Mexican Americans from juries violated the constitutional guarantee of equal protection.

◀ **Creation of the Indian Claims Commission** Flanked by representatives from two different Ute tribes, in 1946 Truman signed a bill enabling Native Americans to claim compensation for lands taken by the U.S. government, saying that the law would "mark the beginning of a new era for our Indian citizens." The commission would ultimately settle 285 cases, although the compensation never matched the land's worth. Bettmann/Getty Images.

The status of indigenous people in the United States was also changing. Some twenty-five thousand Native Americans had left their homes for military service and another forty thousand for work in defense industries. After the war, policymakers began to call for assimilating Native Americans and ending their special relationships with the government—amounting to a reversal of the New Deal emphasis on strengthening tribal governments and preserving indigenous cultures (see chapter 24).

To some officials, influenced by Cold War rhetoric, the communal practices of Native Americans resembled socialism and stifled individual initiative. But there were economic interests at stake as well: Native American tribes held rights to water, land, minerals, and other natural resources that were increasingly attractive to state governments and private entrepreneurs.

In the decade and a half after World War II, the government implemented a three-part Indian policy of compensation, termination, and relocation. In 1946, Congress established the Indian Claims Commission to hear outstanding claims by Native Americans for land taken by the government. When it closed in 1978, the commission had settled 285 cases, with compensation exceeding $800 million. This was only a partial victory for Native Americans, however, since the awards significantly underestimated the land's worth.

The second policy, called termination, also originated in the Truman administration as a pledge to do "nothing for Indians which Indians can do for themselves." Beginning in 1953 under Eisenhower, jurisdiction over tribal land was transferred to state and local entities, ending the trusteeship relationship between Indians and the federal government. The loss of federal hospitals, schools, and other special arrangements devastated Native American tribes. As had occurred after passage of the Dawes Act in 1887 (see chapter 17), corporate interests and private individuals took advantage of the opportunity to purchase Indian land cheaply. The government abandoned termination in the 1960s but only after more than one million acres of Native American land had been transferred to others' hands.

Indian Relocation Program
Federal initiative launched in 1948 to relocate Native Americans on reservations to cities and provide housing assistance, job training, and medical care. More than 100,000 Native Americans would take part, although a good number returned to reservation life and others struggled with urban poverty.

The **Indian Relocation Program**, the third piece of Native American policy, began in 1948 and involved more than 100,000 Native Americans by 1973. The government encouraged Indians to move to cities, where relocation centers were supposed to help with housing, job training, and medical care. The effects were dramatic: The percentage of Native Americans living in urban areas grew from 13.4 in 1950 to 44 in 1970.

Approximately one-third of the Native Americans who moved to urban areas, however, returned to reservations. Most who stayed in cities faced racism, unemployment, poor housing, and the loss of their traditional culture. "I wish we had never left home," said one woman whose husband was out of work. "It's dirty and noisy, and people all around, crowded. . . . It seems like I never see the sky or trees." Reflecting long-standing disagreements among Indians themselves, some who overcame these obstacles applauded the program. But most urban Indians remained poor, and some worried that "we would lose our identity as Indian people, lose our culture and our [way] of living." Within two decades, a national pan-Indian movement—a byproduct of urbanization—emerged to resist assimilation and to demand Native American rights (see chapter 28).

How did Black activists challenge the Supreme Court and the president?

Several factors propelled Black protest in the 1950s. Between 1940 and 1960, more than three million African Americans migrated from the South to areas where they had a political voice. Black leaders publicized how racist practices at home tarnished the U.S. image abroad and handicapped the United States in its competition with the Soviet Union. The very fact of segregation meant that Black activists controlled certain organizational resources, such as Black churches, colleges, and newspapers, where leadership skills could be honed and networks developed.

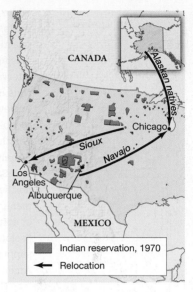

Major Native American Relocations, 1950–1970

The legal strategy of the NAACP reached its crowning achievement with the Supreme Court's ruling in **Brown v. Board of Education** in 1954. Oliver Brown, a World War II veteran in Topeka, Kansas, filed suit because his daughter was barred from the white school near their home, forced instead to attend a Black school more than a mile away. In Virginia, sixteen-year-old Barbara Johns initiated a student strike over wretched conditions in her all-Black high school, leading to another of the suits taken up in *Brown*. The NAACP's lead lawyer, future Supreme Court justice Thurgood Marshall, urged the Court to overturn the "separate but equal" precedent established in *Plessy v. Ferguson* in 1896 (see chapter 21). A unanimous Court, headed by Chief Justice Earl Warren, agreed, declaring that "Separate educational facilities are inherently unequal" and thus violated the Fourteenth Amendment.

Ultimate responsibility for enforcement of the decision lay with President Eisenhower, but he refused to endorse *Brown*. He also kept silent in 1955 when white men murdered Emmett Till, a fourteen-year-old Black boy who had allegedly whistled at a white woman in Mississippi. Eisenhower's own racial prejudice, his preference for limited federal intervention in the states, and his leadership style favoring consensus and gradual progress led him to distance the White House from civil rights issues.

Such inaction fortified southern resistance. In September 1957, Governor Orval Faubus sent Arkansas National Guard troops to block the enrollment of nine Black students at Little Rock's Central High School. He later allowed the students to enter but withdrew the National Guard, leaving the "Little Rock Nine" to face an angry

> **Brown v. Board of Education**
> 1954 Supreme Court ruling that overturned the "separate but equal" precedent established in *Plessy v. Ferguson* in 1896. The Court declared that segregated educational facilities were inherently unequal and thus violated the Fourteenth Amendment.

white mob. "During those years when we desperately needed approval from our peers," Melba Patillo Beals remembered, "we were victims of the most harsh rejection imaginable." As television cameras transmitted the ugly scene, Eisenhower was forced to send regular army troops to Little Rock, the first federal military intervention in the South since Reconstruction. Paratroopers escorted the Little Rock Nine into Central High, staying for the remainder of the school year. Faubus, however, closed the public schools the next fall in order to prevent integration, provoking no further response from the president. White resistance to integration, whether via mob violence or school closings, continued across the South. **(See "Analyzing Historical Evidence: The *Brown* Decision" on page 818.)**

School segregation outside the South was not usually sanctioned by law, but northern school districts found ways to separate Black and white students by manipulating neighborhood boundaries. Even before *Brown*, Black parents in dozens of northern cities had challenged the assignment of their children to inferior "colored" schools. While they had some successes, residential segregation, often supported by federal housing policies, made school segregation a reality for Black Americans in both the North and South.

Civil rights agitation resulted in some congressional and presidential action. Eisenhower ordered the integration of public facilities in Washington, D.C., and on military bases, and he supported the first federal civil rights legislation since Reconstruction. Yet the Civil Rights Acts of 1957 and 1960 were largely symbolic. Baseball star Jackie Robinson spoke for many Black Americans when he wired Eisenhower in 1957, "We disagree that half a loaf is better than none. Have waited this long for a bill with meaning—can wait a little longer." Eisenhower appointed the first Black professional to his White House staff, but E. Frederick Morrow confided in his diary, "I feel ridiculous . . . trying to defend the administration's record on civil rights."

What led to the Montgomery mass protest?

The civil rights movement of the 1950s and 1960s drew on earlier acts of Black resistance. What set it apart was its widespread presence in the South, the large number of participants, their willingness to confront white institutions directly, and their use of nonviolent protest and civil disobedience to bring about change. The Congress of Racial Equality and other groups had experimented with these tactics in the 1940s, organizing to integrate movie theaters, restaurants, and swimming pools in northern cities. In the South, the first sustained protest to claim national attention began in Montgomery, Alabama, on December 1, 1955.

That day, police arrested a Black woman, Rosa Parks, for violating a local segregation ordinance. Riding a crowded bus home from work, she refused to give up her seat in the white section so that a man could sit down. She resisted not because she was physically tired, she recalled; rather she was "tired of giving in." Parks had long been active in the local NAACP, headed by E. D. Nixon, and had sought an opportunity to challenge bus segregation. So had the Women's Political Council (WPC), led by Jo Ann Robinson, an English professor at Alabama State, who had once been humiliated by a bus driver when she accidentally sat in the white section.

▲ **Civil Rights Activism in the North** Black protest had a long history in the North, where African Americans and their allies battled job discrimination and segregation in schools, housing, and public accommodations. Here, demonstrators march outside the Stork Club in New York City in 1951, protesting its refusal to serve the world-famous dancer, singer, and actress Josephine Baker. Note how one of the signs capitalizes on Cold War rhetoric. FPG/Getty Images.

When word came that Parks would fight her arrest, WPC leaders mobilized teachers and students to distribute fliers urging Black residents to boycott the buses. E. D. Nixon called a mass meeting at a Black church, where those assembled founded the Montgomery Improvement Association (MIA). The MIA arranged volunteer carpools and marshaled most of the Black community to sustain what became the yearlong **Montgomery bus boycott**.

Elected to head the MIA was twenty-six-year-old Martin Luther King Jr., a young Baptist pastor with a doctorate in theology from Boston University. A captivating speaker, King addressed mass meetings at Black churches throughout the bus boycott, inspiring courage and commitment by linking racial justice to Christianity. He promised, "If you will protest courageously and yet with dignity and Christian love . . . historians will have to pause and say, 'There lived a great people—a black people—who injected a new meaning and dignity into the veins of civilization.'"

The Black people of Montgomery summoned their courage and determination. Boycotters walked miles or carpooled to get to work, contributed their meager financial resources to the cause, and stood up to intimidation and police harassment. One older woman declared, "I'm not walking for myself, I'm walking for my children and my grandchildren." Authorities arrested several leaders, and a white segregationist firebombed King's house. Yet the boycott persisted until November 1956, when the Supreme Court declared Alabama's laws requiring bus segregation unconstitutional.

Montgomery bus boycott
Yearlong boycott of Montgomery's segregated bus system in 1955–1956 by the city's Black population. The boycott brought Martin Luther King Jr. to national prominence and ended in victory when the Supreme Court declared segregated transportation unconstitutional.

ANALYZING HISTORICAL EVIDENCE

The *Brown* Decision

Responding to lawsuits argued by NAACP lawyers, *Brown v. Board of Education* was the culmination of a series of Supreme Court rulings that chipped away at an earlier Court's decision in *Plessy v. Ferguson* (1896) permitting "separate but equal" public facilities for white and Black Americans.

DOCUMENT 1
Brown v. Board of Education, May 1954

In 1954, Chief Justice Earl Warren delivered the unanimous opinion of the Supreme Court, declaring racial segregation in public education unconstitutional.

It is doubtful that any child may reasonably be expected to succeed in life if he is denied the opportunity of an education. Such an opportunity, if the state has undertaken to provide it, is a right that must be made available to all on equal terms. . . .

We come then to the question presented: Does segregation of children in public schools solely on the basis of race, even though the physical facilities and other "tangible" factors may be equal, deprive the children of the minority group of equal educational opportunities?

We believe that it does. . . . In *McLaurin* [a 1950 case], the Court, in requiring that a Negro admitted to a white graduate school be treated like all other students, again resorted to intangible considerations: ". . . his ability to study, to engage in discussions and exchange views with other students, and, in general, to learn his profession." Such considerations apply with added force to children in grade and high schools. To separate them from others of similar age and qualifications solely because of their race generates a feeling of inferiority as to their status in the community that may affect their hearts and minds in a way unlikely ever to be undone.

We conclude that in the field of public education the doctrine of "separate but equal" has no place. Separate educational facilities are inherently unequal.

Source: *Brown v. Board of Education*, 347 U.S. 483 (1954).

DOCUMENT 2
Southern Manifesto on Integration, March 1956

The Brown *decision outraged many southern white people. In 1956, more than one hundred members of Congress signed a manifesto pledging resistance to the ruling.*

We regard the decision of the Supreme Court in the school cases as a clear abuse of judicial power. It climaxes a trend in the Federal judiciary undertaking to legislate . . . and to encroach upon the reserved rights of the states and the people.

The original Constitution does not mention education. Neither does the Fourteenth Amendment nor any amendment. . . . The Supreme Court of the United States, with no legal basis for such action, undertook to exercise their naked judicial power and substituted their personal political and social ideas for the established law of the land.

This unwarranted exercise of power by the court, contrary to the Constitution, is creating chaos and confusion in the states principally affected. It is destroying the amicable relations between the white and negro races that have been created through ninety years of patient effort by the good people of both races. . . .

We pledge ourselves to use all lawful means to bring about a reversal of this decision which is contrary to the Constitution and to prevent the use of force in its implementation.

Source: "Southern Manifesto on Integration," *Congressional Record*, 84th Congress, 2nd Session, vol. 102, pt. 4 (Washington, D.C.: Government Printing Office, 1956), 4459–60.

In the face of white hostility, Black children carried the burden of implementing the Brown *decision, as these accounts of their experiences in newly integrated schools testify.*

DOCUMENT 3
A High School Boy in Oak Ridge, Tennessee, 1957

I like it a whole lot better than the colored school. You have a chance to learn more and you have more sports. I play forward or guard on the basketball team, only I don't get to participate in all games. Some teams don't mind my playing. Some teams object not because of the fellows on the team, but because of the people in their community. Mostly it's the fans or the board of education that decides against me. . . .

Source: Dorothy Sterling, *Tender Warriors* (New York: Hill and Wang, 1958), 83. Copyright © 1958 by Hill and Wang.

DOCUMENT 4
A High School Girl in the Deep South, May 1966

I chose to go because I felt that I could get a better education here. I knew that the [Black] school that I was then attending wasn't giving me exactly what I should have had. . . . As far as the Science Department was concerned, it just didn't have the chemicals we needed and I just decided to change. When I went over the students there weren't very friendly and when I graduated they still weren't. They didn't want us there and they made that plain, but we went there anyway and we stuck it out.

Source: *In Their Own Words: A Student Appraisal of What Happened after School Desegregation* (Washington, D.C.: Department of Health, Education, and Welfare, Office of Education, 1966), 44.

DOCUMENT 5
A High School Girl in the Deep South, May 1966

The first day a news reporter rode the bus with us. All around us were state troopers. In front of them were federal marshals. When we got to town there were lines of people and cars all along the road. A man without a badge or anything got on the bus and started beating up the newspaper reporter. . . . When we got to the school the students were all around looking through the windows. The mayor said we couldn't come there because the school was already filled to capacity. We turned around and the students started yelling and clapping. When we went back [after obtaining a court order] there were no students there at all. [The white students did not return, so the six black students finished the year by themselves.] The shocking thing was during the graduation ceremonies. All six of the students got together to make a speech. After we finished, I looked around and saw three teachers crying. The principal had tears in his eyes and he got up to make a little speech about us. He said at first he didn't think he would enjoy being around us. You could see in his face that he was really touched.

Source: *In Their Own Words: A Student Appraisal of What Happened after School Desegregation* (Washington, D.C.: Department of Health, Education, and Welfare, Office of Education, 1966), 17–18.

Questions for Analysis

RECOGNIZE VIEWPOINTS: What reasons did the Supreme Court give in favor of desegregation? What reasons did Black students give for wanting to attend integrated schools? How do these reasons differ?

ANALYZE THE EVIDENCE: On what grounds did signers of the "Southern Manifesto" argue that the Supreme Court decision violated the Constitution?

CONSIDER THE CONTEXT: Why did President Eisenhower initially resist desegregation, and what steps did he eventually take to support integration?

King's appearance on the cover of *Time* magazine in February 1957 marked his rapid rise to national and international fame. Black clergy from across the South chose King to head the Southern Christian Leadership Conference (SCLC), newly established to coordinate local protests against segregation and disfranchisement. The prominence of King and other ministers tended to overshadow the substantial numbers of Black women whose grassroots action would be crucial to the movement. King's fame and the media's focus on the South also obscured the national scope of racial injustice. Yet the push for racial equality would dramatically transform both the North and the South in the years to come.

REVIEW

What enabled civil rights to become a mass movement in the 1950s?

Conclusion: What challenges did prosperity mask?

At the American exhibit in Moscow in 1959, the consumer goods that Nixon proudly displayed to Khrushchev spoke to two related themes: American prosperity and superpower rivalry. The era's tremendous economic growth, raising the standard of living for most Americans, was often celebrated as the product of a free enterprise system. But it rested on federal Cold War defense spending as well. The large military outlays that began under Truman helped jump-start postwar prosperity. Eisenhower's continued defense spending, along with housing, highway, and education subsidies, sustained the economic boom.

Prosperity changed the very landscape of the United States. Suburban housing developments sprang up, interstate highways cut up cities and connected the country, farms declined in number but grew in size, and people and industry moved south and west. Not all Americans welcomed these changes, some decrying consumerism and its environmental costs. Nor did all Americans benefit from economic growth. At the height of the affluent society, a shocking forty million people lived in poverty. Material abundance masked other developments as well: persistent racial injustice and rising resistance to it, married women's movement into the labor force, and the stirrings of a youth rebellion.

Compared to the vigorous federal activity of the New Deal years, the Truman and Eisenhower administrations—focused on the Cold War contest—enacted little in the way of landmark legislation. The most important domestic development of the postwar era would come not from elected leaders but from the assertion of citizenship rights by those who had been left outside the affluent society's promise, whether Mexican Americans in Los Angeles or Black Americans in Montgomery and Little Rock. In the 1960s, new leaders would take up the struggle against communism. They would also grapple with unaddressed domestic challenges of racism, poverty, and urban decay. As a new decade dawned, the stage was set for turbulence and conflict.

EXPLAIN WHY IT MATTERS

Servicemen's Readjustment Act (p. 796)

Fair Deal (p. 796)

Taft-Hartley Act (p. 797)

Dixiecrats (p. 797)

Housing Act of 1949 (p. 797)

National Interstate and Defense Highways Act of 1956 (p. 798)

Sun Belt (p. 803)

bracero program (p. 804)

baby boom (p. 807)

Hernandez v. Texas (p. 813)

Indian Relocation Program (p. 814)

Brown v. Board of Education (p. 815)

Montgomery bus boycott (p. 817)

PUT IT ALL TOGETHER

DOMESTIC POLITICS AND POLICY

• How did Truman aim to expand the New Deal, and what prevented him from enacting this agenda?

• What did Eisenhower's "middle way" suggest about American politics in the 1950s?

CULTURAL CURRENTS

• How did prosperity shape living patterns for white working-class and middle-class Americans in the 1950s?

• What developments challenged the celebration of American consumer culture in the 1950s?

CIVIL RIGHTS

• Why was *Brown v. Board of Education* such a pivotal legal ruling in the history of the civil rights movement?

• How and why did the Montgomery bus boycott succeed?

LOOKING BACKWARD, LOOKING AHEAD

• Compare and contrast the culture and society of 1920s with that of 1950s.

• What tensions in 1950s America would become defining political conflicts of the 1960s?

28

RIGHTS, REBELLION, AND REACTION

1960–1974

This chapter discusses the following questions:

- How did Kennedy and Johnson expand the role of government?
- How did the Black freedom movement evolve?
- Why did so many social movements emerge in the 1960s?
- What sparked a new wave of feminism?
- Why and where did the conservative movement gain ground?
- Conclusion: What were the lasting effects of sixties-era liberalism?

▶ **Pauli Murray** Activist, lawyer, poet, professor, and Episcopal priest, Pauli Murray played a leading role in multiple rights movements of the postwar era. She made analogies between racial and gender discrimination and challenged both through powerful legal scholarship that influenced a series of landmark U.S. Supreme Court rulings. Civil rights activist Eleanor Holmes Norton noted that Murray "lived on the edge of history, seeming to pull it along with her." AP Photo.

AN AMERICAN STORY

Even as a child, Pauli Murray resisted Jim Crow, refusing to ride on segregated streetcars and boycotting movie theaters where African Americans were restricted to the balcony. Most of all, Murray detested segregated buses, which "permitted the public humiliation of black people to be carried out in the presence of privileged white spectators." As an adult and civil rights lawyer, Murray waged a battle against all forms of social injustice, playing a key role in the rights revolution of the 1960s.

Anna Pauline Murray was born in 1910 to a family of African, European, and Native American descent and to a lifetime of struggle with her gender and sexual identity. She was orphaned at a young age and lived with relatives in North Carolina. Going north for college, she became a labor activist in New York. In 1938, Murray applied to graduate school at the University of North Carolina, where her white great-great-grandfather had been a trustee, but was rejected on the basis of her race. Several years later, after being arrested for refusing to give up her seat on a bus in Richmond, Virginia, Murray set her sights on law school with "the single-minded intention of destroying Jim Crow."

Denied admission to Harvard because of her sex, Murray was the sole woman in her cohort at Howard University Law School. While a law student, Murray led the first successful sit-in to desegregate restaurants in Washington, D.C., nearly two decades before that tactic would transform the civil rights movement in the South. She also helped frame a successful legal attack on the principle of "separate but equal." Her scholarship underpinned Thurgood Marshall's arguments in the landmark *Brown v. Board of Education* (1954) case.

Graduating first in her class, Murray gained a legal education but also a feminist consciousness; belittled by her male peers, she became a fierce critic of what she termed "Jane Crow." By the 1960s, along with a new generation of feminists, Murray turned her energies to toppling gender discrimination. In 1962, Eleanor Roosevelt invited Murray to serve on President Kennedy's Commission on the Status of Women, where she argued for legal analogies between sex and race. At one point, Murray proposed an "NAACP for women" to feminist Betty Friedan, leading to the founding of the National Organization for Women in 1966.

In 1965, Murray became the first Black recipient of a Yale Law School degree. Her arguments — adopted by Ruth Bader Ginsburg in the 1970s — persuaded the Supreme Court that women were entitled to constitutional protection against discrimination. Murray would go on to a

1972	Title IX bans sex discrimination in education.
1973	Endangered Species Act becomes law.
	Roe v. Wade decided in favor of abortion rights.

history professorship at Brandeis University and later became the first Black woman ordained as an Episcopal priest.

Pauli Murray died before a movement emerged to defend the rights of transgender people, a cause she likely would have embraced both personally and politically. Her legal strategies supported an expansive era of social reform that was carried from grassroots activists all the way to the Supreme Court.

How did Kennedy and Johnson expand the role of government?

At the Democratic National Convention in 1960, John F. Kennedy proclaimed a "New Frontier" that would confront "unsolved problems of peace and war, unconquered pockets of ignorance and prejudice, unanswered questions of poverty and surplus." Four years later, Lyndon B. Johnson invoked a "Great Society" that promised "abundance and liberty for all" and "an end to poverty and racial injustice." Each professed a liberal faith in the federal government to solve social and economic problems.

Prodded by the civil rights movement and assisted by momentous Supreme Court decisions as well as postwar prosperity, liberals' agenda in the 1960s expanded beyond the economic security of the New Deal to include individual rights and racial justice. Johnson won legislation on civil rights, poverty, education, medical care, housing, consumer safety, and environmental protection. This broad agenda also set off political fights. Activists on the left charged that the government had not gone far enough in rectifying social inequalities, while a growing conservative movement pushed back against the growth of federal power.

What were JFK's foreign and domestic priorities?

John F. Kennedy, or JFK, grew up in privilege in Massachusetts, the son of an Irish Catholic businessman who became a New Deal official and the U.S. ambassador to Britain. His distinguished World War II navy record helped Kennedy win election to the House of Representatives in 1946 and to the Senate in 1952. He went on to secure the Democratic presidential nomination in 1960, supported by a powerful political machine, his family's fortune, and a dynamic personal appeal. Kennedy surprised many Democrats by choosing as his running mate Lyndon B. Johnson of Texas, whom liberals disparaged as a typical southern conservative. In the general election, Kennedy narrowly defeated his

Republican opponent, Vice President Richard M. Nixon (**Map 28.1**), who had made his name as an anti-Communist crusader. Black voters contributed to JFK's victory, and Johnson helped carry the South. Kennedy also benefited from the nation's first televised presidential debates, at which he appeared cool and confident beside a nervous and pale Nixon.

At forty-three, JFK was the youngest man and the first Roman Catholic to be elected president. His administration projected energy, idealism, and glamour, while the press kept from the public his serious health problems and extramarital affairs.

At his inauguration, Kennedy called on Americans to serve the common good. "Ask not what your country can do for you," he implored. "Ask what you can do for your country." JFK made these remarks in the context of the superpower struggle, declaring that the United States would "pay any price, bear any burden, meet any hardship, support any friend, oppose any foe to assure the survival and the success of liberty." Especially early in his presidency, Kennedy's commitment to fighting communism abroad—from resisting Castro in Cuba to increasing the U.S. presence in South Vietnam (see chapter 29)—took precedence over rights and reform at home.

Candidate	Electoral Vote	Popular Vote	Percent of Popular Vote
John F. Kennedy (Democrat)	303	34,227,096	49.9
Richard M. Nixon (Republican)	219	34,108,546	49.6
Harry F. Byrd (Independent)	15	501,643	0

MAP 28.1 The Election of 1960

JFK launched the Peace Corps in 1961 in a bid to enhance the reputation of the United States in developing nations. The program recruited young people to open schools, provide basic medical care, and assist with agriculture and small businesses in Latin America, Africa, and Asia. Kennedy, however, failed to persuade Congress to enact legislation to improve education and health care at home. Despite courting Black votes to get elected, Kennedy also refused to take the lead on racial justice. Pledging during the campaign to end segregation in federally subsidized public housing "with the stroke of a pen," Kennedy did not act once in office, leading civil rights groups to mail him pens by the thousands to remind him of his promise. Ultimately, only the bloody confrontations sparked by mass protest prompted him to take a public stand on civil rights.

Still, the idealism of Kennedy's rhetoric inspired many. Moved by the desperate conditions he observed while campaigning in Appalachia, the president brought attention to some of the problems that the affluent society had evaded. After reading Michael Harrington's *The Other America*, which identified more than one in five Americans as "maimed in body and spirit, existing at levels beneath those necessary for human decency," Kennedy pushed poverty onto the national agenda. By 1962, he had won support for a $2 billion urban renewal program, providing job training for the unemployed and incentives to businesses to locate in economically depressed areas. The next year, he asked aides to explore a full-scale attack on poverty. Kennedy also called for an enormous tax cut to increase consumer demand and create jobs.

Kennedy's domestic efforts were in their infancy when he was assassinated on November 22, 1963, as his motorcade passed through Dallas, Texas. Within minutes of the shooting, radio and television broadcast the unfolding horror to the nation. Stunned Americans struggled to understand what had happened. The police arrested Lee Harvey Oswald, who had fired the shots from a nearby building. Two days later, Oswald himself was shot and killed while officers were transferring him from one jail to another. Some claimed that a conspiracy of ultraconservatives or Communists was behind these murders, but a presidential commission eventually concluded that both Oswald and his killer had acted alone.

Kennedy's domestic record was unremarkable in his first two years, but his attention to civil rights, job training, and poverty in 1963 signaled an important shift. Could JFK have persuaded Congress to enact his proposals? It would be up to his vice president to secure and expand the liberal agenda that Kennedy had hinted at.

How did LBJ wage the War on Poverty?

Lyndon B. Johnson, or LBJ, assumed the presidency with a wealth of political experience. Growing up in the Texas Hill Country, Johnson experienced firsthand some of the economic instability of the rural South. As a young man, he taught at a Mexican American school, where the poverty of his students made a lasting impression on him.

Johnson won election in 1937 to the House of Representatives and in 1948 to the Senate, where he served skillfully as Senate majority leader. His modest upbringing, his admiration for Franklin Roosevelt, and his ambition to outdo the New Deal president underpinned LBJ's commitment to reform. The pressure generated by the Black freedom struggle and other social movements also decisively shaped his political agenda.

Johnson excelled behind the scenes, where he could entice, maneuver, or threaten legislators to support his objectives. His persuasive power, the famous "Johnson treatment," became legendary. In his ability to achieve his legislative goals, Johnson had few peers in American history.

Civil Rights Act of 1964
Law that made discrimination in employment, education, and public accommodations illegal. It was the strongest such measure since Reconstruction and included a ban on sex discrimination in employment.

War on Poverty
Set of programs organized through LBJ's Office of Economic Opportunity to reduce poverty through education and training as well as by including the poor in policymaking.

Just days after Kennedy's assassination, Johnson entreated Congress to act so that "John Fitzgerald Kennedy did not live or die in vain." He quickly pushed through Kennedy's tax cut bill, contributing to an economic boom and a drop in unemployment. More remarkable was passage of the **Civil Rights Act of 1964**. The strongest such measure since Reconstruction, the law made discrimination in employment, education, and public accommodations illegal. Given opposition by southern Democrats, its passage required every ounce of Johnson's political skill to pry sufficient votes from Republicans. In the lead-up to the Senate vote, one Republican aide reported that Johnson "never left him alone for thirty minutes."

Antipoverty legislation followed fast on the heels of the Civil Rights Act of 1964. Johnson announced "an unconditional war on poverty" in his January 1964 State of the Union message. In August, Congress passed the Economic Opportunity Act, the opening shot in Johnson's **War on Poverty**. The law authorized ten new programs, allocating $800 million for the first year—or about 1 percent of the federal budget. Many provisions targeted children and youth, including Head Start for preschoolers,

◄ **Johnson in Appalachia** On a public relations tour to promote his Economic Opportunity Act, LBJ visited the family of Tom Fletcher, an unemployed white coal miner in Kentucky. Married and the father of eight children, Fletcher was chosen by the White House to represent the face of American poverty — the roughly 20 percent of the U.S. population who lived on less than $3,000 a year, the poverty threshold for a family of four. Johnson reportedly remarked, "I don't know if I'll pass a single law or get a single dollar appropriated, but before I'm through, no community in America will be able to ignore poverty in its midst." Bettmann/Getty Images.

work-study grants for college students, and the Job Corps for unemployed young people. The Volunteers in Service to America (VISTA) program paid modest wages to those working with the disadvantaged, and a legal services program provided lawyers for the poor.

The most controversial part of the law, the Community Action Program (CAP), required "maximum feasible participation" of the poor themselves in antipoverty projects. Funds were funneled to public and private agencies in an attempt to reach people in need directly and to combat entrenched racial discrimination in local government. Poor people organized to make welfare agencies, school boards, police departments, and housing authorities more accountable to the people they served. Local officials resisted such demands, leading Johnson to back off from genuine representation for the poor. Still, CAP opened opportunities for political leadership and federal funds to those usually excluded from government decision-making.

What were the aims of the Great Society?

As the 1964 election approached, Johnson projected stability and security in the midst of a booming economy—a dramatic contrast to his far-right Republican opponent, Arizona senator Barry M. Goldwater, who attacked the welfare state and entertained the use of nuclear weapons in Vietnam. Johnson achieved a record-breaking 61 percent of the popular vote, and Democrats won resounding majorities in the House and Senate. Still, Goldwater's considerable support marked a growing conservative movement and a looming threat to Democratic control of the South.

Johnson laid out an ambitious vision for what he called the "Great Society," taking aim at the unfinished business of the New Deal and Fair Deal but also pressing beyond it. Thanks to large Democratic majorities in Congress, his own political skills, and grassroots pressure, Johnson achieved legislation on discrimination, poverty, education, medical care, housing, urban development, consumer and environmental protection, and the arts. Reporters called the legislation of the Eighty-Ninth Congress (1965–1966) "a political miracle."

Poverty remained a core focus of Johnson's Great Society. Congress doubled the funding for the Economic Opportunity Act, authorized economic development measures for depressed regions, and allocated more than $1 billion to improve the nation's poorest urban areas. The government offered direct aid as well. A new food stamp program gave those in poverty greater choice in obtaining food, and rent supplements provided alternatives to public housing.

Poor people also formed their own grassroots movements, most prominently the National Welfare Rights Organization. Assisted by antipoverty lawyers, mothers on welfare pushed administrators of Aid to Families with Dependent Children (AFDC) to ease restrictions on welfare recipients and to treat people on low incomes with greater dignity. The number of families receiving assistance jumped from less than one million in 1960 to three million by 1972, a full 90 percent of those eligible.

Johnson's War on Poverty favored expanding individual opportunity—through education, job training, food security, health care, and political empowerment—rather than redistributing income. The Elementary and Secondary Education Act of 1965, a turning point in involving the federal government in K–12 education, channeled funds to local school districts and provided equipment to private and parochial schools serving the poor. That same year, Congress passed the Higher Education Act, vastly expanding federal assistance to colleges and universities for buildings, programs, scholarships, and student loans.

Medicare and Medicaid
Federal support for health care enacted as part of Lyndon Johnson's Great Society. Medicare provided older Americans with universal compulsory medical insurance financed primarily through Social Security taxes. Medicaid authorized federal grants to supplement state-paid medical care for poor people of all ages.

An even greater watershed was the federal government's entry into health care. Faced with a powerful medical lobby opposed to national health insurance, Johnson focused on older Americans, who continued to make up a large portion of the nation's poor. Congress responded in 1965 with the **Medicare** program, providing those age sixty-five and older with universal medical insurance financed largely through Social Security taxes. A separate program, **Medicaid**, used federal grants to supplement state-paid medical care for poor people. By the twenty-first century, these two programs covered 87 million Americans, nearly 30 percent of the population.

◀ **The National Welfare Rights Organization March to End Hunger in 1968** On Mother's Day in 1968, the National Welfare Rights Organization led a 7,000-strong march against hunger through the streets of Washington, D.C. Part of the Poor People's Campaign organized by Martin Luther King Jr. before his death, activists demanded federal funding for full employment, a guaranteed annual income, and low-income housing. Jack Rottier Photograph Collection C0003, Box 8, page 23, Special Collections Research Center. George Mason University Libraries.

Programs such as Medicare fulfilled long-standing liberal goals. But the Great Society's attention to racial discrimination was a break with the past. Advised early on not to waste his political capital on civil rights, Johnson retorted, "What the hell's the presidency for?" Whereas many New Deal programs excluded or discriminated against people of color, the Civil Rights Act of 1964 finally made discrimination in employment, education, and public accommodations illegal. The **Voting Rights Act of 1965** banned literacy tests and other practices used to disqualify Black voters and authorized federal intervention to ensure access to the voting booth.

The Immigration and Nationality Act of 1965 tackled another form of discrimination: quotas based on national origins, which had been installed in 1924 to bar immigrants from areas other than western Europe (see chapter 23). The new law maintained caps on the total number of immigrants, however, and for the first time included the Western Hemisphere in those limits; preference was now given to immediate relatives of U.S. citizens and to those with desirable skills.

Great Society benefits reached well beyond victims of discrimination and the poor. Medicare covered older Americans, regardless of income. Consumer activism led to legislation making cars safer and tightening standards for the food, drug, and cosmetics industries. LBJ insisted that the Great Society meet "not just the needs of the body but the desire for beauty and hunger for community." In 1965, he sent Congress the first presidential message on the environment, obtaining measures to control water and air pollution and to preserve the natural beauty of the American landscape. The National Arts and Humanities Act of 1965 funded artists, musicians, writers, and scholars and brought their work to public audiences.

Assessing Johnson's legislative accomplishments, Senate majority leader Mike Mansfield concluded that the president "has done more than FDR ever did, or ever thought of doing." The flood of reform legislation dwindled after 1966, however, when Democratic majorities in Congress shrank and conservative opposition to government programs gained ground. The Vietnam War dealt the largest blow, diverting Johnson's attention, spawning an antiwar movement that crippled his leadership, and devouring tax dollars that might have been used for reform (see chapter 29).

In 1968, Johnson obtained one more civil rights law, which banned discrimination in housing and jury service. He also signed the National Housing Act of 1968, which authorized an enormous increase in low-income housing: 1.7 million units over three years.

Voting Rights Act of 1965 Law that empowered the federal government to supervise election processes and intervene to ensure access to the voting booth. As a result of the act, Black voting and officeholding in the South shot up, initiating a major transformation in southern politics.

What were the legacies of the Great Society?

Great Society programs like food stamps and Medicaid extended the reach and responsibility of the federal government. Federal expenditures on health, education, and welfare tripled, constituting more than 15 percent of the U.S. budget by 1970.

The result was a significant reduction in poverty. The number of poor Americans, more than 20 percent of the population in 1959, fell to approximately 13 percent in 1968. Those who in Johnson's words "live[d] on the outskirts of hope" found new opportunities. A Mexican American who learned to be a sheet metal worker through a job training program reported, "[My children] will finish high school and maybe go to college. . . . I see my family and I know the chains are broken."

Government spending in the 1960s improved the lives of millions, even if Johnson could not claim victory in the War on Poverty. Older Americans fared better than others. Many male-headed families rose out of poverty, but impoverishment among female-headed families increased. White people escaped poverty faster than did people of color. Great Society programs contributed to a burgeoning Black middle class, yet one in three African Americans remained in poverty (**Figure 28.1**).

Johnson's War on Poverty triggered fierce political debate. Conservative critics charged that the government had overstepped its bounds and that the new programs discouraged individual initiative and fostered family dysfunction by giving "handouts" to the poor. Liberal critics claimed that focusing on training and education wrongly targeted poor people rather than an economic system that could not provide enough adequately paying jobs.

Unlike the New Deal, the Great Society avoided structural reform of the economy. Funded by economic growth rather than new taxes on the wealthy or middle class, Johnson's poverty programs led to no significant redistribution of income. Paid for by prosperity, these programs would become vulnerable in less flush times. The Great Society left a mixed legacy, frustrating lofty liberal aspirations even as it bolstered conservatives' argument that the federal government was incapable of solving pressing social problems.

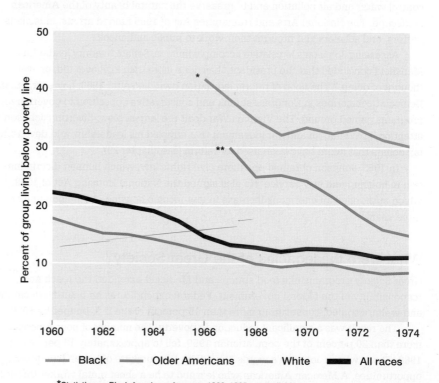

FIGURE 28.1 ▶ Poverty in the United States, 1960–1974 The results of economic growth and the Great Society's attack on poverty are reflected on the graph. Which groups experienced the sharpest decline in poverty, and what might account for the differences among them?

*Statistics on Black Americans for years 1960–1965 not available.
**Statistics on older Americans for years 1960–1966 not available.

How did the courts revolutionize rights?

Led by the Supreme Court under Chief Justice Earl Warren (1953–1969), the judiciary was another instrument of liberal change in the 1960s. In contrast to the federal courts of the Progressive Era and New Deal, which blocked reform, the **Warren Court** often moved ahead of Congress and public opinion, energizing the "rights revolution" of the 1960s. The Court granted new protections to disadvantaged groups and accused criminals, expanding the Constitution's promise of equality and individual rights.

Some of the Court's rulings established federal oversight of areas once left to the states. Following the *Brown v. Board of Education* school desegregation decision of 1954 (see chapter 27), the Court struck down southern states' maneuvers to avoid integration. In *Baker v. Carr* (1963)—which grew out of a complaint that sparsely populated rural districts were often allotted far more representatives than densely populated urban areas—the Court established the principle of "one person, one vote" for state legislatures and for the House of Representatives.

The Court underscored protections for freedom of assembly and speech, including that of protesters. In addition, it announced for the first time a constitutional right to privacy in the birth control case *Griswold v. Connecticut* (1965). A unanimous Court in *Loving v. Virginia* (1967) invalidated state laws banning interracial marriage, citing marriage as one of the "basic civil rights."

In decisions that dramatically altered law enforcement practices, the Warren Court declared that the states, and not just the federal government, were bound by the Bill of Rights. *Gideon v. Wainwright* (1963) established the duty to provide counsel to accused criminals who could not afford to hire a lawyer. *Miranda v. Arizona* (1966) required police officers to inform suspects of their rights upon arrest. The Court overturned convictions based on evidence obtained wrongfully—whether by unlawful arrest, by electronic surveillance, or without a search warrant. While liberals celebrated these rulings as ensuring equal treatment in the criminal justice system, critics accused the justices of "handcuffing the police" and letting criminals go free.

The Court's decisions on religion were even more divisive. A 1963 ruling found that requiring Bible reading and prayer in public schools violated the First Amendment principle of separation of church and state. Later judgments banned official prayer in public schools, even if students were not required to participate. The Court's supporters saw these decisions as protecting the rights of non-Christians and atheists, leaving others free to worship on their own. But the rulings infuriated many Christians. Billboards demanding "Impeach Earl Warren" joined a larger backlash mounting against Great Society liberalism.

Warren Court
Supreme Court under Chief Justice Earl Warren (1953–1969). It expanded the Constitution's promise of equality and individual rights and helped create a "rights revolution" by issuing landmark decisions in civil rights, criminal rights, privacy, reproductive freedom, and separation of church and state.

REVIEW

How did the War on Poverty and the Great Society exemplify a liberal vision of the federal government?

How did the Black freedom movement evolve?

More than anything else, mass protest by Black Americans distinguished the liberalism of the 1960s from that of the New Deal. The civil rights movement shook the nation's conscience, forced federal action, and provided a protest model for other groups. Building on decades of organized resistance to racial injustice, African Americans mobilized to strike down legal segregation and discrimination in the South and to secure voting rights. This "second Reconstruction," a century after the first, hinged on the courage and determination of Black people to stand up to racist violence.

Civil rights activism that focused on the South and on legal rights eventually won widespread acceptance in most of the country. As Black people stepped up protests against racial injustice outside the South and challenged entrenched economic inequality, however, white support for the Black freedom struggle eroded. By the 1970s, the national mass movement had been replaced by an array of local efforts, as civil rights and Black power activists pursued new strategies for liberation.

What strategies did civil rights activists adopt in the 1960s?

The Montgomery bus boycott of 1955–1956 turned a national—and international—spotlight on America's racial divisions and produced a leader in Martin Luther King Jr. (see chapter 27). In the 1960s, Black protest expanded dramatically, as African Americans directly confronted the institutions of an unequal and racially segregated society: retail establishments, public parks and libraries, buses and depots, voting registrars, and police forces.

Massive direct action in the South began in February 1960, when four Black college students in Greensboro, North Carolina, requested service at the whites-only Woolworth's lunch counter. Within days, hundreds of young people joined them, and others launched sit-ins in thirty-one southern cities. From the Southern Christian Leadership Conference headquarters, organizer Ella Baker telephoned her young contacts at Black colleges, asking: "What are you going to do? It's time to move."

Baker helped protesters form a new organization, the **Student Nonviolent Coordinating Committee (SNCC)**. Committed to decision making at the grassroots level, SNCC rejected the top-down leadership of established civil rights organizations, although it embraced King's principles of civil disobedience and nonviolence. Activists were trained to confront their oppressors and stand up for their rights but not to respond if assaulted. Nashville lunch counter protesters preparing for a sit-in were instructed: "Do show yourself friendly on the counter at all times. Do sit straight and always face the counter. Don't strike back or curse back if attacked."

The activists' commitment to nonviolence was tested. Although some cities quietly met protesters' demands, activists more typically encountered violence. Hostile whites poured food over demonstrators, burned them with cigarettes, and pelted them with rocks. Local police were often complicit, attacking protesters with dogs, clubs, fire hoses, and tear gas and arresting thousands.

Student Nonviolent Coordinating Committee (SNCC)
Civil rights organization established by young activists in 1960 in response to the sit-in movement. SNCC rejected the top-down leadership of organizations like the Southern Christian Leadership Conference, although it embraced Martin Luther King Jr.'s principles of civil disobedience and nonviolence.

Another wave of protest began in May 1961, when the Congress of Racial Equality (CORE) organized Freedom Rides to pressure the government to enforce court rulings ordering the integration of public transportation. When a group of white and Black activists reached Alabama, white locals bombed their bus and beat them with baseball bats so fiercely that an observer "couldn't see their faces through the blood." To President Kennedy's pleas for a cooling-off period, CORE leader James Farmer retorted that Black Americans had been "cooling off for 150 years. If we cool off anymore, we'll be in a deep freeze." After a mob attacked the riders in Montgomery, Alabama, Attorney General Robert Kennedy finally dispatched federal marshals to restore order. Nonetheless, Freedom Riders arriving in Jackson, Mississippi, were arrested, and several hundred spent weeks in jail.

In the summer of 1962, SNCC and other groups organized the Voter Education Project to register Black voters in southern states. Fannie Lou Hamer, who went on to become a prominent figure in the civil rights movement, recalled that before these activists arrived in her home state of Mississippi, "I didn't know that a Negro could register and vote." Black citizens constituted a majority in her county but only 1.2 percent of registered voters. Hamer herself passed through a hostile, gun-carrying crowd of white people as she attempted to register.

Although nonviolent themselves, the voting drives, like the Freedom Rides, sparked violent resistance. White southerners bombed Black churches, threw tenant farmers out of their homes, and beat and jailed activists. In June 1963, a white man gunned down Mississippi NAACP leader Medgar Evers in front of his house. Similar violence met King's 1963 campaign in Birmingham, Alabama, to integrate public facilities and open jobs to Black Americans. The police attacked demonstrators, including children, with dogs, cattle prods, and fire hoses—brutalities that television cameras broadcast around the world.

In August 1963, 250,000 Americans flocked to the nation's capital for the March on Washington for Jobs and Freedom, inspired by the strategy of A. Philip Randolph in 1941 (see chapter 25). Speaking from the Lincoln Memorial, King put his indelible stamp on the event. "I have a dream," he repeated, as he imagined the day "when all of God's children . . . will be able to join hands and sing . . . 'Free at last, free at last; thank God Almighty, we are free at last.'"

Activists returned from the march to continued hostility in the South. In 1964, the Mississippi Freedom Summer Project prepared northern Black and white college students to conduct voter registration drives. Opposition was fierce, and by the end of the summer, only twelve hundred new voters had been registered. Southern whites had killed several activists, beaten eighty, arrested more than one thousand, and burned thirty-five Black churches.

Even then, activists could not rely on the support of liberal politicians. When the Mississippi Freedom Democratic Party challenged the all-white delegation sent by the state party to the 1964 Democratic National Convention, its members were rebuffed. Resistance came from the federal government itself, as the Federal Bureau of Investigation spied on King and worked to "expose, disrupt, misdirect, discredit, or otherwise neutralize" Black protest.

Civil Rights Freedom Rides, May 1961

In March 1965, Alabama state troopers used such violent force to turn back a voting rights march from Selma to the state capital of Montgomery that the incident earned the name "Bloody Sunday" and compelled President Johnson to call up the Alabama National Guard to protect the marchers. Battered and hospitalized that day, John Lewis, chairman of SNCC—and later a congressman from Georgia—called the Voting Rights Act of 1965, which passed that October, "every bit as momentous as the Emancipation Proclamation." Referring to the Selma march and to the many years of struggle for the ballot that had preceded it, he said, "we all felt we'd had a part in it."

How did the federal government respond to calls for racial justice?

The Democratic administrations of the 1960s did not lead the way on racial justice. The Voting Rights Act of 1965, like the landmark civil rights legislation that preceded it, was the product of disciplined, persistent, and often bloody protest. Reluctant to alienate white southern voters and their congressional representatives, Kennedy and Johnson tended to move on civil rights only when events gave them little choice.

Yet move they did. The sit-ins and Freedom Rides had not been enough to prompt decisive federal action, but Birmingham was. In June 1963, after scenes of violence against peaceful demonstrators appalled television viewers across the world, Kennedy finally made good on his promise to seek strong antidiscrimination legislation. The Civil Rights Act of 1964, signed by Johnson, was the most important civil rights law since Reconstruction. The act guaranteed equal access for all Americans to public accommodations, public education, employment, and voting, and it extended constitutional protections to Native Americans living on reservations. Title VII of the act outlawed discrimination in employment based on gender as well as race. Because Title VII applied to every aspect of employment, including wages, hiring, and promotion, it represented a major step toward equal opportunity for white women as well as for people of color.

The furious resistance to voter registration drives in the South prompted Johnson to demand legislation to remove "every remaining obstacle to the right and the opportunity to vote," resulting in the Voting Rights Act of 1965. By empowering the federal government to intervene directly to ensure that African Americans could register and vote, the law transformed southern politics. Black voting rates shot up dramatically (**Map 28.2**). In turn, the number of Black Americans holding political office in the South increased from a handful in 1964 to more than one thousand by 1972, translating into tangible benefits for Black communities.

affirmative action
Requirement that employers holding government contracts align their hiring with the available pool of qualified candidates. Established by executive order of President Johnson in 1965, the program intended to counter centuries of discrimination against people of color and women.

Johnson also declared the need to realize equality "not just . . . as a right and theory, but . . . as fact and result." He issued an executive order in 1965 requiring employers holding government contracts to take "**affirmative action**" to ensure equal opportunity. Extended to cover women in 1967, the affirmative action program aimed to counter the effects of centuries of discrimination by requiring employers to act vigorously to align their hiring with the available pool of qualified candidates. While many corporations came to see affirmative action as a good employment practice, the policy became a flashpoint of partisan battles in the 1970s and beyond.

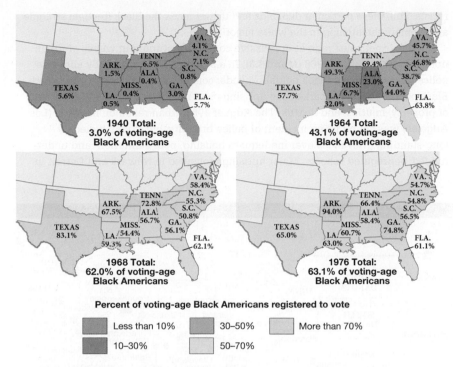

Percent of voting-age Black Americans registered to vote

▣ Less than 10%	▣ 30–50%	▢ More than 70%
■ 10–30%	▢ 50–70%	

MAP 28.2 ▲ Black Voting Rates, 1940–1976 Voting rates of southern Black people increased gradually in the 1940s and 1950s. But they shot up dramatically in the deep South after the Voting Rights Act of 1965 banned literacy tests and provided for federal oversight of registration and voting procedures in order to ensure African Americans' access to the ballot.

Ending racial discrimination in housing was another item on civil rights activists' agenda. But white resistance to neighborhood integration, including in northern, Democratic-leaning cities, was formidable. When Martin Luther King Jr. launched a campaign against de facto segregation in Chicago in 1966, thousands of white people jeered and threw stones at demonstrators. Johnson's efforts to secure a federal open-housing law succeeded only in the wake of King's assassination. The Civil Rights Act of 1968 banned racial discrimination in housing as well as jury selection, and it authorized federal intervention when states failed to protect civil rights workers from violence.

What were the roots of Black power and urban rebellions?

By 1966, Black protest engulfed the entire nation. On the heels of civil rights victories, activists turned to the problem of Black poverty, demanding not just legal equality but also economic justice. Some abandoned nonviolent resistance as a basic principle. None of these developments were brand new. Black people had waged campaigns for decent jobs, housing, and education outside the South since the 1930s. Some Black Americans had always armed themselves in self-defense, skeptical that a passive response to violent attacks would change the hearts of racists. Still, these particular demands and tactics made the Black freedom struggle appear more threatening to the white majority.

Black Americans' rage at oppressive conditions erupted in waves of urban uprisings from 1965 to 1968 (**Map 28.3**). In a situation where virtually all-white police forces patrolled Black neighborhoods, confrontations between police and Black people typically sparked the uprisings and resulted in looting, destruction of property, injuries, and deaths. The August 1965 urban rebellion in Watts (Los Angeles) was set off by an incident of police brutality, but it was fueled by long-standing grievances over inadequate housing, poor sanitation, and under-funded, segregated schools. Major uprisings followed in Newark and Detroit in

MAP ACTIVITY

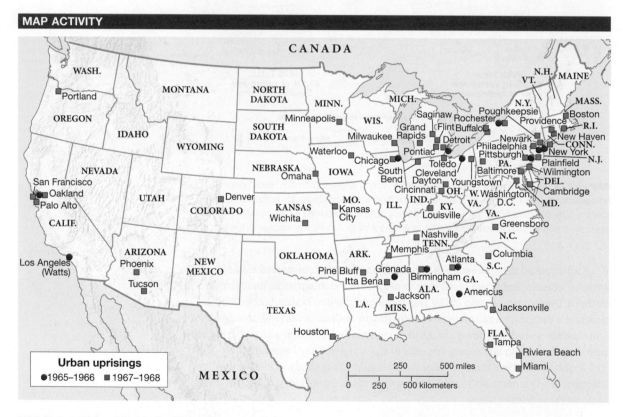

MAP 28.3 ▲ Urban Uprisings, 1965–1968 When a white police officer in the Watts district of Los Angeles struck a twenty-one-year-old Black man, whom he had pulled over for driving drunk, one onlooker shouted, "We've got no rights at all — it's just like Selma." The altercation sparked a five-day uprising. By its end, thirty-four people were dead, more than three thousand were arrested, and scores of businesses had been wiped out by fires and looting. Similar but smaller-scale violence erupted in dozens of cities across the nation during the next three summers.

READING THE MAP: In what regions and cities of the United States were urban uprisings concentrated? What years saw the greatest unrest?

CONNECTIONS: What were the causes of racial conflict in America's cities during this period? Whom did whites generally hold responsible for outbreaks of violence, and why?

July 1967 and in the nation's capital in April 1968. Violence convulsed hundreds of cities, with African Americans suffering most of the casualties.

New voices called for "**Black power**," a term coined by SNCC chairman Stokely Carmichael at a June 1966 rally in Greenwood, Mississippi. In the North, Malcolm X—an activist who while in prison had converted to the Nation of Islam, a religious sect—challenged the ethos of nonviolence. Civil rights leaders, he charged, had failed to protect their communities, and Black Americans would need to act in their own defense against white violence. Proclaiming that Black people needed to separate themselves from "corrupt [white] society," Malcolm X attracted a large following, especially in impoverished urban neighborhoods.

Arguing that Black self-determination could not be achieved through integration—and that even sympathetic white people could not excise their own racism—SNCC expelled its white members. Linking their cause to the colonial struggles and independence movements of people of color around the world, Black radicals believed that African Americans' freedom would come only from control over their own schools, communities, businesses, and political organizations.

Black power became the rallying cry in organizations such as the Black Panther Party for Self-Defense, established in Oakland, California, in 1966 by Huey P. Newton and Bobby Seale to combat police brutality. Armed with rifles and adopting military attire, the Panthers struck fear in many white people. But they also established day care centers, free breakfast and clothing programs, and classes in Black history. The Panthers and other radicals were harassed by the FBI and jailed, with some encounters leaving both Black militants and police dead. Yet Black power's emphasis on self-determination and its critique of American institutions resonated loudly. And

Black power
Collection of efforts in the 1960s and 1970s that emphasized Black self-determination and racial pride rather than integration. Black power advocates encouraged African Americans to assert control over their communities and institutions, with some rejecting the ethos of nonviolence.

◀ **Black Power** Black Panthers organized community centers, where they provided free breakfasts to poor children, distributed party literature, organized protests, and operated "liberation schools." Here, adults and children give the Black power salute outside a Panther school in the Fillmore district of San Francisco in 1969. Such shows of militancy unnerved many white Americans. Bettmann/ Getty Images.

a new emphasis on pride in African and African American culture, captured by the slogan "Black is Beautiful," endured.

The press paid inordinate attention to the Black power movement, which met with a severe backlash from white people. Although the urban rebellions of the mid-1960s erupted spontaneously, many Americans blamed Black militants. By 1966, polls indicated that 85 percent of white Americans—up from 34 percent two years earlier—believed that Black Americans were pressing for too much too quickly.

Martin Luther King Jr. agreed with Black power advocates about the need for economic justice and "a radical reconstruction of society," but he asserted that nonviolence and integration were the means to this end. In 1968, the thirty-nine-year-old leader went to Memphis to support striking municipal sanitation workers. On April 4, he was shot and killed by an escaped white convict. King's assassination triggered riots and protests in one hundred American cities. One speaker at a Boston rally commemorated the civil rights leader who had been "prepared to give his life for justice in America," whereas a pastor from Iowa asked, "Why must we always kill our prophets before we will listen to them?" Into the 1970s, civil rights and Black power activists would continue the difficult work that King and countless other Black women and men had begun.

REVIEW

How and why did the civil rights movement shift its focus in the mid-1960s?

Why did so many social movements emerge in the 1960s?

The civil rights movement's moral claims, protest strategies, and legal victories inspired a multitude of other social movements in the 1960s and 1970s. Native Americans, Latinos, college students, women, gay men and lesbians, and environmentalists all drew on the Black freedom struggle's model. Many of these groups engaged in direct-action protests, demanded new rights, and led cultural pride movements. The challenge they posed to political institutions and cultural values would permanently transform American society.

What were the goals of red power?

Young Native Americans called for "red power" in the late 1960s, reflecting their new militancy as well as the influence of Black radicalism. The termination and relocation programs of the 1950s (see chapter 27), contrary to their intent, had forged a sense of Indian identity across tribal lines and a determination to preserve traditional cultures. Activists pursued cultural recognition as well as economic claims, including rights to natural resources and territory that Native American groups had owned collectively before European settlement.

In 1969, Native American demonstrators captured world attention when several dozen seized Alcatraz Island, an abandoned federal prison in San Francisco Bay, claiming their right of "first discovery" of this land. For nineteen months, they used the occupation to publicize injustices against Native Americans while promoting pan-Indian cooperation. One of the organizers, LaNada War Jack, a member of the Shoshone-Bannock Tribes of the Fort Hall Indian Reservation in Idaho and a student at the University of California, Berkeley, said of the Alcatraz protest, "We were able to reestablish our identity as Indian people, as a culture, as political entities."

In Minneapolis in 1968, two members of the Chippewa tribe, Dennis Banks and George Mitchell, founded the **American Indian Movement (AIM)** to attack the problems faced by the 300,000 Native Americans who lived in urban areas. AIM sought to protect Native Americans from police harassment, to secure antipoverty funds, and to establish "survival schools" to teach Indian history and values. The movement spread quickly. Lakota activist and author Mary Crow Dog wrote that AIM's visit to her South Dakota reservation "loosened a sort of earthquake inside me."

AIM leaders helped organize the "Trail of Broken Treaties" caravan to the nation's capital in 1972, where activists occupied the Bureau of Indian Affairs to protest its policies and interference in Native Americans' lives. In 1973, a much longer siege occurred on the Lakota Sioux reservation in South Dakota. For seventy-two days, AIM took over the village of Wounded Knee, where U.S. troops had massacred more than two hundred Sioux people in 1890 (see chapter 17).

Although these dramatic occupations did not achieve all their specific goals, activists would by the 1970s win the end of relocation and termination policies, greater tribal sovereignty and

American Indian Movement (AIM) Organization established in 1968 to address the problems Native Americans faced in U.S. cities, including poverty and police harassment. AIM pushed to end relocation and termination policies and helped Indians win greater control over their cultures and communities.

▶ **Native Americans Occupy Alcatraz Island** From November 1969 to June 1971, Native American protesters occupied Alcatraz Island in San Francisco Bay. Calling themselves "Indians of All Tribes" to reflect their diversity, they demanded the deed to the island — a response to the taking of Native American lands by white — and the creation of an Indian university, museum, and cultural center. The occupation brought attention to the Native American cause and spurred further activism. Ralph Crane/Getty Images.

control over community services, protection of Native American religious practices, and visibility for their cause. A number of laws and court decisions also restored rights to ancestral lands and compensated tribes for land seized in violation of treaties.

How did the Chicano movement mobilize?

Latinos—the term for an extraordinarily varied population encompassing people of Mexican, Puerto Rican, Caribbean, and other Latin American origins—were the fastest-growing U.S. minority group in the 1960s. Many people of Puerto Rican and Caribbean descent lived in East Coast cities, but more than half of the nation's Latino population—including some six million Mexican Americans—lived in the Southwest. In addition, thousands of undocumented immigrants crossed the border between Mexico and the United States yearly in search of economic opportunity and security from violence.

Political organization of Mexican Americans dated back to the League of United Latin American Citizens (LULAC), founded in 1929, which fought segregation and discrimination through litigation (see chapter 27). In the 1960s, however, young Mexican Americans increasingly rejected traditional politics in favor of direct action. One symbol of this generational change was young activists' adoption of the term *Chicano* (from *mejicano*, the Spanish word for "Mexican").

Chicano movement
Mobilization of Mexican Americans in the 1960s and 1970s to fight for civil rights, economic justice, and political power and to combat police brutality. The movement sought to improve the lives of migrant farmworkers and to end discrimination in employment and education.

The **Chicano movement** drew national attention to California, where Cesar Chavez and Dolores Huerta organized a movement to counter the exploitation of migrant agricultural workers. As the child of migrant farmworkers, Chavez lived in soggy tents, saw his parents cheated by labor contractors, and encountered indifference and discrimination. One teacher, he recalled, "hung a sign on me that said, 'I am a clown, I speak Spanish.'" After serving in World War II, Chavez began to organize voter registration drives among Mexican Americans.

Dolores Huerta grew up in an integrated neighborhood and escaped the farmworkers' grinding poverty but faced stigma based on language and color—one high school teacher challenging Huerta's authorship of an essay because it was so well written. Believing that collective action was the key to progress, she and Chavez founded the United Farm Workers (UFW) union in 1962. To gain leverage for striking workers, the UFW mounted a nationwide boycott of California grapes, winning support from millions of Americans and a wage increase for the workers in 1970. The UFW lost membership during the 1970s but was critical in politicizing Mexican Americans and improving farmworkers' lives.

Others pressed the Equal Employment Opportunity Commission (EEOC) to combat job discrimination against Mexican Americans. After LULAC and the American GI Forum picketed government offices, President Johnson appointed Vicente T. Ximenes as the first Mexican American EEOC commissioner in 1967 and created a special committee on Mexican American issues.

Chicanos rallied under the banner of "brown power" in order to end discrimination in education, gain political access, and combat police brutality. In Denver, Rodolfo "Corky" Gonzales set up "freedom schools" where Chicano children learned Spanish and Mexican American history. The nationalist strains of Chicano protest were evident in La Raza Unida (the United Race), a political party founded in 1970 based on cultural pride and solidarity. Along with Black Americans and Native Americans, Chicanos continued to be disproportionately impoverished, but they gradually won more political offices, more effective enforcement of antidiscrimination legislation, and greater respect for their cultural institutions.

Why did young people join the New Left and counterculture?

Young white people, although comparatively privileged, were also inspired by the Black freedom struggle, and some were radicalized by its critique of American society. Young activists participated in civil rights actions, the antiwar movement, and the new wave of feminism—part of a broader wave of student movements around the globe that challenged establishment institutions.

The central organization of white student protest in the United States was Students for a Democratic Society (SDS). The organization's 1962 Port Huron Statement outlined its purpose, asserting: "We are people of this generation, bred in at least modest comfort, housed now in universities, looking uncomfortably at the world we inherit." Students criticized the complacency of their elders, the remoteness of decision makers, and the powerlessness and alienation generated by a bureaucratic society. SDS aimed to mobilize a "New Left" around the goals of civil rights, peace, and universal economic security. Young conservatives organized around a different set of concerns: the threats of international communism, big government, and incursions on economic freedom

The first large-scale white student protest arose at the University of California, Berkeley, in 1964, when university officials banned students from setting up tables to recruit support for various causes. Led by activists returning from civil rights work in the South, the Free Speech Movement occupied the administration building, and more than seven hundred students were arrested before the California Board of Regents overturned the new restrictions.

Hundreds of student rallies and building occupations followed on campuses across the country as opposition to the Vietnam War mounted and students protested universities' ties with the military. Students also sought to expose the injustices of their own campuses. Women at the University of Chicago charged in 1969 that universities "discriminate against women, impede their full intellectual development, deny them places on the faculty, exploit talented women and mistreat women students." At Howard University, Black students called for a "Black Awareness Research Institute," demanding that academic departments "place more emphasis on how these disciplines may be used to effect the liberation of black people." Across the country, students borrowed sit-ins and other tactics to win curricular reforms such as Black studies and women's studies programs, more financial aid for minority and low-income students, independence from paternalistic rules, and a larger voice in campus decision making. **(See "Analyzing Historical Evidence: Student Protest" on page 842.)**

Student protests sometimes blended into a cultural rebellion against conventional standards of behavior. Drawing on the ideas of the Beats of the 1950s (see chapter 27), the so-called hippies rejected mainstream values such as consumerism, social order, and sexual restraint in search of more authentic experiences. The 1967

ANALYZING HISTORICAL EVIDENCE

Student Protest

A lthough only a minority of college students participated in the protests of the 1960s, a sizable number at all kinds of colleges and universities challenged traditional authorities, criticized established institutions, and demanded a voice in decision making.

DOCUMENT 1
Edward Schwartz, Student Power, October 1967

Student activist Edward Schwartz wrote this statement to represent the views of the National Student Association, the largest college student organization in the 1960s.

Let this principle apply — he who must obey the rule should make it.

Students should make the rules governing dormitory hours, boy-girl visitation, student unions, student fees, clubs, newspapers, and the like. Faculty and administrators should advise — attempt to persuade, even. Yet the student should bear the burden of choice.

Students and faculty should co-decide curricular policy.

Students, faculty, and administration should co-decide admissions policy, overall college policy affecting the community, even areas like university investment. . . . Student power should not be argued on legal grounds. It is not a legal principle. It is an educational principle.

Student power is threatening to those who wield power now, but this is understandable. A student should threaten his administrators outside of class, just as bright students threaten professors inside of class.

Student power ultimately challenges everyone in the university — the students who must decide; the faculty and administrators who must rethink their own view of community relations in order to persuade.

People who say that student power means anarchy imply really that students are rabble who have no ability to form community and to adhere to decisions made by community. Student power is not the negation of rules — it is the creation of a new process for the enactment of rules. Student power is not the elimination of authority, it is the development of a democratic standard of authority.

Source: Excerpt from "He Who Must Obey the Rule Should Make It," from *The University Crisis Reader*, vol. 1, *The Liberal University under Attack*, ed. Immanuel Wallerstein and Paul Starr, pp. 482–84. Copyright © 1971 by Random House, Inc.

DOCUMENT 2
Counterthrust on Student Power, Spring 1967

While the majority of students simply avoided involvement in campus rebellions, some actively criticized the protesters. A leaflet titled "Student Power Is a Farce" reflected the views of Counterthrust, a conservative group at Wayne State University in Michigan.

Our University is being treated to the insanity of Left-Wing students demanding the run of the University. . . . Wayne students are told by the Left that "student power" merely means more democracy on campus. This is an outright lie! Student power is a Left-Wing catchword symbolizing campus militancy and radicalism. In actuality, the Left-Wing, spearheaded by the SDS, want to radically alter the university community. . . .

The Leftists charge a sinister plot by private enterprise to train students for jobs at taxpayers' expense. Evidently it never occurred to the SDS that private enterprise is also the biggest single taxpayer for schools. But, of course, that would require a little thought on the part of the SDS which they have already demonstrated they are incapable of. . . .

The byword of student power–union advocates is Radicalism. . . . Fraternities and student Governments will have no place in student power–unions since both are considered allies of the status quo and thus useless. . . . As responsible Wayne students, we cannot allow our University to be used by Leftists for their narrow purposes. We were invited to this campus by the Michigan Taxpayer to receive an education. Let us honor that invitation.

Source: "Student Power Is a Farce," *Counterthrust*, from *The University Crisis Reader*, vol. 1, *The Liberal University under Attack*, ed. Immanuel Wallerstein and Paul Starr, pp. 487–88. Copyright © 1971 by Random House, Inc.

DOCUMENT 3
Harvard Strike Poster, 1969

This poster referred to a list of demands pinned to the door of the Harvard president's house by members of Students for a Democratic Society. An eight-day strike followed, along with changes to university policy: the reduction of ROTC (the Reserve Officers Training Corps) presence on campus and a student voice in faculty appointments to Afro-American Studies.

STRIKE FOR THE EIGHT DEMANDS STRIKE BECAUSE YOU HATE COPS STRIKE BECAUSE YOUR ROOMMATE WAS CLUBBED STRIKE TO STOP EXPANSION STRIKE TO SEIZE CONTROL OF YOUR LIFE STRIKE TO BECOME MORE HUMAN STRIKE TO RETURN PAINE HALL SCHOLARSHIPS STRIKE BECAUSE THERE'S NO POETRY IN YOUR LECTURES STRIKE BECAUSE CLASSES ARE A BORE STRIKE FOR POWER STRIKE TO SMASH THE CORPORATION STRIKE TO MAKE YOURSELF FREE STRIKE TO ABOLISH ROTC STRIKE BECAUSE THEY ARE TRYING TO SQUEEZE THE LIFE OUT OF YOU STRIKE

HUA 969.100.2 (50), olvwork449770.
Harvard University Archives.

Questions for Analysis

RECOGNIZE VIEWPOINTS: How do the three documents differ in terms of the issues they address? What do they reveal about the range of students' motivations for protesting?

ASK HISTORICAL QUESTIONS: To what extent do your own campus policies and practices suggest that student activism during the 1960s and 1970s succeeded in changing higher education?

CONSIDER THE CONTEXT: In what ways did student protests differ from other social movements of the 1960s?

"Human Be-In" that gathered in San Francisco's Golden Gate Park brought an eclectic group of nonconformists to national attention. Questioning established authority—along with beards and long hair, wildly colorful clothing, and drug use—became a hallmark of the counterculture. Across the country, thousands of radicals renounced private property and established communes in cities or on farms.

Rock and folk music, often carrying insurgent social and political messages, were the backdrop of radical youth culture. "Eve of Destruction," a top hit of 1965, reminded young men of draft age at a time when the voting age was twenty-one, "You're old enough to kill but not for votin'." The 1969 Woodstock Music Festival, attended by 400,000 young people, epitomized the centrality of music to the youth rebellion. Never a movement in a traditional sense, many elements of the counterculture—rock music, jeans, and new social attitudes—filtered into the mainstream. This was especially evident in the liberalization of sexual mores, which, along with the birth control pill (introduced in 1960), fostered the era's "sexual revolution." Cohabitation, premarital sex, and sex outside traditional heterosexual marriage would become both more common and more acceptable in American life.

What and how did gay men and lesbians protest?

More permissive sexual norms did not stretch easily to include tolerance of sexual diversity. Gay men and lesbians in the postwar era typically had escaped discrimination and ostracism only by concealing their identities. Those who couldn't or wouldn't found themselves fired from jobs, arrested for their sexual activities, or accused of "perversion."

In the 1950s, the homophile movement had acted quietly to advance the equal rights of gay people, in part through careful conformity to midcentury norms of respectability. But gays and lesbians organized in new ways in the mid-1960s. In 1965, picketers outside the White House challenged the government's policy of banning gays and lesbians from civil service with signs branding such discrimination "as immoral as discrimination against Negroes and Jews." It took another ten years for the Civil Service Commission to end the policy, but a full-fledged social movement would not wait that long.

A turning point came in 1969 when police conducted a routine raid of a gay bar, the Stonewall Inn, in New York City's Greenwich Village—and gay men and lesbians fought back. "Suddenly, they were not submissive anymore," a police officer remarked. Bolstered by the defiance shown at the **Stonewall riots**, gay men and lesbians launched a host of new advocacy groups, such as the Gay Liberation Front and the National Gay and Lesbian Task Force. As with Black power, gay liberationists pursued equal rights as well as cultural self-determination. Shouts of "gay power" broke out at Stonewall, and activists called for gay men and lesbians to "come out" publicly and proudly.

In 1972, Ann Arbor, Michigan, passed the first antidiscrimination ordinance pertaining to gay men and women, and two years later, Elaine Noble's election to the Massachusetts legislature marked the first time that an openly gay candidate won state office. In 1973, activists succeeded in getting the American Psychiatric Association to withdraw its designation of homosexuality as a disorder. It would take decades for these initial gains to improve conditions for most, but by the mid-1970s, gay men and lesbians had made strides toward equal rights and a society more welcoming of diverse sexualities.

Stonewall riots
Protest set off in 1969 by a police raid of the Stonewall Inn, a gay bar in New York's Greenwich Village. The incident led to the organization of a set of new advocacy groups and energized the Gay Liberation movement.

▶ **Gay Liberation** The Stonewall riots galvanized a generation of young gay men and lesbians, whose ideas and tactics resembled those of other radical movements of the 1960s. Shortly after Stonewall, organizations like the National Gay Task Force and the Gay Liberation Front formed, the latter advertising itself as a "revolutionary group" demanding "complete sexual liberation for all people." The New York Public Library/Art Resource, NY.

What explains the rise of a new environmentalism?

Advocates for the natural environment added their voices to the chorus of social reform in the 1960s and 1970s. Like the conservation movement of the Progressive Era (see chapter 21), the new environmentalists sought to preserve natural areas for recreational and aesthetic purposes and to conserve natural resources. Already in the 1950s, environmental groups had organized to halt construction of dams that would disrupt national parks and wilderness preserves. In the West, population growth and the resulting demands for electricity and water also stirred activists.

The new environmentalists, however, went beyond conservation to question the benefits of economic growth, including the effects of industry and technology on human life and health. Biologist Rachel Carson captured national attention in 1962 with her best seller *Silent Spring*, which vividly described the perils of toxic chemicals, such as the pesticide DDT, to wildlife, plants, and the ecological balance that sustains human life.

The Sierra Club and other older conservation organizations expanded their membership rolls and their agendas, and a host of new environmental groups cropped up. Twenty million Americans took part in the first observation of Earth Day in April 1970, where activists led teach-ins and rallies to raise consciousness about air and water pollution, oil spills, industrial waste, and automobile emissions.

LBJ had signaled federal support for environmental regulations, but it was his successor, Republican president Richard Nixon, who enacted them. Nixon pronounced "clean air, clean water, open spaces . . . the birthright of every American" and urged Congress to "end the plunder of America's natural heritage." In 1970, he created the **Environmental Protection Agency (EPA)** to enforce environmental laws, conduct research, and reduce human health and environmental risks from pollutants. He also signed the landmark Occupational Safety and Health Act (OSHA), protecting workers against job-related accidents and disease; the Clean Air Act of 1970, restricting factory and automobile emissions of carbon dioxide and other pollutants; and the Endangered Species Act of 1973. Congress pressed further, overriding Nixon's veto of the Clean Water Act of 1972, an indication of how decisively the issues raised by environmental activists had moved onto the national agenda.

Environmental Protection Agency (EPA)
Federal agency created by President Nixon in 1970 to enforce environmental laws, conduct environmental research, and reduce health and environmental risks from pollutants.

REVIEW

How did the Black freedom struggle influence other social movements of the 1960s and 1970s?

What sparked a new wave of feminism?

On August 26, 1970, the fiftieth anniversary of woman suffrage, tens of thousands of women across the country—from radical women in jeans to conservatively dressed suburbanites, and from peace activists to politicians—took to the streets. They carried signs reading "Sisterhood Is Powerful" and "Don't Cook Dinner—Starve a Rat Today." Some opposed the war in Vietnam, others demanded racial justice, but women's own liberation was front and center.

Gathering steam in the late 1960s, "second-wave feminism"—a label meant to distinguish it from earlier efforts on behalf of women's rights, including the suffrage movement—reached its high tide in the 1970s and extended into the twenty-first century. By that time, despite a powerful countermovement, women had witnessed remarkable transformations in their legal status, employment opportunities, and public roles, and even their personal and sexual relationships. Popular expectations about appropriate gender roles also shifted dramatically.

What were the causes of feminist protest?

Demographic changes laid the foundations for a resurgence of feminism. During World War II, the importance of women's paid work to the economy and their families challenged traditional views and awakened many female workers, especially those in labor unions, to discrimination in employment. The postwar democratization of higher education also brought more women to college campuses, where their aspirations collided with the confines of domesticity and low-wage, subordinate jobs.

In 1961, Assistant Secretary of Labor Esther Peterson persuaded John F. Kennedy to create the President's Commission on the Status of Women, chaired by Eleanor Roosevelt. Its 1963 report documented widespread discrimination against women in the labor force and recommended remedies ranging from affordable child care to paid maternity leave. Although these policies were not enacted, one of the commission's concerns was addressed even before its report came out, when Congress passed the Equal Pay Act of 1963, making it illegal to pay women less than men for the same work.

Like other movements, second-wave feminism owed much to the Black freedom struggle. By piggybacking onto civil rights measures, women gained protection from employment discrimination (through Title VII of the Civil Rights Act of 1964) and were covered by affirmative action. They soon grew impatient when the government failed to take these new policies seriously. Calling for "an NAACP for women," Betty Friedan, civil rights activist Pauli Murray, several union women, and others founded the **National Organization for Women (NOW)** in 1966.

National Organization for Women (NOW)
Women's civil rights organization formed in 1966. Initially, NOW focused on widening opportunities for women by eliminating gender discrimination in public institutions and the workplace.

At a time when newspapers classified jobs as either "male" or "female" and women could not apply for their own credit cards, NOW set its sights on equal opportunity for women in the male-dominated public arena, including employment, education, medicine, law, and politics. Among other causes, NOW pledged support for the ratification of the Equal Rights Amendment (ERA) to the Constitution, a measure first introduced in 1923 and intended to outlaw differential treatment of men and women under all state and federal laws.

Although NOW elected a Black president, Aileen Hernandez, in 1970, the new feminism's leadership and constituency were predominantly white and middle-class. Women of color criticized white feminists for assuming that white women could speak for all women. Black women, for example, were much more frequently compelled to labor in difficult and dirty jobs for their families' survival. To them, entrance into the paid workforce did not necessarily represent liberation. Feminists struggled with how to build a movement spanning the many constituencies among women: ethnic and racial minorities, labor union members, religious women, rural women, mothers on welfare, lesbians, and more.

How did radical feminism depart from earlier women's movements?

As NOW was getting established, a more radical feminism emerged among young women active in the civil rights struggle and the New Left. These women—often relegated to mundane tasks and sexually exploited by fellow radicals—strained against their second-class status even within movements for social justice. Frustrated when male leaders dismissed and ridiculed their claims of discrimination, some walked out of New Left organizations and created independent women's liberation groups.

Radical feminists first captured national media attention when they picketed the Miss America beauty pageant in 1968. Activists decried being forced "to compete for male approval," describing women as "enslaved by ludicrous 'beauty' standards." Calling their movement "women's liberation," they encouraged public discussion of experiences shrouded in secrecy, such as rape, domestic violence, and abortion. Women formed "consciousness-raising" groups, where they realized that what they had considered to be personal problems reflected an entrenched system of male privilege, or sexism. The slogan of women's liberation, "The personal is political," insisted that sexual relationships, the division of labor in the family, and norms about bodies and beauty were always also relations of power.

Radical feminists differed from the members of NOW in several ways. NOW focused on equal treatment for women in the public sphere; women's liberation targeted women's subordination in the family and in their most intimate relationships. Whereas NOW sought to integrate women into existing institutions, radicals insisted on a total transformation of those institutions and perhaps even a separation from men. Radical feminists also voiced strong support for abortion rights. "Without the full capacity to limit her own reproduction," activist Lucinda Cisler insisted, "a woman's other 'freedoms' are tantalizing mockeries that cannot be exercised." Differences between these two strands of feminism blurred in the 1970s, however, as NOW and other mainstream groups embraced many of the issues raised by radicals.

Feminists of all stripes contended with the media's refusal to take women's grievances seriously. Finding their movement mocked and trivialized, some protesters refused to grant interviews except to female reporters. One solution was to create woman-run media organizations. In 1972, Gloria Steinem and other journalists and writers launched the first mass-circulation magazine for, and controlled by, women. *Ms.: The New Magazine for Women* shunned the recipes and fashion tips typical of women's magazines, instead featuring articles on a broad range of feminist issues.

◀ **No More Miss America, 1968** Demonstrators, organized by the New York Radical Women, march on the Atlantic City Boardwalk to protest the annual Miss America beauty pageant. Protesters circulated a pamphlet titled "No More Miss America." Bettmann/Getty Images.

READING THE IMAGE: What concerns are suggested by the slogans on the picketers' signs? How did these issues differ from those tackled by the National Organization for Women?

CONNECTIONS: What male-controlled social institutions and cultural values did feminists seek to transform?

A host of other organizations devoted to women's heath, abortion rights, and domestic violence cropped up in the decade that followed. After the United Nations declared 1975 International Women's Year, U.S. women also began to take part in global conversations about women's status. As they did, they learned that theirs was often not the most advanced nation when it came to women's welfare or political leadership.

What opposition did feminists encounter?

Feminism altered female aspirations and helped lower barriers to occupations monopolized by men. Between 1960 and 2010, women's share of law and medical degrees shot up from 5 percent and 10 percent, respectively, to approximately 50 percent, although women earned much less than men in those fields. Women gained political offices very slowly; in 2021, they constituted nearly 28 percent of Congress and 30 percent of all state legislators.

Despite outnumbering men in college enrollments and making some inroads into male-dominated occupations, women were still concentrated in low-paying, traditionally female jobs, and a gender gap in earnings persisted. Working women continued to bear primary responsibility for taking care of their homes and families, thereby working a "double shift." Unlike in other industrialized countries, women in the United States were not entitled to paid maternity leave and could not count on government provisions for child care.

By the mid-1970s, feminism faced a powerful countermovement, organized around opposition to the Equal Rights Amendment (see chapter 30). In 1973, the Supreme Court ruled in the landmark *Roe v. Wade* decision that the Constitution protected the right to abortion and that states could not prohibit it in the early stages of pregnancy. The ruling prompted social conservatives—some of whom believed that abortion constituted murder—to organize. Often overlapping with ERA opponents, those drawn to the emerging "right-to-life" movement charged feminism with

Roe v. Wade
1973 Supreme Court ruling that the Constitution protects the right to abortion and prevents states from prohibiting it in the early stages of pregnancy. The decision made abortion a fiercely contested issue between liberals and social conservatives for decades to come.

threatening traditional motherhood and gender roles. Beginning in 1977, abortion foes pressured Congress to restrict the right to abortion by prohibiting coverage under all government-financed health programs. The Supreme Court allowed states to impose additional obstacles.

Despite such resistance, feminists won lasting gains. Title IX of the Education Amendments Act of 1972 banned sex discrimination in all aspects of education, such as admissions, athletics, and hiring. Congress outlawed sex discrimination in credit in 1974, opened U.S. military academies to women in 1976, and prohibited discrimination against pregnant workers in 1978. The Supreme Court struck down laws that treated men and women differently in Social Security, welfare and military benefits, and workers' compensation—rulings based on legal arguments made by future Supreme Court justice Ruth Bader Ginsburg and crafted in part by Pauli Murray.

At the state and local levels, women saw many reforms that radical feminists had put on the public agenda. They won laws requiring police departments and the legal system to treat rape victims more justly and humanely. Activists obtained greater protection and government-funded shelters for victims of domestic violence, along with more effective prosecution of abusers. In perhaps the largest victory of all, many of the feminist causes that appeared radical in the 1960s—from a right to equal pay to the criminalization of marital rape—had won the support of a majority of Americans by the end of the 1970s.

REVIEW

Where did feminists make legal gains? What cultural changes did they seek?

Why and where did the conservative movement gain ground?

Hidden beneath Lyndon B. Johnson's landslide election over the far-right Arizona senator Barry Goldwater in 1964 lay a rising conservative movement, energized by opposition to Black power, student protest, and second-wave feminism. Goldwater defined his goal as "enlarging freedom at home and safeguarding it from the forces of tyranny abroad." His nomination was a victory for conservative activists in the Republican Party who believed that government intervention in the economy hindered prosperity, stifled personal responsibility, and interfered with the right of citizens to determine their own values. Increasingly, they would merge their free enterprise, states' rights, and anti-Communist views with a moral critique of sixties liberalism. Republican Richard Nixon's election to the presidency in 1968 did not immediately overturn liberal policies, but the coordinated actions of conservatives in the 1960s and 1970s paved the way for future victories.

Who joined the grassroots right?

The grassroots movement on the right included middle-class suburban women and men as well as members of the rabidly anti-Communist John Birch Society. These groups assailed big government in domestic affairs but demanded a strong military to eradicate "Godless Communism." Joining them was a key force behind Goldwater's nomination: college students. Gathering at the home of conservative intellectual William F. Buckley in 1960, they formed the Young Americans for Freedom (YAF), a counterpart to radical student groups on the left. In 1966, these same grassroots organizations helped former movie star Ronald Reagan defeat the liberal incumbent governor of California, whom Reagan linked to the Watts riot, student disruptions at the University of California, and rising taxes.

Conservatism flourished in predominantly white, skilled, and economically comfortable communities in the Sun Belt: places such as Orange County, California; Dallas, Texas; and Scottsdale, Arizona, that housed military bases and defense plants. The West harbored a long-standing tradition of individualism and opposition to interference by a remote federal government, despite the Sun Belt's economic dependence on defense spending and federal projects providing water and power for the burgeoning region.

The South, which also benefited from military bases and the space program, shared this antipathy toward the federal government. Hostility to racial equality was, however, much more central to its conservatism. After signing the Civil Rights Act of 1964, President Johnson remarked privately, "I think we just delivered the South to the Republican Party."

Grassroots movements on the right were often triggered by fears about American moral decline and rapid social change. In 1962, for example, Mel and Norma Gabler pressed the Texas Board of Education to ban books in the public schools that they believed undermined "the Christian-Judeo morals, values, and standards as given to us by God through . . . the Bible." New sex education programs were a particular point of contention. The U.S. Supreme Court's liberal decisions on school prayer, abortion, and obscenity further galvanized conservatives in defense of "traditional values."

"Law and order" was another rallying cry of those on the right, reflecting concerns about rising rates of crime in the 1960s but also shifting patterns of decorum. Conservatives tended to link crime, civil disobedience, and antiwar protest to a declining respect for authority in American society. In this vein, a conservative newspaper condemned the sit-in movement as an "incitement to anarchy." Those on the right blamed the social disorder of the era on Supreme Court decisions that "coddled" criminals, permissive attitudes toward protesters, and Great Society programs that seemed to undercut personal responsibility. For one Pennsylvania man, "crime, the streets being unsafe, strikes, the trouble with the colored, all this dope-taking" added up to "a breakdown of the American way of life."

What did the 1968 election mean for liberal reforms?

Opposition to civil rights measures, concern over government spending on the War on Poverty, alarm at the pace of social change, and frustration over the war in

Vietnam (see chapter 29) delivered the White House to Republican Richard M. Nixon in 1968. Although Nixon did not embrace the entire conservative agenda, he sought to rebuild the Republican Party by appealing to disaffected blue-collar and southern white Democrats.

Nixon attacked the Great Society for "pouring billions of dollars into programs that have failed." At the same time during his administration, federal assistance programs such as Social Security, public housing, and food stamps grew, and Congress established Pell grants for low-income students to attend college. Noting the disparity between what Nixon said and what he did, his speechwriter, the archconservative Pat Buchanan, grumbled, "Vigorously did we inveigh against the Great Society, enthusiastically did we fund it."

Nixon's campaign exploited white hostility to Black protest and civil rights policies, but his administration had to answer to the courts and to Congress. In 1968, fourteen years after the *Brown* decision, school desegregation had barely touched the South. Like Eisenhower, Nixon was reluctant to use federal power to compel integration. But the Supreme Court overruled the administration's efforts to delay court-ordered desegregation, with dramatic effects. By 1974, fewer than one in ten southern Black children attended totally segregated schools.

Nixon's administration also implemented affirmative action among federal contractors and unions, and increased loans to minority businesses. Congress took the initiative in other areas, extending the Voting Rights Act of 1965 and strengthening the Civil Rights Act of 1964. In 1971, Congress responded to the youth movement with the Twenty-Sixth Amendment to the Constitution, reducing the voting age to eighteen. In 1973, Nixon signed legislation outlawing discrimination against people with disabilities in all programs receiving federal funds. The president also signed pathbreaking environmental legislation to regulate pollutants in the air and water and established the Environmental Protection Agency.

President Nixon was especially receptive to calls for Native American rights. He told Congress that American Indians were "the most deprived and most isolated minority group . . . the heritage of centuries of injustice." While not bowing to radicals' demands, his administration dealt cautiously with the occupations of Alcatraz and the Bureau of Indian Affairs. Nixon signed measures recognizing claims of Alaskan and New Mexican Indians, restoring tribal status and lands to groups that had lost them through earlier federal policies.

Nixon's response to women's activism was mixed. He vetoed a bill providing federal funds for day care centers, arguing that child care was a matter for the private market rather than the government and warning of the measure's "family-weakening implications." Nixon sided with "defenders of the right to life of the unborn," anticipating the Republican Party's eventual position on abortion laws. Acknowledging a growing feminist movement, however, Nixon signed the landmark Title IX, guaranteeing equality in all aspects of education, and permitted the Labor Department to pursue affirmative action for women.

Nixon's disavowal of New Deal and Great Society programs, although gradual, was significant. Whereas John F. Kennedy had summoned Americans to contribute to the common good, Nixon invited Americans to "ask—not just what will government do for me, but what can I do for myself?" An emphasis on individualism and private enterprise—rather than reliance on the state—would be the calling card of conservative politics in the 1970s and 1980s.

REVIEW

To what extent did Nixon reverse liberal social policies and the expanded role of the federal government?

Conclusion: What were the lasting effects of sixties-era liberalism?

The years between 1960 and 1974 witnessed the most concerted effort to reconcile America's promise of equal opportunity with the reality of vast inequality since the New Deal. Pressed by activists like Pauli Murray, Democratic administrations expanded the liberal agenda to encompass racial justice and individual rights. The lofty rhetoric of Kennedy's New Frontier, the burst of Great Society legislation under Johnson, and the rulings of the Warren Court spoke to a new federal commitment to the social welfare of all Americans.

Johnson's War on Poverty and Great Society were emblematic of these aspirations as well as their limits. Antipoverty programs focused on the poor rather than on income distribution or the creation of adequately paying jobs for all, and they never commanded the resources necessary for a true victory over poverty. Yet some of Johnson's accomplishments were enduring. Federal aid for education and housing became permanent elements of national policy. Medicare and Medicaid continue to provide access to health care for older and poor Americans.

New welfare policies, legal rights and protections, and antidiscrimination measures were secured through organized protest. The Black freedom struggle, from lunch counter sit-ins to Black power, inspired much of this change. Yet it was clear that African Americans' aspirations exceeded white Americans' commitment to genuine equality. While the overturning of crude forms of racism in the South gained wide support, the push for equality in fact as well as in law met powerful resistance.

Feminists, Chicano and red power activists, environmentalists, and gay liberationists, carried the tide of reform into the 1970s. They pushed Nixon's Republican administration to sustain and even extend many liberal programs. At the same time, the rapid social changes and disorder of the era—along with a costly and difficult war in Vietnam—were undermining faith in government and boosting the conservative movement.

EXPLAIN WHY IT MATTERS

Civil Rights Act of 1964 (p. 826)

War on Poverty (p. 826)

Medicare and Medicaid (p. 828)

Voting Rights Act of 1965 (p. 829)

Warren Court (p. 831)

Student Nonviolent Coordinating Committee (SNCC) (p. 832)

affirmative action (p. 834)

Black power (p. 837)

American Indian Movement (AIM) (p. 839)

Chicano movement (p. 840)

Stonewall riots (p. 844)

Environmental Protection Agency (EPA) (p. 845)

National Organization for Women (NOW) (p. 846)

Roe v. Wade (p. 848)

PUT IT ALL TOGETHER

THE GREAT SOCIETY

- What were the most significant domestic achievements of the Johnson administration? What were its most important failures?

- What assumptions about the responsibilities of government underlay Great Society programs?

PROTEST AND REBELLION

- Why was the Black freedom struggle so important to other social movements of the 1960s and 1970s? Were there any other common threads among them?

- What conditions, old and new, spurred second-wave feminism? What kind of reactions did the movement generate?

THE CONSERVATIVE MOVEMENT

- What issues led those on the right to mobilize in the 1960s?

- What Democratic initiatives did Nixon's Republican administration embrace, and why?

LOOKING BACKWARD, LOOKING AHEAD

- How did the African American quest for civil rights in the 1960s differ from that of the 1940s and 1950s?

- What kinds of opposition emerged in the late 1960s to liberal reforms and radical protest? How would that resistance shape politics in the decades that followed?

29

CONFRONTING LIMITS AT HOME AND ABROAD

1961–1979

This chapter discusses the following questions:

- What led to the United States' deepening involvement in Vietnam?
- How did a war abroad provoke a war at home?
- How did U.S. foreign policy change course under Nixon?
- What accounted for Americans' political shift to the right in the 1970s?
- What challenges did the Carter administration face?
- Conclusion: How did the constraints of the 1970s transform U.S. policy and politics?

▶ **A Memorial Service in Vietnam** U.S. soldiers conduct a makeshift funeral service in Vietnam in December of 1965, following a major escalation of the American war in Southeast Asia. The rifles, boots, and helmets stood in for seven of their comrades, killed during a search and destroy mission in the jungle west of Lai Khe. Younger than those who had served in America's prior wars, these men contended with unfamiliar terrain, difficult fighting conditions, uncertain allies, and skeptical civilians. AP Photo/ Henri Huet.

AN AMERICAN STORY

L ieutenant Frederick Downs Jr. grew up on an Indiana farm and enlisted in the army, and a tour of duty in the Vietnam War, after three years of college. Leaving a ten-month-old daughter behind, he completed officer training and shipped out for South Vietnam in September 1967. The infantry platoon leader and his men arrived there "cocky and sure of our destiny, gung ho, invincible."

That confidence was tempered by what they faced in Vietnam. Unlike most of America's previous wars, there was no fixed battlefront, but rather a shifting, confounding search for South Vietnamese rebels and their North Vietnamese allies. In a civil war characterized by guerrilla tactics, Downs and his fellow soldiers struggled to distinguish civilians from combatants and destroyed entire villages simply because they might be used by the enemy.

Downs had faith that his country could win the war but found the South Vietnamese army utterly incompetent. "Maybe the people in Nam are worth saving, but their army isn't worth shit," he wrote in his memoir. Downs won several medals for bravery before his one-year stint in Vietnam ended, a land mine blowing off his left arm and wedging shrapnel into his legs and back.

Downs served in Vietnam at the height of a U.S. engagement sustained by successive Cold War presidents — Truman, Eisenhower, and Kennedy — and dramatically escalated by Lyndon Johnson in 1965. That escalation transformed a civil war among the Vietnamese into America's war, a protracted, destructive, and costly conflict that would take another decade to end. At peak strength in 1968, 543,000 U.S. military personnel served in Vietnam; all told, some 2.6 million saw duty there.

Yet this massive intervention failed to defeat North Vietnam. It also created intense divisions at home, "poisoning the soul of America," in Downs's words. Some Americans supported the goal of a non-Communist South Vietnam and decried only their government's failure to pursue it successfully. Others contended that this objective was neither a vital interest of the United States nor within its capacity or moral right to achieve. Back home in college after months of surgery, Downs encountered a man who asked about the hook descending from his sleeve. When Downs explained that he had lost his arm in Vietnam, the man shot back, "Serves you right."

The war exacted enormous costs. Like Downs, more than 150,000 soldiers suffered severe wounds, and more than 58,000 lost their lives, as did some two million Vietnamese. The war also derailed reform efforts at home, depleted the federal budget, disrupted the economy, kindled domestic discord, and led to the violation of protesters' rights. Defeat in Vietnam hung over a chastened era, one in which American military might — but also U.S. economic prosperity, the expansion of opportunity to all, and even the integrity of the White House — could no longer be assured. Downs had once believed the United States "invincible" and its people "sure of our destiny." Many by the 1970s instead wondered if the nation had lost its way, presenting an opening for the patriotic, optimistic message advanced by Republican Ronald Reagan in 1980.

What led to the United States' deepening involvement in Vietnam?

Renewed Cold War rivalry in Latin America, Europe, and even outer space contributed to the widening of the American engagement in Southeast Asia. So did a fear among U.S. leaders about the consequences, psychological as much as diplomatic, of conceding defeat in the struggle against communism. Building on the policies of their predecessors, Kennedy and Johnson claimed a vital U.S. interest in Vietnam, at first committing just arms and military advisers to the conflict but eventually sending combat troops and launching bombing campaigns. The escalation of the war proceeded even as leaders doubted the capacity of the South Vietnamese army and their own forces' ability to win it. Those who served—younger, poorer, and more likely to be nonwhite than the troops who had fought in World War II or Korea—paid the price.

How did anticommunism shape Kennedy's foreign policy?

John F. Kennedy entered the presidency a vigorous anti-Communist, warning in his inaugural address that the nation faced grave peril: "Each day the crises multiply. . . . Each day we draw nearer the hour of maximum danger." Although the president exaggerated the threat to national security, several developments in the early sixties heightened the sense of crisis. One was Soviet premier Nikita Khrushchev's public encouragement of "wars of national liberation," aligning the Soviet Union with independence movements in the developing world that were often anti-Western, even if they weren't Communist. In 1960 alone, seventeen African nations gained their independence.

Much more than his predecessors, Kennedy supported the aspirations of these new nations, believing the United States could win their people's hearts and minds. This was his rationale for the Peace Corps program (see chapter 28) and the Alliance for Progress, a largely ineffectual effort to help alleviate poverty in Latin America. Kennedy, however, coupled such efforts with an expansion of the elite special forces corps established under Eisenhower to aid groups resisting Communist-leaning movements. These counterinsurgency forces, including the army's Green Berets and the navy's SEALs, were trained to wage guerrilla warfare and equipped with the latest technology.

The first foreign policy crisis Kennedy faced lay in Cuba, just ninety miles off the Florida coast. Fidel Castro's 1959 revolution had moved Cuba into the Soviet orbit, and Eisenhower's Central Intelligence Agency (CIA) had planned an invasion to oust Castro. Kennedy ordered the invasion to proceed in April 1961, sending fourteen hundred anti-Castro exiles trained and armed by the CIA to the Bay of Pigs on the south shore of Cuba. Contrary to U.S. expectations, no popular uprising materialized to support them. Kennedy refused to provide direct military backup, and the invaders quickly fell to Castro's forces in what was painted as a humiliation for the United States.

Just days before the Bay of Pigs invasion, the Soviet Union dealt a psychological blow when a Soviet astronaut became the first human to orbit the earth. Kennedy called for a massive commitment to the space program, with the bold goal of sending a man to the moon by 1970. Congress authorized the Apollo program and boosted appropriations for space exploration. John H. Glenn orbited the earth in 1962, and the United States would by the end of the decade beat the Soviets to the moon, landing two astronauts there in 1969.

Cold War conflict also flared in Europe when Khrushchev demanded an agreement recognizing the existence of two Germanys and threatened U.S. occupation rights and access to West Berlin. The Soviet premier sought to halt the massive exodus of East Germans into West Berlin, a major embarrassment for the Communists. Khrushchev backed off from his threats after East Germany erected the **Berlin Wall** in August 1961 to stem the tide of escapees between the sectors. This concrete barrier between east and west would stand until 1989.

Kennedy used the Berlin crisis to add $3.2 billion to the defense budget, to increase draft calls, and to mobilize the reserves and National Guard. He also doubled the nation's nuclear force within three years, vastly increasing the number of nuclear weapons based in Europe and the supply of intercontinental ballistic missiles (ICBMs). The Soviet Union stepped up its own ICBM program, setting off the most intense arms race in history.

The superpowers came perilously close to using their weapons during the **Cuban missile crisis** in October 1962. When American spy planes captured aerial photographs of Soviet missile launching sites under construction in Cuba, Kennedy placed the military on full alert, announcing that the navy would turn back any Soviet vessel suspected of carrying missiles to Cuba. He warned that any attack launched from Cuba would trigger a full nuclear assault against the Soviet Union.

A terrifying thirteen days followed as the superpowers approached the brink of nuclear war. Disregarding his military advisers, Kennedy refused to bomb the missile sites. Russian ships carrying nuclear warheads toward Cuba turned back, and when one ship crossed the blockade line, the president ordered the navy to follow it rather than confront it. Meanwhile, Kennedy and Khrushchev negotiated an agreement: The Soviets would remove the missiles in exchange for a U.S. promise not to invade the island. Secretly, Kennedy also agreed to remove U.S. missiles from Turkey.

Berlin Wall
Barrier erected by East Germany in 1961 to halt the exodus of East Germans into West Berlin.

Cuban missile crisis
1962 standoff between the Soviet Union and the United States after the Soviets attempted to create a nuclear outpost in Cuba. In a negotiated settlement, the Soviet Union agreed to remove its missiles from Cuba, and the United States agreed to remove its missiles from Turkey.

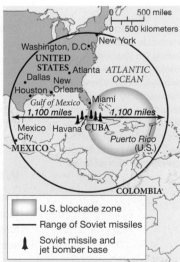

Cuban Missile Crisis, 1962

The episode compelled Kennedy to pursue an easing of hostilities with the Soviet Union. In June 1963, Kennedy stressed what the two superpowers had in common: "We all breathe the same air. We all cherish our children's future and we are all mortal." That year, the United States, the Soviet Union, and Great Britain signed a limited nuclear test ban treaty, reducing the threat of radioactive fallout and raising hopes for further arms reductions.

How did JFK respond to the insurgency in Southeast Asia?

By the time Kennedy took office, more than $1 billion in aid and seven hundred U.S. military advisers had failed to stabilize South Vietnam. Under assault from Communist North Vietnam as well as from rebels within, the U.S.-supported government in Saigon suffered from weak leadership and determined opposition.

The South Vietnamese insurgents—whom Americans derisively called Vietcong—had taken up arms when the Saigon government refused to hold elections. Increasingly, Ho Chi Minh's Communist government in North Vietnam supported the rebels, pledging land reform and the unification of Vietnam. The North constructed a network of infiltration routes, called the Ho Chi Minh Trail, in neighboring Laos and Cambodia, through which it sent people and supplies to help liberate the South (**Map 29.1**). Saigon's forces, the Army of the Republic of Vietnam (ARVN), could not defeat the insurgents. Ngo Dinh Diem, South Vietnam's premier from 1954 to 1963, garnered little support from the South Vietnamese, the majority of whom were Buddhist and saw the Catholic Diem as a corrupt tool of the West.

By 1963, the Saigon government was close to collapse, despite Kennedy's gradual increase of aid and advisers. He, like most American officials, assumed that technology and sheer military power could win in Vietnam. Yet U.S. weapons were ill-suited to guerrilla warfare and surprise attacks by the enemy. They also alienated the very people Americans were fighting for. Thousands of peasants were uprooted. Many others fell victim to bombs containing napalm, a highly flammable substance dropped by the South Vietnamese air force. In 1962, U.S. planes began to spray herbicides such as **Agent Orange** to destroy the insurgents' forest cover and food supply, laying waste to 5.5 million acres of forest and farmland and causing lasting environmental damage.

With tacit permission from Washington, South Vietnamese military leaders in November 1963 executed a coup against Diem. Yet there was no change in U.S. policy. In a speech to be given on the day he was assassinated, Kennedy warned, "We dare not weary of the task." At his death, 16,700 Americans were stationed in Vietnam, and one hundred had died there.

Agent Orange
Herbicide used extensively during the Vietnam War to destroy the hideouts and food supply of South Vietnamese insurgents. Its use was later linked to a wide range of illnesses that U.S. veterans and Vietnamese suffered after the war, including birth defects, cancer, and skin disorders.

Why did LBJ widen the U.S. commitment to Vietnam?

Lyndon B. Johnson's priorities for his presidency were tackling poverty and building the Great Society. Yet he shared the Cold War assumptions underlying Kennedy's foreign policy and continued the massive buildup of nuclear weapons as well as conventional and counterinsurgency forces.

Johnson was determined to foil revolutions like Castro's in Latin America. He sent troops to the U.S.-held Panama Canal Zone to quell an anti-American riot in

MAP ACTIVITY

MAP 29.1 ▶ The Vietnam War, 1964–1975 The United States sent 2.6 million soldiers to Vietnam and spent more than $150 billion on the longest war in American history to that point, but it was unable to prevent the unification of Vietnam under a Communist government.

READING THE MAP: What accords divided Vietnam into two nations? When were these accords signed, and where was the line of division drawn? Through what countries did the Ho Chi Minh Trail pass?

CONNECTIONS: What happened in the Gulf of Tonkin, and how did the United States respond? What was the Tet Offensive, and how did it affect the course of the war?

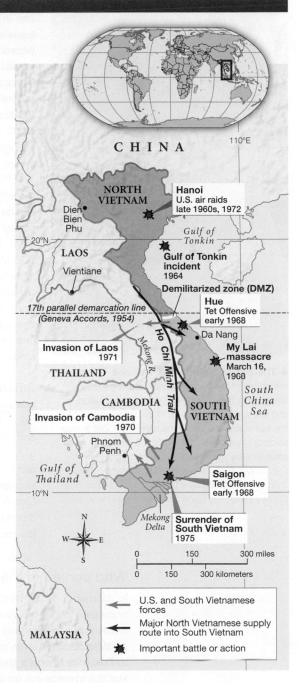

1964. The next year, Johnson ordered twenty thousand soldiers to the Dominican Republic to suppress a revolt, aiming to prevent "another Cuba." No Communists were found among the rebels; moreover, the president had acted without consulting either the Dominicans or the Organization of American States (OAS). This first outright show of U.S. force in Latin America in four decades violated the United States' pledge to respect national sovereignty in the region, generating cries of "Yankee imperialism."

Regarding the struggle in Southeast Asia, some advisers, politicians, and international leaders questioned the wisdom of continued intervention. Most U.S. allies did not consider Vietnam crucial to containing communism and were not prepared to share the military burden. Johnson expressed his own doubts privately: "I don't think it's worth fighting for and I don't think we can get out." Yet like Kennedy, Johnson remembered the political blows that Truman had taken when China fell to communism, and he was determined not "to be the president who saw Southeast Asia go the way China did."

Johnson knew that his South Vietnamese allies were ineffective and that many Vietnamese distrusted the American-supported government. And he agonized over sending young men into combat. Yet he continued to dispatch more military advisers, weapons, and economic aid. In August 1964, based on uncertain reports of North Vietnamese gunboats firing on U.S. destroyers in the Gulf of Tonkin (see Map 29.1), Johnson seized an opportunity to increase the pressure on North Vietnam with air strikes. He won from Congress the Gulf of Tonkin Resolution, which gave the president virtually unlimited authority to "repel any armed attacks against the forces of the United States and to prevent further aggression."

▲ **The Toll on Vietnamese Civilians** The guer-rilla nature of the Vietnam War made it especially devastating for civilians. As many as two million civilians were killed on both sides in the course of the war — almost double the number of Vietnamese soldiers killed — with many villages and agricultural areas entirely destroyed. In this photograph from September 1966, a Vietnamese woman and her children are framed by a U.S. soldier from the First Cavalry Division in Bong Son. AP Images/Henri Huet.

Soon after winning the election of 1964—and believing that a loss in Vietnam would damage his plans for a Great Society at home as well as American credibility in the world—Johnson widened the war. He dismissed reservations expressed by prominent Democrats and rejected peace overtures from North Vietnam tied to American withdrawal and a coalition government in South Vietnam. In 1965, he made the fateful decision to order U.S. troops into combat and to begin sustained bombing of the North. The administration downplayed the import of these policy changes, but they marked a critical turning point. Now it was genuinely America's war.

From 1965 to early 1968, the U.S. military presence grew to more than 500,000 troops as it escalated attacks on North Vietnam and its ally in the South, the National Liberation Front. To minimize protest at home and avoid provoking Chinese or Soviet involvement, Johnson expanded the war slowly but steadily. Eventually, U.S. pilots dropped 643,000 tons of bombs on North Vietnam and more than twice that amount in the South, the total surpassing all the explosives the United States dropped in World War II. The North Vietnamese withstood monthly death tolls of more than two thousand. In South Vietnam, the massive U.S. bombing campaign destroyed villages and fields, turning the former leading rice producer into a rice importer.

On the ground, General William Westmoreland's strategy of attrition was designed to seek out and kill the southern insurgents and members of the North Vietnamese regular army. Officials calculated progress not in territory seized but in "body counts" and "kill ratios"—the number of enemies killed relative to the cost in American and ARVN lives. However, North Vietnam sent in or recruited new Communist forces faster than they could be eliminated. "To win a battle, we had to kill them," explained Lieutenant Frederick Downs Jr. "For them to win, all they had to do was survive." Despite American troops inflicting great losses on the enemy, the war remained a stalemate.

Who served in the Vietnam War?

In contrast to World War II, when the average soldier was twenty-six years old, teenagers fought the Vietnam War. Until the Twenty-Sixth Amendment to the Constitution lowered the voting age from twenty-one to eighteen in 1971, most soldiers could not even vote for the officials who sent them into battle. All the men in Frederick Downs's platoon were between the ages of eighteen and twenty-one, and the average age for all soldiers was nineteen. One eighteen-year-old reflected, "I should have been home getting ready to take a pretty girl to the prom."

The composition of the United States fighting forces in Vietnam was a departure in other ways. Men of all classes had fought in World War II, but in Vietnam the poor and working class constituted about 80 percent of the troops. Privileged youths avoided the

VISUAL ACTIVITY

▶ **Covering the War** Photojournalists and television reporters covered the Vietnam War extensively, bringing images of Southeast Asia and the ravages of war into American living rooms. In the process, they contributed to public debates over the conflict's progress and purpose. Here, a CBS camera crew interviews U.S. soldiers on Tay Ninh Road in 1967. Tim Page/Getty Images.

READING THE IMAGE: What does the photograph suggest about the access of media to military personnel during the war? What impact might live footage of combat and conditions in Vietnam have made on viewers at home and on the growing antiwar movement?

CONNECTIONS: What was the status of U.S. involvement in Vietnam in 1967, the year this photograph was taken? How had that changed from two years earlier?

draft with college deferments or used family connections to get into the National Guard. Sent from Plainville, Kansas, to Vietnam in 1965, Mike Clodfelter could not recall "a single middle-class son of the town's businessmen, lawyers, doctors, or ranchers from my high school graduating class who experienced the Armageddon of our generation."

More than World War II, Vietnam was also a men's war since the United States did not undergo full mobilization. Still, between 7,500 and 11,000 women served in Vietnam, the vast majority of them nurses, many of whom struggled with their helplessness to repair the maimed and dead bodies they attended.

Early in the war, Black Americans constituted a striking 31 percent of combat troops, often choosing the military over the meager opportunities in the civilian economy. Special forces ranger Arthur E. Woodley Jr. recalled, "The only way I could possibly make it out of the ghetto was to be the best soldier I possibly could." Death rates among Black soldiers were also disproportionately high until 1966, when the military adjusted personnel assignments in response to criticism.

Soldiers in previous wars had served "for the duration," but in Vietnam, a soldier served a one-year tour of duty. A commander called it "the worst personnel policy in history," because men had less incentive to fight near the end of their tours, striving merely to stay alive and intact. The young troops faced extremely difficult conditions. Frederick Downs's platoon fought in thick leech-ridden jungles, in rain and oppressive heat, always vulnerable to sniper bullets and land mines. In their hunt for insurgents, the ARVN and American troops killed and wounded thousands of civilians and destroyed their villages. By 1968, nearly 30 percent of the war-scarred population had become refugees. According to Downs, "All Vietnamese had a common desire—to see us go home."

REVIEW

Why did massive amounts of airpower and ground troops fail to bring U.S. victory in Vietnam?

How did a war abroad provoke a war at home?

The failure to stabilize South Vietnam, even as the U.S. military presence and casualties grew, created grave challenges for the administration at home. After 1965, President Johnson fought a war on two fronts as domestic opposition to the war swelled. By 1968, battered both by antiwar critics and by the military's insistence on more troops, Johnson announced a halt to the bombing, a new effort at negotiations, and his decision not to pursue reelection. Demonstrations, violence, and assassinations continued to convulse the increasingly polarized nation, however. Vietnam took center stage in the 1968 election, with voters narrowly electing Republican Richard M. Nixon, who promised to achieve "peace with honor."

What fueled the antiwar movement?

Johnson's authorization of bombing and ground troops transformed previously quiet doubts about the war into a mass movement. In April 1965, Students for a Democratic Society (SDS) recruited twenty thousand people for the first major antiwar demonstration in Washington, D.C. Thousands of students protested against Reserve Officers Training Corps (ROTC) programs, CIA and defense industry recruiters, and military research projects on their campuses. Environmentalists condemned the use of chemical weapons, including the toxic Agent Orange. Women Strike for Peace organized a protest of two thousand at the Pentagon in 1967.

By 1968, antiwar sentiment entered the mainstream, with the *New York Times*, the *Wall Street Journal*, *Life* magazine, civil rights leader Martin Luther King Jr., and popular TV anchorman Walter Cronkite all voicing opposition. Clergy, businesspeople, scientists, and physicians formed their own groups to pressure Johnson to stop the bombing and start negotiations. Antiwar action took diverse forms, including public demonstrations, draft card burnings, and attempts to halt troop trains. The peace movement, although a small fraction of the population, focused media attention on resistance to the war, severely limiting the administration's options. The twenty-year-old consensus around Cold War foreign policy had shattered.

Some Americans refused to serve. The World Boxing Association stripped Muhammad Ali of his heavyweight title when he said he would not "drop bombs and bullets on brown people in Vietnam while so-called negro people in Louisville are treated like dogs." More than 170,000 men gained conscientious objector status and performed nonmilitary duties at home or in Vietnam. About sixty thousand fled the

▲ **Antiwar Leaflet and Button** This leaflet from 1969 and button from 1965 suggest the variety of ways protesters voiced opposition to the Vietnam War. Stuart Lutz/Gado/Getty Images.

country to escape the draft, and more than 200,000 were accused of failing to register or of committing other draft violations.

Some opponents of the war saw the conflict in moral terms. They sought total withdrawal, claiming that their country had no right to interfere in a civil war and to inflict suffering on the Vietnamese people. A larger segment of antiwar protesters believed that the war could not be won at a bearable cost. Working-class people were no more opposed than other groups, but they recognized the class dimensions of both the war and the antiwar movement. A firefighter whose son had died in Vietnam bitterly observed, "It's people like us who give up our sons for the country."

The antiwar movement outraged millions of Americans who supported the war. Some members of the generation who had fought against Hitler could not understand younger people's refusal to support their government. They expressed their anger at war protesters with bumper stickers reading "America: Love It or Leave It."

By 1967, aware that "discontent with the war is now wide and deep," Johnson attempted to silence critics. He equated opposition to the war with communism and assistance to the enemy. His administration deceived the public by making optimistic statements about military progress in Vietnam, concealing officials' doubts. Johnson ordered the CIA to spy on antiwar protesters, and the FBI infiltrated the peace movement in an attempt to disrupt it and spread false information about activists. Even the resort to illegal measures, however, failed to subdue the growing antiwar ranks.

▲ **Mothers against the War** Founded in 1961 to work for nuclear disarmament, Women Strike for Peace began to protest the Vietnam War in 1963. As "concerned housewives" and mothers, members mobilized around the slogan "Not Our Sons, Not Your Sons, Not Their Sons." In February 1967, more than two thousand women protested at the Pentagon, banging on doors that were locked as they approached. Bettmann/Getty Images.

Why was the Tet Offensive a turning point in the war?

The year 1968 was marked by violent confrontations around the world. Antigovernment protests erupted from Mexico City to Paris to Tokyo. In the United States, conflict broke out between so-called hawks who called for intensification of the war and doves who sought de-escalation or withdrawal.

With troop strength nearing half a million and military deaths approaching twenty thousand by the end of 1967, serious doubts about the war penetrated the administration itself. Secretary of Defense Robert McNamara, a principal architect of U.S. involvement, now believed that the North Vietnamese "won't quit no matter how much bombing we do." He feared for the image of the United States, "the world's greatest superpower, killing or seriously injuring

1,000 noncombatants a week, while trying to pound a tiny, backward nation into submission." McNamara left the administration in early 1968 but without voicing his concerns publicly.

A critical turning point in the war and in American public opinion came with the **Tet Offensive**. In January 1968, during Tet, the Vietnamese New Year holiday, the North Vietnamese and southern insurgents launched a campaign of attacks on key cities, every major American base, and the U.S. Embassy in Saigon. The North lost ten times as many soldiers as ARVN and U.S. forces. But Tet was psychologically devastating to the United States, exposing a "credibility gap" between official statements that offered optimistic progress reports to the U.S. public and the reality of a war that America was not close to winning. The attacks created one million more South Vietnamese refugees, and public approval of Johnson's handling of the war plummeted to 26 percent.

In the aftermath of Tet, Johnson conferred with advisers—some of whom had steered Cold War policy since the 1940s—and concluded that it was time to "take steps to disengage." He announced a sharp reduction in the bombing of North Vietnam and an offer to begin peace talks. His popular support and vision for a Great Society in tatters, Johnson added the stunning declaration that he would not run for reelection. The U.S. goal remained a non-Communist South Vietnam, but military strategy would rely more heavily on the South Vietnamese to achieve it.

Although negotiations began in Paris in May 1968, the United States and North Vietnam could not agree on terms, and the fighting continued. Meanwhile, violence escalated at home. Protests struck two hundred college campuses in the spring of 1968. In the bloodiest action, students occupied buildings at Columbia University in New York City, condemning the university's war-related research and its treatment of Black Americans. When negotiations failed, city police stormed the buildings. Scores of demonstrators were injured, and hundreds were arrested. A student strike ensued, prematurely ending the academic year.

How did divisions over Vietnam influence the 1968 election?

In 1968, the violence of the war also marked U.S. electoral politics. In June, two months after the murder of Martin Luther King Jr. and the tumult that followed, antiwar candidate Senator Robert F. Kennedy, campaigning for the Democratic Party's presidential nomination, was killed by a Palestinian Arab refugee angered by the senator's support for Israel.

In August, several thousand demonstrators arrived in Chicago, site of the Democratic National Convention—some to support peace candidate Senator Eugene McCarthy, others to cause disruption. When demonstrators jeered at orders to disperse, police attacked them with tear gas and clubs. Street battles continued for three days, culminating in a police riot where officers turned their weapons even against reporters, peaceful demonstrators, and convention delegates. The bloodshed in Chicago had little effect on the convention's outcome, however. Vice President Hubert H. Humphrey easily defeated the antiwar McCarthy for the Democratic nomination.

In contrast to the turmoil in Chicago, the Republican convention met peacefully and nominated former vice president Richard M. Nixon. The American Independent

---

Tet Offensive
Major campaign of attacks launched throughout South Vietnam in early 1968 by the North Vietnamese and southern insurgents. A turning point in the war, it exposed the disparity between official statements and the reality on the ground, undermining Americans' confidence in their government.

Party introduced a third candidate into the race, nominating staunch segregationist George C. Wallace. The former Alabama governor spoke especially to white working-class voters' dissatisfaction with the reforms and rebellions of the 1960s, stoking their outrage at assaults on patriotism, religion, and traditional values. Nixon cautiously appealed to the resentments that fueled the Wallace campaign, calling for "law and order" and attacking liberal Supreme Court decisions, busing for school desegregation, and student protesters.

The candidates differed little on the central issue of Vietnam. Nixon promised "an honorable end" to the war but did not indicate how to achieve it. Humphrey had serious reservations about U.S. policy in Vietnam but was tied to Johnson's policies and did not air his doubts publicly. Nixon edged out Humphrey by just half a million popular votes but won 301 electoral college votes to Humphrey's 191 and Wallace's 46 (**Map 29.2**). The Democrats maintained control of Congress.

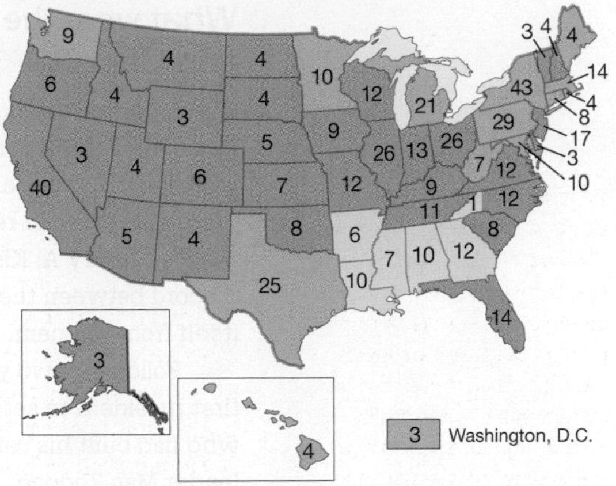

The 1968 election revealed deep cracks in the coalition that had secured Democratic dominance in Washington since the 1930s. Johnson's liberal policies on race shattered a century of Democratic Party rule in the South, which delivered all its electoral votes to Wallace and Nixon. Elsewhere, large numbers of blue-collar workers broke their traditional alliance with the Democrats to vote for Wallace or Nixon, associating the Democratic Party with racial turmoil, poverty programs, changing sexual mores, and failure to turn the tide in Vietnam.

3 | Washington, D.C.

Candidate	Electoral Vote	Popular Vote	Percent of Popular Vote
Richard M. Nixon (Republican)	301	31,770,237	43.4
Hubert H. Humphrey (Democrat)	191	31,270,533	42.7
George C. Wallace (American Independent)	46	9,906,141	13.5

Note: North Carolina split its vote, with one elector voting for Wallace.

MAP 29.2 ▲ The Election of 1968

REVIEW

How did the Vietnam War affect the election of 1968?

How did U.S. foreign policy change course under Nixon?

Having made a name for himself as a vocal anti-Communist in Congress and then as vice president to Eisenhower, President Richard Milhous Nixon was a familiar political figure by 1968. He would also be a transformative one in the realm of world affairs. Diverging from Republican orthodoxy, he made dramatic overtures to the Soviet Union and China and brokered important arms control agreements. Yet anticommunism remained central to Nixon's foreign policy, leading him to back repressive regimes around the world. Despite mounting opposition, the president also aggressively pursued the war in Vietnam, expanding the conflict into Cambodia and Laos. America's longest war would end during his presidency, but Nixon was forced to settle for peace without victory.

What were the results of détente with the Soviet Union and China?

Nixon hoped to make his mark on history by applying his broad understanding of international relations to a changing world. He grasped that the "rigid and bipolar world of the 1940s and 1950s" was changing and that America's European allies were interested in reducing East-West tensions. Nixon and his national security adviser, Henry A. Kissinger, also believed that they could exploit the increasing discord between the Soviet Union and China to help the United States extricate itself from Vietnam.

Following two years of secret negotiations, Nixon in 1972 became the nation's first president to set foot on Chinese soil while in office, an astonishing move by one who had built his career on anticommunism. As the president remarked to Chinese leader Mao Zedong, "Those on the right can do what those on the left only talk about." Although Nixon's visit was largely symbolic, cultural and scientific exchanges followed, and American manufacturers began to find markets in China—small steps toward the rapid globalization of commerce in the 1990s (see chapter 30).

As Nixon and Kissinger had hoped, the warming of U.S.-Chinese relations furthered **détente**, their term for easing conflict with the Soviet Union. Détente did not mean abandoning containment but rather focusing on issues of shared U.S.-Soviet concern in order to foster a stable international order.

Arms control, trade, and stability in Europe were three areas where the superpowers had common interests. In May 1972, Nixon became the first Cold War president to visit Moscow, signing agreements on trade and cooperation in science and space. Most significantly, the United States and Soviet Union signed the **Strategic Arms Limitation Treaty (SALT)** in 1972, halting new production of ICBMs. They also agreed to ban the development of antiballistic missile systems, to prevent both nations from developing a defense secure enough against a nuclear attack to risk a first strike.

In 1975, U.S., Canadian, Soviet, and European leaders signed the historic Helsinki accords that formally recognized the post–World War II boundaries in Europe but also proclaimed "the universal significance of human rights and fundamental freedoms." Dissidents in the Soviet Union and its Eastern European satellites would use this official promise of rights to challenge the Soviet dictatorship and help overthrow it fifteen years later.

Where and why did the United States intervene around the globe?

Despite the thaw in relations with the Soviet Union and China, Nixon and Kissinger continued to view left-wing movements around the world as a threat to U.S. interests. Following a pattern begun by Eisenhower, the Nixon administration ordered his CIA director to destabilize the government of Salvador Allende, a self-proclaimed Marxist who was elected president of Chile in 1970. In 1973, the CIA helped the Chilean military engineer a coup, resulting in Allende's death and a ruthless dictatorship under General Augusto Pinochet.

détente
Term (from the French for "loosening") used for the easing of conflict between the United States and the Soviet Union during the Nixon administration by focusing on issues of common concern, such as arms control and trade.

Strategic Arms Limitation Treaty (SALT)
1972 agreement between the United States and the Soviet Union limiting antiballistic missiles (ABMs) to two each. The treaty prevented either nation from building an ABM defense system so secure against a nuclear attack that it would risk a first strike.

The Nixon administration backed other repressive regimes as well. In southern Africa, it eased pressures on white minority governments that disenfranchised and tyrannized the Black majority. In the Middle East, the United States sent massive arms shipments to support the shah of Iran's harsh regime with an eye on the country's enormous petroleum reserves and its status as a stable anti-Communist ally.

Nixon pursued a delicate balance between defending Israel's security and seeking the goodwill of Arab nations strategically and economically important to the United States. Conflict between Israel and the Arab nations led to the Six-Day War in 1967, with Israel winning a stunning victory, seizing the Sinai Peninsula and Gaza Strip from Egypt, the Golan Heights from Syria, and the West Bank, where hundreds of thousands of Palestinians lived, from Jordan. In October 1973, on the Jewish holiday Yom Kippur, Egypt and Syria retaliated with a surprise attack.

The Nixon administration sided with Israel, prompting Arab nations to organize an oil embargo that resulted in severe shortages in the United States. After Israel repulsed the attack, tensions remained high. The Arab countries refused to recognize Israel, Israel began to settle its citizens in the West Bank and other territories it had seized during the Six-Day War, and no solution could be found for the Palestinian refugees who had been displaced by the creation of Israel in 1948. The conflict continued to simmer, as did anti-American sentiment among Arabs.

Key:
- Israel before 1967
- Land gained by Israel in Six-Day War
- Land returned to Egypt, 1973–1981

Map labels: LEBANON, Beirut, Damascus, SYRIA, Sea of Galilee, Mediterranean Sea, Tel Aviv, GOLAN HEIGHTS, WEST BANK, Amman, Jerusalem, GAZA STRIP, Dead Sea, ISRAEL, Suez Canal, JORDAN, Sinai, Gulf of Suez, EGYPT

Israeli Territorial Gains in the Six-Day War, 1967

How did the Vietnam War end?

Like Johnson, Nixon was determined not to let South Vietnam fall to the Communists, for fear of damaging American credibility. **(See "Analyzing Historical Evidence: Ending the War in Vietnam" on page 868.)** Regardless of the wisdom of the initial intervention, Kissinger asserted, "the commitment of 500,000 Americans has settled the importance of Vietnam. . . . What is involved now is confidence in American promises."

From 1969 to 1972, Nixon and Kissinger pursued a three-pronged approach. First, they tried to expand the South Vietnamese military and strengthen local institutions. Second, Nixon gradually reduced the U.S. presence in Vietnam, although casualties remained high. Together, these tactics were known as "Vietnamization," or the transfer of the fighting of the war to the Vietnamese. Third, the United States replaced U.S. forces with intensive bombing.

In the spring of 1969, Nixon opened a ferocious air war in Cambodia in an attempt to eliminate North Vietnamese sanctuaries there, dropping more than 100,000 tons of bombs. Nixon hid this campaign from Congress and the public for more than a year, ordering an invasion of Cambodia in April 1970. He argued: "If, when the chips are down, the world's most powerful nation . . . acts like a pitiful, helpless giant, the forces of totalitarianism and anarchy will threaten free nations and free institutions throughout the world."

This new phase of the war triggered outrage at home. More than 100,000 protested in Washington, D.C., and students boycotted classes on hundreds of

ANALYZING HISTORICAL EVIDENCE

Ending the War in Vietnam

By 1969, a clear majority of Americans wanted their country out of Vietnam. As these documents suggest, disagreement raged over how to get out and what the consequences of U.S. withdrawal would be.

DOCUMENT 1

Richard M. Nixon Explains His Policy of Vietnamization, November 3, 1969

Elected on the promise of ending the war, Nixon adopted a plan of "Vietnamization": strengthening South Vietnam so that it could take over its own defense and U.S. forces could depart. Here Nixon explains why he chose Vietnamization over immediate withdrawal.

But the question facing us today is: Now that we are in the war, what is the best way to end it?

In January I could only conclude that the precipitate withdrawal of American forces from Vietnam would be a disaster not only for South Vietnam but for the United States and for the cause of peace.

For the South Vietnamese, our precipitate withdrawal would inevitably allow the Communists to repeat the massacres which followed their takeover in the North 15 years before. . . .

For the United States, this first defeat in our Nation's history would result in a collapse of confidence in American leadership, not only in Asia but throughout the world. Three American Presidents have recognized the great stakes involved in Vietnam and understood what had to be done. . . .

For the future of peace, precipitate withdrawal would thus be a disaster of immense magnitude.

— A nation cannot remain great if it betrays its allies and lets down its friends.

— Our defeat and humiliation in South Vietnam without question would promote recklessness in the councils of those great powers who have not yet abandoned their goals of world conquest.

— This would spark violence wherever our commitments help maintain the peace — in the Middle East, in Berlin, eventually even in the Western Hemisphere. . . .

I pledged in my campaign for the Presidency to end the war in a way that we could win the peace. I have initiated a plan of action which will enable me to keep that pledge.

The more support I can have from the American people, the sooner that pledge can be redeemed; for the more divided we are at home, the less likely the enemy is to negotiate at Paris.

Let us be united for peace. Let us also be united against defeat. Because let us understand: North Vietnam cannot defeat or humiliate the United States. Only Americans can do that.

Source: Excerpt from *Public Papers of the Presidents of the United States: Richard Nixon, 1969* (Washington, DC: U.S. Government Printing Office, 1971), 901–9.

DOCUMENT 2

A Vietnam Veteran Urges Congress to End the War, April 22, 1971

John Kerry was a decorated navy lieutenant who served in Vietnam in 1968 and 1969 and later became a U.S. senator, presidential candidate, and secretary of state. He provided this testimony as a leader of Vietnam Veterans against the War.

. . . In our opinion, and from our experience, there is nothing in South Vietnam, nothing which could happen that realistically threatens the United States of America. And to attempt to justify the loss of one American life in Vietnam, Cambodia, or Laos by linking such loss to the preservation of freedom . . . is to us the height of criminal hypocrisy, and it is that kind of hypocrisy which we feel has torn this country apart. . . .

We found that not only was it a civil war, an effort by a people who had for years been seeking their liberation from any colonial influence whatsoever, but also we found that the Vietnamese . . . were hard put to take up the fight against the threat we were supposedly saving them from.

We found most people didn't even know the difference between communism and democracy. They only wanted to work in rice paddies without helicopters strafing them and bombs with napalm burning their villages and tearing their country apart. They wanted everything to do with the war, particularly with this foreign presence of the United States of America, to leave them alone in peace, and they practiced the art of survival by siding with whichever military force was present at a particular time, be it Vietcong, North Vietnamese, or American.

We found also that all too often American men were dying in those rice paddies for want of support from their allies. We saw firsthand how money from American taxes was used for a corrupt dictatorial regime. We saw that many people in this country had a one-sided idea of who was kept free by our flag, as blacks provided the highest percentage of casualties. We saw Vietnam ravaged equally by American bombs as well as by search and destroy missions, as well as by Vietcong terrorism, and yet we listened while this country tried to blame all of the havoc on the Viet Cong. . . .

We watched the U.S. falsification of body counts, in fact the glorification of body counts. We listened while month after month we were told the back of the enemy was about to break. We fought using weapons against "oriental human beings," with quotation marks around that. We fought using weapons against those people

which I do not believe this country would dream of using were we fighting in the European theater. . . .

Now we are told that the men who fought there must watch quietly while American lives are lost so that we can exercise the incredible arrogance of Vietnamizing the Vietnamese. . . .

Each day to facilitate the process by which the United States washes her hands of Vietnam someone has to give up his life so that the United States doesn't have to admit something that the entire world already knows, so that we can't say that we have made a mistake. Someone has to die so that President Nixon won't be, and these are his words, "the first President to lose a war."

We are asking Americans to think about that because how do you ask a man to be the last man to die in Vietnam? How do you ask a man to be the last man to die for a mistake?

Source: Excerpt from *Legislative Proposals Relating to the War in Southeast Asia, Hearings before the U.S. Senate Committee on Foreign Relations,* 92nd Cong. 180–210 (April–May 1971).

Questions for Analysis

SUMMARIZE THE ARGUMENT: Why did Nixon consider it crucial to remain engaged in the war until South Vietnam's freedom from Communist control was assured? What reasons did Kerry give for placing U.S. withdrawal from Vietnam above all other considerations?

RECOGNIZE VIEWPOINTS: Regarding the impact of U.S. actions in Vietnam, which nations or groups most concerned Nixon? Which most concerned Kerry?

CONSIDER THE CONTEXT: How were Nixon and Kerry both correct about what would happen when the United States left Vietnam?

campuses. At a rally at Kent State University in Ohio, National Guard troops opened fire, killing four and wounding ten others. Referring to the killing of white students at the hands of the state, a Black woman in Harlem commented, "They're starting to treat their own children like they treat us." Less than two weeks later, in a confrontation at Jackson State College in Mississippi, police killed two Black students.

Congressional reaction to the invasion of Cambodia revealed deepening concern about abuses of presidential power. In the name of national security, presidents since Franklin Roosevelt had conducted foreign policy without the consent or sometimes even the knowledge of Congress—for example, Eisenhower in Iran and Kennedy in Cuba. But in their determination to win the war in Vietnam, Johnson and Nixon had taken extreme measures to deceive the public and silence critics. The Senate voted to terminate the Gulf of Tonkin Resolution and to cut funds for the Cambodian operation. By the end of June 1970, Nixon had pulled all U.S. troops out of Cambodia.

In 1971, Vietnam veterans became a visible part of the peace movement, the first men in U.S. history to protest a war in which they had fought. They held a public investigation of "war crimes" in Vietnam, rallied in front of the Capitol, and cast away their war medals. In May of that year, veterans numbered among the forty thousand protesters who engaged in civil disobedience in an effort to shut down Washington. Officials made more than twelve thousand arrests, which courts later ruled violations of protesters' rights.

My Lai massacre
U.S. soldiers' killing of an entire village of four hundred Vietnamese civilians in 1968. Covered up by the military, revelations about the massacre came to light during the court-martial of Lieutenant William Calley in 1970.

Revelations about the **My Lai massacre** of 1968, which came to light during the court-martial of Lieutenant William Calley in 1970, further eroded support for the war. During the trial, Americans learned that Calley's company had killed every inhabitant of the hamlet of My Lai—four hundred villagers, nearly all of them old men, women, and children—even though it had encountered no enemy forces. They also learned of the military's cover-up of the massacre for more than a year before a journalist exposed it. Eventually, twelve officers and enlisted men were charged with murder or assault, but only Calley was convicted.

Pentagon Papers
Secret government documents published in 1971 related to an internal study of the Vietnam War. The documents revealed official pessimism about the war despite public assurances about its progress.

Administration policy suffered another blow in 1971 when the *New York Times* published portions of the *Pentagon Papers*, a secret internal study of the war begun in 1967. Nixon attempted to halt further publication, but the Supreme Court ruled this a violation of the First Amendment. Subsequent circulation of the *Pentagon Papers*, which revealed officials' private pessimism about the war's progress even as they made rosy promises, heightened public disillusionment, and undermined the government's credibility. More than 60 percent of Americans polled in 1971 considered it a mistake to have sent American troops to Vietnam; 58 percent believed the war to be immoral.

Military morale sank in the last years of the war. Having been exposed to the antiwar movement at home, many soldiers expressed little faith in their mission. Racial tensions among the troops mounted, and many sought escape in illegal drugs. Enlisted men committed hundreds of "fraggings," or attacks on officers. In a 1971 report, a retired Marine colonel warned: "Our army that now remains in Vietnam [is] near mutinous."

Despite fierce disapproval and protests, Nixon and Kissinger continued to believe that intensive firepower could bring victory in Vietnam. They resumed sustained bombing of the north in 1972, which led to renewed negotiations and a formal peace accord in Paris in early 1973. The agreement required removal of all U.S. troops and military advisers from South Vietnam but allowed North Vietnamese forces to remain. Both sides agreed to return prisoners of war. Nixon called the agreement "peace with honor," but in fact, it allowed only a face-saving withdrawal. Unlike the ending of World War II, remarked an American Legion commander, "There's nothing to celebrate."

After the U.S. withdrawal, fighting resumed immediately among the Vietnamese. In 1975, North Vietnam launched a new offensive, seizing Saigon. The Americans remaining in the country hastily evacuated, along with 150,000 of their South Vietnamese allies. Confusion and tragedy marked the rushed departure. The United States lacked sufficient capacity to evacuate all those who had supported the South Vietnamese government, prompting a U.S. diplomat to remark, "The rest of our lives we will be haunted by how we betrayed those people." Eventually more than 600,000 Vietnamese fled to the United States, but others lost their lives trying to escape, and many who could not get out suffered from political persecution.

What were the legacies of the U.S. defeat in Southeast Asia?

During the four years it took Nixon to end the war, he had expanded the conflict into Cambodia and Laos and launched massive bombing campaigns. Although increasing numbers of legislators criticized the war, Congress never denied the funds to fight it. Only after the peace accords did the legislative branch attempt to reassert its constitutional authority in the making of war. The **War Powers Act** of 1973 required the president to secure congressional approval for any substantial, long-term deployment of troops abroad. The new law, however, did little to reverse the distrust of government that resulted from revelations of U.S. leaders' dishonesty about the war's conduct.

The war produced widespread criticism of the draft from both the left and right. As the United States withdrew from Vietnam, Nixon and Congress agreed to abandon conscription. Military leaders predicted that an all-volunteer army would make for a more disciplined and professional fighting force. Yet ending service as a common obligation would distance most Americans from the horrors of warfare and from the military, whose ranks would disproportionately be filled by poorer Americans and people of color.

Four presidents had declared that the survival of South Vietnam was critical to U.S. containment policy. Yet their predictions that a Communist victory in South Vietnam would set the dominoes toppling did not materialize. Vietnam, Laos, and Cambodia all fell within the Communist camp in the spring of 1975, but the rest of Southeast Asia did not. The fear of a monolithic Communist power dominating Asia was undercut when China and Vietnam reverted to their historically hostile relationship.

The long pursuit of victory in Vietnam complicated the United States' relations with its allies, many of whom had doubted the wisdom of the war. The use of terrifying American military power against a small Asian country also alienated many in the developing world. The war set off turmoil at home, increased presidential power at the expense of congressional authority and public accountability, weakened

War Powers Act
1973 law requiring that the president secure congressional approval for any substantial, long-term deployment of troops abroad. The legislation was an attempt by Congress to reassert its constitutional authority over war making in the aftermath of Vietnam.

TABLE 29.1 Vietnam War Casualties	
United States	
Battle deaths	47,434
Other deaths	10,786
Wounded	153,303
South Vietnam	
Killed in action	110,357
Military wounded	499,026
Civilians killed	415,000
Civilians wounded	913,000
Communist Regulars and Guerrillas	
Killed in action	66,000

Source: U.S. Department of Defense.

the economy, diminished trust in government, and contributed to the downfall of two presidents.

The cruelest legacy of Vietnam fell on those who had served. More than 58,000 Americans lost their lives (**Table 29.1**). For those who survived, the war's pain endured. "The general public just wanted to ignore us," remembered Frederick Downs, while opponents of the war "wanted to argue with us until we felt guilty about what we had done over there." Many veterans believed in the war's aims and felt betrayed by its outcome. Others blamed the government for sacrificing the nation's youth in an immoral, unnecessary war, referring to their dead comrades as having been "wasted." Still others questioned the effects of U.S. power on other nations. A Native American soldier assigned to resettle Vietnamese civilians found it to be "just like when they moved us to the rez [reservation]. We shouldn't have done that."

The Vietnam Veterans Memorial was unveiled in Washington, D.C., in November 1982. Designed by Yale architecture student Maya Lin, the stark, black, V-shaped wall inscribed with the names of men and women lost in the war became one of the most-visited sites in the nation's capital. Veterans themselves, however, often came home to public neglect, with government benefits that were less generous than had been the case in previous wars.

Most soldiers readjusted well to civilian life, but some suffered long after the war ended. The Veterans Administration estimated that nearly one-sixth of the troops suffered from post-traumatic stress disorder, experiencing recurring nightmares, feelings of guilt and shame, violence, substance abuse, and suicidal tendencies. Thirty years after performing army intelligence work in Saigon, Doris Allen "still hit the floor sometimes when [she heard] loud bangs." Some who had served began to report birth defects, cancer, severe skin disorders, and other ailments, linking those illnesses to the deadly poison dioxin in Agent Orange, although it was not until 1991 that Congress acted to provide them with medical assistance.

REVIEW

What were the Vietnam War's legacies for the United States?

What accounted for Americans' political shift to the right in the 1970s?

If the Vietnam War unsettled Americans' faith in their leaders and foreign policy, the era's economic downturn intensified criticism of liberal policies, ranging from social welfare programs to tax rates to school busing. Richard M. Nixon's presidency reflected the impact of the conservative movement as well as the challenges of governing in troubled economic times. The Republican sustained many Great Society social welfare programs and even approved pathbreaking environmental regulations and women's and civil rights measures (see chapter 28). Yet his rhetoric and some of his actions signaled a move to the right. Many Americans would move with him.

Just two years after Nixon won reelection by a huge margin, his abuse of power and efforts to cover up crimes committed by subordinates forced the first presidential resignation in U.S. history. His Republican successor, Gerald R. Ford, served only two years, but the political spectrum continued to shift rightward even when Democrat Jimmy Carter captured the White House in 1976.

How did economic and energy crises affect the nation?

Whereas Eisenhower, Kennedy, and Johnson had all governed during a period of prosperity, Nixon faced a considerably less auspicious economic climate. The enormous increase in U.S. military spending was partly responsible, creating budget deficits. By 1970, both inflation and unemployment had surpassed 6 percent, an unprecedented combination that experts dubbed "stagflation."

Domestic troubles were compounded by the decline of American dominance in the international economy. With Japan and Western Europe fully recovered from the devastation of World War II, foreign cars and electronic equipment now competed favorably with American goods. In 1971, for the first time in decades, the United States imported more than it exported, meaning the nation could no longer back up

▶ **Gas Station Lines** During America's first oil crisis, customers at gas stations encountered around-the-block lines as well as skyrocketing prices, rationing, and signs reading "out of gas." Americans surveyed by pollsters ranked the energy crisis a more pressing concern even than the Watergate scandal. Here, cars line up in New York City on December 23, 1973. AP Photo/Marty Lederhandler.

its currency with gold reserves. Nixon abandoned the gold standard and devalued the dollar to increase exports by making them cheaper. He also intervened in the private marketplace. To protect domestic manufacturers, he imposed a surcharge on most imports and froze wages and prices, thus enabling the government to stimulate the economy without fueling inflation. In the short run, these policies worked. Yet by 1974, unemployment had crept back up and inflation soared.

Skyrocketing energy prices worsened stagflation. During the postwar economic boom, abundant domestic oil deposits and access to cheap Middle Eastern oil had encouraged the manufacture of large cars and building of skyscrapers with no concern for fuel efficiency. By the 1970s, the United States was consuming a stunning one-third of the world's fuel resources.

In the fall of 1973, the United States faced its first energy shortage. Arab nations, furious at the Nixon administration's support of Israel during the Yom Kippur War, cut off oil shipments to the United States. Long lines formed at gas stations, and prices nearly doubled. In response, Nixon authorized temporary emergency measures allocating petroleum and establishing a national 55-mile-per-hour speed limit to save gasoline. The energy crisis eased, but the nation would not easily come to grips with its seemingly unquenchable demand for fuel and dependence on foreign oil.

In what ways did Nixon appeal to the Right?

Nixon's calls for "law and order," his attacks on antiwar protesters, his exploitation of white resistance to integration, and his criticism of the Warren Court were part of a "southern strategy" intended to bring white southerners into the Republican Party. His reelection in 1972 revealed this strategy's success, as well as the growing strength of the conservative movement.

In his 1968 campaign, Nixon billed himself as the candidate of "those who did not indulge in violence, those who did not break the law." A new emphasis on containing crime, begun in Johnson's administration, spoke to fears of social disorder in the aftermath of Black urban uprisings and mass protests. Starting in the 1970s, increased funding for law enforcement and prisons would lead to unparalleled levels of incarceration in the United States and particularly of Black Americans. Nixon also pledged to represent the "forgotten Americans, the non-shouters, the non-demonstrators," a group he called the **"silent majority."** Some of his appeals were racially coded, playing on hostility to new civil rights policies that seemed to favor people of color over white working people.

One of these hot-button issues was busing to achieve school integration. Nixon reluctantly enforced court orders to integrate schools, but only in the South. In northern and western cities, where segregation resulted from housing discrimination and the drawing of school district boundaries, half of all African American children attended nearly all-Black schools. To achieve desegregation, courts began to order busing, the transfer of students between schools in white and Black neighborhoods.

Children had been riding buses to school for decades, but busing in the service of court-mandated racial integration provoked fury. Violence erupted in Boston in 1974 when a district judge ordered busing. The white people most affected came from working-class families. Left in cities abandoned by the more affluent, their children now often rode buses to predominantly Black, overcrowded schools with deficient facilities. Clarence McDonough denounced the liberal officials who bused his "kid half way around Boston so that a bunch of politicians can end up their careers with a clear conscience." Black parents were also conflicted about sending their children on long commutes to schools where white teachers and students might resent their presence. Although white Americans eventually became more accepting of integration, many simply flocked to the white-majority suburbs. After Nixon appointed four new justices, the Supreme Court imposed strict limits on the use of busing to achieve racial balance.

Nixon's judicial appointments would over time weaken other liberal initiatives. He charged the justices of the Warren Court with being "unprecedentedly politically active" and "using their interpretation of the law to remake American society according to their own social, political, and ideological precepts." When Chief Justice Earl Warren resigned in 1969, Nixon replaced him with Warren E. Burger, who was inclined to interpret the Constitution narrowly and to limit government intervention on behalf of individual rights. The Burger Court did however uphold many liberal programs, including affirmative action. Its ruling in *Regents of the University of California v. Bakke* (1978), for example, allowed universities to remedy the results of past discrimination in their admissions policies so long as they did not employ strict quotas and racial classifications.

Nixon's southern strategy and other repercussions of the civil rights revolution ended the Democratic hold on the "solid South." Beginning in 1964, a number of conservative southern Democrats changed their party affiliation; by 2021, Republicans controlled nearly every southern state legislature, governorship, and Senate seat.

What was the Watergate scandal?

Nixon's reelection prospects in 1972 were good. Although the war in Vietnam continued, antiwar protests ebbed with the decrease in American ground forces and

"silent majority"
Richard Nixon's term for those Americans he claimed had been neglected by the liberal establishment in the 1960s in favor of radical protesters and racial and ethnic minorities. Nixon appealed to this group in an effort to attract white northern workers and other traditional Democrats to the Republican Party.

casualties. Nixon's economic initiatives had temporarily checked inflation and unemployment, and his attacks on busing and antiwar protesters had won strong support from the right.

South Dakota senator George S. McGovern was his Democratic opponent, nominated by a diverse slate of women, youthful delegates, and people of color. Republicans portrayed McGovern as a left-wing extremist, tagging him as the candidate of "Acid, Amnesty, and Abortion"—that is, the choice of the counterculture, draft resisters, and feminists. More worrisome for Democrats, McGovern's support for busing, a generous welfare program, and immediate withdrawal from Vietnam alienated some in his own party. Nixon achieved a landslide victory, winning 60.7 percent of the popular vote and every state except Massachusetts. Although the Democrats held on to Congress, Nixon won majorities among traditional Democrats: white southerners, Catholics, urbanites, and blue-collar workers.

The president, however, had little time to savor his triumph, as revelations began to emerge about crimes committed to ensure his victory. During the early-morning hours of June 17, 1972, five men working for Nixon's reelection were discovered breaking into the Democratic Party headquarters in the Watergate complex in Washington, D.C. Nixon and his aides tried to cover up the burglars' connection to his administration, setting in motion the scandal reporters dubbed **Watergate**.

Nixon was not the first president to lie to the public or misuse power. Every president since Franklin D. Roosevelt had enlarged the powers of the office in the name of national security. This expansion of executive powers, commonly referred to as the "imperial presidency," weakened traditional checks and balances on the executive branch and opened the door to abuses. No president, however, had dared go as far as Nixon, who was willing to violate the Constitution to thwart his political opponents.

After investigations by a grand jury and the Senate suggested a cover-up, Nixon accepted official responsibility for Watergate but denied any knowledge of the break-in. He also authorized the appointment of an independent special prosecutor. Meanwhile, a Senate investigating committee uncovered the administration's projects to harass "enemies" through tax audits and other illegal means, implicating the president further. When it was revealed that all conversations in the Oval Office had been taped, a legal battle ensued. Nixon refused to hand

Watergate
Term referring to the 1972 break-in at Democratic Party headquarters in Washington, D.C., by men working for President Nixon's reelection, and Nixon's subsequent efforts to cover it up. The scandal led to the only presidential resignation in American history.

◀ **Watergate** In this drawing, famed political cartoonist Herbert Lawrence Block, known as Herblock, cleverly combined two elements of the Watergate scandal that brought down Nixon. During the investigation, the president declared, "I am not a crook," and the tapes of conversations in the Oval Office that he was forced to turn over to investigators showed an eighteen-minute gap at a critical moment. A 1974 Herblock Cartoon, © The Herb Block Foundation.

over the tapes, citing executive privilege and separation of powers, but the Supreme Court unanimously ruled to order their release.

Nixon's misuse of federal funds and tax evasion also came to light. In August 1973, Vice President Spiro Agnew resigned after having been found to accept bribes while governor of Maryland, and he was replaced by House minority leader Gerald R. Ford of Michigan. The next winter, the House of Representatives began an impeachment investigation, and Nixon was forced to release edited transcripts of the tapes. The transcripts revealed Nixon's orders to aides in March 1973: "I don't give a shit what happens. I want you all to stonewall it, let them plead the Fifth Amendment, cover up or anything else, if it'll save it—save the plan."

In July 1974, the House Judiciary Committee voted to impeach the president on three counts—obstruction of justice, abuse of power, and contempt of Congress— and it seemed certain that the House would follow suit. "The prisons of Georgia are full of people who stole $5 or $10," remarked Georgia state legislator and civil rights activist Julian Bond, "and this man tried to steal the Constitution." To avoid impeachment, Nixon announced his resignation to a national television audience on August 8, 1974—a singular moment in U.S. history.

How did Democrats make gains in the post-Watergate years?

Nixon's successor, Gerald R. Ford, was left to grapple with the aftermath of Watergate as well as severe economic problems. Upon taking office, President Ford announced, "Our long national nightmare is over." But he shocked many Americans one month later by granting Nixon a pardon for any and all offenses he may have committed during his presidency. By contrast, thirty of the former president's associates ultimately pleaded guilty to or were convicted of crimes related to Watergate. Ford's sweeping pardon saved Nixon from nearly certain indictment and trial, provoking a tremendous outcry from Congress and the public.

In contrast to the Republicans' disarray, Democrats made impressive gains in the November congressional elections. Many pledged to guard against the kinds of abuses revealed during Watergate. The Federal Election Campaign Act of 1974 established public financing of presidential campaigns and imposed some restrictions on contributions to curtail the selling of political favors. Congressional legislation had little impact, however. Politicians found other ways of raising money—for example, through political action committees (PACs) that permitted larger contributions than were allowed for individual candidates. The Supreme Court also struck down limitations on campaign spending as violations of freedom of speech. Ever-larger campaign donations flowed to candidates from interest groups, corporations, labor unions, and wealthy individuals.

Congressional investigating committees discovered a host of illegal FBI and CIA activities stretching back to the 1950s, including surveillance of American citizens such as Martin Luther King Jr., harassment of political dissenters, and plots to assassinate Fidel Castro and other foreign leaders. In response to these revelations, President Ford placed new controls on covert operations, and Congress created permanent committees to oversee the intelligence agencies. These measures did little to diminish the public's cynicism about their government, however, nor did they seriously hamstring the CIA.

Dissatisfaction with the Ford administration grew as the nation struggled with stalled economic growth, high unemployment, a foreign trade deficit, and soaring energy prices. Ford carried these burdens into the election campaign of 1976, while contending with a major challenge from the Republican right. Blasting Nixon's and Ford's foreign policy of détente for causing the "loss of U.S. military supremacy," California governor Ronald Reagan came close to capturing the nomination.

The Democrats nominated James Earl "Jimmy" Carter Jr., former governor of Georgia. A graduate of the U.S. Naval Academy, Carter spent seven years as a nuclear engineer in the navy before returning to Plains, Georgia, to run the family peanut farming business. In the wake of Watergate, Carter was an appealing candidate. He carried his own bags, lived modestly, and taught a Bible class at his Baptist church. Carter stressed his faith as a born-again Christian and his distance from the government in Washington. Although he selected liberal senator Walter F. Mondale of Minnesota as his running mate, Carter's nomination nonetheless marked a rightward turn in the Democratic Party.

Ford's failure to tackle the country's economic problems helped Carter win the traditional Democratic coalition of Blacks, organized labor, and ethnic groups and even recapture some of the white southerners who had voted for Nixon in 1972. Still, Carter received just 50 percent of the popular vote to Ford's 48 percent, while Democrats retained substantial margins in Congress.

REVIEW

How did the Nixon administration reflect the growing influence of conservatives in the Republican Party?

What challenges did the Carter administration face?

Democrat Jimmy Carter promised to lead a government that was "competent" as well as "decent, open, fair, and compassionate." He employed less soaring rhetoric than Kennedy or Johnson had, cautioning Americans "that even our great Nation has its recognized limits" and that "we can neither answer all questions nor solve all problems." Carter's humility and personal integrity helped revive trust in the presidency. He made notable advances in environmental and energy policies, championed human rights, and achieved foreign policy successes in the Panama Canal, China, and the Middle East.

Yet the Carter administration's domestic and foreign problems exposed his deficiencies in working with Congress and rallying public opinion. Energy shortages and stagflation worsened as the 1970s progressed. Near the end of Carter's term,

Soviet-American relations deteriorated, new crises emerged in the Middle East, and the economy plummeted, dooming his reelection campaign.

Why did a Democratic president retreat from liberalism?

Carter vowed "to help the poor and aged, to improve education, and to provide jobs," but at the same time "not to waste money." When these goals conflicted, budget balancing took priority over reform. Carter's approach pleased Americans unhappy about their tax dollars being used to benefit the disadvantaged while stagflation eroded their own standard of living. But his fiscal stringency frustrated liberal Democrats pushing for comprehensive welfare reform, national health insurance, and a substantial jobs program.

Carter did fulfill liberals' desire to make government more inclusive by appointing unprecedented numbers of women and people of color to cabinet, judicial, and diplomatic posts. A number of factors, however, thwarted Carter's policy goals. His outsider status helped him win the election but left him without strong ties to party leaders in Congress. Equally significant, the economic problems he inherited—unemployment, inflation, and sluggish growth—confounded economic doctrine. Usually, rising prices accompanied a humming economy with a strong demand for labor. In the 1970s, however, steep inflation and high unemployment occurred simultaneously, enlarging the federal budget deficit. An economist gave the phenomenon an apt title: the "misery index."

As Americans struggled with inflation and unemployment, many found themselves paying higher taxes, especially higher property taxes as the value of their homes increased. Some were incensed to see their taxes fund government programs for people they considered undeserving. In the 1970s, a grassroots antitax movement gathered steam. In 1978, Californians revolted, passing a popular referendum, Proposition 13, which slashed property taxes and limited the state's ability to raise other revenues. What a newspaper called a "primal scream by the People against Big Government" quickly spread to other states.

Carter's response to these economic woes was to cut taxes and to target unemployment through public works and public service jobs programs. Unemployment receded, but then inflation surged. Working people, wrote one journalist, "winced and ached" as their paychecks bought less and less, "hollowing their hopes and dreams, their plans for a house or their children's college education." To curb inflation, Carter curtailed federal spending, and the Federal Reserve Board tightened the money supply. These measures failed to halt inflation, which surpassed 13 percent in 1980; worse, these government policies contributed to rising unemployment.

Carter's refusal to put forward a comprehensive national health insurance plan, long a Democratic priority, announced a retreat from the expansive liberalism of the 1960s. So did his sharp cut of the capital gains tax, which benefited corporations and the wealthy, along with the government's bailout of the auto giant Chrysler to prevent its bankruptcy. Carter also supported proposals to deregulate airlines in 1978 and then the banking, trucking, and railroad industries in 1980—a policy shift in line with conservatives' insistence on a free market and unfettered private enterprise.

Why did energy and the environment capture national attention?

Complicating the battle with stagflation was the nation's enormous energy consumption and dependence on foreign oil. Carter elevated the importance of this issue by establishing the Department of Energy and proposing a wide-ranging conservation program. The **National Energy Act of 1978** penalized manufacturers of gas-guzzling automobiles and provided incentives for conservation and development of alternative fuels, such as wind and solar power. The act, however, fell far short of a long-term, comprehensive solution.

In 1979, a new upheaval in the Middle East, the Iranian revolution, triggered the most severe energy crisis yet. Shortages caused 60 percent of gasoline stations to close down, resulting in long lines and high prices. In response, Congress reduced controls on the oil and gas industry to stimulate American production and imposed a windfall profits tax on producers to redistribute some of the profits they would reap from deregulation.

European nations were no less dependent on foreign oil than was the United States, but they more successfully controlled consumption. They levied high taxes on gasoline, encouraging people to use public transportation and manufacturers to produce more energy-efficient cars. In the automobile-dependent United States, however—with inadequate public transit, a sprawling population, and an aversion to taxes—politicians dismissed that approach. By the end of the century, the United States, with only 6 percent of the world's population, consumed more than 25 percent of global oil production.

A vigorous environmental movement opposed nuclear energy as an alternative fuel, warning of radiation leakage, potential accidents, and the hazards of radioactive waste. In 1976, hundreds of people went to jail for attempting to block construction of a nuclear power plant in Seabrook, New Hampshire. The perils of nuclear energy attracted international attention in March 1979, when a meltdown of the reactor core was narrowly averted at the nuclear facility near Harrisburg, Pennsylvania. Popular opposition and the great expense of building nuclear power plants limited development of the industry.

A disaster at Love Canal in Niagara Falls, New York, brought attention to another set of environmental concerns related to the human costs of unregulated development. Residents suffering high rates of serious illness discovered that their homes sat atop highly toxic waste products from a nearby chemical company. Finally responding to the residents' claims in 1978, the state of New York agreed to help families relocate, and the Carter administration in 1980 created the so-called Superfund: $1.6 billion for cleanup of hazardous wastes left by the chemical industry.

Carter also signed bills to improve clean air and water regulations, to expand the Arctic National Wildlife Refuge (ANWR) preserve in Alaska, and to control strip mining, which left destructive scars on the land. During the 1979 gasoline crisis, Carter attempted to balance the development of domestic fuel sources with environmental concerns, winning legislation to conserve energy and to provide incentives for the development of solar energy and environmentally friendly alternative fuels.

National Energy Act of 1978
Legislation passed during the Carter administration that penalized manufacturers of gas-guzzling automobiles and provided incentives for energy conservation and development of alternative fuels, such as wind and solar power.

How did a focus on human rights alter foreign policy?

"We're ashamed of what our government is as we deal with other nations around the world," Jimmy Carter charged, promising to reverse the history of American support of dictators, secret diplomacy, interference in the internal affairs of other countries, and excessive reliance on military solutions. Human rights formed the cornerstone of his approach.

The Carter administration applied economic pressure on governments that denied their citizens basic rights. The United States, for example, refused aid or trading privileges to nations such as Chile and El Salvador, as well as to the white minority governments of Rhodesia and South Africa. In other cases, however, Carter prioritized strategic and security considerations over human rights principles, invoking no sanctions against repressive governments in Iran, South Korea, and the Philippines. Carter's human rights commitment faced a test when a popular movement overthrew an oppressive dictatorship in Nicaragua. U.S. officials were uneasy about the leftist Sandinistas who led the rebellion and had ties to Cuba. Once the Sandinistas assumed power in 1979, however, Carter held to his human rights stance, recognizing the new government and sending economic aid.

Applying similar principles to the U.S.-controlled Panama Canal, Carter signed a treaty in 1977 providing for its return to Panama in 2000. Supporters viewed the treaty as restitution for the United States' takeover of the territory in 1903. Opponents denounced the loss of the vital waterway. "We bought it, we paid for it, it's ours," claimed Ronald Reagan during the presidential primaries of 1976. Only after a massive effort by the administration would the Senate ratify the Panama Canal treaty.

Carter also nurtured meaningful steps toward peace in the Middle East, seizing on the courage of Egyptian president Anwar Sadat, the first Arab leader to risk his political career by talking directly with Israeli officials. In 1979, Carter invited Sadat and Israeli prime minister Menachem Begin to Camp David, Maryland, where he applied tenacious diplomacy for thirteen days. These talks led to the **Camp David accords**, whereby Egypt became the first Arab state to recognize Israel, and Israel agreed to gradual withdrawal from the Sinai Peninsula, which it had seized in the 1967 Six-Day War (**Map 29.3**).

Camp David accords
Agreements between Egypt and Israel reached at 1979 talks hosted by President Carter at Camp David. In the accords, Egypt became the first Arab state to recognize Israel, and Israel agreed to gradual withdrawal from the Sinai Peninsula.

What new crises did the United States face abroad?

Consistent with his human rights approach, Carter preferred to promote national security through nonmilitary means and initially sought cooperation with the nation's Cold War enemies. In 1979, following up on Nixon's initiatives, he opened formal diplomatic relations with the People's Republic of China and signed a second strategic arms reduction treaty with the Soviet Union.

That same year, however, Carter pursued a military buildup when the Soviet Union invaded neighboring Afghanistan, whose recently installed Communist government was threatened by Muslim opposition. Carter imposed economic sanctions on the Soviet Union, barred U.S. participation in the 1980 Summer Olympic Games in Moscow, and obtained legislation requiring all nineteen-year-old men to register for the draft.

Asserting that Soviet actions in Afghanistan jeopardized oil supplies from the Middle East, the president announced the "Carter Doctrine," threatening the use of any means necessary to prevent an outside force from gaining control of the Persian Gulf. Human rights fell by the wayside as the United States stepped up support for the military dictatorship in neighboring Pakistan, and the CIA funneled secret aid to the Afghan rebels. The thaw in superpower relations that had begun in the 1960s ended.

Events in Iran encouraged this hard-line approach. Generous U.S. arms and aid funneled to the shah had not subdued Iranian dissidents, who still resented the CIA's role in the overthrow of the Mosaddegh government in 1953 (see chapter 26). Opponents of the shah condemned his brutal attempts to quash opposition and detested his adoption of Western culture and values. These grievances fueled a revolution in 1979 that forced him out and brought to power Shiite Islamic fundamentalists led by Ayatollah Ruholla Khomeini.

Carter's decision to allow the shah into the United States for medical treatment enraged Iranians, who believed that the United States would restore him to power, as

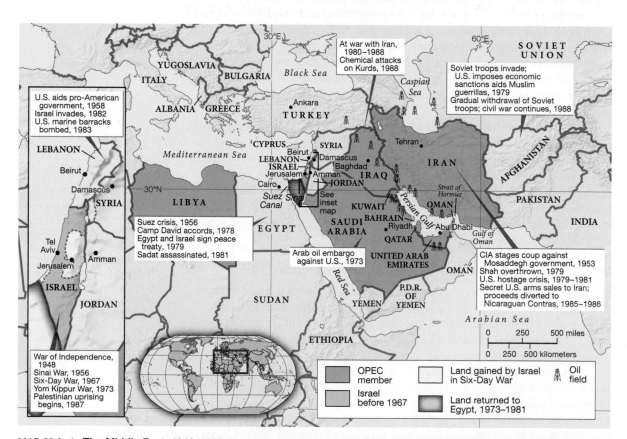

MAP 29.3 ▲ The Middle East, 1948–1989 Preserving access to the rich oil reserves of the Middle East and commitment to the security of Israel were fundamental — and often conflicting — principles of U.S. foreign policy in the region.

▲ **Iran Hostage Crisis** Iranian demonstrators show their support for the militants who seized the U.S. Embassy in Teheran, taking sixty-six Americans hostage. In this photograph from November 13, 1979, demonstrators inside the embassy burn an effigy of Uncle Sam, a reference to the CIA visible on one arm. AP Photo.

it had done in 1953. On November 4, 1979, a crowd broke into the U.S. Embassy in Iran's capital of Teheran and seized sixty-six U.S. diplomats, CIA officers, citizens, and military attachés. Refusing the captors' demands to return the shah to Iran for trial, Carter froze Iranian assets in U.S. banks and placed an embargo on Iranian oil. In April 1980, he sent a small military operation into Iran to rescue the hostages, but the mission failed.

The disastrous rescue attempt and scenes of blindfolded American citizens paraded before TV cameras fed a sense of U.S. impotence, simmering since the defeat in Vietnam. Iran released a handful of the captives (primarily women and Black Americans), but the Iran hostage crisis—lasting 444 days—dominated the news during the 1980 presidential campaign and contributed to Carter's defeat. In a final blow, Iran freed the remaining fifty-two hostages minutes after Carter left office. The hostages boarded a plane in Teheran as his successor, Ronald Reagan, delivered his inaugural address.

Iran hostage crisis
Crisis that began in 1979 after the deposed shah of Iran was allowed into the United States following the Iranian revolution. Protesters broke into the U.S. Embassy in Teheran and took sixty-six Americans hostage, a crisis that lasted 444 days and contributed to Carter losing his bid for reelection in 1980.

REVIEW

How did Carter put into practice his commitment to human rights, and when did this commitment give way to other priorities?

Conclusion: How did the constraints of the 1970s transform U.S. policy and politics?

American military and economic might had suffered severe blows by the 1970s. Defeat in Vietnam did not make the United States the "pitiful, helpless giant" predicted by Nixon, but it did signify a relative decline of U.S. power and the impossibility of implementing containment on a global scale. Overestimating the effectiveness of American technological superiority, U.S. officials badly misjudged the tenacity of a revolutionary movement determined to achieve national independence, and they failed to realize how easily the United States could be perceived as an imperial intruder.

There would be other setbacks—both domestic and geopolitical—in the 1970s, ranging from the Watergate scandal to the Iran hostage crisis. The Vietnam War created deep political fractures and a distrust of the federal government that would linger long after. Large military outlays led to budget deficits, triggering inflation and contributing to ongoing economic crises. Energy shortages and spikes in gasoline prices, along with stagflation in the 1970s announced a decisive end to post–World War II prosperity. Americans chafed against this new age of limits. Some, including a good number of traditional Democrats, responded by voting down taxes, withdrawing their support for sixties-era social welfare programs, and moving rightward in their politics.

CHAPTER REVIEW

EXPLAIN WHY IT MATTERS

Berlin Wall (p. 857)

Cuban missile crisis (p. 857)

Agent Orange (p. 858)

Tet Offensive (p. 864)

détente (p. 866)

Strategic Arms Limitation Treaty (SALT) (p. 866)

My Lai massacre (p. 870)

Pentagon Papers (p. 870)

War Powers Act (p. 871)

"silent majority" (p. 875)

Watergate (p. 876)

National Energy Act of 1978 (p. 880)

Camp David accords (p. 881)

Iran hostage crisis (p. 883)

PUT IT ALL TOGETHER

THE VIETNAM WAR

- What were Kennedy and Johnson's reasons for escalating U.S. involvement in Vietnam?
- How did divisions over the Vietnam War shape politics in the later 1960s?

THE CONSERVATIVE TURN

- What combination of developments contributed to a Republican capturing the presidency in 1968?
- What aspects of Nixon's domestic agenda appealed to conservatives? What aspects of his foreign policy might have concerned them?

GOVERNANCE IN THE 1970s

- How did the economic downturn of the 1970s affect Americans?
- Why did Carter campaign as a Washington "outsider"? How did his domestic policies depart from those of recent Democratic administrations?

LOOKING BACKWARD, LOOKING AHEAD

- How did U.S. policies in the 1950s and 1960s contribute to the energy crises of the 1970s?
- What impact would American dependence on foreign oil have on future U.S. conflicts and commitments abroad?

30

POLITICAL DIVISIONS IN A CONSERVATIVE ERA

1980–2000

This chapter discusses the following questions:

- What conservative goals were realized during Reagan's presidency?
- How did liberals fight the rightward turn?
- Why did the Cold War intensify and how did it end?
- Why did domestic politics become more polarized in the 1990s?
- How did the United States respond to the challenges of globalization?
- Conclusion: What were the legacies of the "Reagan revolution"?

▶ **Phyllis Schlafly** Illinois was one of the most hotly contested states in the battle over ratification of the Equal Rights Amendment. Here, Schlafly rallies ERA opponents in the state capitol in 1975. Schlafly's STOP ERA movement succeeded in Illinois, her home state and the only northern state that failed to ratify the ERA. Despite political activities that required extensive traveling and speaking, Schlafly insisted on referring to herself as a housewife. Bettmann/Getty Images.

AN AMERICAN STORY

One of the "most exciting days" of Phyllis Schlafly's life was hearing Barry Goldwater address the Federation of Republican Women in 1963. In line with other conservatives in that decade, Schlafly insisted that the United States needed not simply to contain communism but to eliminate it. She also wanted to shrink the federal government, especially its role in providing social welfare and enforcing civil rights. In the 1970s, however, Schlafly added new social and cultural issues to the conservative docket, helping build a grassroots movement that would redefine the Republican Party and American politics well into the twenty-first century.

Phyllis Stewart was born in St. Louis in 1924, attended Catholic schools, and worked her way through Washington University testing ammunition at a World War II defense plant. After earning a master's degree in government from Radcliffe College, she worked at the American Enterprise Institute, where she imbibed the think tank's conservatism. Returning to the Midwest, she married Illinois attorney Fred Schlafly and bore six children, saying, "I don't think there's anything as much fun as taking care of a baby."

While insisting that tending a family was a woman's most important career, Schlafly spent much of her time writing or on the road, leading Republican women's organizations and testifying before legislative committees. She ran twice, unsuccessfully, for Congress. In 1964, she wrote *A Choice Not an Echo*, a book promoting Barry Goldwater for president that sold more than three million copies. In 1967, she began publishing a monthly political affairs newsletter, the *Phyllis Schlafly Report*.

In the 1970s, Schlafly began to champion the concerns of Christian conservatives, who had mobilized against rapid changes in family life and gender roles. She spoke out against abortion, homosexuality, and sexual permissiveness, calling for a larger role for religion and traditional morality in public life. Schlafly's ideas resonated with many who opposed sixties-era liberalism, traveling all the way to the White House with Ronald Reagan in 1980.

As president, Reagan addressed the priorities of the traditional right by cutting taxes, government regulations, and social programs and by strengthening the military. He also embraced much of the conservative cultural agenda. Although he faced resistance from feminists, civil rights groups, and environmentalists, Reagan's popularity and policies shifted the entire political spectrum rightward — evident in the campaigns of centrist "new Democrats" and in many initiatives of the Clinton administration during the 1990s.

Another priority of Schlafly's, fighting communism, took a surprising turn in the late 1980s, thanks to a changing situation in the USSR and bold moves by Reagan and his Soviet counterpart, Mikhail Gorbachev. Eastern bloc countries threw off communism with no crackdown from the Soviet leader. Shortly thereafter, the Soviet Union itself was dissolved, leading Reagan's successor, George H. W. Bush, to proclaim the arrival of a "new world order."

Yet new wars abroad and culture wars at home broke out in the 1990s. The United States contended with the challenges of globalization, ethnic conflict, and terrorism even as a polarized electorate and an increasingly deadlocked political system made governance more difficult.

What conservative goals were realized during Reagan's presidency?

Ronald Reagan's inauguration day was marked by the long-awaited release of the American hostages in Iran. The new president pronounced, after a decade of economic and global decline, that "we're too great a nation to limit ourselves to small dreams." Reagan's election in 1980 was the most important turning point in American politics since Franklin D. Roosevelt's election in 1932. His victory established conservatism's dominance in the Republican Party; Democrats adapted by moving toward the right. The United States was not alone in this political shift. Conservatives rose to power in Britain with the election of Prime Minister Margaret Thatcher and in Germany, Canada, and Sweden as well. Social democratic governments elsewhere trimmed their welfare states.

The Reagan administration left a strong imprint on the economy: controlling inflation, deregulating industry, slashing taxes, and generating a staggering federal budget deficit. A fascination with finance and large fortunes characterized popular culture in the 1980s, but poverty increased and economic inequality grew. Although the Reagan era did not see a policy revolution comparable to that of the New Deal, it dealt a strong blow to the once-dominant liberal agenda, fostering antigovernment sentiment and sharply reversing the course of American politics.

How was the Republican Party's agenda changing in the 1980s?

At sixty-nine, Ronald Reagan was the oldest candidate yet nominated for the presidency as well as the first divorcé and former union leader (of the Screen Actors Guild) to hold that office. Gaining national attention first as a movie actor, Reagan was a New Deal Democrat until the 1950s, when he shed that affiliation and became a critic of the liberal state and a national spokesperson for General Electric and free enterprise.

A fervent anti-Communist and prominent supporter of Barry Goldwater in 1964, Reagan's own political career took off when he was elected governor of California in 1966 (see chapter 28). Reagan ran as a conservative, but as governor he displayed flexibility, approving a major tax increase, a strong water pollution bill, and a liberal abortion law. He displayed similar agility during the 1980 presidential campaign, softening his attacks on Social Security, public school funding, and assistance to the poor and choosing the moderate George H. W. Bush as his running mate.

Reagan campaigned in favor of states' rights and against school busing, affirmative action, and welfare fraud. This set of issues, sparked by civil rights gains, had energized Republicans since the Nixon years. Reagan further capitalized on the economic recession and declining U.S. prestige symbolized by the Iran hostage crisis. He asked voters, "Are you better off now than you were four years ago?" Reagan promised to "take government off the backs of the people" and to restore Americans' morale and other nations' respect, a message that resonated with voters.

The 1980 election tested party unity. Indeed, some Republicans balked both at Reagan's nomination and the conservative party platform. After Phyllis Schlafly persuaded the party to reverse its forty-year support for the Equal Rights Amendment, moderate and liberal Republicans protested outside the convention hall. Moderate John B. Anderson, congressman from Illinois, deserted his party to run as an independent. Despite such dissenters, Reagan won the election, with Republicans taking control of the Senate for the first time since the 1950s.

Reagan's victory was a triumph for the grassroots conservative movement that emerged in the 1960s. That movement grew alongside the **New Christian Right**: the politicization of religious conservatives, predominantly Protestants, who had in the past typically refrained from partisan debates. During the 1970s, evangelical and fundamentalist Christian churches drew thousands of new adherents, while mainstream Protestant congregations dwindled. Evangelical ministers such as Pat Robertson preached to huge television audiences, attacking feminism, abortion, and homosexuality and calling for the restoration of traditional "family values." A considerable number of Catholics, such as Schlafly, shared this goal, speaking out against court rulings and laws that seemed to favor moral permissiveness and to undermine religious beliefs.

Conservative political organizations such as the Moral Majority, launched by the Reverend Jerry Falwell in 1979, fought "left-wing, social welfare bills, . . . pornography, homosexuality, [and] the advocacy of immorality in school textbooks." Dr. James Dobson, a psychologist who hosted a popular Christian talk show, founded the Family Research Council in 1983 to lobby Congress for measures to curb abortion, divorce, homosexuality, and single motherhood. The monthly *Phyllis Schlafly Report* helped merge these concerns with the familiar conservative platform of limited government at home and militant anticommunism abroad.

Reagan endorsed the positions of the Christian Right on issues such as abortion and school prayer, but he did not push hard for so-called moral policies. His major achievements instead fulfilled goals of the older right—strengthening the nation's anti-Communist posture and reducing taxes and restraints on free enterprise while criticizing "big government." "Government," Reagan declared in his inaugural address, "is not the solution to our problem; government is the problem."

New Christian Right
Politically active religious conservatives who reshaped the Republican Party in the 1980s through organizations like the Moral Majority. Religious conservatives criticized feminism, opposed abortion and homosexuality, and championed "family values."

▲ **Ronald Reagan Addresses Religious Conservatives** Reagan's victory in 1980 helped to reshape the Republican Party by attracting millions of evangelical Christians to its ranks. In his 1983 address to the National Association of Evangelicals, Reagan called the Soviet Union an "evil empire" and appealed to religious conservatives with strong words about abortion and prayer in the schools, proclaiming that "America is in the midst of a spiritual awakening and a moral renewal." Ronald Reagan Presidential Library.

Reagan, known as "the Great Communicator," was a popular figure, appealing even to Americans who opposed his policies but warmed to his optimism, charisma, and easygoing humor. Ignoring the darker moments of the American past, he presented a version of U.S. history that its citizens could feel good about. Proclaiming that "the era of self-doubt is over," he reassured his fellow citizens that it was "morning in America."

What economic policies did the new administration adopt?

supply-side economics
Economic theory claiming that tax cuts for businesses and individuals, especially the wealthy, encourage investment and production (supply) and stimulate consumption (demand) because individuals can keep more of their earnings. Despite promises to the contrary, supply-side economics during the Reagan administration created a massive federal budget deficit.

Reagan inherited economic problems shared by the Nixon, Ford, and Carter administrations: slow growth, stagflation, and a ballooning trade deficit. His proposed solution was to reduce government intervention, oversight, and spending. He hoped to stimulate the economy by cutting taxes and deregulating industry.

Reagan regarded taxation as a form of theft that prevented Americans from keeping what they had rightfully earned. His first domestic initiative, despite a large budget deficit, was a massive tax cut. To justify it, Reagan relied on a new theory called **supply-side economics**, which held that lowering taxes would actually increase revenue. In theory, businesses would expand, and individuals would work harder because they could keep more of their earnings. The resulting increase in production of goods and services—the supply—would in turn boost demand. Reagan promised that the economy would grow so much that the government would recoup the lost taxes. Instead, it incurred a galloping deficit.

In 1981, Congress passed the Economic Recovery Tax Act, the largest tax reduction in U.S. history. Tax rates were cut from 14 percent to 11 percent for the lowest-income individuals and from 70 percent to 50 percent for the wealthiest, who also benefited from reduced levies on corporations, capital gains, gifts, and inheritances. A second measure, the Tax Reform Act of 1986, slashed taxes still further. Although the 1986 law narrowed loopholes used primarily by the wealthy, affluent Americans saved far more on their tax bills than did average taxpayers, and the distribution of wealth tipped further in favor of the rich.

Rolling back regulations on business was another of Reagan's priorities. Carter had deregulated a number of industries, such as air transportation and banking, while increasing health, safety, and environmental regulations. The Reagan administration, by contrast, pursued across-the-board deregulation. It declined to enforce the Sherman Antitrust Act (see chapter 18), which limited monopolies, allowing an unprecedented number of business mergers and takeovers.

Reagan's administration also loosened regulations protecting employee health and safety and weakened labor unions. When members of the Professional Air Traffic Controllers Organization—one of the few unions to support Reagan in 1980—went on strike in 1981, the president fired them, destroying the union and intimidating organized labor.

Reagan targeted environmental laws, blaming them for the nation's sluggish economic growth. His first secretary of the interior, James Watt, announced, "We will mine more, drill more, cut more timber," as he released federal lands to private use. Meanwhile, the head of the Environmental Protection Agency relaxed enforcement of air and water pollution standards. Of environmentalists, Reagan wisecracked, "I don't think they'll be happy until the White House looks like a bird's nest." Their numbers grew in opposition to his policies, forcing the resignation of several administration officials and blocking full realization of Reagan's deregulatory goals.

Deregulation of the banking industry, begun under Carter with bipartisan support, led to a crisis in the savings and loan (S&L) industry. Some of the newly deregulated S&L institutions extended enormous loans to real estate developers and invested in other high-yield but risky ventures. The lenders reaped lavish profits, and their depositors enjoyed high interest rates. But when real estate values plunged, hundreds of S&Ls went bankrupt, resulting in the largest financial scandal in U.S. history. The government bailout of the industry in 1989 cost American taxpayers more than $100 billion, deepening the federal deficit.

Reagan entered the White House with a pledge to reverse what he billed as the failed and expensive initiatives of the Great Society. Although his proposals to overhaul Social Security were overwhelmingly rejected by Congress, his administration made good on its promise to roll back other social welfare programs. Reagan cut funds for food stamps, job training, and student aid. Hundreds of thousands of people lost benefits in what critics condemned as a "war on the poor."

Increases in defense spending far exceeded the budget savings and, along with the tax cuts, caused the deficit to soar. The nation's debt tripled to $2.3 trillion, with interest payments on the debt consuming one-seventh of all federal expenditures. Despite Reagan's antigovernment rhetoric, both the federal budget and the number of federal employees increased during his presidency.

It took the severest recession since the 1930s to reduce inflation in the U.S. economy. Unemployment approached 11 percent late in 1982, and record numbers of banks and businesses closed. The threat of joblessness further undermined organized labor, forcing unions to make concessions that management insisted were necessary for industry's survival.

In 1983, however, the economy recovered and entered a period of unprecedented growth. That economic upswing and Reagan's own popularity posed a formidable challenge to the Democrats in the 1984 election. They nominated Carter's vice president, Walter F. Mondale, to head the ticket. His precedent-breaking choice of a woman as his running mate—New York representative Geraldine A. Ferraro—did not save the Democrats from a humiliating defeat. Reagan charged his opponents with a fixation on America's failures. Democrats, he claimed, "see an America where every day is April 15th," the deadline for income tax returns, whereas "we see an America where every day is the Fourth of July." Reagan was reelected in a landslide victory, winning 59 percent of the popular vote and every state but Mondale's Minnesota.

Who were the winners and losers in the 1980s economy?

After the economy rebounded in 1983, some Americans won great fortunes. Money making and lavish displays of wealth were splashed across popular culture. Books by business gurus topped best-seller lists, and a new television show, *Lifestyles of the Rich and Famous*, drew large audiences. College students ranked making money as a primary ambition.

Many of the newly wealthy became rich not by producing goods but by moving assets around: manipulating debt and restructuring corporations through mergers and takeovers. Notable exceptions included innovators in the emerging technology sector—like Steve Jobs, who invented the Apple computer in his garage, and Bill Gates, who transformed the software industry with his company Microsoft. Most financial wizards operated within the law, but the 1980s also witnessed a series of criminal convictions for fraud and insider trading.

Older industries faced global pressures, with U.S. manufacturers losing increasing shares of their markets to foreign products, from appliances, machine tools, and electronics to furniture and clothing. Adopting innovative production processes, German and Japanese steel and automobile makers overtook U.S. Steel and General Motors. The weakening of organized labor combined with the decline in manufacturing to erode the position of blue-collar workers. Chicago steelworker Ike Mazo, contemplating the $6-an-hour jobs available to him, fumed, "It's an attack on the living standards of workers."

Service industries expanded but with substantially lower paychecks. The number of full-time workers earning wages below the poverty level ($12,195 for a family of four in 1990) rose from 12 percent to 18 percent of all workers in the 1980s. Increasingly, a second income was needed to stave off economic decline. By 1990, nearly 60 percent of married women with young children worked outside the home, often with limited child care options. Yet even with two incomes, families struggled. The gap between men's and women's annual earnings—an average of $10,000—made things even harder for the 20 percent of U.S. households headed by females.

◄ The Personal Computer
Computers moved into U.S. government agencies and large corporations beginning in the 1950s, but the personal computer was a product of the late 1970s, with the founding of Apple Computers, Inc. Sales of the Apple II computer jumped from $7.8 million in 1978 to $117 million in 1980, with IBM entering the personal computer market the following year. Cold War–era government funding for scientific research and development was partly responsible for the boom in computing and the growth of the high-tech sector of the economy in the 1980s and 1990s. Image Courtesy of The Advertising Archives.

Reagan adhered to a conservative philosophy of "trickle-down" economics, insisting that the benefits of a booming economy would be passed along from the wealthiest to everyone else. Average personal income did rise during his tenure, but the trend toward greater economic inequality that had begun in the 1970s intensified in the 1980s, in part because of Reagan's tax policies. During his presidency, the percentage of Americans living in poverty increased from 11.7 to 13.5—the highest poverty rate in the industrialized world—and homelessness climbed dramatically. Social Security and Medicare helped to stave off destitution among older Americans. Less fortunate were other groups that the economic boom bypassed: people of color, female-headed families, and children, a full one in five of whom lived in poverty.

REVIEW

What factors led to increased economic inequality during the 1980s?

How did liberals fight the rightward turn?

Liberal social movements were on the defensive in the 1980s as the government retreated from a commitment to equal opportunity, a shift reflected in Reagan's federal court appointments. Women, Black Americans, Latinos, and others fought to retain protections they had recently won, while gay men and lesbians made some gains.

What political battles wound up in the courts and Congress?

Ronald Reagan agreed with conservatives that the nation had moved too far in guaranteeing rights to minority groups. Charging "reverse discrimination," conservatives maintained that affirmative action harmed whites, ignoring evidence that people of color and white women still lagged far behind white men in both opportunities and income. Black labor leader Cleveland Robinson pointed to the difficulty of achieving equal opportunity in a faltering economy, calling full employment "the basic ingredient of successful affirmative action." Without it, "you will have both blacks and whites fighting for the same job."

Intense mobilization by civil rights groups, educational leaders, and labor unions — often with support from corporate America — prevented the administration from abandoning affirmative action, and the Supreme Court upheld important antidiscrimination policies. Against Reagan's wishes, Congress extended the Voting Rights Act with veto-proof majorities. The administration, however, was able to limit civil rights enforcement by appointing conservatives to the Justice Department, the Civil Rights Commission, and other agencies, as well as by slashing their budgets.

Congress stepped in to defend antidiscrimination programs after the Justice Department persuaded the Supreme Court to severely weaken Title IX of the Education Amendments Act of 1972, a key law promoting equal opportunity in education. In 1988, Congress passed the Civil Rights Restoration Act over Reagan's veto, banning government funding for any organization that practiced discrimination on the basis of race, color, national origin, sex, disability, or age.

Liberals had once counted upon the federal judiciary as a powerful ally, but the courts were trending toward the right in the 1980s. Appointing half of the 761 federal court judges and three new Supreme Court justices, President Reagan remade the courts with carefully selected candidates who were both younger and more conservative than the federal judiciary as a whole. The full impact of these appointments became clear after Reagan left office, as the Court allowed states to impose restrictions that weakened access to abortion for poor and rural women, reduced protections against employment discrimination, and whittled down legal safeguards against the death penalty.

Why was feminism on the defensive?

Equal Rights Amendment (ERA)
Constitutional amendment passed by Congress in 1972 requiring equal treatment of men and women under federal and state law. Facing fierce opposition from the New Right and the Republican Party, the ERA was defeated as time ran out for state ratification in 1982.

A signal achievement of the New Right in the 1980s was shifting the Republican Party's position on women's rights. For the first time in its history, the party took an explicitly antifeminist tone, opposing the **Equal Rights Amendment (ERA)** and abortion rights, key goals of the women's movement. When the time limit for ratification of the ERA ran out in 1982, conservative activist Phyllis Schlafly and her followers celebrated the defeat of this central feminist objective.

Regrouping, feminists in the 1980s focused more on women's economic and family issues. They found some common ground with the Reagan administration, securing legislation that helped single and divorced mothers collect court-ordered child support payments from absent fathers. Other legislation strengthened women's claims to their husbands' pensions and made it easier for them to qualify for private retirement pensions.

By 1980, American women comprised more than 40 percent of the U.S. workforce, and activists debated how to tackle persistent gender inequality. With new career paths open to them, women were told that they could "have it all": satisfying work lives and family lives both. Yet professional women pointed to an unrealistic "superwoman" image in American society. Women typically were paid less than their male counterparts and were responsible for the majority of housework and child rearing, with little in the way of parental leave or subsidized day care. Working-class women and divorced or single mothers faced different problems, finding themselves more vulnerable financially as the government safety net was trimmed. Given poverty rates that were higher than those of men, women suffered most from Reagan's cuts in social programs.

Reagan's advisers had their own concerns about women, specifically about the gender gap in voting: women's tendency to support liberal and Democratic candidates in larger numbers than did men. Reagan appointed three women to cabinet posts. In 1981, he selected the first woman, Sandra Day O'Connor, a moderate conservative, for the Supreme Court, despite the Christian Right's objection to her support of abortion. But overall, the number of women and people of color in high-level government positions declined.

Although the Reagan administration threw its weight behind abortion restrictions, feminists fought successfully to retain the basic principles of *Roe v. Wade*, supported by narrow majorities on the Supreme Court. They won a key victory from the Court in *Meritor v. Vinson* (1986), which ruled that **sexual harassment** severe or pervasive enough to create a "hostile work environment" constituted sex discrimination. Feminists also made some gains at the state level on such issues as pay equity and sexual and domestic violence.

sexual harassment
Unwelcome or inappropriate sexual remarks or behavior in the workplace. If severe enough to create a "hostile work environment," such harassment was judged to constitute sex discrimination by the Supreme Court in 1986, a victory for the feminist movement.

How did gay men and lesbians secure rights?

In contrast to other social movements, gay and lesbian rights activists won significant victories during the 1980s. Activists were spurred in part by the discovery in 1981 of a devastating disease, **acquired immune deficiency syndrome (AIDS)**, which initially affected gay men disproportionately. Wary of provoking religious conservatives, Reagan refused to prioritize the epidemic or to devote public health resources to combat it, despite the rising death toll, reaching forty thousand by the end of the decade. Outraged activists took to the streets to demand AIDS education, prevention, and treatment. Groups like the AIDS Coalition to Unleash Power (ACT UP), which formed in 1987, successfully pressured Congress to allocate funding to fight the disease.

Since the 1970s, the gay and lesbian rights movement had encouraged closeted gay people to "come out," and this new visibility increased awareness, if not always acceptance, of sexual diversity. Several openly gay politicians won offices, and Democrats began to include gay rights in their party platforms. Activists organized gay rights marches throughout the country, turning out half a million people in New York City in 1987.

acquired immune deficiency syndrome (AIDS)
Disease discovered in 1981 that initially affected gay men disproportionately and brought a heavy death toll. The epidemic became politicized as activists charged the Reagan administration with neglect and demanded research and resources to fight the disease.

◀ **Activists Demand AIDS Funding** Charging that Ronald Reagan's conservative administration had neglected the AIDS epidemic, leaving gay men to perish, groups like ACT UP mobilized to make awareness of the disease unavoidable. "Die-ins" were one tactic that activists used to call attention to the crisis and to demand scientific research and federal resources to fight it. AP Photo/Marcy Nighswander.

Public attitudes about same-sex relationships became more tolerant but remained complex, leading to uneven changes in policies. **(See "Analyzing Historical Evidence: Protecting Gay and Lesbian Rights" on page 898.)** Dozens of cities banned job discrimination against gay men and lesbians, and beginning with Wisconsin in 1982, some states made sexual orientation a protected category under civil rights laws. Local governments and large corporations began to offer health insurance and other benefits to same-sex domestic partners.

Yet a strong countermovement challenged the drive for gay rights. The Christian Right targeted gays and lesbians as symbols of national immorality, with some fundamentalists characterizing the AIDS epidemic as "the wrath of God upon homosexuals." Conservatives succeeded in overturning some gay rights measures, which already lagged far behind protections for women and racial and ethnic minorities. Many states removed antisodomy laws from the books, but in 1986, the Supreme Court upheld the constitutionality of such laws, ruling that the right to privacy did not extend to gay people because their sexual behavior had "no connection" to "family, marriage, or procreation." Until the Court reversed that opinion in 2003, more than a dozen states retained statutes that left gay Americans vulnerable to criminal charges for private consensual behavior.

REVIEW

How did the prospects for progressive reform change during the Reagan years?

Why did the Cold War intensify and how did it end?

The Cold War heated up once again in the 1980s, ending the era of détente. A militant anti-Communist, Reagan accelerated Carter's arms buildup—a response to the Soviet invasion of Afghanistan—and harshly censured the

Soviet Union, calling it "an evil empire." Reagan assisted anti-leftist movements in Asia, Africa, and Central America, even in defiance of Congress, and dispatched troops to the Middle East and the Caribbean. Despite this new aggressiveness—or, some argued, because of it—Reagan presided over the most impressive thaw in the superpower conflict since the Cold War had begun.

What led to renewed militarization in the 1980s?

A fierce critic of containment, détente, and arms reduction talks, Reagan took an unyielding stance against communism. He expanded the military with new bombers and missiles, an enhanced nuclear force in Europe, a larger navy, and a rapid-deployment force. Casting aside the established principle of "mutually assured destruction" as well as scientists' skepticism, Reagan proposed developing a space-based shield that would protect the United States from missile attacks. During his presidency, defense spending averaged $216 billion a year, up from $158 billion in the Carter years and higher even than in the Vietnam era.

Reagan justified the military buildup as a means to negotiate with the Soviets. But his policy of "peace through strength" provoked an outburst of pleas to halt the arms race. In 1982, 700,000 people marched in New York City to demand a "**nuclear freeze**," making it the largest political demonstration in U.S. history.

That same year, the National Conference of Catholic Bishops issued a call for nuclear disarmament. Hundreds of thousands protested across Europe, stimulated by fears of new U.S. missiles scheduled for deployment there in 1983. Protesters marched even in the Soviet Union, intentionally passing in front of the U.S. Embassy to make sure that news of their demonstration could not be censored. A new wave of domestic anxiety about the nuclear threat was evident in the blockbuster television film *The Day After*, which aired on ABC in 1983. More than 100 million tuned in to watch a harrowing fictional portrayal of the aftermath of a nuclear attack on American soil, including graphic portrayals of radiation sickness.

The revived arms race was only one of Americans' concerns on the world stage. Another was the growing threat of terrorism by nonstate organizations that sought to achieve political objectives by attacking civilian populations. Terrorism had a long history, but in the 1970s and 1980s, Americans saw it escalate among groups hostile to Israel and Western policies. In 1972, after the Israeli occupation of the West Bank, Palestinian terrorists had murdered eleven Israeli athletes at the Munich Olympics. In 1982, the terrorist organization Hezbollah, composed of Shiite Muslims and backed by Iran and Syria, arose in Lebanon after Israeli forces invaded to stop the Palestine Liberation Organization (PLO) from using sanctuaries in that country to launch attacks on Israel.

Reagan sent two thousand Marines to Lebanon to join an international peace-keeping mission (see Map 29.3). In 1983, a suicide attack on the U.S. Embassy in the capital of Beirut killed sixty-three people; later that year, a Hezbollah fighter drove an explosives-filled truck into a U.S. barracks there, killing 241 Marines. The attack prompted the withdrawal of U.S. troops, signaling that political violence could affect U.S. policy. Lebanon remained in chaos, while incidents of murder, kidnapping, and hijacking by various Middle Eastern extremist groups continued.

nuclear freeze
Global movement that sought to halt the revived nuclear arms race of the 1980s. Mass protests in Europe and the United States put pressure on the United States and Soviet Union to begin talks on disarmament toward the end of the decade.

ANALYZING HISTORICAL EVIDENCE

Protecting Gay and Lesbian Rights

Beginning in the 1970s, the gay and lesbian rights movement lobbied for antidiscrimination measures. In 1982, Wisconsin became the first state to ban discrimination on the basis of sexual orientation, following several cities that passed gay rights ordinances in the 1970s. By 2022, twenty-two states and the District of Columbia outlawed employment discrimination against gays and lesbians, and more than 250 cities and counties did so.

DOCUMENT 1
Ordinance of the City of Minneapolis, 1974

In 1974, the city council of Minneapolis amended its civil rights ordinance to include discrimination based on sexual orientation.

It is determined that discriminatory practices based on race, color, creed, religion, national origin, sex, or affectional or sexual preference, with respect to employment, labor union membership, housing accommodations, property rights, education, public accommodations, and public services, or any of them, tend to create and intensify conditions of poverty, ill health, unrest, civil disobedience, lawlessness, and vice and adversely affect the public health, safety, order, convenience, and general welfare; such discriminatory practices threaten the rights, privileges, and opportunities of all inhabitants of the city and such rights, privileges, and opportunities are hereby to be declared civil rights.

Source: From *The Rights of Gay People: The Basic ACLU Guide to a Gay Person's Rights*, ed. E. Carrington Boggan et al. (New York: Avon Books, 1975), 251.

DOCUMENT 2
Paul Moore, Letter to the Editor of the *New York Times*, November 23, 1981

Paul Moore, Episcopal bishop of New York, made a religious argument for gay rights.

I quote our diocesan resolution: "Whereas this Convention, without making any judgment on the morality of homosexuality, agrees that homosexuals are entitled to full civil rights. Now therefore be it resolved this Convention supports laws guaranteeing homosexuals all civil rights guaranteed to other citizens." The Bible stands for justice and compassion for all of God's children. To deny

civil rights to anyone for something he or she cannot help is against the clear commandment of justice and love, which is the message of the word of God. As a New Yorker I find it incredible that this great city, populated by more gay persons than any other city in the world, still denies them basic human rights. They make an enormous contribution to the commercial, artistic, and religious life of our city.

Source: Paul Moore, Letter to the Editor of the *New York Times*, November 23, 1981. Courtesy The Archives of the Episcopal Church.

DOCUMENT 3
Vatican Congregation for the Doctrine of the Faith, August 6, 1992

The following statement from the Roman Catholic Church reflected the views of many religious groups that deemed homosexuality immoral.

"Sexual orientation" does not constitute a quality comparable to race, ethnic background, etc., in respect to nondiscrimination. Unlike these, homosexual orientation is an objective disorder and evokes moral concern.

There are areas in which it is not unjust discrimination to take sexual orientation into account, for example, in the placement of children for adoption or foster care, in employment of teachers or athletic coaches, and in military recruitment.

Source: From Vatican Doctrine of the Faith, *Origins*, August 6, 1992. Copyright © Liberia Editrice Vaticana. Reprinted by permission.

DOCUMENT 4
Charles Cochrane Jr., Testimony before the House Subcommittee on Employment Opportunities of the Committee on Education and Labor, January 27, 1982

Congress has considered, but never enacted, legislation banning discrimination on the basis of sexual orientation.

Charles Cochrane Jr., an army veteran and police sergeant, testified on behalf of such a bill.

I am very proud of being a New York City policeman. And I am equally proud of being gay. I have always been gay.

I have been out of the closet for 4 years. November 6 was my anniversary. It took me 34 years to muster enough courage to declare myself openly.

We gays are loathed by some, pitied by others, and misunderstood by most. We are not cruel, wicked, cursed, sick, or possessed by demons. We are artists, business people, police officers, and clergymen. We are scientists, truck drivers, politicians; we work in every field. We are loving human beings who are in some ways different. . . .

During the early years of my association with the New York City Police Department a great deal of energy did go into guarding and concealing my innermost feelings. I believed that I would be subjected to ridicule and harassment were my colleagues to learn of my sexual orientation. Happily, when I actually began to integrate the various aspects of my total self, those who knew me did not reject me.

Then what need is there for such legislation as H.R. 1454? The crying need of others, still trapped in their closets, who must be protected, who must be reassured that honesty about themselves and their lives will not cost them their homes or their jobs. . . .

The bill before you will not act as a proselytizing agent in matters of sexual orientation or preference. It will not include affirmative action provisions. Passage of this bill will protect the inherent human rights of all people of the United States, while in no way diminishing the rights of those who do not see the need for such legislation.

Source: U.S. Congress, House, Committee on Education and Labor, Subcommittee on Employment Opportunities, *Hearing on H.R. 1454 before the U.S. House Subcommittee on Employment Opportunities of the Committee on Education and Labor,* 97th Cong., 2nd sess. (1982), 54–56.

DOCUMENT 5
Carl F. Horowitz, "Homosexuality's Legal Revolution," May 1991

Carl Horowitz, a policy analyst at the Heritage Foundation, a conservative think tank, argued against gay rights.

Homosexual activists have all but completed their campaign to persuade the nation's educational establishment that homosexuality is normal "alternative" behavior, and thus any adverse reaction to it is akin to a phobia, such as fear of heights, or an ethnic prejudice, such as anti-Semitism.

The movement now stands on the verge of fully realizing its use of law to . . . intimidate heterosexuals uncomfortable about coming into contact with it. . . . The movement seeks to win sinecures through the state, and over any objections by "homophobic" opposition. With a cloud of a heavy fine or even a jail sentence hanging over a mortgage lender, a rental agent, or a job interviewer who might be discomforted by them, homosexuals under these laws can win employment, credit, housing, and other economic entitlements. Heterosexuals would have no right to discriminate against homosexuals, but apparently, not vice versa. . . .

Heterosexuals and even "closeted" homosexuals will be at a competitive disadvantage for jobs and housing. . . .

The new legalism will increase heterosexual anger— and even violence—toward homosexuals.

Source: Carl F. Horowitz, "Homosexuality's Legal Revolution," *Freeman,* May 1991.

Questions for Analysis

ANALYZE THE EVIDENCE: Which of these documents discuss how laws protecting gay and lesbian rights would affect heterosexuals? What effects do they anticipate?

CONSIDER THE CONTEXT: In what ways might the civil rights movement have influenced the authors' views on gay and lesbian rights?

RECOGNIZE VIEWPOINTS: What underlying assumptions about gay men and lesbians can you find in the arguments for and against laws to protect their rights?

Following a familiar Cold War script, the Reagan administration also sought to contain leftist movements across the globe. In October 1983, five thousand U.S. troops invaded Grenada (**Map 30.1**), a small Caribbean nation where Marxists had staged a successful coup. In Asia, the United States covertly aided Afghan rebels' war against Afghanistan's Soviet-backed government. In the African nation of Angola, whose government had ties to the Soviet Union and Cuba, the United States armed rebel forces. Reagan also stood with the South African government, despite its brutal suppression of Black protest against apartheid, forcing Congress to override his veto to impose economic sanctions.

What was the Iran-Contra scandal?

Reagan most feared left-wing movements in Central America, which he claimed could "destabilize the entire region from the Panama Canal to Mexico." When a leftist uprising occurred in El Salvador in 1981, the United States sent money and military advisers to prop up its authoritarian government. In neighboring Nicaragua (see Map 30.1), the administration funneled aid to the Contras, an armed coalition seeking to unseat the left-wing Sandinistas, who had toppled a long-standing dictatorship.

Concerned about being drawn into what some saw as "another Vietnam," many Americans opposed U.S. involvement with reactionary forces not supported by the majority of Nicaraguans. Congress repeatedly instructed the president to halt aid to the Contras. But the administration, describing the Contras as "freedom fighters," quietly continued to supply them with weapons and training. Eventually, it also helped to wreck Nicaragua's economy and unseat its president.

Iran-Contra scandal
Reagan administration scandal brought to light in 1986 involving the sale of arms to Iran in exchange for its efforts to secure the release of hostages held in Lebanon and the secret redirection of the proceeds of those sales to the Nicaraguan Contras.

Secret aid to the Contras was part of a larger project that came to be known as the **Iran-Contra scandal**. It began in 1985, when officials of the National Security Council and the CIA covertly arranged to sell arms to Iran, then in the midst of an eight-year war with neighboring Iraq, even while the United States openly supplied Iraq with funds and weapons. The purpose was to get Iran to pressure Hezbollah to release American hostages being held in Lebanon.

Profits from the arms sales were then secretly channeled to the Nicaraguan Contras. Over the objections of his secretaries of state and defense, the president approved the arms sales to Iran, but all three subsequently denied knowing that the proceeds were diverted to the Contras. When news of the affair surfaced in November 1986, the Reagan administration faced serious charges: the president's aides had defied Congress's express ban on military aid to the Contras.

Investigations by an independent prosecutor led to a trial in which seven individuals pleaded guilty or were convicted of lying to Congress and destroying evidence. (One conviction was later overturned on a technicality; President George H. W. Bush pardoned the other six officials.) The independent prosecutor's final report found no evidence that Reagan had broken the law, but it concluded that he had known about the diversion of funds to the Contras and had "knowingly participated or at least acquiesced" in covering up the scandal. Reagan's job approval rating dropped by sixteen points, with 79 percent of Americans opposed to his administration's actions.

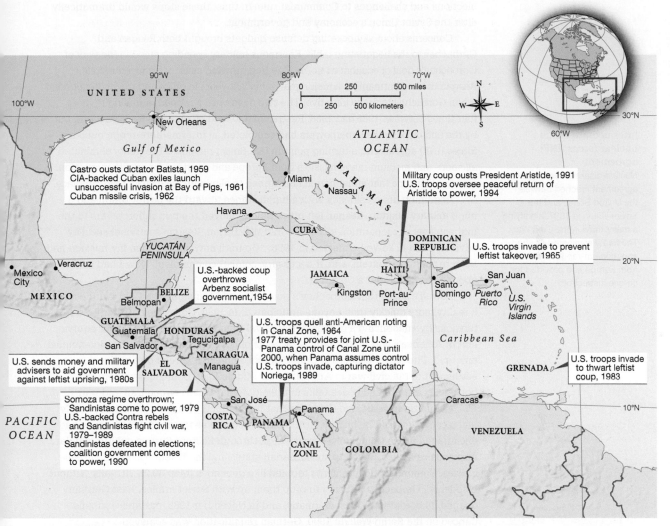

MAP 30.1 ▲ **U.S. Involvement in Latin America and the Caribbean, 1954–1994** During the Cold War, the United States frequently intervened—directly or indirectly—in Central American and Caribbean countries to counter Communist or leftist movements.

How were Soviet-American relations transformed?

The Iran-Contra scandal was soon overshadowed by a momentous reduction in Cold War tensions. The surprising new Soviet-American accord depended both on Reagan's flexibility and profound desire to end the possibility of nuclear war and on an innovative Soviet head of state who recognized that his country's domestic problems required an easing of Cold War antagonism.

When Mikhail Gorbachev assumed power in the Soviet Union in 1985, he was determined to reform a collapsing economy incapable of satisfying basic consumer needs. The new Soviet leader lifted some economic regulations and also proclaimed an era of *glasnost* (greater freedom of expression), eventually allowing contested elections and challenges to Communist rule. In time, these steps would dramatically alter the Soviet Union's economy and government.

Concerns about skyrocketing defense budgets brought both Reagan and Gorbachev to the negotiating table. Enormous military spending stood in the way of Gorbachev's goal of economic reform. Heeding growing calls for arms reductions, Reagan made disarmament a major goal in his last years in office and readily responded when Gorbachev took the initiative. The two developed a rapport, agreeing to meet four times between 1985 and 1988. Reagan had to fend off criticism from the right, but by the end of 1987, the superpowers had completed an **intermediate-range nuclear forces (INF) agreement**, a turning point in U.S.-Soviet relations. The treaty eliminated all short- and medium-range missiles from Europe and provided for on-site inspection. It was the first time that either nation had agreed to eliminate weapons already in place.

Beginning his presidency with a harsh stance toward the Soviet Union and a huge military buildup, Reagan left office having moved the two superpowers to the highest level of cooperation since the Cold War began. Reagan's national security adviser, Colin L. Powell, reflected in 1988, "Up until now, as a soldier, my mission had been to confront, contain, and, if necessary, combat communism. Now I had to think about a world without a Cold War."

Powell's sense that Gorbachev's policies would transform the Cold War became a reality more quickly than anyone anticipated. In 1988, Gorbachev further eased tensions by announcing a gradual withdrawal from Afghanistan, the Soviet equivalent of America's war in Vietnam. New signs of cooperation between the old enemies emerged. The Soviet Union, the United States, and Cuba agreed on a political settlement of the civil war in Angola. In the Middle East, both superpowers supported a cease-fire and peace talks in the eight-year war between Iran and Iraq.

Within three years, the Cold War that had defined global geopolitics for nearly half a century would be history. In 1989, the progressive forces that Gorbachev had encouraged in the Communist world swept through Eastern Europe, where popular uprisings called for an end to authoritarian states and inefficient economic bureaucracies. Communist governments toppled like dominoes (**Map 30.2**), virtually without bloodshed, Gorbachev refusing to prop them up with Soviet armies. East Germany opened its border with West Germany, and in November 1989, ecstatic Germans danced on the Berlin Wall. In 1990, German reunification was achieved.

Soon Poland, Hungary, and other former iron curtain countries lined up to join the North Atlantic Treaty Organization (NATO). Eight former Soviet satellites joined the European Union and the common economic market. Inspired by the liberation of Eastern Europe, republics within the Soviet Union soon established their own independence. With nothing left to govern, Gorbachev resigned. The Soviet Union itself dissolved in 1991 and, with it, the Cold War conflict that had dominated U.S. foreign policy for decades.

How new was the "new world order"?

Republican President George H. W. Bush, elected in 1988 after serving eight years as Reagan's vice president, cheered the dramatic events that ended the Cold War as a victory for the United States. The contest between the free and Communist worlds, it appeared, was finally settled. Bush declared the dawn of a "new world order." Democrats called for a "peace dividend" in the form of defense spending cuts. But

intermediate-range nuclear forces (INF) agreement
Nuclear disarmament agreement reached between the United States and the Soviet Union in 1987, signifying a major thaw in the Cold War. The treaty eliminated all short- and medium-range missiles from Europe and provided for on-site inspection.

MAP ACTIVITY

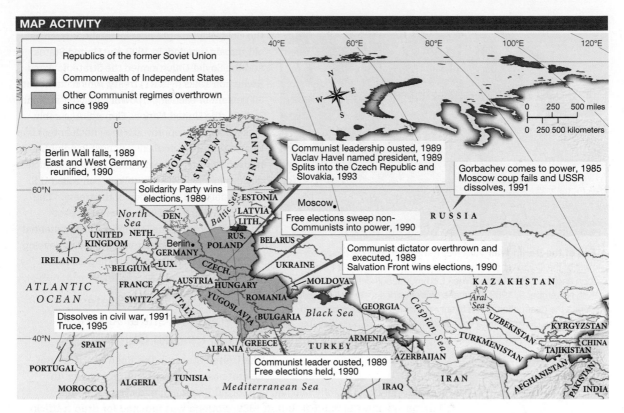

MAP 30.2 ▲ **Events in Eastern Europe, 1985–1995** The overthrow of Communist governments throughout Eastern Europe and the splintering of the Soviet Union into more than a dozen separate nations were among the most momentous developments in world history in the twentieth century.

READING THE MAP: Which country was the first to overthrow its Communist government? Which was the last? In which nations did elections usher in a change in government?

CONNECTIONS: What problems did Mikhail Gorbachev face in 1985, and how did he try to solve them? Why was President Reagan prepared to reach an accommodation with the Soviet leader?

ongoing turmoil in Latin America and the Middle East, along with a new war in the Persian Gulf, dashed hopes that an era of democracy and world peace was at hand.

The United States emerged from the Cold War as the sole superpower at a moment when liberalizing tides seemed to be sweeping the globe. In the early 1990s, democracy came not just to Eastern Europe but also to South Africa, where apartheid was finally defeated. In 1994, voters elected the country's first Black president, Nelson Mandela.

Colin Powell, now chairman of the Joint Chiefs of Staff, joked that he was "running out of villains. I'm down to Castro and Kim Il-sung," referring to the leaders of Cuba and North Korea. Both were still Communist dictatorships, with the latter committed to developing nuclear weapons. China too remained a Communist regime, and in 1989, when thousands of pro-democracy students demonstrated in Beijing's Tiananmen Square, the government responded with a brutal crackdown. Chinese soldiers killed hundreds of protesters, and some ten thousand reformers were arrested.

▲ **Fall of the Berlin Wall**   After 1961, the Berlin Wall became a key symbol of the Cold War and the iron grip of communism over Eastern Europe and the Soviet Union. When Communist authorities opened the wall on November 9, 1989, Germans on both sides rushed to the gate to celebrate the destruction of the twenty-eight-year-old barrier between East and West Berlin. Here, a man takes a pickaxe to a portion of the wall.   Langevin Jacques/Getty Images.

As American leaders would learn, the end of the Cold War brought new instabilities even as old threats receded. In 1990, the United States and the Soviet Union signed the Strategic Arms Reduction Talks (START) treaty, which cut about 30 percent of each superpower's nuclear arsenal. In 1996, the United Nations General Assembly overwhelmingly approved a total nuclear test ban treaty. Yet India and Pakistan, hostile neighbors, refused to sign the treaty, and both tested nuclear devices in 1998. The Republican-controlled U.S. Senate defeated ratification of the treaty. "The post–Cold War world is decidedly not post-nuclear," declared one U.S. official. The potential for rogue nations and terrorist groups to develop nuclear weapons posed an ongoing threat.

Why did the United States intervene in Central America and the Persian Gulf?

The United States in the Bush years did not hesitate to exercise its military power. In Central America, U.S. officials had supported Panamanian dictator Manuel Noriega, an anti-Communist. But in 1989, Noriega was indicted for drug trafficking, and his troops killed an American Marine, leading Bush to order twenty-five thousand military personnel into Panama (see Map 30.1) to capture him. U.S. forces quickly overcame Noriega's troops, at the cost of killing hundreds of Panamanians, including many civilians. Both the United Nations and the Organization of American States condemned the unilateral action by the United States.

Bush's second military engagement, by contrast, rested solidly on international approval. Viewing Iran as America's major enemy in the Middle East, U.S. officials had quietly assisted the Iraqi dictator Saddam Hussein in the Iran-Iraq war from 1980 until its end in 1988. In 1990, struggling with an enormous war debt, Hussein invaded the small country of Kuwait, moving his troops near the Saudi Arabian border. Faced with this threat to the world's largest oil reserves, President Bush ordered a massive military mobilization and assembled an international coalition to stand up to Iraq. Although he invoked principles of national self-determination and international law, access to Middle Eastern oil was also a key concern.

Reflecting the easing of Cold War tensions, the Soviet Union supported a UN embargo on Iraqi oil and authorization for using force if Iraq did not withdraw from Kuwait. The United States deployed more than 400,000 soldiers to Saudi Arabia, joined by 265,000 troops from two dozen other nations, including several Arab states. "The community of nations has

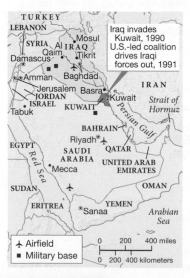

The Persian Gulf War

resolutely gathered to condemn and repel lawless aggression," Bush announced. "With few exceptions, the world now stands as one."

When the UN-imposed deadline for Iraqi withdrawal expired, Bush asked Congress to authorize war. U.S. forces led a forty-day bombing campaign against Iraqi military targets, power plants, oil refineries, and transportation networks. The coalition then stormed into Kuwait and forced Iraqi troops to withdraw, although without deposing Hussein. Instead, U.S. leadership extracted a pledge from him not to rearm or develop weapons of mass destruction and to accept a system of UN inspections.

"By God, we've kicked the Vietnam syndrome once and for all," President Bush exulted when the fighting ended. Most Americans found no moral ambiguity in the **Persian Gulf War** and took pride in their country's display of military might. With the United States steering a coalition in which Arab nations fought beside their former colonial rulers, the war also seemed to signal a new phase of American global leadership.

Yet this "new world order" was more volatile than orderly. Israel, which had endured Iraqi missile attacks, was more secure after the Gulf War, but the Israeli-Palestinian conflict continued to boil. Despite military losses, Hussein remained in power in Iraq and turned his war machine on Iraqi Kurds and Shiite Muslims. Hussein also found ways to conceal arms from UN inspectors, ultimately throwing them out altogether in 1998. And the decision to keep U.S. troops based in Saudi Arabia, the holy land of Islam, fueled the anger and determination of Muslim extremists like Osama bin Laden.

Persian Gulf War
1991 war between Iraq and a U.S.-led international coalition, sparked by the 1990 Iraqi invasion of Kuwait. A forty-day bombing campaign against Iraq, followed by coalition troops storming into Kuwait, brought a quick coalition victory.

REVIEW

How did George H. W. Bush respond to threats to U.S. interests as the Cold War came to an end?

Why did domestic politics become more polarized in the 1990s?

Compared to the dramatic global developments of the late 1980s and early 1990s, President Bush's domestic record was uneventful. He proposed few initiatives of his own, although he signed significant environmental and disability rights legislation. Bush grappled with economic and fiscal problems, some of them resulting from Reagan's policies, but his options were constrained by those in his party who opposed any new taxes.

His successor, Democrat Bill Clinton, operated in a political climate altered by conservative gains. Public opposition to taxes and federal social programs, a Republican-controlled Congress, and the Democratic Party's own move to the center hemmed in his domestic agenda. While Clinton did not completely abandon liberal principles, his administration embraced centrist politics, restricted welfare benefits, failed to enact health care reform, and was placed on the defensive by divisive "culture wars." Given the buoyant economy of the 1990s, Americans elected Clinton to a second term and supported him even when his reckless sexual behavior led to impeachment, crippling his leadership in his final years in office.

How did gridlock become a problem for governing?

The son of a wealthy U.S. senator from New England, George Herbert Walker Bush fought in World War II, served in Congress, and headed the Central Intelligence Agency under Richard Nixon. When Ronald Reagan tapped him for second place on the Republican ticket in 1980, Bush tailored his moderate positions on civil rights, abortion, and the ERA to Reagan's conservative agenda. At the end of Reagan's second term, Republicans rewarded him with the presidential nomination.

In the Democratic primaries in 1988, civil rights leader Reverend Jesse Jackson—whose Rainbow Coalition campaign brought together communities of color, women, workers, and the poor—won several primaries and seven million votes. But the centrist candidate, Massachusetts governor Michael Dukakis, secured the nomination. On election day, Bush won 54 percent of the vote, while the Democrats gained seats in Congress.

Promising "a kinder, gentler nation," President Bush was more inclined than Reagan to support government activity in the private sphere. In 1990, he approved the **Clean Air Act**, the strongest, most comprehensive environmental law in U.S. history.

Some forty million Americans benefited when Bush signed another landmark regulatory measure that year, the **Americans with Disabilities Act (ADA)**, banning discrimination against people with disabilities and requiring that private businesses and public facilities be accessible to them. For Beverly Jones, a court reporter who had lost the use of her legs after an automobile accident in 1984 and found few courthouses wheelchair-accessible, "the passage of the ADA was like opening a door that had been closed to me for so long." Although states like Jones's Tennessee fought the new requirements, the law proved an important step toward equity for people with disabilities.

Bush also needed to satisfy party conservatives, and he would be haunted by a pledge he made on the campaign trail: "Read my lips: No new taxes." Bush vetoed thirty-six bills from Congress, including those extending unemployment benefits, raising taxes, and mandating family and medical leave for workers. Press reports increasingly used the words *stalemate* and *divided government*. Others borrowed the word for a traffic jam, *gridlock*, to characterize the impasse.

Continuing a trend begun during the Reagan years, some states compensated for this paralysis with their own innovations. State legislatures enacted laws to establish parental leave policies, improve food labeling, and protect the environment. Dozens of cities passed ordinances requiring businesses receiving tax abatements to pay wages well above the federal minimum.

The huge federal budget deficit he inherited from Reagan drove Bush in 1990 to abandon his "no new taxes" pledge, enraging conservatives. The new law modestly raised taxes on high-income Americans and increased levies on gasoline, cigarettes, alcohol, and luxury items, while leaving intact most of Reagan's massive tax cuts. Neither the new revenues nor controls on spending curbed the deficit, however,

Clean Air Act
Environmental legislation signed in 1990 by President George H. W. Bush. The act was the strongest and most comprehensive environmental law in the nation's history.

Americans with Disabilities Act (ADA)
Act signed by President George H. W. Bush in 1990 that prohibits discrimination against people with disabilities. The law also required "reasonable accommodation" to ensure accessibility in public facilities and private businesses.

which was boosted by rising costs for Social Security, Medicare, Medicaid, and natural disaster relief.

As had Reagan's, Bush's judicial appointments led to a more conservative Supreme Court. His first nominee was a moderate. But in 1991, when the only Black member of the Court, Thurgood Marshall, retired, Bush nominated Clarence Thomas, a conservative Black American judge who had opposed affirmative action when he headed the Equal Employment Opportunity Commission (EEOC) under Reagan.

Civil rights groups and other liberal organizations fought the nomination. Then Anita Hill, a Black law professor and former EEOC employee, accused Thomas of sexual harassment. Bitter debates broke out over whom to believe and how to weigh dueling charges of racial and sexual discrimination—an indication of how deeply the lines of race and sex continued to divide Americans. Thomas angrily denied the accusation, and the Senate voted narrowly to confirm him. The hearings enraged many women, who denounced male politicians for not taking sexual harassment seriously—and noted that only two women sat in the Senate, a body of one hundred.

What agenda did the "New Democrats" pursue?

Bush's popularity after the Gulf War caused many prominent Democrats to opt out of the presidential race of 1992. But it did not deter William Jefferson "Bill" Clinton, who at age forty-five had served as governor of Arkansas for twelve years. Like Carter in 1976, Clinton and his running mate, Tennessee senator Albert Gore Jr., presented themselves as "New Democrats." Although shaped by the liberal 1960s—he had participated in antiwar protests, smoked marijuana in the 1960s, and married a feminist, Hillary Rodham—Clinton sought to rid his party of its liberal image.

Clinton was a key player in the Democratic Leadership Council, which argued that the party's survival in the post-Reagan years depended on centrist policies, especially regarding the economy. Clinton curried favor with the "forgotten middle class" who "played by the rules." He promised a middle-class tax cut, pledged to reinvigorate the economy, and vowed "to put an end to welfare as we know it." Bush was vulnerable to an unemployment rate of 7 percent and to a challenge from self-made Texas billionaire H. Ross Perot, whose third-party organization revealed Americans' frustrations with the two major parties. Clinton won only 43 percent of the popular vote, Bush 38 percent, and Perot 19 percent—the strongest third-party finish in eighty years (**Map 30.3**).

One sign of the times was Clinton's pronouncement that "the era of big government is over." It reflected the Democratic Party's move to the right, which had begun with Jimmy Carter, as well as conservatives' capture of the terms of debate. It did not, however, signal political harmony. Although he aimed for the middle ground, Clinton's time in office would be marked by intense partisan acrimony. Clinton wanted to restore confidence in government as a force for good without alienating antigovernment voters. But he inherited a huge budget deficit—$4.4 trillion in 1993—which ruled out

▲ **Disability Activism** Decades of advocacy led to the passage of the landmark Americans with Disabilities Act of 1990. When the legislation stalled in Congress in March of that year, hundreds of activists left their wheelchairs and crutches behind, crawling up the Capitol steps to highlight the inaccessibility of the seat of the U.S. government to those with disabilities. Many protesters were arrested during the "Capitol Crawl," but their message was heard and the Act was signed by President George H. W. Bush several months later. Jeff Markowitz/AP Images.

substantial federal initiatives. Clinton was constrained by the Republican-controlled Congress after 1994. Throughout his presidency, he was also burdened by investigations into his past financial activities and private indiscretions.

Despite these obstacles, Clinton achieved a number of reforms for the working poor, women, and environmentalists and used his office to support affirmative action and gay rights. Clinton issued executive orders that eased restrictions on abortion. He also signed several bills that Republicans had previously blocked. In 1993, Congress enacted gun control legislation and the landmark **Family and Medical Leave Act (FMLA)**, which mandated unpaid leave for childbirth, adoption, and family medical emergencies for workers in larger companies. The Violence against Women Act of 1994 authorized $1.6 billion for combating sexual assault and domestic violence. Clinton won stricter air pollution controls and greater protection for national forests and parks. He also secured a minimum-wage increase and a large expansion of aid for college students.

Most significantly, Clinton pushed through a substantial increase in the **Earned Income Tax Credit (EITC)**. Begun in 1975, the EITC implicitly recognized the inability of the free market to secure a living wage for all workers. It gave tax breaks to those who worked full-time at meager pay or, if they owed no taxes, a subsidy to lift their family income above the poverty line. By 2003, some fifteen million low-income families were benefiting from the EITC, which one expert deemed "the largest antipoverty program since the Great Society."

Shortly before Clinton took office, the economy had begun to rebound. Economic expansion, along with spending cuts, tax increases, and declining unemployment, produced in 1998 the first U.S. budget surplus since 1969. Despite this, Clinton failed to achieve one of his key domestic priorities: providing universal health insurance and curbing skyrocketing medical costs. Criticism of his proposal, which had been spearheaded by Hillary Rodham Clinton, as "government-run health care" doomed the initiative. Congress enacted important smaller reforms, such as underwriting health care for five million uninsured children. Yet forty million Americans remained uninsured.

Pledging to make the face of government "look like America," Clinton built on the gradual progress toward political representation that women and people of color had made since the 1960s. Black Americans and women had become mayors in major cities from New York to San Francisco. Virginia had elected the first Black governor since Reconstruction, and Florida the first Latino governor. Clinton's cabinet appointments included six women, three Black Americans, two Latinos, and an Asian American. In 1993, he named the second woman to the Supreme Court: Ruth Bader Ginsburg, whose arguments as an attorney in the 1970s had won major women's rights rulings from that Court.

Family and Medical Leave Act (FMLA)
Law passed in 1993 and signed by President Bill Clinton that mandated unpaid leave for childbirth, adoption, and family medical emergencies for workers in large companies.

Earned Income Tax Credit (EITC)
Federal antipoverty program initiated in 1975 and expanded significantly by President Clinton in 1993. The program assisted the working poor by giving tax breaks to low-income, full-time workers or a subsidy to those who owed no taxes.

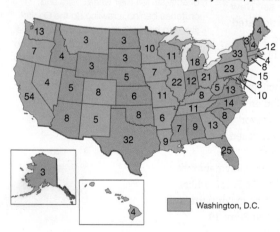

Candidate	Electoral Vote	Popular Vote	Percent of Popular Vote
Bill Clinton (Democrat)	370	44,909,889	43.0
George H.W. Bush (Republican)	168	39,104,545	37.5
Ross Perot (Independent)	0	19,742,267	18.9

MAP 30.3 ▲ The Election of 1992

How did conservative activism shape politics?

The 1994 midterm elections swept away the Democratic majorities in Congress. With Republicans in control of both houses for the first time since 1954, Clinton's agenda was stymied, and he moved to the right politically. Republicans claimed the election results as a mandate for their conservative platform. They pledged to end "government that is too big, too intrusive, and too easy with the public's money," arguing for "a Congress that respects the values and shares the faith of the American family." Their positions on economic and cultural issues would constrain Clinton's remaining years in office.

Led by Speaker of the House Newt Gingrich, antigovernment Republicans attempted to push through a "Contract with America," which called for severe cuts in social, educational, and environmental programs. When budget talks broke down between Clinton and Congress, the government was forced to close down nonessential operations twice in the winter of 1995–1996. Increasingly after 1994, party loyalists rather than policy experts would be selected to lead congressional committees, leading to fewer bills being passed and shrinking bipartisan support for them. Inaction in Congress would add to growing public dissatisfaction with the government.

The most extreme antigovernment sentiment developed far from Washington in the form of grassroots armed militias that championed white Christian supremacy and directed their hostility at institutions ranging from the Internal Revenue Service to the United Nations. The militia movement grew following the passage of new gun control legislation and in response to government agents storming the headquarters of an armed religious cult in Waco, Texas, in April 1993, killing more than eighty. In 1995, on the second anniversary of that event, two militia sympathizers bombed a federal building in Oklahoma City, taking 168 lives in what was at that point the worst terrorist attack in the nation's history.

In the 1990s, hardening attitudes about poverty led to the rollback of the New Deal program Aid to Families with Dependent Children (AFDC), popularly called welfare. Using the term "welfare queen" to stigmatize AFDC recipients and particularly urban Black women, critics put the blame for poverty on the poor themselves and their failures of "personal responsibility." Defenders of AFDC pointed instead to the lack of adequate employment and child care or to the disinvestment that had impoverished America's inner cities—and they noted the far greater subsidies the government provided to other groups, such as large farmers, corporations, and homeowners.

After vetoing two welfare bills proposed by the Republican Congress, Clinton signed a less punitive measure as the 1996 election approached. The Temporary Assistance for Needy Families (TANF) program replaced AFDC. In line with Clinton's declaration that welfare should be "a second chance, not a way of life," it limited welfare payments to two consecutive years, with a lifetime maximum of five years.

Clinton's signature on the new law denied Republicans a partisan issue in the 1996 presidential campaign even as it signaled Democrats' historic retreat from their commitment to poor Americans. The Republican Party also moved to the center, nominating Kansan Robert Dole, a World War II hero and former Senate majority leader. Clinton won 49 percent of the votes; 41 percent went to Dole and 9 percent to third-party candidate Ross Perot. Voters sent a Republican majority back to Congress.

▶ **The End of Welfare** After signing the bill that sharply curtailed government support for poor mothers and their children, Bill Clinton made it a part of his 1996 campaign for reelection. He highlighted the issue especially when campaigning in more conservative regions, as this photo from a campaign stop in Daytona, Florida, shows. Paul J. Richards/AFP/Getty Images.

READING THE IMAGE: What does the poster behind Clinton suggest about the importance of welfare as an issue in 1996? What American values do you think it refers to?

CONNECTIONS: What other programs did Clinton advance to address poverty?

In 1999, Clinton and Congress made a second retreat from the New Deal by further deregulating the financial industry and repealing key aspects of the Glass-Steagall Act, which had been passed in the 1930s to prevent another Great Depression. The Financial Services Modernization Act ended the separation between banking, securities, and insurance services, allowing financial institutions to engage in all three areas—practices that would contribute to the financial meltdown of 2008.

What were the "culture wars"?

Commentators in the 1990s began to talk about the "culture wars," the partisan standoffs that pitted liberals against conservatives on social issues ranging from the teaching of evolution to government funding of the arts. Many of these battles, reflecting the increasing sway of groups like Pat Robertson's Christian Coalition, centered on the changing American family: the high rates of working women, divorce, and unwed mothers, as well as the greater visibility of gay relationships. Hillary Rodham Clinton, a successful lawyer who played a far larger policy role in her husband's administration than had most first ladies, was herself a lightning rod for such issues.

Bowing to conservative pressures and following the advice of military leaders, President Clinton backed away from his promise to lift the ban on gay people in the military. Instead, he instituted a "Don't ask, don't tell" policy, a controversial halfway measure that prohibited discrimination only against service people who did not reveal their sexuality. Cathleen Glover, an army specialist in Arabic who lost her position, as did thousands of other soldiers, lamented, "The army preaches integrity, but asks you to lie to everyone around you." In 1996, Clinton further disappointed gay rights advocates by signing the Defense of Marriage Act (DOMA), prohibiting the federal government from recognizing state-licensed marriages between same-sex couples.

Other battles were prompted by new demands for recognition of ethnic and racial diversity—or "multiculturalism"—in school curricula and public life. Opponents charged that such efforts undermined a common American national identity. Rising immigration rates were politically charged for the same reason. In contrast to earlier arrivals who had come largely from Europe, by the 1980s the vast majority of immigrants came from Asia, Latin America, and the Caribbean. The Immigration and Nationality Act of 1965 passed under Lyndon B. Johnson (see chapter 28) had enabled this change, allowing close relatives of U.S. citizens to enter above the annual ceiling of 270,000 immigrants, thus creating family migration chains. During the Cold War, the United States had also welcomed refugees from communism, including more than 800,000 Cubans and more than 600,000 Vietnamese, Laotians, and Cambodians.

The new immigration was making America an ever more international and multiracial society. The largest numbers of immigrants flocked to California, New York, Texas, Florida, New Jersey, and Illinois, but new immigrants dispersed throughout the country. Taquerias, sushi bars, and Vietnamese restaurants appeared in southeastern and midwestern towns, cable TV companies added Spanish-language stations, and the international sport of soccer soared in popularity. Mixed marriages displayed the growing fusion of cultures, recognized in 2000 on Census Bureau forms, where Americans could for the first time check more than one racial category.

The racial composition of the new immigrants heightened the long-standing wariness of native-born Americans toward newcomers, as did forecasts of a "majority minority" society by 2050. New state laws establishing English as the official language suggested considerable resistance to a changing America. Pressure for restrictive immigration policies stemmed from beliefs that newcomers took jobs from the native-born, suppressed wages by accepting low pay, strained social services, or eroded the dominant culture. In 1994, California voters supported Proposition 187, which denied schooling and public services to undocumented immigrants and their children. Although a judge later struck down that measure, halting illegal immigration would become a mainstay of conservative politics.

Why was Clinton impeached?

Clinton's charisma, his ability to capture the middle ground, and the nation's economic resurgence enabled him to survive scandals and impeachment. Early in his presidency, charges related to firings of White House staff, political use of FBI records, and the Clintons' real estate investments in Arkansas led to an official investigation by an independent prosecutor, Kenneth Starr.

In 1998, Starr began to investigate a charge that Clinton had engaged in sexual relations with a twenty-one-year-old White House intern and lied about it to a federal grand jury. Based on Starr's report, the House of Representatives voted to impeach the president for perjury and obstruction of justice. In 1999, Clinton became only the second president (after Andrew Johnson, in 1868) to be impeached by the House and tried by the Senate.

A majority of Americans condemned the president's behavior but approved of the job he was doing and opposed impeachment. One man remarked, "Let him get a divorce. . . . Don't take him out of office and disrupt the country." Some saw Starr as a fanatic invading individuals' privacy. Others insisted that the president must set a high moral standard and that lying to a grand jury, even over a private matter, was a serious offense. The Senate votes fell far short of the two-thirds majority needed for conviction. Even some Republicans seemed to agree with a Clinton supporter that the president's behavior, though "indefensible, outrageous, unforgivable, shameless," did not warrant his removal from office.

REVIEW

What policies of the Clinton administration moved the Democratic Party to the right?

How did the United States respond to the challenges of globalization?

Clinton's ability to weather impeachment owed much to the robust economy of the 1990s. His two-term presidency witnessed the longest economic boom in history and ended with a budget surplus. America's prosperity was linked to its dominance in a world economy being transformed by globalization: the accelerating integration and interdependence of global markets. Clinton lowered a number of trade barriers, despite heated arguments about whether that was in the country's best interest. Capital, products, information, and people crossed borders in greater numbers and at greater speed.

Clinton agreed with Bush that the United States must retain its position of leadership in the world. But with the collapse of the Cold War, it was unclear whether military defense, economic interests, peacekeeping, or democratization— or some combination of these—ought to guide foreign policy. The president used military force in Somalia, the Middle East, and Eastern Europe; deployed troops in Haiti; and attempted to ease the conflict between Israelis and Palestinians. He also strove to safeguard American interests from terrorist attacks around the world, a challenge in some ways more complex than combating communism.

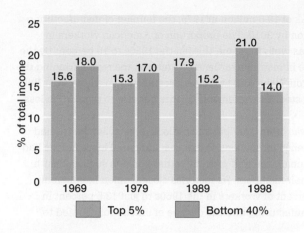

FIGURE 30.1 ◀ **The Growth of Inequality: Changes in Family Income, 1969–1998** For most of the immediate post–World War II period, income increased for all groups on the economic ladder. But after 1969, the income of the poorest families actually declined, while the income of the richest 20 percent of the population grew substantially. Data from the *New York Times*, 1989.

What was the "new economy" and whom did it leave behind?

During the 1990s, the U.S. gross domestic product grew by more than one-third, thirteen million new jobs were created, inflation remained in check, unemployment reached 4 percent—its lowest point in twenty-five years—and the stock market soared.

Clinton's policies contributed to the boom. He made deficit reduction a priority, and in exchange, the Federal Reserve Board and bond market traders encouraged economic expansion by lowering interest rates. Businesses also prospered because they had lowered their costs through corporate restructuring and employee layoffs. Economic problems in Europe and Asia made American firms more competitive in the international market.

Individuals at all income levels benefited, but income inequality, rising since the 1970s, persisted (**Figure 30.1**). More minorities than ever attained middle-class status, but people of color did not participate equally in the economic expansion. In 1999, the median income for white households surpassed $45,000 but was only $29,423 and $33,676 for Black and Latino households, respectively. In 2000, more than 20 percent of Black people and Latinos were poor, in contrast to 7.5 percent of white people.

Some of the economic changes of the 1990s were structural. The computer revolution and the application of new technologies boosted productivity, while the advent of the Internet and the World Wide Web led to talk of a "new economy" tied less to the manufacture of products and more to the flow of information. New communication technologies, from e-mail to cell phones, advanced globalization and transformed daily life.

"Dot-com" companies, computer programming jobs, and money flowed into tech hubs such as California's Silicon Valley as well as Seattle, Austin, and New York. Giant new firms like Amazon and Google attracted frenzied speculation. High-tech stock prices soared, and thousands of new tech start-ups appeared. The tech bubble burst in 2000, but even after the shake-up, the surviving companies generated tremendous wealth. Financial industries also took in an increasing share of economic profits, although neither they nor the high-tech sector accounted for much job growth within the United States.

With computers becoming essential in many job sectors, the demand for highly skilled workers increased. But unskilled laborers faced declining opportunities and wages. Deindustrialization led to a sustained downturn in the old manufacturing centers of Illinois, Michigan, Indiana, Ohio, and Pennsylvania, sharpening regional

Rust Belt
Term referencing the deindustrialization of the former manufacturing core of the United States, stretching from New York to Illinois. The region lost steel and automobile plants as well as population as a result of labor outsourcing and foreign competition beginning in the 1970s.

economic divides. From a peak of 19.6 million in 1979, the number of manufacturing jobs would fall below 12 million by 2010. The proportion of American workers in manufacturing jobs dropped as well: from one-third in the 1950s to 10 percent by the twenty-first century. Once the industrial heartland of America, the region fringing the Great Lakes and stretching from New York to Illinois became known as the **Rust Belt**, a reference not only to stilled steel and automobile plants but also to population loss and urban decay.

Although factory work was often grueling and tedious, blue-collar wages had provided a middle-class existence for millions of families. Industrial labor unions had boosted pay even for the nonunionized and provided other benefits such as health insurance and pensions for their members. As factories closed, union membership plummeted from nearly 30 percent of workers in the 1950s to just 13.5 percent in 2000. Both the decline of manufacturing and the decline of unions contributed to economic insecurity.

Some Rust Belt cities pursued economic revival by building convention centers and casinos; others did so through nontraditional manufacturing or finance. Neither the old nor the new economy provided easy answers for the struggling region.

How did globalization affect the U.S. economy?

The United States experienced the dynamic forces of globalization in many ways. Already in the 1980s, Japanese, European, and Middle Eastern investors had purchased U.S. stocks and bonds, real estate, and corporations. Local communities welcomed foreign capital, and states competed to recruit foreign automobile plants. By the end of the century, the paychecks of nearly four million American workers came from foreign-owned companies such as Honda and BMW.

Paychecks and production traveled in the other direction as well. Whereas in 1960, 96 percent of all shoes bought in the United States were made within the country, nearly all came from abroad by 2000. International competition forced the collapse of some U.S. companies. Others moved production offshore to be closer to foreign markets or to take advantage of cheaper labor in Mexico or Korea and lower safety and environmental standards. An autoworker in Michigan remarked that "corporations are looking for a disposable workforce. . . . No commitment to community; no commitment to country."

In 2004, the 150-year-old company Levi Strauss, whose product had become an iconic American garment in the 1960s, shut down its last plants in the United States, contracting the manufacture of jeans in fifty other countries, from Latin America to Asia. Marivel Gutierez, a side-seam operator in the San Antonio plant, acknowledged that workers in Mexico and elsewhere would benefit, suggesting the globalization of the American dream. "But," she worried, "what happens to our American dream?" Workers like Gutierez stood as reminders that even as many reaped the benefits of free enterprise across national borders, globalization left multitudes of victims in its wake.

Why did Americans debate the benefits of free trade?

Although the process of globalization was centuries old, new communications technologies such as the Internet and cell phones connected nations,

▲ **The Battle of Seattle** Major protests greeted the World Trade Organization conference in Seattle in 1999. A loose coalition of environmentalists, labor unions, consumer activists, advocates for the global poor, anarchists, and nongovernmental organizations took part in the largest antiglobalization demonstration to date. Here a tank drives down a Seattle street amid a sea of protesters and placards. AP Images/Eric Draper.

corporations, and individuals at much faster speeds and much lower costs by the 1990s. Building on efforts by Reagan and Bush, Clinton sought to speed up the growth of a global marketplace by easing restrictions on international commerce.

In 1993 Clinton won congressional approval of the **North American Free Trade Agreement (NAFTA)**, brokered by Bush, which eliminated all tariffs and trade barriers among the United States, Canada, and Mexico. Fearing loss of jobs and industries to Mexico, a majority of Democrats opposed NAFTA, but Republican support ensured approval. In 1994, the Senate ratified the General Agreement on Tariffs and Trade, establishing the **World Trade Organization (WTO)** to enforce substantial tariff and import quota reductions among some 135 member nations.

The free trade issue was intensely contested. Much of corporate America welcomed the elimination of trade barriers and opportunities to lower their taxes. Critics blamed globalization for the loss of good jobs, the weakening of unions and environmental regulations, and the growing gap between the rich and the poor. Demanding "fair trade" rather than simply free trade, they wanted treaties to require decent wage and labor standards and human rights provisions. In 1999, in the "Battle of Seattle," thirty thousand protesters shut down a meeting of the WTO with the cry "no globalization without representation" and demands to end "the enrichment of the few at the expense of all others."

North American Free Trade Agreement (NAFTA)
1993 treaty that eliminated all tariffs and trade barriers among the United States, Canada, and Mexico. NAFTA was opposed by many Democrats but supported by President Clinton and would feature prominently in debates over the benefits and costs of globalization.

World Trade Organization (WTO)
International economic body established in 1994 through the General Agreement on Tariffs and Trade to enforce substantial tariff and import quota reductions. Many corporations welcomed these trade barrier reductions, but critics linked them to job loss and the weakening of unions.

Breakup of Yugoslavia

Globalization controversies centered on unequal power relations between the United States, which dominated the world's industrial core, and developing nations on the periphery. The American company Nike, for example, paid Chinese workers $1.50 per hour to produce shoes that sold for more than $100 in the United States. Yet leaders of developing nations actively sought foreign investment because even those low wages could offer impoverished people a higher standard of living. At the same time, developing countries pointed to American hypocrisy in advocating free trade in industry while heavily subsidizing the U.S. agricultural sector. "When countries like America, Britain and France subsidize their farmers," complained a grower in Uganda, "we get hurt."

Globalization's champions pointed to the cheap consumer goods available to Americans and argued that everyone would benefit in the long run. Opponents focused on the short-term victims. World Bank president James D. Wolfensohn acknowledged that "our challenge is to make globalization an instrument of opportunity and inclusion—not fear."

How did the United States define its role in the post–Cold War world?

The Cold War policy of containment had drawn the United States into protracted civil wars and led it to trample on other nations' sovereignty. But it had provided a durable framework for policymaking. No such framework existed for the 1990s. A central challenge for the Clinton administration was to define principles for deploying U.S. power in the world.

Africa, where civil wars and extreme human suffering rarely evoked a strong U.S. response, was a case in point. In 1992, President Bush had attached U.S. forces to a UN operation in the northern African country of Somalia, where famine and civil war raged. In 1993, President Clinton allowed that humanitarian mission to turn into "nation building," an effort to establish a stable government. Eighteen U.S. soldiers were killed in Somalia, with one soldier's corpse dragged through the streets.

The resulting outcry suggested that most citizens were unwilling to sacrifice American lives when no vital national interest was threatened. Both the United States and the UN stood by in 1994, when more than half a million people were massacred in a violent ethnic civil war in Rwanda. By contrast, Clinton sent American troops into nearby Haiti that same year to restore the nation's democratic government, which had been ousted by a military coup in 1991.

In Eastern Europe, the collapse of communism ignited a severe crisis when ruthless leaders exploited ethnic differences to bolster their power. Yugoslavia splintered into separate states and fell into civil war. Serbian aggression under

President Slobodan Milosevic against Bosnian Muslims—including rape, torture, and mass killings—horrified much of the world. European and U.S. leaders were reluctant to use military force, but U.S. fliers eventually joined NATO in bombing Serbia. Combined with offensives by the Croatian and Bosnian armies, that effort forced Milosevic to the bargaining table, where representatives from Serbia, Croatia, and Bosnia hammered out a peace treaty.

In 1998, new fighting broke out in the southern Serbian province of Kosovo, where ethnic Albanians, who constituted 90 percent of the population, demanded independence. When the Serbian army retaliated, NATO launched a U.S.-led bombing attack on Serbian military and government targets, forcing Milosevic to agree to a settlement. Serbians voted Milosevic out of office in 2000, and he died in 2006 while on trial for genocide by a UN war crimes tribunal.

Elsewhere, Clinton deployed U.S. power when he could send missiles rather than soldiers. He was prepared to act without international support or UN sanction. Clinton bombed Iraq in 1993, when a plot to assassinate former president Bush was uncovered; again in 1996 after Saddam Hussein attacked the Kurds in northern Iraq; and repeatedly between 1998 and 2000, after Hussein expelled UN weapons inspectors. Whereas Bush had acted in the Gulf War with the support of an international force that included Arab states, Clinton acted unilaterally and in the face of Arab opposition.

In August 1998, bombings at the U.S. embassies in Kenya and Tanzania killed twelve Americans and more than 250 Africans. Clinton retaliated with missile attacks on training camps in Afghanistan and facilities in Sudan. His target was Al Qaeda, an Islamist-extremist terrorist network controlled by Osama bin Laden, a Saudi-born millionaire who financed the embassy attacks.

To defuse the Israeli-Palestinian conflict, however, Clinton applied diplomatic rather than military might. In 1993, Norwegian diplomats had brokered an agreement between the head of the Palestine Liberation Organization and the Israeli prime minister to recognize the existence of each other's states. Israel agreed to withdraw from the Gaza Strip and Jericho, allowing for Palestinian self-government there. In July 1994, Clinton presided over another turning point as Israel and Jordan signed a declaration of peace. Yet difficult issues remained, especially control of Jerusalem and the presence of more than 200,000 Israeli settlers in the West Bank, the land seized by Israel in 1967, where three million Palestinians were determined to establish their own state.

Israel and PLO sign accords, 1993
Israel and Jordan sign peace treaty, 1994
Progress of Israeli-Palestinian negotiations halts and violence escalates, 2000
Israel withdraws from Gaza, 2005
Israel at war with Hezbollah in Lebanon, 2006
Israel invades Gaza, 2008

Events in Israel since 1989

REVIEW

What were the major challenges for the Clinton administration on the global stage?

Conclusion: What were the legacies of the "Reagan revolution"?

"Ours was the first revolution in the history of mankind that truly reversed the course of government," boasted Ronald Reagan in his farewell address in 1989. The word *revolution* exaggerated the change, but Reagan's administration did undermine many of the liberal assumptions that had guided American politics since the New Deal, representing the "choice not an echo" that Phyllis Schlafly had called for in 1964.

Antigovernment sentiment grew along with a backlash against the reforms and cultural changes of the 1960s. Reagan's tax cuts, together with hefty increases in defense spending, created a federal deficit crisis that justified cuts in social welfare and made new domestic initiatives unthinkable. These policies contributed to a widening income gap between the rich and the poor, weighing especially heavily on people of color, female-headed families, and children. The new conservative agenda extended through the Bush years and hampered Clinton's domestic reform ambitions. The Democratic president's support for time limits and other restrictions on welfare was the most obvious sign of the country's rightward shift. Yet strong partisan divisions remained, leading to presidential vetoes, government shutdowns, and concerns about a dysfunctional political system.

In the 1990s, Presidents Bush and Clinton grappled with another of Reagan's legacies, the collapse of the Cold War order. As the promising outbreak of democracy in Eastern Europe gave way to ethnic and religious conflicts around the world, there were no obvious answers to the question of when the United States should intervene as a military, diplomatic, or peacekeeping force. In these same years, America became more embedded in the global economy. Products, information, and people crossed borders with accelerating speed and frequency, a development that would also make the nation vulnerable to terrorism. New waves of immigration would likewise alter the face of the American population and the makeup of its culture. Each of these developments would generate fierce debates in the twenty-first century.

CHAPTER REVIEW

EXPLAIN WHY IT MATTERS

New Christian Right (p. 889)

supply-side economics (p. 890)

Equal Rights Amendment (ERA)
(p. 894)

sexual harassment (p. 895)

acquired immune deficiency
syndrome (AIDS) (p. 895)

nuclear freeze (p. 897)

Iran-Contra scandal (p. 900)

intermediate-range nuclear forces
(INF) agreement (p. 902)

Persian Gulf War (p. 905)

Clean Air Act (p. 906)

Americans with Disabilities Act
(ADA) (p. 906)

Family and Medical Leave Act
(FMLA) (p. 908)

Earned Income Tax Credit (EITC)
(p. 908)

Rust Belt (p. 914)

North American Free Trade
Agreement (NAFTA) (p. 915)

World Trade Organization (WTO)
(p. 915)

PUT IT ALL TOGETHER

AMERICA'S MOVE TO THE RIGHT

• What combination of factors helped Ronald Reagan win the presidency?

• What specific conservative goals were fulfilled during the 1980s and 1990s?

LIBERALISM ON THE DEFENSIVE

• What tactics did liberal groups use to resist the conservative turn? How
successful were they?

• How did Bill Clinton's domestic agenda reflect a link to, as well as a departure
from, sixties-era liberalism?

U.S. FOREIGN POLICY

• How and why did U.S. foreign policy change under Reagan?

• What were the major global issues that engaged Americans after the Cold War?
How did the Bush and Clinton administrations respond to them?

LOOKING BACKWARD, LOOKING AHEAD

• How did U.S. foreign policy evolve from the 1950s through the 1990s?

• In what ways have the culture wars of the Clinton years left their mark on
contemporary American politics?

31

AMERICA IN A NEW CENTURY

SINCE 2000

This chapter discusses the following questions:

- How did U.S. foreign and domestic policy shift under George W. Bush?
- What was Obama's reform agenda and what obstacles did he face?
- How were new social movements and new media changing politics?
- What was the significance of Trump's presidency?
- In an intensely divided nation, was there any common ground?
- Conclusion: Was America becoming more or less democratic in the twenty-first century?

▶ **Jose Antonio Vargas** Jose Antonio Vargas, who arrived in the United States from the Philippines as a child, became a successful filmmaker and Pulitzer Prize–winning journalist. He was also, however, an undocumented immigrant. After revealing his citizenship status in 2011, Vargas became a prominent advocate for immigrants' rights. Here, he testifies at a 2013 U.S. Senate hearing on comprehensive immigration reform. AP Photo/Susan Walsh.

AN AMERICAN STORY

In 1993, twelve-year-old Jose Antonio Vargas boarded a U.S.-bound plane, leaving his family in the Philippines behind. The trip was arranged by his mother, who sought a better life for Jose with his maternal grandparents in Mountain View, California.

Vargas quickly found his footing in his new home and school, excelling in spelling bees. At sixteen, he applied for a driver's permit. But when he offered his green card to a clerk as proof of U.S. residency, she handed it back, whispering: "This is fake. Don't come back here again." Only then did Vargas learn that he had been smuggled into the country under a false name and passport.

With the help of his grandfather and that fake passport, Vargas obtained a Social Security number and eventually a driver's license. He worried constantly, however, about his citizenship status, as he watched voters support measures like Proposition 187 in California, which sought to prohibit undocumented immigrants from attending public school or accessing social services. Vargas came out as gay during his senior year of high school but did not dream of divulging his legal status.

As a student, Vargas found he loved language and writing. Securing internships at local newspapers, he went to college and became a successful journalist and documentary filmmaker. Part of a team at the *Washington Post* that won a Pulitzer Prize in 2008, Vargas recalled his grandmother's anxious response to the prestigious award: "What will happen if people find out?"

As a reporter, Vargas steered away from covering immigration, and he carefully shielded his personal story even from close friends. But in 2011, discussions of the DREAM Act, which promoted a path to citizenship for youth who had arrived in the country illegally, inspired him to step out of the shadows. Despite cautions from immigration lawyers about committing "legal suicide," Vargas published an essay revealing his status. A year later, the Obama administration announced a halt to the deportation of undocumented immigrants age thirty and under. Vargas, by then thirty-one, cheered this victory, although he did not qualify.

Undocumented youth were just one flashpoint of fierce partisan struggles in the United States in the new century. Economic uncertainty and resurgent white nationalism contributed to anti-immigrant sentiment, making job losses, border security, and national identity contentious issues. In 2008, even the Democratic presidential nominee, Barack Obama, who was born in Hawai'i, faced questions about his citizenship status from the far-right "birther" movement. In 2016, the Republican candidate, Donald Trump, rallied conservatives with his pledge to "build a wall" along the U.S.-Mexico border.

CHRONOLOGY

2000	George W. Bush pronounced president, following *Bush v. Gore*.
2001	Terrorists attack World Trade Center, Pentagon.
	U.S.-led coalition drives Taliban government out of Afghanistan.
	USA Patriot Act passes.
2002	Department of Homeland Security established.
2003	United States attacks Iraq.
2004	President Bush reelected.
2005	Hurricane Katrina devastates Gulf states.
2007	Great Recession begins.
2008	Barack Obama elected president.
2010	Patient Protection and Affordable Care Act signed.
	United States leaves Iraq, increases troops in Afghanistan.
2011	Osama bin Laden killed.
2012	President Obama reelected.
2013	NSA surveillance of U.S. citizens exposed.
	Black Lives Matter founded.
2015	Same-sex couples gain constitutional right to marriage.
	Paris climate change agreement signed.
2016	Donald Trump elected president.
2017	Women's March launches major protest.
2019	House of Representatives impeaches Trump.
2020	Joseph Robinette Biden Jr. elected president; Trump asserts victory.
	FDA approves COVID-19 vaccines.

Intense debates broke out about what stance the United States, often celebrated as a nation of immigrants, should take toward those fleeing persecution or poverty around the world. Vargas, who worked hard, paid taxes, and claimed no other home, firmly considered himself to be an American. Still, he knew that at any moment he could be deported, writing in a 2018 memoir: "I do not know where I will be when you read this."

How did U.S. foreign and domestic policy shift under George W. Bush?

The dawn of the new century in the United States was marked by tragedy. In September 2001, terrorist attacks in New York City and Washington, D.C., dramatically exposed American vulnerability to political violence—revealing that Islamist terrorism had replaced communism as the primary threat to U.S. security. President George W. Bush sent soldiers into Afghanistan to overthrow the government that had harbored the attackers. In 2003, he went further, opening a second war against Iraq—to much criticism at home and abroad—and sharply reversing long-standing policies of internationalism, multilateralism, and military restraint.

Bush won reelection in 2004, although stability in Iraq and Afghanistan remained elusive. He advanced legislation to improve public school education, subsidize prescription drugs for elderly citizens, and greatly reduce taxes for the wealthy. Serious foreign and domestic crises plagued his second term. His tax cuts, along with new spending, created the largest budget deficit in the nation's history. A financial crisis near the end of Bush's presidency sent the economy into a recession, and Democrats capitalized on widespread dissatisfaction to gain control of Congress in 2006 and the White House in 2008.

Why was the election of 2000 disputed?

The oldest son of former president George H. W. Bush, George W. Bush was the governor of Texas when he won the Republican presidential nomination. Inexperienced in national and international affairs, Bush chose for his running mate a seasoned official, Richard B. Cheney, who had served in three previous Republican administrations.

Many observers predicted that the thriving economy would benefit the Democratic contender, Vice President Al Gore, and he did surpass Bush by more than half a million votes. But Florida's twenty-five electoral college votes would decide the presidency. Bush's tiny margin in Florida prompted an automatic recount of the votes, which eventually gave him an edge of 537 votes in that state. The Democrats asked for hand-counting of Florida ballots in several heavily Democratic counties, where machine errors and confusing ballots may have left thousands of Gore votes unrecorded. The Republicans went to court to try to stop the hand-counts.

The outcome of the election hung in the balance for thirty-six days, as multiple lawsuits made their way to the Supreme Court. Finally, in *Bush v. Gore* (2000), the sharply divided justices ruled five to four against allowing the state of Florida to conduct further recounts. Noting that the conservative justices had abandoned their principle of favoring state over federal authority, Democrats charged partisanship on the Court.

The spectacle of the Supreme Court determining the presidency along partisan lines troubled many observers, including Justice John Paul Stevens, who judged the real loser of the election the "Nation's confidence in the judge as an impartial guardian of the rule of law." Gore, meanwhile, conceded to Bush. For the first time since 1888, a president who failed to win the popular vote took office (**Map 31.1**).

Candidate	Electoral Vote	Popular Vote	Percent of Popular Vote
George W. Bush (Republican)	271	50,456,062	47.8
Al Gore (Democrat)	267	50,996,862	48.4
Ralph Nader (Green Party)	0	2,858,843	2.7
Patrick J. Buchanan (Reform Party)	0	438,760	0.4

MAP 31.1 ▲ **The Election of 2000**

What were the effects of the 9/11 attacks?

On the morning of September 11, 2001, nineteen terrorists hijacked four planes. They flew two of them into the twin towers of New York City's World Trade Center and one into the Pentagon in Washington, D.C.; the fourth crashed in a field in Pennsylvania. Many Americans watched the horrific attacks in real time on television. For weeks thereafter in New York, firefighters and Army Reserve forces sifted through the rubble for bodies. Downtown Manhattan, one man observed, resembled "a war zone." The toxic smoke and ash that filled the air posed their own dangers: By 2018, nearly ten thousand first responders were diagnosed with cancer, and two thousand deaths were linked to 9/11 illnesses.

The attacks—the worst on U.S. soil since those at Pearl Harbor, which had triggered America's entry into World War II—claimed nearly 2,800 lives, including people from ninety different countries. Their impact was felt far beyond the United States. That a handful of terrorists had inflicted tremendous damage on the most powerful nation on earth led Kofi Annan, secretary-general of the United Nations, to declare that "A new insecurity has entered every mind."

The hijackers belonged to Osama bin Laden's **Al Qaeda** international terrorist network, which had attacked U.S. targets in the 1990s. Expressing Islamist extremists' rage at the spread of Western culture and values into the Muslim world, the attacks were also motivated by opposition to the 1991 Persian Gulf War against Iraq, the stationing of American troops in Saudi Arabia, and U.S. support for Israel.

Al Qaeda
Radical Islamist terrorist organization that sought to rid the Middle East of Western, and especially U.S., influence. The organization was responsible for a series of strikes on U.S. targets in the 1990s as well as the September 11, 2001, terrorist attacks.

In the wake of 9/11, President Bush sought a global alliance against terrorism. With NATO support, the United States and Britain began bombing Afghanistan, where Al Qaeda was based, and American forces aided the Northern Alliance, the primary opposition to the radical Muslim Taliban government. By December, the Taliban government was destroyed, but bin Laden eluded capture. Afghans elected a new national government. However, the Taliban retained strength in large parts of the country, contributing to ongoing instability.

How did Americans weigh tensions between security and civil liberties?

Afghanistan

USA Patriot Act
2001 law passed in the wake of 9/11 that gave the government new powers to monitor suspected terrorists and their associates, including the ability to access American citizens' electronic communications and financial records. Critics charged that it represented an unwarranted abridgment of civil rights.

President Bush declared that "ours is a war not against a religion, not against the Muslim faith." Nevertheless, anti-immigrant sentiment in the United States intensified after the September 11 attacks, with those appearing to be Middle Eastern or practicing Islam arousing particular suspicion. Authorities surveilled mosques, carried out "voluntary interviews" with Muslim Americans, and arrested more than one thousand Arabs and Muslims.

A Justice Department study later found that many people with no connection to terrorism spent months in jail, denied their rights as a consequence of racial profiling. Hate crimes against Muslims jumped 1,600 percent by 2002, according to the FBI. Adam Soltani, an Oklahoma college student and president of the Muslim Student Association, saw weekly prayer meetings shrink and realized that "life was not going to be the same for me as a Muslim in America as it had ever been before."

In October 2001, Congress passed the **USA Patriot Act**, giving the government new powers to monitor suspected terrorists, including the ability to indefinitely detain immigrants, to intercept electronic communications, and to access Americans' library and financial records. It was quickly condemned by conservatives and liberals alike. Kathleen MacKenzie, a councilwoman in Ann Arbor, Michigan, explained why the council opposed the Patriot Act: "As concerned as we were about national safety, we felt that giving up [rights] was too high a price to pay." A security official countered, "If you don't violate someone's human rights some of the time, you probably aren't doing your job."

The Total Information Awareness (TIA) program, launched in 2003, similarly attempted to predict and prevent security risks through extensive surveillance of private data such as web browsing histories, phone data, bank deposits, credit card purchases, magazine subscriptions, and medical records. Congress suspended the program's funding after a storm of public criticism, but TIA's data mining software quietly moved into the National Security Agency. A decade past 9/11, the government continued to gather personal information on individual citizens, and the debate over how much liberty Americans ought to sacrifice for the promise of security remained unresolved.

Insisting that presidential powers were virtually limitless in times of national crisis, Bush stretched his authority until he met resistance from the courts and Congress. One of his most controversial steps was to authorize the detention of more than seven hundred prisoners captured in Afghanistan at the U.S. military base at Guantánamo, Cuba, where—until courts acted—those detainees held no rights. Revelations about prisoner torture there led to widespread condemnations of American human rights abuses and calls by the United Nations to close the detention camp. Despite such pressure, Guantánamo remained open.

At home, the U.S. government sought to prevent future terrorist attacks through the most extensive reorganization of the executive branch since the 1947 National Security Act. In 2002, Congress authorized the new **Department of Homeland Security**, combining 170,000 federal employees from twenty-two agencies responsible for various aspects of domestic security. Chief among the department's duties were intelligence analysis; immigration and border security; chemical, biological, and nuclear countermeasures; and emergency preparedness and response.

Department of Homeland Security
Federal agency created in 2002 in response to the 9/11 attacks. In an effort to better coordinate domestic security, the department combined twenty-two existing agencies.

How did the United States wage the "war on terror"?

Bush sought collective action against the Taliban, but on most foreign policy matters he adopted a go-it-alone approach. In addition to violating international rules on the treatment of military prisoners, his administration withdrew from the UN's International Criminal Court and rejected an agreement to enforce bans on biological weapons that all of America's European allies had signed.

Nowhere was the policy of unilateralism more striking than in a new war against Iraq. Addressing West Point graduates in 2002, President Bush proclaimed a new U.S. strategy of preemption, saying: "Traditional concepts of deterrence will not work against a terrorist enemy whose avowed tactics are wanton destruction and the targeting of innocents; whose so-called soldiers seek martyrdom in death and whose most potent protection is statelessness." Because even weak countries and small groups could strike devastating blows to the United States, as Al Qaeda had done on 9/11, the nation had to "be ready for preemptive action."

The president's claim that the United States had the right to start a war was at odds with international law and with many citizens' understanding of American ideals. It distressed most of the nation's allies, who wondered if the United States, with a defense budget and military capacity that far outstripped any other nation's (**Figure 31.1**), had empire-building ambitions.

Nonetheless, Bush worried that Iraq's dictator, Saddam Hussein, was violating UN restrictions on Iraqi development of nuclear, chemical, and biological weapons. In 2002, the United States obtained a UN Security Council resolution demanding that Iraq disarm or face "serious consequences." When Iraq failed to comply, the Bush administration decided on war. Making claims—later proved

United States
$478.2 billion

United Kingdom
$48.3 billion

France
$46.2 billion

Japan
$42.1 billion

China
$41.0 billion

Germany
$33.2 billion

Italy
$27.2 billion

Saudi Arabia
$25.2 billion

Russia
$21.0 billion

India
$20.4 billion

FIGURE 31.1 ▶ Global Comparison: Countries with the Highest Military Expenditures, 2005 During the Cold War, the military budgets of the United States and the Soviet Union were relatively even, but American expenditures would soon far outstrip those of its former enemy as well as any other nation. Even before the Iraq War began in 2003, the U.S. military budget constituted 47 percent of total world military expenditures. Massive defense budgets reflected the determination of Democratic and Republican administrations alike to maintain dominance in the world, even as the capacities of traditional enemies diminished.

false—that Hussein had links to Al Qaeda's terrorist network and held weapons of mass destruction, the president insisted that the immediate threat justified preemptive action. Some ten to fifteen million people around the globe joined antiwar demonstrations in protest. Despite the absence of UN approval and opposition from the Arab world as well as France, Germany, China, and Russia, the United States and Britain invaded Iraq in March 2003, supported by some thirty nations (**Map 31.2**).

MAP ACTIVITY

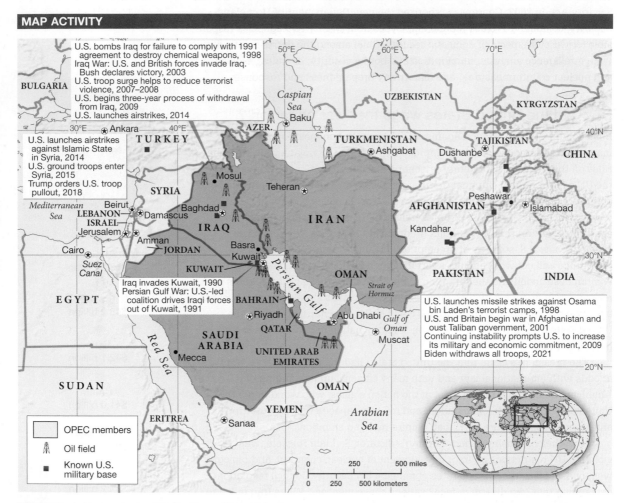

U.S. bombs Iraq for failure to comply with 1991 agreement to destroy chemical weapons, 1998
Iraq War: U.S. and British forces invade Iraq. Bush declares victory, 2003
U.S. troop surge helps to reduce terrorist violence, 2007–2008
U.S. begins three-year process of withdrawal from Iraq, 2009
U.S. launches airstrikes, 2014

U.S. launches airstrikes against Islamic State in Syria, 2014
U.S. ground troops enter Syria, 2015
Trump orders U.S. troop pullout, 2018

Iraq invades Kuwait, 1990
Persian Gulf War: U.S.-led coalition drives Iraqi forces out of Kuwait, 1991

U.S. launches missile strikes against Osama bin Laden's terrorist camps, 1998
U.S. and Britain begin war in Afghanistan and oust Taliban government, 2001
Continuing instability prompts U.S. to increase its military and economic commitment, 2009
Biden withdraws all troops, 2021

OPEC members
Oil field
Known U.S. military base

MAP 31.2 ▲ Events in the Middle East, 1990–2021 Since the end of the Cold War, much of U.S. foreign policy has focused on the Middle East, a region that is rich in oil but politically unstable and where extremist and terrorist organizations have taken root. The Arab League supported the war to liberate Kuwait in 1991, and after September 11, 2001, it also approved of U.S. military operations in Afghanistan. Yet only the countries where the United States had military bases supported the American invasion of Iraq in 2003. Arab hostility toward the United States also reflected the deterioration of Israeli-Palestinian relations after 1999.

READING THE MAP: In what countries are oil sources located? In what countries does the United States have military bases?
CONNECTIONS: What conditions prompted the U.S. military interventions in Iraq and Afghanistan in 1991, 2001, and 2003? What motivated U.S. air strikes against Iraq and Syria in 2014, and why were American ground troops sent to Syria the following year? Did U.S. troop withdrawals — from Iraq in 2011 and Afghanistan a decade later — signify the realization of American goals in the region?

Coalition forces won an easy victory in just over a month, and Bush declared the end of the **Iraq War**. Saddam Hussein was captured, tried by an Iraqi court, and executed. But chaos followed the quick victory. The damage from U.S. bombing was followed by widespread looting, as U.S. troops failed to secure order and provide locals with basic necessities. Some Iraqis wondered what they had gained with the fall of a dictator. "With Saddam there was tyranny, but at least you had a salary to put food on your family's table," remarked one young father. Believing that the U.S. and British forces had been motivated primarily by access to Persian Gulf resources, a Baghdad hospital worker complained, "They can take our oil, but at least they should let us have electricity and water." Five years after the invasion, continuing violence had displaced 1.9 million within Iraq and had caused two million to flee their country.

The administration did not plan adequately for the postwar occupation. The 140,000 American forces there came under attack almost daily from remnants of the former Hussein regime, religious extremists, and hundreds of foreign terrorists now entering the country. By the end of the military occupation, nearly 4,500 U.S. soldiers had lost their lives. Seeking to divide the population, terrorists also launched assaults that killed tens of thousands of Iraqis. Distant from most Americans' concerns, the military occupation faded from newspapers even as the violence there persisted. As a handwritten note on the wall of the government center in Ramadi, Iraq, observed: "America is not at war. The Marine Corps is at war; America is at the mall."

Still, the war was a central issue in the presidential campaign of 2004. U.S. senator John Kerry, the Democratic nominee and a Vietnam veteran who had come to oppose that war as well, criticized Bush's unilateralist actions in Iraq. A slim majority of voters, however, felt Bush would better protect American security than would Kerry, giving the president a 286-to-252 victory in the electoral college, 50.7 percent of the popular vote, and Republican majorities in Congress.

In June 2004, the United States transferred sovereignty to a Shiite-dominated Iraqi government. This failed to satisfy Iraq's other major groups—Sunnis and Kurds—and violence escalated. By 2006, a majority of Americans concluded that the Iraq War had been a mistake. Criticism of the war crossed party lines and included military leaders. The coalition forces had felled a brutal dictator but had been woefully unprepared for what followed. They did not find the weapons of mass destruction or links to Osama bin Laden that had been the Bush administration's rationale for the invasion. Rather, the war unleashed disorder that drew more than one thousand terrorists to Iraq—the place, according to one expert, "for fundamentalists to go . . . to stick it to the West."

The war and occupation exacted a steep price in American and Iraqi lives as well as dollars, costing upward of $750 billion. U.S. relations with other great powers suffered, as did America's global reputation, especially among Arab nations. Shocking revelations of torture and abuse in the Abu Ghraib prison in Iraq, as at Guantánamo, fueled anti-Americanism around the world. The budget deficit swelled, and resources were diverted from other national security challenges, including the stabilization of Afghanistan, the elimination of Al Qaeda, and the threat posed by North Korea's and Iran's pursuit of nuclear weapons.

Iraq War
Preemptive war launched by George W. Bush's administration in 2003 in Iraq, despite the absence of UN approval. Coalition forces won an easy victory, but chaos marked the long U.S. occupation that followed.

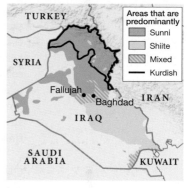

Iraq

Voters responded in 2006, giving Democrats control of Congress for the first time since 1994. A temporary troop surge in Iraq in 2007, along with actions by Iraqi leaders, led to reduced violence, and the administration began planning for the withdrawal of U.S. forces, a task not completed until the end of 2011. Meanwhile, peace eluded the Iraqis, who continued to live amid sectarian turmoil.

What were Bush's domestic successes and failures?

President Bush's economic and cultural agenda was in line with trends in the Republican Party since the Reagan years. He called for tax cuts and the privatization of Social Security and announced his opposition to gay marriage and abortion. Yet Bush, a devout born-again Christian, also promised to govern as a "compassionate conservative." Calling for the Republican Party to embrace the nation's diversity, he appointed Black, Latino, and Asian Americans to his cabinet.

The president's fiscal policies were mostly compassionate to the rich. In 2001, he signed a bill reducing taxes over the next ten years by $1.35 trillion. A 2003 tax law slashed another $320 billion. The laws heavily favored the wealthy by phasing out estate taxes and cutting tax rates on capital gains and dividends. They also provided benefits for married couples and families with children and offered tax deductions for college expenses. The tax cuts helped turn the budget surplus that Bush had inherited from Clinton into a mushrooming federal deficit—the highest in U.S. history up until that point. By 2009, the deficit surpassed $1 trillion as the government struggled to combat a recession. The national debt rose to $9.6 trillion, making the United States increasingly dependent on China and other foreign investors.

Bush weakened environmental protection as part of his larger agenda to reduce government regulation, promote economic growth, and increase energy production. The administration opened millions of wilderness acres to mining, oil, and timber industries, and it relaxed standards under the Clean Air and Clean Water Acts. Along with oil and coal industry lobbyists, Bush declared his skepticism regarding well-established scientific findings about the human-made causes of climate change. To worldwide dismay, the administration withdrew from the Kyoto Protocol, signed in 1997 by 178 nations to reduce greenhouse gas emissions that produce global warming.

Conservatives hailed Bush's two appointments to the Supreme Court. In 2005, John Roberts, who had served in two Republican administrations, was named chief justice. When the moderate Sandra Day O'Connor resigned, Bush's nominee, staunch conservative Samuel A. Alito, was narrowly confirmed. While the Court upheld gay rights and rebuffed the administration by affirming the rights of accused terrorists, it also permitted increasing restrictions on abortion and struck down regulations in the areas of voting rights, gun control, and sex discrimination in employment.

One of the Court's most consequential rulings postdated Bush's time in office: *Citizens United v. Federal Elections Commission* (2010), in which the conservative majority gutted regulation of election campaign financing. Holding that such spending was a form of speech protected by the First Amendment, *Citizens United* opened the floodgates to political contributions by corporations and political action committees.

Citizens United v. Federal Elections Commission Controversial Supreme Court decision of 2010 that ruled federal regulation of election campaign financing a restriction on free speech as protected by the First Amendment. The ruling led to large political contributions by corporations and to the explosion of political action committees.

In contrast to these partisan battles, Bush won support from both Democrats and Republicans for a substantial expansion of the federal government into public education, an unusual move for a conservative. The **No Child Left Behind Act** of 2002 pledged to end, in Bush's words, "the story of children being just shuffled through the system." The law set national standards and imposed penalties on failing schools. The legislation was never adequately funded, however, and school officials criticized its one-size-fits-all approach, as well as its failure to tackle poverty as a source of student deficiencies. A decade later, Congress would return considerable control to states and local districts.

Although health care was traditionally a Democratic issue, in 2003 Bush signed a bill providing prescription drug benefits for the elderly and expanding the role of private insurers in the Medicare system. Most Democrats opposed the legislation because it subsidized private insurers with federal funds, banned imports of low-priced drugs, and prohibited the government from negotiating with drug companies to reduce prices. The law was a boon to the elderly, but medical costs overall continued to soar, and forty million Americans remained uninsured.

One domestic undertaking of the Bush administration found little approval anywhere: its response to natural disaster. In August 2005, **Hurricane Katrina** devastated the coasts of Alabama, Louisiana, and Mississippi, ultimately taking some eighteen hundred lives. The catastrophe that ensued when the levees broke, flooding 80 percent of New Orleans, shook many Americans' faith that the government could protect its own citizens. New Orleans residents who were too old, too poor, or too sick to evacuate spent days waiting on rooftops for help. Others waded in filthy, toxic water or endured extreme heat, food shortages, and general disorder at the centers where they had been told to go for help.

Many judged the federal government's response, managed through the Federal Emergency Management Agency and the new Department of Homeland Security, a failure. "How can we save the world if we can't save our own people?" wondered one Louisianan. The storm displaced more than a million residents of the Gulf Coast

No Child Left Behind Act
2002 legislation championed by President George W. Bush that expanded the role of the federal government in public education. The law required every school to meet annual testing standards, penalized failing schools, and allowed parents to transfer their children out of such schools.

Hurricane Katrina
Hurricane that devastated the coasts of Alabama, Louisiana, and Mississippi in 2005, including the city of New Orleans. The storm displaced more than one million residents of the Gulf Coast region, exposing the vulnerability of poor and Black residents and severe weaknesses in the U.S. response to natural disasters.

◄ **Hurricane Katrina** Residents of the poverty-stricken Lower Ninth Ward of New Orleans pleaded for help in the flooding that followed Hurricane Katrina in August 2005, some waiting as long as five days to be rescued. A historian of the disaster observed, "Americans were not used to seeing their country in ruins, their people in want." Mark Wilson/Getty Images.

region, many of whom were still without stable housing a month after the hurricane hit. A year later, New Orleans had lost half of its population. Many of Katrina's hardest-hit victims were poor and Black, and the disaster starkly highlighted persistent racial inequality in American society.

Soon came a domestic crisis of equal magnitude: a deep economic recession that struck in late 2007. The crisis was rooted in loosened financial regulations under Clinton and regulators' blind eye to predatory lending practices under Bush. The immediate cause was the breakdown of financial institutions that had accumulated trillions of dollars of bad debt, much of it from risky home mortgages. Housing values crashed, leading to more than a million foreclosures in 2008 alone.

As the mortgage crisis rolled through the economy, banking and lending collapsed, shuttering even huge investment firms such as Lehman Brothers. What became known as the **Great Recession** was so severe that Congress passed the $700 billion Troubled Asset Relief Program in 2008 to inject credit into the economy and shore up banks and other businesses.

The financial collapse of 2007–2008 drew comparisons to the Great Depression of the 1930s. It also prompted broad criticism of the deregulation that U.S. leaders of both parties had embraced since the 1970s. The failed Iraq War, the mismanagement of natural disaster, and the foreclosure crisis seriously eroded Bush's support. In 2008, the Democrats would regain power and elect Barack Obama president.

Great Recession
Financial crisis that struck in late 2007 and led to the worst U.S. depression since the 1930s. The crisis was rooted in financial deregulation and predatory lending practices. Housing values and then banking and lending collapsed, prompting the federal government to inject cash into the economy and enact a massive bailout of financial institutions.

REVIEW

What impact did the terrorist attacks on September 11, 2001, have on U.S. foreign policy and life at home?

What was Obama's reform agenda and what obstacles did he face?

Bush's Democratic successor in 2008, President Barack Hussein Obama, sought to change course in both domestic and foreign policy. But first he was confronted with the worst economic crisis that the United States had experienced since the Great Depression. Obama achieved significant antirecession measures and laws to regulate Wall Street as well as major health care reform, but a determined grassroots movement on the Republican right opposed the president at every turn.

In foreign policy, Obama generally sought a less aggressive, more multilateral approach to challenges around the world. His administration drew down U.S. troops in Iraq, reopened diplomatic relations with Cuba, and negotiated a treaty with five major powers and Iran to keep that nation from developing nuclear weapons. But most of the Middle East remained unstable, and the United States seemed increasingly vulnerable to terrorist threats.

Did the 2008 election signal a postracial America?

Obama won an election that represented momentous changes in American politics. The Republican nominee, Senator John McCain of Arizona, a Vietnam War hero, chose as his running mate Alaska governor Sarah Palin, the first Republican woman vice presidential candidate. In the Democratic Party, for the first time, a woman and a Black candidate were the top two contenders, upsetting old notions of whom a president could or should be. In a hard-fought primary battle, Obama edged out New York senator and former first lady Hillary Clinton for the nomination.

In contrast to Clinton, long in the public eye, Obama was a relative newcomer to the national stage, serving just two years in the U.S. Senate before announcing his candidacy. Born in 1961 to a white mother and a Black Kenyan father—a marriage that would have been illegal in many states at that time—Obama was raised in Hawai'i and Indonesia. The first African American to head the *Harvard Law Review*, he settled in Chicago, worked as a community organizer, taught law, served in the Illinois Senate, and won election to the U.S. Senate in 2004. At the age of forty-seven, he won the Democratic presidential nomination with innovative grassroots and Internet organizing and by promising bipartisan cooperation and racial reconciliation. Obama won 53 percent of the popular vote and defeated McCain 365 to 173 in the electoral college, while Democrats increased their majorities in the House and Senate.

Despite the legal victories of the civil rights movement, many had predicted that a Black candidate simply could not win the U.S. presidency. Obama's decisive election in 2008 galvanized progressives, and commentators rushed to announce the dawning of a "postracial" or "color-blind" America that had finally put its troubled history of race relations to rest. *Time* magazine claimed that Martin Luther King Jr.'s dream "is being fulfilled sooner than anyone imagined." A French newspaper declared that "we . . . need to change our preconceptions about American prejudice," adding, "It seems like America could teach us a thing or two about democracy."

Others were not so sure, noting the ugly tenor of the presidential campaign, particularly the false rumors that tagged the Christian and Hawai'ian-born Obama as a Muslim and a noncitizen. The far-right "birther" movement, stoked by future presidential candidate Donald Trump, suggested that the Democratic nominee was ineligible for the presidency because of his purportedly foreign citizenship—and demanded that Obama produce his birth certificate.

During both the campaign and his presidency, Obama treaded cautiously when commenting on race and its legacy in the United States, aware that those reflections, coming from him, could easily be treated as divisive. And the Obama years would provide plenty of evidence of enduring economic inequality and police brutality in Black communities. Still, the 2008 election was by any measure a significant milestone in the history of race and rights in the United States.

What were Obama's domestic aims and accomplishments?

In the 2004 Democratic National Convention address that cemented his status as a rising star in the party, Obama proclaimed that "there is not a liberal America and a conservative America—there is the United States of America. There is not a black America and a white America and Latino America and Asian America—there's the

United States of America." Upon his election, the new president pledged to work across party lines to enact reforms in health care, education, immigration, and the environment.

Instead, the economic crisis that he inherited dominated Obama's early months in office. As the recession spread from financial institutions to other parts of the economy and the world, mortgage foreclosures skyrocketed, major companies went bankrupt, and unemployment climbed, reaching 9.8 percent in late 2010. Obama responded with the American Recovery and Reinvestment Act of 2009, $787 billion worth of spending and tax cuts to stimulate the economy and relieve unemployment. Although it was the largest single spending bill in American history, many experts judged even that infusion of money into the economy as inadequate, given the scope of the crisis.

The Bush administration had shored up the big Wall Street banks and financial institutions at the center of the Great Recession, judging them "too big to fail" without damaging the rest of the economy. Obama likewise orchestrated a federal bailout of General Motors and Chrysler, saving some one million jobs related to the automobile industry but prompting criticism that the government was helping giant corporations at the expense of ordinary Americans. To address the sources of the financial crisis, Congress expanded federal regulation with the Wall Street Reform and Consumer Protection Act in 2010. Nonetheless, the recovery was agonizingly slow, and income inequality reached its highest level since the 1920s.

Beset by economic and environmental crises—like an enormous oil spill in the Gulf of Mexico in 2010—and with a Democratic-controlled Congress for only the first two years of his presidency, Obama's domestic achievements fell short of his ambitions. His judicial appointments of Elena Kagan and Sonia Sotomayor increased the number of women on the Supreme Court to three, with Sotomayor the first-ever Latina justice. He signed legislation that strengthened women's right to equal pay and rolled back some of the Bush tax cuts that had disproportionately favored the wealthy.

The Obama years also saw significant victories for gay rights, including legislation ending discrimination against gay men and lesbians in the military. By the time Obama took office, many large U.S. companies provided health benefits to same-sex domestic partners and included sexual orientation in their nondiscrimination policies. A majority of states banned discrimination in public employment, and many of those laws extended to private employment, housing, and education. Discrimination persisted, but in 2015, the Supreme Court ratified the enormous change in American attitudes toward gay and lesbian rights. In *Obergefell v. Hodges*, the Court declared by a vote of five to four that same-sex couples had a constitutional right to marry, making gay marriage legal in all fifty states.

Obama's paramount achievement was passage of health care reform, sought by Democrats since the 1960s, and which put the United States in step with the majority of industrial nations that subsidized some kind of health care for all citizens. The **Patient Protection and Affordable Care Act** of 2010 required that nearly everyone carry health insurance, and to that end, it provided subsidies and compelled larger businesses to cover their employees. The law also included protections for health care consumers and contained provisions to limit medical costs.

Obergefell v. Hodges
Ruling by the Supreme Court in 2015 declaring that same-sex couples had a constitutional right to marry, making gay marriage legal in all fifty states. The ruling indicated a major shift in American attitudes toward gay and lesbian rights, which had been evolving since the 1970s.

Patient Protection and Affordable Care Act
Sweeping 2010 bill championed by President Barack Obama that established nearly universal health insurance by providing subsidies and compelling larger businesses to offer coverage to employees. The act also imposed new regulations on insurance companies and contained provisions to limit health care costs.

Although liberals failed to get a public option to allow government-managed programs to compete with private insurance plans, the legislation represented the largest expansion of the federal government since the Great Society. It was bitterly resisted by Obama's opponents, one sign of the near-total breakdown of bipartisan cooperation in Congress. Republicans had previously endorsed key elements of the measure, and it resembled Massachusetts's health care program established under Republican governor Mitt Romney. Yet not a single Republican voted for the Affordable Care Act, and most Republican governors impeded its implementation in their states.

Why did partisanship escalate and with what consequences?

Opposition to "Obamacare" (a derisive label later embraced by its supporters), along with the controversial federal bailouts of big corporations, helped fuel a grassroots movement of mostly white, middle-class, and older voters. The **Tea Party movement,** borrowing its name from the Revolutionary-era Boston Tea Party that protested "taxation without representation," was funded by billionaire conservatives and fostered by right-wing media, particularly Fox News, the nation's most-watched partisan cable news network. Supporters complained of an overreaching government and of their values being displaced. As one put it, "The government is taking over everything—I want my freedom back." Most Tea Party activists defended Social Security and Medicare as benefits they had earned, but they resisted any new federal taxes or entitlement programs.

An intensely polarized Congress posed a roadblock to further economic legislation, and frustrated Obama's efforts to reform environmental and immigration policy. The president carried the burden of a nearly 8 percent unemployment rate into the 2012 election, where he faced Republican Mitt Romney. With the electorate deeply divided over the proper role of the federal government, Obama won easily in the electoral college, with 332 votes to Romney's 206, and captured 51 percent of the popular vote. Following the 2014 midterm elections, however, Republicans took over both houses of Congress.

Republicans used their majority to thwart Obama's agenda. In response, the president employed executive authority to raise the minimum wage for federal workers and to chip away at some of the racial injustices in the criminal justice system. Calling undocumented immigrants like Jose Antonio Vargas "Americans in their heart, in their minds, in every single way but one: on paper," the president issued an executive order protecting immigrant youth from deportation when legislation to that effect, the DREAM Act, stalled in Congress. He likewise stiffened curbs on motor vehicle and power plant emissions and encouraged alternative energy development. Obama also helped make possible a landmark climate change agreement, signed in Paris in 2015 by 195 nations, that pledged action to reduce carbon emissions.

Executive authority only went so far, however. When Obama nominated Merrick Garland for a spot on the Supreme Court upon the death of sitting justice Antonin Scalia in early 2016, the conservative congressional leadership pushed back. Garland was a moderate who had been praised by Republicans. Yet the Senate majority leader, backed by all the Republicans on the Senate Judiciary Committee, barred a vote on

Tea Party movement
Political movement of mostly white, middle-class, and older voters that was funded by billionaire conservatives and fostered by right-wing media. Sparked by opposition to financial bailouts and the Affordable Care Act under Obama, its followers protested what they saw as government overreach.

Garland's nomination, arguing that the next president—not the current one, who had nearly a year left in office—should select the new justice. It was a startling, unprecedented partisan move and a major defeat for Obama. Although Democrats railed against this tactic, the seat would remain unfilled until after the election of 2016.

What were the results of a multilateral approach to foreign policy?

Obama criticized much of his predecessor's foreign policy, which Bush had described as a "global war on terror." Obama believed that concept exaggerated the threat, justified disastrous decisions like the invasion of Iraq, sacrificed American ideals in the pursuit of security, and distracted attention from serious problems at home.

Yet once in office, Obama continued some of Bush's initiatives. His pledge to close the detention center at Guantánamo met resistance in Congress, and thirty-nine prisoners remained there, without rights, in 2022—twenty-seven of them never charged with any crime. The president also greatly increased the use of unmanned drone strikes in other countries, killing hundreds of people, both terrorists and innocent citizens—actions condemned by human rights advocates.

Obama pursued the Bush administration's plan to withdraw from Iraq. When the last U.S. troops departed in 2011, terrorist violence and sectarian strife only grew stronger. Despite his pledge to bring home all troops from Afghanistan, Obama dispatched fifty thousand more, acknowledging that he could not end the longest military operation in American history. Those troops would finally withdraw, two presidential administrations later, in 2021.

In a dramatic mission in May 2011, however, U.S. special forces killed Osama bin Laden, who was hiding in Pakistan. Celebrated as a U.S. victory in a conflict with few such milestones, bin Laden's removal weakened but did not destroy Al Qaeda and its offshoots.

Obama was awarded the Nobel Peace Prize in 2009 for his "extraordinary efforts to strengthen international diplomacy and cooperation between people" and especially for his promise to regain the trust of Muslim nations. But he was confronted with difficult decisions about the U.S. role in the Middle East—in particular, how much and what kind of intervention in the region could bring stability without the charge of American domination.

In 2011, popular uprisings, collectively referred to as the "Arab Spring," sought to wrest reforms from entrenched dictators in Tunisia, Egypt, Libya, and Syria. Each nation was troubled by internal divisions, decades of official corruption, and neglect of people's basic needs. Moreover, terrorists operated in each country, hoping to exploit the situation to install a radical fundamentalist Islamic state. The uprising toppled Libya's dictator, Muammar al-Gaddafi, but little progress was made toward stability, constitutional government, equal rights, and economic security in the region. Protests in Syria turned into a civil war that took more than 200,000 lives and sent four million Syrians into exile, creating a refugee crisis in Europe.

The calamity of the Iraq War and the desire to repair America's international reputation made Obama wary of intervention, even as chaos and violence continued in Libya, Syria, and Yemen. The rise of the Islamic State in Iraq and Syria (ISIS) (see Map 31.2), a more brutal and effective offspring of Al Qaeda, created further turmoil. By 2016, ISIS controlled key areas of Iraq and Syria and was linked to or inspired terrorist attacks on civilians in Egypt, Turkey, France, Belgium, and the United States—in both San Bernardino, California, and Orlando, Florida. Reluctant to commit the U.S. military beyond air strikes and some special forces on the ground, the Obama administration was criticized for indecisiveness and "leading from behind."

Preferring to attack problems with diplomacy, in 2015 Obama worked with China, Russia, France, the United Kingdom, and Germany to secure a treaty with Iran to prevent it from developing nuclear weapons. Believing that Iran could not be trusted, Republicans had pushed for sanctions rather than negotiations, and their harsh condemnation of the Iran nuclear deal reflected Americans' sharp disagreements about how to protect national security.

That same year, Obama determined to "bury the last remnant of the Cold War in the Americas" by opening diplomatic relations with Cuba. Fighting the new wars of the post-9/11 era, however, would create dilemmas at home as well as abroad. Leaks of classified information by National Security Agency (NSA) contractor Edward Snowden in 2013 revealed that Obama's administration had maintained Bush's surveillance of U.S. citizens. The NSA, it was reported, had secretly collected data about millions of Americans' communications with the assistance of major telephone and Internet providers. The news launched a national debate about the constitutionality of mass surveillance and the secret intelligence courts that oversaw it.

Judging Snowden a traitor, some argued that protecting the nation from terrorist attacks was worth any incursion on individual liberty. Others praised Snowden as a whistleblower who had courageously unveiled the NSA's trampling of Americans' rights. The episode focused attention on how new technologies threatened citizens' privacy in the twenty-first century, whether through data mining and online profiling or the use of drones and sensors. In the wake of Snowden's exposé, Americans ranked government infringement of civil liberties a greater concern than potential terrorist attacks for the first time in a decade. Outrage about the NSA's bulk collection of telephone records also triggered bipartisan congressional efforts to rein in the agency's intelligence apparatus or make it more accountable—a rare point of agreement in a polarized Washington.

REVIEW

What were the successes and failures of Obama's presidency?

How were new social movements and new media changing politics?

G ridlock in governing was only part of the story of American politics in the twenty-first century. An array of activists used new media and organizing tools to press for social change in a flourishing of grassroots protest.

Although many of the issues were enduring—income inequality, civil rights, police brutality, and sexual harassment—they received fresh attention. Some newer causes gained support as well, from the self-determination of transgender people to the rights of undocumented immigrants. Despite steep resistance, activists also won victories, whether through concrete reforms or by changing the public conversation.

Why and how did progressives mobilize around economic equality?

By the twenty-first century, long-range developments were reshaping Americans' economic prospects. Globalization continued to transform the U.S. economy through foreign capital and investment, the influx of immigrants, and the outsourcing of jobs—the latter development hastened by Bush's lowering of more trade barriers through the Central American–Dominican Republic Free Trade Agreement of 2005.

The bailout of huge financial institutions during the Great Recession, along with the declining fortunes of working-class Americans, produced some of the strongest political challenges to income inequality in decades. A grassroots protest movement

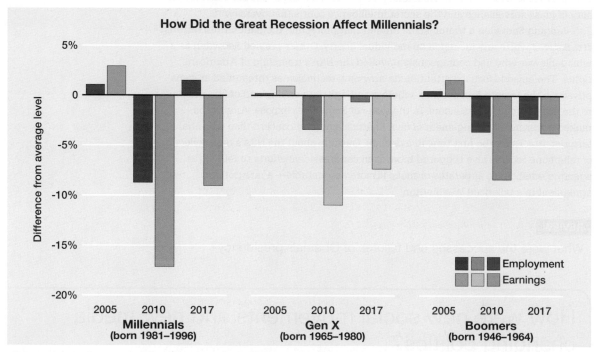

FIGURE 31.2 ▲ Economic Prospects of Millennials Millennials (born 1981–1996) are the most educated and diverse generation of Americans yet. But they have also experienced slower economic growth than any other generation in U.S. history, leading to lower earnings, smaller savings, more debt, and delayed milestones such as home ownership — as this comparison to the earning and employment rates of Generation X (born 1965–1980) and Boomers (born 1946–1964) reveals.

Data from: https://www.washingtonpost.com/business/2020/05/27/millennial-recession-covid/

calling itself **Occupy Wall Street** began in 2011 in New York City. Beginning with a small group camped out in the city's financial district, the movement took off, sparking rallies all over the country. Many were drawn to the Occupy slogan championing "the 99 percent"—that is, nearly everyone—over the "1 percent": shorthand for the wealthiest Americans who, activists claimed, exerted outsize control over both economic and political affairs. Occupy's attacks on monopolies and unearned wealth carried echoes of the progressive movement a century earlier (see chapter 21).

The youthful Occupy movement responded to stagnating wages and the replacement of union positions by low-paid, insecure jobs on the one hand, and the concentration of wealth in the stock market and in the hands of the very rich on the other. Millennials, those born between 1981 and 1996, were particularly affected by the Great Recession (**Figure 31.2**). By the time of the first Occupy protest, for example, the average income of the wealthiest 1 percent in America was $1.2 million per year. One study of the fifty largest employers of low-wage workers in the United States found that executive compensation averaged $9.4 million, with $175 billion returned to shareholders over a period of five years.

Attention to these stark inequalities, the most pronounced in the industrial world, galvanized a campaign to raise the federal hourly minimum wage, which had stood at $7.25 since 2009. Some 4.5 million workers earned wages at or below that minimum, and they labored in the fastest-growing occupations in the United States, from food service and retail work to in-home health care. As a security guard at New York's JFK airport who made $1,000 a month observed, "Half of the money goes to rent. After all of my expenses I don't have anything left. . . . I can't explain how much I need the minimum wage to increase."

A coalition of labor unions and community organizations led rallies in more than thirty cities in 2012 to raise the minimum wage. Strikes and civil disobedience targeted major low-wage employers such as Walmart and McDonald's. Activists achieved some remarkable successes. In 2014, Seattle raised its citywide minimum wage to $15 per hour, the highest in the nation, with other states and cities following suit.

The economic pain of globalization, along with the erosion of economic security in rural America, the Rust Belt, and elsewhere, had unpredictable effects. It increased the appeal of populist movements across the political spectrum, bolstering the candidacies of two atypical presidential contenders in 2016: Democratic socialist Bernie Sanders and real estate mogul Donald Trump.

What new rights movements emerged in the twenty-first century?

Civil rights causes gained momentum as well, raising questions about the limits of justice and inclusion in what had become a far more pluralistic American society. Following the passage of the Americans with Disabilities Act in 1990, for example, activists called upon U.S. society not simply to prevent discrimination against those differently abled but to recognize and honor multiple kinds of ability, including respect for neurodiversity.

Building on the legal and social victories of the gay liberation movement, transgender people demanded that gender identity be treated not as a biological

Occupy Wall Street
Grassroots protest movement that began in 2011 in New York City and quickly spread across the nation. Its activists championed economic justice for "the 99 percent" over the "1 percent," targeting inequalities of wealth, the economic insecurity of America's workers, and the disproportionate influence of wealthy individuals and corporations on economic and political affairs.

given but as something for each individual to determine. Advocates for those with fluid or nonbinary (neither male nor female) gender identities established new practices around flexible pronouns and inclusive language. A number of celebrities who came out as transgender brought new visibility to the movement. But activism around transgender rights and the very idea of nonbinary identities also generated intense backlash. Conservative state legislatures proposed "bathroom bills" that sought to preserve traditional gender distinctions in restrooms and laws banning trans women from sports teams and athletic competitions.

The boundaries of national belonging would be tested by the surprising eruption in 2006 of a movement in support of undocumented immigrants' rights, prompted by a Republican bill that sought to criminalize assistance to those in the country without papers. These demonstrations were some of the largest in U.S. history, including a "Day Without Immigrants" protest in southern California, which called attention to the essential economic work performed by the undocumented. Some activists, who called themselves DREAMers, launched a national "coming out" campaign in 2010 by publicly declaring their undocumented status. Their actions would both inspire Jose Antonio Vargas and put considerable pressure on Congress to create a path to legal residency.

What sparked the Black Lives Matter movement?

Among the most visible of the new social movements—and with the highest stakes: life or death—was in fact a continuation of a long struggle against the unequal and often violent policing of Black communities. It was ignited by the 2012 killing of Trayvon Martin, an unarmed Black teen in Florida, by a white "neighborhood watch" member, who was then acquitted. **Black Lives Matter** was founded the following year to push back against racism in policing and to advocate for the political and economic empowerment of Black people "in a world where Black lives are systematically and intentionally targeted for demise."

Black Lives Matter
Movement founded in 2013 in response to police shootings and killings of unarmed Black Americans. The organization protested racism in policing, advocated criminal justice reform, and called for the political and economic empowerment of Black people.

When Michael Brown, an unarmed eighteen-year-old, was shot and killed by police in Ferguson, Missouri, in 2014, activists flocked to that city, mounting weeks of protests. Polls revealing racial gaps in attitudes toward law enforcement, as well as the appearance of a countermovement calling itself "Blue Lives Matter," made clear that not all Americans agreed that police brutality was an urgent issue. Confrontations between protesters and the state police and National Guard in Ferguson recalled the urban rebellions of the 1960s, leading some to question how far the post–civil rights United States had traveled in overcoming its painful racial history.

After Ferguson, Black Lives Matter became a national movement. The shooting or killing of Black Americans by the police—often with no repercussions for the officers involved—was the target of demonstrations in more than one hundred cities, including New York City, Cleveland, Baltimore, and North Charleston. What became the Movement for Black Lives drew attention to the devastating toll of violence on people of color as well the need for as criminal justice reform. Clashes between Black civilians and white officers captured on smartphones spread quickly through social media, and a flurry of laws mandating body cameras for police officers hinted at the evolving use of new technologies in social movements.

How did social media tools transform political activism?

Barack Obama's presidential campaign in 2008 was one of the first to harness the power of online organizing to reach voters. As Internet access and smartphones spread rapidly, activists would increasingly turn to digital networks to organize protests and broadcast stories and images.

The Occupy and Black Lives Matter movements depended on social media platforms to coordinate the activities of strangers and even the discussion of high-level policy matters. Social media also played a notable part in the Arab Spring of 2011, with protesters garnering international support as much through Facebook and Twitter as through traditional print and broadcast media.

In the years that followed, political issues often gained traction most swiftly online. A movement against sexual harassment and assault, #MeToo, made waves in 2017—and ended some powerful men's careers—by exposing the extent of workplace abuse women experienced in Hollywood, the restaurant industry, journalism, and corporate America more broadly. The campaign, organized in order to "give people a sense of the magnitude of the problem," was conducted largely through Twitter posts by female celebrities and was followed by millions. While some denounced the public outing of inappropriate behavior as "cancel culture," there was no doubting the attention the campaign brought to enduring gender inequities in the workplace.

Social media platforms offered activists new leverage. Responding to a mass shooting in 2018 at a Parkland, Florida, high school that left seventeen dead—one of a series of school shootings that shook the nation—students took it upon themselves

▲ **Black Lives Matter Protest** Sparked by the killing of Black youths but fueled by long-standing resentment of the violent policing of African American communities, the Black Lives Matter movement grew rapidly through street demonstrations as well as online circulation of news and images. Here, a protester stands in front of St. Louis police outfitted in riot gear after a "not guilty" verdict was handed down in an officer's murder trial in 2017. REUTERS/Lawrence Bryant.

to break through congressional inaction on gun control laws. Launching the organization #NeverAgain, inspired by #MeToo, youthful activists used their social media accounts to keep the tragedy in the news and to coordinate school walkouts as well as a national "March for Our Lives." One of them, X (formerly Emma) González, had accrued 1.2 million Twitter followers less than a month after the Parkland massacre. That year, sixty-seven new gun safety laws were passed in twenty-six states and the District of Columbia, reforms that many credited to young activists.

Social media had become critical for attracting visibility and support to political causes. Some worried, however, that these platforms had significant downsides as a medium for public discussion because of their capacity to filter news, polarize views, and spread misinformation—problems that would become increasingly evident in the electoral arena.

REVIEW

How did new technologies affect social activism?

What was the significance of Trump's presidency?

The election of 2016 was among the most surprising in American history, leaving pundits at a loss to explain how a candidate with no prior political experience and best known to voters for his reality television show had captured the U.S. presidency. Once in office, Trump proved to be as unpredictable and unconventional a president as he had been a candidate. With an erratic style, including contacting foreign leaders personally and announcing policy changes via tweets, Trump's White House was unlike any other that Americans could remember.

During his single but eventful term, Trump secured a major corporate tax cut, rolled back environmental protections, withdrew from major international agreements, launched a trade war with China, and installed numerous conservative judges. More consequential in some ways was his flouting of the norms of his office and of democratic discourse. Trump relished attacks on opponents, never adopting the unifying tone typical of past presidents. Refusing to denounce rising white nationalism and anti-immigrant sentiment, he fanned racial tensions and was a uniquely divisive presence in American politics, his approval ratings never climbing higher than 50 percent. The Trump administration was beset early on by investigations into corruption, leading to the resignations and arrests of a series of his close aides and associates. The end of his presidency would be dominated by a public health crisis and then a political one: the COVID-19 pandemic and Trump's refusal to accept the results of the 2020 election.

How did the 2016 election disrupt expectations?

Donald Trump was not expected to win the Republican nomination in 2016. A billionaire New York City real estate developer and reality TV star, he had traveled in celebrity circles since the 1980s and frequently speculated about a run for president. Trump had changed his political party affiliation several times before registering as a Republican in 2009. As a candidate in 2015, Trump endorsed key tenets of modern conservatism: cutting taxes, relaxing environmental regulations, and restricting abortion. Initially scorned by the Republican Party establishment, he went on to defeat sixteen other hopefuls in the primaries, drawing much of his support directly from social media followers and fans.

Unprecedented for a major party's presidential nominee, Trump had no prior government or military service. His opponent, Hillary Clinton, had served as a U.S. senator and secretary of state as well as First Lady for eight years. The election was historic, with a woman heading the Democratic ticket. Clinton had bested another unusual candidate for the nomination: Bernie Sanders, a senator from Vermont and Democratic socialist who campaigned on a platform of economic justice that inspired many young voters.

The 2016 campaign season was a study in contrasts. Clinton developed detailed position papers on many issues and ran on her extensive record of public service. Trump, on the other hand, spoke off the cuff and often inaccurately, avoiding specifics. The fact that Trump did not sound like a traditional politician was part of his draw for voters, particularly as compared to Hillary Clinton, who had been part of the Democratic establishment for decades and was intensely disliked by Republicans. Trump's attacks on the mainstream media, which he claimed to be stacked against him, also seemed to resonate.

Most experts gave Trump little or no chance of winning the presidency. In nearly every pre-election poll, Clinton was predicted to be the victor. In the end, she did win the popular vote by a margin of nearly 2.9 million votes (**Map 31.3**). But Trump's narrow edge in several key Rust Belt states—Michigan, Ohio, and Pennsylvania—secured his stunning upset victory in the electoral college. It was the second time a Republican had won the electoral but not the popular vote in the twenty-first century.

Trump's win was the product of several long-term developments. In a populist and nationalist appeal that struck a chord with white conservatives, he railed against immigration, unfair trade policies, and the loss of American jobs, pledging to "Make America Great Again." Evangelical resentment toward progressive movements centered on race and gender propelled his campaign. So did the power of celebrity, structural features of the U.S. electoral system, persistent sexism, and widespread frustration with politics-as-usual.

Given the unexpected outcome, the electoral college and the 2016 election itself came under scrutiny, especially the vulnerability of the American voting system to hackers. Charges of electoral interference by Russian interests via cyberattacks circulated widely. Concerns about the effects of disinformation campaigns, or "fake news," and evidence

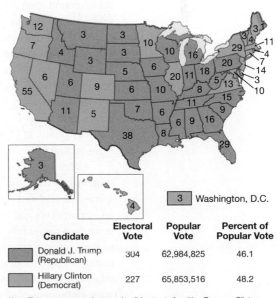

| 3 | Washington, D.C. |

Candidate	Electoral Vote	Popular Vote	Percent of Popular Vote
Donald J. Trump (Republican)	304	62,984,825	46.1
Hillary Clinton (Democrat)	227	65,853,516	48.2

Note: There were seven electors who did not vote for either Trump or Clinton.

MAP 31.3 ▲ The Election of 2016

of improper data sharing between a social media company and a political consulting firm—the Facebook/Cambridge Analytica scandal of 2018—raised further alarms about the integrity of U.S. democratic processes.

Following a campaign laced with what many considered to be racist and nativist rhetoric, as well as by revelations of Trump's sexual misconduct, the new president was greeted by nationwide protests as he took office. The Women's March, which gathered in Washington, D.C., the day after Trump's inauguration in 2017, was one of the largest such events in U.S. history. Yet one of the most striking aspects of Trump's presidency would be how differently Americans in a deeply divided electorate regarded it. Whereas Democrats viewed the state of national politics and foreign policy with mounting apprehension, Trump's conservative base remained fiercely loyal to the forty-fifth president.

Why were right-wing populism and white nationalism on the rise?

Trump's election was part of a broader international swing toward right-wing populism. Populist movements on the right gained ground in Europe, one reaction to the economic insecurity wrought by globalization. In the United States, nationalist and anti-immigrant sentiment accompanied calls for border security and protectionist trade policy. In his somber inaugural address, Trump tapped into these concerns, referencing the "rusted-out factories scattered like tombstones across the landscape of our nation," and the "millions upon millions of American workers left behind."

The wealthiest occupant of the White House in U.S. history, one who had managed to evade paying millions of dollars in personal income taxes, Donald Trump was an unlikely spokesman for the down-and-out. But his signature issues—lowering taxes, negotiating for better trade deals, and halting illegal immigration—aligned with workers' unease about their economic futures.

Part of that unease stemmed from the tremendous surge of immigration the United States experienced in the late twentieth and early twenty-first centuries. Some who came to the United States were drawn by the promise of economic opportunity; others, including many Central Americans, had been displaced by U.S. policies and military interventions. By 2014, the United States' 42.2 million immigrants comprised 13.2 percent of the population. Latinos constituted the largest U.S. minority group, at 55 million, or 17 percent of the population, although after 2010 more immigrants came from Asia than from Latin America.

As had been the case throughout U.S. history, these newcomers were targets of economic resentment. Like their predecessors, the majority of post-1965 immigrants were unskilled and poor. They took the lowest-paying jobs, constituting nearly half of all farmworkers and housekeepers. Mexican immigrants, for example, constituted more than two-thirds of crop workers in 2015. Yet a significant number were highly skilled workers, sought after by burgeoning high-tech industries. In 2000, approximately 40 percent of all immigrants who entered the United States had a college education. By 2006, nearly one-third of all software developers were foreign-born, as were 28 percent of all physicians.

Americans expressed particular hostility toward undocumented immigrants like Jose Antonio Vargas, even though the nation depended on their low-paid labor.

VISUAL ACTIVITY

▲ **Deindustrialization** Detroit, with its major auto manufacturing plants and plentiful union jobs that lifted many families into the middle class, was a powerhouse of the midcentury U.S. economy. This factory was the home of Fisher Body Works, which operated from 1919 to 1984, building Cadillacs and Buicks for General Motors as well as military planes during World War II. By 2015, when this photograph was taken, it had long been shuttered. matt_ragen/Alamy.

READING THE IMAGE: What does the condition of this former factory suggest about the fortunes of the Rust Belt in the global economy of the twenty-first century? What story would its presence in Detroit tell to a laborer? Why did Donald Trump make images of such factories a theme of his presidential campaign?
CONNECTIONS: What forces led to the decline of American manufacturing in the 1970s and after?

Under George W. Bush, illegal entry at the U.S-Mexico border had come under new scrutiny. His successors—Democrat and Republican alike—would greatly expand the U.S. Border Patrol, aggressively deporting undocumented immigrants at the rate of roughly 400,000 a year. By 2016, the number of undocumented immigrants in the country was in fact the lowest it had been in a decade, estimated at 10.7 million.

Determined to further curb illegal immigration, Trump authorized the separation of children from their families in government detention camps at the U.S.-Mexico border, an outcome decried as inhumane. He capitalized on anti-immigrant and antiforeign sentiment in other ways as well. One of his first moves as president was to call for a ban on travel to the United States by citizens of majority-Muslim countries, in what seemed to many a return to an earlier America's ethnic and religious profiling. Although lower courts struck down two iterations of the travel ban, the Supreme Court upheld a modified version in 2018. The FBI under Trump targeted immigrants and Muslims rather than white supremacists and domestic terrorists, even though the agency acknowledged that the latter were more often responsible for violence and deaths.

Critics detected racism in these policies as well as in Trump's actions and statements. When Black athletes kneeled during the playing of the national anthem to protest racial discrimination and police brutality, the president rebuked them as unpatriotic, suggesting that National Football League quarterback Colin Kaepernick "find a country that works better for him." He implied that four Democratic congress-women of color, three born in the United States and one originally from Somalia, were not truly American, taunting them to return to the "crime infested" countries they came from.

Trump's refusal in 2017 to condemn a white nationalist rally in Charlottesville, Virginia, during which a young female protester was killed, caused particular alarm. His remark that there were "very fine people on both sides" of the conflict brought denunciations from outside and inside his party. The president seemed reluctant to alienate a like-minded section of his base, the so-called alt right, which espoused violent extremism and white supremacy. Indeed, studies found that it became more common for Americans to openly express racist views during the Trump years.

Racial tensions surfaced in public contests over the nation's past, from the removal of Confederate statues to the place of slavery in the teaching of American history. Racism's legacy in the present, meanwhile, was plain in continued police killings of Black Americans. George Floyd's murder in Minneapolis in May 2019, caused by an officer kneeling on his back and neck for nine minutes and twenty-nine seconds, was captured on video, triggering mass protests across the United States and the world. Floyd's dying words, "I can't breathe," became a rallying cry for the movement against police brutality. Breonna Taylor's death by shooting in Louisville, Kentucky, at the hands of white officers the following March prompted an urgent national conversation about police reform. But the issue, like many others during Trump's tenure, would prove divisive, with conservatives and liberals unable even to agree that it needed solving.

What was Trump's record in office?

Trump's anti-establishment tendencies and distrust of traditional experts often led him to fill government positions not with experienced staffers but with novices and people personally loyal to him, including his daughter and son-in-law. Volatility characterized his administration. Trump's National Security Advisor, Michael Flynn, resigned less than one month into office. Flynn's departure (and later arrest) was soon followed by Trump's controversial firing of FBI director James Comey; the replacement of his chief of staff; the arrests of his campaign chairman, several other advisers, and his personal lawyer; and the resignations of his secretary of state, EPA head, attorney general, and secretary of defense. Trump's dissolving of the office responsible for global health security and biodefense in 2018 would later be blamed for America's lack of preparation for the COVID-19 pandemic.

Trump himself seemed determined to use his office to deepen fissures among Americans. He relished attacks on adversaries, from the news media—whom he tagged as "enemies of the people"—to members of Congress and even members of his own administration. Gaps between Republicans and Democrats widened on nearly every issue. Nowhere was the chasm larger than in approval rates for Trump, which over the course of his term averaged 86 percent for registered Republicans but only 6 percent for registered Democrats—the largest divide for any president since modern polling had begun.

In the policy arena, Trump took up core issues on the Republican docket, securing a massive corporate tax cut and reining in banking regulations while reversing environmental protections, including opening the Arctic National Wildlife Refuge to oil drilling. He signed the United States Space Force Act, creating the first new military service in seventy years. Reflecting continuing partisan battles over sexual and cultural matters, he also issued a ban on transgender individuals serving in the military.

Trump made good on a promise to install a raft of conservative justices, earning praise from the religious right, who sought to overturn constitutional protections for abortion. Democratic senators furiously protested Trump's nominees for the Supreme Court, Neil Gorsuch and Brett Kavanaugh, the latter of whom was accused of sexual misconduct by three women during his confirmation hearings. When Ruth Bader Ginsberg died near the end of Trump's term, Republicans rushed through the confirmation of a final conservative justice, Amy Coney Barrett, just eight days before Trump left office. The resulting 6-3 conservative majority on the Supreme Court was likely to be one of his administration's most enduring legacies.

On two of his biggest promises, however, Trump faltered. Although he had pledged to repeal "Obamacare," the president had not grasped how popular federally guaranteed health insurance was and how difficult it would be politically for some in his own party to oppose it. Multiple attempts to derail the Affordable Care Act failed, although the administration did succeed in modifying some of its provisions.

Another of Trump's oft-repeated campaign promises was the construction of a physical wall at the U.S.-Mexican border to stem illegal immigration, but this effort stalled as well. When, after the midterm elections in 2018, a Democratic-controlled House refused to fund a border wall, the standoff between Trump and Congress triggered the longest government shutdown in U.S. history, stretching for thirty-five days during the winter of 2018–19 and stranding many federal workers without pay. With Democrats unwilling to budge, Trump then attempted an end run around Congress, declaring a national emergency at the country's southern border in order to release the necessary funds.

With this focus on threats to national identity and security, the humanitarian functions of government seemed to slip in importance. When two major hurricanes devastated Puerto Rico—a U.S. territory—in 2017, leaving much of the island without access to power, food, and water, the Trump administration was criticized for its slow and ineffectual response. In California, where a series of massive wildfires caused enormous destruction, federal assistance came grudgingly, and only after Trump rebuked the state's forest management practices.

▲ **California Fires** A man stands on a rooftop in Camarillo, California, surveying approaching flames in May 2013. West Coast wildfires grew in number and intensity over the next decade, the result of climate change: rising temperatures, longer and more severe drought conditions, and drier terrain. In 2020, California recorded its worst wildfire season on record, and in 2021 alone more than 2.5 million acres across the state burned. David McNew/Getty Images.

In what ways did the United States retreat from global leadership?

Nowhere was Donald Trump's departure from the norms of past administrations more dramatic than in the conduct of foreign affairs, where he showed an impatience with traditional diplomacy and sought instead to speak directly to Kim Jong Un, North Korea's dictator, and to meet privately with Russian president Vladimir Putin. Trump shocked many when he sided with Putin over U.S. intelligence officials regarding evidence of Russian interference in the 2016 election and when he spoke admiringly of Turkey's and Brazil's authoritarian leaders. Trump cut the budget of the State Department and sidelined advisers there in favor of following his own instincts or those of close political advisers. Despite boasts of bringing his businessman's "art of the deal" to the conduct of foreign policy, Trump's personal diplomacy did not immediately advance U.S. economic or military objectives.

The Trump administration's most significant impact on world affairs was in its retreat from U.S. global leadership. On the campaign trail, Trump outlined an "America First" policy, whereby U.S. interests, particularly economic interests, would be foremost. In office, he called upon the nation's allies to compensate the United States for its role in their defense. He sought import tariffs on foreign goods, setting off trade disputes with the European Union, Canada, and, most consequentially, China. Trump also showed little interest in traditional U.S. human rights policies.

More generally, Trump's administration stepped back from U.S. commitments and alliances abroad, among them the Trans-Pacific Partnership trade negotiations, the Iran nuclear deal, and the Paris climate agreement. Trump also unilaterally recognized Jerusalem as the capital of Israel and announced the withdrawal of U.S. troops from Syria, prompting the resignation of his secretary of defense. Such moves undercut his own foreign policy team and provoked sharp criticism from other world leaders. America's international reputation suffered badly. Some experts wondered if an era of U.S. global leadership, embraced by Americans in the post–World War II years, was ending—and looked to France or Germany to step into that role.

Meanwhile, a Justice Department probe investigating Russian interference in the 2016 election and its potential connections to the Trump campaign hung over the administration. By early 2019, several of Trump's associates had pleaded guilty to criminal charges related to campaign finance violations, tax fraud, and lying under oath. But it was a whistleblower's report that Trump had sought out the assistance of a foreign leader, Ukraine's president, to influence the upcoming 2020 election that led the Democratic-majority House of Representatives to bring two articles of impeachment against Trump—for abuse of power and obstruction of Congress. He would be only the third president to be impeached in U.S. history (after Andrew Johnson in 1868 and Bill Clinton in 1998). The Senate, voting along party lines, acquitted him.

REVIEW

What social and political conflicts emerged in the Trump years? To what extent did Trump himself contribute to them?

In an intensely divided nation, was there any common ground?

T he final year of Trump's presidency and the first year of his successor's would be consumed by a public health crisis of major proportions, the global **COVID-19** pandemic. Arriving in the United States in early 2020, a new virus dramatically altered life during the next two years, causing staggering levels of illness, death and economic damage but also intense political fights over scientific expertise, health protocols, and government oversight.

The only American president ever to be impeached twice, Trump would also face a political crisis of his own making: his supporters' assault on the U.S. Capitol following Trump's false statements about the 2020 election. In the riot's aftermath, Americans worried not just about partisan battles—which had been a constant of national politics since the 1990s—but about the future of their democracy. Democrat Joe Biden would make national unity a theme of his new administration, but bipartisanship and a common civic culture remained elusive.

COVID-19
Life-threatening respiratory illness caused by a new coronavirus identified in 2019, SARS-CoV-2. The highly contagious virus and its variants sparked a global pandemic, causing millions of deaths and upending economies, schools, and daily life around the world.

How did COVID-19 reveal inequalities and rifts among Americans?

No sooner had Trump faced down impeachment in early 2020 than his administration encountered a new threat—the emergence of a novel coronavirus, SARS-CoV-2, and the disease that would come to be known as COVID-19. First reported in China in late 2019, the virus spread swiftly through the tightly connected world of the twenty-first century. Two cases identified in Washington State in January 2020 were the beginning of a fast-moving health crisis in the United States that had not abated two years later.

On March 11, 2020, the World Health Organization (WHO) declared the COVID-19 a global pandemic. Two days later, Trump announced a national emergency, prompting schools, colleges, sports teams, public events, and restaurants and other businesses to shut down. Health protocols were formulated by the Centers for Disease Control and Prevention (CDC), including social distancing, masking, quarantining, and contact tracing. Almost overnight, Americans' work lives, social interactions, and travel patterns were completely upended (**Figure 31.3**).

Trump's handling of the pandemic drew mixed reviews. He created a federal task force to deal with the crisis, placing Vice President Mike Pence in charge, and signed legislation providing $2 trillion in aid to hospitals as well as small businesses and state and local governments. Trump also invested substantially in vaccine development through Operation Warp Speed, which supported multiple different scientific trials simultaneously so as to find an effective barrier to the virus as quickly as possible.

But the president also withdrew U.S. funding from the WHO and flouted the public health recommendations of the CDC. Often declining to wear a mask and

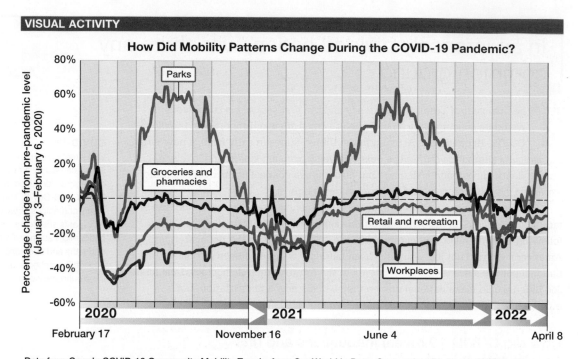

Data from Google COVID-19 Community Mobility Trends, from Our World in Data: Coronavirus Pandemic (COVID-19).

FIGURE 31.3 ▲ Pandemic Mobility Patterns In early 2020, and across the next two years, the COVID-19 pandemic led to dramatic shifts in Americans' movements due to shelter-in-place orders, travel restrictions, social distancing guidelines, and remote work practices.

READING THE FIGURE: What places did Americans visit more often, less often, and about the same during the pandemic — and what do these patterns suggest? Why does the shape of the line for parks differ from the others?
CONNECTIONS: Why did different groups within the United States have diverging experiences of the pandemic? What changes to daily life due to COVID-19 were likely to be fleeting, and which enduring?

underplaying the seriousness of the disease, he encouraged his supporters to follow suit. Trump publicized ineffective and even dangerous cures, undermined Dr. Anthony Fauci, a lead member of the White House Coronavirus Task Force, and endangered his own bodyguards and staff members when he contracted COVID-19 in October 2020. Regularly referring to the coronavirus as the "Chinese virus" because of its point of origin, Trump was further criticized for contributing to the uptick in anti-Asian slurs and violence during the pandemic.

The disease inflicted great suffering in the United States, which in the first spring of the pandemic became the global leader in reported deaths. During Trump's tenure, 400,000 Americans died of COVID-19, with daily fatality rates often higher than the entire toll from either the Pearl Harbor or 9/11 attacks. By March 2022, more than a year into President Biden's term, the death toll was nearly one million. The pandemic created enormous strain on working parents with school-age children, who suddenly had to balance jobs with remote learning, and on children themselves. And it demanded great sacrifices from health care workers who toiled long hours in grim conditions—and early on, often without adequate protective gear to shield them from the virus.

The pandemic exacted enormous economic and social costs. Unemployment hit 14.8 percent by April 2020, a post–World War II high, and Trump would as a result be the first president to leave office with fewer Americans employed than when he came in. The economic effects of the shutdown were, however, vastly uneven. Better-off Americans, cushioned by savings and often able to work remotely on videoconferencing platforms like Zoom, were better able to weather the pandemic than essential but low-income workers—grocery clerks, bus and subway drivers, and service staff of all kinds—who had no choice but to work in person and risk exposure to the virus. Racial disparities in vulnerability to the disease underscored unequal access to health care. Age-adjusted data revealed that Latinos, Black Americans, and Native Americans died from COVID-19 at roughly twice the rate of white Americans.

One bright spot was scientists' rapid development of highly effective mRNA vaccines, which became available in December of 2020 and proved in the year to follow to work even against the disease's mutations. One medical researcher described that accomplishment as "historic, momentous, the greatest biomedical triumph yet."

But convincing Americans to get the vaccine and then a booster when available was another matter. Some were already distrustful of the government; some were made more so by disinformation campaigns waged on social media about the vaccine or claims that COVID-19 was a hoax; still others were uncertain about how to weigh the risks of the disease against the risk of a new vaccine. Despite its wealth and easy access to doses of the vaccine, by 2022 the United States ranked sixty-seventh among nations in the proportion of its population that was fully vaccinated.

Clashing perspectives on vaccines and on the pandemic itself reflected the problematic way information now circulated in public life. Nearly three-quarters of Americans said in 2019 that the two political parties disagreed not just on matters of policy or ideology but about what constituted "basic facts." That conservatives and liberals increasingly consumed their news from different sources was a large part of the explanation. Many blamed Trump for disseminating misinformation and disinformation through social media—a problem Americans by 2019 ranked more worrisome than terrorism, racism, or illegal immigration. **(See "Analyzing Historical Evidence: New Media: Bad for Democracy?" on page 950.)** The president's penchant for falsehoods and conspiracy theories would eventually get him permanently banned from the Twitter platform.

The pandemic exposed deep rifts in civic culture. Rather than coming together in the face of the biggest public health crisis in a century, Americans at times seemed to turn on one another. Ugly fights broke out between those who supported masking and social distancing and those who scorned health protocols; between teachers who felt unsafe returning to classrooms and parents and lawmakers who wanted children back in school; and between groups that supported vaccine mandates as the only path to containing the virus and those that championed citizens' freedom to make their own medical decisions, free of government interference.

ANALYZING HISTORICAL EVIDENCE

New Media: Bad for Democracy?

Americans have long seen the free press as a protector of democratic society. The rise of cable television, the Internet, and social media in the late twentieth and early twenty-first centuries challenged this view. While some predicted that these platforms would enhance public deliberation, others worried about the potential for new media to become an echo chamber, to spread misinformation, and to undermine democracy.

DOCUMENT 1
Cass Sunstein, *Republic.com*, 2001

Sunstein, a legal scholar who later worked in the Obama administration, noted in 2001 the growing trend of filtered news and considered what it would mean for democratic deliberation.

When the power to filter is unlimited, people can decide, in advance and with perfect accuracy, what they will and will not encounter. They can design something very much like a communications universe of their own choosing.

Our communications market is rapidly moving in the direction of this apparently utopian picture. As of this writing, many newspapers, including the *Wall Street Journal*, allow readers to create "personalized" electronic editions, containing exactly what they want, and excluding what they do not want. . . .

Many of us are applauding these developments, which obviously increase individual convenience and entertainment. But in the midst of the applause, we should insist on asking some questions. How will the increasing power of private control affect democracy? How will the Internet, the new forms of television, and the explosion of communications options alter the capacity of citizens to govern themselves? What are the social preconditions for a well-functioning system of democratic deliberation, or for individual freedom itself?

Source: Cass R. Sunstein, *Republic.com* (Princeton, NJ: Princeton University Press, 2001), pp. 5, 7–8.

DOCUMENT 2
Clay Shirky, *Here Comes Everybody*, 2008

Shirky, a writer and thinker about Internet technologies, enthused about the possibilities of social media to bring

people together in new ways outside of traditional political or economic institutions.

We now have communications tools that are flexible enough to match our social capabilities, and we are witnessing the rise of new ways of coordinating action that take advantage of that change. . . . [W]e are living in the middle of a remarkable increase in our ability to share, to cooperate with one another, and to take collective action, all outside the framework of traditional institutions and organizations. . . . The effects are going to be . . . widespread and momentous. . . .

. . . The current change, in one sentence, is this: most of the barriers to group action have collapsed, and without those barriers, we are free to explore new ways of gathering together and getting things done.

Source: Clay Shirky, *Here Comes Everybody: The Power of Organizing without Organizations* (New York: Penguin Press, 2008), pp. 20–22.

DOCUMENT 3
Julian Sanchez, "A Coda on Closure," 2010

Sanchez, a senior fellow at the libertarian Cato Institute, elaborated on earlier comments he made regarding a right-wing "reality . . . defined by a multimedia array of interconnected and cross promoting conservative blogs, radio programs, magazines, and of course, Fox News."

There is . . . reason to think that more consciously conservative news outlets could serve as a valuable counterweight to a professional class of journalists who largely self-identify as liberals. But in practice, I believe, it has instead become worryingly untethered from reality as the impetus to satisfy the demand for red meat overtakes any motivation to report accurately. That does not mean conservatives are completely cut off from outside information

. . . but it tends to be approached in roughly the same spirit we might read the Korean Central News Agency. The press are no longer seen as even biased refs in the public debate, but as members of one team or another in a conflict whose only referee is victory. . . . At its worst it manifests as a willingness to hold and circulate factually false beliefs that a simple search ought to explode.

Source: Julian Sanchez, "A Coda on Closure," juliansanchez.com, April 22, 2010.

DOCUMENT 4
Kathleen Hall Jamieson, *Cyberwar*, 2018

Jamieson, a communications scholar, surveyed the evidence on Russian tampering with American social media sites and news reports during the 2016 presidential election.

A sampling of the outward signs of the Russian cyberwar reveals its range. One hundred and twenty-six million Americans were exposed to Russian-trafficked content on Facebook. At least 1.4 million Twitter users were subjected to the wiles of Kremlin-tied trolls and bots feigning allegiance to American values while, according to an assessment by the US intelligence agencies, bent on fomenting dissent among US citizens and defeating one of the two major party candidates. . . . The electoral systems of twenty-one states by one count and thirty-nine by another were hacked. In locales from Florida to Minnesota, individuals unwittingly helped the Russians organize rallies. . . .

Although there was not a Russian behind every tree in 2016, there was one behind some high-volume social media accounts and sites. Facebook, Instagram, Twitter, YouTube, and Tumblr were among the tech giants that unwittingly became conduits for Russian propaganda. Those in charge of them not only didn't anticipate the malign uses to which their systems could be put, but also failed to identify and thwart the illegal troll efforts to influence voters. The glacial pace with which the platforms uncovered and disclosed election-related abuse does not invite confidence in their readiness to prevent a sequel.

Source: Kathleen Hall Jamieson, *Cyberwar: How Russian Hackers and Trolls Helped Elect a President: What We Don't, Can't and Do Know* (New York: Oxford University Press, 2018), pp. 10–11, 218.

DOCUMENT 5
A Study on the Spread of "False News," *Science*, 2018

An extensive scientific study of how stories circulate on Twitter found that inaccurate information traveled faster, more deeply, and more broadly than did accurate news — especially in the case of political stories.

[B]oth true and false information spreads rapidly through online media. Defining what is true and false has become a common political strategy, replacing debates based on a mutually agreed on set of facts. . . .

When we analyzed . . . dynamics of true and false rumors, we found that falsehood diffused significantly farther, faster, deeper, and more broadly than the truth in all categories of information. . . .

False political news . . . was more viral than any other category of false information.

Source: Soroush Vosoughi, Deb Roy, and Sinan Aral, "The Spread of True and False News Online," *Science* 359 (March 9, 2018): 1146–51.

Questions for Analysis

SUMMARIZE THE ARGUMENT: What problems and possibilities arose with new media, according to these authors? How does each link the communication of information to democratic society?

CONSIDER THE CONTEXT: Do you notice any distinctions between the writings from earlier and later time periods? How and why have discussions about new media changed since 2001?

ASK HISTORICAL QUESTIONS: Does the debate over new media resemble in any way earlier U.S. debates over radio or television? What are the similarities and differences?

How did the 2020 election lead to an attack on the U.S. Capitol?

The 2020 election was conducted in the midst of the COVID-19 pandemic and before any vaccines had been approved, spurring a major shift toward mail-in voting. Democrat Joe Biden, Obama's vice president—who had managed, after early setbacks in the primaries, to secure the nomination with the help of Black voters—challenged incumbent Donald Trump.

Despite the pandemic, 160 million Americans voted, the highest turnout rate in 120 years. Voters were highly motivated to get to the polls, with a reported nine out of ten registered Democrats and Republicans convinced that "lasting harm" to the nation would result if their favored candidate did not prevail. Marbili Walters, a Venezuelan-born Trump supporter, lamented that "voting for someone else should not feel like we are at war." Many viewed the election with trepidation, fearing civil unrest, whatever the outcome.

The volume of mailed ballots was expected to slow the tally after the polls closed on election day. The next morning, however, Trump proclaimed victory, even though millions of votes were still to be counted. Four days later, the election was called for Biden, the Democrat winning 306 electoral votes to Trump's 232 and racking up a 7 million popular vote advantage.

Trump had early on hedged on committing to a peaceful transfer of power—a core value of American democracy that had never been challenged. And even before the election, he had sowed doubts about its results by attacking the integrity of mail-in ballots and impugning the security of voting processes in general. After Biden was declared the winner, Trump charged that massive voter fraud had robbed him of a "landslide victory." He then launched a series of legal challenges to the tally in states that had tipped to Biden, but could furnish no convincing evidence of fraud. Court after court, including the highest court in the land, dismissed Trump's assertions as baseless. Nevertheless, supporters trusted his repeated false claims, three-quarters of them in January 2021 indicating their belief that Trump was either definitely or "probably" the rightful winner of the election.

The consequences of Trump's words alarmed the nation and the entire democratic world. On January 6, 2021, Trump spoke at a "Stop the Steal" rally in Washington, D.C., organized to protest the official certification of Biden's election that day. Afterward, several thousand attendees—mostly white, some of them carrying Confederate flags—swarmed the Capitol Building where Congress was meeting, breaking into the building, vandalizing property, and assaulting 138 police officers. Five people were killed during the riot and many more were injured.

Americans of all political opinions recoiled at the violent attack on the Capitol. One House Republican called the riot "an unconstitutional attempt led by the president of the United States to overturn an American election and reinstall himself in power illegitimately." The president of France, Emmanuel Macron, rushed to reassure the world that "we believe in the strength of our democracies. We believe in the strength of American democracy." A week after the riot, Trump was impeached by the House of Representatives for a second time, on the charge of "inciting insurrection," with ten Republicans voting in support. Although he would again be acquitted, his unprecedented two impeachment trials testified to the turmoil Trump had brought to U.S. politics. As he left office, his approval ratings bottomed out, falling to just 29 percent.

Trump never officially conceded defeat in the 2020 election. And in a final breach of protocol, he declined to attend Biden's inauguration—the first time a president had done so in a century and a half. Instead, Trump boarded a plane bound for Florida to begin his post-presidential life. He would be gone but not forgotten, looming large over the Republican Party and immediately toying with the possibility of a 2024 presidential run.

Soon enough, partisan interpretations of the **U.S. Capitol riot** and the impeachment would gain ground. So too would other attacks on democratic institutions. In the weeks and months following the election, Republican state legislatures sought to enact restrictions on voting by mail, which had contributed to the historic turnout in 2020. Voting list purges, reductions in the number of polling stations, especially in majority-Democratic and -Black precincts, and other measures portrayed as shoring up the integrity of elections were proposed by legislators—despite numerous studies concluding that the 2020 election had in fact been highly secure, with minimal instances of fraud.

U.S. Capitol riot
Attack by supporters of President Trump on the U.S. Capitol Building on January 6, 2021, in an effort to halt the certification of Joe Biden's electoral college victory in the presidential race of 2020. Several thousand attendees at a "Stop the Steal" rally broke into and vandalized the Capitol Building, assaulting and injuring more than a hundred police officers and causing five deaths.

▲ **U.S. Capitol Attack** Following a "Stop the Steal" rally protesting the official ratification of Joe Biden's victory in the 2020 presidential election, several thousand Trump supporters swarmed the U.S. Capitol on January 6, 2021. The protesters would go on to break into and occupy the Capitol Building, vandalize property, and assault police, injuring 138 officers and leading to several deaths. The unprecedented event drew immediate condemnation across political lines, although partisan interpretations soon diverged. Samuel Corum/Getty Images.

How did crises shape the early Biden administration?

Joseph Robinette Biden Jr. stepped into office in some of the most difficult circumstances in modern U.S. history—including the ongoing public health emergency, an economy badly damaged by COVID-19, and the fallout from a violent attempt to overturn a democratic election just weeks before he took office. Deep tensions around racial justice, continuing strife over immigration at the nation's southern border, and ever more pressing evidence of environmental calamity compounded the challenge.

The oldest person yet to be elected to the presidency at seventy-eight, Biden was equipped with five decades of experience in public service: thirty-six years as a U.S. senator from Delaware, two prior runs for president, and eight years as vice president to Barack Obama. Biden was a devout Catholic, just the second to occupy the office of the presidency. He had struggled for much of his life with a stutter and had endured a string of family tragedies that shaped his faith in compassionate leadership. Biden ran for office in 2020, he said, because "we are in the battle for the soul of this nation." He promised Americans the return of a traditional head of state, pledging his commitment to decency and to unifying the nation. After the tumult of Trump's presidency, Biden inspired the confidence of key U.S. allies such as Britain, Germany, and France.

In his choice of Kamala Harris as his running mate—the first female, Black, and South Asian vice president—Biden underscored the importance of diversity to his administration as well as his departure from the racial divisiveness of his predecessor. He appointed an unprecedented number of women and people of color to key positions, including Deb Haaland as secretary of the interior, the first Native American to serve as a Cabinet secretary. And he followed through on his vow to nominate the first Black woman, Ketanji Brown Jackson, to the Supreme Court.

Biden made fighting COVID-19 his first priority: requiring masks on public transportation, reopening schools, and rolling out a national vaccination campaign. He targeted July 4, 2021, as the date by which his administration would be able to declare victory over the pandemic, but this goal would be dashed by the new and highly contagious Delta and then Omicron variants of the coronavirus. By March 2022, an estimated 8.5 million Americans had lost a close family member to COVID-19 and others suffered from debilitating and poorly understood long-term symptoms, often referred to as "long" or "long-haul" COVID.

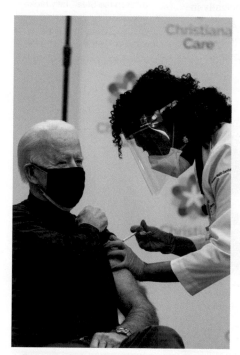

▲ **Biden Receives Vaccine** A month before taking office, Joe Biden received a first dose of the new COVID-19 vaccine. Biden made fighting the pandemic a priority of his campaign, which included following public health protocols on masking, quarantining, social distancing, and school and business closures — guidelines the Trump administration had sometimes fought or ignored. By publicizing his shot, the president-elect hoped to advertise the safety of the vaccine and the new administration's trust in scientific expertise. ALEX EDELMAN/Getty Images.

A moderate Democrat for most of his career, Biden would as president endorse the most extensive set of progressive reforms in a generation: a major infrastructure bill, investments in clean energy, and remedies for systematic racism in housing, the criminal justice system, and voting rights. Counting on his extensive experience in the Senate, Biden also promised that he would be able to achieve bipartisan consensus. This claim was tested early on by his coronavirus relief package: Congress delivered $1.9 trillion in relief but without a single Republican in support.

Biden did secure a bipartisan infrastructure law. But with a small Democratic majority in the House of Representatives and an evenly divided Senate, his efforts to strengthen voting rights and support working families were uphill battles. Biden was also faced with the most conservative Supreme Court since the 1930s. Fulfilling a long-standing goal of the Right, the justices overturned *Roe v. Wade* and constitutional protections for abortion in 2022. Like his recent predecessors, Biden used executive actions to achieve some of his goals—for example, rejoining the Paris Climate Agreement on his first day in office and reversing many of Trump's environmental actions.

In foreign policy, Biden's first major decision fulfilled his campaign pledge to withdraw U.S. troops from Afghanistan, first sent there in 2001 as a response to the 9/11 attacks. In April 2021, he announced that it was "time to end America's longest war" and for "American troops to come home." Biden stated that the United States would no longer use its military to "remake other countries," a reference to three previous administrations' rationales for intervention in both Afghanistan and Iraq. He would be severely criticized for the chaotic evacuation of troops, civilians, and Afghan allies, during which thirteen American service members died. With U.S. troops gone, the Afghan government quickly collapsed and the Taliban seized control, leading to a refugee crisis as thousands fled the country.

Biden signaled that going forward, his administration would be focused on cybersecurity as well as economic competition with Russia and China. In 2022, however, Russia invaded its neighbor Ukraine—which had been part of the Soviet Union until it won its independence in 1991. More than five million refugees fled Ukraine in the first two months of attacks. Russia's actions raised fears of a major European land war as well as renewed hostilities between the United States and its former Cold War enemy. Biden coordinated with NATO allies to respond to the invasion with economic sanctions and revoked Russia's trade status. The conflict revealed cracks in the post-1989 international order. Only time would tell how it would affect America's role in world affairs—but the invasion made clear that trade wars and cyberattacks would not completely supplant traditional wars in the twenty-first century.

Refugee Flow from Ukraine (as of April 2022)

REVIEW

What did the policies of the early Biden administration suggest about the future of U.S. commitments at home and abroad?

Conclusion: Was America becoming more or less democratic in the twenty-first century?

From the 9/11 attacks on the Pentagon and World Trade Center to the ongoing threat of COVID-19, the twenty-first century held new challenges on the world stage for the United States. International terrorism and instability in the Middle

East lent urgency to the long-standing question of how the United States should act beyond its borders. Unilateralism and preemption under Bush, the more multilateral approach of Obama, and an "America First" agenda under Trump each had vocal critics.

President Biden would seek to restore both traditional alliances and the mantle of American global leadership. It remained uncertain, however, whether the United States would be able to retain its status as the leader of the world's democracies. Climate change remained a looming global threat, with the United States ranking as one of the world's largest emitters of greenhouse gases. Major natural and environmental disasters, from floods to fires, underscored ways in which the most powerful nation on earth both contributed to and was affected by global developments.

Questions stemming from within the United States were no easier. The sense of common national purpose born of the 9/11 attacks in 2001 turned out to be a brief pause in the escalating partisan combat in Congress and the broader culture. The COVID-19 pandemic uncovered what often seemed like two opposed Americas divided by ideology, media, and basic understandings of their country. Disruptive politics, disinformation campaigns, rollbacks in voting rights, racial inequality, and a growing sense of the fragility of national norms and institutions made some Americans question whether U.S. democracy itself would survive.

Far-right movements, including nativism and white nationalism, were on the rise—one response to profound economic distress as globalization continued to reshape American society and low-wage, insecure work became the norm for many. But there were countercurrents in the explosion of progressive grassroots movements and the increasingly diverse makeup of the nation's political leadership, including after 2018 the first two Muslim women and first two Native American women to serve in the U.S. Congress. Debates over who belonged in the United States and to whom America belonged—posed by groups as different as Tea Party organizers, Black Lives Matter activists, and DREAMers—were not new but rather the latest chapter in the nation's unfolding story.

CHAPTER REVIEW

EXPLAIN WHY IT MATTERS

Al Qaeda (p. 923)

USA Patriot Act (p. 924)

Department of Homeland Security (p. 925)

Iraq War (p. 927)

Citizens United v. Federal Elections Commission (p. 928)

No Child Left Behind Act (p. 929)

Hurricane Katrina (p. 929)

Great Recession (p. 930)

Obergefell v. Hodges (p. 932)

Patient Protection and Affordable Care Act (p. 932)

Tea Party movement (p. 933)

Occupy Wall Street (p. 937)

Black Lives Matter (p. 938)

COVID-19 (p. 947)

U.S. Capitol riot (p. 953)

PUT IT ALL TOGETHER

THE POST-9/11 WORLD

- How were American international relations affected by the events of September 11, 2001?
- What impact did the "war on terror" have on civil liberties at home and on the U.S. observance of human rights?

SOCIAL JUSTICE

- How did activists seek to address continuing racial inequality in the twenty-first century? In what areas had race relations made the most — and the least — progress?
- What prompted the formation of movements like Occupy Wall Street and #MeToo, and what tactics did they use to further their goals?

DIVIDED DEMOCRACY

- How did political polarization affect governance during the Obama, Trump, and Biden administrations?
- What divisions in American life did the COVID-19 pandemic expose?

LOOKING BACKWARD, LOOKING AHEAD

- Compare the place of the United States in the world in 1945, 1989, and today.
- Defend or refute the following statement: In fifty years' time, the United States will still be the most powerful nation in the world.

DIRECTORY

APPENDIX I
Documents

APPENDIX II
Government and Demographics

DOCUMENTS

THE DECLARATION OF INDEPENDENCE

In Congress, July 4, 1776,

THE UNANIMOUS DECLARATION OF THE THIRTEEN UNITED STATES OF AMERICA

When in the course of human events, it becomes necessary for one people to dissolve the political bands which have connected them with another, and to assume, among the powers of the earth, the separate and equal station to which the laws of nature and of nature's God entitle them, a decent respect to the opinions of mankind requires that they should declare the causes which impel them to the separation.

We hold these truths to be self-evident, that all men are created equal; that they are endowed by their Creator with certain unalienable rights; that among these, are life, liberty, and the pursuit of happiness. That, to secure these rights, governments are instituted among men, deriving their just powers from the consent of the governed; that, whenever any form of government becomes destructive of these ends, it is the right of the people to alter or to abolish it, and to institute a new government, laying its foundation on such principles, and organizing its powers in such form, as to them shall seem most likely to effect their safety and happiness. Prudence, indeed, will dictate that governments long established, should not be changed for light and transient causes; and, accordingly, all experience hath shown, that mankind are more disposed to suffer, while evils are sufferable, than to right themselves by abolishing the forms to which they are accustomed. But, when a long train of abuses and usurpations, pursuing invariably the same object, evinces a design to reduce them under absolute despotism, it is their right, it is their duty, to throw off such government and to provide new guards for their future security. Such has been the patient sufferance of these colonies, and such is now the necessity which constrains them to alter their former systems of government. The history of the present King of Great Britain is a history of repeated injuries and usurpations, all having, in direct object, the establishment of an absolute tyranny over these States. To prove this, let facts be submitted to a candid world: He has refused his assent to laws the most wholesome and necessary for the public good.

He has forbidden his governors to pass laws of immediate and pressing importance, unless suspended in their operation till his assent should be obtained; and, when so suspended, he has utterly neglected to attend to them.

He has refused to pass other laws for the accommodation of large districts of people, unless those people would relinquish the right of representation in the legislature; a right inestimable to them, and formidable to tyrants only.

He has called together legislative bodies at places unusual, uncomfortable, and distant from the depository of their public records, for the sole purpose of fatiguing them into compliance with his measures.

He has dissolved representative houses repeatedly for opposing, with manly firmness, his invasions on the rights of the people.

He has refused, for a long time after such dissolutions, to cause others to be elected; whereby the legislative powers, incapable of annihilation, have returned to the people at large for their exercise; the state remaining in the mean-time exposed to all the danger of invasion from without, and convulsions within.

He has endeavored to prevent the population of these States; for that purpose, obstructing the laws for naturalization of foreigners, refusing to pass others to encourage their migration hither, and raising the conditions of new appropriations of lands.

He has obstructed the administration of justice, by refusing his assent to laws for establishing judiciary powers.

He has made judges dependent on his will alone, for the tenure of their offices, and the amount and payment of their salaries.

He has erected a multitude of new offices, and sent hither swarms of officers to harass our people, and eat out their substance.

He has kept among us, in times of peace, standing armies, without the consent of our legislature.

He has affected to render the military independent of, and superior to, the civil power.

He has combined, with others, to subject us to a jurisdiction foreign to our Constitution, and unacknowledged by our laws; giving his assent to their acts of pretended legislation:

For quartering large bodies of armed troops among us:

For protecting them by a mock trial, from punishment, for any murders which they should commit on the inhabitants of these States:

For cutting off our trade with all parts of the world:

For imposing taxes on us without our consent:

For depriving us, in many cases, of the benefit of trial by jury:

For transporting us beyond seas to be tried for pretended offences:

For abolishing the free system of English laws in a neighboring province, establishing therein an arbitrary government, and enlarging its boundaries, so as to render it at once an example and fit instrument for introducing the same absolute rule into these colonies:

For taking away our charters, abolishing our most valuable laws, and altering, fundamentally, the powers of our governments:

For suspending our own legislatures, and declaring themselves invested with power to legislate for us in all cases whatsoever.

He has abdicated government here, by declaring us out of his protection, and waging war against us.

He has plundered our seas, ravaged our coasts, burnt our towns, and destroyed the lives of our people.

He is, at this time, transporting large armies of foreign mercenaries to complete the works of death, desolation, and tyranny, already begun, with circumstances of cruelty and perfidy scarcely paralleled in the most barbarous ages, and totally unworthy the head of a civilized nation.

He has constrained our fellow citizens, taken captive on the high seas, to bear arms against their country, to become the executioners of their friends, and brethren, or to fall themselves by their hands.

He has excited domestic insurrections amongst us, and has endeavored to bring on the inhabitants of our frontiers, the merciless Indian savages, whose known rule of warfare is an undistinguished destruction of all ages, sexes, and conditions.

In every stage of these oppressions, we have petitioned for redress; in the most humble terms; our repeated petitions have been answered only by repeated injury. A prince, whose character is thus marked by every act which may define a tyrant, is unfit to be the ruler of a free people.

Nor have we been wanting in attention to our British brethren. We have warned them, from time to time, of attempts made by their legislature to extend an unwarrantable jurisdiction over us. We have reminded them of the circumstances of our emigration and settlement here. We have appealed to their native justice and magnanimity, and we have conjured them, by the ties of our common kindred, to disavow these usurpations, which would inevitably interrupt our connections and correspondence. They, too, have been deaf to the voice of justice and consanguinity. We must, therefore, acquiesce in the necessity which denounces our separation, and hold them as we hold the rest of mankind, enemies in war, in peace, friends.

We, therefore, the representatives of the United States of America, in general Congress assembled, appealing to the Supreme Judge of the world for the rectitude of our intentions, do, in the name, and by authority of the good people of these colonies, solemnly publish and declare, that these united colonies are, and of right ought to be, free and independent states: that they are absolved from all allegiance to the British Crown, and that all political connection between them and the state of Great Britain is, and ought to be, totally dissolved; and that, as free and independent states, they have full power to levy war, conclude peace, contract alliances, establish commerce, and to do all other acts and things which independent states may of right do. And, for the support of this declaration, with a firm reliance on the protection of Divine Providence, we mutually pledge to each other our lives, our fortunes, and our sacred honor.

The foregoing Declaration was, by order of Congress, engrossed, and signed by the following members:

JOHN HANCOCK

New Hampshire
Josiah Bartlett
William Whipple
Matthew Thornton

Massachusetts Bay
Samuel Adams
John Adams
Robert Treat Paine
Elbridge Gerry

Rhode Island
Stephen Hopkins
William Ellery

Connecticut
Roger Sherman
Samuel Huntington
William Williams
Oliver Wolcott

New York
William Floyd
Phillip Livingston
Francis Lewis
Lewis Morris

New Jersey
Richard Stockton
John Witherspoon
Francis Hopkinson
John Hart
Abraham Clark

Pennsylvania
Robert Morris
Benjamin Rush
Benjamin Franklin
John Morton
George Clymer
James Smith

George Taylor
James Wilson
George Ross

Delaware
Caesar Rodney
George Read
Thomas M'Kean

Maryland
Samuel Chase
William Paca
Thomas Stone
Charles Carroll,
  of Carrollton

North Carolina
William Hooper
Joseph Hewes
John Penn

South Carolina
Edward Rutledge
Thomas Heyward, Jr.
Thomas Lynch, Jr.
Arthur Middleton

Virginia
George Wythe
Richard Henry Lee
Thomas Jefferson
Benjamin Harrison
Thomas Nelson, Jr.
Francis Lightfoot Lee
Carter Braxton

Georgia
Button Gwinnett
Lyman Hall
George Walton

Resolved, That copies of the Declaration be sent to the several assemblies, conventions, and committees, or councils of safety, and to the several commanding officers of the continental troops; that it be proclaimed in each of the United States, at the head of the army.

THE CONSTITUTION OF THE UNITED STATES*

Agreed to by Philadelphia Convention, September 17, 1787. Implemented March 4, 1789.

Preamble

We the people of the United States, in order to form a more perfect union, establish justice, insure domestic tranquility, provide for the common defense, promote the general welfare, and secure the blessings of liberty to ourselves and our posterity, do ordain and establish this Constitution for the United States of America.

Article I

Section 1 All legislative powers herein granted shall be vested in a Congress of the United States, which shall consist of a Senate and a House of Representatives.

Section 2 The House of Representatives shall be composed of members chosen every second year by the

---

*Passages no longer in effect are in italic type.

people of the several States, and the electors in each State shall have the qualifications requisite for electors of the most numerous branch of the State Legislature.

No person shall be a Representative who shall not have attained to the age of twenty-five years, and been seven years a citizen of the United States, and who shall not, when elected, be an inhabitant of that State in which he shall be chosen.

Representatives and direct taxes shall be apportioned among the several States which may be included within this Union, according to their respective numbers, *which shall be determined by adding to the whole number of free persons, including those bound to service for a term of years and excluding Indians not taxed, three-fifths of all other persons.* The actual enumeration shall be made within three years after the first meeting of the Congress of the United States, and within every subsequent term of ten years, in such manner as they shall by law direct. The number of Representatives shall not exceed one for every thirty thousand, but each State shall have at least one Representative; *and until such enumeration shall be made, the State of New Hampshire shall be entitled to choose three, Massachusetts eight, Rhode Island and Providence Plantations one, Connecticut five, New York six, New Jersey four, Pennsylvania eight, Delaware one, Maryland six, Virginia ten, North Carolina five, South Carolina five, and Georgia three.*

When vacancies happen in the representation from any State, the Executive authority thereof shall issue writs of election to fill such vacancies.

The House of Representatives shall choose their Speaker and other officers; and shall have the sole power of impeachment.

Section 3 The Senate of the United States shall be composed of two Senators from each State, *chosen by the legislature thereof,* for six years; and each Senator shall have one vote.

Immediately after they shall be assembled in consequence of the first election, they shall be divided as equally as may be into three classes. The seats of the Senators of the first class shall be vacated at the expiration of the second year, of the second class at the expiration of the fourth year, and of the third class at the expiration of the sixth year, so that one-third may be chosen every second year; *and if vacancies happen by resignation or otherwise, during the recess of the legislature of any State, the Executive thereof may make temporary appointments until the next meeting of the legislature, which shall then fill such vacancies.*

No person shall be a Senator who shall not have attained to the age of thirty years, and been nine years a citizen of the United States, and who shall not, when elected, be an inhabitant of that State for which he shall be chosen.

The Vice-President of the United States shall be President of the Senate, but shall have no vote, unless they be equally divided.

The Senate shall choose their other officers, and also a President pro tempore, in the absence of the Vice-President, or when he shall exercise the office of President of the United States.

The Senate shall have the sole power to try all impeachments. When sitting for that purpose, they shall be on oath or affirmation. When the President of the United States is tried, the Chief Justice shall preside: and no person shall be convicted without the concurrence of two-thirds of the members present.

Judgment in cases of impeachment shall not extend further than to removal from the office, and disqualification to hold and enjoy any office of honor, trust or profit under the United States: but the party convicted shall nevertheless be liable and subject to indictment, trial, judgment and punishment, according to law.

Section 4 The times, places and manner of holding elections for Senators and Representatives shall be prescribed in each State by the legislature thereof; but the Congress may at any time by law make or alter such regulations, except as to the places of choosing Senators.

The Congress shall assemble at least once in every year, and such meeting *shall be on the first Monday in December, unless they shall by law appoint a different day.*

Section 5 Each house shall be the judge of the elections, returns and qualifications of its own members, and a majority of each shall constitute a quorum to do business; but a smaller number may adjourn from day to day, and may be authorized to compel the attendance of absent members, in such manner, and under such penalties, as each house may provide.

Each house may determine the rules of its proceedings, punish its members for disorderly behavior, and with the concurrence of two-thirds, expel a member.

Each house shall keep a journal of its proceedings, and from time to time publish the same, excepting such parts as may in their judgment require secrecy; and the yeas and nays of the members of either house on any question shall, at the desire of one-fifth of those present, be entered on the journal.

Neither house, during the session of Congress, shall, without the consent of the other, adjourn for more than three days, nor to any other place than that in which the two houses shall be sitting.

Section 6 The Senators and Representatives shall receive a compensation for their services, to be ascertained by law and paid out of the treasury of the United States. They shall in all cases except treason, felony and breach of the peace, be privileged from arrest during their attendance at the session of their respective houses, and in going to and returning from the same; and for any speech or debate in either house, they shall not be questioned in any other place.

No Senator or Representative shall, during the time for which he was elected, be appointed to any civil office under the authority of the United States, which shall have been created, or the emoluments whereof shall have been increased, during such time; and no person holding any office under the United States shall be a member of either house during his continuance in office.

Section 7 All bills for raising revenue shall originate in the House of Representatives; but the Senate may propose or concur with amendments as on other bills.

Every bill which shall have passed the House of Representatives and the Senate, shall, before it become a law, be presented to the President of the United States; if he approve he shall sign it, but if not he shall return it with objections to that house in which it shall have originated, who shall enter the objections at large on their journal, and proceed to reconsider it. If after such reconsideration two-thirds of that house shall agree to pass the bill, it shall be sent, together with the objections, to the other house, by which it shall likewise be reconsidered, and, if approved by two-thirds of that house, it shall become a law. But in all such cases the votes of both houses shall be determined by yeas and nays, and the names of the persons voting for and against the bill shall be entered on the journal of each house respectively. If any bill shall not be returned by the President within ten days (Sundays excepted) after it shall have been presented to him, the same shall be a law, in like manner as if he had signed it, unless the Congress by their adjournment prevent its return, in which case it shall not be a law.

Every order, resolution, or vote to which the concurrence of the Senate and House of Representatives may be necessary (except on a question of adjournment) shall be presented to the President of the United States; and before the same shall take effect, shall be approved by him, or being disapproved by him, shall be repassed by two-thirds of the Senate and House of Representatives, according to the rules and limitations prescribed in the case of a bill.

Section 8 The Congress shall have power

To lay and collect taxes, duties, imposts, and excises, to pay the debts and provide for the common defense and general welfare of the United States; but all duties, imposts and excises shall be uniform throughout the United States;

To borrow money on the credit of the United States;

To regulate commerce with foreign nations, and among the several States, and with the Indian tribes;

To establish an uniform rule of naturalization, and uniform laws on the subject of bankruptcies throughout the United States;

To coin money, regulate the value thereof, and of foreign coin, and fix the standard of weights and measures;

To provide for the punishment of counterfeiting the securities and current coin of the United States;

To establish post offices and post roads;

To promote the progress of science and useful arts by securing for limited times to authors and inventors the exclusive right to their respective writings and discoveries;

To constitute tribunals inferior to the Supreme Court;

To define and punish piracies and felonies committed on the high seas and offences against the law of nations;

To declare war, grant letters of marque and reprisal, and make rules concerning captures on land and water;

To raise and support armies, but no appropriation of money to that use shall be for a longer term than two years;

To provide and maintain a navy;

To make rules for the government and regulation of the land and naval forces;

To provide for calling forth the militia to execute the laws of the Union, suppress insurrections and repel invasions;

To provide for organizing, arming, and disciplining the militia, and for governing such part of them as may be employed in the service of the United States, reserving to the States respectively the appointment of the officers, and the authority of training the militia according to the discipline prescribed by Congress;

To exercise exclusive legislation in all cases whatsoever, over such district (not exceeding ten miles square) as may, by cession of particular States, and the acceptance of Congress, become the seat of the government of the United States, and to exercise like authority over all places purchased by the consent of the legislature of the State, in which the same shall be, for erection of forts, magazines, arsenals, dock-yards, and other needful buildings;—and

To make all laws which shall be necessary and proper for carrying into execution the foregoing powers, and all other powers vested by this Constitution in the government of the United States, or in any department or officer thereof.

Section 9 *The migration or importation of such persons as any of the States now existing shall think proper to admit shall not be prohibited by the Congress prior to the year one thousand eight hundred and eight; but a tax or duty may be imposed on such importation, not exceeding ten dollars for each person.*

The privilege of the writ of habeas corpus shall not be suspended, unless when in cases of rebellion or invasion the public safety may require it.

No bill of attainder or ex post facto law shall be passed.

No capitation, or other direct, tax shall be laid, unless in proportion to the census or enumeration herein before directed to be taken.

No tax or duty shall be laid on articles exported from any State.

No preference shall be given by any regulation of commerce or revenue to the ports of one State over those of another; nor shall vessels bound to, or from, one State be obliged to enter, clear, or pay duties in another.

No money shall be drawn from the treasury, but in consequence of appropriations made by law; and a regular statement and account of the receipts and expenditures of all public money shall be published from time to time.

No title of nobility shall be granted by the United States: and no person holding any office of profit or trust under them, shall, without the consent of the Congress, accept of any present, emolument, office, or title, of any kind whatever, from any king, prince, or foreign state.

Section 10 No State shall enter into any treaty, alliance, or confederation; grant letters of marque and reprisal; coin money; emit bills of credit; make anything but gold and silver coin a tender in payment of debts; pass any bill of attainder, ex post facto law, or law impairing the obligation of contracts, or grant any title of nobility.

No State shall, without the consent of Congress, lay any imposts or duties on imports or exports, except what may be absolutely necessary for executing its inspection laws: and the net produce of all duties and imposts, laid by any State on imports or exports, shall be for the use of the treasury of the United States; and all such laws shall be subject to the revision and control of the Congress.

No State shall, without the consent of Congress, lay any duty of tonnage, keep troops, or ships of war in time of peace, enter into any agreement or compact with another State, or with a foreign power, or engage in war, unless actually invaded, or in such imminent danger as will not admit of delay.

Article II

Section 1 The executive power shall be vested in a President of the United States of America. He shall hold his office during the term of four years, and, together with the Vice-President, chosen for the same term, be elected as follows:

Each State shall appoint, in such manner as the legislature thereof may direct, a number of electors, equal to the whole number of Senators and Representatives to which the State may be entitled in the Congress; but no Senator or Representative, or person holding an office of trust or profit under the United States, shall be appointed an elector.

The electors shall meet in their respective States, and vote by ballot for two persons, of whom one at least shall not be an inhabitant of the same State with themselves. And they shall make a list of all the persons voted

for, and of the number of votes for each; which list they shall sign and certify, and transmit sealed to the seat of government of the United States, directed to the President of the Senate. The President of the Senate shall, in the presence of the Senate and House of Representatives, open all the certificates, and the votes shall then be counted. The person having the greatest number of votes shall be the President, if such number be a majority of the whole number of electors appointed; and if there be more than one who have such majority, and have an equal number of votes, then the House of Representatives shall immediately choose by ballot one of them for President; and if no person have a majority, then from the five highest on the list said house shall in like manner choose the President. But in choosing the President the votes shall be taken by States, the representation from each State having one vote; a quorum for this purpose shall consist of a member or members from two-thirds of the States, and a majority of all the States shall be necessary to a choice. In every case, after the choice of the President, the person having the greatest number of votes of the electors shall be the Vice-President. But if there should remain two or more who have equal votes, the Senate shall choose from them by ballot the Vice-President.

The Congress may determine the time of choosing the electors, and the day on which they shall give their votes; which day shall be the same throughout the United States.

No person except a natural-born citizen, *or a citizen of the United States at the time of the adoption of this Constitution*, shall be eligible to the office of President; neither shall any person be eligible to that office who shall not have attained to the age of thirty-five years, and been fourteen years a resident within the United States.

In cases of the removal of the President from office or of his death, resignation, or inability to discharge the powers and duties of the said office, the same shall devolve on the Vice-President, and the Congress may by law provide for the case of removal, death, resignation, or inability, both of the President and Vice-President, declaring what officer shall then act as President, and such officer shall act accordingly, until the disability be removed, or a President shall be elected.

The President shall, at stated times, receive for his services a compensation, which shall neither be increased nor diminished during the period for which he shall have been elected, and he shall not receive within that period any other emolument from the United States, or any of them.

Before he enter on the execution of his office, he shall take the following oath or affirmation: — "I do solemnly swear (or affirm) that I will faithfully execute the office of the President of the United States, and will to the best of my ability preserve, protect and defend the Constitution of the United States."

Section 2 The President shall be commander in chief of the army and navy of the United States, and of the militia of the several States, when called into the actual service of the United States; he may require the opinion, in writing, of the principal officer in each of the executive departments, upon any subject relating to the duties of their respective offices, and he shall have power to grant reprieves and pardons for offences against the United States, except in cases of impeachment.

He shall have power, by and with the advice and consent of the Senate, to make treaties, provided two-thirds of the Senators present concur; and he shall nominate, and by and with the advice and consent of the Senate, shall appoint ambassadors, other public ministers and consuls, judges of the Supreme Court, and all other officers of the United States, whose appointments are not herein otherwise provided for, and which shall be established by law: but Congress may by law vest the appointment of such inferior officers, as they think proper, in the President alone, in the courts of law, or in the heads of departments.

The President shall have power to fill up all vacancies that may happen during the recess of the Senate, by granting commissions which shall expire at the end of their next session.

Section 3 He shall from time to time give to the Congress information of the state of the Union, and recommend to their consideration such measures as he shall judge necessary and expedient; he may, on extraordinary occasions, convene both houses, or either of them, and in case of disagreement between them, with respect to the time of adjournment, he may adjourn them to such time as he shall think proper; he shall receive ambassadors and other public ministers; he shall take care that the laws be faithfully executed, and shall commission all the officers of the United States.

Section 4 The President, Vice-President and all civil officers of the United States shall be removed from office on impeachment for, and on conviction of, treason, bribery, or other high crimes and misdemeanors.

Article III

Section 1 The judicial power of the United States shall be vested in one Supreme Court, and in such inferior courts as the Congress may from time to time ordain and establish. The judges, both of the Supreme and inferior courts, shall hold their offices during good behavior, and shall, at stated times, receive for their services a compensation which shall not be diminished during their continuance in office.

Section 2 The judicial power shall extend to all cases, in law and equity, arising under this Constitution, the laws of the United States, and treaties made, or which shall be made, under their authority; — to all cases affecting ambassadors, other public ministers and consuls; — to all cases of admiralty and maritime jurisdiction; — to controversies to which the United States shall be a party; — to controversies between two or more States; — *between a State and citizens of another State*; — between citizens of different States; — between citizens of the same State claiming lands under grants of different States, and between a State, or the citizens thereof, and foreign states, citizens or subjects.

In all cases affecting ambassadors, other public ministers and consuls, and those in which a State shall be party, the Supreme Court shall have original jurisdiction. In all the other cases before mentioned, the Supreme Court shall have appellate jurisdiction, both as to law and fact, with such exceptions, and under such regulations, as the Congress shall make.

The trial of all crimes, except in cases of impeachment, shall be by jury; and such trial shall be held in the State where said crimes shall have been committed; but when not committed within any State, the trial shall be at such place or places as the Congress may by Law have directed.

Section 3 Treason against the United States shall consist only in levying war against them, or in adhering to their enemies, giving them aid and comfort. No person shall be convicted of treason unless on the testimony of two witnesses to the same overt act, or on confession in open court.

The Congress shall have power to declare the punishment of treason, but no attainder of treason shall work corruption of blood, or forfeiture except during the life of the person attainted.

Article IV

Section 1 Full faith and credit shall be given in each State to the public acts, records, and judicial proceedings of every other State. And the Congress may by general laws prescribe the manner in which such acts, records, and proceedings shall be proved, and the effect thereof.

Section 2 The citizens of each State shall be entitled to all privileges and immunities of citizens in the several States.

A person charged in any State with treason, felony, or other crime, who shall flee from justice, and be found in another State, shall on demand of the executive authority of the State from which he fled, be delivered up, to be removed to the State having jurisdiction of the crime.

No Person held to service or labor in one State, under the laws thereof, escaping into another, shall, in consequence of any law or regulation therein, be discharged from such service or labor, but shall be delivered up on claim of the party to whom such service or labor may be due.

Section 3 New States may be admitted by the Congress into this Union; but no new State shall be formed or erected within the jurisdiction of any other State; nor any State be formed by the junction of two or more States, or parts of States, without the consent of the legislatures of the States concerned as well as of the Congress.

The Congress shall have power to dispose of and make all needful rules and regulations respecting the territory or other property belonging to the United States; and nothing in this Constitution shall be so construed as to prejudice any claims of the United States, or of any particular State.

Section 4 The United States shall guarantee to every State in this Union a republican form of government, and shall protect each of them against invasion; and on application of the legislature, or of the executive (when the legislature cannot be convened), against domestic violence.

Article V

The Congress, whenever two-thirds of both houses shall deem it necessary, shall propose amendments to this Constitution, or, on the application of the legislatures of two-thirds of the several States, shall call a convention for proposing amendments, which, in either case, shall be valid to all intents and purposes, as part of this Constitution, when ratified by the legislatures of three-fourths of the several States, or by conventions in three-fourths thereof, as the one or the other mode of ratification may be proposed by the Congress; provided *that no amendments which may be made prior to the year one thousand eight hundred and eight shall in any manner affect the first and fourth clauses in the ninth section of the first article*; and that no State, without its consent, shall be deprived of its equal suffrage in the Senate.

Article VI

All debts contracted and engagements entered into, before the adoption of this Constitution, shall be as valid against the United States under this Constitution, as under the Confederation.

This Constitution, and the laws of the United States which shall be made in pursuance thereof; and all treaties made, or which shall be made, under the authority of the United States, shall be the supreme law of the land; and the judges in every State shall be bound thereby, anything in the Constitution or laws of any State to the contrary notwithstanding.

The Senators and Representatives before mentioned, and the members of the several State legislatures, and all executive and judicial officers, both of the United States and of the several States, shall be bound by oath or affirmation to support this Constitution; but no religious test shall ever be required as a qualification to any office or public trust under the United States.

Article VII

The ratification of the conventions of nine States shall be sufficient for the establishment of this Constitution between the States so ratifying the same.

Done in convention by the unanimous consent of the States present, the seventeenth day of September in the year of our Lord one thousand seven hundred and eighty-seven and of the Independence of the United States of America the twelfth. In witness whereof we have hereunto subscribed our names.

GEORGE WASHINGTON
President and Deputy from Virginia

New Hampshire
John Langdon
Nicholas Gilman

Massachusetts
Nathaniel Gorham
Rufus King

Connecticut
William Samuel Johnson
Roger Sherman

New York
Alexander Hamilton

New Jersey
William Livingston
David Brearley
William Paterson
Jonathan Dayton

Pennsylvania
Benjamin Franklin
Thomas Mifflin
Robert Morris
George Clymer
Thomas FitzSimons
Jared Ingersoll
James Wilson
Gouverneur Morris

Delaware
George Read
Gunning Bedford, Jr.
John Dickinson
Richard Bassett
Jacob Broom

Maryland
James McHenry
Daniel of St. Thomas
   Jenifer
Daniel Carroll

Virginia
John Blair
James Madison, Jr.

North Carolina
William Blount
Richard Dobbs Spaight
Hugh Williamson

South Carolina
John Rutledge
Charles Cotesworth
   Pinckney
Charles Pinckney
Pierce Butler

Georgia
William Few
Abraham Baldwin

AMENDMENTS TO THE CONSTITUTION WITH ANNOTATIONS
(including the six unratified amendments)

▶ *IN THEIR EFFORT TO GAIN Antifederalists' support for the Constitution, Federalists frequently pointed to the inclusion of Article 5, which provides an orderly method of amending the Constitution. In contrast, the Articles of Confederation, which were universally recognized as seriously flawed, offered no means of amendment. For their part, Antifederalists argued that the amendment process was so "intricate" that one might as easily roll "sixes an hundred times in succession" as change the Constitution.*

The system for amendment laid out in the Constitution requires that two-thirds of both houses of Congress agree to a proposed amendment, which must then be ratified by three-quarters of the legislatures of the states. Alternatively, an amendment may be proposed by a convention called by the legislatures of two-thirds of the states. Since 1789, members of Congress have proposed thousands of amendments. Besides the seventeen amendments added since 1789, only the six "unratified" ones included here were approved by two-thirds of both houses and sent to the states for ratification.

Among the many amendments that never made it out of Congress have been proposals to declare dueling, divorce, and interracial marriage unconstitutional as well as proposals to establish a national university, to acknowledge the sovereignty of Jesus Christ, and to prohibit any person from possessing wealth in excess of $10 million.*

Among the issues facing Americans today that might lead to constitutional amendment are efforts to balance the federal budget, to limit the number of terms elected officials may serve, to limit access to or prohibit abortion, to establish English as the official language of the United States, and to prohibit flag burning. None of these proposed amendments has yet garnered enough support in Congress to be sent to the states for ratification.

Although the first ten amendments to the Constitution are commonly known as the Bill of Rights, only Amendments 1–8 actually provide guarantees of individual rights. Amendments 9 and 10 deal with the structure of power within the constitutional system. The Bill of Rights was promised to appease Antifederalists

who refused to ratify the Constitution without guarantees of individual liberties and limitations to federal power. After studying more than two hundred amendments recommended by the ratifying conventions of the states, Federalist James Madison presented a list of seventeen to Congress, which used Madison's list as the foundation for the twelve amendments that were sent to the states for ratification. Ten of the twelve were adopted in 1791. The first on the list of twelve, known as the Reapportionment Amendment, was never adopted (see page A-13). The second proposed amendment was adopted in 1992 as Amendment 27 (see page A-24).

Amendment I

Congress shall make no law respecting an establishment of religion, or prohibiting the free exercise thereof; or abridging the freedom of speech, or of the press; or the right of the people peaceably to assemble, and to petition the government for a redress of grievances.

▶ *The First Amendment is a potent symbol for many Americans. Most are well aware of their rights to free speech, freedom of the press, and freedom of religion and their rights to assemble and to petition, even if they cannot cite the exact words of this amendment.*

The First Amendment guarantee of freedom of religion has two clauses: the "free exercise clause," which allows individuals to practice or not practice any religion, and the "establishment clause," which prevents the federal government from discriminating against or favoring any particular religion. This clause was designed to create what Thomas Jefferson referred to as "a wall of separation between church and state." In the 1960s, the Supreme Court ruled that the First Amendment prohibits prayer (see Engel v. Vitale, *online) and Bible reading in public schools.*

Although the rights to free speech and freedom of the press are established in the First Amendment, it was not until the twentieth century that the Supreme Court began to explore the full meaning of these guarantees. In 1919, the Court ruled in Schenck v. United States *(online) that the government could suppress free expression only where it could cite a "clear and present danger." In a*

**Richard B. Bernstein,* Amending America *(New York: Times Books, 1993), 177–81.*

decision that continues to raise controversies, the Court ruled in 1990, in Texas v. Johnson, that flag burning is a form of symbolic speech protected by the First Amendment.

Amendment II

A well-regulated militia being necessary to the security of a free State, the right of the people to keep and bear arms shall not be infringed.

◆ ◆ ◆

▶ Fear of a standing army under the control of a hostile government made the Second Amendment an important part of the Bill of Rights. Advocates of gun ownership claim that the amendment prevents the government from regulating firearms. Proponents of gun control argue that the amendment is designed only to protect the right of the states to maintain militia units.

In 1939, the Supreme Court ruled in United States v. Miller that the Second Amendment did not protect the right of an individual to own a sawed-off shotgun, which it argued was not ordinary militia equipment. Since then, the Supreme Court has refused to hear Second Amendment cases, while lower courts have upheld firearms regulations. Several justices currently on the bench seem to favor a narrow interpretation of the Second Amendment, which would allow gun control legislation. The controversy over the impact of the Second Amendment on gun owners and gun control legislation will certainly continue.

Amendment III

No soldier shall, in time of peace, be quartered in any house without the consent of the owner, nor in time of war, but in a manner to be prescribed by law.

◆ ◆ ◆

▶ The Third Amendment was extremely important to the framers of the Constitution, but today it is nearly forgotten. American colonists were especially outraged that they were forced to quarter British troops in the years before and during the American Revolution. The philosophy of the Third Amendment has been viewed by some justices and scholars as the foundation of the modern constitutional right to privacy. One example of this can be found in Justice William O. Douglas's 1965 opinion in Griswold v. Connecticut (online).

Amendment IV

The right of the people to be secure in their persons, houses, papers, and effects, against unreasonable searches and seizures, shall not be violated, and no warrants shall issue but upon probable cause, supported by oath or affirmation, and particularly describing the place to be searched, and the persons or things to be seized.

◆ ◆ ◆

▶ In the years before the Revolution, the houses, barns, stores, and warehouses of American colonists were ransacked by British authorities under "writs of assistance," or general warrants. The British, thus empowered, searched for seditious material or smuggled goods that could then be used as evidence against colonists who were charged with a crime only after the items were found. The first part of the Fourth Amendment protects citizens from "unreasonable" searches and seizures.

The Supreme Court has interpreted this protection as well as the words search and seizure in different ways at different times. At one time, the Court did not recognize electronic eavesdropping as a form of search and seizure, though it does today. At times, an "unreasonable" search has been almost any search carried out without a warrant, but in the two decades before 1969, the Court sometimes sanctioned warrantless searches that it considered reasonable based on "the total atmosphere of the case."

The second part of the Fourth Amendment defines the procedure for issuing a search warrant and states the requirement of "probable cause," which is generally viewed as evidence indicating that a suspect has committed an offense.

The Fourth Amendment has been controversial because the Court has sometimes excluded evidence that has been seized in violation of constitutional standards. The justification is that excluding such evidence deters violations of the amendment, but doing so may allow a guilty person to escape punishment.

Amendment V

No person shall be held to answer for a capital, or otherwise infamous crime, unless on a presentment or indictment of a grand jury, except in cases arising in the land or naval forces, or in the militia, when in actual service in time of war or public danger; nor shall any person be subject for the same offence to be twice put in jeopardy of life or limb; nor shall be compelled in any criminal case to be a witness against himself, nor be deprived of life, liberty, or property, without due process of law; nor shall private property be taken for public use without just compensation.

♦ ♦ ♦

▶ *The Fifth Amendment protects people against government authority in the prosecution of criminal offenses. It prohibits the state, first, from charging a person with a serious crime without a grand jury hearing to decide whether there is sufficient evidence to support the charge and, second, from charging a person with the same crime twice. The best-known aspect of the Fifth Amendment is that it prevents a person from being "compelled . . . to be a witness against himself." The last clause, the "takings clause," limits the power of the government to seize property.*

Although invoking the Fifth Amendment is popularly viewed as a confession of guilt, a person may be innocent yet still fear prosecution. For example, during the Red-baiting era of the late 1940s and 1950s, many people who had participated in legal activities that were associated with the Communist Party claimed the Fifth Amendment privilege rather than testify before the House Un-American Activities Committee because the mood of the times cast those activities in a negative light. Since "taking the Fifth" was viewed as an admission of guilt, those people often lost their jobs or became unemployable. (See chapter 26.) Nonetheless, the right to protect oneself against self-incrimination plays an important role in guarding against the collective power of the state.

Amendment VI

In all criminal prosecutions, the accused shall enjoy the right to a speedy and public trial, by an impartial jury of the State and district wherein the crime shall have been committed, which district shall have been previously ascertained by law, and to be informed of the nature and cause of the accusation; to be confronted with the witnesses against him; to have compulsory process for obtaining witnesses in his favor, and to have the assistance of counsel for his defence.

♦ ♦ ♦

▶ *The original Constitution put few limits on the government's power to investigate, prosecute, and punish crime. This process was of great concern to*

the early Americans, however, and of the twenty-eight rights specified in the first eight amendments, fifteen have to do with it. Seven rights are specified in the Sixth Amendment. These include the right to a speedy trial, a public trial, a jury trial, a notice of accusation, confrontation by opposing witnesses, testimony by favorable witnesses, and the assistance of counsel.

Although this amendment originally guaranteed these rights only in cases involving the federal government, the adoption of the Fourteenth Amendment began a process of applying the protections of the Bill of Rights to the states through court cases such as Gideon v. Wainwright *(1963) (online).*

Amendment VII

In suits at common law, where the value in controversy shall exceed twenty dollars, the right of trial by jury shall be preserved, and no fact tried by a jury shall be otherwise reexamined in any court of the United States, than according to the rules of the common law.

♦ ♦ ♦

▶ *This amendment guarantees people the same right to a trial by jury as was guaranteed by English common law in 1791. Under common law, in civil trials (those involving money damages) the role of the judge was to settle questions of law and that of the jury was to settle questions of fact. The amendment does not specify the size of the jury or its role in a trial, however. The Supreme Court has generally held that those issues be determined by English common law of 1791, which stated that a jury consists of twelve people, that a trial must be conducted before a judge who instructs the jury on the law and advises it on facts, and that a verdict must be unanimous.*

Amendment VIII

Excessive bail shall not be required, nor excessive fines imposed, nor cruel and unusual punishments inflicted.

♦ ♦ ♦

▶ *The language used to guarantee the three rights in this amendment was inspired by the English Bill of Rights of 1689. The Supreme Court has not had a lot to say about "excessive fines." In recent years, it has agreed that, despite the provision against "excessive bail," persons who are believed to be dangerous to others can be held without bail even before they have been convicted.*

Although opponents of the death penalty have not succeeded in using the Eighth Amendment to achieve the end of capital punishment, the clause regarding "cruel and unusual punishments" has been used to prohibit capital punishment in certain cases (see Furman v. Georgia, *1972, online) and to require improved conditions in prisons.*

Amendment IX

The enumeration in the Constitution, of certain rights, shall not be construed to deny or disparage others retained by the people.

♦ ♦ ♦

▶ *Some Federalists feared that inclusion of the Bill of Rights in the Constitution would allow later generations of interpreters to claim that the people had surrendered any rights not specifically enumerated there. To guard against this, Madison added language that became the Ninth Amendment. Interest in this heretofore largely ignored amendment revived in 1965 when it was used in a concurring opinion in* Griswold v. Connecticut *(online). While Justice William O. Douglas called on the Third Amendment to support the right to privacy in deciding that case, Justice Arthur Goldberg, in the concurring opinion, argued that the right to privacy regarding contraception was an unenumerated right that was protected by the Ninth Amendment.*

In 1980, the Court ruled that the right of the press to attend a public trial was protected by the Ninth Amendment. While some scholars argue that modern judges cannot identify the unenumerated rights that the framers were trying to protect, others argue that the Ninth Amendment should be read as providing a constitutional "presumption of liberty" that allows people to act in any way that does not violate the rights of others.

Amendment X

The powers not delegated to the United States by the Constitution, nor prohibited by it to the States, are reserved to the States respectively, or to the people.

♦ ♦ ♦

▶ *The Antifederalists were especially eager to see a "reserved powers clause" explicitly guaranteeing the states control over their internal affairs. Not surprisingly, the Tenth Amendment has been a frequent battleground in the struggle over states' rights and federal supremacy. Prior to the Civil War, the Democratic Republican*

Party and Jacksonian Democrats invoked the Tenth Amendment to prohibit the federal government from making decisions about whether people in individual states could own slaves. The Tenth Amendment was virtually suspended during Reconstruction following the Civil War. In 1883, however, the Supreme Court declared the Civil Rights Act of 1875 unconstitutional on the grounds that it violated the Tenth Amendment. Business interests also called on the amendment to block efforts at federal regulation.

The Court was inconsistent over the next several decades as it attempted to resolve the tension between the restrictions of the Tenth Amendment and the powers the Constitution granted to Congress to regulate interstate commerce and levy taxes. The Court upheld the Pure Food and Drug Act (1906), the Meat Inspection Acts (1906 and 1907), and the White Slave Traffic Act (1910), all of which affected the states, but struck down an act prohibiting interstate shipment of goods produced through child labor. Between 1934 and 1935, a number of New Deal programs created by Franklin D. Roosevelt were declared unconstitutional on the grounds that they violated the Tenth Amendment. (See chapter 24.) As Roosevelt appointees changed the composition of the Court, the Tenth Amendment was declared to have no substantive meaning. Generally, the amendment is held to protect the rights of states to regulate internal matters such as local government, education, commerce, labor, and business, as well as matters involving families such as marriage, divorce, and inheritance within the state.

Unratified Amendment

Reapportionment Amendment (proposed by Congress September 25, 1789, along with the Bill of Rights)
After the first enumeration required by the first article of the Constitution, there shall be one Representative for every thirty thousand, until the number shall amount to one hundred, after which the proportion shall be so regulated by Congress, that there shall be not less than one hundred Representatives, nor less than one Representative for every forty thousand persons, until the number of Representatives shall amount to two hundred; after which the proportion shall be so regulated by Congress, that there shall not be less than two hundred Representatives, nor more than one Representative for every fifty thousand persons.

▶ *If the Reapportionment Amendment had passed and remained in effect, the House of Representatives today would have more than 5,000 members rather than 435.*

Amendment XI

[Adopted 1798]

The judicial power of the United States shall not be construed to extend to any suit in law or equity, commenced or prosecuted against one of the United States by citizens of another State, or by citizens or subjects of any foreign state.

◆ ◆ ◆

▶ *In 1793, the Supreme Court ruled in favor of Alexander Chisholm, executor of the estate of a deceased South Carolina merchant. Chisholm was suing the state of Georgia because the merchant had never been paid for provisions he had supplied during the Revolution. Many regarded this Court decision as an error that violated the intent of the Constitution.*

Antifederalists had long feared a federal court system with the power to overrule a state court.

When the Constitution was being drafted, Federalists had assured worried Antifederalists that section 2 of Article 3, which allows federal courts to hear cases "between a State and citizens of another State," did not mean that the federal courts were authorized to hear suits against a state by citizens of another state or a foreign country. Antifederalists and many other Americans feared a powerful federal court system because they worried that it would become like the British courts of this period, which were accountable only to the monarch. Furthermore, Chisholm v. Georgia *prompted a series of suits against state governments by creditors and suppliers who had made loans during the war.*

In addition, state legislators and Congress feared that the shaky economies of the new states, as well as the country as a whole, would be destroyed, especially if loyalists who had fled to other countries sought reimbursement for land and property that had been seized. The day after the Supreme Court announced its decision, a resolution proposing the Eleventh Amendment, which overturned the decision in Chisholm v. Georgia, *was introduced in the U.S. Senate.*

Amendment XII

[Adopted 1804]

The electors shall meet in their respective States, and vote by ballot for President and Vice-President, one of whom, at least, shall not be an inhabitant of the same State with themselves; they shall name in their ballots the person voted for as President, and in distinct ballots the person voted for as Vice-President, and they shall make distinct lists of all persons voted for as President, and of all persons voted for as Vice-President, and of the number of votes for each, which lists they shall sign and certify, and transmit sealed to the seat of government of the United States, directed to the President of the Senate; — the President of the Senate shall, in the presence of the Senate and House of Representatives, open all the certificates and the votes shall then be counted; — the person having the greatest number of votes for President shall be the President, if such number be a majority of the whole number of electors appointed; and if no person have such majority, then from the persons having the highest numbers not exceeding three on the list of those voted for as President, the House of Representatives shall choose immediately, by ballot, the President. But in choosing the President, the votes shall be taken by States, the representation from each State having one vote; a quorum for this purpose shall consist of a member or members from two-thirds of the States, and a majority of all the States shall be necessary to a choice. And if the House of Representatives shall not choose a President whenever the right of choice shall devolve upon them, before the fourth day of March next following, then the Vice-President shall act as President, as in the case of the death or other constitutional disability of the President.

The person having the greatest number of votes as Vice-President shall be the Vice-President, if such number be a majority of the whole number of electors appointed; and if no person have a majority, then from the two highest numbers on the list the Senate shall choose the Vice-President; a quorum for the purpose shall consist of two-thirds of the whole number of Senators, and a majority of the whole number shall be necessary to a choice. But no person constitutionally ineligible to the office of President shall be eligible to that of Vice-President of the United States.

◆ ◆ ◆

▶ *The framers of the Constitution disliked political parties and assumed that none would ever form. Under the original system, electors chosen by the states would each vote for two candidates. The candidate who won the most votes would become president, while the person who won the second-highest number of votes would become vice president. Rivalries between Federalists and Antifederalists led to the formation of political parties, however, even before George Washington had left office. Though Washington was elected unanimously in 1789 and 1792, the elections of 1796 and 1800 were procedural disasters because of party maneuvering (see chapters 9 and 10). In 1796, Federalist John Adams was chosen as president, and his great rival, the Antifederalist Thomas Jefferson (whose party was called the Republican Party), became his vice president. In 1800, all the electors cast their two votes as one of two party blocs. Jefferson and his fellow Republican nominee, Aaron Burr, were tied with 73 votes each. The contest went to the House of Representatives, which finally elected Jefferson after 36 ballots. The Twelfth Amendment prevents these problems by requiring electors to vote separately for the president and vice president.*

Unratified Amendment

Titles of Nobility Amendment (proposed by Congress May 1, 1810)

If any citizen of the United States shall accept, claim, receive or retain any title of nobility or honor or shall, without the consent of Congress, accept and retain any present, pension, office or emolument of any kind whatever, from any emperor, king, prince or foreign power, such person shall cease to be a citizen of the United States, and shall be incapable of holding any office of trust or profit under them or either of them.

◆ ◆ ◆

▶ *This amendment would have extended Article 1, section 9, clause 8 of the Constitution, which prevents the awarding of titles by the United States and the acceptance of such awards from foreign powers without congressional consent. Historians speculate that general nervousness about the power of the emperor Napoleon, who was at that time extending France's empire throughout Europe, may have prompted the proposal. Though it fell one vote short of ratification, Congress and the American people thought the proposal had been ratified, and it was included in many nineteenth-century editions of the Constitution.*

The Civil War and Reconstruction Amendments (Thirteenth, Fourteenth, and Fifteenth Amendments)

▶ *In the four months between the election of Abraham Lincoln and his inauguration, more than 200 proposed*

constitutional amendments were presented to Congress as part of a desperate attempt to hold the rapidly dissolving Union together. Most of these were efforts to appease the southern states by protecting the right to own slaves or by disfranchising Black Americans through constitutional amendment. None were able to win the votes required from Congress to send them to the states. The relatively innocuous Corwin Amendment seemed to be the only hope for preserving the Union by amending the Constitution.

The northern victors in the Civil War tried to restructure the Constitution just as the war had restructured the nation. Yet they were often divided in their goals. Some wanted to end slavery; others hoped for social and economic equality regardless of race; others hoped that extending the power of the ballot box to former slaves would help create a new political order. The debates over the Thirteenth, Fourteenth, and Fifteenth Amendments were bitter. Few of those who fought for these changes were satisfied with the amendments themselves; fewer still were satisfied with their interpretation. Although the amendments put an end to the legal status of slavery, it took nearly a hundred years after the amendments' passage before most of the descendants of former slaves could begin to experience the economic, social, and political equality the amendments had been intended to provide.

Unratified Amendment

Corwin Amendment (proposed by Congress March 2, 1861)

No amendment shall be made to the Constitution which will authorize or give to Congress the power to abolish or interfere, within any State, with the domestic institutions thereof, including that of persons held to labor or service by the laws of said State.

◆ ◆ ◆

▶ *Following the election of Abraham Lincoln, Congress scrambled to try to prevent the secession of the slaveholding states. House member Thomas Corwin of Ohio proposed the "unamendable" amendment in the hope that by protecting slavery where it existed, Congress would keep the southern states in the Union. Lincoln indicated his support for the proposed amendment in his first inaugural address. Only Ohio and Maryland ratified the Corwin Amendment before it was forgotten.*

Amendment XIII

[Adopted 1865]

Section 1 Neither slavery nor involuntary servitude, except as a punishment for crime whereof the party shall have been duly convicted, shall exist within the United States, or any place subject to their jurisdiction.

Section 2 Congress shall have power to enforce this article by appropriate legislation.

♦ ♦ ♦

▶ *Although President Lincoln had abolished slavery in the Confederacy with the Emancipation Proclamation of 1863, abolitionists wanted to rid the entire country of slavery. The Thirteenth Amendment did this in a clear and straightforward manner. In February 1865, when the proposal was approved by the House, the gallery of the House was newly opened to Black Americans who had a chance at last to see their government at work. Passage of the proposal was greeted by wild cheers from the gallery as well as tears on the House floor, where congressional representatives openly embraced one another.*

The problem of ratification remained, however. The Union position was that the Confederate states were part of the country of thirty-six states. Therefore, twenty-seven states were needed to ratify the amendment. When Kentucky and Delaware rejected it, backers realized that without approval from at least four former Confederate states, the amendment would fail. Lincoln's successor, President Andrew Johnson, made ratification of the Thirteenth Amendment a condition for southern states to rejoin the Union. Under those terms, all the former Confederate states except Mississippi accepted the Thirteenth Amendment, and by the end of 1865 the amendment had become part of the Constitution and slavery had been prohibited in the United States.

Amendment XIV

[Adopted 1868]

Section 1 All persons born or naturalized in the United States, and subject to the jurisdiction thereof, are citizens of the United States and of the State wherein they reside. No State shall make or enforce any law which shall abridge the privileges or immunities of citizens of the United States; nor shall any State deprive any person of life, liberty, or property, without due process of law; nor deny to any person within its jurisdiction the equal protection of the laws.

Section 2 Representatives shall be appointed among the several States according to their respective numbers, counting the whole number of persons in each State, excluding Indians not taxed. But when the right to vote at any election for the choice of Electors for President and Vice-President of the United States, Representatives in Congress, the executive and judicial officers of a State, or the members of the legislature thereof, is denied to any of the male inhabitants of such State, being twenty-one years of age and citizens of the United States, or in any way abridged, except for participation in rebellion, or other crime, the basis of representation therein shall be reduced in the proportion which the number of such male citizens shall bear to the whole number of male citizens twenty-one years of age in such State.

Section 3 No person shall be a Senator or Representative in Congress, or Elector of President and Vice-President, or hold any office, civil or military, under the United States, or under any State, who, having previously taken an oath, as a member of Congress, or as an officer of the United States, or as a member of any State legislature, or as an executive or judicial officer of any State, to support the Constitution of the United States, shall have engaged in insurrection or rebellion against the same, or given aid or comfort to the enemies thereof. Congress may, by a vote of two-thirds of each house, remove such disability.

Section 4 The validity of the public debt of the United States, authorized by law, including debts incurred for payment of pensions and bounties for services in suppressing insurrection or rebellion, shall not be questioned. But neither the United States nor any State shall assume or pay any debt or obligation incurred in aid of insurrection or rebellion against the United States, or any claim for the loss or emancipation of any slave; but all such debts, obligations, and claims shall be held illegal and void.

Section 5 The Congress shall have power to enforce, by appropriate legislation, the provisions of this article.

♦ ♦ ♦

▶ *Without Lincoln's leadership in the reconstruction of the nation following the Civil War, it soon became clear that the Thirteenth Amendment needed additional constitutional support. Less than a year after Lincoln's assassination, Andrew Johnson was ready to bring the former Confederate states back into the Union with few changes in their governments or politics. Anxious Republicans drafted the Fourteenth Amendment to prevent that from happening. The most important provisions of this complex amendment made all native-born or naturalized persons American citizens and prohibited states from abridging the "privileges or immunities" of citizens; depriving them of "life, liberty, or property, without due process of law"; and denying them "equal protection of the laws." In essence, it made all former slaves citizens and protected the rights of all citizens against violation by their own state governments.*

As occurred in the case of the Thirteenth Amendment, former Confederate states were forced to ratify the amendment as a condition of representation in the House and the Senate. The intentions of the Fourteenth Amendment and the ways those intentions should be enforced have been the most debated point of constitutional history. The terms due process *and* equal protection *have been especially troublesome. Was the amendment designed to outlaw racial segregation? Or was the goal simply to prevent the leaders of the rebellious South from gaining political power?*

The framers of the Fourteenth Amendment hoped Article 2 would produce Black voters who would increase the power of the Republican Party. The federal government, however, never used its power to punish states for denying Black people their right to vote. Although the Fourteenth Amendment had an immediate impact in giving Black Americans citizenship, it did nothing to protect them from the vengeance of white people once Reconstruction ended. In the late nineteenth and early twentieth centuries, section 1 of the Fourteenth Amendment was often used to protect business interests and strike down laws protecting workers on the grounds that the rights of "persons" (that is, corporations) were protected by "due process." More recently, the Fourteenth Amendment has been used to justify school desegregation and affirmative action programs, as well as to dismantle such programs.

Amendment XV

[Adopted 1870]

Section 1 The right of citizens of the United States to vote shall not be denied or abridged by the United States or by any State on account of race, color, or previous condition of servitude.

Section 2 The Congress shall have power to enforce this article by appropriate legislation.

◆ ◆ ◆

▶ *The Fifteenth Amendment was the last major piece of Reconstruction legislation. While earlier Reconstruction acts had already required Black suffrage in the South, the Fifteenth Amendment extended Black voting rights to the entire nation. Some Republicans felt morally obligated to do away with the double standard between North and South since many northern states had stubbornly refused to enfranchise Black people. Others believed that the freedman's ballot required the extra protection of a constitutional amendment to shield it from white counterattack. But partisan advantage also played an important role in the amendment's passage, since Republicans hoped that by giving the ballot to northern Blacks, they could lessen their political vulnerability.*

Many women's rights advocates had fought for the amendment. They had felt betrayed by the inclusion of the word "male" in section 2 of the Fourteenth Amendment and were further angered when the proposed Fifteenth Amendment failed to prohibit denial of the right to vote on the grounds of sex as well as "race, color, or previous condition of servitude." In this amendment, for the first time, the federal government claimed the power to regulate the franchise, or vote. It was also the first time the Constitution placed limits on the power of the states to regulate access to the franchise. Although ratified in 1870, the amendment was not enforced until the twentieth century.

The Progressive Amendments (Sixteenth, Seventeenth, Eighteenth, and Nineteenth Amendments)

▶ *No amendments were added to the Constitution between the Civil War and the Progressive Era. America was changing, however, in fundamental ways. The rapid industrialization of the United States after the Civil War led to many social and economic problems. Hundreds of amendments were proposed, but none received enough support in Congress to be sent to the states. Some scholars believe that regional differences and rivalries were so strong during this period that it was almost impossible to gain a consensus on a constitutional amendment. During the Progressive Era, however, the Constitution was amended four times in seven years.*

Amendment XVI

[Adopted 1913]

The Congress shall have power to lay and collect taxes on incomes, from whatever source derived, without apportionment among the several States, and without regard to any census or enumeration.

◆ ◆ ◆

▶ *Until passage of the Sixteenth Amendment, most of the money used to run the federal government came from customs duties and taxes on specific items, such as liquor. During the Civil War, the federal government taxed incomes as an emergency measure. Pressure to enact an income tax came from those who were concerned about the growing gap between rich and poor in the United States. The Populist Party began campaigning for a graduated income tax in 1892, and support continued to grow. By 1909, thirty-three proposed income tax amendments had been presented in Congress, but lobbying by corporate and other special interests had defeated them all. In June 1909, the growing pressure for an income tax, which had been endorsed by Presidents Roosevelt and Taft, finally pushed an amendment through the Senate. The required thirty-six states had ratified the amendment by February 1913.*

Amendment XVII

[Adopted 1913]

Section 1 The Senate of the United States shall be composed of two Senators from each State, elected by the people thereof, for six years; and each Senator shall have one vote. The electors in each State shall have the qualifications requisite for electors of [voters for] the most numerous branch of the State legislatures.

Section 2 When vacancies happen in the representation of any State in the Senate, the executive authority of such State shall issue writs of election to fill such vacancies: Provided, that the Legislature of any State may empower the executive thereof to make temporary appointments until the people fill the vacancies by election as the Legislature may direct.

Section 3 This amendment shall not be so construed as to affect the election or term of any Senator chosen before it becomes valid as part of the Constitution.

◆ ◆ ◆

▶ *The framers of the Constitution saw the members of the House as the representatives of the people and the members of the Senate as the representatives of the states. Originally senators were to be chosen by the state legislators. According to reform advocates, however, the growth of private industry and transportation conglomerates during the Gilded Age had created a network of corruption in which wealth and power were exchanged for influence and votes in the Senate. For example, Senator Nelson Aldrich, who represented Rhode Island in the late nineteenth and early twentieth centuries, was known as "the senator from Standard Oil" because of his open support of special business interests.*

Efforts to amend the Constitution to allow direct election of senators had begun in 1826, but since any proposal had to be approved by the Senate, reform seemed impossible. Progressives tried to gain influence in the Senate by instituting party caucuses and primary elections, which gave citizens the chance to express their choice of a senator who could then be officially elected by the state legislature. By 1910, fourteen of the country's thirty senators received popular votes through a state primary before the state legislature made its selection. Despairing of getting a proposal through the Senate, supporters of a direct election amendment had begun in 1893 to seek a convention of representatives from two-thirds of the states to propose an amendment that could then be ratified. By 1905, thirty-one of forty-five states had endorsed such an amendment. Finally, in 1911, despite extraordinary opposition, a proposed amendment passed the Senate; by 1913, it had been ratified.

Amendment XVIII

[Adopted 1919; repealed 1933 by Amendment XXI]

Section 1 After one year from the ratification of this article the manufacture, sale, or transportation of intoxicating liquors within, the importation thereof into, or the exportation thereof from the United States and all territory subject to the jurisdiction thereof, for beverage purposes, is hereby prohibited.

Section 2 The Congress and the several States shall have concurrent power to enforce this article by appropriate legislation.

Section 3 This article shall be inoperative unless it shall have been ratified as an amendment to the Constitution by the legislatures of the several States, as provided by the Constitution, within seven years from the date of the submission thereof to the States by the Congress.

◆ ◆ ◆

▶ *The Prohibition Party, formed in 1869, began calling for a constitutional amendment to outlaw alcoholic beverages in 1872. A prohibition amendment was first proposed in the Senate in 1876 and was revived eighteen times before 1913. Between 1913 and 1919, another thirty-nine attempts were made to prohibit liquor in the United States through a constitutional amendment. Prohibition became a key element of the progressive agenda as reformers linked alcohol and drunkenness to numerous social problems, including the corruption of immigrant voters. While opponents of such an amendment argued that it was undemocratic, supporters claimed that their efforts had widespread public support. The admission of twelve "dry" western states to the Union in the early twentieth century and the spirit of sacrifice during World War I laid the groundwork for passage and ratification of the Eighteenth Amendment in 1919. Opponents added a time limit to the amendment in the hope that they could thus block ratification, but this effort failed. (See also Amendment XXI.)*

Amendment XIX

[Adopted 1920]

Section 1 The right of citizens of the United States to vote shall not be denied or abridged by the United States or by any State on account of sex.

Section 2 Congress shall have the power to enforce this article by appropriate legislation.

◆ ◆ ◆

▶ *Advocates of women's rights tried and failed to link woman suffrage to the Fourteenth and Fifteenth Amendments. Nonetheless, the effort for woman suffrage continued. Between 1878 and 1912, at least one and sometimes as many as four proposed amendments were introduced in Congress each year to grant women the right to vote. While over time women won very limited voting rights in some states, at both the state and federal levels opposition to an amendment for woman suffrage remained very strong. President Woodrow Wilson and other officials felt that the federal government should not interfere with the power of the states in this matter. Others worried that granting suffrage to women would*

encourage ethnic minorities to exercise their own right to vote. And many were concerned that giving women the vote would result in their abandoning traditional gender roles. In 1919, following a protracted and often bitter campaign of protest in which women went on hunger strikes and chained themselves to fences, an amendment was introduced with the backing of President Wilson. It narrowly passed the Senate (after efforts to limit the suffrage to white women failed) and was adopted in 1920 after Tennessee became the thirty-sixth state to ratify it.

Unratified Amendment

Child Labor Amendment (proposed by Congress June 2, 1924)

Section 1 The Congress shall have power to limit, regulate, and prohibit the labor of persons under eighteen years of age.

Section 2 The power of the several States is unimpaired by this article except that the operation of State laws shall be suspended to the extent necessary to give effect to legislation enacted by Congress.

◆ ◆ ◆

▶ *Throughout the late nineteenth and early twentieth centuries, alarm over the condition of child workers grew. Opponents of child labor argued that children worked in dangerous and unhealthy conditions, that they took jobs from adult workers, that they depressed wages in certain industries, and that states that allowed child labor had an economic advantage over those that did not. Defenders of child labor claimed that children provided needed income in many families, that working at a young age developed character, and that the effort to prohibit the practice constituted an invasion of family privacy.*

 In 1916, Congress passed a law that made it illegal to sell goods made by children through interstate commerce. The Supreme Court, however, ruled that the law violated the limits on the power of Congress to regulate interstate commerce. Congress then tried to penalize industries that used child labor by taxing such goods. This measure was also thrown out by the Court. In response, reformers set out to amend the Constitution. The proposed amendment was ratified by twenty-eight states, but by 1925, thirteen states had rejected it. Passage of the Fair Labor Standards Act in 1938, which was upheld by the Supreme Court in 1941, made the amendment irrelevant.

Amendment XX

[Adopted 1933]

Section 1 The terms of the President and Vice-President shall end at noon on the 20th day of January, and the terms of Senators and Representatives at noon on the 3rd day of January, of the years in which such terms would have ended if this article had not been ratified; and the terms of their successors shall then begin.

Section 2 The Congress shall assemble at least once in every year, and such meeting shall begin at noon on the 3rd day of January, unless they shall by law appoint a different day.

Section 3 If, at the time fixed for the beginning of the term of the President, the President-elect shall have died, the Vice-President-elect shall become President. If a President shall not have been chosen before the time fixed for the beginning of his term, or if the President-elect shall have failed to qualify, then the Vice-President-elect shall act as President until a President shall have qualified; and the Congress may by law provide for the case wherein neither a President-elect nor a Vice-President-elect shall have qualified, declaring who shall then act as President, or the manner in which one who is to act shall be selected, and such person shall act accordingly until a President or Vice-President shall have qualified.

Section 4 The Congress may by law provide for the case of the death of any of the persons from whom the House of Representatives may choose a President whenever the right of choice shall have devolved upon them, and for the case of the death of any of the persons from whom the Senate may choose a Vice-President whenever the right of choice shall have devolved upon them.

Section 5 Sections 1 and 2 shall take effect on the 15th day of October following the ratification of this article.

Section 6 This article shall be inoperative unless it shall have been ratified as an amendment to the Constitution by the Legislatures of three-fourths of the several States within seven years from the date of its submission.

◆ ◆ ◆

▶ *Until 1933, presidents took office on March 4. Since elections are held in early November and electoral votes are counted in mid-December, this meant that more than three months passed between the time a new president was elected and when he took office. Moving the inauguration to January shortened the transition period and allowed Congress to begin its term closer to the time of the president's inauguration. Although this seems like a minor change, an amendment was required because the Constitution specifies terms of office. This amendment also deals with questions of succession in the event that a president-elect or vice president-elect dies before assuming office. Section 3 also clarifies a method for resolving a deadlock in the electoral college.*

Amendment XXI

[Adopted 1933]

Section 1 The eighteenth article of amendment to the Constitution of the United States is hereby repealed.

Section 2 The transportation or importation into any State, Territory, or Possession of the United States for delivery or use therein of intoxicating liquors, in violation of the laws thereof, is hereby prohibited.

Section 3 This article shall be inoperative unless it shall have been ratified as an amendment to the Constitution by conventions in the several States, as provided in the Constitution, within seven years from the date of the submission thereof to the States by the Congress.

◆ ◆ ◆

▶ *Widespread violation of the Volstead Act, the law enacted to enforce prohibition, made the United States a nation of lawbreakers. Prohibition caused more problems than it solved by encouraging crime, bribery, and corruption. Further, a coalition of liquor and beer manufacturers, personal liberty advocates, and constitutional scholars joined forces to challenge the amendment. By 1929, thirty proposed repeal amendments had been introduced in Congress, and the Democratic Party made repeal part of its platform in the 1932 presidential campaign. The Twenty-First Amendment was proposed in February 1933 and ratified less than a year later. The failure of the effort to enforce prohibition through a constitutional amendment has often been cited by opponents of subsequent efforts to shape public virtue and private morality.*

Amendment XXII

[Adopted 1951]

Section 1 No person shall be elected to the office of the President more than twice, and no person who has held the office of President, or acted as President, for more than two years of a term to which some other person was elected President shall be elected to the office of President more than once. But this article shall not apply to any person holding the office of President when this Article was proposed by the Congress, and shall not prevent any person who may be holding the office of President, or acting as President, during the term within which this Article becomes operative from holding the office of President or acting as President during the remainder of such term.

Section 2 This article shall be inoperative unless it shall have been ratified as an amendment to the Constitution by the legislatures of three-fourths of the several States within seven years from the date of its submission to the States by the Congress.

◆ ◆ ◆

▶ *George Washington's refusal to seek a third term of office set a precedent that stood until 1912, when former president Theodore Roosevelt sought, without success, another term as an independent candidate. Democrat Franklin Roosevelt was the only president to seek and win a fourth term, though he did so amid great controversy. Roosevelt died in April 1945, a few months after the beginning of his fourth term. In 1946, Republicans won control of the House and the Senate, and early in 1947 a proposal for an amendment to limit future presidents to two four-year terms was offered to the states for ratification. Democratic critics of the Twenty-Second Amendment charged that it was a partisan posthumous jab at Roosevelt.*

    Since the Twenty-Second Amendment was adopted, however, the only presidents who might have been able to seek a third term, had it not existed, were Republicans Dwight Eisenhower, Ronald Reagan, and George W. Bush, and Democrat Bill Clinton. Since 1826, Congress has entertained 160 proposed amendments to limit the president to one six-year term. Such amendments have been backed by fifteen presidents, including Gerald Ford and Jimmy Carter.

Amendment XXIII

[Adopted 1961]

Section 1 The District constituting the seat of Government of the United States shall appoint in such manner as the Congress may direct: A number of electors of President and Vice-President equal to the whole number of Senators and Representatives in Congress to which the District would be entitled if it were a State, but in no event more than the least populous State; they shall be in addition to those appointed by the States, but they shall be considered for the purposes of the election of President and Vice-President, to be electors appointed by a State; and they shall meet in the District and perform such duties as provided by the twelfth article of amendment.

Section 2 The Congress shall have the power to enforce this article by appropriate legislation.

▶ *When Washington, D.C., was established as a federal district, no one expected that a significant number of people would make it their permanent and primary residence. A proposal to allow citizens of the district to vote in presidential elections was approved by Congress in June 1960 and was ratified on March 29, 1961.*

Amendment XXIV

[Adopted 1964]

Section 1 The right of citizens of the United States to vote in any primary or other election for President or Vice-President, for electors for President or Vice-President, or for Senator or Representative in Congress, shall not be denied or abridged by the United States or any State by reason of failure to pay any poll tax or other tax.

Section 2 The Congress shall have the power to enforce this article by appropriate legislation.

◆ ◆ ◆

▶ *In the colonial and Revolutionary eras, financial independence was seen as necessary to political independence, and the poll tax was used as a requirement for voting. By the twentieth century, however, the poll tax was used mostly to bar poor people, especially southern Blacks, from voting. While conservatives complained that the amendment interfered with states' rights, liberals thought that the amendment did not go far enough because it barred the poll tax only in national elections and not in state or local elections. The amendment was ratified in 1964, however, and two years later, the Supreme Court ruled that poll taxes in state and local elections also violated the equal protection clause of the Fourteenth Amendment.*

Amendment XXV

[Adopted 1967]

Section 1 In case of the removal of the President from office or of his death or resignation, the Vice-President shall become President.

Section 2 Whenever there is a vacancy in the office of the Vice-President, the President shall nominate a Vice-President who shall take office upon confirmation by a majority vote of both Houses of Congress.

Section 3 Whenever the President transmits to the President pro tempore of the Senate and the Speaker of the House of Representatives his written declaration that he is unable to discharge the powers and duties of his office, and until he transmits to them a written declaration to the contrary, such powers and duties shall be discharged by the Vice-President as Acting President.

Section 4 Whenever the Vice-President and a majority of either the principal officers of the executive departments or of such other body as Congress may by law provide, transmit to the President pro tempore of the Senate and the Speaker of the House of Representatives their written declaration that the President is unable to discharge the powers and duties of his office, the Vice-President shall immediately assume the powers and duties of the office as Acting President.

Thereafter, when the President transmits to the President pro tempore of the Senate and the Speaker of the House of Representatives his written declaration that no inability exists, he shall resume the powers and duties of his office unless the Vice-President and a majority of either the principal officers of the executive department[s] or of such other body as Congress may by law provide, transmit within four days to the President pro tempore of the Senate and the Speaker of the House of Representatives their written declaration that the President is unable to discharge the powers and duties of his office. Thereupon Congress shall decide the issue, assembling within forty-eight hours for that purpose if not in session. If the Congress, within twenty-one days after receipt of the latter written declaration, or, if Congress is not in session, within twenty-one days after Congress is required to assemble, determines by two-thirds vote of both Houses that the President is unable to discharge the powers and duties of his office, the Vice-President shall continue to discharge the same as Acting President; otherwise, the President shall resume the powers and duties of his office.

◆ ◆ ◆

▶ *The framers of the Constitution established the office of vice president because someone was needed to preside over the Senate. The first president to die in office was William Henry Harrison, in 1841. Vice President John Tyler had himself sworn in as president, setting a precedent that was followed when seven later presidents died in office. The assassination of President James A. Garfield in 1881 posed a new problem, however. After he was shot, the president was incapacitated for two months before he died; he was unable to lead the country, while his vice president, Chester A. Arthur, was unable to assume leadership. Efforts to resolve questions of succession in the event of a presidential disability thus began with the death of Garfield.*

In 1963, the assassination of President John F. Kennedy galvanized Congress to action. Vice President Lyndon Johnson was a chain-smoker with a history of heart trouble. According to the 1947 Presidential Succession Act, the two men who stood in line to succeed him were the seventy-two-year-old Speaker of the House and the eighty-six-year-old president of the Senate. There were serious concerns that any of these men might become incapacitated while serving as chief executive. The first time the Twenty-Fifth Amendment was used, however, was not in the case of presidential death or illness but during the Watergate crisis. When Vice President Spiro T. Agnew was forced to resign following allegations of bribery and tax violations, President Richard M. Nixon appointed House minority leader Gerald R. Ford vice president. Ford became president following Nixon's resignation eight months later and named Nelson A. Rockefeller as his vice president. Thus, for more than two years, the two highest offices in the country were held by people who had not been elected to them.

Amendment XXVI

[Adopted 1971]

Section 1 The right of citizens of the United States, who are eighteen years of age or older, to vote shall not be denied or abridged by the United States or by any State on account of age.

Section 2 The Congress shall have power to enforce this article by appropriate legislation.

◆ ◆ ◆

▶ *Efforts to lower the voting age from twenty-one to eighteen began during World War II. Recognizing that those who were old enough to fight a war should have some say in the government policies that involved them in the war, Presidents Eisenhower, Johnson, and Nixon endorsed the idea. In 1970, the combined pressure of the antiwar movement and the demographic pressure of the baby boom generation led to a Voting Rights Act lowering the voting age in federal, state, and local elections.*

In Oregon v. Mitchell (1970), the state of Oregon challenged the right of Congress to determine the age at which people could vote in state or local elections. The Supreme Court agreed with Oregon. Since the Voting Rights Act was ruled unconstitutional, the Constitution had to be amended to allow passage of a law that would lower the voting age. The amendment was ratified in a little more than three months, making it the most rapidly ratified amendment in U.S. history.

Unratified Amendment

Equal Rights Amendment (proposed by Congress March 22, 1972; seven-year deadline for ratification extended to June 30, 1982)

Section 1 Equality of rights under the law shall not be denied or abridged by the United States or by any State on account of sex.

Section 2 The Congress shall have the power to enforce, by appropriate legislation, the provisions of this article.

Section 3 This amendment shall take effect two years after the date of ratification.

◆ ◆ ◆

▶ *In 1923, soon after women had won the right to vote, Alice Paul, a leading activist in the woman suffrage movement, proposed an amendment requiring equal treatment of men and women. Opponents of the proposal argued that such an amendment would invalidate laws that protected women and would make women subject to the military draft. After the Civil Rights Act of 1964 was adopted, protective workplace legislation was removed anyway.*

The renewal of the women's movement, as a byproduct of the civil rights and antiwar movements, led to a revival of the Equal Rights Amendment (ERA) in Congress. Disagreements over language held up congressional passage of the proposed amendment, but on March 22, 1972, the Senate approved the ERA by a vote of 84 to 8, and it was sent to the states. Six states ratified the amendment within two days, and by the middle of 1973 the amendment seemed well on its way to adoption, with thirty of the needed thirty-eight states having ratified it. In the mid-1970s, however, a powerful "Stop ERA" campaign developed. The campaign portrayed the ERA as a threat to "family values" and traditional relationships between men and women. Although thirty-five states ultimately ratified the ERA, five of those state legislatures voted to rescind ratification, and the amendment was never adopted.

Unratified Amendment

D.C. Statehood Amendment (proposed by Congress August 22, 1978)

Section 1 For purposes of representation in the Congress, election of the President and Vice-President, and article V of this Constitution, the District constituting the seat of government of the United States shall be treated as though it were a State.

Section 2 The exercise of the rights and powers conferred under this article shall be by the people of the District constituting the seat of government, and as shall be provided by Congress.

Section 3 The twenty-third article of amendment to the Constitution of the United States is hereby repealed.

Section 4 This article shall be inoperative, unless it shall have been ratified as an amendment to the Constitution by the legislatures of three-fourths of the several states within seven years from the date of its submission.

◆ ◆ ◆

▶ *The 1961 ratification of the Twenty-Third Amendment, giving residents of the District of Columbia the right to vote for a president and vice president, inspired an effort to give residents of the district full voting rights. In 1966, President Lyndon Johnson appointed a mayor and city council; in 1971, D.C. residents were allowed to name a nonvoting delegate to the House; and in 1981, residents were allowed to elect the mayor and city council. Congress retained the right to overrule laws that might affect commuters, the height of federal buildings, and selection of judges and prosecutors. The district's nonvoting delegate to Congress, Walter Fauntroy, lobbied fiercely for a congressional amendment granting statehood to the district. In 1978, a proposed amendment was approved and sent to the states. A number of states quickly ratified the amendment, but, like the ERA, the D.C. Statehood Amendment ran into trouble.*

Opponents argued that section 2 created a separate category of "nominal" statehood. They argued that the federal district should be eliminated and that the territory should be reabsorbed into the state of Maryland. Although these theoretical arguments were strong, some scholars believe that racist attitudes toward the predominantly Black population of the city were also a factor leading to the defeat of the amendment.

Amendment XXVII

[Adopted 1992]

No law, varying the compensation for the services of the Senators and Representatives, shall take effect, until an election of Representatives shall have intervened.

◆ ◆ ◆

▶ *While the Twenty-Sixth Amendment was the most rapidly ratified amendment in U.S. history, the Twenty-Seventh Amendment had the longest journey to ratification. First proposed by James Madison in 1789 as part of the package that included the Bill of Rights, this amendment had been ratified by only six states by 1791. In 1873, however, it was ratified by Ohio to protest a massive retroactive salary increase by the federal government. Unlike later proposed amendments, this one came with no time limit on ratification.*

In the early 1980s, Gregory D. Watson, a University of Texas economics major, discovered the "lost" amendment and began a single-handed campaign to get state legislators to introduce it for ratification. In 1983, it was accepted by Maine. In 1984, it passed the Colorado legislature. Ratifications trickled in slowly until May 1992, when Michigan and New Jersey became the thirty-eighth and thirty-ninth states, respectively, to ratify. This amendment prevents members of Congress from raising their own salaries without giving voters a chance to vote them out of office before they can benefit from the raises.

GOVERNMENT AND DEMOGRAPHICS

Presidential Elections

Year	Candidates	Parties	Popular Vote	Percentage of Popular Vote	Electoral Vote	Percentage of Voter Participation
1789	**GEORGE WASHINGTON (VA)***				69	
	John Adams				34	
	Others				35	
1792	**GEORGE WASHINGTON (VA)**				132	
	John Adams				77	
	George Clinton				50	
	Others				5	
1796	**JOHN ADAMS (MA)**	Federalist			71	
	Thomas Jefferson	Democratic-Republican			68	
	Thomas Pinckney	Federalist			59	
	Aaron Burr	Dem.-Rep.			30	
	Others				48	
1800	**THOMAS JEFFERSON (VA)**	Dem.-Rep.			73	
	Aaron Burr	Dem.-Rep.			73	
	John Adams	Federalist			65	
	C. C. Pinckney	Federalist			64	
	John Jay	Federalist			1	
1804	**THOMAS JEFFERSON (VA)**	Dem.-Rep.			162	
	C. C. Pinckney	Federalist			14	
1808	**JAMES MADISON (VA)**	Dem.-Rep.			122	
	C. C. Pinckney	Federalist			47	
	George Clinton	Dem.-Rep.			6	
1812	**JAMES MADISON (VA)**	Dem.-Rep.			128	
	DeWitt Clinton	Federalist			89	
1816	**JAMES MONROE (VA)**	Dem.-Rep.			183	
	Rufus King	Federalist			34	
1820	**JAMES MONROE (VA)**	Dem.-Rep.			231	
	John Quincy Adams	Dem.-Rep.			1	
1824	**JOHN Q. ADAMS (MA)**	Dem.-Rep.	108,740	30.5	84	26.9
	Andrew Jackson	Dem.-Rep.	153,544	43.1	99	
	William H. Crawford	Dem.-Rep.	46,618	13.1	41	
	Henry Clay	Dem.-Rep.	47,136	13.2	37	

*State of residence when elected president.

Year	Candidates	Parties	Popular Vote	Percentage of Popular Vote	Electoral Vote	Percentage of Voter Participation
1828	**ANDREW JACKSON (TN)**	Dem.-Rep.	647,286	56.0	178	57.6
	John Quincy Adams	National Republican	508,064	44.0	83	
1832	**ANDREW JACKSON (TN)**	Dem.-Rep.	687,502	55.0	219	55.4
	Henry Clay	National Republican	530,189	42.4	49	
	John Floyd	Independent			11	
	William Wirt	Anti-Mason	33,108	2.6	7	
1836	**MARTIN VAN BUREN (NY)**	Democratic	765,483	50.9	170	57.8
	W. H. Harrison	Whig			73	
	Hugh L. White	Whig	739,795	49.1	26	
	Daniel Webster	Whig			14	
	W. P. Mangum	Independent			11	
1840	**WILLIAM H. HARRISON (OH)**	Whig	1,274,624	53.1	234	78.0
	Martin Van Buren	Democratic	1,127,781	46.9	60	
	J. G. Birney	Liberty	7,069		—	
1844	**JAMES K. POLK (TN)**	Democratic	1,338,464	49.6	170	78.9
	Henry Clay	Whig	1,300,097	48.1	105	
	J. G. Birney	Liberty	62,300	2.3	—	
1848	**ZACHARY TAYLOR (LA)**	Whig	1,360,099	47.4	163	72.7
	Lewis Cass	Democratic	1,220,544	42.5	127	
	Martin Van Buren	Free-Soil	291,263	10.1	—	
1852	**FRANKLIN PIERCE (NH)**	Democratic	1,601,274	50.9	254	69.6
	Winfield Scott	Whig	1,386,580	44.1	42	
	John P. Hale	Free-Soil	155,825	5.0	—	
1856	**JAMES BUCHANAN (PA)**	Democratic	1,836,169	45.3	174	78.9
	John C. Frémont	Republican	1,341,264	33.1	114	
	Millard Fillmore	American	874,534	21.6	8	
1860	**ABRAHAM LINCOLN (IL)**	Republican	1,866,452	39.9	180	81.2
	Stephen A. Douglas	Democratic	1,375,157	29.4	12	
	John C. Breckinridge	Democratic	847,953	18.1	72	
	John Bell	Union	590,631	12.6	39	
1864	**ABRAHAM LINCOLN (IL)**	Republican	2,213,665	55.1	212	73.8
	George B. McClellan	Democratic	1,805,237	44.9	21	
1868	**ULYSSES S. GRANT (IL)**	Republican	3,012,833	52.7	214	78.1
	Horatio Seymour	Democratic	2,703,249	47.3	80	
1872	**ULYSSES S. GRANT (IL)**	Republican	3,597,132	55.6	286	71.3
	Horace Greeley	Democratic; Liberal Republican	2,834,125	43.9	66	

Year	Candidates	Parties	Popular Vote	Percentage of Popular Vote	Electoral Vote	Percentage of Voter Participation
1876	**RUTHERFORD B. HAYES (OH)**	Republican	4,036,298	47.9	185	81.8
	Samuel J. Tilden	Democratic	4,288,590	51.0	184	
1880	**JAMES A. GARFIELD (OH)**	Republican	4,454,416	48.5	214	79.4
	Winfield S. Hancock	Democratic	4,444,952	48.1	155	
1884	**GROVER CLEVELAND (NY)**	Democratic	4,874,986	48.5	219	77.5
	James G. Blaine	Republican	4,851,981	48.3	182	
1888	**BENJAMIN HARRISON (IN)**	Republican	5,439,853	47.9	233	79.3
	Grover Cleveland	Democratic	5,540,309	48.6	168	
1892	**GROVER CLEVELAND (NY)**	Democratic	5,555,426	46.1	277	74.7
	Benjamin Harrison	Republican	5,182,690	43.0	145	
	James B. Weaver	People's	1,029,846	8.5	22	
1896	**WILLIAM McKINLEY (OH)**	Republican	7,104,779	51.1	271	79.3
	William J. Bryan	Democratic-People's	6,502,925	47.7	176	
1900	**WILLIAM McKINLEY (OH)**	Republican	7,207,923	51.7	292	73.2
	William J. Bryan	Dem.-Populist	6,358,133	45.5	155	
1904	**THEODORE ROOSEVELT (NY)**	Republican	7,623,486	57.9	336	65.2
	Alton B. Parker	Democratic	5,077,911	37.6	140	
	Eugene V. Debs	Socialist	402,283	3.0	—	
1908	**WILLIAM H. TAFT (OH)**	Republican	7,678,908	51.6	321	65.4
	William J. Bryan	Democratic	6,409,104	43.1	162	
	Eugene V. Debs	Socialist	420,793	2.8	—	
1912	**WOODROW WILSON (NJ)**	Democratic	6,293,454	41.9	435	58.8
	Theodore Roosevelt	Progressive	4,119,538	27.4	88	
	William H. Taft	Republican	3,484,980	23.2	8	
	Eugene V. Debs	Socialist	900,672	6.1	—	
1916	**WOODROW WILSON (NJ)**	Democratic	9,129,606	49.4	277	61.6
	Charles E. Hughes	Republican	8,538,221	46.2	254	
	A. L. Benson	Socialist	585,113	3.2	—	
1920	**WARREN G. HARDING (OH)**	Republican	16,143,407	60.5	404	49.2
	James M. Cox	Democratic	9,130,328	34.2	127	
	Eugene V. Debs	Socialist	919,799	3.4	—	
1924	**CALVIN COOLIDGE (MA)**	Republican	15,725,016	54.0	382	48.9
	John W. Davis	Democratic	8,386,503	28.8	136	
	Robert M. La Follette	Progressive	4,822,856	16.6	13	
1928	**HERBERT HOOVER (CA)**	Republican	21,391,381	57.4	444	56.9
	Alfred E. Smith	Democratic	15,016,443	40.3	87	
	Norman Thomas	Socialist	881,951	2.3	—	

Year	Candidates	Parties	Popular Vote	Percentage of Popular Vote	Electoral Vote	Percentage of Voter Participation
1932	**FRANKLIN D. ROOSEVELT (NY)**	Democratic	22,821,857	57.4	472	56.9
	Herbert Hoover	Republican	15,761,841	39.7	59	
	Norman Thomas	Socialist	881,951	2.2	—	
	William Z. Foster	Communist	102,991	0.3	—	
1936	**FRANKLIN D. ROOSEVELT (NY)**	Democratic	27,751,597	60.8	523	61.0
	Alfred M. Landon	Republican	16,679,583	36.5	8	
	William Lemke	Union	882,479	1.9	—	
1940	**FRANKLIN D. ROOSEVELT (NY)**	Democratic	27,244,160	54.8	449	62.5
	Wendell Willkie	Republican	22,305,198	44.8	82	
1944	**FRANKLIN D. ROOSEVELT (NY)**	Democratic	25,602,504	53.5	432	55.9
	Thomas E. Dewey	Republican	22,006,285	46.0	99	
1948	**HARRY S. TRUMAN (MO)**	Democratic	24,105,695	49.5	303	53.0
	Thomas E. Dewey	Republican	21,969,170	45.1	189	
	J. Strom Thurmond	States' Rights	1,169,021	2.4	39	
	Henry A. Wallace	Progressive	1,156,103	2.4	—	
1952	**DWIGHT D. EISENHOWER (NY)**	Republican	33,936,252	55.1	442	63.3
	Adlai Stevenson	Democratic	27,314,992	44.4	89	
1956	**DWIGHT D. EISENHOWER (NY)**	Republican	35,575,420	57.6	457	60.6
	Adlai Stevenson	Democratic	26,033,066	42.1	73	
	Other	—	—		1	
1960	**JOHN F. KENNEDY (MA)**	Democratic	34,227,096	49.9	303	62.8
	Richard M. Nixon	Republican	34,108,546	49.6	219	
	Other	—	—		15	
1964	**LYNDON B. JOHNSON (TX)**	Democratic	43,126,506	61.1	486	61.7
	Barry M. Goldwater	Republican	27,176,799	38.5	52	
1968	**RICHARD M. NIXON (NY)**	Republican	31,770,237	43.4	301	60.9
	Hubert H. Humphrey	Democratic	31,270,533	42.7	191	
	George Wallace	American Indep.	9,906,141	13.5	46	
1972	**RICHARD M. NIXON (NY)**	Republican	47,169,911	60.7	520	55.2
	George S. McGovern	Democratic	29,170,383	37.5	17	
	Other	—	—		1	
1976	**JIMMY CARTER (GA)**	Democratic	40,830,763	50.1	297	53.5
	Gerald R. Ford	Republican	39,147,793	48.0	240	
	Other	—	1,575,459	2.1	—	
1980	**RONALD REAGAN (CA)**	Republican	43,901,812	51.0	489	54.0
	Jimmy Carter	Democratic	35,483,820	41.0	49	
	John B. Anderson	Independent	5,719,722	7.0	—	
	Ed Clark	Libertarian	921,188	1.1	—	

Year	Candidates	Parties	Popular Vote	Percentage of Popular Vote	Electoral Vote	Percentage of Voter Participation
1984	**RONALD REAGAN (CA)**	Republican	54,455,075	59.0	525	53.1
	Walter Mondale	Democratic	37,577,185	41.0	13	
1988	**GEORGE H. W. BUSH (TX)**	Republican	47,946,422	54.0	426	50.2
	Michael S. Dukakis	Democratic	41,016,429	46.0	112	
1992	**WILLIAM J. CLINTON (AR)**	Democratic	44,909,889	43.0	370	55.9
	George H. W. Bush	Republican	39,104,545	37.5	168	
	H. Ross Perot	Independent	19,742,257	18.9	—	
1996	**WILLIAM J. CLINTON (AR)**	Democratic	47,401,185	49.2	379	49.0
	Robert Dole	Republican	39,197,469	40.7	159	
	H. Ross Perot	Independent	8,085,294	8.4	—	
2000	**GEORGE W. BUSH (TX)**	Republican	50,456,062	47.8	271	51.2
	Al Gore	Democratic	50,996,862	48.4	267	
	Ralph Nader	Green Party	2,858,843	2.7	—	
	Patrick J. Buchanan	Reform Party	438,760	0.4	—	
2004	**GEORGE W. BUSH (TX)**	Republican	61,872,711	50.7	286	60.3
	John F. Kerry	Democratic	58,894,584	48.3	252	
	Other	—	1,582,185	1.3	—	
2008	**BARACK OBAMA (IL)**	Democratic	69,456,897	52.9	365	56.8
	John McCain	Republican	59,934,314	45.7	173	
2012	**BARACK OBAMA (IL)**	Democratic	65,899,660	51.1	332	57.5
	Willard Mitt Romney	Republican	60,932,152	47.2	206	
2016	**DONALD J. TRUMP (NY)**	Republican	62,984,825	46.1	304**	61.4
	Hillary Clinton	Democratic	65,853,516	48.2	227	
	Gary Johnson	Libertarian	4,489,221	3.3	—	
	Jill Stein	Green Party	1,457,216	1.1	—	
2020	**JOSEPH R. BIDEN (DE)**	Democratic	81,268,924	51.3	306	66.8
	Donald J. Trump	Republican	74,223,234	46.9	232	
	Jo Jorgensen	Libertarian	1,865,724	1.2	—	
	Howie Hawkins	Green Party	405,035	0.3	—	

**There were seven electors who did not vote for either Trump or Clinton.

U.S. Supreme Court Justices

Name	Service	Appointed by	Name	Service	Appointed by
John Jay*	1789–1795	Washington	John M. Harlan	1877–1911	Hayes
James Wilson	1789–1798	Washington	William B. Woods	1880–1887	Hayes
John Blair	1789–1796	Washington	Stanley Matthews	1881–1889	Garfield
John Rutledge	1790–1791	Washington	Horace Gray	1882–1902	Arthur
William Cushing	1790–1810	Washington	Samuel Blatchford	1882–1893	Arthur
James Iredell	1790–1799	Washington	Lucius Q. C. Lamar	1888–1893	Cleveland
Thomas Johnson	1791–1793	Washington	**Melville W. Fuller**	1888–1910	Cleveland
William Paterson	1793–1806	Washington	David J. Brewer	1889–1910	B. Harrison
John Rutledge†	1795	Washington	Henry B. Brown	1890–1906	B. Harrison
Samuel Chase	1796–1811	Washington	George Shiras	1892–1903	B. Harrison
Oliver Ellsworth	1796–1799	Washington	Howell E. Jackson	1893–1895	B. Harrison
Bushrod Washington	1798–1829	J. Adams	Edward D. White	1894–1910	Cleveland
Alfred Moore	1799–1804	J. Adams	Rufus W. Peckham	1896–1909	Cleveland
John Marshall	1801–1835	J. Adams	Joseph McKenna	1898–1925	McKinley
William Johnson	1804–1834	Jefferson	Oliver W. Holmes	1902–1932	T. Roosevelt
Henry B. Livingston	1806–1823	Jefferson	William R. Day	1903–1922	T. Roosevelt
Thomas Todd	1807–1826	Jefferson	William H. Moody	1906–1910	T. Roosevelt
Gabriel Duval	1811–1836	Madison	Horace H. Lurton	1910–1914	Taft
Joseph Story	1811–1845	Madison	Charles E. Hughes	1910–1916	Taft
Smith Thompson	1823–1843	Monroe	Willis Van Devanter	1910–1937	Taft
Robert Trimble	1826–1828	J. Q. Adams	**Edward D. White**	1910–1921	Taft
John McLean	1829–1861	Jackson	Joseph R. Lamar	1911–1916	Taft
Henry Baldwin	1830–1844	Jackson	Mahlon Pitney	1912–1922	Taft
James M. Wayne	1835–1867	Jackson	James C. McReynolds	1914–1941	Wilson
Roger B. Taney	1836–1864	Jackson	Louis D. Brandeis	1916–1939	Wilson
Philip P. Barbour	1836–1841	Jackson	John H. Clarke	1916–1922	Wilson
John Catron	1837–1865	Van Buren	**William H. Taft**	1921–1930	Harding
John McKinley	1837–1852	Van Buren	George Sutherland	1922–1938	Harding
Peter V. Daniel	1841–1860	Van Buren	Pierce Butler	1923–1939	Harding
Samuel Nelson	1845–1872	Tyler	Edward T. Sanford	1923–1930	Harding
Levi Woodbury	1845–1851	Polk	Harlan F. Stone	1925–1941	Coolidge
Robert C. Grier	1846–1870	Polk	**Charles E. Hughes**	1930–1941	Hoover
Benjamin R. Curtis	1851–1857	Fillmore	Owen J. Roberts	1930–1945	Hoover
John A. Campbell	1853–1861	Pierce	Benjamin N. Cardozo	1932–1938	Hoover
Nathan Clifford	1858–1881	Buchanan	Hugo L. Black	1937–1971	F. Roosevelt
Noah H. Swayne	1862–1881	Lincoln	Stanley F. Reed	1938–1957	F. Roosevelt
Samuel F. Miller	1862–1890	Lincoln	Felix Frankfurter	1939–1962	F. Roosevelt
David Davis	1862–1877	Lincoln	William O. Douglas	1939–1975	F. Roosevelt
Stephen J. Field	1863–1897	Lincoln	Frank Murphy	1940–1949	F. Roosevelt
Salmon P. Chase	1864–1873	Lincoln	**Harlan F. Stone**	1941–1946	F. Roosevelt
William Strong	1870–1880	Grant	James F. Byrnes	1941–1942	F. Roosevelt
Joseph P. Bradley	1870–1892	Grant	Robert H. Jackson	1941–1954	F. Roosevelt
Ward Hunt	1873–1882	Grant	Wiley B. Rutledge	1943–1949	F. Roosevelt
Morrison R. Waite	1874–1888	Grant	Harold H. Burton	1945–1958	Truman

*Chief Justices appear in bold type.
†Acting Chief Justice; Senate refused to confirm appointment.

Name	Service	Appointed by	Name	Service	Appointed by
Frederick M. Vinson	1946–1953	Truman	Sandra Day O'Connor	1981–2006	Reagan
Tom C. Clark	1949–1967	Truman	**William H. Rehnquist**	1986–2005	Reagan
Sherman Minton	1949–1956	Truman	Antonin Scalia	1986–2016	Reagan
Earl Warren	1953–1969	Eisenhower	Anthony M. Kennedy	1988–2018	Reagan
John Marshall Harlan	1955–1971	Eisenhower	David H. Souter	1990–2009	G. H. W. Bush
William J. Brennan Jr.	1956–1990	Eisenhower	Clarence Thomas	1991–	G. H. W. Bush
Charles E. Whittaker	1957–1962	Eisenhower	Ruth Bader Ginsburg	1993–2020	Clinton
Potter Stewart	1958–1981	Eisenhower	Stephen G. Breyer	1994–2022	Clinton
Byron R. White	1962–1993	Kennedy	**John G. Roberts Jr.**	2005–	G. W. Bush
Arthur J. Goldberg	1962–1965	Kennedy	Samuel A. Alito Jr.	2006–	G. W. Bush
Abe Fortas	1965–1969	L. Johnson	Sonia Sotomayor	2009–	Obama
Thurgood Marshall	1967–1991	L. Johnson	Elena Kagan	2010–	Obama
Warren E. Burger	1969–1986	Nixon	Neil M. Gorsuch	2017–	Trump
Harry A. Blackmun	1970–1994	Nixon	Brett M. Kavanaugh	2018–	Trump
Lewis F. Powell Jr.	1972–1988	Nixon	Amy Coney Barrett	2020–	Trump
William H. Rehnquist	1972–1986	Nixon	Ketanji Brown Jackson	2022–	Biden
John Paul Stevens	1975–2010	Ford			

Admission of States to the Union

State	Date of Admission	State	Date of Admission
Delaware	December 7, 1787	Michigan	January 16, 1837
Pennsylvania	December 12, 1787	Florida	March 3, 1845
New Jersey	December 18, 1787	Texas	December 29, 1845
Georgia	January 2, 1788	Iowa	December 28, 1846
Connecticut	January 9, 1788	Wisconsin	May 29, 1848
Massachusetts	February 6, 1788	California	September 9, 1850
Maryland	April 28, 1788	Minnesota	May 11, 1858
South Carolina	May 23, 1788	Oregon	February 14, 1859
New Hampshire	June 21, 1788	Kansas	January 29, 1861
Virginia	June 25, 1788	West Virginia	June 19, 1863
New York	July 26, 1788	Nevada	October 31, 1864
North Carolina	November 21, 1789	Nebraska	March 1, 1867
Rhode Island	May 29, 1790	Colorado	August 1, 1876
Vermont	March 4, 1791	North Dakota	November 2, 1889
Kentucky	June 1, 1792	South Dakota	November 2, 1889
Tennessee	June 1, 1796	Montana	November 8, 1889
Ohio	March 1, 1803	Washington	November 11, 1889
Louisiana	April 30, 1812	Idaho	July 3, 1890
Indiana	December 11, 1816	Wyoming	July 10, 1890
Mississippi	December 10, 1817	Utah	January 4, 1896
Illinois	December 3, 1818	Oklahoma	November 16, 1907
Alabama	December 14, 1819	New Mexico	January 6, 1912
Maine	March 15, 1820	Arizona	February 14, 1912
Missouri	August 10, 1821	Alaska	January 3, 1959
Arkansas	June 15, 1836	Hawai'i	August 21, 1959

Population

FROM AN ESTIMATED 4,600 white inhabitants in 1630, the country's population grew to a total of more than 331 million in 2020. The U.S. census, first conducted in 1790, counted both free and enslaved Black people but did not include Native Americans until 1860. The years 1790 to 1900 saw the most rapid population growth, with an average increase of 25 percent to 35 percent per decade.

In addition to "natural" growth (birthrate exceeding death rate), immigration was also a factor in that rise, especially between 1840 and 1860, 1880 and 1890, and 1900 and 1910. The twentieth century witnessed slower growth, partly a result of 1920s immigration restrictions and a decline in the birthrate, especially during the depression era and the 1960s and 1970s.

Population Growth, 1630–2020

Year	Population	Percent Increase	Year	Population	Percent Increase
1630	4,600	—	1830	12,866,020	33.5
1640	26,600	473.3	1840	17,069,453	32.7
1650	50,400	89.1	1850	23,191,876	35.9
1660	75,100	49.0	1860	31,443,321	35.6
1670	111,900	49.1	1870	39,818,449	26.6
1680	151,500	35.4	1880	50,155,783	26.0
1690	210,400	38.9	1890	62,947,714	25.5
1700	250,900	19.3	1900	75,994,575	20.7
1710	331,700	32.2	1910	91,972,266	21.0
1720	466,200	40.5	1920	105,710,620	14.9
1730	629,400	35.0	1930	122,775,046	16.1
1740	905,600	43.9	1940	131,669,275	7.2
1750	1,170,800	30.0	1950	150,697,361	14.5
1760	1,593,600	36.1	1960	179,323,175	19.0
1770	2,148,100	34.8	1970	203,302,031	13.4
1780	2,780,400	29.4	1980	226,542,199	11.4
1790	3,929,214	41.3	1990	248,718,302	9.8
1800	5,308,483	35.1	2000	281,422,509	13.1
1810	7,239,881	36.4	2010	308,745,538	9.7
1820	9,638,453	33.1	2020	331,449,281	7.4

Sources: *Historical Statistics of the U.S.* (1960); *Historical Statistics of the U.S., Colonial Times to 1970* (1975); *Statistical Abstract of the U.S., 1996* (1996); *Statistical Abstract of the U.S., 2003* (2003); and United States Census (2010, 2020).

Major Trends in Immigration, 1820–2020

THE EXTENT AND NATURE of immigration to the United States have varied greatly over time. During the first major influx, between 1840 and 1860, newcomers hailed primarily from northern and western Europe. From 1880 to 1915, when rates soared even more dramatically, the profile changed, with 80 percent of the "new immigration" coming from central, eastern, and southern Europe. Following World War I, strict quotas reduced the flow considerably, with notable falloff during the Great Depression and World War II. The sources of immigration during the last half century have changed significantly, a result of geopolitical developments and

U.S. actions around the globe as well as changes to the immigration law in 1965 that dismantled the national quota system. Since then, the number of immigrants in the United States has more than quadrupled, with the majority of arrivals coming from Latin America, the Caribbean, and Asia. The 1980s and 1990s brought more immigrants to the United States than in any period since the early twentieth century. Latinos constituted the largest group, although more new arrivals after 2010 came from Asia. By 2020, immigrants were 13.7 percent of the U.S. population, slightly below the record high of 14.8 percent in 1890.

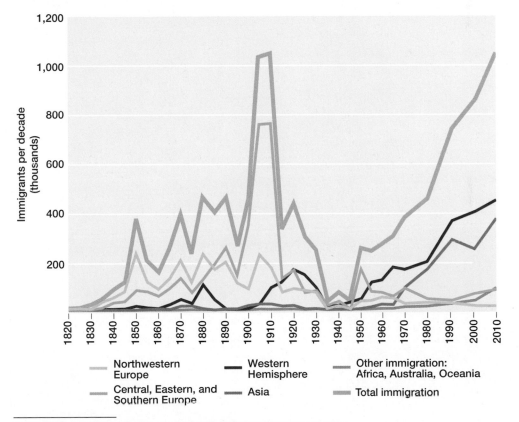

Data from *Historical Statistics of the U.S., Colonial Times to 1970* (1975); *Statistical Abstract of the U.S., 1999* (1999); *Statistical Abstract of the U.S., 2011* (2011); and Abby Budiman, "Key Findings about U.S. Immigrants," *Pew Research Center* (2020).

GLOSSARY

acquired immune deficiency syndrome (AIDS) Disease discovered in 1981 that initially affected gay men disproportionately and created a heavy death toll. The epidemic became politicized as activists charged the Reagan administration with neglect and demanded research and resources to fight the disease.

affirmative action Requirement that employers holding government contracts align their hiring with the available pool of qualified candidates. Established by executive order of President Johnson in 1965, the program was intended to counter centuries of discrimination against people of color and women.

Agent Orange Herbicide used extensively during the Vietnam War to destroy the hideouts and food supply of South Vietnamese insurgents. Its use was later linked to a wide range of illnesses that U.S. veterans and Vietnamese suffered after the war, including birth defects, cancer, and skin disorders.

Agricultural Adjustment Act (AAA) New Deal legislation passed in May 1933 aimed at cutting agricultural production and raising crop prices.

Al Qaeda Radical Islamic terrorist organization that sought to rid the Middle East of Western, and especially U.S., influence. The organization was responsible for a series of attacks on U.S. targets in the 1990s as well as the September 11, 2001, terrorist attacks.

American Expeditionary Force (AEF) U.S. armed forces under the command of General John Pershing who fought under a separate American command in Europe during World War I. They helped defeat Germany when they entered the conflict in full force in 1918.

American Federation of Labor (AFL) Organization created by Samuel Gompers in 1886 that coordinated the activities of craft unions throughout the United States. The AFL worked to achieve immediate benefits for skilled workers. Its narrow goals for unionism became popular after the Haymarket bombing.

American Indian Movement (AIM) Organization established in 1968 to address the problems Native Americans faced in U.S. cities, including poverty and police harassment. AIM pushed to end relocation and termination policies and helped Indians win greater control over their cultures and communities.

Americans with Disabilities Act (ADA) Act signed by President George H. W. Bush in 1990 that banned discrimination against the disabled. The law also required handicapped accessibility in public facilities and private businesses.

appeasement British strategy aimed at avoiding a war with Germany by not objecting to Hitler's territorial aggressions.

baby boom Surge in the American birthrate between 1945 and 1965, which peaked in 1957 with 4.3 million births. The baby boom both reflected and promoted Americans' postwar prosperity.

Battle of the Little Big Horn 1876 battle begun when American cavalry under George Armstrong Custer attacked an encampment of Native Americans from several tribes who refused to remove to a reservation. Indian warriors led by Crazy Horse and Sitting Bull annihilated the American soldiers, but their victory was short lived.

Battle of Midway June 3–6, 1942, naval battle in the Central Pacific in which American forces surprised and defeated the Japanese fleet planning to invade Midway Island.

Berlin Wall Barrier erected by East Germany in 1961 to halt the exodus of East Germans into West Berlin.

birth control movement Movement launched in 1915 by Margaret Sanger in New York City's Lower East Side. Birth control advocates hoped that contraception would alter social and political power relationships. By having fewer babies, the working class could constrict the size of the workforce, thus making possible higher wages, and at the same time refuse to provide soldiers for the world's armies.

black codes Laws passed by state governments in the South in 1865 and 1866 that sought to keep formerly enslaved people subordinate to whites peopl. At the core of the black codes lay the desire to force freedmen back to the plantations.

Black Hills Mountains in western South Dakota and northeast Wyoming that are sacred to the Lakota Sioux. In the 1868 Treaty of Fort Laramie, the United States guaranteed Indians control of the Black Hills, but it broke its promise after gold was discovered there in 1874.

Black Lives Matter Movement founded in 2013 in response to police shootings and killings of unarmed Black Americans. The organization protested racism in policing, advocated criminal justice reform, and called for the political and economic empowerment of Black people.

Black Power Collection of efforts in the 1960s and 1970s that emphasized Black self-determination and racial pride rather than integration. Black power advocates encouraged African Americans to assert control over their communities and institutions, with some rejecting the ethos of nonviolence.

Bolshevik Russian revolutionary. Bolsheviks forced Czar Nicholas II to abdicate and seized power in Russia in 1917. In a separate peace with Germany, the Bolshevik government withdrew Russia from World War I.

Bonus Marchers World War I veterans who marched on Washington, D.C., in 1932 to peacefully lobby for immediate payment of the pension ("bonus") promised them in 1924. President Herbert Hoover feared that the veterans would set off riots and sent the U.S. Army to evict them from the city.

bossism Pattern of urban political organization that arose in the late nineteenth century in which an often corrupt "boss" maintains an inordinate level of power through command of a political machine that distributes services to its constituents.

Boxer uprising Uprising in China led by the Boxers, an antiforeign society, in which 30,000 Chinese converts and 250 foreign Christians were killed. An international force rescued foreigners in Beijing, and European powers imposed the humiliating Boxer Protocol on China in 1901.

***bracero* program** Program begun in 1942 permitting Mexicans temporary entrance into the United States as agricultural laborers. Until the program ended in 1964, more than 100,000 Mexicans entered the United States each year.

Brown v. Board of Education 1954 Supreme Court ruling that overturned the "separate but equal" precedent established in *Plessy v. Ferguson* in 1896. The Court declared that separate educational facilities were inherently unequal and thus violated the Fourteenth Amendment.

Camp David accords Agreements between Egypt and Israel reached at 1979 talks hosted by President Carter at Camp David. In the accords, Egypt became the first Arab state to recognize Israel, and Israel agreed to gradual withdrawal from the Sinai Peninsula.

Carlisle Indian School Institution established in Pennsylvania in 1879 to educate and assimilate Native Americans. It pioneered the "outing system," in which Indian students were sent to live with white families in order to accelerate acculturation.

carpetbaggers Southerners' pejorative term for northern migrants who sought opportunity in the South after the Civil War. Northern migrants formed an important part of the southern Republican Party.

Central Intelligence Agency (CIA) Agency created by the National Security Act of 1947 to expand the government's espionage capacities. The CIA attempted to thwart communism through covert activities, including propaganda, sabotage, economic warfare, and support for anti-Communist forces around the world.

Chicano movement Mobilization of Mexican Americans in the 1960s and 1970s to fight for civil rights, economic justice, and political power and to combat police brutality. The movement sought to improve the lives of migrant farmworkers and to end discrimination in employment and education.

Chinese Exclusion Act 1882 law that effectively barred Chinese immigration and set a precedent for further immigration restrictions. The Chinese population in America dropped sharply as a result of the passage of the act, which was fueled by racial and cultural animosities.

Citizens United v. Federal Elections Commission Controversial Supreme Court decision of 2010 that ruled federal regulation of election campaign financing was a restriction on free speech as protected by the First Amendment. The ruling led to large political contributions by corporations and to the explosion of political action committees.

Civil Rights Act of 1866 Legislation passed by Congress in 1866 that nullified the black codes and affirmed that Black Americans should have equal benefit of the law. President Andrew Johnson vetoed this expansion of Black rights and federal authority, but Congress later overrode his veto.

Civil Rights Act of 1964 Law that made discrimination in employment, education, and public accommodations illegal. It was the strongest such measure since Reconstruction and included a ban on sex discrimination in employment.

civil service reform Effort in the 1880s to end the spoils system and reduce government corruption. The Pendleton Civil Service Act of 1883 created the Civil Service Commission to award government jobs under a merit system that required examinations for office and made it impossible to remove jobholders for political reasons.

Civilian Conservation Corps (CCC) Federal relief program established in March 1933 that provided jobs on conservation projects to millions of unemployed young men and a token number of women.

Clean Air Act Environmental legislation signed in 1990 by President George H. W. Bush. The act was the strongest and most comprehensive environmental law in the nation's history.

Comanchería Native American empire based on trade in horses, hides, guns, and captives that stretched from the Canadian plains to Mexico in the eighteenth century. By 1865, fewer than five thousand Comanches lived in the empire, which ranged from west Texas north to Oklahoma.

Compromise of 1877 Informal agreement in which Democrats agreed not to block Rutherford Hayes's inauguration and to deal fairly with freedmen. In return, Hayes vowed not to use the army to uphold the remaining Republican regimes in the South and to provide the South with substantial federal subsidies for railroads. The compromise brought the Reconstruction era to an end.

Comstock Lode Silver ore deposit discovered in 1859 in Nevada. Discovery of the Comstock Lode touched off a mining rush that brought a diverse population into the region and led to the establishment of a number of boomtowns, including Virginia City, Nevada.

Congress of Industrial Organizations (CIO) Coalition of mostly unskilled workers formed in 1935 that mobilized massive union organizing drives in major industries.

containment Foreign policy strategy that committed the United States to resisting the expansion of the Soviet Union and communism during the Cold War.

court-packing plan Law proposed by Franklin Roosevelt to add one new Supreme Court justice for each existing judge who had served for ten years and who was over the age of seventy.

COVID-19 pandemic Life-threatening respiratory illness caused by a new coronavirus, SARS-CoV-2, identified in 2019. The highly contagious virus and its variants sparked a global pandemic, causing millions of deaths and upending economies, schools, and daily life around the world.

Coxey's army Unemployed men who marched to Washington, D.C., in 1894 to urge Congress to enact a public works program to end unemployment. Jacob S. Coxey of Ohio led the most publicized contingent. The movement failed to force federal relief legislation.

Cripple Creek miners' strike of 1894 Strike led by the Western Federation of Miners in response to an attempt to lengthen their workday to ten hours. With the support of local businessmen and the Populist governor of Colorado, the miners successfully maintained an eight-hour day.

Cuban missile crisis 1962 standoff between the Soviet Union and the United States after the Soviets attempted to create a nuclear outpost in Cuba. In a negotiated settlement, the Soviet Union agreed to remove its missiles from Cuba, and the United States agreed to remove its missiles from Turkey.

cult of domesticity Nineteenth-century belief that women's place was in the home, where they should create havens for their families. This sentimentalized ideal led to an increase in the hiring of domestic servants and freed white middle-class women to spend time in pursuits outside the home.

D-Day The Allied invasion of northern France on June 6, 1944, opening a second front against the Germans.

Dawes Allotment Act 1887 law that divided up reservations and allotted parcels of land to individual Native Americans as private property. In the end, the U.S. government sold almost two-thirds of "surplus" Indian land to white settlers. The Dawes Act dealt a crippling blow to traditional tribal culture.

Democrats Political party that evolved out of the Democratic Republicans after 1834. Strongest in the South and West, the Democrats embraced Andrew Jackson's vision of limited government, expanded political participation for white men, and the promotion of an ethic of individualism.

Department of Homeland Security Federal agency created in 2002 in response to the 9/11 attacks. In an effort to better coordinate domestic security, the department combined twenty-two existing agencies.

détente Term (from the French for "loosening") used for the easing of conflict between the United States and the Soviet Union during the Nixon administration by focusing on issues of common concern, such as arms control and trade.

Dixiecrats Group of southern Democrats who defected from their party during the 1948 convention when it passed a liberal civil rights plank, suggesting the difficulty the Democratic Party would have in keeping both white southerners and Black Americans in its ranks.

domino theory Theory of containment expressed by President Eisenhower in the context of Vietnam. Using the metaphor of dominoes, he warned that the fall of one government to communism would lead neighboring countries to fall as well.

Double V campaign World War II campaign in America to attack racism at home and abroad.

Earned Income Tax Credit (EITC) Federal antipoverty program initiated in 1975 and expanded significantly by President Clinton in 1993. The program assisted the working poor by giving tax breaks to low-income, full-time workers or a subsidy to those who owed no taxes.

Eighteenth Amendment (prohibition) Constitutional amendment banning the manufacture, transportation, and sale of alcohol. Congress passed the amendment in December 1917, and it went into effect in January 1920.

Ellis Island Immigration facility opened in 1892 in New York Harbor that processed new immigrants coming into New York City. In the late nineteenth century, some 75 percent of European immigrants to America came through New York.

Environmental Protection Agency (EPA) Federal agency created by President Nixon in 1970 to enforce environmental laws, conduct environmental research, and reduce health and environmental risks from pollutants.

Equal Rights Amendment (ERA) Constitutional amendment passed by Congress in 1972 requiring equal treatment of men and women under federal and state laws. Facing fierce opposition from the New Right and the Republican Party, the ERA was defeated as time ran out for state ratification in 1982.

Fair Deal President Truman's domestic agenda, little of it enacted, for extending the New Deal through universal health care, federally protected civil rights, public assistance for housing, and federal aid to education.

Family and Medical Leave Act (FMLA) Law passed in 1993 and signed by President Bill Clinton that mandated unpaid leave for childbirth, adoption, and family medical emergencies for workers in large companies.

family economy Economic contributions of multiple members of a household that were necessary to the survival of the family. From the late nineteenth century into the twentieth, many working-class families depended on the wages of all family members, regardless of sex or age.

Farmers' Alliance Movement to form local organizations to advance farmers' collective interests that gained wide popularity in the 1880s. Over time, farmers' groups consolidated into the Northwestern Farmers' Alliance and the Southern Farmers' Alliance. In 1892, the Farmers' Alliance gave birth to the People's Party.

Federal Deposit Insurance Corporation (FDIC) Federal agency that guaranteed the government would reimburse bank depositors if their banks failed.

fee-based governance System where public employees receive a percentage of fees, taxes, bounties, and subsidies collected. For example, postmasters got a small percentage on the stamps they sold.

Fifteenth Amendment Constitutional amendment passed in February 1869 prohibiting states from depriving any citizen of the right to vote because of "race, color, or previous condition of servitude." It extended Black suffrage nationwide.

finance capitalism Investment sponsored by banks and bankers that typified the American business scene at the end of the nineteenth century. After the panic of 1893, bankers stepped in and reorganized major industries to stabilize them, leaving power concentrated in the hands of a few influential capitalists.

fireside chats Series of informal radio addresses Franklin Roosevelt made to the nation in which he explained New Deal initiatives.

first transcontinental railroad Railroad completed in 1869 that was the first to span the North American continent. Built in large part by Chinese laborers in the West, this railroad, followed soon by others, opened access to new areas in the West, fueling land speculation and actively recruiting settlers.

Five-Power Naval Treaty of 1922 Treaty that committed Britain, France, Japan, Italy, and the United States to a reduction of naval forces, producing the world's greatest success in disarmament up to that time.

Fourteen Points Woodrow Wilson's plan, proposed in 1918, to create a new democratic world order with lasting peace. Wilson's plan affirmed basic liberal ideals, supported the right to self-determination, and called for the creation of a League of Nations. Wilson compromised on his plan at the 1919 Paris peace conference, and the U.S. Senate refused to ratify the resulting treaty.

Fourteenth Amendment Constitutional amendment passed in 1866 that made all native-born or naturalized persons U.S. citizens and prohibited states from abridging the rights of national citizens. The amendment hoped to provide a guarantee of equality before the law for Black citizens.

free Black An African American person who was not enslaved. State legislatures stemmed the growth of the free Black population and shrank the liberty of free Black people.

free silver Term used in the late nineteenth century by those who that advocated minting silver dollars in addition to supporting the gold standard and the paper currency backed by gold. Poor farmers from the West and South hoped this would result in inflation, effectively providing them with debt relief. Western silver barons wanted the government to buy silver and mint silver dollars, thereby raising the price of silver.

Freedmen's Bureau Government organization created in March 1865 to distribute food and clothing to destitute southerners and to ease the transition from enslaved to free person.

Ghost Dance Religion founded in 1889 by Paiute shaman Wovoka. It combined elements of Christianity and traditional Native American religion and served as a nonviolent form of resistance for Indians in the late nineteenth century. The Ghost Dance frightened white people and was violently suppressed.

GI Bill of Rights Legislation passed in 1944 authorizing the government to provide World War II veterans with funds for education, housing, and health care, as well as loans to start businesses and buy homes.

Gilded Age Period of enormous economic growth and ostentatious displays of wealth during the last quarter of the nineteenth century. Industrialization dramatically changed U.S. society and created a newly dominant group of rich entrepreneurs and an impoverished working class.

global migration Movement of populations across large distances such as oceans and continents. In the late nineteenth century, large-scale immigration from southern and eastern Europe into the United States contributed to the growth of cities and changes in American demographics.

good neighbor policy Foreign policy announced by Roosevelt in 1933 that promised the United States would not interfere in the internal or external affairs of another country.

gospel of wealth The idea that the financially successful should use their wisdom, experience, and wealth to help the poor. Andrew Carnegie promoted this view in an 1889 essay in which he maintained that the wealthy should serve as stewards of society as a whole.

Great Migration Movement of a half million Black people from their homes in the South to find economic and social opportunity in the North, spurred by acute labor shortages in northern industrial cities during World War I.

Great Railroad Strike A violent multicity strike that began in 1877 with West Virginia railroad brakemen who protested against sharp wage reductions and quickly spread to include roughly 600,000 workers. President Rutherford B. Hayes used federal troops to break the strike. Following the strike's failure, union membership surged.

Great Recession Financial crisis that struck in late 2007 and led to the worst U.S. depression since the 1930s. The crisis was rooted in financial deregulation and predatory lending practices. Housing values and then banking and lending collapsed, prompting the federal government to inject cash into the economy and enact a massive bailout of financial institutions.

Haymarket bombing May 4, 1886, conflict in which both workers and policemen were killed or wounded during a labor demonstration in Chicago. The violence began when someone threw a bomb into the ranks of police at the gathering. The incident created a backlash against labor activism.

Hernandez v. Texas 1954 Supreme Court decision ruling that the systematic exclusion of Mexican Americans from juries violated the constitutional guarantee of equal protection.

Holocaust German genocide of Europe's Jews, along with others the Nazis deemed "undesirable."

Homestead Act of 1862 Act that promised 160 acres in the trans-Mississippi West free to any citizen or prospective citizen who settled on the land for five years. The act spurred American settlement of the West. Altogether, nearly one-tenth of the United States was granted to settlers.

Homestead lockout 1892 lockout of workers at the Homestead, Pennsylvania, steel mill after Andrew Carnegie refused to renew the union contract and workers prepared to strike. Union supporters attacked the Pinkerton National Detective Agency guards hired to protect the mill, but the National Guard soon broke the strike.

House Un-American Activities Committee (HUAC) Congressional committee prominent during the early years of the Cold War that investigated Americans for disloyalty to the government or associations with Communists.

Housing Act of 1949 Law authorizing the construction of 810,000 units of government housing. This landmark effort marked the first significant commitment of the federal government to meet the housing needs of the poor.

Hurricane Katrina Hurricane that devastated the coasts of Alabama, Louisiana, and Mississippi in 2005, including the city of New Orleans. The storm displaced more than one million residents of the Gulf Coast region, exposing the vulnerability of poor and Black residents and severe weaknesses in the U.S. response to natural disasters.

Indian Relocation Program Federal initiative launched in 1948 to relocate Indians on reservations to cities and provide housing assistance, job training, and medical care. More than 100,000 Native Americans would take part, although a good number returned to reservation life and others struggled with urban poverty.

Industrial Workers of the World (IWW) Umbrella union and radical political group founded in 1905 that was dedicated to organizing unskilled workers to oppose capitalism. Nicknamed the Wobblies, the IWW advocated direct action by workers, including sabotage and general strikes, in hopes of triggering a widespread workers' uprising.

intermediate-range nuclear forces (INF) agreement Nuclear disarmament agreement reached between the United States and the Soviet Union in 1987, signifying a major thaw in the Cold War. The treaty eliminated all short- and medium-range missiles from Europe and provided for on-site inspection.

internment camps Makeshift prison camps to which Americans of Japanese descent were sent as a result of Franklin Roosevelt's Executive Order 9066, issued in February 1942.

Interstate Commerce Commission (ICC) Federal regulatory agency designed to oversee the railroad industry. Congress created it through the 1887 Interstate Commerce Act after the Supreme Court decision in *Wabash v. Illinois* (1886) effectively denied states the right to regulate railroads. The ICC proved weak and did not immediately pose a threat to the industry.

Interstate Highway and Defense System Act of 1956 Law authorizing the construction of a national highway system. Promoted as essential to national defense and a spur to economic growth, the act accelerated the movement of people and goods and changed the nature of American communities.

Iran-Contra scandal Reagan administration scandal brought to light in 1986 involving the sale of arms to Iran in exchange for its efforts to secure the release of hostages held in Lebanon and the secret redirection of the proceeds of those sales to the Nicaraguan Contras.

Iran hostage crisis Crisis that began in 1979 after the deposed shah of Iran was allowed into the United States following the Iranian revolution. Iranians broke into the U.S. embassy in Teheran and took sixty-six Americans hostage, a crisis that lasted 444 days and contributed to Carter losing his bid for reelection in 1980.

Iraq War Preemptive war launched by George W. Bush's administration in 2003 in Iraq, despite the absence of UN approval. Coalition forces won an easy victory, but chaos marked the long U.S. occupation that followed.

iron curtain Metaphor coined by Winston Churchill in 1946 to describe the line dividing Soviet-controlled countries in Eastern Europe from democratic nations in Western Europe.

Jim Crow System of racial segregation in the South lasting from after the Civil War into the twentieth century. Jim Crow laws segregated Black people in public facilities such as trains and streetcars, curtailed their voting rights, and denied other basic civil rights.

Johnson-Reed Act 1924 law that severely restricted immigration to the United States to no more than 161,000 a year, with quotas for each European nation. The racist restrictions were designed to staunch the flow of immigrants from southern and eastern Europe and from Asia.

Knights of Labor The first mass organization of America's working class. Founded in 1869, the Knights of

Labor attempted to bridge the boundaries of ethnicity, gender, ideology, race, and occupation to build a "universal brotherhood" of all workers.

Korean War Conflict between North Korean forces supported by China and the Soviet Union and South Korean and U.S.-led United Nations forces over the country's partition. The war, lasting from 1950 to 1953, was the first instance of the United States sending troops into battle to implement containment.

Ku Klux Klan Secret society that first thwarted Black freedom after the Civil War but was reborn in 1915 to fight against perceived threats posed by Black people, immigrants, radicals, feminists, Catholics, and Jews. The new Klan spread well beyond the South in the 1920s.

League of Nations International organization proposed in Woodrow Wilson's Fourteen Points that was designed to secure enduring peace and collective security through peaceful means. The U.S. Senate refused to ratify the Treaty of Versailles, and the United States never became a member of the league.

Lend-Lease Act Legislation in 1941 that enabled Britain to obtain arms from the United States without cash but with the promise to reimburse the United States when the war ended.

Lusitania British passenger liner torpedoed by a German U-boat on May 7, 1915. The attack killed 1,198 passengers, including 128 Americans, challenging American neutrality and moving the United States a step closer to entering World War I.

Manhattan Project Top-secret project authorized by Franklin Roosevelt in 1942 to develop an atomic bomb.

Marshall Plan Aid program begun in 1948 to help European economies recover from World War II. By 1953, the United States had provided $13 billion to sixteen Western European nations, boosting its own economy in the process.

McCarthyism Name given to Senator Joseph McCarthy's campaign in the early 1950s to expose Communist infiltration of the U.S. government. Many of those accused of Communist sympathies were blacklisted or lost their jobs, although most did not in fact belong to the Communist Party.

Medicare and Medicaid Federal support for health care enacted as part of Lyndon Johnson's Great Society. Medicare provided older Americans with universal compulsory medical insurance financed primarily through Social Security taxes. Medicaid authorized federal grants to supplement state-paid medical care for poor people of all ages.

military-industrial complex Term used by President Eisenhower used to refer to the influence of the military establishment and defense contractors on U.S. government and policy.

Military Reconstruction Act Congressional act of March 1867 that initiated military rule of the South. Congressional reconstruction divided the ten unreconstructed Confederate states into five military districts, each under the direction of a Union general. It also established the procedure by which unreconstructed states could reenter the Union.

Montgomery bus boycott Yearlong boycott of Montgomery's segregated bus system in 1955–1956 by the city's Black American population. The boycott brought Martin Luther King Jr. to national prominence and ended in victory when the Supreme Court declared segregated transportation unconstitutional.

muckraking Early-twentieth-century style of journalism that exposed the corruption of big business and government. Theodore Roosevelt coined the term after a character in *Pilgrim's Progress* who was too busy raking muck to notice higher things.

mutually assured destruction (MAD) Term for the standoff between the United States and the Soviet Union based on the assumption that a nuclear first strike by either nation would result in massive retaliation and mutual destruction for both.

My Lai massacre U.S. soldiers' killing of an entire village of four hundred Vietnamese civilians in 1968. Covered up by the military, revelations about the massacre came to light during the court-martial of Lieutenant William Calley in 1970.

National American Woman Suffrage Association (NAWSA) Organization formed in 1890 that united the National Woman Suffrage Association and the American Woman Suffrage Association. The NAWSA pursued state-level campaigns to gain the vote for women. With successes in Idaho, Colorado, and Utah, woman suffrage had become more accepted by the 1890s.

National Energy Act of 1978 Legislation passed during the Carter administration that penalized manufacturers of gas-guzzling automobiles and provided incentives for energy conservation and development of alternative fuels, such as wind and solar power.

National Interstate and Defense Highways Act of 1956 Law authorizing the construction of a national interstate highway system. Promoted as essential to national defense and a spur to economic growth, the act accelerated the movement of people and goods and changed the nature of American communities.

National Organization for Women (NOW) Women's civil rights organization formed in 1966. Initially, NOW focused on widening opportunities for women by eliminating gender discrimination in public institutions and the workplace.

National Recovery Administration (NRA) Federal agency established in June 1933 to promote industrial recovery by the adoption of codes that set prices, minimized competition, and allowed workers to organize in unions.

neutrality acts Legislation passed between 1935 and 1937 that sought to avoid entanglement in foreign wars while protecting trade.

New Christian Right Politically active religious conservatives who reshaped the Republican Party in the 1980s through organizations like the Moral Majority. Religious conservatives criticized feminism, opposed abortion and homosexuality, and championed "family values."

New Deal coalition Political coalition that supported Franklin Roosevelt's New Deal and the Democratic Party.

"The New Freedom" Woodrow Wilson's 1912 campaign slogan, which reflected his belief in limited government and states' rights. Wilson promised to use antitrust legislation to eliminate big corporations and to improve opportunities for small businesses and farmers.

"The New Nationalism" Theodore Roosevelt's 1912 campaign slogan, which reflected his commitment to federal planning and regulation. Roosevelt wanted to use the federal government to act as a "steward of the people" to regulate giant corporations.

New Negro Term referring to Black artist who challenged American racial hierarchy. The New Negro emerged in New York City in the 1920s in what became known as the Harlem Renaissance, which produced dazzling literary, musical, and artistic talent.

new woman Alternative image of womanhood that came into the American mainstream in the 1920s. The mass media frequently portrayed young, college-educated women who drank, smoked, and wore skimpy dresses. New women also challenged American convictions about separate spheres for women and men and the sexual double standard.

Nineteenth Amendment (woman suffrage) Constitutional amendment granting women the vote. Congress passed the amendment in 1919, and it was ratified in August 1920. Like proponents of prohibition, the advocates of woman suffrage triumphed by linking their cause to the war.

No Child Left Behind Act 2002 legislation championed by President George W. Bush that expanded the role of the federal government in public education. The law required every school to meet annual testing standards, penalized failing schools, and allowed parents to transfer their children out of such schools.

North American Free Trade Agreement (NAFTA) 1993 treaty that eliminated all tariffs and trade barriers among the United States, Canada, and Mexico. NAFTA was supported by President Clinton and would feature prominently in debates over the benefits and costs of globalization.

North Atlantic Treaty Organization (NATO) Military alliance formed in 1949 among the United States, Canada, and Western European nations to counter any possible Soviet threat. It represented an unprecedented commitment by the United States to go to war if any of its allies were attacked.

NSC 68 Secret government report of 1950 warning that national survival required a massive military buildup. The Korean War led to nearly all of the expansion called for in the report, so that by 1952 defense spending consumed nearly 70 percent of the federal budget.

nuclear freeze Global movement that sought to halt the revived nuclear arms race of the 1980s. Mass protests in Europe and the United States put pressure on the United States and Soviet Union to begin talks on disarmament toward the end of the decade.

Obergefell v. Hodges Ruling by the Supreme Court in 2015 declaring that same-sex couples had a constitutional right to marry, making gay marriage legal in all fifty states. The ruling indicated a major shift in American attitudes toward gay and lesbian rights, which had been evolving since the 1970s.

Occupy Wall Street Grassroots protest movement that began in 2011 in New York City and quickly spread across the nation. Its activists championed economic justice for "the 99 percent" over the "1 percent," targeting inequalities of wealth, the economic insecurity of America's workers, and the disproportionate influence of wealthy individuals and corporations on economic and political affairs.

Open Door policy Policy successfully insisted upon by Secretary of State John Hay in 1899–1900 recommending that the major powers of the United States, Britain, Japan, Germany, France, and Russia all have access to trade with China and that Chinese sovereignty be maintained.

Patient Protection and Affordable Care Act Sweeping 2010 bill championed by President Barack Obama that established nearly universal health insurance by providing subsidies and compelling larger businesses to offer coverage to employees. The act also imposed new regulations on insurance companies and contained provisions to limit health care costs.

Pentagon Papers Secret government documents published in 1971 related to an internal study of the Vietnam War. The documents revealed official pessimism about the war despite public assurances about its progress.

People's Party (Populist Party) Political party formed in St. Louis in 1892 by the Farmers' Alliance to advance the goals of the Populist movement. Populists sought economic democracy, promoting land, electoral, banking, and monetary reform. Republican victory in the presidential election of 1896 effectively destroyed the People's Party.

Persian Gulf War 1991 war between Iraq and a U.S.-led international coalition, sparked by the 1990 Iraqi invasion of Kuwait. A forty-day bombing campaign against Iraq, followed by coalition troops storming into Kuwait, brought a quick coalition victory.

Plessy v. Ferguson 1896 Supreme Court ruling that upheld the legality of racial segregation. According to the ruling, blacks could be segregated in separate schools, restrooms, and other facilities as long as the facilities were "equal" to those provided for whites.

plutocracy A society ruled by the rich.

progressivism A reform movement that often advocated government activism to mitigate the problems created by urban industrialism. Progressivism reached its peak in 1912 with the creation of the Progressive

Party. The term *progressivism* has come to mean any general effort advocating for social justice programs.

prohibition The ban on the manufacture and sale of alcohol that went into effect in January 1920 with the Eighteenth Amendment. Prohibition proved almost impossible to enforce. By the end of the 1920s, most Americans wished it to end, and it was finally repealed in 1933.

Pullman boycott Nationwide railroad workers' boycott of trains carrying Pullman cars in 1894 after Pullman workers, suffering radically reduced wages, joined the American Railway Union (ARU) and union leaders were fired in response. The boycott ended after the U.S. Army fired on strikers and ARU leader Eugene Debs was jailed.

Reconstruction Finance Corporation (RFC) Federal agency established by Herbert Hoover in 1932 to help American industry by lending government funds to endangered banks and corporations, which Hoover hoped would benefit people at the bottom through trickle-down economics. In practice, this strategy provided little help to the poor.

Red Cloud's War A conflict touched off when gold discoveries in Montana led settlers to invade Lakota lands. Chief Red Cloud, along with Crazy Horse, fought the incursion and was successful in forcing the army to abandon its forts on the Bozeman Trail and sign the second Treaty of Fort Laramie in 1868 reserving the Black Hills for the Lakota.

Red scare Widespread fear of internal subversion and Communist revolution that swept the United States in 1919 and resulted in suppression of dissent. Wartime repression of free speech, labor unrest, postwar recession, the difficult peacetime readjustment, and the Soviet establishment of the Comintern all contributed to the scare.

Redeemers Name taken by southern Democrats who harnessed white rage during Reconstruction in order to overthrow Republican rule and Black political power and thus, they believed, save southern civilization.

reform Darwinism Sociological theory developed in the 1880s that argued humans could speed up evolution by altering their environment. A challenge to the laissez-faire approach of social Darwinism, reform Darwinism insisted that the liberal state should play an active role in solving social problems.

reservations Land assigned by the federal government to American Indians in the 1860s to reduce tensions between Indians and western settlers. With meager government rations, Native Americans faced a life of poverty and starvation.

Roe v. Wade 1973 Supreme Court ruling that the Constitution protects the right to abortion and prevents states from prohibiting it in the early stages of pregnancy. The decision made abortion a fiercely contested issue between liberals and social conservatives for decades to come.

Roosevelt Corollary Theodore Roosevelt's 1904 follow-up to the Monroe Doctrine in which he declared that the United States had the right to intervene in Latin America to stop "brutal wrongdoing" and protect American interests. The corollary warned European powers to keep out of the Western Hemisphere.

Rust Belt Term referencing the deindustrialization of the former manufacturing core of the United States, stretching from New York to Illinois. The region lost steel and automobile plants as well as population as a result of labor outsourcing and foreign competition beginning in the 1970s.

scalawag A derogatory term that southerners applied to southern white Republicans, who were seen as traitors to the South. Most were yeoman farmers.

Schenck v. United States 1919 Supreme Court decision that upheld the conviction of socialist Charles Schenck for urging resistance to the draft during wartime. It established a "clear and present danger" test for restricting free speech.

Scopes trial 1925 trial of John Scopes, a biology teacher in Dayton, Tennessee, for violating his state's ban on teaching evolution. The trial created a nationwide media frenzy and came to be seen as a showdown between urban and rural values.

Scottsboro Boys Nine Black youths who were arrested for the alleged rape of two white women in Scottsboro, Alabama, in 1931. After an all-white jury sentenced the young men to death, the Communist Party took action that saved them from the electric chair.

Selective Service Act Law enacted in 1940 requiring all men who would be eligible for a military draft to register in preparation for the possibility of a future conflict.

Servicemen's Readjustment Act Act, popularly known as the GI Bill, that provided tuition benefits, unemployment benefits, loan assistance, and medical care to World War II veterans, in an attempt to ease the transition from a wartime economy.

settlement houses Settlements established in poor neighborhoods beginning in the 1880s. Reformers like Jane Addams and Lillian Wald believed that only by living among the poor could they help bridge the growing class divide. College-educated women formed the backbone of the settlement house movement.

sexual harassment Unwelcome or inappropriate sexual remarks or behavior in the workplace. If severe enough to create a "hostile work environment," such harassment was judged to constitute sex discrimination by the Supreme Court in 1986, a victory for the feminist movement.

sharecropping Labor system that emerged in the South during Reconstruction. Under this system, planters divided their plantations into small farms that freedmen rented, paying with a share of each year's crop. Sharecropping gave Black farmers some freedom, but they remained dependent on white landlords and country merchants.

Sherman Antitrust Act 1890 act that outlawed pools and trusts, ruling that businesses could no longer enter into agreements to restrict competition. Government inaction, combined with the Supreme Court's narrow reading of the act in the *United States v. E. C. Knight Company* (1895) decision, undermined the law's effectiveness.

"silent majority" Richard Nixon's term for those Americans he claimed had been neglected by the liberal establishment in the 1960s in favor of radical protesters and minorities. Nixon appealed to this group in an effort to attract white northern workers and other traditional Democrats to the Republican Party.

Sinophobia Hostility and discrimination towards Chinese people, often based in racial prejudice and fear.

social Darwinism A social theory popularized in the late nineteenth century by Herbert Spencer and William Graham Sumner. Proponents believed that only relentless competition could produce social progress and that wealth was a sign of "fitness" and poverty a sign of "unfitness" for survival.

social gospel A vision of Christianity that saw its mission as not simply to reform individuals but to reform society. Emerging in the early twentieth century, it offered a powerful corrective to social Darwinism and the gospel of wealth, which fostered the belief that riches signaled divine favor.

Social Security New Deal program created in August 1935 that was designed to provide a modest income for elderly people as well as modest unemployment insurance.

Socialist Party Political party formed in 1900 that advocated cooperation over competition and promoted the breakdown of capitalism. Its members, who were largely middle-class and native-born, saw both the Republican and the Democratic parties as hopelessly beholden to capitalism.

Spanish-American War 1898 war between Spain and the United States that began as an effort to free Cuba from Spain's colonial rule. This popular war left the United States an imperial power in control of Cuba and colonies in Puerto Rico, Guam, and the Philippines.

spoils system System in which politicians doled out government positions to their loyal supporters. This patronage system led to widespread corruption during the Gilded Age.

Sputnik First man-made satellite to circle the earth, launched by the Soviets in 1957. It created fears that the Soviets were ahead of the United States not only in missile development and space exploration but also in science and education.

Stonewall riots Protest set off in 1969 by a police raid of the Stonewall Inn, a gay bar in New York's Greenwich Village. The incident led to the organization of a set of new advocacy groups and energized the Gay Liberation movement.

Strategic Arms Limitation Treaty (SALT) 1972 agreement between the United States and the Soviet Union limiting antiballistic missiles (ABMs) to two each. The treaty prevented either nation from building an ABM defense system so secure against a nuclear attack that it would risk a first strike.

Student Nonviolent Coordinating Committee (SNCC) Civil rights organization established by young activists in 1960 in response to the sit-in movement. SNCC rejected the top-down leadership of organizations like the Southern Christian Leadership Conference, although it embraced Martin Luther King Jr.'s principles of civil disobedience and nonviolence.

Sun Belt Name applied to the Southwest and South, which grew rapidly after World War II as a center of defense industries and nonunionized labor.

supply-side economics Economic theory claiming that tax cuts for businesses and individuals, especially the wealthy, encourage investment and production (supply) and stimulate consumption (demand) because individuals can keep more of their earnings. Despite promises to the contrary, supply-side economics during the Reagan administration created a massive federal budget deficit.

sweatshop A small room used for clothing piecework beginning in the late nineteenth century. As mechanization transformed the garment industry with the introduction of foot-pedaled sewing machines and mechanical cloth-cutting knives, independent tailors were replaced with sweatshop workers hired by contractors to sew pieces into clothing.

Taft-Hartley Act Law passed by the Republican-controlled Congress in 1947 that amended the Wagner Act and placed restrictions on organized labor, making it more difficult for unions to organize workers.

Tea Party movement Political movement of mostly white, middle-class, and older voters that was funded by billionaire conservatives and fostered by right-wing media. Sparked by opposition to financial bailouts and the Affordable Care Act under Obama, its followers protested what they saw as an overreaching government.

Teapot Dome Nickname for the scandal in which Interior Secretary Albert Fall accepted $400,000 in bribes for leasing oil reserves on public land in Teapot Dome, Wyoming. It was part of a larger pattern of corruption that marred Warren G. Harding's presidency.

Tet Offensive Major campaign of attacks launched throughout South Vietnam in early 1968 by the North Vietnamese and southern insurgents. A turning point in the war, it exposed the disparity between official statements and the war's reality, shaking Americans' confidence in the government.

Triple Alliance Early-twentieth-century alliance among Germany, Austria-Hungary, and Italy, which was formed as part of a complex network of military and diplomatic agreements intended to prevent war in Europe by balancing power.

Triple Entente Early-twentieth-century alliance among Great Britain, France, and Russia. The Triple Entente stood opposed to the Triple Alliance.

Truman Doctrine President Truman's commitment to "support free peoples who are resisting attempted subjugation by armed minorities or by outside pressures." First applied to Greece and Turkey in 1947, it became the justification for U.S. intervention into many countries during the Cold War.

trust A system in which corporations give shares of their stock to trustees who hold the stocks "in trust" for their stockholders, thereby coordinating the industry to ensure profits to the participating corporations and to curb competition.

"typewriters" Women who were hired by businesses in the decades after the Civil War to keep records and conduct correspondence, often using equipment such as typewriters.

Uncle Tom's Cabin Enormously popular antislavery novel written by Harriet Beecher Stowe and published in 1852. It helped to solidify northern sentiment against slavery and to confirm white southerners' sense that no sympathy remained for them in the free states.

underconsumption When factories and farms produce more than consumers can buy, causing factories to lay off workers and farmers to lose markets for their crops.

U.S. Capitol riot Attack by supporters of President Trump on the U.S. Capitol Building on January 6, 2021, in an effort to halt the certification of Joseph R. Biden's electoral college victory in the presidential race of 2020. Several thousand attendees at a "Stop the Steal" rally broke into and vandalized the Capitol Building, assaulting and injuring more than a hundred police officers and causing five deaths.

USA Patriot Act 2001 law passed in the wake of 9/11 that gave the government new powers to monitor suspected terrorists and their associates, including the ability to access American citizens' electronic communications and financial records. Critics charged that it represented an unwarranted abridgment of civil rights.

Versailles treaty Treaty signed on June 28, 1919, that ended World War I. The agreement redrew the map of the world and assigned Germany sole responsibility for the war, saddling it with a debt of $33 billion in war damages. Many Germans felt betrayed by the treaty.

Voting Rights Act of 1965 Law that empowered the federal government to supervise election processes and to intervene to ensure access to the voting booth. As a result of the act, Black voting and officeholding in the South shot up, initiating a major transformation in southern politics.

Wagner Act 1935 law that guaranteed industrial workers the right to organize into unions.

War on Poverty Set of programs organized through LBJ's Office of Economic Opportunity, to ameliorate poverty through education and training as well as by including the poor in policymaking.

War Powers Act 1973 law requiring that the president secure congressional approval for any substantial long-term deployment of troops abroad. The legislation was an attempt by Congress to reassert its constitutional authority over war making in the aftermath of Vietnam.

Warren Court Supreme Court under Chief Justice Earl Warren (1953–1969). It expanded the Constitution's promise of equality and individual rights and helped create a "rights revolution" by issuing landmark decisions in civil rights, criminal rights, privacy, reproductive freedom, and separation of church and state.

Watergate Term referring to the 1972 break-in at Democratic Party headquarters in Washington, D.C., by men working for President Nixon's reelection, and Nixon's subsequent efforts to cover it up. The scandal led to the only presidential resignation in American history.

welfare capitalism Popular programs for workers sponsored by employers in the 1920s. Some businesses improved safety and sanitation inside factories. They also instituted paid vacations and pension plans. This encouraged loyalty to companies and discouraged independent labor unions.

Woman's Christian Temperance Union (WCTU) All-women organization founded in 1874 to advocate total abstinence from alcohol. The WCTU provided important political training for women, which many used in the suffrage movement.

Works Progress Administration (WPA) Federal New Deal program established in 1935 that provided government-funded public works jobs to millions of unemployed Americans during the Great Depression.

World Trade Organization (WTO) International economic body established in 1994 through the General Agreement on Tariffs and Trade to enforce substantial tariff and import quota reductions. Many corporations welcomed these trade barrier reductions, but critics linked them to job loss and the weakening of unions.

World's Columbian Exposition World's fair held in Chicago in 1893 that attracted millions of visitors. The elaborately designed pavilions of the "White City" included exhibits of technological innovation and of cultural exoticism. They embodied an urban ideal that contrasted with the realities of Chicago life.

Wounded Knee 1890 massacre of Sioux Indians by the Seventh Cavalry at Wounded Knee Creek, South Dakota. Sent to suppress the Ghost Dance, the soldiers opened fire on the Sioux as they attempted to surrender. More than two hundred Sioux men, women, and children were killed in this last episode in the "Indian wars."

yellow journalism Term first given to sensationalistic newspaper reporting and cartoon images rendered in yellow. A circulation war between William Randolph Hearst's *New York Journal* and Joseph Pulitzer's *New York World* provoked the tactics of yellow journalism that fueled popular support for the Spanish-American War in 1898.

Young Americans for Freedom (YAF) Organization of conservative college students formed in 1960 in opposition to international communism and government interference in the economy. YAF was a key force behind far-right candidate Barry Goldwater securing the Republican presidential nomination in 1964.

INDEX

A NOTE ABOUT THE INDEX:
Names of individuals appear in **boldface**.
Letters in parentheses following pages refer to:
(b)   boxed feature
(f)   figures, including charts and graphs
(i)   illustrations, including photographs and artifacts
(m)   maps
(t)   tables

ABOUT THE AUTHORS

James L. Roark (Ph.D., Stanford University) is Samuel Candler Dobbs Professor Emeritus of American History at Emory University. He received his university's Emory Williams Distinguished Teaching Award, and in 2001–2002 he was Pitt Professor of American Institutions at Cambridge University. He has written *Masters without Slaves: Southern Planters in the Civil War and Reconstruction* and coauthored *Black Masters: A Free Family of Color in the Old South* with Michael P. Johnson. He has also co-edited *No Chariot Let Down: Charleston's Free People of Color on the Eve of the Civil War* with Michael P. Johnson.

Michael P. Johnson (Ph.D., Stanford University) is Professor of History at Johns Hopkins University. His publications include *Toward a Patriarchal Republic: The Secession of Georgia*; *Abraham Lincoln, Slavery, and the Civil War: Selected Speeches and Writings*; and *Reading the American Past: Selected Historical Documents*, the documents reader for *The American Promise*. He has also coedited *No Chariot Let Down: Charleston's Free People of Color on the Eve of the Civil War* with James L. Roark.

François Furstenberg (Ph.D., Johns Hopkins University) is Professor of History at Johns Hopkins University. From 2003–2014 he taught at the Université de Montréal. His publications include *In the Name of the Father: Washington's Legacy, Slavery, and the Making of a Nation*; and *When the United States Spoke French: Five Refugees who Shaped a Nation*.

Patricia Cline Cohen (Ph.D., University of California, Berkeley) is Professor Emeritus of History at the University of California, Santa Barbara, where she received the Distinguished Teaching Award in 2005–2006. She has written *A Calculating People: The Spread of Numeracy in Early America* and *The Murder of Helen Jewett: The Life and Death of a Prostitute in Nineteenth-Century New York*, and she has coauthored *The Flash Press: Sporting Male Weeklies in 1840s New York*.

Sarah Stage (Ph.D., Yale University) has taught U.S. history at Williams College and the University of California, Riverside, and she was a visiting professor at Beijing University and Szechuan University. Currently she is Professor of Women's Studies at Arizona State University. Her books include *Female Complaints: Lydia Pinkham and the Business of Women's Medicine* and *Rethinking Home Economics: Women and the History of a Profession*.

Susan M. Hartmann (Ph.D., University of Missouri) is Arts and Humanities Distinguished Professor Emeritus of History at Ohio State University. In 1995 she won the university's Exemplary Faculty Award in the College of Humanities. Her publications include *Truman and the 80th Congress*; *The Home Front and Beyond: American Women in the 1940s*; *From Margin to Mainstream: American Women and Politics since 1960*; and *The Other Feminists: Activists in the Liberal Establishment*.

Sarah E. Igo (Ph.D., Princeton University) is the Andrew Jackson Professor of American History and Director of American Studies at Vanderbilt University. Previously, she was an associate professor at the University of Pennsylvania, where she won the Richard S. Dunn Award for Distinguished Teaching in 2003. She is the author of *The Averaged American: Surveys, Citizens and the Making of a Mass Public* and *The Known Citizen: A History of Privacy in Modern America*.